LINCOLN CHRISTIAN UNIVERSITY

ASSESSMENT

In Special and Inclusive Education

Eleventh Edition

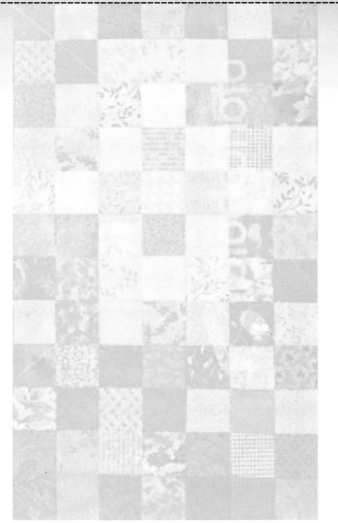

John Salvia
The Pennsylvania State University

James E. Ysseldyke
University of Minnesota

Sara Bolt
Michigan State University

 WADSWORTH
CENGAGE Learning™

Australia • Brazil • Japan • Korea • Mexico • Singapore • Spain • United
Kingdom • United States

Assessment: In Special and Inclusive Education,
Eleventh Edition

John Salvia, James Ysseldyke, Sara Bolt

Acquisition Editor: Christopher Shortt

Marketing Manager: Kara Parsons

Development Editor: Julia Giannotti

Associate Media Editor: Ashley Cronin

Assistant Editor: Diane Mars

Editorial Assistant: Linda Stewart

Media Editor: Mary Noel

Marketing Coordinator: Andy Yap

Senior Content Project Manager, Editorial
Production: Margaret Park Bridges

Art and Design Manager: Jill Haber

Manufacturing Buyer: Arethea L. Thomas

Senior Rights Acquisition Account Manager:
Katie Huha

Text Researcher: Mary Dalton-Hoffman

Production Service: Matrix Productions

Senior Photo Editor: Jennifer Meyer Dare

Cover Designer: Alisa Aronson Graphic Design

Cover Image Credit: © iStockphoto.com/Emilia Kun

Compositor: Integra

© 2010, 2007 Wadsworth, Cengage Learning

ALL RIGHTS RESERVED. No part of this work covered by the copyright
herein may be reproduced, transmitted, stored, or used in any form or by any
means graphic, electronic, or mechanical, including but not limited to photocopying,
recording, scanning, digitizing, taping, Web distribution, information networks,
or information storage and retrieval systems, except as permitted under Section
107 or 108 of the 1976 United States Copyright Act, without the prior written
permission of the publisher.

For product information and technology assistance, contact us at
Cengage Learning Academic Resource Center, 1-800-423-0563.

For permission to use material from this text or product,
submit all requests online at **www.cengage.com/permissions.**
Further permissions questions can be e-mailed to
permissionrequest@cengage.com.

Library of Congress Control Number: 2008938346

ISBN-13: 978-0-547-13437-6

ISBN-10: 0-547-13437-1

Wadsworth
10 Davis Drive
Belmont, CA 94002-3098
USA

Cengage Learning products are represented in Canada by Nelson Education, Ltd.

For your course and learning solutions, visit **www.cengage.com.**

Purchase any of our products at your local college store or at our preferred online store
www.ichapters.com.

Printed in the United States of America
1 2 3 4 5 6 7 13 12 11 10 09

CONTENTS

122909

Part 2 Assessment in Classrooms 95

Part 4 Using Assessment Results to Make Educational Decisions   337

PREFACE

As indicated by the title of the eleventh edition, *Assessment: In Special and Inclusive Education*, we continue to be concerned about assessing the performance and progress of students with disabilities regardless of whether their education occurs in general or special education settings. Since the initial publication of *Assessment* in 1978, educational and psychological assessment of students with disabilities has changed dramatically. Sweeping federal legislation has guaranteed the rights of students with disabilities to free and appropriate public education; students and their parents are guaranteed a variety of meaningful legal protections throughout the evaluation process. The quality of tests has improved dramatically. Where once it could be difficult to find a device that had sufficient reliability, validity, and normative data for use in making important educational decisions on behalf of students, teachers and psychologists now have numerous such devices from which to choose.

At the same time, information science has changed. Colleges and universities have gone from a "hard copy" to digital institutions. The Internet has more information than a scholar can pore through in a lifetime, and now users are not tied to a fixed terminal. The Internet is accessible anywhere there is wifi or a wireless telephone signal.

Clearly, the time had come for *Assessment* to change, and the eleventh edition has changed substantially. We have streamlined the text and we make far greater use of our website. There is a new, student-friendly design and new features are introduced. The statistical and measurement content now focuses on information commonly needed in schools; the more technical information in earlier editions has moved to our website. The number of specific tests reviewed has been reduced to the most commonly used tests; reviews of less frequently used tests (as well as dated tests) have moved to our website. We have added new chapters on managing assessment in classrooms, uses of technology in assessment, and communicating assessment results. We have incorporated much of the content from "Testing Students with Limited English Proficiency," "Assessing Instructional Ecology," and "Assessing Response to Instruction" into other chapters; we have also placed those chapters on our website for students who prefer the information in that form. Finally, we dropped three other chapters ("Portfolio Analysis," "Assessment of Intelligence: Group Tests," and "Assessment of Sensory Acuity") because, although important, we felt they were peripheral to the focus of the book. However, two of those chapters are available on the website, and some of the content of the third has been incorporated into other chapters.

Many of the same philosophical differences continue to divide the assessment community. Disputes continue over the value of standardized and unstandardized test administration, objective and subjective scoring, generalizable and nongeneralizable measurement, interpersonal and intrapersonal comparisons, and so forth. After carefully considering the various approaches to assessment, we remain committed to approaches that facilitate data-based decision making. Thus we believe students and society are best served by the objective, reliable, and valid assessment of student abilities and of meaningful educational results.

Our position is based on several conclusions. First, the IDEA requires objective assessment, largely because it usually leads to better decision making. Second, we are encouraged by the substantial improvement in assessment devices and practices over the past twenty-plus years. Third, although some alternatives are merely unproven, other innovative approaches to assessment—especially those that celebrate subjectivity—have severe shortcomings that have been understood since the early 1900s. Fortunately, much of the initial enthusiasm for those approaches is already beginning to wane. Fourth, we believe it is unwise to abandon effective procedures without substantial evidence that the proposed alternatives really are better. Too often, we learned that an educational innovation was ineffective after it had failed far too many students.

From the first edition, we tried to make *Assessment* a comprehensive book that was suitable for novice and expert. We provided comprehensive coverage of measurement concepts, commonly used tests, and important educational decisions. We explained the calculation of descriptive statistics (e.g., means and standard deviations), basic measurement statistics (reliability coefficients), and advanced measurement statistics (e.g., reliability of predicted differences). We reviewed most of the commonly used devices that were current. We explained the types of decisions that educators make in the process of identifying and serving students with disabilities. And we discussed the role of assessment accountability decisions. As education law evolved, as measurement theory developed, as more tests were introduced, successive editions of *Assessment* grew.

Audience for This Book

Assessment: In Special and Inclusive Education, Eleventh Edition, is intended for a first course in assessment taken by those whose careers require understanding and informed use of assessment data. The primary audience is made up of those who are or will be teachers in special education at the elementary or secondary level. The secondary audience is the large support system for special educators: school psychologists, child development specialists, counselors, educational administrators, nurses, preschool educators, reading specialists, social workers, speech and language specialists, and specialists in therapeutic recreation. Additionally, in today's reform climate, many classroom teachers enroll in the assessment course as part of their own professional development. In writing for those who are taking their first course in assessment, we have assumed no prior knowledge of measurement and statistical concepts.

Purpose

Students with disabilities have the right to an appropriate evaluation and to an appropriate education in the least restrictive educational environment. Those who assess have a tremendous responsibility; assessment results are used to make decisions that directly and significantly affect students' lives. Those who assess are responsible for knowing the devices and procedures they use and for understanding the limitations of those devices and procedures. Decisions regarding a student's eligibility for special education and related services must be based on valid information; decisions about how and where to educate students with disabilities must be based on valid data.

The New Edition

Coverage

The eleventh edition continues to offer straightforward and clear coverage of basic assessment concepts, evenhanded evaluations of standardized tests in each domain, and illustrations of applications to the decision-making process. Most chapters have been updated, and several have been revised substantially. The organization of the eleventh edition has changed. We now have four parts: Assessment: An Overview, Assessment in Classrooms, Assessment Using Formal Measures, and Using Assessment Results to Make Educational Decisions.

New Pedagogical Features

Each chapter starts out with the **new** clearly stated chapter goals and list of key terms. Main headings throughout the chapter are then linked to the chapter goal that they address. These elements promote active reading and learning.

The **new** Scenario in Assessment feature connects the concepts highlighted in the chapter to the real-life classroom. In this feature, students read vignettes that describe assessment situations in which new teachers might find themselves.

Tests Reviewed

One of the most notable changes is a reduction in the number of tests reviewed in Part 3. We have opted to place tests that are less frequently used on our website, http://www.cengage.com/education/salvia.

There are several new and revised tests and measures in the book, including the Woodcock–Johnson–III Normative Update: Tests of Cognitive Abilities and Tests of Achievement (WJ-III NU); Peabody Picture Vocabulary Test–Fourth Edition; TerraNova, Third Edition; STAR Reading; KeyMath–3 Diagnostic Assessment; Test of Language Development: Primary–Fourth Edition; Test of Language Development: Intermediate–Fourth Edition; Test of Written Language–Fourth Edition; and AIMSweb. These new tests are indicated by an asterisk in the list of all tests reviewed in this edition, which appears on the inside front cover and first page of this book.

New Chapters

The following are brand-new chapters to this edition:

- Chapter 1, "Introduction: The Context for Assessment in Schools and Current Assessment Practices"
- Chapter 3, "Test Scores and How to Use Them," combines the fundamental information from previous chapters on "Descriptive Statistics," "Norms," and "Quantification of Test Performance."

■ Chapter 4, "Technical Adequacy," combines the fundamental information from previous chapters on "Reliability" and "Validity."

■ Chapter 8, "Managing Classroom Assessment," explains the characteristics of effective testing programs with special emphasis on monitoring students' responses to instruction, how to manage regular classroom assessments, and how to make classroom decisions using student progress data.

■ Chapter 14, "Using Measures of Intelligence," combines three previous chapters ("Assessment of Intelligence: An Overview," "Assessment of Intelligence: Group Tests," and Assessment of Intelligence: Individual Tests").

■ Chapter 19, "Using Technology-Enhanced Measures," explains and provides examples of the use of technology for both continuous and periodic progress monitoring; it also describes classroom response systems, classroom observation systems, and programs used to score tests and write reports.

■ Chapter 23, "Communicating Assessment Information," discusses communication between school teams and parents about assessment and decision making. It includes information about the characteristics of effective school teams, the types of teams commonly formed in school settings, strategies for effectively communicating assessment information to parents, how assessment information is communicated and maintained in written formats, and various related rules concerning data collection and record keeping.

Organization

Part 1, "Assessment: An Overview," places testing in the broader context of assessment: In Chapter 1, "Introduction: The Context for Assessment in Schools and Current Assessment Practices," we describe assessment as a multifaceted process. The kinds of decisions made using assessment data are delineated, and basic terminology and concepts are introduced. In Chapter 2, "Legal and Ethical Considerations in Assessment," we describe the ways assessment practices are regulated and mandated by legislation and litigation. In Chapter 3, "Test Scores and How to Use Them," we describe the commonly used ways to quantify test performance and provide interpretative data. In Chapter 4, "Technical Adequacy," we explain the basic measurement concepts of reliability and validity. In Chapter 5, "Using Test Adaptations and Accommodations," we discuss how tests can be adapted to accommodate students with disabilities and English Language Learners.

Part 2, "Assessment in Classrooms," provides readers with fundamental knowledge necessary to conduct assessments in the classrooms. Chapter 6, "Assessing Behavior Through Observation," explains the major concepts in conducting systematic observations of student behavior. Chapter 7, "Teacher-Made Tests of Achievement," provides a systematic overview of tests that teachers can create to measure students' learning and progress in the curriculum. Chapter 8, "Managing Classroom Assessment," is devoted to helping educators plan assessment programs that are efficient and effective in the use of both teacher and student time.

In Part 3, "Assessment Using Formal Measures," we provide information about the abilities and skills most commonly tested in the schools. Part 3 begins with Chapter 9, "How to Evaluate a Test." This chapter is a primer on what to look for when considering the use of a commercially produced test. The next nine chapters in Part 3, provide an overview of the domain and reviews of the most frequently used measures: Chapter 10 (Assessment of Academic Achievement with

Multiple-Skill Devices), Chapter 11, (Using Diagnostic Reading Measures), Chapter 12 (Using Diagnostic Mathematics Measures), Chapter 13 (Using Measures of Oral and Written Language), Chapter 14 (Using Measures of Intelligence), Chapter 15 (Using Measures of Perceptual and Perceptual–Motor Skills), Chapter 16 (Using Measures of Social and Emotional Behavior), Chapter 17 (Using Measures of Adaptive Behavior), and Chapter 18 (Using Measures of Infants, Toddlers, and Preschoolers). Part 3 concludes with Chapter 19, "Using Technology-Enhanced Assessments," which describes computerized approaches to testing and systematic observation.

In Part 4, "Using Assessment Results to Make Educational Decisions," we discuss the most important decisions educators make on behalf of students with disabilities. In Chapter 20, "Making Instructional Decisions," we discuss the decisions that are made prior to a student's referral for special education and those that are made in special education settings. In Chapter 21, "Making Special Education Eligibility Decisions," we discuss the role of multidisciplinary teams and the process for determining a student's eligibility for special education and related services. In Chapter 22, "Making Accountability Decisions," we explain the legal requirements for states and districts to meet the standards of *No Child Left Behind* and *IDEA*, achievement standards, and important considerations in making accountability decisions. In Chapter 23, "Communicating Assessment Information," we provide an overview of communicating with school teams and parents about assessment and decision making, and include information about the characteristics of effective school teams, strategies for effectively communicating assessment information to parents, and the rules concerning data collection and record-keeping.

Instructor and Student Websites

These websites extend the textbook content and provide resources for further exploration into assessment practices. There are chapters and test reviews from previous editions, appendixes, and additional resources helpful for students and instructors.

Visit www.cengage.com/education/salvia for additional tests and resources. Test development is an ongoing process. It is our intent to review new tests as they become available and to place the reviews on the website.

Acknowledgments

Over the years, many people have assisted in our efforts. In the preparation of this edition, we express our sincere appreciation to Julia Giannotti for her assistance throughout the development of this edition. We remain indebted to Lisa Mafrici, senior developmental editor, and Loretta Wolozin, who sponsored eight of the previous editions. We also appreciate the assistance of Heidi Triezenberg for her work on the Instructor's Resource Manual with Test Items, which accompanies this text.

John Salvia
Jim Ysseldyke
Sara Bolt

ASSESSMENT

PART 1

Assessment: An Overview

School personnel regularly use assessment information to make important decisions about students. Part 1 of this text looks at basic considerations in psychological and educational assessment of students, and introduces concepts and principles that constitute a foundation for informed and critical use of assessment information.

Chapter 1 provides a description of the kinds of decisions made using assessment information, and considers the ways in which assessment impacts society, children, and their education. Chapter 2 includes a description of the major laws that affect assessment in schools, and describes ethical considerations in best assessment practices. Chapter 3 includes a description of the kinds of scores one obtains from tests and a set of considerations on how to use those scores. It is intended for the person with little or no background in descriptive statistics; it contains a discussion of the major concepts necessary for understanding most of the remaining chapters in this part and later parts of the book.

Chapter 4 is focused on the technical adequacy of tests. The main focus is on reliability (the important concept that scores are fallible, and the amount of error associated with scores) and validity (the extent to which a test or other procedure leads to valid inferences about tested performance). Validity is the most important and inclusive aspect of a test's technical adequacy.

Chapter 5 includes a description of important considerations in adapting tests to accommodate the specific needs of students with disabilities and English language learners.

Introduction: The Context for Assessment in Schools and Current Assessment Practices

Chapter Goals

1 Know the definition of assessment and how assessment differs from testing.

2 Know the importance that assessment plays in school and society, including the kinds of consequences that assessments can have.

3 Know the types of assessment decisions made by educators.

4 Identify important considerations (including why we assess and how assessment practices are evolving) as you prepare to learn about assessment in special and inclusive education.

Key Terms

assessment

inclusive education

competence enhancement

testing

capacity building

screening decisions

progress monitoring
  decisions

individual goals

state standards

No Child Left Behind Act

Individuals with Disabilities
  Education Improvement
  Act

resource allocation
  decisions

eligibility decisions

program evaluation
  decisions

accountability decisions

adequate yearly
  progress

instructional environment

observation

professional judgment

recollection

Assessment
The process used to understand + address individual differences of students.

EDUCATION IS INTENDED TO PROVIDE ALL STUDENTS WITH THE SKILLS AND competencies they need to enhance their lives and the lives of their fellow citizens. This function would be extremely difficult even if all students entered school with the same abilities and competencies and even if students learned in the same way and at the same rate. However, they do not.

Some are very smart, and some are not; some have mastered much of the first-grade curriculum before they enter school, whereas others need unusual amounts of help to learn the same material; some are fluent in English, and others are not; many have appropriate school behavior, and some do not. Also, the students attending schools today are a much more diverse group than in the past. Today's classrooms are multicultural, multiethnic, and multilingual. Students demonstrate a significant range of academic skills; in some large urban environments, for example, 75 percent of sixth graders are reading more than 2 years below grade level, and there is as much as a 10-year range in skill level in math in a sixth-grade classroom. More than 200,000 infants and toddlers, and more than 6.5 million children and youth with disabilities (approximately 13 percent of the school-age population) receive special education and related services. Most of these children and youth are attending schools in their own neighborhoods—this was not always the case in the past—and fewer students with disabilities are in separate buildings or separate classes, instead learning in classes with their peers. Thus, the focus of this book is on students in special and inclusive education.

In the United States, there are two major expectations for schools: excellence and equity. It is expected that students will work toward and achieve high standards, and it is expected that *all* students will do so. All students are entitled to a free and appropriate public education. The job of schools and the personnel who work in them is twofold: We are to enhance the competence of all students, and we are to build the capacity of systems (broadly conceived as communities, schools, parents and caregivers, and service agencies) to meet the needs of individual students.

School personnel are confronted with the significant challenge of meeting the needs of a very diverse group of students. This is why assessment is such an important activity. Assessment is the process that professionals use to understand and address individual differences in the schools. Assessment is a problem analysis and problem-solving activity that enables school personnel to identify students' current level of skills, target instruction at students' personal levels, monitor student progress and make adjustments in instruction, and evaluate the extent to which students have met instructional goals. One purpose of assessment is to help plan instructional activities that will take students from wherever they are in skill acquisition and move them toward where we want them to be (competence enhancement). Another purpose of assessment is to let us know how schools are doing with all students and to help us build the capacity of schools to enhance student competence (capacity building).

1   Assessment Defined

Assessment is a process of collecting data for the purpose of making decisions about students or schools. School personnel use assessment information to make decisions about what students have learned, what and where they should be taught, and the kinds of related services (for example, speech and language services, and psychological services) they need. Throughout their professional careers, teachers, guidance counselors, school social workers, school psychologists, and school administrators are required to give, score, and interpret a wide variety of tests. Because professional school personnel routinely receive test information from their colleagues within the schools and from professionals outside the schools, they need a working knowledge of important aspects of testing.

School personnel also use assessment information to make decisions about schools. School districts increasingly are being held accountable for the performance of their pupils. Parents, the general public, legislators, and bureaucrats want to know the extent to which students are profiting from their schooling experiences. Federal education policy contains specific expectations for states to develop high educational standards and to use tests to measure the extent to which students meet the standards.

When we assess students, we measure their competence. Specifically, we measure their progress toward attaining those competencies that their schools or parents want them to master. In schools, we are concerned about competence in three domains in which teachers provide interventions: academic, behavioral (including social), and physical. Historically, the focus of assessment has been on measuring student progress toward instructional goals and on diagnosing the need for special programs and related services. For example, we may want to know whether Antoine needs special education services to help him in developing his reading skills (need for service in an academic domain), whether Claude's behavior in class is sufficiently atypical to require special treatments or interventions (behavioral domain), or the extent to which Ellen is developing physically at a normal rate (measuring progress in the physical domain).

In this text, we address primarily the use of assessment information to make educational decisions about individual students and groups. We also describe the use of tests in making accountability decisions for schools and school systems. Our coverage of assessments is broad, including both formal and informal assessments, multiple methods for collecting information, and the many purposes for which the collected information is used.

2 The Importance of Assessment in School and Society

Assessment touches everyone's life. It especially affects the lives of people who work with children and youth and who work in schools. As you begin your study of the assessment of students, consider the following ways in which assessment affects people's lives:

- You learn that as part of the state certification process, you must take tests that assess your knowledge of teaching practices, learning, and child development.
- Mr. and Mrs. Johnson receive a call from their child's third-grade teacher, who says he is concerned about Morgan's performance on a reading test. He would like to refer Morgan for further testing to determine whether Morgan has a learning disability.
- Mr. and Mrs. Erffmeyer tell you that their son is not eligible for special education services because he scored "too high" on an intelligence test.
- In response to publication of test results showing that U.S. students rank low in comparison to students in other industrialized nations, the U.S. Secretary of Education issues a call for more rigorous educational standards for all students.
- The superintendent of schools in a large urban district learns that only 40 percent of the students in her school district passed the state graduation test.
- Your local school district asks for volunteers to serve on a task force to design a measure of technological literacy to use as a test with students.

Everyone thinks they are an expert on education, and assessment is one of the most hotly debated issues among not only educators but also the general public. People react strongly when test scores are used to make interpersonal comparisons in which they or those they love look inferior. We expect parents to react strongly when test scores are used to make decisions about their children's life opportunities—for example, whether or not their child could enter college, pass a class, be promoted to the next grade, receive special education, or be placed in a program for gifted and talented students. Unwanted outcomes often lead to questions about the kinds of tests used, the skills or behaviors they measure, and their technical adequacy. Probably no other activity that takes place in education brings with it so many challenges. Testing plays a critical role in schools and in society. Entire communities are keenly interested when test scores from their schools are reported and compared with scores from schools in other communities. Often, tests are used to make high-stakes decisions that may have a direct and significant effect on the continued funding of schools and school systems. The joint committee of three professional associations that developed a set of standards for test construction and use has addressed the importance of testing:

> Educational and psychological testing are among the most important contributions of behavioral science to our society, providing fundamental and significant improvements over previous practices. Although not all tests are well developed nor are all testing practices wise and beneficial, there is extensive evidence documenting the effectiveness of well-constructed tests for uses supported by validity

What is the difference between assessment + testing?

evidence. The proper use of tests can result in wiser decisions about individuals and programs than would be the case without their use and also can provide a route to broader and more equitable access to education and employment. The improper use of tests, however, can cause considerable harm to test-takers and other parties affected by test-based decisions. (American Educational Research Association, American Psychological Association, & National Council on Measurement in Education, 1999, p. 1).

3 Types of Assessment Decisions Made by Educators

Educational assessment decisions address problems. Some of these assessment decisions involve problem identification (deciding whether there is a problem), whereas others address problem analysis and problem solving. Most educational problems begin as discrepancies between our expectations for students and their actual performance. Students may be discrepant academically (they are not learning to read as fast as they are expected), behaviorally (they are not acting as they are expected), or physically (they are not able to sense or respond as expected). At some point, a discrepancy is sufficiently large that it is seen as a problem rather than benign human variation. The crossover point between a discrepancy and a problem is a function of many factors: the importance of the discrepancy (for example, inability to print a letter versus forgetting to dot the "i"), the intrusiveness of the discrepancy (for example, a throat-clearing tic versus shouting obscenities in class), and so forth. Other assessment decisions address problem solving (addressing questions of how to solve problems and thereby improve students' education). Table 1.1 lists the kinds of decisions school personnel make using assessment information.

TABLE 1.1	Decisions Made Using Assessment Information
Screening	Are there unrecognized problems?
Progress monitoring	Is the student making adequate progress? ■ Toward individual goals ■ Toward state standards
Instructional planning and modification	What can we do to enhance competence and build capacity, and how can we do it?
Resource allocation	Are additional resources needed?
Eligibility for special education services	Is the student eligible for special education and related services?
Program evaluation	Are the instructional programs that are being used effective?
Accountability decisions	Does what we do lead to desired outcomes?

Important to identify physical, academic & behavior problems early

Screening Decisions: Are There Unrecognized Problems?

Educators now recognize that it is very important to identify physical, academic, or behavior problems early in students' school careers. Early identification enables us to develop interventions that may alleviate or eliminate later difficulties. Educators also understand that it is important to screen for specific conditions such as visual difficulties because prescription of corrective lenses enables students to be more successful in school. School personnel engage in universal screening (they test everyone) for some kinds of potential problems. All young children are screened for vision or hearing problems with the understanding that identification of sensory problems allows us to prescribe corrective measures (glasses, contacts, hearing aids, or amplification equipment) that will alleviate the problems. All students are required to have a physical examination, and most students are assessed for "school readiness" prior to entrance into school.

Progress Monitoring Decisions: Is the Student Making Adequate Progress?

School personnel assess students for the purpose of making two kinds of progress monitoring decisions: (1) Is the student making adequate progress toward individual goals? and (2) Is the student making adequate progress toward state standards?

Monitoring Progress Toward Individual Goals

School personnel regularly assess the specific skills that students do or do not have in specific academic content areas such as decoding words, comprehending what they read, performing math calculations, solving math problems, or writing. We want to know whether the student's rate of acquisition will allow the completion of all instructional goals within the time allotted (for example, by the end of the school year or by the completion of secondary education). The data are collected for the purpose of making decisions about what to teach and the level at which to teach. For example, students who have mastered single-digit addition need no further instruction (although they may still need practice) in single-digit addition. Students who do not demonstrate those skills need further instruction. The specific goals and objectives for students who receive special education services are listed in their individualized educational programs (IEPs).

The focus in assessment is helping students move toward the competencies we want them to attain so that we can modify instruction or interventions that are not meeting desired effects. Progress may be monitored continuously or periodically to ensure students have acquired the information and skills being taught, can maintain the newly acquired skills and information over time, and can appropriately generalize the newly acquired skills and information. The IEPs of students who receive special education services must contain statements of the methods that will be used to assess their progress toward attaining these goals. In any case, the information is used to make decisions about whether the instruction or intervention is working and whether there is a need to alter instruction.

Monitoring Progress Toward State Standards

School personnel set goals/standards/expectations for performance of schools, classes, and individual students. All states have identified academic content and performance standards that specify what students are expected to learn in reading, mathematics, social studies, science, and so forth. Some students may have additional goals. Students with significant cognitive disabilities may be required to work toward a set of alternative achievement standards, or standards may be modified for students with disabilities that interfere with their movement toward state goals or standards (this is discussed in detail in Chapter 22). Moreover, states are required by law to have in place a system of assessments aligned with their goals/standards/expectations. The assessments that are used to identify the standing of groups are also used to ascertain if individuals have met or exceeded state standards/goals.

Instructional Planning and Modification Decisions: What Can We Do to Enhance Competence and Build Capacity, and How Can We Do It?

Inclusive education teachers are able to take a standard curriculum and plan instruction based on it. Although curricula vary from district to district—largely as a function of the values of community and school—they are appropriate for most students at a given age or grade level. However, what should teachers do for those students who differ significantly from their peers or from district standards in their academic and behavioral competencies? These students need special help to benefit from classroom curriculum and instruction, and school personnel must gather data to plan special programs for these students.

Three kinds of decisions are made in instructional planning: (1) what to teach, (2) how to teach it, and (3) what expectations are realistic. Deciding what to teach is a content decision usually made on the basis of a systematic analysis of the skills that students do and do not have. Scores on tests and other information help teachers decide whether students have specific competencies. Test information may be used to determine placement in reading groups or assignment to specific compensatory or remedial programs. Teachers also use information gathered from observations and interviews in deciding what to teach. They obtain information about how to teach by trying different methods of teaching and monitoring students' progress toward instructional goals. Finally, decisions about realistic expectations are always inferences, based largely on observations of performance in school settings and performance on tests.

One of the provisions of the No Child Left Behind Act, the major federal law governing delivery of elementary and secondary education, states that schools are to use "evidence-based" instructional practices. There are a number of interventions with empirical evidence to support their use with students with special needs. A number of websites are devoted to evidence-based teaching, including the following: U.S. Department of Education (www.ed.gov/index.jhtml), Campbell Collaboration (www.campbellcollaboration.org), and What Works Clearinghouse (www.whatworks.ed.gov).

Resource Allocation Decisions: Are Additional Resources Necessary?

Assessment results may indicate that individual students need special help or enrichment. These students may be referred to a teacher assistance team,[1] or they may be referred for evaluation to a multidisciplinary team that will decide whether these students are entitled to special education services. School personnel gather data on student sensory difficulties or on academic skills for the purpose of deciding whether or not additional resources are necessary. They also use assessment information to make decisions about how to enlist parents, schools, teachers or community agencies in enhancing student competence.

When it is clear that many or all students require additional programs or support, system change and increased capacity may be indicated. Clear examples of building the capacity of schools to meet student needs include preschool education for all, federal funding to increase student competence in math and science, and federal requirements for school personnel to develop individualized plans to guide the transition from high school to postschool employment.

Eligibility for Special Education Services Decisions: Is the Student Eligible for Special Education and Related Services?

School personnel use assessment information to make decisions about whether students are eligible for special education and related services. Before a student may be declared eligible for special education services, he or she must be shown to be exceptional (have a disability or a gift or talent) *and* to have special learning needs. It is not enough to be disabled *or* to have special learning needs. Students can be disabled and not require special education services. Students can have special learning needs but not meet the state criteria for being declared disabled. For example, there is no federal mandate for provision of special education services to students with behavior disorders, and in many states students with behavior disorders are not eligible for special education services (students need to be identified as emotionally disturbed to receive special education services). Students who receive special education (1) have diagnosed disabilities and (2) need special education services to achieve educational outcomes.

In addition to the classification system employed by the federal government, every state has an education code that specifies the kinds of students considered disabled. States may have different names for the same disability. For example, in California, some students are called "deaf" or "hard of hearing"; in other states, such as Colorado, the same kinds of students are called "hearing impaired." States

---

[1]Two kinds of teams typically operate in schools. The first, usually composed of teachers only, is designed as a first line of assistance to help classroom teachers solve problems with individual students in their class. These teams, often called teacher assistance teams, mainstream assistance teams, or schoolwide assistance teams, meet regularly to brainstorm possible solutions to problems teachers confront. The second kind of team is the multidisciplinary team that is required by law for purposes of making special education eligibility decisions. These teams are usually made up of a principal, regular and special education teachers, and related services personnel such as school psychologists, speech and language pathologists, occupational therapists, and nurses. These teams have different names in different places. Most often, they are called child study teams, but in Minneapolis, for example, they are called special education referral committees or IEP teams.

*Students who receive special education
1) have diagnosed disabilities
2) need special educational services to achieve educational outcomes.*

may expand special education services to provide for students with disabilities that are not listed in the Individuals with Disabilities Education Improvement Act (IDEA), but states may not exclude from services the disabilities listed in the IDEA. Some states consider gifted students to be exceptional and entitled to special education services; other states do not.

Program Evaluation: Are Instructional Programs Effective?

Assessment data are collected to evaluate specific programs. Here the emphasis is on gauging the effectiveness of the curriculum in meeting the goals and objectives of the school. School personnel typically use this information for schoolwide curriculum planning. For example, schools can compare two approaches to teaching in a content area by (1) giving tests at the beginning of the year, (2) teaching comparable groups two different ways, and (3) giving tests at the end of the year. By comparing students' performances before and after, the schools are able to evaluate the effectiveness of the two competing approaches.

The process of assessing educational programs can be complex if numerous students are involved and if the criteria for making decisions are written in statistical terms. For example, an evaluation of two instructional programs might involve gathering data from hundreds of students and comparing their performances and applying many statistical tests. Program costs, teacher and student opinions, and the nature of each program's goals and objectives might be compared to determine which program is more effective. This kind of large-scale evaluation probably would be undertaken by a group of administrators working for a school district. Of course, program evaluations can be much less formal. For example, Martha is a third-grade teacher. When Martha wants to know the effectiveness of an instructional method she is using, she does her own evaluation. Recently, she wanted to know whether phonics instruction in reading is better than using flashcards to teach word recognition. She used both approaches for 2 weeks and found that students learned to recognize words much more rapidly when she used a phonics approach.

Accountability Decisions: Does What We Do Lead to Desired Outcomes?

Under the provisions of the No Child Left Behind Act, schools, school districts, and state education agencies are now held accountable for individual student performance and progress. School districts must report annually to their state's department of education the performance of all students, including students with disabilities, on tests the state requires students to take. By law, states, districts, and individual schools must demonstrate that the students they teach are making adequate yearly progress (AYP). When it is judged by the state that a school is not making AYP, or when specified subgroups of students (disadvantaged students, students with disabilities, or specific racial/ethnic groups) are not making AYP, sanctions are applied. The school is said to be a school in need of improvement. When schools fail to make AYP for 2 years, parents of the children who attend those schools are permitted to transfer their children to other schools that are not considered in need of improvement. When the school fails to make AYP for 3 years, students are entitled to supplemental educational services (usually after-school tutoring). Failure to make AYP for longer periods of time results in increasing sanctions until finally the state can take over the school or district and reconstitute it.

4 Important Things to Think About as You Read and Study This Textbook

There are a number of things to think about as you proceed through this book. In this section, we describe several things to bear in mind.

The Type of Decision Determines the Type of Information Needed

In assessing students, it is critical to think about the kind of decision you are making. Different kinds of decisions require different kinds of assessments (both different tests and different assessment processes). For example, if one is attempting to decide whether Millie meets the state eligibility criteria for being classified mentally retarded, it would be necessary to administer an individual intelligence test. If one is attempting to plan an instructional program for Millie, who is mentally retarded, it is not necessary to administer an intelligence test. Rather, we need to know the specific skills that she does and does not have. Such information is best obtained by assessing her level of skill attainment or achievement. Finally, if one wants to know whether Millie is making progress in her instructional program, progress monitoring provides this information.

Focus on Alterable Behaviors

After we decide a student is eligible for special education services, our focus should be on assessment of alterable behaviors (behaviors that can be changed). Educators can work to enhance student competence in reading, math, writing, and other academic content areas. They can change the way they teach students to decode words or to write in complete sentences. As educators, we can change what happens in school. As citizens, we can work to change what happens outside of school.

Assess Instruction Before Assessing Learners

When a student is experiencing difficulty in school, two related and complementary types of assessment should be performed. First, the instruction a student has received is assessed to ascertain whether the student's difficulties stem from inappropriate curriculum or inadequate teaching. When instruction is found to be inadequate, the student should be given appropriate instruction to determine whether it alleviates the difficulty. When appropriate instruction fails to remediate the difficulty, further assessment of the student is carried out. Each approach is described in this section.

Assessing Instruction

Until the early 1980s, most assessment activities in school settings consisted of efforts to assess the learner. Yet school personnel often have difficulty developing instructional recommendations solely on the basis of information about the characteristics of students. Englemann, Granzin, and Severson (1979) recommended that assessment begin with instructional diagnosis "to determine aspects of instruction that are inadequate, to find out precisely how they are inadequate, and to imply what must be done to correct their inadequacy" (p. 361). In this approach, assessment consists of systematic analysis of instruction in terms of its appropriateness for the learner. Two dimensions are usually considered when instruction is assessed: instructional challenge and instructional environment.

Instructional Challenge   For instruction to be effective, it must be possible for the learner, with a reasonable effort, to master the information (the facts, skills, behaviors, or processes) being taught. If the degree to which information challenges a learner is thought of as a continuum, we can think of material as ranging from too easy (unchallenging), through approximately right in degree of difficulty (appropriately challenging), to too difficult (overly challenging). School personnel endeavor to match instruction so that there is an appropriate level of challenge—usually approximately 90 percent known to 10 percent unknown. To do so, they must know the level of skill development of the learner. Thus, they typically gather data on the skills that students do and do not have. Then they plan instruction matched to the students' skill level.

Instructional Environment   Instruction involves more than appropriate curriculum. It is a complex activity, the outcomes of which depend on the interaction of many factors. Recognition of this fact has led to efforts to assess the qualitative nature of students' instructional environments (Ysseldyke & Christenson, 2002). In doing so, educators gather information on the extent to which evidence-based components of effective instruction are present in the instruction that individual students receive. Two dimensions of instruction (classroom management and learning management) are worth describing here.

Classroom management: Classroom management refers to a collection of organizational goals centered on using time wisely in order to maximize learning and on maintaining a safe classroom environment that is conducive to student learning. In classrooms that are poorly organized, students lose learning opportunities because of disruptions by other students, ineffective grouping, poor transitions between activities, and so forth. In contrast, well-organized classrooms have clearly stated and well-understood procedures, consistent consequences for student behavior, and student freedom within a structured environment.

Learning management: The organization and management of the classroom to ensure learning require careful attention to detail. Essentially, teachers must oversee the learning situation. Effective teachers (1) demonstrate what is to be learned and then provide adequate opportunities for meaningful rehearsal and guided and independent practice with appropriate materials until skills become automatic; (2) give students immediate, specific, and corrective feedback about their performances and provide opportunities to correct mistakes; (3) reinforce desired outcomes; and (4) stress understanding, application, and transfer of information.

Assessing Learners

When students have received appropriate instruction but are still experiencing academic or behavioral problems, school personnel usually begin to assemble existing information to document the nature of the problem (that is, to identify specific learning strengths and weaknesses) and to generate hypotheses about the problem's likely solution. They do so using observations, recollections, tests, and professional judgments.

Assessment Is Broader Than Testing

School personnel sometimes equate testing and assessment. Testing consists of administering a particular set of questions to an individual or group of individuals to obtain a score. That score is the end product of testing. A test is only one of several assessment techniques or procedures for gathering information. During the process of assessment, data from observations, recollections, tests, and professional judgments all come into play.

Observations

Observations can provide highly accurate, detailed, verifiable information not only about the person being assessed but also about the surrounding contexts. Observations can be categorized as either nonsystematic or systematic. In *nonsystematic*, or informal, observation, the observer simply watches an individual in his or her environment and notes the behaviors, characteristics, and personal interactions that seem significant. In *systematic observation*, the observer sets out to observe one or more precisely defined behaviors. The observer specifies observable events that define the behavior and then counts the frequency or measures the frequency, duration, amplitude, or latency of the behaviors.

Recollections

Recalled observations and interpretations of behavior and events are frequently used as an additional source of information. People who are familiar with the student can be very useful in providing information through interviews and rating scales. Interviews can range in structure from casual conversations to highly structured processes in which the interviewer has a predetermined set of questions that are asked in a specified sequence. Generally, the more structured the interview, the more accurate are the comparisons of the results of several different interviews. Rating scales can be considered the most formal type of interview. Rating scales allow questions to be asked in a standardized way and to be accompanied by the same stimulus materials, and they provide a standardized and limited set of response options.

Tests

A *test* is a predetermined set of questions or tasks for which predetermined types of behavioral responses are sought. Tests are particularly useful because they permit tasks and questions to be presented in exactly the same way to each person tested. Because a tester elicits and scores behavior in a predetermined and consistent manner, the performances of several different test takers can be compared, no matter who does the testing. Hence, tests tend to make many contextual factors in assessment consistent for all those tested. The price of this consistency is that the predetermined questions, tasks, and responses may not be equally relevant to all students. Tests yield two types of information—quantitative and qualitative. *Quantitative data* are the actual scores achieved on the test. An example of quantitative data is Lee's score of 80 on her math test. *Qualitative data* consist of other observations made while a student is tested; they tell us how Lee achieved her score. For example, Lee may have solved all of the addition and subtraction problems with the exception of those that required regrouping. When tests are used, we usually want to know both the scores and how the student earned those scores.

Professional Judgments

The judgments and assessments made by others can play an important role in assessment. Diagnosticians occasionally seek out other professionals to complement their own skills and background. Thus, referring a student to various specialists (hearing specialists, vision specialists, reading teachers, and so on) is a common and desirable practice in assessment. Judgments by teachers, counselors, psychologists, and practically any other professional school employee may be useful in particular circumstances.

Expertise in making judgments is often a function of familiarity with the student being assessed. Teachers regularly express professional judgments; for example, teacher comments on a student's report card represent a teacher's judgment.

Assessments Have Consequences

Decisions in school frequently have important, and occasionally lifelong, consequences. The procedures for gathering data and conducting assessments are matters that are rightfully of great concern to the general public—both individuals who are directly affected by the assessments (such as parents, students, and classroom teachers) and individuals who are indirectly affected (for example, taxpayers and elected officials). These matters are also of great concern to individuals and agencies that license or certify assessors to work in the schools. Finally, these matters are of great concern to the assessment community. For convenience, the concerns of these groups are discussed separately; however, the reader should recognize that many of the concerns overlap and are not the exclusive domain of one group or another.

Concerns of the General Public

The individuals who are affected by educational decisions are rightly concerned about assessment procedures. They want, and deserve, good decisions. However, any decision can have undesired consequences. Decision making creates "haves" and "have-nots." Most people who take a test for a driver's license pass the test; some people fail the test and are denied driving privileges. College entrance tests determine admission for some students and exclusion for others. In the same way, decisions about special and remedial education have consequences. Some consequences are desired, such as extra services for students who are entitled to special education. Other consequences are unwanted, such as denial of special education services or diminished self-esteem resulting from a disability label. Concerns of laypeople generally surface when the educational decisions have undesired consequences and are viewed as undemocratic, elitist, or simply unfair.

Concerns of Certification Boards

Certification and licensure boards establish standards to ensure that assessors are appropriately qualified to conduct assessments.[2] Test administration, scoring, and interpretation require different degrees of training and expertise, depending on the kind of test being administered. All states certify teachers and psychologists who work in the schools; all states require formal training, and some require competency testing. Although most teachers can readily administer or learn to administer group intelligence and achievement tests, as well as classroom assessments of achievement, a person must have considerable training to score and interpret most individual intelligence and personality tests. Therefore, when pupils are tested, we should be able to assume that the person doing the testing has adequate training to conduct the testing correctly (that is, establish rapport, administer the test correctly, score the test, and accurately interpret the test).

Not All Assessments Are Equal

Tests are samples of behavior. Different tests sample different behavior, and tests differ in their technical adequacy. It is important when interpreting test results that users take into serious account the kinds of behaviors sampled by the tests and the tests' technical adequacy. You will learn by reading this text the kinds of tests that are available for use in educational settings, the kinds of behaviors sampled by tests that are said to assess the same domain (for example, reading), and the technical adequacy of the tests. We focus on the extent to which students who are assessed are representative of those on whom and for whom a test was built. We also focus on the extent to which tests provide consistent results (are reliable) and actually measure what their authors say they measure (validity). When tests do not meet professional standards, we say so. Assessment is a process of collecting data for the purpose of making decisions about students. It is critical that it be done correctly and that those who assess students do so with technical accuracy, fidelity, and integrity.

Assessment Practices Are Dynamic

Educational personnel regularly change their assessment practices. New federal or state laws, regulations, or guidelines specify and, in some cases, mandate new assessment practices. New tests become available, and old ones go away. States change their special education eligibility criteria, and technological advances enable us to gather data in new and more efficient ways. Also, the population of students

---

[2]These boards also sanction professionals for practicing beyond their competence.

Scenario in Assessment

Ima and Mohammed

Ima

Ima Tryun is an eighth grader who was retained in first grade. Ima has been identified as a student with a learning disability in the area of written communication/basic reading skills. Ima attends school regularly and has an integrated special/regular instruction schedule. He receives resource services and in-class support for mathematics, science, and social studies taken in the general education classroom.

Ima reads on a third-grade level. His writing is hampered by his inability to spell. He has wonderful ideas and communicates them well. With the use of a tape recorder, Ima is able to record his ideas. His writing skills are improving with his reading skills. Ima shows excellent auditory comprehension and his attention to task is above average. He actively participates in class activities and discussions. Ima exhibits low self-esteem toward school. However, he will ask for and accept help from teachers. He is well accepted by his peers and is "looked up to."

1. Does Ima have a problem? If so, what is it?
2. What kinds of assessment decisions do you need to make about teaching Ima?
3. What kinds of further information do you need in order to teach Ima? How might you gather that information?
4. How might you change the way you teach Ima or the way he responds to you?

Mohammed

It is May 12. The year is nearly over (well, at least you are on a downhill slope to summer vacation). The prin-cipal walks Mohammed into your room and says to Mohammed, "This is your new teacher, just do what she says and all will be ok." A Somalian interpreter is present and communicates this to Mohammed. He also lets you know that Mohammed arrived in the United States 3 weeks ago and just moved to your town yesterday. The interpreter tells you that he has no clue whether Mohammed ever went to school in his native Somalia, and there are no educational records. The principal says, "That's why we put this kid in your class rather than in Roger's or Audrey's section. You are the best; you'll figure out what to do." You rethink year end. You already have most of the struggling students in your class. You feel dumped on. You know you have four students who likely will not pass benchmark tests by the end of the year, and you already have students who speak three different languages.

What would you do?

1. Does Mohammed have a problem? If so, what is it?
2. What issues do you face in attempting to deal with Mohammed and his educational needs in the context of a classroom in which you have others who are struggling and you do not want to ignore the needs of those who are doing just fine?
3. Would it matter what grade or subject matter content you are teaching?
4. What kinds of assessment decisions do you need to make about teaching Mohammed?
5. What kinds of information do you need in order to do an effective job of teaching Mohammed?

attending schools changes, bringing new challenges to educational personnel who are working to enhance the academic and behavioral competence of all students. We address the dynamic nature of assessment by maintaining a website for this book. On that website we can inform you of changes that take place in laws, instruments, practices, or procedures.

5 Important Considerations as You Prepare to Learn About Assessment in Special and Inclusive Education in Today's School

Why Learn About Assessment?

Educational professionals must assess. Assessment is a critical practice engaged in for the purpose of matching instruction to the level of students' skills, monitoring student progress, modifying instruction, and working hard to enhance student competence. It is a critical component of teaching, and thus it is necessary that teachers have good skills in assessment and good understanding of assessment information.

Although assessment can be a scary topic for practicing professionals as well as individuals training to become professionals, learning the different important facets helps people become less apprehensive. Educational assessments always have consequences that are important for students and their families. We can expect that good assessments lead to good decisions—decisions that facilitate a student's progress toward the desired goal (especially long term) of the student becoming a happy, well-adjusted, independent, productive member of society. Poor assessments can slow that progress, stop progress, and sometimes reverse progress. The assessment process is also scary because there is so much to know; a student of assessment can easily get lost in the details of measurement theory, legal requirements, teaching implications, and national politics. Things were much simpler when the first edition of this book was published in 1978. The federal legislation and court cases that governed assessment were minimal. Some states had various legal protections for the assessment of students; others did not. There were many fewer tests used with students in special education, and many of them were technically inadequate (that is, they lacked validity for various reasons). Psychologists decided if a student was entitled to special education, and students did not have IEPs. Back then, the major problems we addressed were how to choose a technically adequate test, how to use it appropriately, and how to interpret test scores correctly. Although the quality of published tests has increased dramatically throughout the years, there are still poor tests being used.

Things are more complex today. Federal law regulates the assessment of children for and in special education. Educators and psychologists have many more tools at their disposal—some excellent, some not so good. Educators and psychologists must make more difficult decisions than ever before. For example, the law recognizes more disabilities, and educators need to be able to distinguish important differences among disabilities.

Measurement theory and scoring remain difficult but integral parts of assessment. Failure to understand the basic requirements for valid measurement or the precise meaning of test scores inescapably leads to faulty decision making.

Assessment results often bring unwanted news to the community, parents, students, and teachers. Because property values fluctuate with the perceived quality of the local schools, bad news about how students are doing in schools brings bad news to the real estate market. Parents never want to hear that their children are not succeeding or that their children's prospects for adult life are limited. Students do not want to hear that they are different or not doing as well as their peers; they

With increased standards in assessment has student learning increased?

certainly do not want to be called handicapped or disabled. Teachers do not want to hear that their instruction has not produced learning or that their classroom management techniques are adding to a student's inappropriate classroom behavior. Inadequate student achievement often leads teachers to deny that student achievement really is inadequate; educators proclaim that tests measure trivial knowledge (not the important things they teach), that they decontextualize knowledge, making it fragmented and artificial, and so on. Other teachers accept their students' failures (for example, the teachers burn out). The good teachers work harder (for example, learn instructional techniques that actually work and individualize instruction).

Good News: Significant Improvements in Assessment Have Happened and Continue to Happen

The good news is that there have been significant improvements in assessment since the first edition of *Assessment* in 1978. Assessment is evolving in a number of important ways.

- Methods of test construction have changed.
- New kinds of statistical analyses have enabled test authors to do a better job of building their assessments.
- Skills and abilities that we assess have changed as theory and knowledge have evolved. We recognize attention deficit disorder and autism as separate disabilities; intelligence tests reflect theories of intelligence.
- Good new assessment methods have worked their way into practice: systematic observation, functional assessment, curriculum-based measurement, curriculum-based assessment, and technology-enhanced assessment and instructional management.
- Advancements in technology are making the collection, storage, and analysis of assessment data much more manageable and user-friendly.
- Federal laws prescribe the procedures that schools must follow in conducting assessments and hold schools more accountable for the assessments they conduct.

We have every reason to expect that assessment practices will continue to change for the better.

CHAPTER COMPREHENSION QUESTIONS

Write your answers to each of the following questions, and then compare your responses to the text.

1. Define assessment and state how it differs from testing.

2. What role does assessment play in school and society?

3. What are the kinds of assessment decisions educators make?

4. Identify four important considerations in why we assess and how assessment practices are evolving as you prepare to learn about assessment in special and inclusive education.

2 Legal and Ethical Considerations in Assessment

Chapter Goals

1 Understand the major laws that affect assessment, along with the specific provisions (for example, individualized education program, least restrictive environment, and due process provisions) of the laws.

2 Understand the ethical standards for assessment that have been developed by professional associations, and consider examples of ethical and unethical assessment practices.

Key Terms

Education for All Handicapped Children Act

Individuals with Disabilities Education Act

Elementary and Secondary Education Act

individualized education program

least restrictive environment

due process

ethical principles of psychologists

code of conduct for psychologists

beneficence

evidence-based instructional practice

National Association of
School Psychologists'
*Principles for Professional
Ethics*

National Education Association's *Code of Ethics of
the Education
Profession*

No Child Left Behind Act

nondiscriminatory
assessment

protection in evaluation
procedures (PEPs)

Public Law 94-142

Section 504 of the
Rehabilitation Act
of 1973

standards for educational
and psychological
testing

MUCH OF THE PRACTICE OF ASSESSING STUDENTS IS THE DIRECT RESULT OF federal laws, court rulings, and professional standards and ethics. Federal laws mandate that students be assessed before they are entitled to special education services. Federal laws also mandate that there be an individualized education program for every student with a disability; that instructional objectives for each of these students be derived from a comprehensive individualized assessment; and that states provide an annual report to the U.S. Department of Education on the academic performance of all students, including students with disabilities. Professional associations (for example, the Council for Exceptional Children, the National Association of School Psychologists, and the American Psychological Association) specify standards for good professional practice and ethical principles to guide the behavior of those who assess students.

1   Laws

Prior to 1975, there was no federal requirement that students with disabilities attend school, or that schools should make an effort to teach students with disabilities. Requirements were on a state-by-state basis, and they differed and were applied differently in the states. Since the mid-1970s, the delivery of services to students in special and inclusive education has been governed by federal laws. An important federal law, called Section 504 of the Rehabilitation Act of 1973, gave individuals with disabilities equal access to programs and services funded by federal monies. In 1975, Congress passed the Education for All Handicapped Children Act (Public Law 94-142), which included many instructional and assessment requirements. The law was reauthorized, amended, and updated in 1986, 1990, 1997, and 2004. In 1990, the law was given a new name: the Individuals with Disabilities Education Act (IDEA). To reflect contemporary practices, Congress replaced references to "handicapped children" with "children with disabilities." In the 2004 reauthorization, the law was again retitled the Individuals with Disabilities Education Improvement Act to highlight the fact that the major intent of the law is to improve educational services for students with disabilities.

One other federal law, the 2001 Elementary and Secondary Education Act (commonly referred to as the No Child Left Behind Act (NCLB)), is especially important to contemporary assessment practices. Table 2.1 lists the federal laws that are especially important to assessment practices, and the major new provisions of each of the laws are highlighted.

TABLE 2.1	Major Federal Laws and Their Key Provisions Relevant to Assessment
Act	**Provisions**
Section 504 of the Rehabilitation Act of 1973 (Public Law 93-112)	It is illegal to deny participation in activities or benefits of programs, or to in any way discriminate against a person with a disability solely because of the disability.
	Individuals with disabilities must have equal access to programs and services.
	Auxiliary aids must be provided to individuals with impaired speaking, manual, or sensory skills.
Education for All Handicapped Children Act of 1975 (Public Law 94-142)	Students with disabilities have the right to a free, appropriate public education.
	Schools must have on file an individualized education program for each student determined to be eligible for services under the act.
	Parents have the right to inspect school records on their children. When changes are made in a student's educational placement or program, parents must be informed. Parents have the right to challenge what is in records or to challenge changes in placement.
	Students with disabilities have the right to be educated in the least restrictive educational environment.
	Students with disabilities must be assessed in ways that are considered fair and nondiscriminatory. They have specific protections.
1986 Amendments to the Education for All Handicapped Children Act (Public Law 99-457)	All rights of the Education for All Handicapped Children Act are extended to preschoolers with disabilities.
	Each school district must conduct a multidisciplinary assessment and develop an individualized family service plan for each preschool child with a disability.
Individuals with Disabilities Education Act of 1990 (Public Law 101-476)	This act reauthorizes the Education for All Handicapped Children Act.
	Two new disability categories (traumatic brain injury and autism) are added to the definition of students with disabilities.
	A comprehensive definition of transition services is added.
1997 Amendments to the Individuals with Disabilities Education Act (IDEA; Public Law 105-17)	These amendments add a number of significant provisions to IDEA and restructure the law.
	A number of changes in the individualized education program and participation of students with disabilities in state and district assessments are mandated.
	Significant provisions on mediation of disputes and discipline of students with disabilities are added.
2001 Elementary and Secondary Education Act (No Child Left Behind Act; Public Law 107-110)	Targeted resources are provided to help ensure that disadvantaged students have access to a quality public education (Funds Title 1).
	The act aims to maximize student learning, provide for teacher development, and enhance school system capacity.
	The act requires states and districts to report on annual yearly progress for all students, including students with disabilities.
	The act provides increased flexibility to districts in exchange for increased accountability.
	The act gives parents whose children attend schools on state "failing schools list" for 2 years the right to transfer their children to another school.
	Students in "failing schools" for 3 years are eligible for supplemental education services.
2004 Reauthorization of IDEA	New approaches are introduced to prevent overidentification by race or ethnicity.
	State must have measurable annual objectives for students with disabilities.
	Districts are not required to use severe discrepancy between ability and achievement in identifying learning disabled students.

Section 504 of the Rehabilitation Act of 1973

Section 504 of the Rehabilitation Act of 1973 prohibits discrimination against persons with disabilities. The act states:

> No otherwise qualified handicapped individual shall, solely by reason of his handicap, be excluded from the participation in, be denied the benefits of, or be subjected to discrimination in any program or activity receiving federal financial assistance.

If the Office of Civil Rights (OCR) of the U.S. Department of Education finds that a state education agency (SEA) or local education agency (LEA) is not in compliance with Section 504, and that a state or district chooses not to act to correct the noncompliance, the OCR may withhold federal funds from that SEA or LEA.

Most of the provisions of Section 504 were incorporated into and expanded in the Education for All Handicapped Children Act of 1975 (Public Law 94-142) and are a part of the Individuals with Disabilities Education Improvement Act of 2004. Section 504 is broader than those other acts because its provisions are not restricted to a specific age group or to education. Section 504 is the law most often cited in court cases involving either employment of people with disabilities or appropriate education in colleges and universities for students with disabilities. Section 504 has been used to secure services for students with conditions not formally listed in the disabilities education legislation.

Major Assessment Provisions of the Individuals with Disabilities Education Improvement Act

When Congress passed the Education for All Handicapped Children Act in 1975, it included four major requirements relative to assessment: (1) an individualized education program (IEP) for each student with a disability, (2) protection in evaluation procedures, (3) education in the least restrictive appropriate environment (LRE), and (4) due process rights. The provisions of federal law continued with the 2004 reauthorized Individuals with Disabilities Education Improvement Act.

The Individualized Education Program Provisions

Public Law 94-142 (the Education for All Handicapped Children Act of 1975) specified that all students with disabilities have the right to a free, appropriate public education and that schools must have an IEP for each student with a disability. In the IEP, school personnel must specify the long-term and short-term goals of the instructional program. IEPs must be based on a comprehensive assessment by a multidisciplinary team. We stress that assessment data are collected for the purpose of helping team members specify the components of the IEP. The team must specify not only goals and objectives but also plans for implementing the instructional program. They must specify how and when progress toward accomplishment of objectives will be evaluated. Figure 2.1 illustrates an IEP for a student in a Minnesota school district. Note that specific assessment activities that form the basis of the program are listed, as are specific instructional goals or objectives. IEPs are to be formulated by a multidisciplinary child study team that meets with the parents. Parents have the right to agree or disagree with the contents of the program.

FIGURE 2.1
An Individualized Education
Program

INDIVIDUALIZED EDUCATION PROGRAM

11/11/08
Date

Thompson   _J._

STUDENT: Last Name   First   Middle

                                              5.3   8/4/98
School of Attendance   Home School   Grade Level   Birthdate/Age

_____
School Address   School Telephone Number

Child Study Team Members

                                        LD Teacher
                                        Case Manager
Homeroom teacher   _Parents_
Name   Title   Name   Title
Facilitator (school psychologist)
Name   Title   Name   Title
Speech pathologist
Name   Title   Name   Title

Summary of Assessment Results

IDENTIFIED STUDENT NEEDS: _Reading from last half of_
DISTAR II – present performance level

LONG-TERM GOALS: _To improve reading achievement level by at_
least one year's gain. To improve math achievement to grade level.
To improve language skills by one year's gain.

SHORT-TERM GOALS: _Master Level 4 vocabulary and reading_
skills. Master math skills in basic curriculum. Master
spelling words from Level 3 list. Complete units 1-9 from
Level 3 curriculum.

MAINSTREAM MODIFICATIONS: _____

(continued)

FIGURE 2.1
An Individualized Education
Program (*continued*)

Description of Services to Be Provided

Type of service	Teacher	Starting date	Amt. of time per day	OBJECTIVES AND CRITERIA FOR ATTAINMENT
SLD Level III	LD Teacher	11/11/08	2½ hrs	*Reading: Will know all vocabulary through the "Honeycomb" level. Will master skills as presented through DISTAR II. Will know 123 sound-symbols presented in "Sound Way to Reading."* *Math: Will pass all tests at basic 4 level.* *Spelling: 5 words each week from Level 3 list.* *Language: Will complete units 1–9 of the grade 4 language program. Will also complete supplemental units from "Language Step by Step."*

General education classes	Teacher	Amt. of time per day	OBJECTIVES AND CRITERIA FOR ATTAINMENT
		3½ hrs	*Out-of-seat behavior: Sit attentively and listen during general education class discussions. A simple management plan will be implemented if he does not meet this expectation. General education modifications of social studies: Will keep a folder in which he expresses through drawing the topics his class will cover. Modified district social studies curriculum. No formal testing will be done. An oral reader will read text to him, and oral questions will be asked.*

The following equipment, and other changes in personnel, transportation, curriculum, methods, and educational services will be made:

DISTAR II reading program spelling Level 3; "Sound Way to Reading" program; vocabulary tapes

Substantiation of least restrictive alternatives: *The planning team has determined the student's academic needs are best met with direct SLD support in reading, math, language, and spelling.*

Anticipated Length of Plan: ___1 yr___   The next periodic review will be held: ___May 2009___

☐ I do approve this program placement and the above IEP

☐ I do not approve this placement and/or the IEP

☐ I request a conciliation conference

_____
PARENT/GUARDIAN

_____
PRINCIPAL or Designee

Lee

Lee is a young man with autism whose achievements belie his disability. An African American graduate of a public high school, Lee was valedictorian of his class, went on to college, earned a degree, and entered the world of work. Lee is one of many young people who have benefited from the landmark law we now know as the Individuals with Disabilities Education Act (IDEA).

Congress enacted what was then the Education for All Handicapped Children Act (Public Law 94-142) on November 29, 1975. The law was intended to support states and localities in protecting the rights of, meeting the individual needs of, and improving the results for infants, toddlers, children, and youths with disabilities and their families.

Before IDEA, many children like Lee were denied access to education and opportunities to learn. For example, in 1970, U.S. schools educated only one in five children with disabilities, and many states had laws excluding certain students, including children who were deaf, blind, emotionally disturbed, or mentally retarded, from its schools.

Today, thanks to IDEA, early intervention programs and services are provided to more than 200,000 eligible infants and toddlers and their families, while about 6.5 million children and youths receive special education and related services to meet their individual needs. More students with disabilities are attending schools in their own neighborhoods—schools that may not have been open to them previously. And fewer students with disabilities are in separate buildings or separate classrooms on school campuses, and are instead learning in classes with their peers.

When President Bush and Congress set out to reauthorize the IDEA legislation in 2004, they made sure it called for states to establish goals for the performance of children with disabilities that are aligned with each state's definition of "adequate yearly progress" under the No Child Left Behind Act of 2001 (NCLB). Together, NCLB and IDEA hold schools accountable for making sure students with disabilities achieve high standards. In the words of Secretary Spellings, "The days when we looked past the underachievement of these students are over. No Child Left Behind and the IDEA 2004 have not only removed the final barrier separating special education from general education, they also have put the needs of students with disabilities front and center. Special education is no longer a peripheral issue. It's central to the success of any school."

IDEA is now aligned with the important principles of NCLB in promoting accountability for results, enhancing the role of parents, and improving student achievement through instructional approaches that are based on scientific research. While IDEA focuses on the needs of individual students and NCLB focuses on school accountability, both laws share the goal of improving academic achievement through high expectations and high-quality education programs.

Through these efforts, we are reaching beyond physical access to the education system toward achieving full access to high-quality curricula and instruction to improve education outcomes for children and youths with disabilities.

Evidence that this approach is working can be found in the increase in the number of students with disabilities graduating from high school instead of dropping out. The National Longitudinal Transition Study-2 (NLTS2), which documented the experiences of a national sample of students with disabilities over several years as they moved from secondary school into adult roles, shows that the incidence of students with disabilities completing high school rather than dropping out increased by 17 percentage points between 1987 and 2003.

During the same period, their postsecondary education participation more than doubled to 32 percent. In 2003, 70 percent of students with disabilities who had been out of school for up to 2 years had paying jobs, compared to only 55 percent in 1987. Employment and independence are important pieces of the American Dream. In today's world, getting there depends on having the foundation of a good education. Through IDEA and NCLB, students with disabilities have the support that they need to be the best they can be.

Source: U.S. Department of Education (www.ed.gov/policy/speced/leg/idea/history30.html).

In the 1997 amendments, Congress mandated a number of changes to the IEP. The core IEP team was expanded to include both a special education teacher and a general education teacher. The 1997 law also specified that students with disabilities are to be included in state- and districtwide assessments and that states must report annually on the performance and progress of all students, including students with disabilities. The IEP team must decide whether the student will take the assessments with or without accommodations or take an alternate or modified assessment.

Protection in Evaluation Procedures Provisions

Congress included a number of specific requirements in Public Law 94-142. These requirements were designed to protect students and help ensure that assessment procedures and activities would be fair, equitable, and nondiscriminatory. Specifically, Congress mandated eight provisions:

1. Tests are to be selected and administered so as to be racially and culturally nondiscriminatory.
2. To the extent feasible, students are to be assessed in their native language or primary mode of communication (such as American Sign Language or communication board).
3. Tests must have been validated for the specific purpose for which they are used.
4. Tests must be administered by trained personnel in conformance with the instructions provided by the test producer.
5. Tests used with students must include those designed to provide information about specific educational needs, not just a general intelligence quotient.
6. Decisions about students are to be based on more than their performance on a single test.
7. Evaluations are to be made by a multidisciplinary team that includes at least one teacher or other specialist with knowledge in the area of suspected disability.
8. Children must be assessed in all areas related to a specific disability, including—where appropriate—health, vision, hearing, social and emotional status, general intelligence, academic performance, communicative skills, and motor skills.

In passing the 1997 amendments and the 2004 amendments, Congress reauthorized these provisions.

Least Restrictive Environment Provisions

In writing the 1975 Education for All Handicapped Children Act, Congress wanted to ensure that, to the greatest extent appropriate, students with disabilities would be placed in settings that would maximize their opportunities to interact with students without disabilities. Section 612(S)(B) states:

> To the maximum extent appropriate, handicapped children . . . are educated with children who are not handicapped, and that special classes, separate schooling, or other removal of handicapped children from the regular educational environment occurs only when the nature or the severity of the handicap is such that education in regular classes with the use of supplementary aids and services cannot be achieved satisfactorily.

The LRE provisions arose out of court cases in which state and federal courts had ruled that when two equally appropriate placements were available for a student with a disability, the most normal (that is, least restrictive) placement was preferred. The LRE provisions were reauthorized in all revisions of the law.

Due Process Provisions

In Public Law 94-142, Congress specified the procedures that schools and school personnel would have to follow to ensure due process in decision making. Specifically, when a decision affecting identification, evaluation, or placement of a student with disabilities is to be made, the student's parents or guardians must be given both the opportunity to be heard and the right to have an impartial due process hearing to resolve conflicting opinions.

Schools must provide opportunities for parents to inspect the records that are kept on their children and to challenge material that they believe should not be included in those records. Parents have the right to have their child evaluated by an independent party and to have the results of that evaluation considered when psychoeducational decisions are made. In addition, parents must receive written notification before any education agency can begin an evaluation that might result in changes in the placement of a student.

In the 1997 amendments to IDEA, Congress specified that states must offer mediation as a voluntary option to parents and educators as an initial part of dispute resolution. If mediation is not successful, either party may request a due process hearing. The due process provisions were reauthorized in the 2004 IDEA.

The No Child Left Behind Act of 2001

The No Child Left Behind Act of 2001 is the reform of the federal Elementary and Secondary Education Act. Signed into law on January 8, 2002, the act has several major provisions that affect assessment and instruction of students with disabilities and disadvantaged students. The law requires stronger accountability for results by specifying that states must have challenging state educational standards, test children in grades 3–8 every year, and specify statewide progress objectives that ensure proficiency of every child by grade 12. The law also provides increased flexibility and local control, specifying that states can decide their standards and procedures but at the same time must be held accountable for results. Parents are given expanded educational options under this law, and students who are attending schools judged to be "failing schools" have the right to enroll in other public schools, including public charter schools. A major provision of this law is called "putting reading first," a set of provisions ensuring all-out effort to have every child reading by the end of third grade. These provisions provide funding to schools for intensive reading interventions for children in grades K–3. Finally, the law specifies that all students have the right to be taught using "evidence-based instructional methods"—that is, teaching methods proven to work. The provisions of this law require that states include all students, among them students with disabilities and English-language learners, in their statewide accountability systems.

2004 Reauthorization of IDEA

The Individuals with Disabilities Education Act was reauthorized in 2004. Several of the new requirements of the law have special implications for assessment of students with disabilities. After much debate, Congress removed the requirement that students must have a severe discrepancy between ability and achievement in order to be considered as having a learning disability. It replaced this provision with permission to states and districts to use data on student responsiveness to intervention in making service eligibility decisions. We provide an extensive discussion of assessing response to intervention in Chapter 8. Congress also specified that states must have measurable goals, standards, or objectives for all students with disabilities.

2 Ethical Considerations

Professionals who assess students have the responsibility to engage in ethical behavior. Most professional associations have put together sets of standards to guide the ethical practice of their members; many of these standards relate directly to assessment practices. In publishing ethical and professional standards, the associations express serious concern and commitment to promoting high technical standards for assessment instruments and high ethical standards for the behavior of individuals who work with assessments. Here, we cite a number of important ethical considerations, borrowing heavily from the American Psychological Association's (2002) *Ethical Principles of Psychologists and Code of Conduct*, the National Association of School Psychologists' (2002) *Principles for Professional Ethics*, and the National Education Association's *Code of Ethics of the Education Profession*. We have not cited the standards explicitly, but we have distilled from them a number of broad ethical principles that guide assessment practice and behavior.

Beneficence

Beneficence, or responsible caring, means educational professionals do things that are likely to maximize benefit to students, or at least do no harm. This means that educational professionals always act in the best interests of the students they serve. The assessment of students is a social act that has specific social and educational consequences. Those who assess students use assessment data to make decisions about the students, and these decisions can significantly affect an individual's life opportunities. Those who assess students must accept responsibility for the consequences of their work, and they must make every effort to be certain that their services are used appropriately. In short, they are committed to the application of professional expertise to promote improvement in the quality of life available to the student, family, school, and community. For the individual who assesses students, this ethical standard may mean refusing to engage in assessment activities that are desired by a school system but that are clearly inappropriate.

Recognition of the Boundaries of Professional Competence

Those who are entrusted with the responsibility for assessing and making decisions about students have differing degrees of competence. Not only must professionals regularly engage in self-assessment to be aware of their own limitations but also they should recognize the limitations of the techniques they use. For individuals, this sometimes means refusing to engage in activities in areas in which they lack competence. It also means using techniques that meet recognized standards and engaging in the continuing education necessary to maintain high standards of

"As a professional who will assess students, it is imperative that you accept responsibility for the consequences of your work and work to offset any negative consequences of your work." what does this mean? what negative consequences

competence. As a professional who will assess students, it is imperative that you accept responsibility for the consequences of your work and work to offset any negative consequences of your work.

As schools become increasingly diverse, professionals must demonstrate sensitivity in working with people from different cultural and linguistic backgrounds and with children who have different types of disabling conditions. Assessors should have experience working with students of diverse backgrounds and should demonstrate competence in doing so, or they should refrain from assessing and making decisions about such students.

Respect for the Dignity of Persons

Respect for the dignity of persons means that educational professionals respect students' right to privacy and confidentiality, and that they assess in fair and non-discriminatory ways.

Privacy and Confidentiality of Information

Those who assess students regularly obtain a considerable amount of very personal information about those students. Such information must be held in strict confidence. A general ethical principle held by most professional organizations is that confidentiality may be broken only when there is clear and imminent danger to an individual or to society. Results of pupil performance on tests must not be discussed informally with school staff members. Formal reports of pupil performance on tests must be released only with the permission of the persons tested or their parents or guardians.

Those who assess students are to make provisions for maintaining confidentiality in the storage and disposal of records. When working with minors or other persons who are unable to give voluntary informed consent, assessors are to take special care to protect these persons' best interests.

Fairness and Nondiscrimination in Assessment

Those who assess students are responsible for selecting and administering tests in a fair and nonbiased manner. Assessment approaches must be selected that are valid and that provide an accurate representation of students' skills and abilities rather than of their disabilities. Tests are to be selected and administered so as to be racially and culturally nondiscriminatory, and students should be assessed in their native language or primary mode of communication (for example, Braille or communication boards).

Adherence to Professional Standards on Assessment

A joint committee of the American Educational Research Association, the American Psychological Association, and the National Council on Measurement in Education (1999) published a document titled *Standards for Educational and Psychological Testing*. These standards specify a set of requirements for test development and use. It is imperative that those who develop tests behave in accordance with the standards, and that those who assess students use instruments and techniques that meet the standards.

In Parts 3 and 4 of this text, we review commonly used tests and discuss the extent to which those tests meet the standards specified in *Standards for Educational and Psychological Testing*. We provide information to help test users make informed judgments about the technical adequacy of specific tests. There is no federal or state agency that acts to limit the publication or use of technically inadequate tests. Only by refusing to use technically inadequate tests will users force developers to improve them. After all, if you were a test developer, would you continue to publish a test that few people purchased and used? Would you invest your company's resources to make changes in a technically inadequate test that yielded a large annual profit to your firm if people continued to buy and use it the way it was?

 Test Security

Those who assess students are expected to maintain test security. It is expected that assessors will not reveal to others the content of specific tests or test items. At the same time, assessors must be willing and able to back up with test data decisions that may adversely affect individuals.

CHAPTER COMPREHENSION QUESTIONS

Write your answers to each of the following questions, and then compare your responses to the text.

1. What three major laws affect assessment practices?

2. How do the major components of IDEA (individualized educational plan, least restrictive environment, protection in evaluation procedures, and due process) affect assessment practices?

3. How do the broad ethical principles of beneficence, competence boundaries, respect for the dignity of persons, confidentiality, and fairness affect assessment practices?

> 3. The results of the assessment(s) are held confidentially by the person assessing the student until permission has been given to share the results.

3

Test Scores and How to Use Them

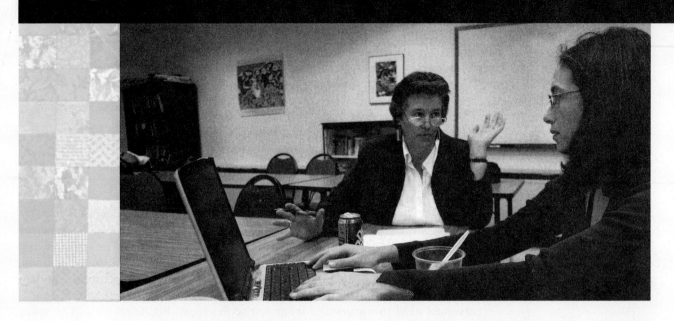

Chapter Goals

1 Understand the basic quantitative concepts that deal with scales of measurement, characteristics of distributions, average scores, measures of dispersion, and correlation.

2 Understand how student performances are scored objectively using percent correct accuracy, fluency, and retention.

3 Understand how test performances are made meaningful through criterion-referenced, achievement standards-referenced, and norm-referenced interpretations.

4 Understand that norms are constructed to be proportionally representative of the population in terms of important personal characteristics (for example, gender and age), contain a large number of people, be representative of today's population, and be relevant for the purposes of assessment.

Key Terms

ordinal scale	objective scoring	age equivalent
equal-interval scale	subjective scoring	grade equivalent
mean	percent correct	percentile ranks (percentiles)
variance	accuracy	
standard deviation	instructional level	standard scores
skew	frustration level	z scores
kurtosis	independent level	T scores
mode	fluency	IQs
median	retention	normal curve equivalents (NCEs)
range	criterion-referenced	
variance	achievement standards-referenced	stanines
correlation coefficient	norm-referenced	norms

THIS CHAPTER IS AN INTRODUCTION TO SOME OF THE BASIC QUANTITATIVE concepts used in assessment. More information about descriptive statistics, test scores, and norms is available for download on the student website. There you will find more detailed explanations, information about how various scores or statistics are calculated, and information about more advanced topics. School personnel need to understand what test scores mean because they will be using test scores throughout their professional careers. Correct interpretations of scores can lead to good decision making, whereas incorrect interpretations cannot. To illustrate, suppose you are a teacher and learn that 65 percent of the students in your class earned scores of "proficient" in reading when they took the state test last spring; 22 percent of your students earned scores of "basic." You are told that Willis has an IQ of 87 and is considered a "slow learner," and that he scored at the 22nd percentile on a measure of vocabulary. Elaine is said to have a grade equivalent of 4.2 on a math test. You are also told that your class scored at the state median on a measure of writing. Obviously, this information is supposed to mean something to you and could affect how you will teach. What do these scores mean? How do they affect the instructional decisions you will make?

1 Basic Quantitative Concepts

The basic quantitative concepts for beginning students deal with scales of measurement, characteristics of sets of scores, average scores, measures of dispersion, and correlation.

Scales of Measurement

Assessment in the real world is a quantitative activity. The type of mathematical operations that can be properly done depends on the nature of the score. There are four types of scores: nominal, ordinal, ratio, and equal interval (Stevens, 1951). The four scales differ in the relationship between possible consecutive values on the measurement continuum, for example, the difference between 1 and 2 inches on a ruler. In education and psychology, ordinal and equal interval are by far the most commonly used scales; nominal and ratio scales are fairly rare.[1]

Ordinal scales order things from better to worse or from worse to better (for example, good, better, best, or novice, intermediate, and expert). On ordinal scales, the magnitude of the difference between adjacent values is unknown and unlikely to be equal. Thus, we cannot determine how much better an *intermediate* performance is than a *novice* performance or if the difference between *novice* and *intermediate* is the same as the difference between *intermediate* and *expert*. Because the differences between adjacent values are unknown and presumed unequal, ordinal scores cannot be added together or averaged.

Equal-interval scales also order things from better to worse. However, unlike ordinal scales, the magnitude of the difference between adjacent values is known and is equal. Examples of equal-interval scales in everyday life include the measurement of time, length, weight, and so forth. Because the differences between adjacent values are equal, equal-interval scores can be added, subtracted, multiplied, and divided.

Characteristics of Distributions

Sets of equal-interval scores (for example, student scores on a classroom test) can be described in terms of four characteristics: mean, variance, skew, and kurtosis. Each of these characteristics can be calculated, although there is no need for us to go into their calculations. The *mean* is the arithmetic average of the scores (for example, the mean height for U.S. women is their average height). The *variance* describes the distance between each score and every other score in the set. These characteristics are very important and are discussed repeatedly throughout this book.

Skew refers to the symmetry of a distribution of scores. In a symmetrical set of scores, the scores above the mean mirror the scores below the mean. When a test is easy and many students earn high scores, whereas only a few students earn low scores, the distribution of scores is not symmetrical; it is skewed. There are more scores above the mean and more extreme scores below the mean, as shown in Figure 3.1 (left). The opposite happens when a test is difficult; many students earn low scores, whereas a few students earn high scores. There are more scores below the mean and more extreme scores above the mean, as shown in Figure 3.1 (right).

Kurtosis describes the peakedness of a curve—that is, the rate at which a curve rises and falls. Relatively flat distributions spread out test takers and are called *platykurtic*. (The prefix *plat-* means flat, as in platypus or plateau.) Relatively fast-rising distributions do not spread out test takers and are called *leptokurtic*. Figure 3.2 illustrates a platykurtic and a leptokurtic curve.

---

[1]On *nominal scales*, adjacent values have no inherent relationship; they merely name values on the scale (for example, male and female or telephone numbers that name a specific telephone). Thus, it makes no sense to find the average value on a nominal scale; for example, there is no meaning for a number that is the average of the telephone numbers of all of one's friends. *Ratio scales* are equal-interval scales that have an absolute and logical zero, whereas equal-interval scales do not. For example, 0°C is not the absence of heat, nor is 0°F. Because equal-interval scales do not have a logical zero, ratios using equal-interval (or ordinal, of course) data make no sense; for example, 100°C is not twice as hot as 50°C. Ratio scales do have an absolute zero. Thus, if John weighs 300 pounds and Bob weighs 150 pounds, John weighs twice as much as Bob.

FIGURE 3.1
Positive and
Negative Skews

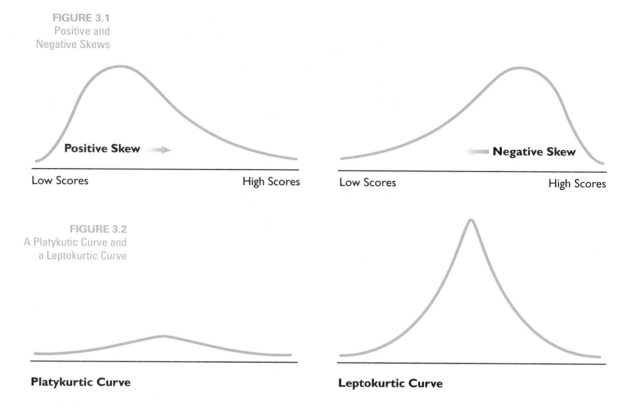

FIGURE 3.2
A Platykutic Curve and
a Leptokurtic Curve

Platykurtic Curve   **Leptokurtic Curve**

Average Scores

An average gives us a general description of how a group as a whole performed. There are three different averages: mode, median, and mean.

The *mode* is defined as the score most frequently obtained. A mode (if there is one) can be found for data on a nominal, ordinal, ratio, or equal-interval scale. Distributions may have two modes (if they do, they are called "bimodal distributions"), or they may have more than two.

The *median* is the point in a distribution above which are 50 percent of test takers (not test scores) and below which are 50 percent of test takers (not test scores). Medians can be found for data on ordinal, equal-interval, and ratio scales; they must not be used with nominal scales. The median score may or may not actually be earned by a student.

The *mean* is the arithmetic average of the scores in a distribution and is the most important average for use in assessment. It is the sum of the scores divided by the number of scores; the symbol $\bar{X}$. The mean, like the median, may or may not be earned by any child in the distribution. Means should be computed only for data equal-interval (and ratio) scales.

Measures of Dispersion

Dispersion tells us how scores are spread out above and below the average score. Three measures of dispersion are range, variance, and standard deviation. The *range* is the distance between the extremes of a distribution, including the extremes; it is the highest score less the lowest score plus 1. Range is a relatively crude measure of dispersion because it is based on only two pieces of information. Range can be calculated with ordinal data (for example, "ratings ranged from excellent to poor") and equal-interval data.

The variance and the standard deviation are the most important indexes of dispersion. The *variance* (symbolized as S^2 or σ^2) is a numerical index describing the dispersion of a set of scores around the mean of the distribution.[2] Because the variance is an average, the number of cases in the set or the distribution does not affect it. Large sets of scores may have large or small variances; small sets of scores may have large or small variances. Also, because the variance is measured in terms of distance from the mean, it is not related to the actual value of the mean. Distributions with large means may have large or small variances; distributions with small means may have large or small variances.

The *standard deviation* (symbolized as S or σ) is the positive square root of the variance.[3] It is frequently used as a unit of measurement in much the same way that an inch or a ton is used as a unit of measurement. When scores are equal interval, they can be measured in terms of standard deviation units from the mean. The advantage of measuring in standard deviations is that when the distribution is normal, we know exactly what proportion of cases occurs between the mean and the particular standard deviation. As shown in Figure 3.3, approximately 34 percent of the cases in a normal distribution always occur between the mean and one standard deviation (S) either above or below the mean. Thus, approximately 68 percent of all cases occur between one standard deviation below and one standard deviation above the mean (34% + 34% = 68%). Approximately 14 percent of the cases occur between one and two standard deviations below the mean or between one and two standard deviations above the mean. Thus, approximately 48 percent of all cases occur between the mean and two standard deviations either above or below the mean (34% + 14% = 48%). Approximately 96 percent of all cases occur between two standard deviations above and two standard deviations below the mean.

As shown by the positions and values for scales A, B, and C in Figure 3.3, it does not matter what the values of the mean and the standard deviation are. The relationship holds for various obtained values of the mean and the standard deviation. For scale A, where the mean is 25 and the standard deviation is 5, 34 percent of the scores occur between the mean (25) and one standard deviation below the mean (20) or between the mean and one standard deviation above the mean (30). Similarly, for scale B, where the mean is 50 and the standard deviation is 10, 34 percent of the cases occur between the mean (50) and one standard deviation below the mean (40) or between the mean and one standard deviation above the mean (60).

Correlation

Correlation quantifies relationships between variables. *Correlation coefficients* are numerical indexes of these relationships. They tell us the extent to which any two variables go together—that is, the extent to which changes in one variable are

---

[2] S^2 is the symbol for the variance of a sample, whereas σ^2 is the symbol for the variance of a population.

[3] S is the symbol for the standard deviation of a sample, whereas σ is the symbol for the standard deviation of a population.

FIGURE 3.3
Scores on Three Scales,
Expressed in Standard
Deviation Units

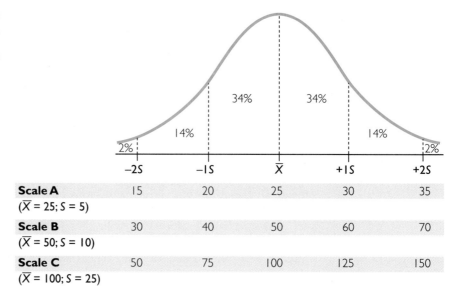

	−2S	−1S	X̄	+1S	+2S
Scale A (X̄ = 25; S = 5)	15	20	25	30	35
Scale B (X̄ = 50; S = 10)	30	40	50	60	70
Scale C (X̄ = 100; S = 25)	50	75	100	125	150

reflected by changes in the second variable. These coefficients are used in measurement to estimate both the reliability and the validity of a test. Correlation coefficients can range in value from .00 to either +1.00 or −1.00. The sign (+ or −) indicates the direction of the relationship; the number indicates the magnitude of the relationship. A correlation coefficient of .00 between two variables means that there is no relationship between the variables. The variables are independent; changes in one variable are not related to changes in the second variable. A correlation coefficient of either +1.00 or −1.00 indicates a perfect relationship between two variables. Thus, if you know a person's score on one variable, you can predict that person's score on the second variable without error. Correlation coefficients between .00 and 1.00 (or −1.00) allow some prediction, and the greater the coefficient, the greater its predictive power.

2   Scoring Student Performance

Tests are structured situations in which predetermined materials are presented to an individual in a predetermined manner in order to evaluate that individual's responses. How a person's responses are scored and interpreted depends on the materials used, the intent of the test author, and the diagnostician's intention.

Objective Versus Subjective Scoring

There are two approaches to scoring a student's response: objective and subjective. By *objective scoring*, we mean scoring that is based on observable qualities and not influenced by emotion, guess, or personal bias. By *subjective scoring*, we mean scoring that is not based on observable qualities but relies on personal impressions and private criteria. The clear intent of the Individuals with Disabilities Education Act is to require objective measurement (*Federal Register* 71(156), August 14, 2006).

There is simply no doubt that objective measurement is less likely to be influenced by extraneous factors such as a student's race, gender, appearance, religion, or even name. When multiple examiners or observers use objective scoring procedures to evaluate student performance, they obtain the same scores. This is not the case when subjective scoring procedures are used. Although some educators advocate celebrating subjectivity in scoring, we should be skeptical of scores associated with global ratings, scoring rubrics, and portfolio assessments.

Summarizing Student Performance

When a single behavior or skill is of interest and assessed only once, evaluators usually employ a dichotomous scoring scheme: right or wrong, present or absent, and so forth. Typically, the correct or right option of the dichotomy is defined precisely; the other option is defined by default. For example, a correct response to "$1 + 2 = ?$" might be defined as "3, written intelligibly, written after the $=$ sign, and written in the correct orientation"; a wrong response would be one that fails to meet one or more of the criteria for a correct response.

A single response can also be awarded partial credit that can range along a continuum from completely correct to completely incorrect. For example, a teacher might objectively score a student response and give partial credit for a response because the student used the correct procedures to solve a mathematics problem even though the student made a computational error. Partial credit can be useful when trying to document slow progress toward a goal. For example, in a life-skills curriculum, a teacher might scale the item "drinking from a cup without assistance" as shown in Table 3.1. Of course, each point on the continuum requires a definition for the partial credit to be awarded.

When an evaluation is concerned with multiple items, a tester may simply report how a student performed on each and every item. More often, however, the tester summarizes the student's performance over all the test items to provide an index of total performance. The sum of correct responses is usually the first summary index computed.

Although the number correct provides a limited amount of information about student performance, it lacks important information that provides a context for understanding that performance. Five summary scores are commonly used to provide a more meaningful context for the total score: the percent correct, percent accuracy, and the rate of correct response, fluency, and retention.

Percent correct is widely used in a variety of assessment contexts. The percent correct is calculated by dividing the number correct by the number possible and

TABLE 3.1	Drinking from a Cup	
Level	**Definition**	
Well	Drinks with little spilling or assistance	
Acceptably	Dribbles a few drops	
Learning	Requires substantial prompting or spills	
Beginning	Requires manual guidance	

multiplying that quotient by 100. This index is best used with *power tests*—tests for which students have sufficient time to answer all of the questions.

Accuracy is the number of correct responses divided by the number of attempted responses multiplied by 100. Accuracy is appropriately used when an assessment procedure precludes a student from responding to all items.[4] For example, a teacher may ask a student to read orally for 2 minutes, but it may not be possible for that student (or any other student) to read the entire passage in the time allotted. Thus, Benny may attempt 175 words in a 350-word passage in 2 minutes; if he reads 150 words correctly, his percentage correct would be approximately 86 percent—that is, $100 \times (150/175)$.

Percentages are given verbal labels that are intended to facilitate instruction. The two most commonly used labels are "mastery" and "instructional level." *Mastery* divides the percentage continuum in two: Mastery is generally set at 90 or 95 percent correct, and nonmastery is less than the level of mastery. The criterion for mastery is arbitrary, and in real life we frequently set the level for mastery too low.

Instructional level divides the percentage range into three segments: frustration, instructional, and independent levels. When material is too difficult for a student, it is said to be at the *frustration level*; this level is usually defined as material for which a student knows less than 85 percent of it. An *instructional level* provides a degree of challenge where a student is likely to be successful, but success is not guaranteed; this level is usually defined by student responses between 85 and 95 percent correct. The *independent level* is defined as the point where a student can perform without assistance; this level is usually defined as student performance of more than 95 percent correct. For example, in reading, students who decode more than 95 percent of the words should be able to read a passage without assistance; students who decode between 85 and 95 percent of the words in a passage should be able to read and comprehend that passage with assistance; and students who cannot decode 85 percent of the words in a passage will probably have great difficulty decoding and comprehending the material, even with assistance.[5]

Fluency is the number of correct responses per minute. Teachers often want their students to have a supply of information at their fingertips so that they can respond fluently (or automatically) without thinking. For example, teachers may want their students to recognize sight words without having to sound them out, recall addition facts without having to think about them, or supply Spanish words for their English equivalents. Criterion rates for successful performance are usually determined empirically. For example, readers with satisfactory comprehension usually read connected prose at rates of 100 or more words per minute (Mercer & Mercer, 1985). Readers interested in desired rates for a variety of academic skills are referred to Salvia and Hughes (1990).

Retention refers to the percentage of learned information that is recalled. Retention may also be termed recall, maintenance, or memory of what has been learned. Regardless of the label, it is calculated in the same way: Divide the number recalled by the number originally learned, and multiply that ratio by 100. For example, if Helen learned 40 sight vocabulary words and recalled 30 of them 2 weeks

---

[4]A situation in which there are more opportunities to respond than time to respond is termed a *free operant*. Free operant situations arise in assessments that are timed to allow the opportunity for unlimited increases in rate.

[5]Students should not be given homework (independent practice) until they are at the independent level.

later, her retention would be 75 percent—that is, $100 \times (30/40)$. Because forgetting becomes more likely as the interval between the learning and the retention assessment increases, retention is usually qualified by the period of time between attainment of mastery and assessment of recall. Thus, Helen's retention would be stated as 75 percent over a 2-week period.

3 Interpretation of Test Performance

There are three common ways to interpret an individual student's performance in special and inclusive education: criterion-referenced, standards-referenced, and norm-referenced.

Criterion-Referenced Interpretations

When we are interested in a student's knowledge about a single fact, we compare a student's performance against an objective and absolute standard (criterion) of performance. Thus, to be considered criterion-referenced, there must be a clear, objective criterion for each of the correct responses to each question or to each portion of the question if partial credit is to be awarded.

Achievement Standards-Referenced Interpretations

In large-scale assessments, school districts must ascertain the degree to which they are meeting state and national achievement standards. To do so, states specify the qualities and skills that competent learners need to demonstrate. These indices consist of four components.

- Levels of performance: The entire range of possible student performances (from very poor to excellent) is divided into a number of bands or ranges. Verbal labels that are attached to each of these ranges indicate increasing levels of accomplishment. For example, an *emerging* performance is less accomplished than an *advanced* performance, whereas an *advanced* performance is less accomplished than a *proficient* performance.
- Objective criteria: Each level of performance is defined by precise, objective descriptions of student accomplishment relative to the task. These descriptions can be quantified.
- Examples: Examples of student work at each level are provided. These examples illustrate the range of performance within each level.
- Cut scores: Cutoff scores are provided. These scores provide quantitative criteria that clearly delineate student performance level.

Norm-Referenced Interpretations

Sometimes testers are interested in knowing how a student's performance compares to the performances of other students—usually students of similar demographic characteristics (age, gender, grade in school, and so forth). In order to make this type of comparison, a student's score is transformed into a *derived score*. There are two types of derived scores: developmental scores and scores of relative standing.

Scenario in Assessment

Mr. Stanley

Mr. Stanley is a first-year special education teacher who teaches intermediate-level children with learning problems in a district elementary school. His school's principal asked him to participate in a multidisciplinary team meeting for a student who has been experiencing serious learning difficulties. Because Mr. Stanley had never participated in an initial evaluation before and was a bit nervous, he asked the school psychologist what would happen at the meeting. The psychologist told him that she (the psychologist) would go over the student's test results, specifically her scores on the Wechsler Intelligence Scale for Children (IV) and the Woodcock–Johnson Tests of Achievement (III). She also told him to expect that parents and the general education teacher would provide their input to the process.

To prepare for the meeting, Mr. Stanley looked up the Wechsler and Woodcock–Johnson tests in his college assessment text. Therein he reviewed what behaviors the tests sampled and the derived scores he could expect to see reported. At the meeting, the psychologist reported the percentiles and standard scores earned by the student, and Mr. Stanley knew exactly what each meant. With this knowledge, he was able to participate meaningfully in the team's discussion of the student's disability and possible need for special education.

Developmental Scores

There are two types of developmental scores: developmental equivalents and developmental quotients. *Developmental equivalents* may be age equivalents or grade equivalents. Developmental scores are based on the average performance of individuals of a given age or grade. Suppose the average performance of 10-year-old children on a test was 27 correct. Furthermore, suppose that Horace answered 27 questions correctly. Horace answered as many questions correctly as the average of 10-year-old children. He would earn an age equivalent of 10 years. An *age equivalent* means that a child's raw score is the average (the median or mean) performance for that age group. Age equivalents are expressed in years and months; a hyphen is used in age scores (for example, 7-1 for 7 years, 1 month old). If the test measured mental ability, Horace's score would have a mental age; if the test measured language, it would be called a language age. A *grade equivalent* means that a child's raw score is the average (the median or mean) performance for a particular grade. Grade equivalents are expressed in grades and tenths of grades; a decimal point is used in grade scores (for example, 7.1). Age-equivalent and grade-equivalent scores are interpreted as a performance equal to the average of X-year-olds and the average of Xth graders' performance, respectively.

The interpretation of age and grade equivalents requires great care. Five problems occur in the use of developmental scores.

1. *Systematic misinterpretation:* Students who earn an age equivalent of 12-0 have merely answered as many questions correctly as the average for children 12 years of age. They have not necessarily performed as a 12-year-old child would; they may well have attacked the problems in a different way or demonstrated a different performance pattern from many 12-year-old

students. For example, a second grader and a ninth grader might both earn grade equivalents of 4.0, but they probably have not performed identically. We have known for more than 30 years that younger children perform lower level work with greater accuracy (for instance, successfully answered 38 of the 45 problems attempted), whereas older children attempt more problems with less accuracy (for instance, successfully answered 38 of the 78 problems attempted) (Thorndike & Hagen, 1978).

2. *Need for interpolation and extrapolation:* Average age and grade scores are estimated for groups of children who are never tested. Interpolated scores are estimated for groups of students between groups actually tested. For example, students within 30 days of their eighth birthday may be tested, but age equivalents are estimated for students who are 8-1, 8-2, and so on. Extrapolated scores are estimated for students who are younger and older than the children tested. For example, a student may earn an age equivalent of 5-0 even though no child younger than 6 was tested.

3. *Promotion of typological thinking:* An average 12-0 pupil is a statistical abstraction. The average 12-year-old is in a family with 1.2 other children, 0.8 of a dog, and 2.3 automobiles; in other words, the average child does not exist. Average 12-0 children more accurately represent a range of performances, typically the middle 50 percent.

4. *Implication of a false standard of performance:* Educators expect a third grader to perform at a third-grade level and a 9-year-old to perform at a 9-year-old level. However, the way equivalent scores are constructed ensures that 50 percent of any age or grade group will perform below age or grade level because half of the test takers earn scores below the median.

5. *Tendency for scales to be ordinal, not equal interval:* The line relating the number correct to the various ages is typically curved, with a flattening of the curve at higher ages or grades. Figure 3.4 is a typical developmental curve. Because the scales are ordinal and not based on equal interval units, scores on these scales should not be added or multiplied in any computation.

To interpret a developmental score (for example, a mental age), it is usually helpful to know the age of the person whose score is being interpreted. Knowing developmental age as well as chronological age (CA) allows us to judge an individual's relative performance. Suppose that Ana earns a mental age (MA) of 120 months. If Ana is 8 years (96 months) old, her performance is above average. If she is 35 years old, however, it is below average. The relationship between developmental age and chronological age is often quantified as a developmental quotient. For example, a *ratio IQ* is

$$IQ = MA \text{ (in months)} \times 100 \div CA \text{ (in months)}$$

All the problems that apply to developmental levels also apply to developmental quotients.

Percentile Family

Percentile ranks (*percentiles*) are derived scores that indicate the percentage of people whose scores are at or below a given raw score. Although percentiles are

FIGURE 3.4
Mean Number Correct for 10 Age
Groups: An Example of Arriving
at Age-Equivalent Scores

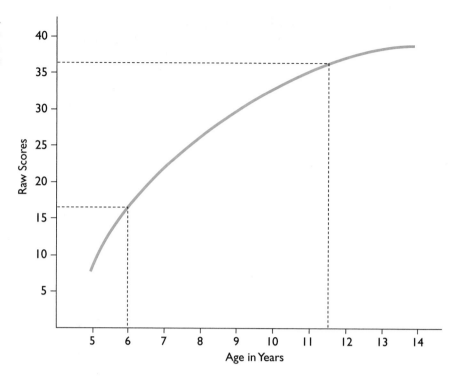

easily calculated, test authors usually provide tables that convert raw scores on a test to percentiles for each age or grade of test takers. Interpretation of percentiles is straightforward. If Bill earns a percentile of 48 on a test, Bill's test score is equal to or better than those of 48 percent of the test takers. (It is also correct to say that 53 percent of the test takers earned scores equal to or better than that of Bill.) Theoretically, percentiles can range from 0.1 to 99.9—that is, a performance that is equal to or better than those of one-tenth of 1 percent of the test takers to a performance that is equal to or better than those of 99.9 percent of the test takers. The 50th percentile rank is the median.

Occasionally, a score is reported within a percentile band. The two most common are deciles and quartiles:

■ *Deciles* are bands of percentiles that are 10 percentile ranks in width; each decile contains 10 percent of the norm group. The first decile is percentiles wide, from 0.1 to 9.9; the second ranges from 10 to 19.9; the tenth decile goes from 90 to 99.9.

■ *Quartiles* are bands of percentiles that are 25 percentiles wide; each quartile contains 25 percent of the norm group. The first quartile contains percentile from 0.1 to 24.9; the fourth quartile contains the ranks 75 to 99.9.

Percentiles allow us to compare the performances of several students even when they differ in age or grade. For example, it is not particularly helpful to know that George is 70 inches tall, Bridget is 6 feet 3 inches tall, Bruce is 1.93 meters tall, and Alexandra is 177.8 centimeters tall. It is much simpler to compare their heights when the measurements are in the same units. Converting their heights to feet and inches, we see that George is 5 feet 10 inches, Bridget is 6 feet 3 inches,

Bruce is 6 feet 4 inches, and Alexandra is 5 feet 10 inches. Percentiles put raw scores into comparable units. Similarly, it is not particularly helpful to know that George got 75 percent correct on the spelling portion of a group-administered test of achievement, 56 percent correct on the reading comprehension portion, and 63 percent on the mathematics portion. Without knowing how other students scored, such information offers little, if any, insight into George's achievement. However, converting the percents correct into percentiles allows direct and easy comparison: 54th percentile in spelling, 47th percentile in reading comprehension, and 61st percentile in mathematics. The major disadvantage of percentiles is that they are not equal-interval scores. Therefore, they cannot be added together or subtracted from one another. Thus, it would be incorrect to say that George is 7 percentiles better in reading comprehension than in spelling, although it is correct to say that George did relatively better in spelling than in reading comprehension.

Standard Score Family

Standard scores are derived scores with a predetermined mean and standard deviation. The most basic standard score is the z distribution. In the distribution of z scores, the mean is always equal to 0.[6] In the distribution of z scores, the standard deviation is always equal to 1.[7] Thus, regardless of the mean and standard deviation of the raw (obtained) scores, z scores transform those scores into a new distribution with a mean of 0 and a standard deviation of 1. Positive scores are above the mean; negative scores are below the mean. The larger the number, the more above or below the mean is the score. z scores are interpreted as being X number of standard deviations above or below the mean. When the distribution of scores is bell shaped or normal, we know the exact percentile that corresponds to a z score.

In assessment, it is customary to transform z scores into different standard scores with predetermined means and standard deviations. Four such scores are common in assessment: T scores, IQs, normal curve equivalents, and stanines.

- A *T score* is a standard score with a mean of 50 and a standard deviation of 10. A person earning a T score of 40 scored one standard deviation below the mean, whereas a person earning a T score of 60 scored one standard deviation above the mean.

- *IQs* are standard scores with a mean of 100 and a standard deviation of 15.[8] A person earning an IQ of 85 scored one standard deviation below the mean, whereas a person earning an IQ of 115 scored one standard deviation above the mean.[9]

---

[6]This transformation is achieved by subtracting the mean of the obtained scores from each obtained score.

[7]This transformation is achieved by dividing the difference between the obtained score less the mean of the obtained scores by the obtained standard deviation.

[8]Some older tests have standard deviations that are 16 or another value.

[9]When it was first introduced, the IQ was defined as the ratio of mental age to chronological age, multiplied by 100. Statisticians soon found that MA has different variances and standard deviations at different chronological ages. Consequently, the same ratio IQ has different meanings at different ages—the same ratio IQ corresponds to different z scores and percentiles at different ages. To remedy this situation, scientist stopped using ratio IQs and began converting scores to standard scores.

▪ *Normal curve equivalents* (NCEs) are standard scores with a mean equal to 50 and a standard deviation equal to 21.06. Although the standard deviation may at first appear strange, this scale divides the normal curve into 100 equal intervals.

▪ *Stanines* (short for standard nines) are standard-score bands that divide a distribution into nine parts. The first stanine includes all scores that are 1.75 standard deviations or more below the mean, and the ninth stanine includes all scores 1.75 or more standard deviations above the mean. The second through eighth stanines are each 0.5 standard deviation in width, with the fifth stanine ranging from 0.25 standard deviations below the mean to 0.25 standard deviations above the mean.

Standard scores are frequently more difficult to interpret than percentile scores because the concepts of means and standard deviations are not widely understood by people without some statistical knowledge. Thus, standard scores may be more difficult for students and their parents to understand. Aside from this disadvantage, standard scores offer all the advantages of percentiles plus an additional advantage: Because standard scores are equal-interval, they can be combined (for example, added or averaged).[10]

Concluding Comments on Derived Scores

Test authors provide tables to convert raw scores into derived scores. Thus, test users do not have to calculate derived scores. Standard scores can be transformed into other standard scores readily; they can be converted to percentiles without conversion tables only when the distribution of scores is normal. In normal distributions, the relationship between percentiles and standard scores is known. Figure 3.5 compares various standard scores and percentiles for normal distributions. When the distribution of scores is not normal, conversion tables are necessary in order to convert percentiles to standard scores (or vice versa). These conversion tables are test specific, so only a test author can provide them. Moreover, conversion tables are always required in order to convert developmental scores to scores of relative standing, even when the distribution of test scores is normal. If the only derived score available for a test is an age equivalent, then there is no way for a test user to convert raw scores to percentiles. However, age or grade equivalents can be converted back to raw scores, which can be converted to standard scores if the raw score mean and standard deviation are provided.

---

[10]Standard scores also solve another subtle problem. When scores are combined in a total or composite, the elements of that composite (for example, 18 scores from weekly spelling tests that are combined to obtain a semester average) do not count the same (that is, they do not carry the same weight) unless they have equal variances. Tests that have larger variances contribute more to the composite than tests with smaller variances. When each of the elements has been standardized into the same standard scores (for example, when each of the weekly spelling tests has been standardized as z scores), the elements (that is, the weekly scores) will carry exactly the same weight when they are combined. Moreover, the only way a teacher can weight tests differentially is to standardize all the tests and then multiply by the weight. For example, if a teacher wished to count the second test as three times the first test, the scores on both tests would have to be standardized, and the scores on the second test would then be multiplied by three before the scores were combined.

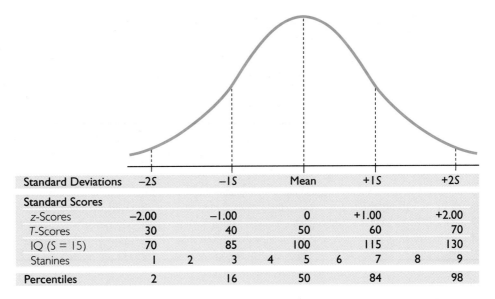

Standard Deviations	−2S		−1S		Mean		+1S		+2S
Standard Scores									
z-Scores	−2.00		−1.00		0		+1.00		+2.00
T-Scores	30		40		50		60		70
IQ (S = 15)	70		85		100		115		130
Stanines	1	2	3	4	5	6	7	8	9
Percentiles	2		16		50		84		98

The selection of the particular type of score to use and to report depends on the purpose of testing and the sophistication of the consumer. In our opinion, developmental scores should never be used. Both laypeople and professionals readily misinterpret these scores. In order to understand the precise meaning of developmental scores, the interpreter must generally know both the mean and the standard deviation and then convert the developmental score to a more meaningful score, a score of relative standing. Various professional organizations (for example, the International Reading Association, the American Psychological Association, the National Council on Measurement in Education, and the Council for Exceptional Children) also hold very negative official opinions about developmental scores and quotients.

Standard scores are convenient for test authors. Their use allows an author to give equal weight to various test components or subtests. Their utility for the consumer is twofold. First, if the score distribution is normal, the consumer can readily convert standard scores to percentile ranks. Second, because standard scores are equal-interval scores, they are useful in analyzing strengths and weaknesses of individual students and in research.

We favor the use of percentiles. These unpretentious scores require the fewest assumptions for accurate interpretation. The scale of measurement need only be ordinal, although it is very appropriate to compute percentiles on equal-interval or ratio data. The distribution of scores need not be normal; percentiles can be computed for any shape of distribution. Professionals, parents, and students readily understand them. Most important, however, is the fact that percentiles tell us nothing more than what any norm-referenced derived score can tell us—namely, an individual's relative standing in a group. Reporting scores in percentiles may remove some of the aura surrounding test scores, and it permits test results to be presented in terms users can understand.

Scenario in Assessment

Kate

Kate returned from her first day of classes at the junior high school and told her parents about her classes. All seemed to be just what she expected except for her math class: None of her friends were in the class, and she already knew how to do all the math the teacher talked about teaching them that year. Her father called the school the next day and was able to meet with Kate's counselor that afternoon. The counselor explained that math class was tracked on the basis of the students' IQs, and since Kate's IQ was less than 100 she was put into the slowest math group.

Because all of Kate's previous intelligence tests were well above average, her dad asked to see the actual results of her test. The counselor produced the computer printout with all of his students' IQs, covered the names of all students except for Kate's, and showed Kate's dad the printout. Sure enough, the number next to his daughter's name was 95. When her dad scanned up the column to the heading, he found the word "percentile." The counselor had read a percentile as a standard score, and his error made quite a difference. Kate's IQ was not 95; it was 124. She did not belong in the slowest math group; she belonged in pre-algebra.

Knowing the meaning of derived scores is essential when educational decisions are based on those scores.

4 Norms

Normative groups allow us to compare one person's performance to the performance of others. Whenever we make such a comparison, it is important to know who those other persons are. For example, suppose Kareem earned a percentile rank of 50 on an intelligence test. If the norm group comprised only students enrolled in programs for the mentally retarded, a score at the 50th percentile would indicate limited intellectual ability. However, if the norm group consisted of individuals enrolled in programs for the gifted, Kareem's score would indicate superior intellectual ability. If we wanted to know Kareem's general intellectual ability, it would make sense to compare his test performance to a representative sample of all children.

It is also important that a person's performance is compared to that of an appropriate group. Normative comparisons can range from national to local, with local being a school district, a specific school, or even a specific classroom. To illustrate the latter, suppose a teacher (Ms. Lane) may be concerned that Mike is not participating sufficiently in classroom discussions. To verify that concern, she could select two or three students who are participating at appropriate levels—not the best participants but satisfactory participants. During the next day or two, she could then count the number of times Mike offered a contribution to a discussion and compare his participation with that of the three comparison students. The performance of the comparison students is, by her definition, satisfactory. If Mike's performance is comparable to theirs, his performance is also satisfactory.

Often, larger school districts develop norms by administering an achievement test that matches their curricula to all their students. Then districtwide means and standard deviations can be used to convert individual scores to standard scores. This information allows two useful comparisons. First, the achievement of individual students can be compared to that of other students in the district in order to identify students in need of additional services, either remedial or enriching. Second, standard scores averaged by school allow school-by-school comparisons that can identify schools in which achievement is generally a problem. Whole states do essentially the same thing to evaluate the educational attainment by school districts.

Unlike local norms where an entire population of students is tested, national norms always involve sampling, and it is essential that we know the characteristics and abilities of the people sampled. Obviously, the accuracy and meaningfulness of a derived score for one student is inextricably tied to the characteristics of the norm sample. Thus, "it is important that the reference populations be carefully and clearly described" (American Educational Research Association [AERA], American Psychological Association, & National Council on Measurement in Education, 1999, p. 51).[11] This description is absolutely essential for test users to judge if a test taker can be reasonably compared to the individuals within the norm sample. Representativeness hinges on two questions: (1) Does the norm sample contain individuals with relevant characteristics and experiences? and (2) Are the characteristics and experiences present in the sample in the same proportion as they are in the population of reference?[12]

Important Characteristics

What makes a characteristic relevant depends on the construct being measured. Some characteristics have a clear logical and empirical relationship to a person's development and are important for any psychoeducational construct.

Gender

Some differences between males and females may be relevant in understanding a student's test score. For example, girls tend to physically develop faster than boys during the first year or two, and many more boys have delayed maturation than do girls during the preschool and primary school years. After puberty, men tend to be bigger and stronger than women. In addition to physical differences, gender role expectations may differ and systematically limit the types of activities in which a child participates because of modeling, peer pressure, or the responses of significant adults.

Nevertheless, on most psychological and educational tests, gender differences are small, and the distributions of scores of males and females tend to overlap considerably. When gender differences are minor, norm groups clearly should contain the appropriate proportions of males (approximately 48 percent) and females (approximately 52 percent)—the proportion found in the general U.S. population. However, when gender differences are substantial, the correct course of action depends on the purpose of the normative comparison. If a test

[11]In practice, it is also impossible to test the entire population because the membership of the population is constantly changing. Fortunately, the characteristics of a population can be accurately estimated from the characteristics of a representative sample.

[12]Characteristics expressed by less than 1 or 2 percent of the population may not be represented accurately.

is intended to identify students with developmental lags and if gender differences are pronounced, it is better to have separate norms for males and females. For example, if 3-year-old Aaron earns a percentile of 45 on a developmental test that has both boys and girls in the norms, his score indicates that his development is slightly behind that of other children. However, he may actually be doing well for a boy at that age. On the other hand, if the purpose is to identify the students with the best background for advanced placement in a subject where there are gender differences, it is probably better to have a single norm sample composed of males and females.

Age

Chronological age is an important consideration for developmental skills and abilities. Norms for tests of ability compare the performances of individuals of essentially the same age. It would make no sense to compare the running performance of a 2-year-old to that of a 4-year-old.

We have known for more than 40 years that different psychological abilities develop at different rates.[13] When an ability or skill is developing rapidly (for example, locomotion in infants and toddlers), the age range of the norm group must be much less than 1 year. Thus, on scales used to assess infants and young children, we often see norms in 3-month ranges. For children of school age, differences of less than a few months are usually unimportant. Thus, we typically see norms in 6-month and 12-month ranges. After an ability has matured, there may be no meaningful differences over several years. As a result, we often see norms in 10-year ranges on adult scales. Therefore, although 1-year norms are most common, developmental theory and research can suggest norms of lesser or greater age ranges.

Grade in School

All achievement tests should measure learned facts and concepts that have been taught in school. The more grades completed by students (that is, the more schooling), the more they should have been taught. Thus, the most useful norm comparisons are usually made to students of the same grade, regardless of their ages.[14] It is also important to note that students of different ages are present in most grades; for example, some 7-year-old children may not be enrolled in school, some may be in kindergarten, some in first grade, some in second grade, and some even in third grade.

Acculturation of Parents

Acculturation is an imprecise concept that refers to an understanding of the language (including conventions and pragmatics), history, values, and social conventions of society at large. Nowhere are the complexities of acculturation more readily illustrated than in the area of language. Acculturation requires people to know more than standard American English; they must also know the appropriate contexts for various words and idioms, appropriate volume and distance between speaker and listener, appropriate posture to indicate respect, and so forth.

---

[13]See, for example, Guilford (1967, pp. 417–426).
[14]In situations in which students are not grouped by grade, it may be necessary to use age comparisons.

Because acculturation is a broad and somewhat diffuse construct, it is difficult to define or measure precisely. Typically, test authors use the educational or occupational attainment (socioeconomic status) of the parents as a general indication of the level of acculturation of the home. The socioeconomic status of a student's parents is strongly related to that student's scores on all sorts of tests—intelligence, achievement, adaptive behavior, social functioning, and so forth. The children of middle- and upper-class parents have tended to score higher on such tests (see Gottesman, 1968; Herrnstein & Murray, 1994). Whatever the reasons for class differences in child development, norm samples certainly must include all segments of society (in the same proportion as in the general population) in order to be representative.

Race and Cultural Identity

Race and culture are particularly relevant to our discussion of norms for two reasons. First, the scientific and educational communities have often been insensitive and occasionally blatantly racist and classist. Second, differences in *tested* achievement and ability persist among races and cultural groups, although these differences continue to narrow.[15] Inclusion of individuals of all racial, cultural, and socioeconomic groups is important for two reasons. First, to the extent that individuals of different groups undergo cultural experiences that differ even within a given social class and geographic region, norm samples that exclude (or underrepresent) one group are unrepresentative of the total population. Second, if individuals from various groups are excluded from field tests of test items, various statistics used in test development may be inaccurate,[16] and the test's scaling may be in error.

Geography

There are systematic differences in the attainment of individuals living in different geographic regions of the United States, and various psychoeducational tests reflect these regional differences. Most consistently, the average scores of individuals living in the southeastern United States (excluding Florida) are often lower than the average scores of individuals living in other regions of the country. Moreover, community size, population density, and changes in population have also been related to academic and intellectual development.

There are several seemingly logical explanations for many of these relationships. For example, educational attainment is related to educational expenditures, and there are regional differences in the financial support of public education. Well-educated young adults tend to move away from communities with limited employment and cultural opportunities. When brighter and better educated individuals leave a community, the average intellectual ability and educational attainment in that community decline, and the average ability and attainment of the communities to which the brighter individuals move increase. Regardless of the reasons for geographical differences, test norms should include individuals from all geographic regions, as well as from urban, suburban, and rural communities.

[15]We also note that perhaps as much as 90 percent of observed racial and cultural differences can be attributed to socioeconomic differences.
[16]For example, item difficulty estimates (p values) and various item-total correlations.

Intelligence

A representative sample of individuals in terms of their level of intellectual functioning is essential for standardizing an intelligence test and most other kinds of tests, including tests of achievement, linguistic or psycholinguistic ability, perceptual skills, and perceptual–motor skills. In the development of norms, it is essential to test the full range of intellectual ability. Limiting the sample to students enrolled in and attending school (usually general education classes) restricts the norms. Failure to consider individuals with mental retardation in standardization procedures introduces systematic bias into test norms by underestimating the population mean and standard deviation.

Proportional Representation

Implicit in the preceding discussion of characteristics of people in a representative normative sample is the idea that various kinds of people should be included in the sample in the same proportion as they occur in the general population. No matter how test norms are constructed, test authors should systematically compare the relevant characteristics of the population and their standardization samples. Although we frequently use the singular (that is, norm sample or group) when discussing norms, it is important to understand that tests have multiple normative samples. For example, an achievement test intended for use with students in kindergarten through twelfth grade has 13 norm groups (1 for each grade). If that achievement test has separate norms for males and females at each grade, then there are 26 norm groups. When we test a second-grade boy, we do not compare his performance with the performances of all students in the total norm sample. Rather, we compare the boy's performance with that of other second graders (or of other second-grade boys if there are separate norms for boys and girls). Thus, the preceding discussions of representatives and the number of subjects apply to each specific comparison group within the norms—not to the aggregated or combined samples. Representativeness should be demonstrated for each comparison group.

Number of Subjects

The number of participants in a norm sample is important for several reasons. First, the number of subjects should be large enough to guarantee stability. If a sample is very small, another group of participants might have a different mean and standard deviation. Second, the number of participants should be large enough to represent infrequent characteristics. For example, if approximately 1 percent of the population is Native American, a sample of 25 or 50 people will be unlikely to contain even 1 Native American. Third, there should be enough subjects so that there can be a full range of derived scores. In practice, 100 participants in each age or grade is considered the minimum.

Age of Norms

For a norm sample to be representative, it must represent the current population. Levels of skill and ability change over time. Skilled athletes of today run faster, jump higher, and are stronger than the best athletes of a generation ago. Some of the improvement can be attributed to better training, but some can also be attributed to better nutrition and societal changes. Similarly, intellectual and educational performances have increased from generation to generation, although these increases are neither steady nor linear.

For example, on norm-referenced achievement tests, considerably more than half the students score above the average after the test has been in use 5–7 years.[17] In such cases, the test norms are clearly dated because only half the population can ever be above the median. Although some increase in tested achievement can be attributed to teacher familiarity with test content, there is little doubt that some of the changes represent real improvement in achievement.

The important point is that old norms tend to estimate a student's relative standing in the population erroneously because the old norms are too easy. The point at which norms become outdated will depend in part on the ability or skill being assessed. With this caution, it seems to us that approximately 15 years is the maximum useful life for norm samples used in ability testing; 7 years appears to be the maximum for norm life for achievement tests. Although test publishers should ensure that up-to-date norms are readily available, test users ultimately are responsible for avoiding the inappropriate use of out-of-date norms (AERA et al., 1999, p. 59).

Relevance of Norms

Norms must provide comparisons that are relevant to the purpose of assessment. National norms are the most appropriate if we are interested in knowing how a particular student is developing intellectually, perceptually, linguistically, or physically. Norms developed on a particular portion of the population may be meaningful in special circumstances. Local norms can be useful in ascertaining the degree to which individual students have profited from their schooling in the local school district as well as in retrospective interpretations of a student's performance. Norms based on particular groups may be more relevant than those based on the population as a whole. For example, the American Association on Mental Retardation's Adaptive Behavior Scale was standardized on individuals who were mentally retarded; aptitude tests are often standardized on individuals in specific trades or professions. The utility of special population norms is similar to the utility of local norms: They are likely to be more useful in retrospective comparisons than in future predictions because unless we know how the special population corresponds to the general population, predictions may not be appropriate. In addition, "norms that are presented should refer to clearly described groups. These groups should be the ones with whom users of the test will ordinarily wish to compare the people who are tested" (AERA et al., 1997, p. 33).

[17]See, for example, Linn, Graue, and Sanders (1990).

CHAPTER COMPREHENSION QUESTIONS

Write your answers to each of the following questions, and then compare your responses to the text.

1. Compare and contrast the two scales of measurement most commonly used in educational and psychological measurement.

2. Explain the following terms: mean, median, mode, variance, skew, and correlation coefficient.

3. Explain the statistical meaning of the following scores: percentile, z score, IQ, NCE, age equivalent, and grade equivalent.

4. Why is the acculturation of the parents of students in normative samples important?

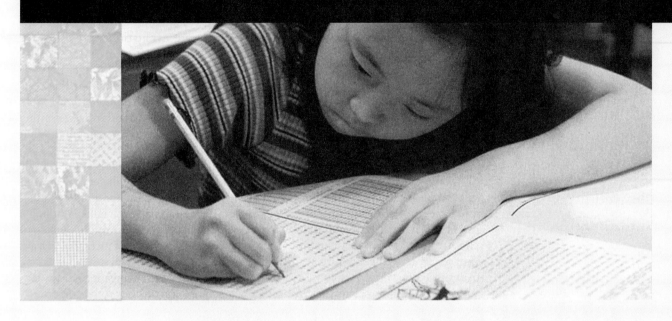

Chapter Goals

1 Understand the basic concept of reliability, including error in measurement, reliability coefficients, standard error of measurement, estimated true scores, and confidence intervals.

2 Understand the general concept of validity, how tests are validated, factors affecting general reliability, and responsibility for valid assessment.

measurement error

reliability coefficient

item reliability

alternate form reliability

internal consistency

stability

interobserver agreement

simple agreement

point-to-point agreement

standard error of measurement

estimated true scores

confidence intervals

validity

content validity

concurrent criterion-related validity

predictive criterion-related validity

construct validity

systematic bias

1   Reliability

NONE OF US WOULD CONSIDER HAVING HEART SURGERY ON THE BASIS OF A diagnostic test known for its inaccuracy. Although educational decisions are not this dramatic, every day school personnel select, create, and use assessment procedures that lead to educational decisions. Accurate evaluation results lead to good decision making, whereas inaccurate results cannot. To illustrate, suppose you learn that other teachers would count as correct test responses that you have marked incorrect, that students earned good grades on their weekly spelling tests but made numerous errors in their written work, and that students who were earning A's in reading were scoring at the 30th percentile on standardized reading tests. What do these things suggest about the accuracy of your assessments? What do they suggest about the decisions based on these assessments?

When we test students, we want to get accurate information that is unlikely to be misinterpreted. The very nature of schooling presumes students will generalize what they have learned to situations and contexts outside of the school and after graduation. Except for school-specific rules (for example, no running in the halls), nothing a student learns in school would have any value unless it generalized to life outside of school. When we test students or otherwise observe their performances, we always want to be able to generalize what we observe in a variety of ways. Moreover, we want those generalizations to be accurate—to be reliable. We also want to draw conclusions about their performances, and we want those conclusions to be correct.

Error in Measurement

In educational and psychological measurement, there are two types of error. *Systematic* or *predictable error* (also called bias) is error that affects a person's (or group's) score in one direction. Bias inflates people's measured abilities above their true abilities. For example, suppose a teacher used only multiple-choice tests with a class of boys and girls. Since boys, as a group, tend to do better on this type of test, the boys' abilities may be somewhat overestimated due to the way their knowledge was measured. Bias can also deflate people's measured abilities above their true abilities. The girls' abilities may be somewhat underestimated due to the use of multiple-choice tests that tested their knowledge; they may well have scored higher on an essay examination. The other type of error is *random error*; its direction and magnitude cannot be known for an individual test taker. This type of error can just as easily raise as lower estimates of student's ability or knowledge. Reliability refers to the relative absence of random error present during measurement.

The Reliability Coefficient

The reliability coefficient is a special use of a correlation coefficient. The symbol for a correlation coefficient (r) is used with two identical subscripts (for example, r_{xx} or r_{aa}) to indicate a reliability coefficient. The reliability coefficient indicates the proportion of variability in a set of scores that reflects true differences among individuals. If there is relatively little error, the ratio of true-score variance to obtained-score variance approaches a reliability index of 1.00 (perfect reliability); if there is a relatively large amount of error, the ratio of true-score variance to obtained-score variance approaches .00 (total unreliability). Thus, a test with a reliability coefficient of .90 has relatively less error of measurement and is more reliable than a test with a reliability coefficient of .50. Subtracting the proportion of true-score variance from 1 yields the proportion of error variance in the distribution of scores. Thus, if the reliability coefficient is .90, 10 percent of the variability in the distribution is attributable to error.

All other things being equal, we want to use the most reliable procedures and tests that are available. Since perfectly reliable devices are quite rare, the choice of test becomes a question of minimum reliability or the specific purpose of assessment. We recommend that the standards for reliability presented in Table 4.1 be used in applied settings.

Three Types of Reliability

In educational and psychological assessment, we are concerned with three types of reliability or generalizations: generalization to other similar items, generalization to other times, and generalization to other observers. These three generalizations have different names (that is, item reliability, stability, and interobserver agreement) and are separately estimated by different procedures.

Item Reliability   It is seldom possible or practical to administer all possible test items of interest. Instead, testers use a sample of items (that is, a subset of items) from all the possible items (that is, the domain of items). We would like to assume that students' performances on the sample of items are similar to their performances on all the items if it were possible or practical to administer all items. When our generalizations about student performance on a domain are correctly generalized from performance on the test, the test is said to be reliable. Sometimes our sample of test items leads us to overestimate a student's knowledge or ability; in such cases, the sample is unreliable. Sometimes our sample of test items leads us to underestimate a student's knowledge or ability; in such cases, the sample is unreliable.

There are two main approaches to estimating the extent to which we can generalize to different samples of items: alternate-form reliability and internal consistency.

Alternate-form reliability requires two or more forms of the same test. These forms (1) measure the same trait or skill to the same extent and (2) are standardized on the same population. Alternate forms offer essentially equivalent tests (but not identical items); sometimes, in fact, they are called equivalent forms. The means and

---

TABLE 4.1	Standards for Reliability

1. If test scores are to be used for administrative purposes and are reported for groups of individuals, a reliability of .60 should be the minimum. This relatively low standard is acceptable because group means are not affected by a test's lack of reliability.

2. If weekly (or more frequent) testing is used to monitor pupil progress, a reliability of .70 should be the minimum. This relatively low standard is acceptable because random fluctuations can be taken into account when a behavior or skill is measured often.

3. If the decision being made is a screening decision (for example, a recommendation for further assessment), there is still a need for higher reliability. For screening devices, we recommend an .80 standard.

4. If a test score is to be used to make an important decision concerning an individual student (for example, tracking or special education placement), the minimum standard should be .90.

Scenario in Assessment

George and Jules

George and Jules were going to have a test on World War II in their history class. George concentrated his efforts on the causes and consequences of the war. Jules reviewed his notes and then watched the movie "Patton." The next day, the boys took the history test, which contained three short-answer questions and one major essay question, "Discuss Patton's role in the European theater of war." George got a "C" on his test; Jules got an "A." George complained that his test score was not an accurate reflection of what he knew about the war and that it was unfair because it did not address the war's causes and consequences. On the other hand, Jules was very pleased with his score even though it would have been considerably lower if the teacher had asked a different question. The test did not provide a reliable estimate of either's knowledge of World War II.

variances for the alternate forms are assumed to be (or should be) the same. In the absence of error of measurement, any subject would be expected to earn the same score on both forms. To estimate the reliability of two alternate forms of a test (for example, form A and form B), a large sample of students is tested with both forms. Half the subjects receive form A and then form B; the other half receive form B and then form A. Scores from the two forms are correlated. The resulting correlation coefficient is a reliability coefficient.

Internal consistency is the second approach to estimating the extent to which we can generalize to different test items. It does not require two or more test forms. Instead, after a test is given, it is split into two halves that are correlated to produce an estimate of reliability. For example, suppose we wanted to use this method to estimate the reliability of a 10-item test. The results of this hypothetical test are presented in Table 4.2. After administering the test to a group of students, we divide the test into two 5-item tests by summing the even-numbered items and the odd-numbered items for each student. This creates two alternate forms of the test, each containing one half of the total number of test items. We can then correlate the sums of the odd-numbered items with the sums of the even-numbered items to obtain an estimate of the reliability of each of the two halves. This procedure for estimating a test's reliability is called a *split-half reliability estimate*.

It should be apparent that there are many ways to divide a test into two equal-length tests. The aforementioned 10-item test can be divided into many different pairs of 5-item tests. If the 10 items in our full test are arranged in order of increasing difficulty, both halves should contain items from the beginning of the test (that is, easier items) and items from the end of the test (that is, more difficult items). There are many ways of dividing such a test (for example, grouping items 1, 4, 5, 8, and 9 and items 2, 3, 6, 7, and 10). The most common way to divide a test is by odd-numbered and even-numbered items (see the columns labeled "Evens Correct" and "Odds Correct" in Table 4.2).

A better method of estimating internal consistency was developed by Cronbach (1951) and is called coefficient alpha. *Coefficient alpha* is the average split-half correlation based on all possible divisions of a test into two parts. In practice,

| TABLE 4.2 | | | | | | Hypothetical Performance of 20 Children on a 10-Item Test | | | | | | | |

	Items										Totals		
Child	1	2	3	4	5	6	7	8	9	10	Total Test	Evens Correct	Odds Correct
1	+	+	+	−	+	−	−	−	+	−	5	1	4
2	+	+	+	+	−	+	+	+	−	+	8	5	3
3	+	+	−	+	+	+	+	−	+	+	8	4	4
4	+	+	+	+	+	+	+	+	−	+	9	5	4
5	+	+	+	+	+	+	+	+	+	−	9	4	5
6	+	+	−	+	−	+	+	+	+	+	8	5	3
7	+	+	+	+	+	−	+	−	+	+	8	3	5
8	+	+	+	−	+	+	+	+	+	+	9	4	5
9	+	+	+	+	+	+	−	+	+	+	9	5	4
10	+	+	+	+	+	−	+	+	+	+	9	4	5
11	+	+	+	+	+	−	+	−	−	−	6	2	4
12	+	+	−	+	+	+	+	+	+	+	9	5	4
13	+	+	+	−	−	+	−	+	−	−	5	3	2
14	+	+	+	+	+	+	+	−	+	+	9	4	5
15	+	+	−	+	+	−	−	−	−	−	4	2	2
16	+	+	+	+	+	+	+	+	+	+	10	5	5
17	+	−	+	−	−	−	−	−	−	−	2	0	2
18	+	−	+	+	+	+	+	+	+	+	9	4	5
19	+	+	+	+	−	+	+	+	+	+	9	5	4
20	+	−	−	−	−	+	−	+	−	−	3	2	1

there is no need to compute all possible correlation coefficients; coefficient alpha can be computed from the variances of individual test items and the variance of the total test score.

Coefficient alpha can be used when test items are scored pass–fail or when more than 1 point is awarded for a correct response. An earlier, more restricted method of estimating a test's reliability, based on the average correlation between all possible split halves, was developed by Kuder and Richardson. This procedure, called *KR-20*, is coefficient alpha for dichotomously scored test items (that is, items that can be scored only right or wrong).

Stability   When students have learned information and behavior, we want to be confident that students can access that information and demonstrate those behaviors at times other than when they are assessed. We would like to be able to generalize today's test results to other times in the future. Educators are interested in many human traits and characteristics that, theoretically, change very little over time. For example, children diagnosed as colorblind at age 5 years are expected to be diagnosed as colorblind at any time in their lives. Colorblindness is an inherited trait that cannot be corrected. Consequently, the trait should be perfectly stable. When an assessment identifies a student as colorblind on one occasion and not colorblind on a later occasion, the assessment is unreliable.

Other traits are developmental. For example, people's heights will increase from birth through adulthood. The increases are relatively slow and predictable. Consequently, we would not expect many changes in height over a 2-week period. Radical changes in people's heights (especially decreases) over short periods of time would cause us to question the reliability of the measurement device. Most educational and psychological characteristics are conceptualized much as height is conceptualized. For example, we expect reading achievement to increase with length of schooling but to be relatively stable over short periods of time, such as 2 weeks. Devices used to assess traits and characteristics must produce sufficiently consistent and stable results if those results are to have practical meaning for making educational decisions. When our generalizations about student performance on a domain are correctly generalized from one time to another, the test is said to be stable or have test–retest reliability. Obviously, the notion of stability excludes changes that occur as the result of systematic interventions to change the behavior. Thus, if a test indicates that a student does not know the long vowel sounds and we teach those sounds to the student, the change in the student's test performance would not be considered a lack of reliability.

The procedure for obtaining a stability coefficient is straightforward. A large number of students are tested and then retested after a short period of time (preferably 2 weeks later). The students' scores from the two administrations are then correlated, and the obtained correlation coefficient is the stability coefficient.

Interobserver Agreement   We would like to assume that if any other comparably qualified examiner were to give the test, the results would be the same—we would like to be able to generalize to similar testers. Suppose Ms. Amig listened to her students say the letters of the alphabet. It would not be very useful if she assigned Barney a score of 70 percent correct, whereas another teacher (or education professional) who listened to Barney awarded a score of 50 percent correct or 90 percent correct for the same performance. When our scoring or other observations agree with those of comparably trained observers who observe the same phenomena at the same time, the observations are said to have interobserver reliability or agreement.[1] Ms. Amig would like to assume that any other education professional would score her students' responses in the same way.

---

[1]Agreement among observers has several different names. Observers can be referred to as testers, scorers, or raters; it depends on the nature of their actions. Agreement can also be called reliability.

There are two very different approaches to estimating the extent to which we can generalize to different scorers: a correlational approach and a percentage of agreement approach. The correlational approach is similar to estimating reliability with alternate forms, which was previously discussed. Two testers score a set of tests independently. Scores obtained by each tester for the set are then correlated. The resulting correlation coefficient is a reliability coefficient for scorers.

Percentage of agreement is more common in classrooms and applied behavioral analysis. Instead of the correlation between two scorers' ratings, a percentage of agreement between raters is computed. There are four ways of calculating percent agreement. The first two types of agreement we discuss are the most common, but the last two are more common in research publications.

Simple agreement is calculated by dividing the smaller number of occurrences by the larger number of occurrences and multiplying the quotient by 100. For example, suppose Ms. Amig and her teacher's aide, Ms. Carter, observe Sam on 20 occasions to determine how frequently he is on task during reading instruction. The results of their observations are shown in Table 4.3. Ms. Amig observes 12 occasions when Sam is on task, whereas Ms. Carter observes 10 occasions. Simple agreement is 83 percent; that is, $100 \times (10/12)$.

The second type of percent agreement, *point-to-point agreement*, is a more precise way of computing percentage of agreement because each data point is considered. Point-to-point agreement is calculated by dividing the number of observations for which both observers agree (occurrence and nonoccurrence) by the total number of observations and multiplying the quotient by 100. Using data shown in Table 4.3, there are 14 occasions when Ms. Amig's and Ms. Carter's observations agree. Point-to-point agreement is 70 percent; that is, $100 \times (14/20)$.

The two other indices of percent agreement are agreement for occurrence and kappa. Explanations of these indices and their calculation are available in the download material.

Concluding Comments About the Reliability Coefficient

Generalization to other items, times, and observers are independent of each other. Therefore, each index of reliability provides information about only a part of the error associated with measurement.

In school settings, item reliability is not a problem when we test students on the entire domain (for example, naming all upper and lower case letters of the alphabet). Item reliability should be estimated when we test students on a sample of items from the domain (for example, a 20-item test on multiplication facts that is used to infer master on all facts). Interscorer reliability is usually not a problem when our assessments are objective and our criteria for a correct response clear (for example, a multiple-choice test). Interscorer reliability should be assessed whenever subjective or qualitative criteria are used to score student responses (for example, using a scoring rubric to assess the quality of written responses). When students are assessed frequently with interchangeable tests or probes, stability is usually assessed directly prior to intervention by administering tests on 3 or more days until the student's performance has stabilized.[2] If a test is given once, its stability should be estimated, although in practice teachers seldom estimate the stability of their tests.

---

[2]The period during which students are assessed prior to observation is generally called the baseline.

TABLE 4.3		Observations of Sam's On-Task Behavior During Reading, Where "−" Is Off Task and "+" Is On Task	
Observation	**Ms. Amig**	**Ms. Carter**	**Observers Agree**
1	+	+	Yes
2	−	−	Yes
3	−	+	No
4	+	+	Yes
5	+	+	Yes
6	−	−	Yes
7	−	−	Yes
8	−	+	No
9	+	+	Yes
10	+	−	No
11	−	−	Yes
12	+	+	Yes
13	+	+	Yes
14	+	+	Yes
15	−	−	Yes
16	+	−	No
17	+	+	Yes
18	−	−	Yes
19	+	−	No
20	+	−	No
Total No. of Occurrences	12	10	14

Standard Error of Measurement

The *standard error of measurement* (SEM) is another index of test error. The SEM is the average standard deviation of error distributed around a person's true score. Although we can compute standard errors of measurement for scorers, times, and item samples, SEMs for scorers are seldom calculated.

To illustrate, suppose we wanted to assess students' emerging skill in naming letters of the alphabet using a 10-letter test. There are many samples of 10-letter tests that could be developed. If we constructed 100 of these tests and tested just one kindergartner, we would probably find that the distribution of scores for that kindergartner was approximately normal. The mean of that distribution would be the student's true score. The distribution around the true score would be the result of imperfect samples of letters; some letter samples would overestimate the pupil's ability, and others would underestimate it. Thus, the variance around the mean would be the result of error. The standard deviation of that distribution is the standard deviation of errors attributable to sampling and is called the standard error of measurement.

When students are assessed with norm-referenced tests, they are typically tested only once. Therefore, we cannot generate a distribution similar to those shown in Figure 4.1. Consequently, we do not know the test taker's true score or the variance of the measurement error that forms the distribution around that person's true score. By using what we know about the test's standard deviation and its reliability for items, we can estimate what that error distribution would be. However, when estimating the error distribution for one student, test users should understand that the SEM is an average; some standard errors will be greater than that average, and some will be less.

Equation 4.1 is the general formula for finding the SEM. The SEM equals the standard deviation of the obtained scores (S) multiplied by the square root of 1 minus the reliability coefficient. The type of unit (IQ, raw score, and so forth) in which the standard deviation is expressed is the unit in which the SEM is expressed. Thus, if the test scores have been converted to T scores, the standard deviation is in T score units and is 10; the SEM is also in T score units. From Equation 4.1, it is apparent that as the standard deviation increases, the SEM increases, and as the reliability coefficient decreases, the SEM increases.

$$\text{SEM} = S\sqrt{1 - r_{xx}} \qquad (4.1)$$

The SEM provides information about the certainty or confidence with which a test score can be interpreted. When the SEM is relatively large, the uncertainty is large; we cannot be very sure of the individual's score. When the SEM is relatively small, the uncertainty is small; we can be more certain of the score.

FIGURE 4.1
The Standard Error of Measurement: The Standard Deviation of the Error Distribution Around a True Score for One Subject

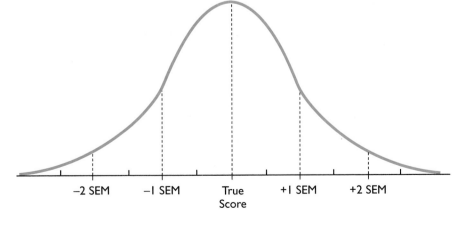

−2 SEM   −I SEM   True Score   +I SEM   +2 SEM

Estimated True Scores

An obtained score on a test is not the best estimate of the true score because obtained scores and errors are correlated. Scores above the test mean have more "lucky" error (error that raises the obtained score above the true score), whereas scores below the mean have more "unlucky" error (error that lowers the obtained score below the true score). An easy way to understand this effect is to think of a test on which Mike guesses on several test items. If all Mike's guesses are correct, he has been very lucky and earns a score that is not representative of what he truly knows. However, if all his guesses are incorrect, Mike has been unlucky and earns a score that is lower than a score that represents what he truly knows.

Confidence Intervals

Although we can never know a person's true score, we can estimate the likelihood that a person's true score will be found within a specified range of scores. This range is called a *confidence interval*. Confidence intervals have two components. The first component is the score range within which a true score is likely to be found. For example, a range of 80 to 90 indicates that a person's true score is likely to be contained within that range. The second component is the level of confidence, generally between 50 and 95 percent. The level of confidence tells us how certain we can be that the true score will be contained within the interval. Thus, if a 90 percent confidence interval for Jo's IQ is 106 to 112, we can be 90 percent sure that Jo's true IQ is between 106 and 112. It also means that there is a 5 percent chance her true IQ is higher than 112 and a 5 percent chance her true IQ is lower than 106. To have greater confidence would require a wider confidence interval.

Sometimes confidence intervals are implied. A score may be followed by a "±" and a number (for example, 109 ± 2). Unless otherwise noted, this notation implies a 68 percent confidence interval with the number following the ± being the SEM. Thus, the lower limit of the confidence interval equals the score less the SEM (that is, $109 - 2$) and the upper limit equals the score plus the SEM (that is, $109 + 2$). The interpretation of this confidence interval is that we can be 68 percent sure that the student's true score is between 107 and 111.

Another confidence interval is implied when a score is given with the probable error (PE) of measurement. For example, a score might be reported as 105 PE ± 1. A PE yields 50 percent confidence. Thus, 105 PE ± 1 means a 50 percent confidence interval that ranges from 104 to 106. The interpretation of this confidence interval is that we can be 50 percent sure that the student's true score is between 104 and 106; 25 percent of the time the true score will be less than 104, and 25 percent of the time the true score will be greater than 106.

2 Validity

Validity refers to "the degree to which evidence and theory support the interpretation of test scores entailed by proposed uses of tests" (American Educational Research Association [AERA], American Psychological Association, & National Council on Measurement in Education, 1999, p. 9). Validity is therefore the most fundamental

Elmwood Area School District

The Elmwood Area School District has adopted a child-centered, conceptual mathematics investigations curriculum that stresses problem solving as well as writing and thinking about mathematics. Students are expected to discover mathematical principles and explain them in writing. In the spring, the district administered the TerraNova achievement test for the purpose of determining whether students were learning what the district intended for them to learn. Much to its dismay, the mean scores on the mathematics subtests were substantially below average, and many students previously thought to be doing well in school were referred to determine if they had a specific learning disability in mathematics calculation. After the school psychologists completed their initial review of student records, the problem became clear. The TerraNova, although generally a good test, did not measure what was being taught in the Elmwood Area School District. Because mathematical calculations were not emphasized (or even systematically taught), Elmwood students had not had the same opportunities to learn as students in other districts. TerraNova was not a valid test within the school district, although it was appropriately used in many others. The validity of a test is validity for the specific child being assessed.

consideration in developing and evaluating tests and other assessment procedures. Although much of the discussion that follows is necessarily general, it must always be remembered that all questions of validity are specific to the individual student being tested. The specific question that must always be asked is whether the testing process leads to correct inferences about a specific person in a specific situation for a specific purpose.

A test that leads to valid inferences in general or about most students may not yield valid inferences about a specific student. Two circumstances illustrate this. First, unless a student has been systematically acculturated in the values, behavior, and knowledge found in the public culture of the United States, a test that assumes such cultural information is unlikely to lead to appropriate inferences about that student. Consider, for example, the inappropriateness of administering a verbally loaded intelligence test to a recent U.S. immigrant. Correct inferences about this person's intellectual ability cannot be drawn from the testing because the intelligence test requires not only proficiency in English but also proficiency in U.S. culture and mores.

Second, unless a student has been systematically instructed in the content of an achievement test, a test assuming such academic instruction is unlikely to lead to appropriate inferences about that student's ability to profit from instruction. It would be inappropriate to administer a standardized test of written language (which counts misspelled words as errors) to a student who has been encouraged to use inventive spelling and reinforced for doing so. It is unlikely that the test results would lead to correct inferences about that student's ability to profit from systematic instruction in spelling.

General Validity

Because it is impossible to validate all inferences that might be drawn from a test performance, test authors typically validate just the most common inferences. Thus, test users should expect some information about the degree to which each commonly encouraged inference has (or lacks) validity. Although the validity of each inference is based on all the information that accumulates over time, test authors are expected to provide some evidence of a test's validity for specific inferences at the time the test is offered for use.

In addition, test authors should validate the inferences for groups of students with whom the test will typically be used.

Methods of Validating Test Inferences

The process of gathering information about the appropriateness of inferences is called validation. Several types of evidence can be considered (AERA et al., 1999, pp. 11–17).[3]

▒ Evidence related to test content: Test content refers to "the themes, wording, and format of the items, tasks, or question on a test, as well as the guidelines for procedures regarding administration and scoring" (AERA et al., 1999, p. 11).

▒ Evidence related to internal structure: Internal structure refers to the number of dimensions or components within a domain that are represented on the test. For example, if a test developer theorized that there were several components of intelligence, one would rightly expect the resulting test to contain several components of intelligence.

▒ Evidence of the relationships between the test and other performances: The relationship to other performances refers to the accuracy with which test scores predict performance on the same type of test or other similar tests.

▒ Evidence of convergent and discriminant power: Convergent power refers to a test's ability to produce scores similar to those produced by other tests of the same ability or skills. Discriminant power refers to a test's ability to produce scores different from those produced by other tests of a different ability or skill.

▒ Evidence of the consequences of testing: Tests are administered with the expectation that some benefit will be realized either to the test taker or to the organization requiring the test. In education, the possible benefits include the selection of efficacious instruction, materials, and placements. "A fundamental purpose of validation is to indicate whether these specific benefits are likely to be realized. Thus, in the case of a test used in a placement decision, the validation would be informed by evidence that alternative placements, in fact, are differentially beneficial to the persons and the institution" (AERA et al., 1999, p. 16).

Historically, the types of evidence under consideration have been categorized as follows: evidence of content validity, evidence of criterion-related validity, and

---

[3]AERA et al. (1999) also recognize evidence based on response processes that are usually described by test takers. This sort of evidence has not been widely accepted in special and inclusive education, perhaps because it can be difficult to obtain reliably from children and individuals with disabilities. Therefore, we do not deal with response processes in this text.

evidence of construct validity. Indeed, most test authors still use these categories. Therefore, we use these three categories in our discussions of validity in this chapter. Specifically, we consider evidence related to test content as content validity; evidence of the relationships between the test and other performances as criterion-related validity; and evidence related to internal structure, evidence of convergent and discriminant power, and evidence of the consequences of testing as construct validity. (We have already discussed in preceding chapters other evidence of a test's validity—namely, the meaning of test scores, reliability, the adequacy of the test's standardization, and, when applicable, the test's norms.)

Content Validity

Content validity refers to the extent to which a test's items actually represent the domain or universe to be measured. It is a major source of evidence for the validation for any educational or psychological test and many other forms of assessment (such as observations and ratings). Evidence of valid content is especially important in the measurement of achievement and adaptive behavior. Whether experts or those who use the tests examine the content, the judgment about a test's validity requires a clear definition of the domain or universe represented.[4]

Appropriateness of Included Items   In examining the appropriateness of the items included in a test, we must ask: Is this an appropriate test question, and does this test item really measure the domain or construct? Consider the four test items from a hypothetical primary (kindergarten through grade 2) arithmetic achievement test presented in Figure 4.2. The first item requires the student to read and add two single-digit numbers, the sum of which is less than 10. This seems to be an appropriate item for an elementary arithmetic achievement test. The second item requires the student to complete a geometric progression. Although this item is mathematical, the skills and knowledge required to complete the question correctly are not taught in any elementary school curriculum by the second grade. Therefore, the question should be rejected as an invalid item for an arithmetic achievement test to be used with children from kindergarten through the second grade. The third item likewise requires the student to read and add two single-digit numbers, the sum of which is less than 10. However, the question is written in Spanish. Although the content of the question is suitable (this is an elementary addition problem), the method of presentation requires language skills that most U.S. students do not have. Failure to complete the item correctly could be attributed either to the fact that the child does not know Spanish or to the fact that the child does not know that $3 + 2 = 5$. Test givers should conclude that the item is not valid for an arithmetic test for children who do not read Spanish. The fourth item requires that the student select the correct form of the Latin verb *amare* ("to love"). Clearly, this is an inappropriate item for an arithmetic test and should be rejected as invalid.

Content Not Included   Test content must be examined to ascertain if important content is not included. For example, the validity of any elementary arithmetic test would be questioned if it included only problems requiring the addition of single-digit numbers with a sum less than 10. Educators would reasonably expect an arithmetic

---

[4]There are statistical procedures that can be used by test authors to help validate the content validity of a test. See download.

FIGURE 4.2
Sample Multiple-Choice
Questions for a Primary
Grade (K–2) Arithmetic
Achievement Test

1. Three and six are _____.
   a. 4
   b. 7
   c. 8
   d. 9

2. What number follows in this series?
   1, 2.5, 6.25, _____
   a. 10
   b. 12.5
   c. 15.625
   d. 18.50

3. ¿Cuántos son tres y dos? _____
   a. 3
   b. 4
   c. 5
   d. 6

4. Ille puer puellas _____.
   a. amo
   b. amat
   c. amamus

test to include a far broader sample of tasks (for example, addition of two- and three-digit numbers, subtraction, understanding of the process of addition, and so forth). An incomplete assessment results in an incomplete and invalid appraisal.

How Content Is Measured   How we assess content directly influences the results of assessment. For example, when students are tested to determine if they know the sum of two single-digit numbers, their knowledge can be evaluated in a variety of ways. Children might be required to recognize the correct answer in a multiple-choice array, supply the correct answer, demonstrate the addition process with manipulatives, apply the proper addition facts in a word problem, or write an explanation of the process they followed in solving the problem.

This aspect of validity is currently being hotly debated by those favoring constructed responses such as extended answers, performances, or demonstrations. Current theory and research methods as they apply to trait or ability congruence under different methods of measurement are still emerging. Much of the current methodology grew out of Campbell and Fiske's (1959) early work and is beyond the scope of this text. However, there is an emerging consensus that the methods used to assess student knowledge or ability should closely parallel those used in instruction.

Criterion-Related Validity

Criterion-related validity refers to the extent to which a person's performance on a criterion measure can be estimated from that person's performance on the assessment procedure being validated. This prediction is usually expressed as a correlation between the assessment procedure (for example, a test) and the criterion. The correlation coefficient is termed a *validity coefficient.* Two types of criterion-related validity are commonly described: concurrent validity and predictive validity. These terms denote the time at which a person's performance on the criterion measure is obtained.

Concurrent Criterion-Related Validity   *Concurrent criterion-related validity* refers to how accurately a person's current performance (for example, test score) estimates that person's performance on the criterion measure at the same time.

A basic concurrent criterion-related validity question is: Does a person's performance measured with a new or experimental test allow the accurate estimation of that person's performance on a criterion measure that has been widely accepted as valid? For example, if the Acme Ruler Company manufactures yardsticks, how do we know that a person's height, as measured by an Acme yardstick, is that person's true height? How do we know that the "Acme foot" is really a foot? The logical criterion measure is "the foot" maintained by the National Bureau of Standards. We can take several things to the bureau and measure them with both the Acme foot and the standard foot. If the two sets of measurements correspond closely (that is, are highly correlated and have very similar means and standard deviations), we can conclude that the Acme foot is a valid measure of length.

Similarly, if we are developing a test of achievement, we can ask: How does knowledge of a person's score on our achievement test allow the estimation of that person's score on a criterion measure? How do we know that our new test really measures achievement? Again, the first step is to find a valid criterion measure. However, there is no National Bureau of Standards for educational tests. Therefore, we must turn to a less-than-perfect criterion. There are two basic choices: (1) other achievement tests that are presumed to be valid and (2) judgments of achievement by teachers, parents, and students. We can, of course, use both tests and judgments. If our new test presents evidence of content validity and elicits test scores corresponding closely (correlating significantly) to judgments and scores from other achievement tests that are presumed to be valid, we can conclude that there is evidence for our new test's criterion-related validity.

Predictive Criterion-Related Validity   *Predictive criterion-related validity* refers to how accurately a person's current performance (for example, test score) estimates that person's performance on the criterion measure at a later time. Thus, concurrent and predictive criterion-related validity refer to the temporal sequence by which a person's performance on some criterion measure is estimated on the basis of that person's current assessment; concurrent and predictive validity differ in the time at which scores on the criterion measure are obtained.

Suppose Acme Ruler Company decides to diversify and manufacture tests of color vision. How do we know that a diagnosis of colorblindness made on the basis of the Acme test is accurate? How do we know that an Acme-based diagnosis will correspond to next month's diagnosis made by an ophthalmologist? We can test several children with the Acme test, schedule appointments with an ophthalmologist, and compare the Acme-based diagnoses with the ophthalmologist's diagnoses. If the Acme test accurately predicts the ophthalmologist's diagnoses, we can conclude that the Acme test is a valid measure of color vision. Similarly, if we are developing a test to assess reading readiness, we can ask: Does knowledge of a student's score on our reading readiness test allow an accurate estimation of the student's actual readiness for subsequent instruction? How do we know that our test really assesses reading readiness? Again, the first step is to find a valid criterion measure. In this case, the student's initial progress in reading can be used. Reading progress can be assessed by a reading achievement test (presumed to be valid) or by teacher judgments of reading ability or reading readiness at the time reading instruction is actually begun. If our reading readiness test has content validity and corresponds closely with either later teacher judgments of readiness or validly assessed reading skill, we can conclude that ours is a valid test of reading readiness.

Construct Validity

Construct validity refers to the extent to which a procedure or test measures a theoretical trait or characteristic. Construct validity is especially important for measures of process, such as intelligence or scientific inquiry. To provide evidence of construct validity, a test author must rely on indirect evidence and inference. The definition of the construct and the theory from which the construct is derived allow us to make certain predictions that can be confirmed or disconfirmed. In a real sense, we do not validate inferences from tests or other assessment procedures; rather, we conduct experiments to demonstrate that the inferences are not valid. The continued inability to disconfirm the inferences in effect validates the inferences.

For example, intellectual ability is generally believed to be developmental. We could hypothesize that if we were to conduct an investigation, intelligence test scores would be correlated with chronological age. If we found that a test of intelligence did not correlate with chronological age, this finding would cast serious doubt on the test as a measure of intelligence. (The experiment would disconfirm the test as a measure of intelligence.) However, the presence of a substantial correlation between chronological age and scores on the test does not confirm that the test is a measure of intelligence.[5] Gradually, the test developer accumulates evidence that the test continues to act in the way that it would if it were a valid measure of the construct. As the research evidence accumulates, the developer can make a stronger claim to construct validity.

Factors Affecting General Validity

Whenever an assessment procedure fails to measure what it purports to measure, validity is threatened. Consequently, any factor that results in measuring "something else" affects validity. Both unsystematic error (unreliability) and systematic error (bias) threaten validity.

Reliability

Reliability sets the upper limit of a test's validity, so reliability is a necessary but not a sufficient condition for valid measurement. Thus, all valid tests are reliable, unreliable tests are not valid, and reliable tests may or may not be valid. The validity of a particular procedure can never exceed the reliability of that procedure because unreliable procedures measure error; valid procedures measure the traits they are designed to measure.

Systematic Bias

Several systematic biases can limit a test's validity. The following are among the most common.

---

[5]Many test authors systematically ensure that their tests will be correlated with age by requiring that each item correlate positively with age or grade and passing. Also, in addition to intelligence, many other abilities correlate with chronological age—for example, achievement, perceptual abilities, and language skills.

Method of Measurement   Students' tested performance can be affected by the way in which they are tested. Skills can be assessed in a variety of ways (for example, by demonstration, description, and explanation). Each of the different ways could yield somewhat different assessments of student achievement.

Enabling Behaviors   Enabling behaviors and knowledge are skills and facts that a person must rely on to demonstrate a target behavior or knowledge. For example, to demonstrate knowledge of causes of the American Civil War on an essay examination, a student must be able to write. The student cannot produce the targeted behavior (the written answer) without the enabling behavior (writing). Similarly, knowledge of the language of assessment is crucial. Many of the abuses in assessment are directly attributable to examiners' failures in this area. For example, intelligence testing in English of non-English-speaking children at one time was sufficiently commonplace that a group of parents brought suit against a school district (*Diana v. State Board of Education*, 1970). Students who are deaf are routinely given the Performance subtests of the Wechsler Adult Intelligence Scales (Baumgardner, 1993) even though they cannot hear the directions. Children with communication disorders are often required to respond orally to test questions. Such obvious limitations in or absences of enabling behaviors are frequently overlooked in testing situations, even though they invalidate the test's inferences for these students.

Differential Item Effectiveness   Test items should work the same way for various groups of students. Jensen (1980) discussed several empirical ways to assess item effectiveness for different groups of test takers. First, we should expect that the relative difficulty of items is maintained across different groups. For example, the most difficult item for males should also be the most difficult item for females, the easiest item for whites should be the easiest item for nonwhites, and so forth. We should also expect that reliabilities and validities will be the same for all groups of test takers.

The most likely explanation for items having differential effectiveness for different groups of people is differential exposure to test content. Test items may not work in the same ways for students who experience different acculturation or different academic instruction. For example, standardized achievement tests presume that the students who are taking the tests have been exposed to similar curricula. If teachers have not taught the content being tested, that content will be more difficult for their students (and inferences about the students' ability to profit from instruction will probably be incorrect).

Systematic Administration Errors

Unless a test is administered according to the standardized procedures, the inferences based on the test are invalid. Suppose Ms. Williams wishes to demonstrate how effective her teaching is by administering an intelligence test and an achievement test to her class. She allows the students 5 minutes less than the standardized time limits on the intelligence test and 5 minutes more on the standardized achievement test. The result is that the students earn higher achievement test scores (because they had too much time) and lower intelligence test scores (because they did not have enough time). The inference that less intelligent students have learned more than anticipated is not valid.

Scenario in Assessment

Crina

Crina was born in Eastern Europe and spent most of the first 10 years of her life in an orphanage, where she looked after younger children. She was adopted shortly before her 11th birthday by an Ohio family. The only papers that accompanied Crina to the United States were her passport, baptismal certificate, and letter from the orphanage stating that Crina's parents were deceased.

Crina's adoptive parents learned some of Crina's language, and Crina tried to learn English in the months before she was enrolled in the local school system. When she was enrolled in the local public school, she was placed in an age-appropriate regular classroom and received additional support from an English as a Second Language (ESL) teacher.

Things did not go well. Crina did not adapt to the school routine, had virtually no understanding of any content area, and was viewed as essentially unteachable. She spent most of her school time trying to help the teacher by neatening up the room, passing out materials, running errands, and so forth. Within Crina's first week in school, her teacher sought additional help from the ESL teacher, the school principal, and the school psychologist. Although all offered suggestions, none of them seemed to work; the school was unable to find a native speaker of Crina's language. Within the first month of school, Crina was referred to a child study team that in turn referred her for psychological and educational assessment.

The school psychologist administered the current Wechsler Intelligence Scale for Children and the Wechsler Individual Achievement Test, although both tests are administered in English. Crina did much better on tests that did not require her to speak or understand English—for example, block designs. Her estimated IQ was in the 40s and her achievement was so low that no derived scores were available.

Given her age and the extent of her needs, the school team recommended that she be placed in a life skills class with other moderately retarded students. Crina's mother rejected that placement because Crina had already mastered most of the life skills she would be taught there; at the orphanage, she cleaned,

cooked, bathed and tended younger children, and so forth. In addition, her mother believed more verbal students than the ones in the life skills class would be better language models for Crina. Basically, her mother wanted a program of basic academics that would be more appropriate—a program in which Crina could learn to read and write English, learn basic computational skills, make friends, and become acculturated.

For reasons that were never entirely clear, the school refused to compromise and the dispute went to a due process hearing. The mother obtained an independent educational evaluation. Her psychologist assessed Crina's adaptive behavior; because the test had limited validity due to Crina's unique circumstances, the psychologist estimated that Crina was functioning within the average range for a person her age. Her psychologist also administered a nonverbal test of intelligence—one that neither required her to understand verbal directions nor to make verbal responses. With the same caveats, Crina was again estimated to be functioning in the average range for a person her age. To make a long story short, the school lost; Crina and her parents won.

The Moral. All validity is local. The district followed its policies for providing the teacher with support, for providing Crina with support, for convening a multidisciplinary team, and so forth. The tests administered by the school were generally reliable, valid, and well normed. However, they were not appropriate for Crina and her unique circumstances. Obviously, she lacked the language skills, cultural knowledge, and academic background to be assessed validly by the tests given by the school. Although the tests given by the parents' psychologist were better, they still had to be considered minimum estimates of her abilities due to the cultural considerations.

A Happy Ending. Crina learned enough English during the next several years to develop friendships, to read and write enough to be gainfully employed, and to leave school feeling positive about the experience and her accomplishments.

Norms

Scores based on the performance of unrepresentative norms lead to incorrect estimates of relative standing in the general population. To the extent that the normative sample is systematically unrepresentative of the general population in either central tendency or variability, the differences based on such scores are incorrect and invalid.

Responsibility for Valid Assessment

The valid use of assessment procedures is the responsibility of both the author and the user of the assessment procedure. Test authors are expected to present evidence for the major types of inferences for which the use of a test is recommended, and a rationale should be provided to support the particular mix of evidence presented for the intended uses (AERA et al., 1997, p. 13). Test users are expected to ensure that the test is appropriate for the specific students being assessed.

CHAPTER COMPREHENSION QUESTIONS

Write your answers to each of the following questions, and then compare your responses to the text.

1. Explain the concept of measurement error.

2. What does a reliability coefficient of .75 tell you about true-score variability and error variability?

3. Compare and contrast item reliability, stability, and interobserver agreement.

4. What is the difference between simple agreement and point-to-point agreement, and when might you use each appropriately?

5. What is a standard error of measurement?

6. Explain the two types of criterion-related validity.

7. What is construct validity?

8. Explain three factors that can affect a test's validity.

5 Using Test Adaptations and Accommodations

Chapter Goals

1 Understand four reasons why you should be concerned with test adaptations and accommodations.

2 Be familiar with universal design and know how the principles of universal design can be applied to promote accessible testing.

3 Know eight factors to consider when deciding whether test changes are necessary and, if so, which test changes might be appropriate.

4 Know two categorization schemes for accommodations, including one associated with accommodation type and one associated with accommodation validity.

5 Know accommodation guidelines you can use in making accommodation decisions for eligibility testing.

6 Know accommodation guidelines you can use in making accommodation decisions for accountability testing.

Key Terms

accommodation

limited English proficiency/
English language
learners

universal design for
assessment

presentation
accommodations

response accommodations

setting accommodations

scheduling
accommodations

native language
accommodations

English language
accommodations

test translations

ALTHOUGH THE USE OF WELL-DESIGNED STANDARDIZED TESTS CAN ENHANCE assessment decision making, it does not result in optimal measurement for every student. In fact, for some students, the way that a test is administered under standardized conditions may actually prohibit their demonstration of true knowledge and skill. For instance, some standardized test conditions require that students express their answers orally in English; this can make it difficult for students who are English language learners (ELLs) to demonstrate their knowledge. Some tests require that students print their answers in a test booklet; this can make it difficult for students with motor impairments to demonstrate their knowledge. Clearly, changes in test conditions may be needed. However, some changes can have a negative impact on the validity of test scores. Educators must attend to the kinds of adaptations that can be made without compromising the technical adequacy of tests. In this chapter, we consider issues associated with adapting tests and providing accommodations for students with disabilities and those who are ELLs.

1 Why Be Concerned About Testing Adaptations?

Changes in Student Population

The diversity of students attending today's schools is mind-boggling. When most people think of diversity, they think of race and ethnicity. Clearly, schools are more racially and ethnically diverse. However, they are becoming more diverse in other ways that concern assessment personnel. In large city school systems throughout the United States, students speak more than 50 different languages and dialects as their primary language. Diversity of language has created challenges in making instruction and assessment accessible to all students. Students enter school these days with a very diverse set of academic background experiences and opportunities. Within the same classroom, students often vary considerably in their academic skill development. A clear challenge for all educational professionals is the design of instruction that will accommodate this vast range in skill development and, similarly, the use of assessments that will capture the large range in student skills.

Since the mid-1970s, considerable attention has been focused on including all students in neighborhood schools and general education settings. Much attention has been focused on including students who are considered developmentally, physically, or emotionally impaired. As federal and state officials make educational policies, they are now compelled to make them for all children and youth, including those with severe disabilities. Also, as policymakers attempt to develop practices that will result in improved educational results, they rely on data from district- and state-administered tests. However, relying on assessment data presents challenges associated with deciding whom to include in the multiple kinds of assessments and the kinds of changes that can be made to include them.

Although meaningful assessment of the skills of such a diverse student population is challenging, it is clear that all students need to be included in large-scale assessment programs. If students are excluded from large-scale assessments, then the data on which policy decisions are made represent only part of the school population. If students are excluded from accountability systems, they may also be denied access to the general education curriculum. If data are going to be gathered on all students, then major decisions must be made regarding the kinds of data to be collected and how tests are to be modified or adapted to include students with special needs. Historically, there has been widespread exclusion of students with disabilities from state and national testing (Thompson & Thurlow, 2001; McGrew, Thurlow, Shriner, & Spiegel, 1992). Participation in large-scale assessments is now recognized by many educators and parents as a critical element of equal opportunity and access to education. Thurlow and Thompson (2004) report that all states now require participation of all students. However, many questions remain about which participation and accommodation strategies are the best for particular students.

Changes in Educational Standards

Part of major efforts to reform or restructure schools has been a push to specify high standards for student achievement and an accompanying push to measure the extent to which students meet those high standards. It is expected that schools will include students with disabilities and ELLs in assessments, especially assessments completed for accountability purposes.

State education agencies in nearly every state are engaging in critical analyses of the standards, objectives, outcomes, results, skills, or behaviors that they want students to demonstrate upon completion of school. Content area professional agencies, such as the National Council of Teachers of Mathematics and the National Science Foundation, have developed sets of standards in specific content areas, such as math, geography, and science. As they do so, they must decide the extent to which standards should be the same for students with and without disabilities. In Chapter 22, you will learn about current state efforts to develop alternate achievement standards and modified achievement standards for students with disabilities. Development of standards is not enough. Groups that develop standards must develop ways of assessing the extent to which students are meeting the standards.

The Need for Accurate Measurement

It is critical that the assessment practices used for gathering information on individual students provide accurate information. Without accommodations, testing runs the risk of being unfair for certain students. Some test formats make it more difficult for students with disabilities to understand what they are supposed to do or what the response requirements are. Because of their disabilities, some students find it impossible to respond in a way that can be evaluated accurately.

It Is Required by Law

By law, students with disabilities have a right to be included in assessments used for accountability purposes, and accommodations in testing should be made to enable them to participate. This legal argument is derived largely from the Fourteenth Amendment to the U.S. Constitution (which guarantees the right to equal protection and to due process of law). The Individuals with Disabilities Education Act (IDEA) guarantees the right to education and to due process. Also, Section 504 of the Rehabilitation Act of 1973 indicates that it is illegal to exclude people from participation solely because of a disability.

The Americans with Disabilities Act of 1992 mandates that all individuals must have access to exams used to provide credentials or licenses. Agencies administering tests must provide either auxiliary aids or modifications to enable individuals with disabilities to participate in assessment, and these agencies may not charge the individual for costs incurred in making special provisions. Adaptations that may be provided include an architecturally accessible testing site, a distraction-free space, or an alternative location; test schedule variation or extended time; the use of a scribe, sign language interpreter, reader, or adaptive equipment; and modifications of the test presentation or response format.

The 1997 and 2004 IDEA mandate that states include students with disabilities in their statewide assessment systems. The necessary accommodations are to be provided to enable students to participate. By July 2000, states were to have available alternate assessments. These are to be used by students who are unable to participate in the regular assessment even with accommodations. Alternate assessments are substitute ways of gathering data, often by means of portfolios or performance measures. The No Child Left Behind Act of 2001 included a requirement that states report annually on the performance and progress of all students, and this principle was reiterated in the 2004 reauthorization of IDEA. Furthermore, results are to be disaggregated by subgroups (for example, those with limited English proficiency and those with disabilities) when sufficient numbers of students within these subgroups are present for the results to be reliable.

Although all of the previously discussed legal requirements are associated with assessment used for accountability purposes, there are other legal requirements associated with making test changes when making eligibility decisions. Within IDEA, there are particular procedures that are to be followed when assessing ELLs for the purpose of eligibility determination. Section 300.304(c)(1)(i–ii)(a)(2) states,

> Assessments and other evaluation materials used [to make special education eligibility decisions] (i) are selected and administered so as not to be discriminatory on a racial or cultural basis; (ii) are provided and administered in the child's native language or other mode of communication and in the form most likely to yield accurate information on what the child knows and can do academically, developmentally, and functionally, unless it is clearly not feasible to so provide or administer.

This principle is echoed in §300.306(b) of IDEA, which forbids a student to be identified as in need of special educational services if the determining factor is limited proficiency in English.

Scenario in Assessment

Amy

Amy is a student with a visual impairment that does not quite meet the definition of legal blindness. Her teacher provides her with accommodations during instruction. For example, Amy's seat is positioned in class directly under the large fluorescent light fixture, the spot considered by the teacher to have the brightest light. On several occasions when Amy has expressed difficulty seeing, the teacher has provided her with a special desk lamp that brightens her work surface. The teacher tries to arrange the daily schedule so that work that requires lots of vision (for example, reading) occurs early in the day. In doing so, her teacher hopes that Amy experiences less eye strain. Similar accommodations are made in classroom testing, and on the day of the state test the following testing accommodations are provided for Amy:

- She is tested in an individual setting, where extra bright light shines directly on her test materials.

- The test is administered on three separate mornings rather than over an entire day. This helps minimize her eye strain.

- The test is administered with frequent breaks because of fatigue to eyes created by extra bright light and intense strain at deciphering text.

- The teacher uses a copy machine to enlarge the print on pages requiring reading.

- A scribe records Amy's responses to avoid extra time and eye strain trying to find the appropriate location for a response and to give the response.

However, it is important to note that if the goal of assessment is to ascertain a student's current level of functioning in English, and for the purpose of accountability for students' English language skill development, then it would be appropriate to test the student in English.

In this chapter, we first describe the concept of universal design that can be applied to improve assessment for all students as well as reduce (but certainly not eliminate) the need for making challenging decisions about accommodation use. Next, we describe many factors that may contribute to a student's need for accommodations, as well as accommodations that may address those needs. Finally, we offer recommendations for making accommodation decisions.

As you read this chapter, remember that the major objective of assessment is to benefit students. Assessment can do so either by enabling us to develop interventions that help a child achieve the objectives of schooling or by informing local, state, and national policy decisions that benefit all students, including those with diverse needs.

2 The Importance of Promoting Test Accessibility

The extent to which test adaptations and accommodations are needed depends in part on the way in which an assessment program is designed. When test development involves careful consideration of the unique needs of all students who may eventually participate, less "after-the-fact" changes in test conditions will be needed. Application of the principles of universal design can improve accessibility, such that appropriate testing for all students is promoted.

Concept of Universal Design

Universal design is a concept that was first applied in architectural design. Wheelchair ramps and curb cuts are features that were determined to be helpful when architects considered the many unique needs of individuals with disabilities while designing buildings and their surrounding areas.

The Center for Universal Design has provided the following definition and seven principles of universal design:

> Universal design is the design of products and environments to be usable by all people, to the greatest extent possible, without the need for adaptation or specialized design.

Seven Principles of Universal Design

- Equitable use: The design is useful and marketable to people with diverse abilities.
- Flexibility in use: The design accommodates a wide range of individual preferences and abilities.
- Simple and intuitive: Use of the design is easy to understand, regardless of the user's experience, knowledge, language skills, or current concentration level.
- Perceptible information: The design communicates necessary information effectively to the user, regardless of ambient conditions or the user's sensory abilities.
- Tolerance for error: The design minimizes hazards and the adverse consequences of accidental or unintended actions.
- Low physical effort: The design can be used efficiently and comfortably and with a minimum of fatigue.
- Size and space for approach and use: Appropriate size and space is provided for approach, reach, manipulation, and use regardless of user's body size, posture, or mobility.

> From http://www.design.ncsu.edu/cud/about_ud/udprinciplestxt.htm. Reprinted by permission of the Center for Universal Design.

Applying Universal Design in Test Development and Use

Following a review of the principles put forth by the Center for Universal Design, the National Center on Educational Outcomes identified several elements of universal design that could be incorporated in the design of large-scale assessment programs (Thompson, Johnstone, & Thurlow, 2002). These include the following:

1. Inclusive assessment population
2. Precisely defined constructs
3. Accessible, nonbiased items
4. Amenable to accommodations
5. Simple, clear, and intuitive instructions and procedures
6. Maximum readability and comprehensibility
7. Maximum legibility

According to IDEA 2004, states must incorporate the principles of universal design in the development of their assessment programs.

Universal Design Applications Promote Better Testing for All

Although universal design stems from a desire to address the unique needs of particular individuals, it often improves assessment for many other students too. Just as wheelchair ramps can be extremely helpful to those of us who opt to use rolling carts to lug our many materials into buildings, universally designed assessment programs can facilitate better test measurement for a variety of students. For example, when test directions are simplified, this has the potential to promote better understanding by students both with and without special needs. When the legibility of items is improved, all students can exert fewer cognitive resources on deciphering item content and more resources on the specific processes or skills that the test is intended to measure.

Although application of universal design can reduce the need for accommodations among some students, it is not likely to eliminate the need for changes to address other unique student needs. In the following section, we describe factors that should be considered when determining whether an adaptation or accommodation might be needed.

3 Factors to Consider in Making Accommodation Decisions

Six factors can impede getting an accurate picture of students' abilities and skills during assessment: (1) the students' ability to understand assessment stimuli, (2) the students' ability to respond to assessment stimuli, (3) the nature of the norm group, (4) the appropriateness of the level of the items (sufficient basal and ceiling items), (5) the students' exposure to the curriculum being tested (opportunity to learn), and (6) the nature of the testing environment. It is also important to take into consideration cultural and linguistic differences when thinking about students' individual accommodation needs.

Ability to Understand Assessment Stimuli

Assessments are considered unfair if the test stimuli are in a format that, because of a disability, the student does not understand. For example, tests in print are considered unfair for students with severe visual impairments. Tests with oral directions are considered unfair for students with hearing impairments. In fact, because the law requires that students be assessed in their primary language and because the primary language of many deaf students is not English, written assessments in English are considered unfair and invalid for many deaf students. When students cannot understand test stimuli because of a sensory or mental limitation that is unrelated to what the test is targeted to measure, accurate measurement of the targeted skills is hindered by the sensory or mental limitation. Such a test is invalid, and failure to provide an accommodation is illegal.

Ability to Respond to Assessment Stimuli

Tests typically require students to produce a response. For example, intelligence tests require verbal, motor (pointing or arranging), or written (including multiple-choice) responses. To the extent that physical or sensory limitations inhibit accurate responding, these test results are invalid. For example, some students with cerebral palsy may lack sufficient motor ability to arrange blocks. Others may have sufficient motor ability but have such slowed responses that timed tests are inappropriate estimates of their abilities. Yet others may be able to respond quickly but expend so much energy that they cannot sustain their efforts throughout the test. Not only are test results invalid in such instances but also the use of such test results is proscribed by federal law.

Normative Comparisons

Norm-referenced tests are standardized on groups of individuals, and the performance of the person assessed is compared with the performance of the norm group. To the extent that the test was administered to the student differently than the way it was administered to the norm group, you must be very careful in interpreting the results. Adaptations of measures require changing either stimulus presentation or response requirements. The adaptation may make the test items easier or more difficult, and it may change the construct being measured. Although qualitative or criterion-referenced interpretations of such test performances are often acceptable, norm-referenced comparisons can be flawed. *Standards for Educational and Psychological Testing* (American Educational Research Association, American Psychological Association, & National Council on Measurement in Education, 1999) specifies that when tests are adapted, it is important that there is validity evidence for the change that is made. Otherwise, it is important to describe the change when reporting the score and to use caution in score interpretation.

Appropriateness of the Level of the Items

Tests are often developed for students who are in specific age ranges or who have a particular range of skills. They can sometimes seem inappropriate for students who are either very high or very low functioning compared to their age-mates. Assessors are tempted to give out-of-level tests when an age-appropriate test contains either an insufficient number of easy items or not enough easy items for the student being assessed. Of course, when out-of-level tests are given and norm-referenced interpretations are made, the students are compared with a group of students who differ from them. We have no idea how same-age or same-grade students would perform on the given test. Out-of-level testing may be appropriate to identify a student's current level of educational performance or to evaluate the effectiveness of instruction with a student who is instructed out of grade level. It is inappropriate for accountability purposes.

Exposure to the Curriculum Being Tested (Opportunity to Learn)

One of the issues of fairness raised by the general public is the administration of tests that contain material that students have not had an opportunity to learn. This same issue applies to the making of accommodation decisions. Students with sensory impairments have not had an opportunity to learn the content of test items that use verbal or auditory stimuli. Students receiving special education services who have not had adequate access to the general education curriculum have not had the same opportunity to master the general education curriculum.

To the extent that students have not had an opportunity to learn the content of the test (that is, they were absent when the content was taught, the content is not taught in the schools in which they were present, or the content was taught in ways that were not effective for the students), they probably will not perform well on the test. Their performance will reflect more a lack of opportunity to learn than limited skill and ability.

Environmental Considerations

Students should be tested in settings in which they can demonstrate maximal performance. If students cannot easily gain access to a testing setting, this may diminish their performance. Tests should always be given in settings that students with disabilities can access with ease. The settings should also be quiet enough to minimize distractibility. Also, because fatigue is an issue, tests should be given in multiple short sessions (broken up with breaks) so students do not become overly tired.

Cultural Considerations

Many students with limited English proficiency come from cultures that are very different from the public culture of the United States. As a result, whenever a test relies on a student's cultural knowledge to test some area of achievement or aptitude, the test will necessarily be invalid because it will also test the student's knowledge of U.S. culture.

In some cultures, children are expected to speak minimally to adults or authority figures; elaboration or extensive verbal output may be viewed as disrespectful. In some cultures, answering questions may be viewed as self-aggrandizing, competitive, and immodest. These cultural values work against students in most testing situations. Male–female relations are also subject to cultural differences. Female students may be hesitant to speak to male teachers; male students (and their fathers) may not view female teachers as authority figures. Children may be hesitant to speak to adults from other cultures, and testers may be reluctant to encourage or say "no" to children whose culture is unfamiliar. Children new to the United States may have been traumatized by civil strife and therefore be wary of or frightened by strangers. It may therefore be difficult for an examiner to establish rapport with a student who has limited English proficiency. Some evidence suggests that children do better with examiners of the same race and cultural background (Fuchs & Fuchs, 1989).

Immigrant students and their families may have little experience with the types of testing done in U.S. schools. Consequently, these students may lack test-taking skills. Finally, doing well on tests may not be as valued within the first cultures of immigrant students.

Whereas some students from different cultural backgrounds may be relatively quick to assimilate with U.S. culture, other students may not. There are a variety of factors that may play a role in determining how quickly such students become familiar and integrated within U.S. culture. Some are immigrants or children of immigrants who have come to the United States seeking a better life. Others are fleeing repressive governments in their nation of origin. Some have plans to remain in the United States, whereas others are in the country just temporarily. Some have a large network of individuals nearby who speak their native language, whereas others do not. All of these factors may play a role in the student's motivation and need to be knowledgeable of U.S. culture, which may in turn relate to his or her performance on tests in the United States. As a result, merely knowing the student's time of arrival in the United States may not be enough to help gauge whether he or she is familiar enough with U.S. culture; these other factors need to be taken into consideration.

Linguistic Considerations

The overwhelming majority of classroom and commercially prepared tests are administered in English. Students who do not speak or read English cannot access the content and respond to these tests. Although a student with limited English proficiency may speak some English, knowing enough English for some social conversation is not the same as knowing enough English for instruction or for the nuances of highly abstract concepts that may be included as a part of testing. To assess students' knowledge, skills, or abilities, students must have sufficient fluency in the language of the test. Although this proposition is logical and quite easy to say, the difficult part is in the doing. It is particularly challenging given the many different languages and language programs that are used in U.S. schools today, as well as the differences in rates of English language acquisition among students with different background characteristics.

Bilingual Students

"Bilingual" implies equal proficiency in two languages. Nevertheless, young children must learn which language to use with specific people. For example, they may be able to switch between English and Spanish with their siblings, speak only Spanish with their grandparents, and use only English with their older sister's husband, who still has not learned Spanish. Although children can switch between languages, sometimes in midsentence, they are seldom truly bilingual.

When students grow up in a home in which two languages are spoken, they are seldom equally competent or comfortable in using both languages, regardless of the context or situation. These students tend to prefer one language or the other for specific situations or contexts. For example, Spanish may be spoken at home and in the neighborhood, whereas English is spoken at school. Moreover, when two languages are spoken in the home, the family may develop a hybrid language borrowing a little from each. For example, in Spanish *caro* means "dear," and *car* in English means "automobile." In some bilingual homes (and communities), *caro* comes to mean "automobile." These speakers may not be speaking "proper" Spanish or English, although they have no problem communicating.

These factors enormously complicate the testing of bilingual students. Some bilingual students may understand academic questions better in English, but the language in which they answer can vary. If the content was learned in English, they may be better able to answer in English. However, if the answer calls for a logical explanation or an integration of information, they may be better able to answer in their other language. Finally, it cannot be emphasized strongly enough that language dominance is not the same as language competence for testing purposes. Because a student knows more Spanish than English does not mean that the student knows enough Spanish to be tested in that language.

English as a Second Language

It is critical to distinguish between social/interpersonal uses of language and cognitive/academic uses. Students learning English as a second language usually need at least 2 years to develop social and interpersonal communication skills. However, they require 5 or 6 years to develop language sufficient for cognitive and academic proficiency (Cummins, 1984). Thus, after even 3 or 4 years of schooling, students who demonstrate few problems with English usage in social situations still probably lack sufficient language competence to be tested in English.

At least three factors can affect the time required for students to attain cognitive and academic sufficiency in English.

1. Age: Young children are programmed to learn language. At approximately 12 to 14 years of age, learning another language becomes much more difficult. Thus, all things being equal, one should expect younger students to acquire English faster than older students.

2. Immersion in English: The more contexts in which English is used, the faster will be its acquisition. Thus, a student's learning of English as a second language will depend in part on the language the parents speak at home. If the native language is spoken at home, progress in English will be slower. This creates a dilemma for parents who want their children to learn (or remember) their first language and also learn English.

3. Similarity to English: Languages can vary along several dimensions. The phonology may be different. The 44 speech sounds of English may be the same as or different from the speech sounds of other languages. For example, Xhosa (an African language) has three different click sounds, whereas English has none. English lacks the sound equivalent of the Spanish *ñ*, the Portuguese *-nh*, and the Italian *-gn*. The orthography may be different. English uses the Latin alphabet. Other languages may use different alphabets (for example, Cyrillic) or no alphabet (Mandarin). English does not use diacritical marks; whereas other languages do. The letter-sound correspondences may be different. The letter *h* is silent in Spanish but pronounced as an English *r* in one Brazilian dialect. The grammar may be different. Whereas English tends to be noun dominated, other languages tend to be verb dominated. Word order varies. Adjectives precede nouns in English, but they follow nouns in Spanish. The more language features the second language has in common with the first language, the easier it is to learn the second language.

There are certainly many things to take into consideration when determining whether a test change is needed for a particular student, and what the most appropriate test change might be. Now that you have had an opportunity to consider many unique characteristics of students that may make it difficult for them to demonstrate knowledge through testing, we will consider changes that have the potential to make tests more accessible to individual children with unique needs.

Photo 5.1
A student uses a computer magnifier to read books and an augmentative keyboard to write.

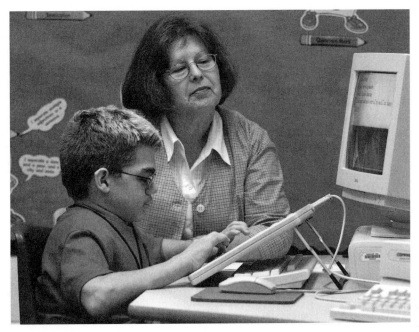

4 Categories of Testing Accommodations

An accommodation is any change in testing materials or procedures that enables students to participate in assessments so that their abilities with respect to what is intended to be measured can be more accurately assessed. There are four general types of accommodations:

- Presentation (for example, repeat directions, read aloud)
- Response (for example, mark answers in book, point to answers)
- Setting (for example, study carrel, separate room, special lighting)
- Timing/schedule (for example, extended time, frequent breaks, multiple days)

In addition, ELL accommodations are sometimes categorized as follows:

- English language (for example, simplifying the English language in the stem of an item, providing a customized English dictionary that includes definitions for difficult words on the test)
- Native language (for example, providing a side-by-side test translation, providing directions in the student's native language)
- Other (for example, extended time, small group testing)

Concern about accommodation applies to individually administered and large-scale testing. The concerns are legal (Is an individual sufficiently disabled to require taking an accommodated test?), technical (To what extent can we adapt measures and still have technically adequate tests?), and political (Is it fair to give accommodations to some students, yet deny them to others?).

It is important to recognize that the appropriateness of an accommodation will depend on the skills targeted for measurement, as well as the types of decisions that are intended to be made. Although it may initially appear to you that it is easy to determine exactly which accommodations allow for better measurement of targeted skills and fair and appropriate assessment, people actually tend to disagree on which accommodations maintain the validity of tests, making it a more complicated issue. Based on input from a variety of stakeholders (that is, teachers, state assessment directors, and researchers), one test publisher has created a framework for accommodations and classified common accommodations into one of three categories: accommodations that have no impact on test validity, accommodations that may affect validity, and accommodations that are known to affect validity (CTB/McGraw-Hill, 2004). Extended descriptions of these categories, as well as accommodations that are considered to fit within these categories, are provided in Figure 5.1.

FIGURE 5.1
Categories of Testing Accommodations

Category 1 The accommodations listed in category 1 are not expected to influence student performance in a way that alters the interpretation of either criterion- or norm-referenced test scores. Individual student scores obtained using category 1 accommodations should be interpreted in the same way as the scores of other students who take the test under default conditions. These students' scores may be included in summaries of results without notation of accommodation(s).

Presentation

- Use visual magnifying equipment
- Use a large-print edition of the test
- Use audio amplification equipment
- Use markers to maintain place
- Have directions read aloud
- Use a tape recording of directions
- Have directions presented through sign language
- Use directions that have been marked with highlighting

Response

- Mark responses in test booklet
- Mark responses on large-print answer document
- For selected-response items, indicate responses to a scribe
- Record responses on audio tape (except for constructed-response writing tests)
- For selected-response items, use sign language to indicate response
- Use a computer, typewriter, Braille writer, or other machine (for example, communication board) to respond
- Use template to maintain place for responding
- Indicate response with other communication devices (for example, speech synthesizer)
- Use a spelling checker except with a test for which spelling will be scored

Setting

- Take the test alone or in a study carrel
- Take the test with a small group or different class
- Take the test at home or in a care facility (for example, hospital), with supervision

- Use adaptive furniture
- Use special lighting and/or acoustics

Timing/scheduling

- Take more breaks that do not result in extra time or opportunity to study information in a test already begun
- Have flexible scheduling (for example, time of day and days between sessions) that does not result in extra time or opportunity to study information in a test already begun

ELL specific

- Spelling aids, such as spelling dictionaries (without definitions) and spell/grammar checkers, provided for a test for which spelling and grammar conventions will not be scored
- Computer-based written response mode for constructed response items other than for a writing test. For a writing test, computer writing aids are disabled (for example, grammar and spelling checks) that interfere with what is to be scored
- Computer-based testing with glossary without content-related definitions
- Bilingual word list, customized dictionaries (word-to-word translations), and glossary provided for words that are not content related
- Format clarification of test
- Directions clarified
  - Directions explained/clarified in English
  - Directions explained/clarified in native language
- Both oral and written directions in English provided
- Both oral and written directions in native language provided
- Directions translated into native language, including audiotaped directions

Category 2 Category 2 accommodations may have an effect on student performance that should be considered when interpreting individual criterion- and norm-referenced test scores. In the absence of research demonstrating otherwise, scores and any consequences or decisions associated with them should be interpreted in light of the accommodation(s) used.

Presentation

- Have stimulus material, questions, and/or answer choices read aloud, except for a reading test
- Use a tape recorder for stimulus material, questions, and/or answer choices, except for a reading test
- Have stimulus material, questions, and/or answer choices presented through sign language, except for a reading test
- Communication devices (for example, text talk converter), except for a reading test
- Use a calculator or arithmetic tables, except for a mathematics computation test

Response

- Use graph paper to align work
- For constructed-response items, indicate responses to a scribe, except for a writing test

Timing/scheduling

- Use extra time for any timed test
- Take more breaks that result in extra time for any timed test

(*continued*)

(Figure 5.1 *continued*)

- ▦ Extend the timed section of a test over more than one day, even if extra time does not result
- ▦ Have flexible scheduling that results in extra time

ELL specific

- ▦ Test items read aloud in linguistically clarified* English on a test other than a reading test
- ▦ Test items read aloud in native language on a test other than a reading test
- ▦ Test items read aloud in English on a test other than a reading test
- ▦ Audiotaped test items provided in English on a test other than a reading test
- ▦ Test that is linguistically clarified in English for words not related to content on nonreading (for example, words defined or explained) in English
- ▦ Oral response in English using a scribe for tests other than a writing test**
- ▦ Written response in native language translated into English for tests other than a writing test**
- ▦ Audiotaped test items provided in native language version provided for content other than reading and writing test
- ▦ Side-by-side bilingual test or translated version provided for content other than reading and writing tests

* Linguistic clarifications are developed and provided by test publisher, not by test administrator.
** These may be appropriate, but not feasible, for most ELL students.

Category 3 Category 3 accommodations change what is being measured and are likely to have an effect that alters the interpretation of individual criterion- and norm-referenced scores. This occurs when the accommodation is strongly related to the knowledge, skill, or ability being measured (for example, having a reading comprehension test read aloud). In the absence of research demonstrating otherwise, criterion- and norm-referenced test scores and any consequences or decisions associated with them should be interpreted not only in light of the accommodation(s) used but also in light of how the accommodation(s) may alter what is measured.

Presentation

- ▦ Use Braille or other tactile form of print
- ▦ On a reading (decoding) test, have stimulus material, questions, and/or answer choices presented through sign language
- ▦ On a reading (decoding) test, use a text-talk converter, where the reader is required to construct meaning and decode words from text
- ▦ On a reading (decoding) test, use a tape recording of stimulus material, questions, and/or answer choices
- ▦ Have directions, stimulus material, questions, and/or answer choices paraphrased
- ▦ For a mathematics computation test, use of a calculator or arithmetic tables
- ▦ Use a dictionary, where language conventions are assessed

Response

- ▦ For a constructed-response writing test, indicate responses to a scribe
- ▦ Spelling aids, such as spelling dictionaries (without definitions) and spell/grammar checkers, provided for a test for which spelling and grammar conventions will be scored
- ▦ Use a dictionary to look up words on a writing test

From *Guidelines for Inclusive Test Administration 2005,* p. 8. Copyright © 2004 by CTB/McGraw-Hill LLC. Reproduced with permission of The McGraw-Hill Companies, Inc.

Research continues to be conducted on accommodations to refine and provide justification for how these accommodations are assigned to the various validity categories. We emphasize throughout this book the importance of considering test purpose and the decisions that assessment is intended to inform when deciding what assessment tools to use. Deciding whether a particular accommodation is appropriate for testing is no different. When deciding on accommodation appropriateness, careful attention must be paid to what the test is intended to measure and what decisions are intended to be made with the results.

Progress is rapid in designing and validating test accommodations. You are advised to visit the website for the National Center on Educational Outcomes (http://cehd.umn.edu/nceo) to read the latest research and publications on state and national practice in testing accommodations.

5 Recommendations for Making Accommodation Decisions During Eligibility Testing

There are major debates about the kinds of accommodations that should be permitted in testing. There are also major arguments about the extent to which accommodations in testing destroy the technical adequacy of tests. We first provide recommendations for making accommodation decisions on tests that are commonly used to make decisions about individuals (for example, eligibility and instructional planning for exceptional children). Then, we provide recommendations for making accommodation decisions on tests that are typically administered at the group level and used for accountability purposes.

The issues in making accommodation decisions extend to more than screening and accountability. In fact, they play a major role in decisions about exceptionality, special need, eligibility, and instructional planning. We think there are some reasonable guidelines for best practice in making decisions about individuals, and we offer associated guidelines here.

Students with Disabilities

- Conduct all assessments in the student's primary language or mode of communication. The mode of communication is that normally used by the person (such as sign language, Braille, or oral communication). Loeding and Crittenden (1993, p. 19) note that for students who are deaf, the primary communication mode is either a visual–spatial, natural sign language used by members of the American Deaf Community called American Sign Language (ASL) or a manually coded form of English, such as Signed English, Pidgin Sign English, Seeing Essential English, Signing Exact English, or Sign-Supported Speech/English. Therefore, they argue, "traditional paper-and-pencil tests are inaccessible, invalid, and inappropriate to the deaf student because the tests are written in English only."

- Make accommodations in format when the purpose of testing is not substantially impaired. It should be demonstrated that the accommodations assist the individual in responding but do not provide content assistance (for example, a scribe should record the response of the person being tested—not interpret what the person says, include his or her additional knowledge, and then record a response). Personal assistants who are provided during testing, such as readers, scribes, and interpreters, should be trained in how to provide associated accommodations to ensure proper administration.

▪ Make normative comparisons only with groups whose membership includes students with background sets of experiences and opportunities like those of the students being tested.

Students with Limited English Proficiency

Lack of progress in learning English is the most common reason students with limited English proficiency are referred to ascertain eligibility for special education (Figueroa, 1990). It seems that most teachers do not understand that it usually takes several years to acquire sufficient fluency to be fully functional academically and cognitively in English. The fundamental principle when assessing students with limited English proficiency is to ensure that the assessment materials and procedures used actually assess students' target knowledge, skill, or ability, and that it is not influenced by their inability (or limited ability) to understand and use English. Three basic approaches have been used to assess students whose English is sufficiently limited to make eligibility testing in English inappropriate: using nonverbal tests, testing in the student's native language, and not testing at all. The strengths and weaknesses of each of these approaches are discussed.

Use Nonverbal Tests

Several nonverbal tests are available for testing intelligence. This type of test is believed to reduce the effects of language and culture on the assessment of intellectual abilities. Nonverbal tests do not, however, completely eliminate the effects of language and culture. Some tests involve oral directions, but the remaining aspects of the test do not require students to comprehend or express their responses in a particular language. Some tests (for example, the Comprehensive Test of Nonverbal Intelligence) allow testers to use either oral or pantomime directions. A few tests are exclusively nonverbal (for example, the Leiter International Performance Scale) and do not require language for directions or responses.

Because students' skills in language comprehension usually precede their skills in language production, performance tests with oral directions might be useful with some students. However, the testers should have objective evidence that a student sufficiently comprehends academic language for the test to be valid, and such evidence is generally not available. Tests that do not rely on oral directions or responses are more useful because they do not make any assumptions about students' language competence. However, other validity issues cloud the use of performance tests in the schools. For example, the nature of the tasks on nonverbal intelligence tests is usually less related to success in school than are the tasks on verbal intelligence tests.

Moreover, some cultural considerations are beyond the scope of directions and responses. For example, the very nature of testing may be more familiar in U.S. culture than in the cultures of other countries. When students are familiar with the testing process, they are likely to perform better. As another example, students from other cultures may respond differently to adults in authority, and these differences may alter estimates of their ability derived from tests. Thus, although performance and nonverbal tests may be a better option than verbal tests administered in English, they are not without problems.

Test in the Student's Native Language

There are several ways to test students using directions and materials in their native language. Commercial tests may have been developed in the student's native language. If such tests are not available, testers may locate a foreign-language version of the test. If foreign-language versions are not available, testers may be able to translate a test from English to the student's native language, either on their own or through use of an interpreter.

Use Commercially Translated Tests   Several tests are currently available in language versions other than English—most frequently, Spanish. These tests run the gamut from those that are translated to those that are renormed and those that are reformatted for another language and culture. The difference among these approaches is significant.

When tests are only translated, we can assume that the child understands the directions and the questions. However, the questions may be of different difficulty in U.S. culture and the English language for two reasons. First, the difficulty of the vocabulary can vary from language to language. For example, reading *cat* in English is different from reading *gato* in Spanish. *Cat* is a three-letter, one-syllable word containing two of the first three letters of the English alphabet; *gato* is a four-letter, two-syllable word with the first, seventh, fifteenth, and twentieth letters of the alphabet. The frequency of *cat* in each language is likely different, as is the popularity of cats as house pets.

The second reason that translated questions may be of different difficulty is that the difficulty of the content can vary from culture to culture because children from different cultures have not had the same opportunity to learn the information. For example, suppose we asked Spanish-speaking students from Venezuela, Cuba, and California who attended school in the United States to identify Simón Bolívar, Ernesto "Che" Guevara, and César Chávez. We could speculate that the three groups of students would probably identify the three men with different degrees of accuracy. The students from California would be most likely to recognize Chávez as an American labor organizer but less frequently recognize Bolívar and Guevara. Students from Venezuela would likely recognize Bolívar as a liberator of South America more often than would students from Cuba and the United States. Students from Cuba would be more likely to recognize Guevara as a revolutionary than would students from the other two countries. Thus, the difficulty of test content is embedded in culture.

Also, when tests are translated, we cannot assume that the psychological demands made by test items remain the same. For example, an intelligence test might ask a child to define *peach*. A child from equatorial South America may never have eaten, seen, or heard of a peach, whereas U.S. students are quite likely to have seen and eaten peaches. For U.S. students, the psychological demand of identifying a peach is to recall the biological class and essential characteristics of something they have experienced. For South American children, the item measures their knowledge of an exotic fruit. For U.S. children, the test would measure intelligence; for South American children, the test would measure achievement.

Some of the problems associated with a simple translation of a test can be circumvented if the test is renormed on the target population and items are reordered in terms of their translated difficulties. For example, to use the Wechsler Intelligence Scale for Children, fourth edition, effectively with Spanish-speaking Puerto Ricans, the test could be normed on a representative sample of Spanish-speaking Puerto Rican students. Based on the performance of the new normative sample, the items could be reordered as necessary. However, renorming and reordering do not reproduce the psychological demands made by test items in English.

Develop and Validate a Version of the Test for Each Cultural/Linguistic Group   Given the problems associated with translations, tests developed in the student's language and culture are clearly preferable to those that are not. For example, suppose one wished to develop a version of the Wechsler Intelligence Scale for Children *para los Niños de Cuba*. Test items could be developed within the Cuban American culture according to the general framework of the Wechsler scale. Specific items might or might not be the same. The new test would then need to be validated. For example, factor-analytic studies could be undertaken to ascertain whether the same four factors underlie the new test (that is, verbal comprehension, perceptual organization, freedom from distractibility, and processing speed).

Although they may be preferable, culture- and language-specific tests are not economically justifiable for test publishers except in the case of the very largest minorities—for example, Spanish-speaking students with much U.S. acculturation. The cost of standardizing a test is sizable, and the market for intelligence tests in, for example, Hmong, Ilocano, or Gujarathi is far too small to offset the development costs. Even if such tests were made, they would require someone familiar with the language to administer to students. For Spanish-speaking students, many publishers offer both English and Spanish versions. Some of these are translations, others are adaptations, and still others are independent tests. Test users must be careful to assess the appropriateness of the Spanish version to make sure that it is culturally appropriate for the test taker.

Use an Interpreter   If the tester is fluent in the student's native language or if a qualified interpreter is available, it is possible (although undesirable) to administer tests that are interpreted for a student with limited English proficiency. Interpretations can occur on an as-needed basis. For example, the tester can translate or interpret directions or test content and answer questions in the student's native language. Although interpretation is an appealing, simple approach, it presents numerous problems. In addition to the problems associated with the commercial availability of translations, the accuracy of the interpretation is unknown.

Do Not Test

Not all educational decisions and not all assessments require testing. For students with limited English proficiency from a variety of cultures, testing for the purpose of determining eligibility is usually a bad idea. However, the school cannot overlook the possibility that students with limited English proficiency are really handicapped beyond their English abilities.

Determination of disability can be made without psychological or educational testing. The determination of sensory or physical disability can be readily made with the use of interpreters. Students or their parents need little proficiency in English for professionals to determine if a student has a traumatic brain injury, other health impairments, or orthopedic, visual, or auditory disabilities. Disabilities based on impaired social function (such as emotional disturbance and autism) can be identified through direct observation of a student or interviews with family members (using interpreters if necessary), teachers, and so forth.

The appraisal of intellectual ability is required to identify students with mental retardation. When students have moderate to severe forms of mental retardation, it may be possible to determine that they have limited intellectual ability without ever testing. For example, direct observation may reveal that a student has not acquired language (either English or the native language), communicates only by pointing and making grunting noises, is not toilet trained, and engages in inappropriate play whether judged by standards of the primary culture or by standards of U.S. culture. The student's parents may recognize that the student is much slower than their other children and would be judged to have mental retardation in their native culture. In this case, parents may want special educational services for their child. In such a situation, identification would not be impeded by the student's (or parents') lack of English. However, students with mild mental retardation do not demonstrate such pronounced developmental delays; rather, their disability is relative and not easily separated from their limited proficiency in English.

The identification of students with specific learning disabilities seems particularly difficult. IDEA 2004 requires that various conditions be considered indicative of a specific learning disability only if the student has been "provided with learning experiences and instruction appropriate for the child's age or state-approved grade-level standards" and that the condition is not a result of cultural disadvantage. Clearly, these conditions can rarely be met for students with limited English proficiency, especially when the students are also culturally diverse and have only attended U.S. public schools for a short period of time.

Finally, limited English proficiency should not be considered a speech or language impairment. Although it is quite possible for a student with limited English to have a speech or language impairment, that impairment would also be present in the student's native language. Speakers of the student's native language, such as the student's parents, could verify the presence of stuttering, impaired articulation, or voice impairments; the identification of a language disorder would require a fluent speaker of the child's native language.

When it is not possible to determine whether a student has a disability, students with limited English proficiency who are experiencing academic difficulties still need to have services besides special education available. Districts should have programs in English as a second language that could continue to help students after they have acquired social communication skills.

6 Recommendations for Making Accommodation Decisions During Accountability Testing

Many other accommodation recommendations can be implemented when collecting assessment data to make decisions about groups of students, specifically for the purpose of making accountability decisions. It is important to note that most states include language in their laws or regulations specifying the content areas for which students with limited English proficiency can be tested in a different language, as well as the number of years following enrollment in a U.S. public school during which they can take accountability tests in an alternate language. Students with limited English proficiency are typically required to take an annual test of their English language proficiency. These test results are used to determine whether they (as a group) are making progress in English language development and to hold schools accountable for providing effective English language development programs for those students who need them. Clearly, providing a native language accommodation on such tests would be highly inappropriate.

Thurlow, Elliott, and Ysseldyke (2003) suggest the following recommendations about accommodation decision making for the purpose of accountability:

- States and districts should have written guidelines for the use of accommodations in large-scale assessments used for accountability purposes.

- Decisions about accommodations should be made by one or more persons who know the student, including the student's strengths and weaknesses.

- Decision makers should consider the student's learning characteristics and the accommodations currently used during classroom instruction and classroom testing.

- The student's category of disability or program setting should not influence the decision.

- The goal is to ensure that accommodations have been used by the student prior to their use in an assessment—generally, in the classroom during instruction and in classroom testing situations. New accommodations should not be introduced for the district- or statewide assessment.

- The decision is made systematically, using a form that lists questions to answer or variables to consider in making the accommodation decision. Ideally, classroom data on the effects of accommodations are part of the information entered into decisions. Decisions and the reasons for them should be noted on the form.

- Decisions about accommodations should be documented on the student's individualized educational program.

- Parents should be involved in the decision by either participating in the decision-making process or being given the analysis of the need for accommodations and by signing the form that indicates accommodations that are to be used.[1]

- Accommodation decisions made to address individual student needs should be reconsidered at least once a year, given that student needs are likely to change over time.

[1]Adapted from Thurlow, Elliott, and Ysseldyke (2003), pp. 46–47, with permission.

Scenario in Assessment

Patricia

Patricia is an eighth-grade student who moved to the United States from Mexico City 5 years ago. While in Mexico City, she attended a grade school from the time that she was 5 years old until she was 9 years old, when she moved to the United States. When she arrived in the United States, she was offered services through a sheltered English program. Because she had developed many academic skills in Spanish during her time in Mexico City, the team involved in making decisions about how she would participate in the statewide assessment program decided that it would be most appropriate for her to have a side-by-side English/Spanish version of the math test. The following year, she had made substantial progress in developing her English skills, particularly her conversational skills. Although she had received her math instruction primarily in English over the course of the year, she was still having trouble understanding some English words associated with academic concepts. Therefore, the team decided to alter her accommodation slightly and offer her a customized dictionary that provided English definitions for some of the more difficult words presented on the test. After 2 years, she had made great gains in her English language development. Thus, the team decided it would be possible for her to participate using the English language test version in isolation, but extended time was offered to her because it sometimes took her slightly more time to process language in her still relatively new language of English. This year, she is very skilled in comprehending the English language, and the team has agreed that it is best for her to participate in the large-scale math test with no accommodations.

CHAPTER COMPREHENSION QUESTIONS

Write your answers to each of the following questions, and then compare your responses to the text or the study guide.

1. What are four reasons why you should be concerned with test adaptations and accommodations?

2. How can the principles of universal design be applied to promote accessible testing for all students?

3. Describe at least six factors to be considered when deciding whether test changes are necessary and what test changes may be appropriate.

4. Describe two schemes for categorizing accommodations, and provide examples of accommodations that might fit each category within those categorization schemes.

5. What are some accommodation guidelines to use in making eligibility decisions?

6. What are some accommodation guidelines to use in making accountability decisions?

PART 2

Assessment in Classrooms

The development of assessment has *never* been static, and its improvement has seldom been merely incremental. Scientific positivism was embraced by the mental-testing (such as intelligence tests) movement, and objective (scientific) tests gained widespread acceptance during the first half of the twentieth century. By the 1960s, however, experience with the use of norm-referenced, objectively scored tests suggested that they had a variety of technical shortcomings. A subsequent flurry of activity produced norm-referenced tests with greater reliability and substantially better norms. Nonetheless, educators frequently used these tests in inappropriate ways (for example, to plan and evaluate instruction).

As educators learned that these tests could not be used effectively to facilitate many classroom decisions, other assessment procedures were developed. Thus systematic observation procedures, so successful in experimental psychology, were adopted for classroom use. Similarly, there was renewed interest in the development of teacher-made tests. Although systematic observation and teacher-made tests were widely accepted and effectively used, many educators were still dissatisfied with the perceived limitations of these assessment techniques. During the late 1970s and 1980s, interest grew in assessing instruction and what went on in the classroom (rather than student abilities and skills). By the early 1990s, more subjective and qualitative approaches to assessment were advocated and tried.

Educational assessment may appear to have come full circle, but educators have gotten off at different points. Thus today there is no shortage of opinions about how classroom assessments ought to be conducted. Some educators still rely on norm-referenced achievement tests to plan and evaluate instruction; some rely on systematic observation; some rely on teacher-made tests and curriculum-based assessment; some rely on subjective and qualitative judgments to assess classroom learning; and some rely on a combination of approaches.

In Part 2 of this text, we discuss the approaches most likely to be used by classroom teachers. We do not consider these approaches to be informal or unstandardized. They are frequently formal: Students know that they are being assessed and that the assessments count for something. They are also frequently standardized: Students receive the same directions and tasks, and their responses are frequently scored using the same criteria. These approaches to assessment are used most frequently by classroom teachers, but we recognize that some specialists (such as school psychologists and speech and language therapists) may also use these approaches.

Part 2 begins with Chapter 6, on observation, which provides a general overview of basic considerations and good practice. Chapter 7 provides an overview of objective and performance measures constructed by teachers. Chapter 8 gives you a set of steps and procedures for preparing for and managing mandated tests, monitoring progress, and interpreting data. The chapter concludes with a description of the Iowa problem-solving model used in the Heartland Area Education Agency.

6

Assessing Behavior Through Observation

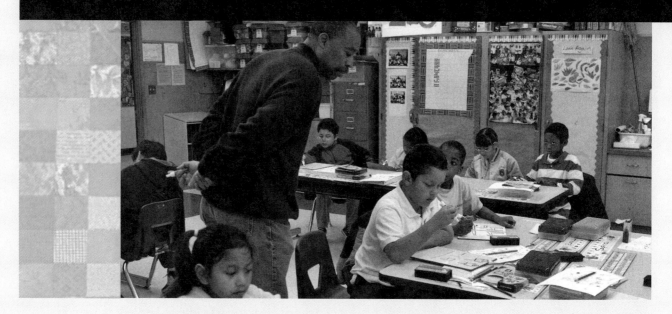

Chapter Goals

1 Understand the general considerations in conducting the conditions of observation, defining behaviors to be observed, behavioral topographies and functions, and measurable characteristics of behavior.

2 Understand that observations require careful sampling of contexts, times, and behaviors.

3 Understand that conducting systematic observations requires careful preparation, precise data gathering, procedures for summarizing data, and criteria for evaluating the observed performances.

Key Terms

qualitative observation	unobtrusive observations	function of behavior
quantitative observation	contrived observations	duration
aided observation	naturalistic observations	latency
obtrusive observations	topography of behavior	frequency

amplitude   whole-interval sampling   social comparison

behavioral contexts   partial-interval sampling   social tolerance

continuous recording   momentary time sampling   aimline

1 General Considerations

TEACHERS ARE CONSTANTLY MONITORING THEMSELVES AND THEIR STUDENTS. Sometimes they are just keeping an eye on things to make sure that their classrooms are safe and goal oriented, to anticipate disruptive or dangerous situations, or just to keep track of how things are going in a general sense. Often, teachers notice behavior or situations that seem important and require their attention: The fire alarm has sounded, Harvey has a knife, Betty is asleep, Jo is wandering around the classroom, and so forth. In other situations, often as a result of their general monitoring, teachers look for very specific behavior to observe: social behavior that should be reinforced, attention to task, performance of particular skills, and so forth.

Systematic observations are also used to inform placement and instructional decisions. When assessment does not rely on permanent products (that is, written examinations and physical creations such as a table in shop or a dinner in home economics), observation is usually involved. Clearly, social behavior, learning behavior (for example, attention to task), and aberrant behavior (for example, hand flapping) are all suitable targets of systematic observation. Obviously, behavior can be an integral part of assessing physical and mental states, physical characteristics, and educational handicaps as well as monitoring student progress and attainment.

There are two basic approaches to observation: qualitative and quantitative. *Qualitative observations* can describe behavior as well as its contexts (that is, antecedents and consequences). These observations usually occur without predetermining the behaviors to be observed or the times and contexts in which to observe. Instead, an observer monitors the situation and memorializes the observations in a narrative, the most common form being anecdotal records. Good anecdotal records contain a complete description of the behavior and the context in which it occurred and can set the stage for more focused and precise *quantitative observations*.

We stress behavioral observation, a quantitative approach to observation. Measuring behavior through observation is distinguished by five steps that occur in advance of the actual observations: (1) The behavior is defined precisely and objectively, (2) the characteristics of the behavior (for example, frequency) are specified, (3) procedures for recording are developed, (4) the times and places for observation are selected and specified, and (5) procedures are developed to assess interobserver agreement. Beyond these defining characteristics, behavioral observations can vary on a number of dimensions.

Handwritten margin notes:

Qualitative observations
Describe behavior as well as its contexts

Measuring Behaviors through observ.
1) Behavior defined precisely + objectively
2) Characteristics of behavior are specified
3) Procedures for recording are developed
4) Time + Place 4 observ. selected + specified
5) Procedures developed to assess interobserver agreement

Scenario in Assessment

Zack, Part 1

Ms. Lawson notices that during sustained silent reading time Zack seems to be walking around the room a lot and disturbing students who are reading. When she tells him to return to his seat, he always does, but he does not seem to remain there for long. She decides to keep an eye on him and to document his behavior before developing a more systematic intervention.

She notes the context, antecedents, consequences, and specifics of Zack's behavior. Figure 6.1 contains the first 3 days of relevant notes.

FIGURE 6.1
Observations of Zack's Behavior

Day:	Monday
Context:	Sustained Silent Reading—all students in own seats. Zack was on task for activities other than independent seat work.
Antecedents:	I tell class to take out their novels and begin reading where they had left off on Friday.
Behavior:	Zack takes out his novel, but does not open it. He fidgets a minute or two and then gets out of seat, wanders around the room, talks to Cindy and Marie.
Consequences:	Girls initially ignore Zack, then tell to go away, Zack giggles, and I scold him and tell him to return to his seat. Zack is falling behind in reading.
Day:	Tuesday
Context:	Science Activity Center—students working on time unit.
Antecedents:	Students are asked to write up their observations from their measurement experiments independently.
Behavior:	Zack requires help to find his lab book. After writing a few words, he gets up to sharpen his pencil but ends up strolling around the room. Again talks to Cindy and Marie.
Consequences:	Girls complain that Zack is bothering them again, Zack says he was just asking them about the project. I tell him to get back to work or he will get a time out. Zack is falling behind in science.
Note:	Zack was on task for activities other than independent seat work.
Day:	Wednesday
Context:	Sustained Silent Reading—all students in own seats.
Antecedents:	I tell class to take out their novels and begin reading where they had left off on Monday.
Behavior:	Zack puts his head down on the open pages of his novel. After about 5 minutes, he gets up and wanders around again.
Consequences:	Time out. Zack is far behind peers in completing his novel.
Note:	Zack was again on task for activities other than independent seat work.

Live or Aided Observation

Quantitative analysis of behavior can occur in real time or after the behavior has occurred by means of devices such as video or audio recorders that can replay, slow down, or speed up records of behavior. Observation can be enhanced with equipment (for example, a telescope), or it can occur with only the observer's unaided senses.

Obtrusive Versus Unobtrusive Observation

Observations are called obtrusive when it is obvious to the person being observed that he or she is being observed. The presence of an observer makes observation obvious; for example, the presence of a practicum supervisor in the back of the classroom makes it obvious to student teachers that they are being observed. The presence of observation equipment makes it obvious; for example, a video camera with a red light lit makes it obvious that observation is occurring. Something added to a situation can signal that someone is observing. For example, a dark, late-model, four-door sedan idling on the side of the road with a radar gun protruding from the driver's window makes it obvious to approaching motorists that they are being observed, or a flickering light and noise coming from behind a mirror in a testing room indicate to test takers that there is someone or something watching from behind the mirror.

When observations are unobtrusive, the people being observed do not realize they are being watched. Observers may pretend that they are not observing or observe from hidden positions. They may use telescopes to watch from afar. They may use hidden cameras and microphones.

Unobtrusive observations are preferable for two reasons. First, people are reluctant to engage in certain types of behavior if another person is looking. Thus, when antisocial, offensive, or illegal behaviors are targeted for assessment, observation should be conducted surreptitiously. Behavior of these types tends not to occur if they are overtly monitored. For example, Billy is unlikely to steal Bob's lunch money when the teacher is looking, and Rodney is unlikely to spray-paint gang graffiti on the front doors of the school when other students are present.

Likewise, if people are being observed, they are reluctant to engage in highly personal behaviors in which they must expose private body parts. In these instances, the observer should obtain the permission of the person or the person's guardian before conducting such observations. Moreover, a same-sex observer who does not know the person being observed (and whom the person being observed does not know) should conduct the observations.

The second reason that unobtrusive observations are preferable is that the presence of an observer alters the observation situation. Observation can change the behavior of those in the observation situation. For example, when a principal sits in the back of a probationary teacher's classroom to conduct an annual evaluation, both the teacher's and the students' behavior may be affected by the principal's presence. Students may be better behaved or respond more enthusiastically in the mistaken belief that the principal is there to watch them. The teacher may write on the chalkboard more frequently or give more positive reinforcement than usual in the belief that the principal values those techniques. Observation can also eliminate other types of behavior. For example, retail stores may mount circuit TV cameras and video monitors in obvious places to let potential thieves know that they are being watched constantly and to try to discourage shoplifting.

When the target behavior is not antisocial, offensive, highly personal, or undesirable, obtrusive observation may be used provided the persons being observed have been desensitized to the observers and/or equipment. It is fortunate that most people quickly become accustomed to observers in their daily environment—especially if observers make themselves part of the surroundings by avoiding eye contact, not engaging in social interactions, remaining quiet and not moving around, and so on. Observation and recording can become part of the everyday classroom routine. In any event, obtrusive observation should not begin until the persons to be observed are desensitized and are acting in their usual ways.

Contrived Versus Naturalistic Observation

Contrived observations occur when a situation is set up before a student is introduced into it. For example, a playroom may be set up with toys that encourage aggressive play (such as guns or punching-bag dolls) or with items that promote other types of behavior. A child may be given a book and told to go into the room and read or may simply be told to wait in the room. Other adults or children in the situation may be confederates of the observer and may be instructed to behave in particular ways. For example, an older child may be told not to share toys with the child who is the target of the observation, or an adult may be told to initiate a conversation on a specific topic with the target child.

In contrast, naturalistic observations occur in settings that are not contrived. For example, specific toys are not added to or removed from a playroom; the furniture is arranged as it always is arranged.

Defining Behavior

Behavior is usually defined in terms of its topography, its function, and its characteristics. The function that a behavior serves in the environment is not directly observable, whereas the characteristics and topography of behavior can be measured directly.

Topography of Behavior

Behavioral topography refers to the way a behavior is performed. For example, suppose the behavior of interest is holding a pencil to write and we are interested in Patty's topography for that behavior. The topography is readily observable: Patty holds the pencil at a 45-degree angle to the paper, grasped between her thumb and index finger; she supports the pencil with her middle finger; and so forth. Paul's topography for holding a pencil is quite different. Paul holds the pencil between his great toe and second toe so that the point of the pencil is toward the sole of his foot, and so forth.

Function of Behavior

The function of a behavior is the reason a person behaves as he or she does or the purpose the behavior serves. Obviously, the reason for a behavior cannot be observed; it can only be inferred. Sometimes, a person may offer an explanation of a behavior's function—for example, "I was screaming to make him stop." We can accept the explanation of the behavior's function if it is consistent with the circumstances, or we can reject the explanation of the function when it is not consistent with the circumstances or is unreasonable. Other times, we can infer a behavior's function from its consequences. For example, Johnny stands screaming at the rear door of his house until his mother opens the door; then he runs into the back yard and stops screaming. We might infer that the function of Johnny's screaming is to have the door opened. Behavior typically serves one or more of five functions: (1) social attention/communication; (2) access to tangibles or preferred activities; (3) escape, delay, reduction, or avoidance of aversive tasks or activities; (4) escape or avoidance of other individuals; and (5) internal stimulation (Carr, 1994).

Measurable Characteristics of Behavior

The measurement of behavior, whether individual behavior or a category of behavior, is based on four characteristics: duration, latency, frequency, and amplitude. These characteristics can be measured directly (Shapiro & Kratochwill, 2000).

Duration

Behaviors that have discrete beginnings and endings may be assessed in terms of their *duration*—that is, the length of time a behavior lasts. The duration of a behavior is usually standardized in two ways: average duration and total duration. For example, in computing average duration, suppose that Janice is out of her seat four times during a 30-minute activity, and the durations of the episodes are 1 minute, 3 minutes, 7 minutes, and 5 minutes. In this example, the average duration is 4 minutes—that is, $(1 + 3 + 7 + 5)/4$. To compute Janice's total duration, we add $1 + 3 + 7 + 5$ to conclude that she was out of her seat a total of 16 minutes. Often, total duration is expressed as a rate by dividing the total occurrence by the length of an observation. This proportion of duration is often called the "prevalence of the behavior." In the preceding example, Janice's prevalence is .53 (that is, 16/30).

Latency

Latency refers to the length of time between a signal to perform and the beginning of the behavior. For example, a teacher might ask students to take out their books. Sam's latency for that task is the length of time between the teacher's request and Sam's placing his book on his desk. For latency to be assessed, the behavior must have a discrete beginning.

Frequency

For behaviors with discrete beginnings and endings, we often count *frequency*—that is, the number of times the behaviors occur. When behavior is counted during variable time periods, frequencies are usually converted to rates. Using rate of behavior allows observers to compare the occurrence of behavior across different time periods and settings. For example, three episodes of out-of-seat behavior in 15 minutes may be converted to a rate of 12 per hour.

Alberto and Troutman (2005) suggest that frequency should not be used under two conditions: (1) when the behavior occurs at such a high rate that it cannot be counted accurately (for example, many stereotypic behaviors, such as foot tapping, can occur almost constantly) and (2) when the behavior occurs over a prolonged period of time (for example, cooperative play during a game of *Monopoly*).

Amplitude

Amplitude refers to the intensity of the behavior. In many settings, amplitude can be measured precisely (for example, with noise meters). However, in the classroom, it is usually estimated with less precision. For example, amplitude can be estimated using a rating scale that calibrates the amplitude of the behavior (for example, crying might be scaled as "whimpering," "sobbing," "crying," and "screaming"). Amplitude may also be calibrated in terms of its objective or subjective impact on others. For example, the objective impact of hitting might be scaled as "without apparent physical damage," "resulting in bruising," and "causing bleeding." More subjective behavior ratings estimate the internal impact on others; for example, a student's humming could be scaled as "does not disturb others," "disturbs students seated nearby," or "disturbs students in the adjoining classroom."

Selecting the Characteristic to Measure

The behavioral characteristic to be assessed should make sense; we should assess the most relevant aspect of behavior in a particular situation. For example, if Burl is wandering around the classroom during the reading period, observing the duration of that behavior makes more sense than observing the frequency, latency, or amplitude of the behavior. If Camilla's teacher is concerned about her loud utterances, amplitude may be the most salient characteristic to observe. If Molly is always slow to follow directions, observing her latency makes more sense than assessing the frequency or amplitude of her behavior. For most behaviors, however, frequency and duration are the characteristics measured.

2 Sampling Behavior

As with any assessment procedure, we can assess the entire domain if it is finite and convenient. If it is not, we can sample from the domain. Important dimension for sampling behavior include the contexts in which the behaviors occur, the times at which the behaviors occur, and the behaviors themselves.

Contexts

When specific behaviors become the targets of intervention, it is useful to measure the behavior in a variety of contexts. Usually, the sampling of contexts is purposeful rather than random. We might want to know, for example, how Jesse's behavior in the resource room differs from his behavior in the general education classroom. Consistent or inconsistent performance across settings and contexts can provide useful information about what events might set the occasion for the behavior. Differences between the settings in which a behavior does and does not occur can provide potentially useful hypotheses about *setting events* (that is, environmental events that set the occasion for the performance of an action) and *discriminative stimuli* (that is, stimuli that are consistently present when a behavior is reinforced and that come to bring out behavior even in the absence of the original reinforcer).[1]

---

[1]Discriminative stimuli are not conditioned stimuli in the Pavlovian sense that they elicit reflexive behavior. Discriminative stimuli provide a signal to the individual to engage in a particular behavior because that behavior has been reinforced in the presence of that signal.

Bringing behavior under the control of a discriminative stimulus is often an effective way of modifying it. For example, students might be taught to talk quietly (to use their "inside voice") when they are in the classroom or hallway.

Similarly, consistent or inconsistent performance across settings and contexts can provide useful information about how the consequences of a behavior are affecting that behavior. Some consequences of a behavior maintain, increase, or decrease behavior. Thus, manipulating the consequences of a behavior can increase or decrease its occurrence. For example, assume that Joey's friends usually laugh and congratulate him when he makes a sexist remark and that Joey is reinforced by his friends' behavior. If his friends could be made to stop laughing and congratulating him, Joey would probably make fewer sexist remarks.

Times

With the exception of some criminal acts, few behaviors are noteworthy unless they happen more than once. Behavioral recurrence over time is termed *stability* or *maintenance*. In a person's lifetime, there are almost an infinite number of times to exhibit a particular behavior. Moreover, it is probably impossible and certainly unnecessary to observe a person continuously during his or her entire life. Thus, temporal sampling is always performed, and any single observation is merely a sample from the person's behavioral domain.

Time sampling always requires the establishment of blocks of time, termed *observation sessions*, in which observations will be made. A session might consist of a continuous period of time (for example, one school day). More often, sessions are discontinuous blocks of time (for example, every Monday for a semester or during daily reading time).

Continuous Recording

Observers can record behavior continuously within sessions. They count each occurrence of a behavior in the observation session; they can time the duration or latency of each occurrence within the observation session.

When the observation session is long (for example, when it spans several days), continuous sampling can be very expensive and is often intrusive. Two options are commonly used to estimate behavior in very long observation sessions: the use of rating scales to make estimates and time sampling. In the first option, rating scales are used to estimate one (or more) of the four characteristics of behavior. Following are some examples of such ratings:

- *Frequency:* A parent might be asked to rate the frequency of a behavior. How often does Patsy usually pick up her toys—always, frequently, seldom, never?

- *Duration:* A parent might be asked to rate how long Bernie typically watches TV each night—more than 3 hours, 2 or 3 hours, 1 or 2 hours, or less than 1 hour?

- *Latency:* A parent might be asked to rate how quickly Marisa usually responds to requests—immediately, quickly, slowly, or not at all (ignores requests)?

- *Amplitude:* A parent might be asked to rate how much of a fuss Jessica usually makes at bedtime—screams, cries, begs to stay up, or goes to bed without fuss?

In the second observation option, duration and frequency are sampled systematically during prolonged observation intervals. Three different sampling plans have been advocated: whole-interval recording, partial-interval recording, and momentary time sampling.

Time Sampling

Continuous observation requires the expenditure of more resources than does discontinuous observation. Therefore, it is common to observe for a sample of times within an observation session.

In *interval sampling*, an observation session is subdivided into intervals during which behavior is observed. Usually, observation intervals of equal length are spaced equally through the session, although the recording and observation intervals need not be the same length. Three types of interval sampling and scoring are common.

1. In *whole-interval* sampling, a behavior is scored as having occurred only when it occurs throughout the entire interval. Thus, it is scored only if it is occurring when the interval begins and continues through the end of the interval.

2. *Partial-interval sampling* is quite similar to whole-interval recording. The difference between the two procedures is that in partial-interval recording, an occurrence is scored if it occurs during any part of the interval. Thus, if a behavior begins before the interval begins and ends within the interval, an occurrence is scored; if a behavior starts after the beginning of the interval, an occurrence is scored; if two or more episodes of behavior begin and end within the interval, one occurrence is scored.

3. *Momentary time sampling* is the most efficient sampling procedure. An observation session is subdivided into intervals. If a behavior is occurring at the last moment of the interval, an occurrence is recorded; if the behavior is not occurring at the last moment of the interval, a nonoccurrence is recorded. For example, suppose we observe Robin during her 20-minute reading period. We first select the interval length (for example, 10 seconds). At the end of the first 10-second interval, we observe if the behavior is occurring; at the end of the second 10-second interval, we again observe. We continue observing until we have observed Robin at the end of the 60th 10-second interval.

Salvia and Hughes (1990) have summarized a number of studies investigating the accuracy of these time-sampling procedures. Both whole-interval and partial-interval sampling procedures provide inaccurate estimates of duration and frequency.[2] Momentary time sampling provides an unbiased estimate of the proportion of time that is very accurate when small intervals are used (that is, 10- to 15-second intervals). Continuous recording with shorter observation sessions is the better method of estimating the frequency of a behavior.

---

[2]Suen and Ary (1989) have provided procedures whereby the sampled frequencies can be adjusted to provide accurate frequency estimates, and the error associated with estimates of prevalence can be readily determined for each sampling plan.

Behaviors

Teachers and psychologists may be interested in measurement of a particular behavior or a constellation of behaviors thought to represent a trait (for example, cooperation). When an observer views a target behavior as important in and of itself, only that specific behavior is observed. However, when a specific behavior is thought to be one element in a constellation of behaviors, other important behaviors within the constellation must also be observed in order to establish the content validity of the behavioral constellation. For example, if taking turns on a slide were viewed as one element of cooperation, we should also observe other behaviors indicative of cooperation (such as taking turns on other equipment, following the rules of games, and working with others to attain a common goal). Each of the behaviors in a behavioral constellation can be treated separately or aggregated for the purposes of observation and reporting.

Observations are usually conducted on two types of behavior. First, we regularly observe behavior that is desirable and that we are trying to increase. Behavior of this type includes all academic performances (for example, oral reading or science knowledge) and prosocial behavior (for example, cooperative behavior or polite language). Second, we regularly observe behavior that is undesirable or may indicate a disabling condition. These behaviors are harmful, stereotypic, inappropriately infrequent, or inappropriate at the times exhibited.

- *Harmful behavior:* Behavior that is self-injurious or physically dangerous to others is almost always targeted for intervention. Self-injurious behavior includes such actions as head banging, eye gouging, self-biting or self-hitting, smoking, and drug abuse. Potentially harmful behavior can include leaning back in a desk or being careless with reagents in a chemistry experiment. Behaviors harmful to others are those that directly inflict injury (for example, hitting or stabbing) or are likely to injure others (for example, pushing other students on stairs or subway platforms, bullying, or verbally instigating physical altercations). Unusually aggressive behavior may also be targeted for intervention. Although most students will display aggressive behavior, some children go far beyond what can be considered typical or acceptable. These students may be described as hot-tempered, quick-tempered, or volatile. Overly aggressive behavior may be physical or verbal. In addition to the possibility of causing physical harm, high rates of aggressive behavior may isolate the aggressor socially.

- *Stereotypic behavior:* Stereotypic behaviors, or stereotypies (for example, hand flapping, rocking, and certain verbalizations such as inappropriate shrieks), are outside the realm of culturally normative behavior. Such behavior calls attention to students and marks them as abnormal to trained psychologists or unusual to untrained observers. Stereotypic behaviors are often targeted for intervention.

- *Infrequent or absent desirable behavior:* Incompletely developed behavior, especially behavior related to physiological development (for example, walking), is often targeted for intervention. Intervention usually occurs when development of these behaviors will enable desirable functional skills or social acceptance. Shaping is usually used to develop absent behavior, whereas reinforcement is used to increase the frequency of behavior that is within a student's repertoire but exhibited at rates that are too low.

■ *Normal behavior exhibited in inappropriate contexts:* Many behaviors are appropriate in very specific contexts but are considered inappropriate or even abnormal when exhibited in other contexts. Usually, the problems caused by behavior in inappropriate contexts are attributed to lack of stimulus control. Behavior that is commonly called "private" falls into this category; elimination and sexual activity are two examples. The goal of intervention should be not to get rid of these behaviors but to confine them to socially appropriate conditions. Behavior that is often called "disruptive" also falls into this category. For example, running and yelling are very acceptable and normal when exhibited on the playground; they are disruptive in a classroom.

A teacher may decide on the basis of logic and experience that a particular behavior should be modified. For example, harmful behavior should not be tolerated in a classroom or school, and behavior that is a prerequisite for learning academic material must be developed. In other cases, a teacher may seek the advice of a colleague, supervisor, or parent about the desirability of intervention. For example, a teacher might not know whether certain behavior is typical of a student's culture. In yet other cases, a teacher might rely on the judgments of students or adults as to whether a particular behavior is troublesome or distracting for them. For example, are others bothered when Bob reads problems aloud during arithmetic tests? To ascertain whether a particular behavior bothers others, teachers can ask students directly, have them rate disturbing or distracting behavior, or perhaps use sociometric techniques to learn whether a student is being rejected or isolated because of his or her behavior. The sociometric technique is a method for evaluating the social acceptance of individual pupils and the social structure of a group: Students complete a form indicating their choice of companions for seating, work, or play. Teachers look at the number of times an individual student is chosen by others. They also look at who chooses whom.

For infrequent prosocial behavior or frequent disturbing behavior, a teacher may wish to get a better idea of the magnitude and pervasiveness of the problem before initiating a comprehensive observational analysis. Casual observation can provide information about the frequency and amplitude of the behavior; carefully noting the antecedents, consequences, and contexts may provide useful information about possible interventions if an intervention is warranted. If casual observations are made, anecdotal records of these casual observations should be maintained.

3   Conducting Systematic Observations

Preparation

Careful preparation is essential to obtaining accurate and valid observational data that are useful in decision making. Five steps should guide the preparation for systematic observation:

1. *Define target behaviors.*

- Use definitions that describe behavior in observable terms.
- Avoid references to internal processes (for example, understanding or appreciating).

- Anticipate potentially difficult discriminations and provide examples of instances and noninstances of the behavior. Include subtle instances of the target behavior, and use related behaviors and behavior with similar topographies as noninstances.
- State the characteristic of the behavior that will be measured (for example, frequency or latency).

2. *Select contexts.* Observe the target behavior systematically in at least three contexts: the context in which the behavior was noted as troublesome (for example, in reading instruction), a similar context (for example, in math instruction), and a dissimilar context (for example, in physical education or recess).

3. *Select an observation schedule.*
   - Choose the session length. In the schools, session length is usually related to instructional periods or blocks of time within an instructional period (for example, 15 minutes in the middle of small-group reading instruction).
   - Decide between continuous and discontinuous observation. The choice of continuous or discontinuous observation will depend on the resources available and the specific behaviors that are to be observed. When very low-frequency behavior or behavior that must be stopped (for example, physical assaults) is observed, continuous recording is convenient and efficient. For other behavior, discontinuous observation is usually preferred, and momentary time sampling is usually the easiest and most accurate for teachers and psychologists to use. When a discontinuous observation schedule is used, the observer requires some equipment to signal exactly when observation is to occur. The most common equipment is a portable audiocassette player and a tape with pure tones, recorded at the desired intervals. One student or several students in sequence may be observed. For example, three students can be observed in a series of 5-second intervals. An audiotape would signal every 5 seconds. On the first signal, Henry would be observed; on the second signal, Joyce would be observed; on the third signal, Bruce would be observed; on the fourth signal, Henry would be observed again; and so forth.

4. *Develop recording procedures.* The recording of observations must also be planned. When a few students are observed for the occurrence of relatively infrequent behaviors, simple procedures can be used. The behaviors can be observed continuously and counted using a tally sheet or a wrist counter. When time sampling is used, observations must be recorded for each time interval; thus, some type of recording form is required. In the simplest form, the recording sheet contains identifying information (for example, name of target student, name of observer, date and time of observation session, and observation-interval length) and two columns. The first column shows the time interval, and the second column contains space for the observer to indicate whether the behavior occurred during each interval. More complicated recording forms may be used for multiple behaviors and/or multiple students. When multiple behaviors are observed, they are often given code numbers. For example, "out of seat" might be coded as 1, "in seat but off task" might be coded as 2, "in seat and on task" might be coded as 3, and "no opportunity to observe" might be coded as 4. Such codes should be

included on the observation record form. Figure 6.2 shows a simple form on which to record multiple behaviors of students. The observer writes the code number(s) in the box corresponding to the interval. Complex observational systems tend to be less accurate than simple ones. Complexity increases as a function of the number of different behaviors that are assessed and the number of individuals who are observed. Moreover, both the proportion of target individuals to total individuals and the proportion of target behaviors observed to the number of target behaviors to be recorded also have an impact on accuracy. The surest way to reduce inaccuracies is to keep things relatively simple.

5. *Select the means of observation.* The choice of human observers or electronic recorders will depend on the availability of resources. If electronic recorders are available and can be used in the desired environments and contexts, they may be appropriate when continuous observation is warranted. If other personnel are available, they can be trained to observe and record the target behaviors accurately. Training should include didactic instruction in defining the target behavior, the use of time sampling (if it is to be used), and the way in which to record behavior, as well as practice in using the observation system.

FIGURE 6.2
A Simple Recording Form for Three Students and Two Behaviors

Observer: *Mr. Kowalski*

Date: *2/15/08*

Times of observation: *10:15 to 11:00*

Observation interval: *10 sec*

Instructional activity: *Oral reading*

Students observed:

S1 = *Henry J.*

S2 = *Bruce H.*

S3 = *Joyce W.*

Codes:

1 = out of seat
2 = in seat but off task
3 = in seat, on task
4 = no opportunity to observe

	S1	S2	S3
1	____	____	____
2	____	____	____
3	____	____	____
4	____	____	____
5	____	____	____
.			
.			
.			
179	____	____	____
180	____	____	____

Training is always continued until the desired level of accuracy is reached. Observers' accuracy is evaluated by comparing each observer's responses with those of the others or with a criterion rating (usually a previously scored videotape). Generally, very high agreement is required before anyone can assume that observers are ready to conduct observations independently. Ultimately, the decision of how to collect the data should also be based on efficiency. For example, if it takes longer to desensitize students to an obtrusive video recorder than it takes to train observers, then human observers are preferred.

Data Gathering

Observers should prepare a checklist of equipment and materials that will be used during the observation and assemble everything that is needed, including an extra supply of recording forms, spare pens or pencils, and something to write on (for example, a clipboard or tabletop). When electronic recording is used, equipment should be checked before every observation session to make sure it is in good working condition, and the observer should bring needed extras (for example, batteries, signal tapes, and recording tapes). Also, before the observation session, the observer should check the setting to locate appropriate vantage points for equipment or furniture. During observation, care should be taken to conduct the observations as planned. Thus, the observer should make sure that he or she adheres to the definitions of behavior, the observation schedules, and recording protocols. Careful preparation can head off trouble.

As with any type of assessment information, two general sources of error can reduce the accuracy of observation. Random error can result in over- or underestimates of behavior. Systematic error can bias the data in a consistent direction—for example, behavior may be systematically overcounted or undercounted.

Random Error

Random errors in observation and recording usually affect observer agreement. Observers may change the criteria for the occurrence of a behavior, they may forget behavior codes, or they may use the recording forms incorrectly. Because changes in agreement can signal that something is wrong, the accuracy of observational data should be checked periodically. The usual procedure is to have two people observe and record on the same schedule in the same session. The two records are then compared, and an index of agreement (for example, point-to-point agreement) is computed. Poor agreement suggests the need for retraining or for revision of the observation procedures. To alleviate some of these problems, we can provide periodic retraining and allow observers to keep the definitions and codes for target behaviors with them. Finally, when observers know that their accuracy is being systematically checked, they are usually more accurate. Thus, observers should not be told when they are being observed but to expect their observations to be checked.

One of the most vexing factors affecting the accuracy of observations is the incorrect recording of correctly observed behavior. Even when observers have applied the criterion for the occurrence of a behavior correctly, they may record their decision incorrectly. For example, if 1 is used to indicate occurrence and 0 is used to indicate nonoccurrence, the observer might accidentally record 0 for a behavior that has occurred. Inaccuracy can be attributed to three related factors.

1. *Lack of familiarity with the recording system:* Observers definitely need practice in using a recording system when several behaviors or several students are to be observed. They also need practice when the target behaviors are difficult to define or when they are difficult to observe.

2. *Insufficient time to record:* Sufficient time must be allowed to record the occurrence of behavior. Problems can arise when using momentary time sampling if the observation intervals are spaced too closely (for example, 1- or 5-second intervals). Observers who are counting several different high-frequency behaviors may record inaccurately. Generally, inadequate opportunities for observers to record can be circumvented by electronic recording of the observation session; when observers can stop and replay segments of interest, they essentially have unlimited time to observe and record.

3. *Lack of concentration:* It may be difficult for observers to remain alert for long periods of time (for example, 1 hour), especially if the target behavior occurs infrequently and is difficult to detect. Observers can reduce the time that they must maintain vigilance by either taking turns with several observers or recording observation sessions for later evaluation. Similarly, when it is difficult to maintain vigilance because the observational context is noisy, busy, or otherwise distracting, electronic recording may be useful in focusing on target subjects and eliminating ambient noise.

Systematic Error

Systematic errors are difficult to detect. To minimize error, four steps can be taken.

1. *Guard against unintended changes in the observation process.*[3] When assessment is carried out over extended periods of time, observers may talk to each other about the definitions that they are using or about how they cope with difficult discriminations. Consequently, one observer's departure from standardized procedures may spread to other observers. When the observers change together, modifications of the standard procedures and definitions will not be detected by examining interobserver agreement. Techniques for reducing changes in observers over time include keeping the scoring criteria available to observers, meeting with the observers on a regular basis to discuss difficulties encountered during observation, and providing periodic retraining. Surprisingly, even recording equipment can change over time. Audio signal tapes (used to indicate the moment a student should be observed) may stretch after repeated uses; a 10-second interval may become an 11-second interval. Similarly, the batteries in playback units can lose power, and signal tapes may play more slowly. Therefore, equipment should be cleaned periodically, and signal tapes should be checked for accuracy.

2. *Desensitize students.* The introduction of equipment or new adults into a classroom, as well as changes in teacher routines, can signal to students that observations are going on. Overt measurement can alter the target behavior

---

[3]Technically, general changes in the observation process over time are called instrumentation problems.

Minimize errors
1) Guard against unintended changes in the observation process
2) Desensitize students
3) Minimize observer expectancies
4) Motivate observers

or the topography of the behavior. Usually, the pupil change is temporary. For example, when Janey knows that she is being observed, she may be more accurate, deliberate, or compliant. However, as observation becomes a part of the daily routine, students' behavior usually returns to what is typical for them. This return to typical patterns of behavior functionally defines desensitization. The data generated from systematic observation should not be used until the students who are observed are no longer affected by the observation procedures and equipment or personnel. However, sometimes the change in behavior is permanent. For example, if a teacher was watching for the extortion of lunch money, Robbie might wait until no observers were present or might demand the money in more subtle ways. In such cases, valid data would not be obtained through overt observation, and either different procedures would have to be developed or the observation would have to be abandoned.

3. *Minimize observer expectancies.* Sometimes, what an observer believes will happen affects what is seen and recorded. For example, if an observer expects an intervention to increase a behavior, that observer might unconsciously alter the criteria for evaluating that behavior or might evaluate approximations of the target behavior as having occurred. The more subtle or complex the target behavior, the more susceptible it may be to expectation effects. The easiest way to avoid expectations during observations is for the observer to be blind to the purpose of the assessment. When video- or audiotapes are used to record behavior, the order in which they are evaluated can be randomized so that observers do not know what portion of an observation is being scored. When it is impossible or impractical to keep observers blind to the purpose, the importance of accurate observation should be stressed and such observation rewarded.

4. *Motivate observers.* Inaccurate observation is sometimes attributed to lack of motivation on the part of an observer. Motivation can be increased by providing rewards and feedback, stressing the importance of the observations, reducing the length of observation sessions, and not allowing observation sessions to become routine.

 ## Data Summarization

Depending on the particular characteristic of behavior being measured, observational data may be summarized in different ways. When duration or frequency is the characteristic of interest, observations are usually summarized as rates (that is, the prevalence or the number of occurrences per minute or other time interval). Latency and amplitude should be summarized statistically by the mean and the standard deviation or by the median and the range. All counts and calculations should be checked for accuracy.

4 Criteria for Evaluating Observed Performances

Once accurate observational data have been collected and summarized, they must be interpreted. Behavior is interpreted in one of two ways. For some behavior, its presence or absence is compared to an absolute criterion. Behaviors evaluated in this way include unsafe and harmful behavior, illegal behavior, and so forth.

1. Often, we interpret behavior by comparing it to the behavior of others. For example, knowing that 6-year-old Marie is out of seat 10 percent of the time during instruction in content areas is not readily interpretable. Behavior rates can be evaluated in several ways.

2. Normative data may be available for some behavior or, in some cases, data from behavior rating scales and tests can provide general guidelines.

3. Social comparisons can be made using a peer whose behavior is considered appropriate. The peer's rate of behavior is then used as the standard against which to evaluate the target student's rate of behavior.

The social tolerance for a behavior can also be used as a criterion. For example, the degree to which different rates of out-of-seat behavior disturb a teacher or peers can be assessed. Teachers and peers could be asked to rate how disturbing is the out-of-seat behavior of students who exhibit different rates of behavior. In a somewhat different vein, the contagion of the behavior to others can be a crucial consideration in teacher judgments of unacceptable behavior. Thus, the effects of different rates of behavior can be assessed to determine whether there is a threshold above which other students initiate undesirable behavior.

We also use progress toward objectives or goals as the standard with which to evaluate behavior. A common and useful procedure is graphing data against an aimline. As shown in Figure 6.3, an aimline connects a student's measured behavior at the start of an intervention with the point (called an aim) representing the terminal behavior and the date by which that behavior should be attained. When the goal is to accelerate a desirable behavior (Figure 6.3A), student performances above the aimline are evaluated as good progress. When the goal is to decelerate an undesirable behavior (Figure 6.3B), student performances below the aimline are evaluated as good progress. Good progress is progress that meets or exceeds the desired rate of behavior change.

FIGURE 6.3
Aimlines for Accelerating and Decelerating Behavior

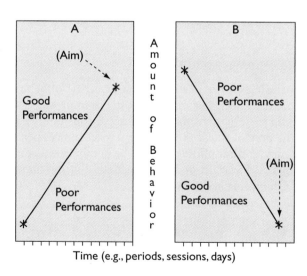

Time (e.g., periods, sessions, days)

Scenario in Assessment

Zack, Part 2

Ms. Lawson has previously collected anecdotal information that suggests that Zack has a problem staying on task and in his seat when independent work is required regardless of the subject matter or time of day. Before conducting systematic observations of Zack's *wanderings*, Ms. Lawson defines precisely what she means by wandering. She defines it as "walking around classroom during seatwork assignments." She specifically excludes leaving his seat with her permission. She decides to count the frequency of both wandering and compliance during seatwork throughout the day for 4 days—Monday through Thursday. In addition, to have interpretive data, she decides to observe two other boys who she considers generally well behaved but not exceptionally so.

Ms. Lawson decides to record the behavior unobtrusively by using a wrist counter and transferring the frequencies to a chart after the students have left for the day. Fortunately, she has a student teacher who can make simultaneous observations in order to check reliability. However, she must first meet with the student teacher to discuss the definition of wandering and the procedures used to record behavior. Because the target behavior was so easy to observe and the procedures so simple, reliability was not thought to be a major issue. She would like to determine the function of Zack's wandering. The likely functions seemed to be avoidance from an unpleasant task or social attention, but more information would be needed to reach a conclusion.

Each day, Ms. Lawson and her student teacher transferred the frequencies of the number of times Zack and the two comparison boys wandered the room. She calculated simple agreement and transferred her frequencies to the graph shown in Figure 6.4.

The results were as expected. Simple agreement between Ms. Lawson and her student teacher was always 100 percent. The boys who were observed for social comparison seldom wandered, and Zack wandered approximately 20 percent of the time.

FIGURE 6.4
Comparison of Zack and Peer Wanderings

CHAPTER COMPREHENSION QUESTIONS

Write your answers to each of the following questions, and then compare your responses to the text or the study guide.

1. What five steps should you follow in preparing to conduct systematic quantitative observations?

2. What is the difference between a behavior's topography and function?

3. What characteristics of behavior (for example, amplitude) can be observed?

4. Explain the three ways in which behavior can be sampled and identify which is the best way.

5. What can an observer do to minimize or prevent errors in observations?

6. Explain the four ways in which behavior can be interpreted.

7 Teacher-Made Tests of Achievement

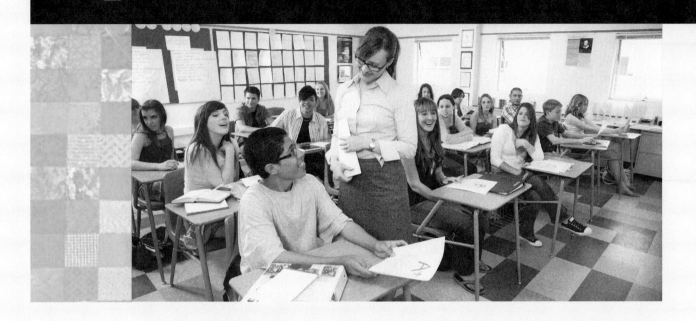

Chapter Goals

1 Understand that teacher-made tests can be used to ascertain skill development, monitor instruction, document instructional problems, and make summative judgments.

2 Understand that teacher-made tests vary on the dimensions of content specificity, testing frequency, and testing formats.

3 Know that considerations in preparing tests include selecting specific areas of the curriculum, writing relevant questions, organizing and sequencing items, developing formats for presentation and response modes, writing directions for administration, developing systematic procedures for scoring responses, and establishing criteria to interpret student performance.

4 Know that response formats use different types of questions and have special considerations for students with disabilities.

5 Understand that assessment in the core achievement areas of reading, mathematics, spelling, and writing differs for beginning and advanced students.

6 Understand the potential sources of difficulty in the use of teacher-made tests.

HISTORICALLY, TEACHER-MADE TESTS HAVE NOT BEEN HELD IN HIGH REGARD. FOR example, some measurement specialists (for example, Thorndike & Hagen, 1978) cite carefully prepared test items as an advantage of commercially available norm-referenced achievement tests. By implication, careful preparation of questions may not be a characteristic of teacher-made tests. In addition, adjectives such as "informal" or "unstandardized" have been used to describe teacher-made tests. As a group, however, teacher-made tests cannot be considered informal because they are not given haphazardly or casually. They cannot be considered unstandardized because students usually receive the same materials and directions, and the same criteria are usually used in correcting student answers. Although there is a place for commercially available norm-referenced achievement tests, we think that their value has been overestimated. Indeed, teacher-made tests can be better suited to evaluation of student achievement than are commercially prepared, norm-referenced achievement tests.

Achievement refers to what has been directly taught and learned by a student. It is different from attainment (what has been learned anywhere). Teachers are in the best position to know what has been (or at least should be) taught in their classrooms. This simple fact stands in sharp contrast to commercially prepared tests that are not designed to assess achievement within specific curricula (see, for example, Crocker, Miller, & Franks, 1989) or to meet a specific state's standards. Rather, these tests are intentionally constructed to have general applicability so that they can be used with students in almost any curriculum or broad state standards. Moreover, it is clear that various curriculum series differ from one another in the particular educational objectives covered, the performance level expected of students, and the sequence of objectives; for example, DISTAR mathematics differs from Scott, Foresman mathematics (Shriner & Salvia, 1988). Even within the same curriculum series, teachers modify instruction to provide enrichment or remedial instruction. Thus, two teachers using the same curriculum series and trying to meet the same state standards may offer different instruction. Although teachers may not construct tests that match the curriculum and state standards, they are the only ones capable of knowing precisely what has been taught and what level of performance is expected from students. Consequently, they are the only ones who can match testing to instruction.

In addition, teacher-made tests are usually designed to assess what students are learning or have learned. Commercially prepared, norm-referenced tests are designed to assess which students know more and which students know less (that is, to discriminate among test takers on the basis of what they know). Thus, teachers include enough items on their tests to make valid estimates of what students have learned, whereas developers of norm-referenced tests try to include the minimum number of test items that allow reliable discrimination. This difference between teacher-made and commercially prepared tests has two important consequences. First, because teacher-made tests can include many more items (even all of the items of interest), they can be much more sensitive to small but important changes in student learning. For example, a teacher-made test that included all of the addition facts could show whether a student has learned nine addition facts in the past 2 days; norm-referenced tests usually assess all of the mathematical operations and necessarily have only a few addition problems so that this level of specificity is not possible to attain with them. Also, teacher-made tests can show what content requires additional instruction and student practice; norm-referenced tests cannot. Finally, teacher-made tests can indicate when students have mastered an instructional goal so instruction can be provided on new objectives; norm-referenced tests cannot.

In short, teachers need tests that reflect what they are teaching and are sensitive to changes in student achievement.[1] We strongly recommend that the assessments be objective—that is, based on observable phenomena and minimally affected by a variety of subjective factors. The use of objective methods is not merely a matter of personal preference. Federal regulations require that students with disabilities be evaluated using objective procedures.[2] This chapter provides a general overview of objective practices for teachers who develop their own tests for classroom assessment in the core areas of reading, mathematics, spelling, and written language.

1 Uses

Teachers regularly set aside time to assess their pupils for a variety of purposes. Most commonly, they make up tests to ascertain the extent to which their students have learned or are learning what has been taught or assigned. Student achievement is the basis on which teachers make decisions about student skill development, student progress, instructional problems, and grades. Often, an assessment can be used for more than one purpose. For example, assessments made to monitor instruction can be aggregated for use in making summative judgments.

Ascertain Skill Development

A student's level of skill development is a fundamental consideration in planning instruction. We want to know what instructional objectives our students have met in order to decide what things we should be teaching our students. Obviously, if students have met an instructional objective, we should not waste their time by continuing to teach what they have already learned. Rather, we should build on their learning by extending their learning (for example, planning for generalization of learning) or moving on to the next objective in the instructional sequence. Also, students who meet objectives so rapidly that they are being held back by slower peers can be grouped for enrichment activities or faster-paced instruction;

---

[1]Teachers assess frequently to detect changes in student achievement. However, frequent testing with exactly the same test usually produces a practice effect. Unless there are multiple forms for a test, student learning may be confused with practice effect.

[2]Note that general educators are often trained in more subjective and holistic approaches, and the difference in approaches can cause many problems when general and special educators work together to provide an education for all students in an inclusive classroom.

slower students can be grouped so that they can learn necessary concepts to the point of mastery without impeding the progress of their faster-learning peers.

Monitor Instruction

The extent to which any lesson, program, or intervention will be effective with a specific student within a specific educational context cannot be known *a priori*. Although we know what techniques are generally effective with most students, those techniques may not work as well (or at all) with specific students because of their unique characteristics, the characteristics of their teachers, or the context in which the instruction occurs. Teachers can teach and hope that their students have learned, or they can check throughout the learning process to make sure that their students are learning correctly and efficiently.

The evidence is overwhelming that learning is much more efficient when student errors and misunderstandings are caught early and corrected. Catching student errors early saves time; students then do not have to unlearn incorrect material before learning the correct information or skill. Catching student errors early also means that they do not get left behind. Early detection of student errors is above all humane. Student achievement during instruction can be used to inform decisions about altering instruction, grouping students, evaluating teaching performance, and perhaps referring students to other educational specialists for additional instructional services.

Teachers should not rely on a single test or observation to monitor progress. It is better to collect data systematically and frequently and then to assemble the results into a readily interpretable format such as graphs. Thus, progress monitoring involves (1) collecting and analyzing data to ascertain student progress toward mastery of specific skills or general outcomes and (2) using the data collected to make instructional decisions—that is, "data-driven decision making." Progress can be readily seen when student responses are graphed. When correct responses are plotted against an aimline,[3] progress is indicated when student performance is consistently above the aimline. Figure 7.1 shows an example of satisfactory performance as judged from an aimline graph. When correct responses and errors are plotted in the same graph, satisfactory performance is indicated in four ways, as shown in Figure 7.2. Correct responses increase and/or errors decrease. The data in these two figures indicate clearly that the student is making good progress.

A different way to think about documenting student progress is with *celeration*, a word coined to describe the trend of data. Celeration quantifies the degree of student progress over time. White and Haring (1980) provided a method of calculating celeration that is still in use. To illustrate, suppose that a teacher had obtained data on a student's rate of oral reading each day for 10 consecutive days. The teacher would first need to find the medians for the first and second half of the days (that is, week 1 and week 2). The smaller median would be divided by the larger median. If the smaller median occurred in the first half (week), a multiplication sign (×) is placed before the decimal; if the smaller median occurred in the second half (week), a division sign (÷) is used.

---

[3]Recall from Chapter 6 that an aimline connects a student's measured behavior at the start of an intervention with the point (called an aim) representing the terminal behavior and the date by which that behavior should be attained.

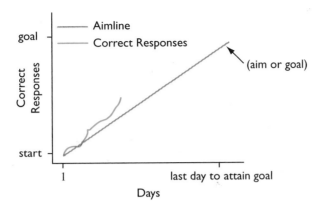

FIGURE 7.1
Satisfactory Progress Judged from an Aimline Graph

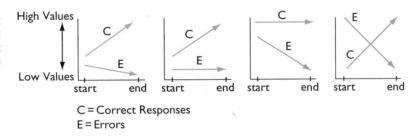

FIGURE 7.2
Satisfactory Progress Judged from a Graph of Correct Responses and Errors

C = Correct Responses
E = Errors

Document Instructional Problems

Instructional problems are indicated primarily by a lack of progress toward instructional goals.[4] Evidence on the nature and degree of the problem should be gathered systematically through testing, observation, or analysis of permanent products such as worksheets. Teachers should not rely on a single test or observation as documentation of an instructional problem. The better way is to collect data systematically and frequently. Here, too, it is usually helpful to assemble the results into graphs, from which lack of progress can be readily seen. When correct responses are plotted against an aimline, lack of progress is indicated when student performance is consistently below the aimline. Figure 7.3 shows an example of poor performance as judged from an aimline graph. When correct responses and errors are plotted in the same graph, poor performance is indicated in four ways, as shown in Figure 7.4. Correct responses are not increasing and/or errors are increasing. Teachers can also calculate the celeration of student performance; ÷ celeration would indicate an instructional problem.

Make Summative Judgments

Summative judgments are categorized into two classes: judgments about general student attainment and judgments about teaching effectiveness. General student attainment is generally synonymous with the grade assigned to that student for a particular marking period. How grades are determined varies considerably from school district to school district. In some districts, there are districtwide policies

---

[4]Instructional problems are also indicated when students must spend inordinate amounts of time outside the classroom to succeed or when they develop undesirable behaviors that suggest frustration or anxiety.

FIGURE 7.3
Aimline Graph Showing Lack
of Student Progress

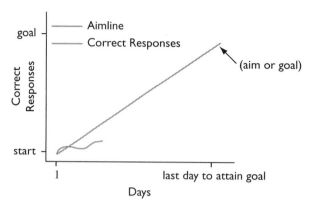

FIGURE 7.4
Graphs Showing Correct
Responses and Errors

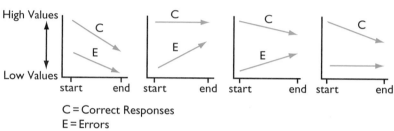

C = Correct Responses
E = Errors

that define each grade (for example, to earn an *A* students must average 92 percent or more on all tests). Teachers may differ on how they weight tests (for example, quizzes may count less than tests). We take no position on what should be included in a student's grade. What we do recommend is that the basis of a student's grade be carefully explained at the beginning of the year (or marking period) so that all students know how they will be graded. We also recommend that grades be as objective as possible so that they avoid any hint of bias or favoritism.

Judgments about teaching effectiveness should be made on the basis of student achievement. When many students in a classroom fail to learn material, teachers should suspect that something is wrong with their materials, their techniques, or some other aspect of instruction. For example, the students may have lacked prerequisite concepts or skills, or the instruction may be too fast paced or poorly sequenced. Teachers working with students with special needs are obligated by law and ethical standards to modify their instruction when it is not working.

2   Dimensions of Academic Assessment

Assessments differ along several dimensions: content specificity, frequency, and response quantification. Different purposes can require different degrees of specificity, different frequency, and different formats.

Content Specificity

By *content*, we mean simply the domain within which the testing will occur. When we think of teacher-made tests, we generally think of academic domains such as reading, arithmetic, spelling, and so forth. However, the domain to be tested can include supplementary curricula (for example, study skills).

By *specificity*, we mean the parts of the domain to be assessed. Any domain can be divided and subdivided into smaller and more precise chunks of content. For example, in reading we are unlikely to want to assess every possible thing within the domain of reading. Therefore, we would break down reading into the part or chunk in which we were interested in assessing: beginning reading, one-syllable words, one-syllable words with short vowel sounds, one-syllable words with short a, consonant-short a-consonant words, consonant-short a-specific consonants (-t, -n, and -r), and so forth.

The specificity of an assessment depends on the purpose of the assessment. Especially at the beginning of a school year or when a new student joins a class, educators want to know a student's level of skill development—what the student knows and does not know—in order to plan instruction. In this case, an appropriate assessment will begin with a broad sample of content to provide an estimate of student knowledge of the various topics that have been and will be covered. Areas in which a student lacks information or skills will be assessed with more precise procedures to identify the exact areas of deficiency so that appropriate remedial instruction can be provided.

When teachers assess to monitor instruction and document problems, their assessments are very specific. They should assess what they teach to ascertain if students have learned what was taught. If students are learning word families (for example, "bat," "cat," "fat," and "hat"), they should be testing on their proficiency with the word families they have been taught.

Testing Frequency

The time students have in school is finite, and time spent in testing is time not spent in other important activities. Therefore, the frequency of testing and the duration of tests must be balanced against the other demands on student and teacher time.

Most teacher-made tests are used to monitor instruction and assign grades. Although the frequency of assessment varies widely in practice, the research evidence is clear that more frequent assessments (two or more times a week) are associated with better learning than are less frequent assessments. When students are having difficulty learning or retaining content, teachers should measure performance and progress more frequently. Frequent measurement can provide immediate feedback about how students are doing and pinpoint the skills missing among students.[5] The more frequent the measurement, the quicker you can adapt instruction to ensure that students are making optimal progress. However, frequent measurement is only helpful when it can immediately direct teachers as to what to teach next or how to teach next. To the extent that teachers can use data efficiently, frequent assessment is valuable; if it consists simply of frequent measurement with no application, then it is not valuable. Student deficits in skill level and progress may dictate how frequently measurement should occur: Students with substantial deficits are monitored more frequently to ensure that instructional methods are effective. Those who want to know more about how expected rate is set or about the specific procedures used to monitor student progress are referred to Hintze, Christ, and Methe (2005), Hosp and Hosp (2003), or Shinn (1989).

[5]Many of the new measurement systems, such as those employing technology-enhanced assessments, call for continuous measurement of pupil performance and progress. They provide students with immediate feedback on how they are doing, give teachers daily status reports indicating the relative standing of all students in a class, and identify areas of skill deficits.

Broader assessments used for grading are given at the end of units or marking periods and cover considerable content. Thus, they must either be very general or be a limited sample of more specific content. In either case, the results of such assessments do not provide sufficiently detailed information about what a student knows and does not know for teachers to plan remediation.

Testing Formats

When a teacher wants either to compare (1) the performance of several students on a skill or set of skills or (2) one pupil's performances on several occasions over time, the assessments must be the same. Standardization is the process of using the same materials, procedures (for example, directions and time allowed to complete a test), and scoring standards for each test taker each time the test is given. Without standardization, observed differences could be reasonably attributed to differences in testing procedures. Almost any test can be standardized if it results in observable behavior or a permanent product (for example, a student's written response).

The first step in creating a test is knowing what knowledge and skills a student has been taught and how they have been taught. Thus, teachers will need to know the objectives, standards, or outcomes that they expect students to work toward mastering, and they will need to specify the level of performance that is acceptable.

Test formats can be classified along two dimensions: (1) the modality through which the item is presented—test items usually require a student to look at or to listen to the question, although other modalities may be substituted, depending on the particulars of a situation or on characteristics of students—and (2) the modality through which a student responds—test items usually require an oral or written response, although pointing responses are frequently used with students who are nonverbal. Teachers may use "see–write," "see–say," "hear–write," and "hear–say" to specify the testing modality dimensions.

In addition, "write" formats can be of two types. *Selection formats* require students to indicate their choice from an array of possible answers (usually termed response options). True–false, multiple-choice, and matching are the three common selection formats. However, they are not the only ones possible; for example, students may be required to circle incorrectly spelled words or words that should be capitalized in text. Formats requiring students to select the correct answer can be used to assess much more than the recognition of information, although they are certainly useful for that purpose. They can also be used to assess students' understanding, their ability to draw inferences, and their correct application of principles. Select questions are not usually well suited for assessing achievement at the levels of analysis, synthesis, and evaluation.

Supply formats require a student to produce a written or an oral response. This response can be as restricted as the answer to a computation problem or a one-word response to the question, "When did the potato famine begin in Ireland?" Often, the response to supply questions is more involved and can require a student to produce a sentence, a paragraph, or several pages.

As a general rule, supply questions can be prepared fairly quickly, but scoring them may be very time-consuming. Even when one-word responses or numbers are requested, teachers may have difficulty finding the response on a student's test paper, deciphering the handwriting, or correctly applying criteria for awarding points. In contrast, selection formats usually require a considerable amount of time to prepare, but once prepared, the tests can be scored quickly and by almost anyone.

The particular formats teachers choose are influenced by the purposes for testing and the characteristics of the test takers. Testing formats are essentially bottom up or top down. Bottom-up formats assess the mastery of specific objectives to allow generalizations about student competence in a particular domain. Top-down formats survey general competence in a domain and assess in greater depth those topics for which mastery is incomplete. For day-to-day monitoring of instruction and selecting short-term instructional objectives, we favor bottom-up assessment. With this type of assessment, a teacher can be relatively sure that specific objectives have been mastered and that he or she is not spending needless instructional time teaching students what they already know. For determining starting places for instruction with new students and for assessing maintenance and generalization of previously learned material, we favor top-down assessment. Generally, this approach should be more efficient in terms of teachers' and students' time because broader survey tests can cover a lot of material in a short period of time.

For students who are able to read and write independently, see–write formats are generally more efficient for both individual students and groups. When testing individual students, teachers or teacher aides can give the testing materials to the students and can proceed with other activities while the students are completing the test. Moreover, when students write their responses, a teacher can defer correcting the examinations until a convenient time.

See–say formats are also useful. Teacher aides or other students can listen to the test takers' responses and can correct them on the spot or record them for later evaluation. Moreover, many teachers have access to electronic equipment that can greatly facilitate the use of see–say formats (for example, audio or video recorders).

The hear–write format is especially useful with selection formats for younger students and students who cannot read independently. This format can also be used for testing groups of students and is routinely used in the assessment of spelling when students are required to write words from dictation. With other content, teachers can give directions and read the test questions aloud, and students can mark their responses. The primary difficulty with a hear–write format with groups of students is the pacing of test items; teachers must allot sufficient time between items for slower-responding students to make their selections.

Hear–say formats are most suitable for assessing individual students who do not write independently or who write at such slow speeds that their written responses are unrepresentative of what they know. Even with this format, teachers need not preside over the assessment; other students or a teacher aide can administer, record, and perhaps evaluate the student's responses.

3 Considerations in Preparing Tests

Teachers need to build skills in developing tests that are fair, reliable, and valid. The following kinds of considerations are important in developing or preparing tests.

Selecting Specific Areas of the Curriculum

Tests are samples of behavior. When narrow skills are being assessed (for example, spelling words from dictation), either all the components of the domain should be tested (in this case, all the assigned spelling words) or a representative sample should be selected and assessed. The qualifier "representative" implies that an appropriate number of easy and difficult words—and of words from the beginning, middle, and end of the assignment—will be selected. When more complex domains are assessed, teachers should concentrate on the more important facts or relationships and avoid the trivial.

Writing Relevant Questions

Teachers must select and use enough questions to allow valid inferences about students' mastery of short-term or long-term goals, and attainment of state standards. Nothing offends test takers quite as much as a test's failure to cover material they have studied and know, except perhaps their own failure to guess what content a teacher believes to be important enough to test. In addition, fairness demands that the way in which the question is asked be familiar and expected by the student. For example, if students were to take a test on the addition of single-digit integers, it would be a bad idea to test them using a missing-addend format (for example, "$4 + \_\_\_\_ = 7$") unless that format had been specifically taught and was expected by the students.

Organizing and Sequencing Items

The organization of a test is a function of many factors. When a teacher wants a student to complete all the items and to indicate mastery of content (a power test), it is best to intersperse easy and difficult items. When the desire is to measure automaticity or the number of items that can be completed within a specific time period (a timed test), it is best to organize items from easy to difficult. Pages of test questions or problems to be solved should not be cluttered.

Developing Formats for Presentation and Response Modes

Different response formats can be used within the same test, although it is generally a good idea to group together questions with the same format. Regardless of the format used, the primary consideration is that the test questions be a fair sample of the material being assessed.

Writing Directions for Administration

Regardless of question format, the directions should indicate clearly what a student is to do—for example, "Circle the correct option," "Choose the best answer," and "Match each item in column b to one item in column a." Also, teachers should explain what, if any, materials may be used by students, any time limits, any unusual scoring procedures (for example, penalties for guessing), and point values when the students are mature enough to be given questions that have different point values.

Developing Systematic Procedures for Scoring Responses

As discussed in the opening paragraphs of this chapter, teachers must have predetermined and systematic criteria for scoring responses. However, if a teacher discovers an error or omission in criteria, the criteria should be modified. Obviously, previously scored responses must be rescored with the revised criteria.

Establishing Criteria to Interpret Student Performance

Teachers should specify in advance the criteria they will use for assigning grades or weighting assignments. For example, they may want to specify that students who earn a certain number of points on a test will earn a specific grade, or they may want to assign grades on the basis of the class distribution of performance. In either case, they must specify what it takes to earn certain grades or how assignments will be evaluated and weighted.

4 Response Formats

There are two basic types of test format. Selection formats require students to recognize a correct answer that is provided on the test. Supply formats require students to produce correct answers.

Selection Formats

Three types of selection formats are commonly used: multiple-choice, matching, and true–false. Of the three, multiple-choice questions are clearly the most useful.

Multiple-Choice Questions

Multiple-choice questions are the most difficult to prepare. These questions have two parts: (1) a *stem* that contains the question and (2) a response set that contains both the correct answer, termed the *keyed response*, and one or more incorrect options, termed *distractors*. In preparing multiple-choice questions, teachers should generally follow these guidelines:

■ Keep the response options short and of approximately equal length. Students quickly learn that longer options tend to be correct.

■ Keep material that is common to all options in the stem. For example, if the first word in each option is "the," it should be put into the stem and removed from the options.

A poorly worded question:
A lasting contribution of the Eisenhower presidency was the creation of

    a. the communication satellite system

    b. the interstate highway system

    c. the cable TV infrastructure

    d. the Eisenhower tank

Better wording:
A lasting contribution of the Eisenhower presidency was the creation of the

    a. communication satellite system

    b. interstate highway system

    c. cable TV infrastructure

    d. Eisenhower tank

▪ Avoid grammatical tip-offs. Students can discard grammatically incorrect options. For example, when the correct answer must be plural, alert students will disregard singular options; when the correct answer must be a noun, students will disregard options that are verbs.

A poorly constructed question:
A(n) _____ test measures what a student has learned that has been taught in school.

    a. achievement

    b. intelligence

    c. social

    d. portfolio

A better constructed question:
_____ tests measure what a student has learned that has been taught in school.

    a. achievement

    b. intelligence

    c. social

    d. portfolio

▪ Avoid implausible options. In the best questions, distractors should be attractive to students who do not know the answer. Common errors and misconceptions are often good distractors.

A poorly constructed question:
Which of the following persons was NOT a candidate of the Republican Party for President of the United States in the 2007/2008 primaries?

    a. Bart Simpson

    b. Mitt Romney

    c. Mike Huckabee

    d. Rudy Giuliani

A better constructed question:
Which of the following persons was NOT a candidate of the Republican Party for President of the United States in the 2007/2008 primaries?

    a. John Edwards

    b. Mitt Romney

    c. Mike Huckabee

    d. Rudy Giuliani

■ Make sure that one and only one option is correct. Students should not have to read their teacher's mind to guess which wrong answer is the least wrong or which right answer is the most correct.

A poorly constructed question:
Which of the following persons was NOT a candidate of the Republican Party for President of the United States in the 2007/2008 primaries?

   a. John Edwards
   b. Mitt Romney
   c. Mike Huckabee
   d. Joseph Biden

A better constructed question:
Which of the following persons was NOT a candidate of the Republican Party for President of the United States in the 2007/2008 primaries?

   a. John Edwards
   b. Mitt Romney
   c. Mike Huckabee
   d. Rudy Giuliani

■ Avoid interdependent questions. Generally, it is bad practice to make the selection of the correct option dependent on getting a prior question correct.

An early question:
Which of the following persons was a candidate of the Democrat Party for President of the United States in the 2007/2008 primaries?

   a. Tom Tancredo
   b. Mitt Romney
   c. Mike Huckabee
   d. Joseph Biden

A subsequent dependent question:
The candidate in the preceding question was or is a

   a. governor
   b. member of the U.S. House of Representatives
   c. U.S. senator
   d. U.S. ambassador to Russia

■ Avoid options that indicate multiple correct options (for example, "all the above" or "both a and b are correct"). These options often simplify the question.

A poorly constructed question:
Which of the following persons was a candidate of the Democrat Party for President of the United States in the 2007/2008 primaries?

   a. John Edwards
   b. Mitt Romney
   c. both a and b are correct
   d. Ron Paul

A better constructed question:
Which of the following persons was NOT a candidate of the Democrat Party for President of the United States in the 2007/2008 primaries?

   a. John Edwards

   b. Mitt Romney

   c. Ron Paul

   d. Rudy Giuliani

▓ Avoid similar incorrect options. Students who can eliminate one of the two similar options can readily dismiss the other one. For example, if citrus fruit is wrong, lemon must be wrong.

A poorly constructed question:
Eisenhower's inspiration for the interstate highway system was the

   a. Ohio Turnpike

   b. modern German autobahns

   c. Pennsylvania Turnpike

   d. Alcan Highway

A better constructed question:
Eisenhower's inspiration for the interstate highway system was the

   a. ancient Roman highways

   b. modern German autobahns

   c. Pennsylvania Turnpike

   d. Alcan Highway

▓ Make sure that one question does not provide information that can be used to answer another question.

An early question:
A lasting contribution of the Eisenhower presidency was the creation of

   a. the communication satellite system

   b. the interstate highway system

   c. the cable TV infrastructure

   d. the Eisenhower tank

A later question that answers a prior question:
Eisenhower's inspiration for the interstate highway system was the

   a. ancient Roman highways

   b. modern German autobahns

   c. Pennsylvania Turnpike

   d. Alcan Highway

▓ Avoid using the same words and examples that were used in the students' texts or in class presentations.

▓ Vary the position of the correct response in the options. Students will recognize patterns of correct options (for example, when the correct answers to a sequence of questions are a, b, c, d, a, b, c, d) or a teacher's preference for a specific position (usually c).

When appropriate, teachers can make multiple-choice questions more challenging by asking students to recognize an instance of a rule or concept, by requiring students to recall and use material that is not present in the question, or by increasing the number of options. (For younger children, three options are generally difficult enough. Older students can be expected to answer questions with four or five options.) In no case should teachers deliberately mislead or trick students.

Matching Questions

Matching questions are a variant of multiple-choice questions in which a set of stems is simultaneously associated with a set of options. Generally, the content of matching questions is limited to simple factual associations (Gronlund, 1985). Teachers usually prepare matching questions so that there are as many options as stems, and an option can be associated only once with a stem in the set. Although we do not recommend their use, there are other possibilities: more options than stems, selection of all correct options for one stem, and multiple use of an option.[6] These additional possibilities increase the difficulty of the question set considerably.

In general, we prefer multiple-choice questions to matching questions. Almost any matching question can be written as a series of multiple-choice questions in which the same or similar options are used. Of course, the correct response will change. However, teachers wishing to use matching questions should consider the following guidelines:

- Each set of matching items should have some dimension in common (for example, explorers and dates of discovery). This makes preparation easier for the teacher and provides the student with some insight into the relationship required to select the correct option.
- Keep the length of the stems approximately the same, and keep the length and grammar used in the options equivalent. At best, mixing grammatical forms will eliminate some options for some questions; at worst, it will provide the correct answer to several questions.
- Make sure that one and only one option is correct for each stem.
- Vary the sequence of correct responses when more than one matching question is asked.
- Avoid using the same words and examples that were used in the students' texts or in class presentations.

It is easier for a student when questions and options are presented in two columns. When there is a difference in the length of the items in each column, the longer item should be used as the stem. Stems should be placed on the left and options on the right, rather than stems above with options below them. Moreover, all the elements of the question should be kept on one page. Finally, teachers often allow students to draw lines to connect questions and options. Although this has the obvious advantage of helping students keep track of where their answers

---

[6]Scoring for these options is complicated. Generally, separate errors are counted for selecting an incorrect option and failing to select a correct option. Thus, the number of errors can be very large.

should be placed, erasures or scratch-outs can be a headache to the person who corrects the test. A commercially available product (Learning Wrap-Ups) has cards printed with stems and answers and a shoelace with which to "lace" stems to correct answers. The correct lacing pattern is printed on the back, so it is self-correcting. Teachers could make such cards fairly easily as an alternative to trying to correct tests with lots of erasures.

True–False Statements

In most cases, true–false statements should simply not be used. Their utility lies primarily in assessing knowledge of factual information, which can be better assessed with other formats. Effective true–false items are difficult to prepare. Because guessing the correct answer is likely—it happens 50 percent of the time—the reliability of true–false tests is generally low. As a result, they may well have limited validity. Nonetheless, if a teacher chooses to use this format, a few suggestions should be followed:

■ Avoid specific determiners such as "all," "never," "always," and so on.

■ Avoid sweeping generalizations. Such statements tend to be true, but students can often think of minor exceptions. Thus, there is a problem in the criterion for evaluating the truthfulness of the question. Attempts to avoid the problem by adding restrictive conditions (for example, "with minor exceptions") either render the question obviously true or leave a student trying to guess what the restrictive condition means.

■ Avoid convoluted sentences. Tests should assess knowledge of content, not a student's ability to comprehend difficult prose.

■ Keep true and false statements approximately the same length. As is the case with longer options on multiple-choice questions, longer true–false statements tend to be true.

■ Balance the number of true and false statements. If a student recognizes that there are more of one type of statement than of the other, the odds of guessing the correct answer will exceed 50 percent.

Special Considerations for Students with Disabilities

In developing and using items that employ a selection format, teachers must pay attention to individual differences among students, particularly to disabilities that might interfere with performance. The individualized educational programs (IEPs) of students with disabilities often contain needed accommodations and adaptations. Prior to testing, it is always a good idea to double-check student's IEPs to make sure that any required accommodations and adaptations have been made. For example, students who have skill deficits in remembering things for short periods of time, or who do not attend well to verbally or visually presented information, may need multiple-choice tests with fewer distractors. Students who have difficulty with the organization of visually presented material may need to have matching questions rewritten as multiple-choice questions. Remember, it is important to assess the skills that students have, not the effects of disability conditions.

Scenario in Assessment

Barry

Ms. Johnson is a special education teacher in a middle school. One of her students, Barry, has an IEP that provides for him to take adapted content area tests. Mr. Blumfield sends Ms. Johnson a social studies test that he will be giving in 8 days so that she can adapt it. The test contains both multiple-choice (five options) and true–false tests. Mr. Blumfield plans to allow students the entire period (37 minutes) to complete their tests.

Ms. Johnson has several concerns about the test. In her experience with Barry, she has found that he requires untimed and shorter tests and some questions must be read to him. In addition, when supply tests are used, he requires a couple of modifications. He cannot understand true–false questions and he has unusual difficulty when there are more than three options on multiple-choice questions. Therefore, she schedules a meeting with Mr. Blumfield to discuss her adaptation of his test.

Mr. Blumfield has 127 students, and 8 of these students have IEPs. Therefore, Ms. Johnson begins the meeting by reminding him that Barry's IEP provides for the adaptation of content area tests. She also tells Mr. Blumfield that she is willing to make the adaptations but will need some guidance from him. The first thing she wants to learn is the important content—the questions assessing the major ideas and important facts that Mr. Blumfield has stressed in his lessons. The next thing she wants to learn is which questions can be deleted.

Then Ms. Johnson explains how she will adapt the test:

- She will modify the content by deleting relatively unimportant ideas and concepts; she will retain all of the major ideas and important concepts.

- She will replace true–false questions that assess major ideas with multiple-choice questions that get at the same information.

- She will reduce the number of distractors in multiple-choice questions from five to three.

- She will reorder test items by grouping questions about related content together and ordering questions from easy to difficult whenever possible.

She also explains that she will read to Barry any part of the test that he requests, and that the test will not be timed so he may not finish in one period. Finally, she offers to score the test for Mr. Blumfield.

Barry earns a B+ on the adapted teacher-made test.

Supply Formats

It is useful to distinguish between items requiring a student to write one- or two-word responses (such as fill-in questions) and those requiring more extended responses (such as essay questions). Both types of items require careful delineation of what constitutes a correct response (that is, criteria for scoring). It is generally best for teachers to prepare criteria for a correct response at the time they prepare the question. In that way, they can ensure that the question is written in such a way as to elicit the correct types of answers—or at least not to mislead students—and perhaps save time when correcting exams. (If teachers change criteria for a correct response after they have scored a few questions, they should rescore all previously scored questions with the revised criteria.)

Fill-In Questions

Aside from mathematics problems that require students to calculate an answer and writing spelling words from dictation, fill-in questions require a student to complete a statement by adding a concept or fact—for example, "_____ arrived in America in 1492." Fill-ins are useful in assessing knowledge and comprehension objectives; they are not useful in assessing application, analysis, synthesis, or evaluation objectives. Teachers preparing fill-in questions should follow these guidelines:

■ Keep each sentence short. Generally, the less superfluous information in an item, the clearer the question will be to the student and the less likely it will be that one question will cue another.

■ If a two-word answer is required, teachers should use two blanks to indicate this in the sentence.

■ Avoid sentences with multiple blanks. For example, the item "In the year _____, _____ discovered _____" is so vague that practically any date, name, and event can be inserted correctly, even ones that are irrelevant to the content; for example, "In the year 1999, Henry discovered girls."

■ Keep the size of all blanks consistent and large enough to accommodate readily the longest answer. The size of the blank should not provide a clue about the length of the correct word.

The most problematic aspect of fill-in questions is the necessity of developing an appropriate response bank of acceptable answers. Often, some student errors may consist of a partially correct response; teachers must decide which answers will receive partial credit, full credit, and no credit. For example, a question may anticipate "Columbus" as the correct response, but a student might write "that Italian dude who was looking for the shortcut to India for the Spanish king and queen." In deciding how far afield to go in crediting unanticipated responses, teachers should look over test questions carefully to determine whether the student's answer comes from information presented in another question (for example, "The Spanish monarch employed an Italian sailor to find a shorter route to").

Extended Responses

Essay questions are most useful in assessing comprehension, application, analysis, synthesis, and evaluation objectives. There are two major problems associated with extended response questions. First, teachers are generally able to sample only a limited amount of information because answers may take a long time for students to write. Second, extended-essay responses are the most difficult type of answer to score. To avoid subjectivity and inconsistency, teachers should use a scoring key that assigns specific point values for each element in the ideal or criterion answer. In most cases, spelling and grammatical errors should not be deducted from the point total. Moreover, bonus points should not be awarded for particularly detailed responses; many good students will provide a complete answer to one question and spend any extra time working on questions that are more difficult for them.

Finally, teachers should be prepared to deal with responses in which a student tries to bluff a correct answer. Rather than leave a question unanswered, some students may answer a related question that was not asked, or they may structure their response so that they can omit important information that they cannot remember or never knew. Sometimes, they will even write a poem or a treatise on why the question asked is unimportant or irrelevant. Therefore, teachers must be very specific about how they will award points, stick to their criteria unless they discover that something is wrong with them, and not give credit to creative bluffs.

Teachers should also be very precise in the directions that they give so that students will not have to guess what responses their teachers will credit. Following are a number of verbs (and their meanings) that are commonly used in essay questions. It is often worthwhile to explain these terms in the test directions to make sure that students know what kind of answer is desired.

- *Describe*, *define*, and *identify* mean to give the meaning, essential characteristics, or place within a taxonomy.
- *List* means to enumerate and implies that complete sentences and paragraphs are not required unless specifically requested.
- *Discuss* requires more than a description, definition, or identification; a student is expected to draw implications and elucidate relationships.
- *Explain* means to analyze and make clear or comprehensible a concept, event, principle, relationship, and so forth; thus, *explain* requires going beyond a definition to describe the hows or whys.
- *Compare* means to identify and explain similarities between two or among more things.
- *Contrast* means to identify and explain differences between two or among more things.
- *Evaluate* means to give the value of something and implies an enumeration and explanation of assets and liabilities, pros and cons.

Finally, unless students know the questions in advance, teachers should allow students sufficient time for planning and rereading answers. For example, if teachers believe that 10 minutes is necessary to write an extended essay to answer a question that requires original thinking, they might allow 20 minutes for the question. The less fluent the students are, the greater is the proportion of time that should be allotted.

Special Considerations in Assessing Students with Disabilities

In developing items that employ a supply format, teachers must pay attention to individual differences among learners, particularly to disabilities that may interfere with performance. For example, students who write very slowly can be expected to have difficulty with fill-in or essay questions. Students who have considerable difficulty expressing themselves in writing will probably have difficulty completing or performing well on essay examinations. Teachers should make sure that they have included the adaptations and accommodations required in student IEPs.

5 Assessment in Core Achievement Areas

The assessment procedures used by teachers are a function of the content being taught, the criterion to which content is to be learned (such as 80 percent mastery), and the characteristics of the students. With primary-level curricula in core areas, teachers usually want more than knowledge from their students; they want the material learned so well that correct responses are automatic. For example, teachers do not want their students to think about forming the letter "a," sounding out the word "the," or using number lines to solve simple addition problems such as "$3 + 5 =$"; they want their students to respond immediately and correctly. Even for intermediate-level materials, teachers seek highly proficient responding from their students, whether that performance involves performing two-digit multiplication, reading short stories, writing short stories, or writing spelling words from dictation. However, teachers in all grades, but especially in secondary schools, are also interested in their students' understanding of vast amounts of information about their social, cultural, and physical worlds, as well as their acquisition and application of critical thinking skills. The assessment of skills taught to high degrees of proficiency is quite different from the assessment of understanding and critical thinking skills.

In the following sections, core achievement areas are discussed in terms of three important attributes: the skills and information to be learned within the major strands of most curricula, the assessment of skills to be learned to proficiency, and the assessment of understanding of information and concepts. Critical thinking skills are usually embedded within content areas and are assessed in the same ways as understanding of information is assessed—with written multiple-choice and extended-essay questions.

Reading

Reading is usually divided into decoding skills and comprehension. The specific behaviors included in each of these subdomains will depend on the particular curriculum and its sequencing.

Beginning Skills

Beginning decoding relies on students' ability to analyze and manipulate sounds and syllables in words (Stanovich, 2000). Instruction in beginning reading can include letter recognition, letter–sound correspondences, sight vocabulary, phonics, and, in some curricula, morphology. Automaticity is the goal for the skills to be learned. See–say (for example, "What letter is this?") and hear–say (for example, "What sound does the letter make?") formats are regularly used for both instruction and assessment. During students' acquisition of specific skills, teachers should first stress the accuracy of student responses. Generally, this concern translates into allowing a moment or two for students to think about their responses. A generally accepted criterion for completion for early learning is 90 to 95 percent correct. As soon as accuracy has been attained (and sometimes before), teachers change their criteria from accurate responses to fast and accurate responses. For see–say formats, fluent students will need no thinking time for simple material; for example, they should be able to respond as rapidly as teachers can change stimuli to questions such as "What is this letter?" Once students accurately decode letters and letter combinations fluently, the emphasis shifts to fluency or the automatic retrieval of words. Fluency is a combination of speed and accuracy and is widely viewed as a fundamental prerequisite for reading comprehension (National Institute of Child Health and Human Development, 2000a, 2000b).

For beginners, reading comprehension is usually assessed in one of three ways: by assessing students' retelling, their responses to comprehension questions, or their rate of oral reading. The most direct method is to have students retell what

Robert

Robert has learned the basic alphabetic principles—letter sound associations, sound blending, and basic phonic rules. However, his reading fluency is very slow. This lack of fluency makes comprehension difficult and also causes problems for him in completing his work in the times allotted. His IEP contains an annual goal of increasing his fluency to 100 words per minute with two or fewer errors in material written at his grade level. Mr. Williams, his special education teacher, developed a program that relied on repeated readings. He had recently read an article by Therrien (2004) that indicated the important aspects of repeated reading to follow in his program. He decided to check fluency daily using brief probes.

After Mr. Williams determined the highest level reading materials that Robert could read with 95 percent accuracy, he prepared a series of 200-word passages at that level and one-third higher levels up to Robert's actual grade placement. Each passage formed a logical unit and began with a new paragraph. The vocabulary was representative of Robert's reading level, and passage comprehension did not rely on preceding material that was not read. He prepared two copies of each passage and placed each in an acetate cover. (This allowed him to indicate errors directly on the passage and then to wipe both copies clean after testing for reuse at another time.)

Mr. Williams then prepared instructions for Robert: "I want to see how fast you can read material the first time and a second or third time. I want you to read as fast as you can without making errors. If you don't know a word, just skip it. I'll tell you the word when you are done. Then I'll ask you to reread the passage. When I say start, you begin reading. After 1 minute, I'll say stop and you stop reading. Do you have any questions?"

Mr. Williams gave Robert two practice readings that he did not score. This gave Robert some experience with the process. He then began giving Robert daily probes, entered Robert's rate on the first reading, and connected the data points for the same passage on different days. When Robert could read three consecutive probes at the target rate the first time, Mr. Williams increased the reading level of the material (for example, days 13, 14, and 15). The intervention would end when Robert was reading grade-level materials fluently—the third level above where the intervention started.

As shown in Figure 7.5, Robert made steady progress, both within reading levels and between reading levels. Mr. Williams was pleased with the intervention and would continue with it until it was no longer working or Robert had achieved the goal.

FIGURE 7.5
Robert's Progress in Reading

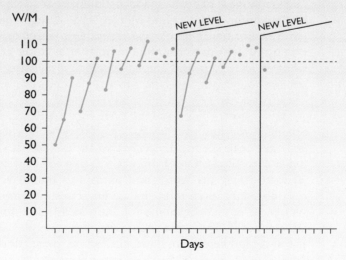

they have read without access to the reading passage. Retold passages may be scored on the basis of the number of words recalled. Fuchs, Fuchs, and Maxwell (1988) have offered two relatively simple scoring procedures that appear to offer valid indications of comprehension. Retelling may be conducted orally or in writing. With students who have relatively undeveloped writing skills, retelling should be oral when it is used to assess comprehension, but it may be in writing as a practice or drill activity. Teachers can listen to students retell, or students can retell using tape recorders so that their efforts can be evaluated later.

A second common method of assessing comprehension is to ask students questions about what they have read. Questions should address main ideas, important relationships, and relevant details. Questions may be in supply or selection formats, and either hear–say or see–write formats can be used conveniently. As with retelling, teachers should concentrate their efforts on the gist of the passage.

A third convenient, although indirect, method of assessing reading comprehension is to assess the rate of oral reading. One of the earliest attempts to explain the relationship between rate of oral reading and comprehension was offered by LaBerge and Samuels (1974), who noted that poor decoding skills created a bottleneck that impeded the flow of information, thus impeding comprehension. The relationship makes theoretical sense: Slow readers must expend their energy decoding words (for example, attending to letters, remembering letter–sound associations, blending sounds, or searching for context cues) rather than concentrating on the meaning of what is written. Not only is the relationship between reading fluency and comprehension logical but also empirical research supports this relationship (Freeland, Skinner, Jackson, McDaniel, & Smith, 2000; National Institute of Child Health and Human Development, 2000a, 2000b; Sindelar, Monda, & O'Shea, 1990).

Therefore, teachers probably should concentrate on the rate of oral reading regularly with beginning readers. To assess reading rate, teachers should have students read for 2 minutes from appropriate materials. The reading passage should include familiar vocabulary, syntax, and content; the passage must be longer than the amount any student can read in the 2-minute period. Teachers have their own copy of the passage on which to note errors. The number of words read correctly and the number of errors made in 2 minutes are each divided by 2 to calculate the rate per minute. Mercer and Mercer (1985) suggest a rate of 80 words per minute (with two or fewer errors) as a desirable goal for reading words from lists and a rate of 100 words per minute (with two or fewer errors) for words in text. See Chapter 13 for a more complete discussion of errors in oral reading.

Advanced Skills

Students who have already mastered basic sight vocabulary and decoding skills generally read silently. Emphasis for these students shifts, and new demands are made. Decoding moves from oral reading to silent reading with subvocalization (that is, saying the words and phrases to themselves) to visual scanning without subvocalization; thus, the reading rates of some students may exceed 1,000 words per minute. Scanning for main ideas and information may also be taught systematically. The demands for reading comprehension may go well beyond the literal comprehension of a passage; summarizing, drawing inferences, recognizing and understanding symbolism, sarcasm, irony, and so forth may be systematically taught. For these advanced students, the gist of a passage is usually more important than the details. Teachers of more advanced students may wish to score retold passages on the basis of main ideas, important relationships, and details recalled correctly and the number of errors (that is, ideas, relationships, and details omitted plus the insertion of material not included in the passage). In such cases, the different types of information can be weighted differently, or the use of comprehension strategies (for example, summarization) can be encouraged. However, read–write assessment formats using multiple-choice and extended-essay questions are more commonly used.

Informal Reading Inventories

When making decisions about referral or initial placement in a reading curriculum, teachers often develop *informal reading inventories* (IRIs), which assess decoding and reading comprehension over a wide range of skill levels within the specific reading curricula used in a classroom. Thus, they are top-down assessments that span several levels of difficulty.

IRIs are given to locate the reading levels at which a student reads independently, requires instruction, and is frustrated. Techniques for developing IRIs and the criteria used to define independent, instructional, and frustration reading levels vary. Teachers should use a series of graded reading passages that range from below a student's actual placement to a year or two above the actual placement. If a reading series prepared for several grade levels is used, passages can be selected from the beginning, middle, and end of each grade. Students begin reading the easiest material and continue reading until they can decode less than 85 percent of the words. Salvia and Hughes (1990) recommend an accuracy rate of 95 percent for independent reading and consider 85 to 95 percent accuracy the level at which a student requires instruction.

Mathematics

The National Council of Teachers of Mathematics has adopted standards for pre-kindergarten through secondary education. These standards deal with both content (that is, Number, Measurement, Algebra, Geometry, and Data and Statistics) and process (that is, Reasoning, Representation, Problem Solving, Connections, and Communication). Special education tends to share the goals of the National Mathematics Panel (2008), which has stressed computational proficiency and fluency in basic skills. In noninclusive special education settings, math content is generally stressed (that is, readiness skills, vocabulary and concepts, numeration, whole-number operations, fractions and decimals, ratios and percentages, measurement, and geometry) (Salvia & Hughes, 1990). At any grade level, the specific skills and concepts included in each of these subdomains will depend on the state standards and the particular curriculum and its sequencing. Mathematics curricula usually contain both problem sets that require only computations and word problems that require selection and application of the correct algorithm as well as computation. The difficulty of application problems goes well beyond the difficulty of the computation involved and is related to three factors: (1) the number of steps involved in the solution (for example, a student might have to add and then multiply; Caldwell & Goldin, 1979),

(2) the amount of extraneous information (Englert, Cullata, & Horn, 1987), and (3) whether the mathematical operation is directly implied by the vocabulary used in the problem (for example, words such as *and* or *more* imply addition, whereas words such as *each* may imply division; see Bachor, Stacy, & Freeze, 1986). Although reading level is popularly believed to affect the difficulty of word problems, its effect has not been clearly established (see Bachor, 1990; Paul, Nibbelink, & Hoover, 1986).

Beginning Skills

The whole-number operations of addition, subtraction, multiplication, and division are the core of the elementary mathematics curriculum. Readiness for beginning students includes such basics as classification, one-to-one correspondence, and counting. Vocabulary and concepts are generally restricted to quantitative words (for example, "same," "equal," and "larger") and spatial concepts (for example, left, above, and next to). Numeration deals with writing and identifying numerals, counting, ordering, and so forth.

See–write is probably the most frequently used assessment format for mathematical skills, although see–say formats are not uncommon. For content associated with readiness, vocabulary and concepts, numeration, and applications, matching formats are commonly used. Accuracy is stressed, and 90 to 95 percent correct is commonly used as the criterion. For computation, accuracy and fluency are stressed in beginning mathematics; teachers do not stop their instruction when students respond accurately, but they continue instruction to build automaticity. Consequently, a teacher may accept somewhat lower rates of accuracy (that is, 80 percent).

When working toward fluency, teachers usually use probes. Probes are small samples of behavior. For example, in assessment of skill in addition of single-digit numbers, a student might be given only five single-digit addition problems. Perhaps the most useful criterion for math probes assessing computation is the number of correct digits (in an answer) written per minute, not the number of correct answers per minute. The actual criterion rate will depend on the operation, the type of material (for example, addition facts versus addition of two-digit numbers with regrouping), and the characteristics of the particular students. Students with motor difficulties may be held to a lower criterion or assessed with see–say formats. For see–write formats, students may be expected to write answers to addition and subtraction problems at rates between 50 and 80 digits per minute and to write answers to simple multiplication and division problems at rates between 40 and 50 digits per minute (Salvia & Hughes, 1990).

Advanced Skills

The more advanced mathematical skills (that is, fractions, decimals, ratios, percentages, and geometry) build on whole-number operations. These skills are taught to levels of comprehension and application. Unlike those for beginning skills, assessment formats are almost exclusively see–write, and accuracy is stressed over fluency, except for a few facts such as "half equals 0.5 equals 50 percent." Teachers must take into account the extent to which specific student disabilities will interfere with performance of advanced skills. For example, difficulties in sequencing of information and in comprehension may interfere with students' performance on items that require problem solving and comprehension of mathematical concepts.

Spelling

Although spelling is considered by many to be a component of written language, in elementary school it is generally taught as a separate subject. Therefore, we treat it separately in this chapter.

Spelling is the production of letters in the correct sequence to form a word. The specific words that are assigned as spelling words may come from several sources: spelling curricula, word lists, content areas, or a student's own written work. In high school and college, students are expected to use dictionaries and to spell correctly any word they use. Between that point and approximately fourth grade, spelling words are typically assigned, and students are left to their own devices to learn them. In the first three grades, spelling is usually taught systematically using phonics, morphology, rote memorization, or some combination of the three approaches.

Teachers may assess mastery of the prespelling rules associated with the particular approach they are teaching. For example, when a phonics approach is used, students may have to demonstrate mastery of writing the letters associated with specific vowels, consonants, consonant blends, diphthongs, and digraphs. Teachers assess mastery of spelling in at least four ways:

1. *Recognition response:* The teacher provides students with lists of alternative spellings of words (usually three or four alternatives) and reads a word to the student. The student must select the correct spelling of the dictated word from the alternatives. Emphasis is on accuracy.

2. *Spelling dictated single words:* Teachers dictate words, and students write them down. Although teachers often give a spelling word and then use it in a sentence, students find the task easier if just the spelling word is given (Horn, 1967). Moreover, the findings from research performed in 1988 suggest that a 7-second interval between words is sufficient (Shinn, Tindall, & Stein, 1988).

3. *Spelling words in context:* Students write paragraphs using words given by the teacher. This approach is as much a measure of written expression as of spelling. The teacher can also use this approach in instruction of written language by asking students to write paragraphs and counting the number of words spelled correctly.

4. *Students' self-monitoring of errors:* Some teachers teach students to monitor their own performance by finding and correcting spelling errors in the daily assignments they complete.

Written Language

Written language is no doubt the most complex and difficult domain for teachers to assess. Assessment differs widely for beginners and advanced students. Once the preliminary skills of letter formation and rudimentary spelling have been mastered, written-language curricula usually stress both content and style (that is, grammar, mechanics, and diction).

Beginning Skills

The most basic instruction in written language is penmanship, in which the formation and spacing of uppercase (capital) and lowercase printed and cursive letters are taught. Early instruction stresses accuracy, and criteria are generally qualitative. After accuracy has been attained, teachers may provide extended practice to move students toward automaticity. If this is done, teachers will evaluate performance on the basis of students' rates of writing letters. Target rates are usually in the range of 80 to 100 letters per minute for students without motor handicaps.

Once students can fluently write letters and words, teachers focus on teaching students to write content. For beginners, content generation is often reduced to generation of words in meaningful sequence. Teachers may use story starters (that is, pictures or a few words that act as stimuli) to prompt student writing. When the allotted time for writing is over, teachers count the number of words or divide the number of words by the time to obtain a measure of rate. Although this sounds relatively easy, decisions as to what constitutes a word must be made. For example, one-letter words are seldom counted.

Teachers also use the percentage of correct words to assess content production. To be considered correct, the word must be spelled correctly, be capitalized if appropriate, be grammatically correct, and be followed by the correct punctuation (Isaacson, 1988). Criteria for an acceptable percentage of correct words are still the subject of discussion. For now, social comparison, by which one student's writing output is compared with the output of students whose writing is judged acceptable, can provide teachers with rough approximations. Teaching usually boils down to focusing on capitalization, simple punctuation, and basic grammar (for example, subject–verb agreement). Teachers may also use multiple-choice or fill-in tests to assess comprehension of grammatical conventions or rules.

Advanced Skills

Comprehension and application of advanced grammar and mechanics can be tested readily with multiple-choice or fill-in questions. Thus, this aspect of written language can be assessed systematically and objectively. The evaluation of content generation by advanced students is far more difficult than counting correct words. Teachers may consider the quality of ideas, the sequencing of ideas, the coherence of ideas, and consideration of the reading audience. In practice, teachers use holistic judgments of content (Cooper, 1977). In addition, they may point out errors in style or indicate topics that might benefit from greater elaboration or clarification. Objective scoring of any of these attributes is very difficult, and extended scoring keys and practice are necessary to obtain reliable judgments, if they are ever attained. More objective scoring systems for content require computer analysis and are currently beyond the resources of most classroom teachers.

6   Potential Sources of Difficulty in the Use of Teacher-Made Tests

To be useful, teacher-made tests must avoid three pitfalls: (1) relying on a single summative assessment, (2) using nonstandardized testing procedures, and (3) using technically inadequate assessment procedures. The first two are easily avoided; avoiding the third is more difficult.

First, teachers should not rely solely on a single summative assessment to evaluate student achievement after a course of instruction. Such assessments do not provide teachers with information they can use to plan and modify sequences of instruction. Moreover, minor technical inadequacies can be magnified when a single summative measure is used. Rather, teachers should test progress toward educational objectives at least two or three times a week. Frequent testing is most important when instruction is aimed at developing automatic or fluent responses in students. Although fluency is most commonly associated with primary curricula, it is not restricted to reading, writing, and arithmetic. For example, instruction in foreign languages, sports, and music is often aimed at automaticity.

Second, teachers should use standardized testing procedures. To conduct frequent assessments that are meaningful, the tests that are used to assess the same objectives must be equivalent. Therefore, the content must be equivalent from test to test; moreover, test directions, kinds of cues or hints, testing formats, criteria for correct responses, and type of score (for example, rates or percentage correct) must be the same.

Third, teachers should develop technically adequate assessment procedures. Two aspects of this adequacy are especially important: content validity and reliability. The tests must have content validity. There should seldom be problems with content validity when direct performances are used. For example, the materials used in determining a student's rate of oral reading should have content validity when they come from that student's reading materials; tests used to assess mastery of addition facts will have content validity because they assess the facts that have been taught. A problem with content validity is more likely when teachers use tests to assess achievement outside of the tool subjects (that is, other than reading, math, and language arts).

Although only teachers can develop tests that truly mirror instruction, teachers must not only know what has been taught but also prepare devices that test what has been taught. About the only way to guarantee that an assessment covers the content is to develop tables of specifications for the content of instruction and testing. However, test items geared to specific content may still be ineffective.

Careful preparation in and of itself cannot guarantee the validity of one question or set of questions. The only way a teacher can know that the questions are good is to field test the questions and make revisions based on the field test results. Realistically, teachers do not have time for field testing and revision prior to giving a test. Therefore, teachers must usually give a test and then delete or discount poor items. The poor items can be edited and the revised questions used the next time the examination is needed. In this way, the responses from one group of students become a field test for a subsequent group of students. When teachers use this approach, they should not return tests to students because students may pass questions down from year to year.

The tests must also be reliable. Interscorer agreement is a major concern for any test using a supply format but is especially important when extended responses are evaluated. Agreement can be increased by developing precise scoring guides for all questions of this type and by sticking with the criteria. Interscorer agreement should not be a problem for tests using select or restricted fill-in formats. For select and fill-in tests, internal consistency is of primary concern. Unfortunately, very few people can prepare a set of homogeneous test questions the first time. However, at the same time that they revise poor items, teachers can delete or revise items to increase a test's homogeneity (that is, delete or revise items that have correlations with the total score of .25 or less). Additional items can also be prepared for the next test.

CHAPTER COMPREHENSION QUESTIONS

Write your answers to each of the following questions, and then compare your responses to the text or the study guide.

1. Explain three potential advantages of teacher-made tests.

2. How do skill attainment and progress monitoring differ?

3. Explain content specificity.

4. Explain why frequent testing is valuable.

5. Give examples of a see–write, see–say, hear–write, and see–write formats.

6. Explain six common errors to avoid in developing multiple-choice tests.

7. Explain three things a teacher can do to prepare better matching questions.

8. Explain three things a teacher can do to prepare better true–false questions.

9. Explain three ways in which reading comprehension can be assessed.

10. Explain three ways of assessing spelling.

11. Why is fluency an important dimension to assess in beginning skills?

8 Managing Classroom Assessment

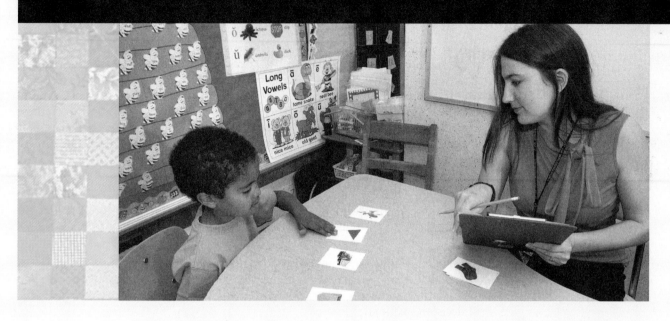

Chapter Goals

1 Know three characteristics of effective testing programs.

2 Be familiar with a process for putting a classroom assessment management program in place.

3 Understand various ways for setting goals and making decisions using progress monitoring data.

4 Be familiar with several systemwide efforts that involve systematic collection, analysis, and use of student progress monitoring data.

Key Terms

mandated tests	aimline	goal line
progress monitoring	trendline	decision-making rules
celeration charts		

EXCEPT FOR INDIVIDUAL EVALUATIONS CONDUCTED BY SPECIALISTS SUCH AS psychologists and speech therapists, classroom teachers are responsible for most testing conducted in schools. When districts want group achievement tests on all of their students (or those in particular grades), teachers are the ones who administer these tests in their classrooms. When the state requires all students to complete standards-based assessments, teachers are the ones who administer these tests in their classrooms. Beyond these mandated assessments, teachers routinely test to monitor student progress and ascertain the degree of student achievement on units and so forth.

Testing to monitor student progress during and after instruction is best when tests are carefully planned, thoughtfully managed, and fully incorporated into the classroom routines. In short, testing should be an easy and natural part of classroom life. Teachers should plan their testing programs at the beginning of the year. Good testing programs have three characteristics: efficiency, ease, and integration.

▮ *Efficiency.* Time spent in testing (including administration, scoring, and record keeping) is time not spent teaching and learning. Therefore, good assessment plans provide for the minimum assessments that are sufficient for decision making.

▮ *Ease.* Easy testing programs from the teacher's perspective are those that minimize teacher time and effort in all aspects of testing (that is, preparation, administration, scoring, and record keeping). The easiest testing programs are those that can be carried out by paraprofessionals or by the students. Easy testing programs from the student's perspective are those with which students are familiar, comfortable, and confident. Thus, it is important to set expectations about how assessment works in the classroom, how people are to behave, and so on early in the school year and reinforce these expectations periodically.

▮ *Integration.* Assessment activities can be integrated into the school day in two ways. First, teachers can monitor pupil performance during instructional activities. For example, basic skill drills can be structured to provide useful assessment information about accuracy and fluency. Second, teachers can establish a regular schedule for brief assessments, such as daily 1-minute oral reading probes. Making assessments frequent and part of the regular classroom routine has the added benefit of reducing student anxiety associated with higher stakes testing.

1 Preparing for and Managing Mandated Tests

When districtwide and statewide assessments are conducted, they generally occur within classrooms. Teachers usually have advance notice about when various mandated tests will occur, how long they will take, and how they are to be administered. Teachers should become thoroughly familiar with expectations for their role, and they should be thoroughly prepared with backup supplies of pencils, timers, answer sheets (if allowed), and so forth. Teachers should also provide their students with advanced knowledge in such a way as to reduce anxiety about these tests without diminishing their importance. For example, it is a good idea to tell students that all students in the district or all students in their grade are taking the test and that the tests are designed to help the district do a good job teaching all of the students.

In addition to these general considerations, teachers should check all of their students' individualized educational programs (IEPs) to verify that each student is required to take the assessment and what, if any, adaptations or accommodations must be provided. Teachers should also check their students' IEPs to determine whether any student is to receive an alternate assessment and if individual students need any alternate assessment accommodations.

2 Preparing for and Managing Progress Monitoring

Even the most extensively researched curriculum and teaching techniques may not work with every student. Moreover, there is currently no way to discern the students for whom the curriculum or methods will be effective from those for whom the educational procedures will not work. The only way to know if educational procedures are effective is to determine if they were effective. That is, we can know if what we have done has worked, but we cannot know this before we do it. Thus, teachers are faced with a choice: They can either teach and hope that their instruction will work or they can teach and measure if their instruction has worked. We advocate the latter approach.

Monitoring student achievement allows teachers the chance to reteach unlearned material, provide alternative content or methods for those students who have not learned, or get additional help for them. Moreover, student progress should be monitored frequently enough to allow early detection and error correction. Errors that are caught late in the learning process are much more difficult to correct because students have practiced the incorrect responses. Finally, the monitoring procedures must be sensitive to incremental changes in student achievement. Of all the ways teachers can monitor student learning, we prefer continuous (that is, daily or several times per week) and systematic monitoring rather than periodic monitoring (that is, assessing student knowledge after instruction of large amounts of content or after several weeks of instruction).

Lack of time is the primary reason given by teachers for not measuring frequently or well. However, advanced planning and extra work in the beginning will save countless hours during the school year. Teachers can do five things to make assessment less time-consuming for themselves and their students: establish testing routines, create assessment stations, prepare and organize materials, maintain assessment files, and involve other adults and students in the assessment process when possible.

Establish Routines

Establishing a consistent testing routine brings predictability for students. If students know they will be taking a brief vocabulary test in Spanish class each Friday or a timer will be used for the 2-minute quiz at the start of math class every

Tuesday and Thursday, they will require progressively fewer cues and less time to get ready to take the quizzes. For younger students, it helps to use the same cues that a quiz is coming. For example, "OK students, it's time for a math probe. Clear your desks except for a pencil." Similarly, if the test-taking rules are the same every time, student compliance becomes easier to obtain and maintain. For example, when teaching an assessment course to college students, we do not allow them to wear baseball caps (some write notes inside the bill), we allow them to use calculators (but not those with alphanumeric displays because notes can be programmed into them), students must sit in every other file so that there is no one to their immediate left or right, and we do not return the exams to students (to allow the reuse of questions without fear of students having a file of previous questions), although we do go over the exam with students individually if they wish. After the first exam or two, students know the rules and seldom need to be reminded.

To the extent feasible, the same directions and cues should be used. For example, a teacher might always announce a quiz in the same way: "Quiz time. Get ready." Directions for specific tests and quizzes may vary by content. For example, for an oral reading probe the teacher may say, "When I say 'start,' begin reading at the top of the page. Try to read each word. If you don't know the word, you can skip it or I'll read it for you. At the end of a minute, I'll say 'stop.'" A teacher can use similar directions for a math probe: "Write your name at the top of the paper. When I say 'start,' begin writing your answers. Write neatly. If you don't know an answer, you can skip it. At the end of a minute, I'll say 'stop.'"

Create Assessment Stations

An assessment station is a place where individual testing can occur within a classroom. An assessment station should be large enough for an adult and student to work comfortably and be free of distractions. Stations are often placed in the back of the classroom, with chairs or desks facing the back wall and portable dividers walling off the left and right sides of the workspace.

Assessment stations allow classroom testing to occur concurrently with other classroom activities. They allow a teacher or an aide to test students or students to self-test. Student responses can be corrected during or after testing.

Prepare Assessment Materials

The first consideration in preparing assessment materials is that the assessment must match the instruction. Unless there is a good match between what is taught and what is tested, test results will lack validity. The best way for assessments to match curriculum is to use the actual content and formats that are used in instruction. For example, to assess mastery of addition facts that have been taught as number sentences, one would assess using number sentences as shown in Figure 8.1.[1]

If generic assessment devices are already available, there is no reason not to use them if they are appropriate. By appropriate, we mean that they represent measurement of the skills and knowledge that are part of the student's instruction. One advantage to using existing assessment devices is that many have been developed to ensure that the probes are of similar difficulty level across a year such that they can truly measure student progress over time. Now that Internet

---

[1] Obviously, if testing is done to assess generalization or application of material, test content and perhaps formats will vary from those used during instruction.

FIGURE 8.1
Matching Math Content to
Assessment

How Addition Facts Are Taught

2 + 5 = _____   6 + 3 = _____   4 + 4 = _____

How Addition Facts Should Be Tested

6 + 3 = _____   4 + 4 = _____   2 + 5 = _____

How Addition Facts Should Not Be Tested

6 + _____ = 9   4   What are 2 and 5? _____

                       +4

access is practically universal, teachers only need to go to their favorite search engine and search for reading, writing, or math probes. They will find numerous sites that generate a variety of probes. However, it is important to recognize that not all existing probes are developed such that they are of equal difficulty level. Although there is evidence suggesting that various progress monitoring tools in reading are reliable and sensitive to student achievement gains, much less research has been conducted to demonstrate that existing tools in other areas (for example, math and writing) have adequate reliability for measuring progress over time. The National Center on Student Progress Monitoring provides information on whether various existing tools meet standards for effective progress monitoring (see http://www.studentprogress.org/chart/chart.asp).

Computer software can be used to facilitate probe and quiz preparation. For example, Microsoft Word has a feature that provides summary data for print documents, including the number of words and the reading level. Any spreadsheet program allows the interchange of rows and columns so that a practically infinite number of parallel probes for word reading or math calculations can be created.

There is no need for teachers to create new assessment materials when they test the same content during subsequent semesters unless, of course, their instruction has changed enough to necessitate changing their tests. Tests, probes, projects, and other assessment devices take time to develop, and it is more efficient to use them again rather than start over. Like any other teaching material, tests may require revision. Sometimes a seemingly wonderful story starter used to measure writing skills does not work well with students. It is generally better to start the revision process while the problems or ideas are fresh—that is, immediately after a teacher has noticed that the tests are not working well. Sometimes all that is needed is a comment on the test that documents the problem. For example, "students didn't like the story starter." Sometimes the course of action is obvious: "Words are too small—need bigger font and more space between words." If possible, teachers should make the revisions to the assessment materials as soon as they have a few moments of free time. Otherwise, the problems may be forgotten until the next time the teacher wants to use the test.

Organize Materials

When assessment materials have been developed and perhaps revised, the major management problem is retrieval—both remembering that there are materials and where those materials are located. This problem is solved by organizing materials and maintaining a filing system.

One organizational strategy is to use codes. Teachers commonly color code tests and teaching materials. For example, instructional and assessment materials for oral reading might be located in folders with red tabs, whereas those for math may have blue tabs. Within content areas or units, codes may be based on instructional goals. For example, in reading, a teacher may have 10 folders with red tabs for regular C–V–C (consonant–short vowel–consonant) words. Student materials may be kept in different locations, such as a filing cabinet for reading probes with different drawers for different goals. Once the materials have been organized, teachers need only resupply their files at the beginning of each year (or semester in secondary schools).

Involve Others

The process of assessment mainly requires professional judgment at two steps: (1) creating the assessment device and the procedures for its administration and (2) interpreting the results of the assessment. The other steps in the assessment process are routine and require only minimal training, not extensive professional expertise. Thus, although teachers must develop and interpret assessments, other adults or the students can be trained to conduct the assessments. Getting help with the actual administration of a test or probe frees teachers to perform other tasks that require professional judgment or skills while still providing the assessment data needed to guide instruction.

Data Displays

After performances are scored, they must be recorded. Although tables and grade books are commonly used, they are not nearly as useful as charts and graphs. These displays greatly facilitate interpretation and decision making. There are two commonly used types of charts: equal interval and standard celeration charts. Both types of chart share common graphing conventions as shown in Figure 8.2.

FIGURE 8.2
Graphing Conventions

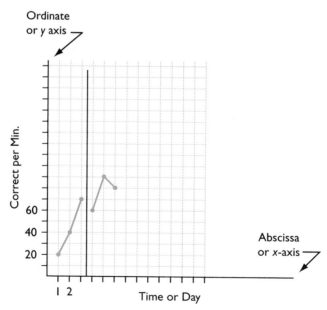

Scenario in Assessment

Phil Self-Administers a Probe

After instruction and guided practice, Phil knows how to take his reading probes. He goes to the assessment center and follows the steps posted on the divider.

1. He checks his probe schedule and sees that he is supposed to take 2-minute oral reading probe No. 17.

2. He goes to the file, gets a copy of the probe, and lays it face up on the desk. He inserts a blank audio cassette into the tape recorder and rewinds to the beginning of the tape.

3. After locating the 3-minute timer on the desk, he starts recording.

4. He says the probe number and then sets the timer for 2 minutes.

5. He reads aloud into the tape recorder until the timer rings.

6. He stops the tape recorder, ejects it, and places it in the inbox on his teacher's desk.

Phil then returns to his seat and begins working. At a convenient time, his teacher or the aide gets a copy of the probe that Phil read, slides it into an acetate cover, and notes errors on the cover, tallies the errors, calculates Phil's scores, and enters them on his chart. Then the teacher rewinds Phil's tape, wipes the acetate cover clean, and places the probe back into the file for reuse.

- The vertical (y) axis indicates the amount of the variable (that is, its frequency, percent correct, rate of correct responses, and so forth). The axis is labeled (for example, correct responses per minute).

- The horizontal (x) axis indicates time, usually sessions or days. The axis is labeled (for example, school days).

- Dots represent performances on specific days; a dot's location on the chart is the intersection of the day or session in which the performance occurred and the amount (for example, rate) of performance.

- Dots for performances on the same behavior or skill are connected. For example, performance in orally reading material written at the beginning first-grade level would be connected; performance in orally reading material written at the middle first-grade level would be connected but not connected to the performances on beginning first-grade material.

- Vertical lines separate different types of performances or different intervention conditions.

- Charts contain identifying data, such as the student's name and the objective being measured.

Two types of charts are used in special education: equal-interval charts and standard celeration charts. The difference between the two types of charts concerns the calibration of the vertical axis.

Equal-interval charts are most likely to be familiar to beginning educators. On these charts, the differences between adjacent points are additive and equal.

The difference between one and two correct is the same as the difference between 50 and 51 correct. Figure 8.2 is an equal-interval graph.

Standard celeration charts (also called standard behavior charts, semilogarithmic charts, or seven cycle charts) are based on the principle that changes (increases or decreases) in the frequency of behavior within a specified time (for example, number of correct responses per minute) are multiplicative, not additive. That is, the change from one correct to two correct is 100 percent and is the same as the change from 50 to 100. On daily celeration charts, the abscissa (*x*-axis) is divided into 140 days (that can be used as sessions). On the ordinate (*y*-axis), frequencies range from one per day to thousands per minute. A line from the bottom left corner of the chart to the top right corner indicates behavior that has doubled; any line parallel to that diagonal line similarly indicates behavior that has doubled. A line from the top left corner of the chart to the bottom right corner indicates that the behavior has reduced by half, and any diagonal line that is parallel to that line also indicates the behavior has halved. Figure 8.3 is a standard celeration day chart.

Although standard celeration charts allow one to see percentage change directly, it does not appear to matter which type of graph is used in terms of student achievement (Fuchs & Fuchs, 1987).

The benefits of charting student progress have been well documented since the 1960s. In general, students whose teachers chart pupil behavior have better achievement than students whose teachers do not chart. Students who chart their

FIGURE 8.3
Standard Celeration Chart

own performance have better achievement than students who do not chart their achievement. Finally, achievement tends to be best when both teachers and students chart pupil progress (see, for example, Fuchs & Fuchs, 1986).

3 Interpreting Data: Decision-Making Rules

Charting of data on student progress can help educators discern whether a student is making progress. After a baseline performance level is established, goals are typically set to assist with decision making. Goals may be set to ensure students reach the level of proficiency needed for them to be developmentally on track for a particular learning outcome (benchmark approach), or they can be set using anticipated rates of growth established through prior research investigations, such as those described in Fuchs, Fuchs, Hamlett, Walz, & Germann (1993).

Results from brief tests such as those frequently used to monitor progress can fluctuate, making it difficult to know whether the student is making progress toward meeting a goal. Sometimes fluctuations in performance are due to variations in the difficulty level of the test presented, sometimes they are due to student characteristics unrelated to what the test is intended to measure (for example, interest level and concentration level), and sometimes they are due to changes in student achievement, which are what you are intending to detect.

If a student is not improving in achievement at a rate needed to meet a predetermined goal, it is important that changes be made in instruction. However, given that there may be substantial fluctuation in the measures taken, how can we truly know whether the student is failing to make progress? Several decision-making strategies have been developed to help make appropriate decisions using progress monitoring data.

Four-point rule: Once a goal or aimline has been drawn, each data point collected after the determination of initial performance should be plotted soon after each probe is administered. If four consecutive data points fall below the goal line, a teaching change or intervention is considered warranted.

Parallel rule: Educators can draw an aimline as previously discussed. After several data points are collected, the trend in the student's performance can be compared to the aimline. If the instructional goal is the acquisition of a skill, the desired trendline is above the aimline and should be parallel or rise more steeply than the aimline. If the trendline does not meet the above criteria, instruction should be modified.

4 Model Progress Monitoring Projects

As people have recognized the benefits of frequent measurement of student learning, many educational systems have implemented systemwide changes that support progress monitoring efforts and have provided intervention as needed to those students who are not making adequate progress. The reauthorization of the Individuals with Disabilities Education Act in 2004 indicated that Response-to-Intervention can be used to identify students in need of special education services, so many educational agencies are incorporating systematic procedures for managing progress monitoring data and using such data to make a variety of decisions. Table 8.1 provides information on some projects that have supported such efforts. An expanded description of an educational agency that has been involved in systematic progress monitoring and using the collected data to inform decision making, namely the Heartland Area Education Agency, is provided in the following section.

Heartland Area Education Agency and the Iowa Problem-Solving Model

School personnel in the Heartland Education Agency in central Iowa were among the first in the nation to implement a formal model of problem solving that included direct and frequent assessment of student response to instruction. The model began to be implemented in approximately 1990 as part of an effort by the Iowa Department of Education to move away from a traditional service delivery model in which students were identified as having a disability based primarily on results from commercial norm-referenced testing and toward a problem-solving model in which the goal was to identify what interventions worked for a student and possibly qualify a student for services if it was identified that special education services were necessary for the student to make progress. The problem-solving model was initially implemented with individual students, but now many Iowa schools are also using problem solving to analyze data and target intervention toward schoolwide problems.

The Iowa problem-solving model had its origins in early work on behavioral consultation (Bergan, 1977; Tharp & Wetzel, 1969), and formal steps in problem solving were used with individual students. The steps are illustrated in Figure 8.4. When students experience academic difficulties, education professionals conduct an assessment to ascertain the difference between expected and actual student behavior or performance. Data are collected in an effort to clearly define the problem, determine why it is occurring, and identify an intervention that has a high likelihood of success. A plan is developed for addressing the problem, the plan is implemented, and the plan is evaluated using data from progress monitoring. "The process of defining problems, developing plans, implementing plans, and evaluating effectiveness is used with a greater degree of specificity and with additional resources as the intensity and severity of problems increases" (Grimes & Kurns, 2003).

In the past, this process has been applied at four different levels to address individual student problems of varying severity and need for resources. Recently, the model has been refined to address problems from a schoolwide perspective using a three-tier overlay to the traditional four-tier model. Core instruction is considered the "universal intervention," or the set of experiences that students receive in general education. It is argued that "the most efficient manner of improving student performance is through the provision of an effective core curriculum and then early determination of performance gaps for students whose performance is not keeping pace with expectations" (Grimes & Kurns, 2003).

TABLE 8.1				Projects Involving Systematic Progress Monitoring in School Districts		
Agency or Project	**Location**	**Areas Targeted**	**Grades Targeted**	**Decisions Made Using Progress Monitoring Data**[a]	**When Was the Associated Project Started?**	**Source with More Information**
Heartland Area Education Agency	Various districts in central Iowa	Reading, writing, math, social–behavioral, task-related behavior	PreK–12	Screening, progress monitoring, instructional planning, resource allocation program evaluation, eligibility	First applied in the early 1990s	Grimes & Kurns (2003)
Ohio Intervention Based Assessment	Various districts throughout Ohio	Learning and behavior	Elementary	Progress monitoring, eligibility	First systematically applied in the early 1990s	McNamara (1998)
Minneapolis Problem-Solving Model	Minneapolis public schools	Academic and behavior	Elementary and secondary	Screening, progress monitoring, eligibility	1994	Marston, Muyskens, Lau, & Canter (2003)
Pennsylvania Instructional Support Teams	Mandated in school districts in Pennsylvania prior to 1997	Academic and behavior	Elementary	Progress monitoring for selected students prior to full evaluation	1990	Kovaleski & Glew (2006)
Michigan Integrated Behavior and Learning Support Initiative	Various schools throughout Michigan	Academic and behavior	Elementary	Screening, progress monitoring, instructional planning, program evaluation	2003	http://www.cenmi.org/miblsi

[a]The decisions listed in this column were based on documents that were publicly available at the time this chapter was written. Since that time, the model programs may have published documents about other decisions for which they were using progress data or they may have added other decisions.

Tier 2, sometimes called secondary intervention (we labeled it targeted instruction), consists of (1) implementation of specific educational interventions for students experiencing academic and behavior problems and (2) systematic assessment of the extent to which those interventions are successful in enabling the student to improve in functioning and to be more like his or her peers. Tier 3

FIGURE 8.4
Problem-Solving Process

SOURCE: From Grimes, J. and Kurns, S. (2003). *Response to Intervention: Heartland's model of prevention and intervention.* National Center on Learning Disabilities and Responsiveness to Intervention Symposium sponsored by NCLD, Kansas City, MO, December 4–5, 2003. Reprinted by permission of Jeff Grimes.

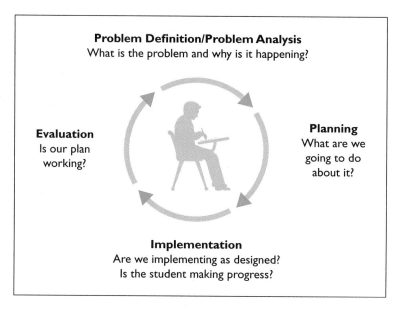

interventions are intensive interventions for students who do not profit from tier 2 interventions, and they may include special education services. The Heartland problem-solving approach is shown in Figure 8.5.

Assessment within the Heartland problem-solving model typically consists of periodic measurement of the progress of all students in general education settings. Devices such as the Dynamic Indicators of Basic Early Literacy Skills (DIBELS) (Good & Kaminski, 2002) are administered periodically (several times a year), and students who fail to perform as well as their peers are identified for

FIGURE 8.5
Heartland Problem-Solving Approach

SOURCE: Heartland Area Education Agency, Johnston, Iowa. Reprinted by permission.

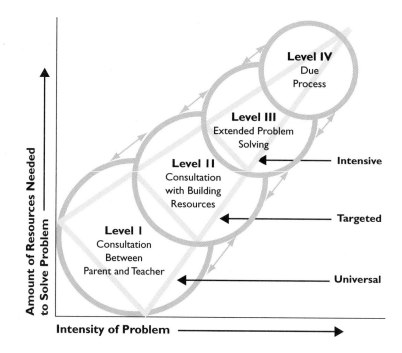

problem-solving intervention within tier 2 or tier 3 of the schoolwide model. It is possible at tier 1 to engage in continuous assessment of the progress of all students toward state or district standards. The technology exists for enabling school personnel to do this (for example, using Accelerated Math or Yearly Progress Pro) on a continuous rather than periodic basis. Within Heartland, school teams are developed to systematically examine schoolwide student performance data in relationship to the school curriculum, instruction, and environment in order to identify whether intervention is needed and how intervention could most effectively be targeted.

The needs of many students who fail to demonstrate satisfactory performance and progress according to tier 1 schoolwide data collection devices are referred for additional assessment at tier 2. This typically includes approximately 10 to 15 percent of the school population. Interventions are selected by school personnel to target identified needs, and progress is monitored on a biweekly or monthly basis using tools such as DIBELS or curriculum-based measurement methodologies derived from the early work of Deno, D. Fuchs, L. Fuchs, and Shinn (Deno, 1985; Deno & Fuchs, 1987; Shinn, 1989; L. Fuchs et al., 1984). Teams working through the problem-solving process at tier 2 may include professionals with greater expertise in curriculum-based evaluation (CBE; Howell & Nolet, 2000) to assist with analyzing problems and developing interventions.

For those who fail to make appropriate progress using tier 2 intervention, assessment at tier 3 may occur, and it typically involves the expertise of a specialist (school psychologist, educational consultant, or social worker) in the given area of concern. CBE is used to more systematically examine the nature of the individual pupil's problem and to collect data that can link to a potentially highly effective intervention. Progress is measured very frequently (at least once weekly) using curriculum-based measurement techniques, and the intervention is modified as needed. Special education support may be considered for students requiring a continued high level of support to make adequate progress.

CHAPTER COMPREHENSION QUESTIONS

Write your answers to each of the following questions, and then compare your responses to the text or the study guide.

1. Name and describe three characteristics of effective testing programs.

2. What are three resources that you can use for setting up a plan for managing data collection and analysis in a classroom?

3. Provide two methods for setting goals and two methods for making decisions using progress monitoring data.

4. Describe two projects that have been implemented on a systemwide level to encourage collection, analysis, and use of classroom assessment data.

PART 3

Assessment: Using Formal Measures

The chapters in Part 3 describe the most common domains in which assessment of processes (or abilities) and products (or skills) are conducted. With the exception of "How to Evaluate a Test" (Chapter 9), each chapter in this part focuses on a different process or skill domain and opens with an explanation of why the domain is assessed. We next provide a general overview of the components of the domain (that is, the behaviors that are usually assessed) and then discuss the more commonly used tests within the domain. Each chapter concludes with some suggestions for coping with problems in assessing the domain, and a set of chapter comprehension questions.

The criteria we used in selecting and reviewing specific tests warrant some discussion. First, in selecting tests we could not, and did not, include all the available measures for each domain. Rather, we tried to select representative and commonly used devices in each area. We moved some reviews that were included in previous editions of this textbook to the website for the book. And, as new tests become available, we will review them and include the reviews on the website. Readers interested in tests not reviewed in this book may want to consult the website first, then consult books devoted entirely to test reviews, such as Buros's *Mental Measurements Yearbooks*.

Second, in evaluating the technical adequacy of each test, we restricted our evaluation to information in the test manuals. There were two reasons for this decision: (1) As stated in the *Standards for Educational and Psychological Testing* (AERA et al., 1999), test authors are responsible for providing all necessary technical information in their test manuals. The test authors must have some basis for claiming that their tests are valid. Therefore, we searched the manuals for technical information that supports the test authors' contentions. (2) An attempt to include the vast body of research literature on commonly used tests would have resulted in a multivolume opus that would be impossible to publish as a current work. Entire books have been written on the subject of using and interpreting single tests.

In reviewing each test, we always use the same format. We describe the general format of the test and the specific behaviors that the test is designed to sample; these descriptions allow the reader to evaluate the extent to which specific tests sample the domain. Next, we describe the kinds of scores that the test provides for the practitioner; this gives information about the meaning and interpretation of those scores. Subsequently, we examine the standardization sample for each test; this enables the reader to judge—recalling the discussion in Chapter 3, "Test Scores and How to Use Them"— the adequacy of the norm group and evaluate the appropriateness of each test for use with specific populations of students. After that, we evaluate the evidence of reliability and validity for each test, using the standards set forth in Chapter 4, "Technical Adequacy." Finally, we give a summary of each test.

We urge our readers to examine the research on tests in which they might be interested. Test users are ultimately responsible for test selection and interpretation. Thus, if you are considering using a particular test that has incomplete or inadequate technical characteristics, it is your responsibility to demonstrate its validity. Current research may provide the support you need to demonstrate the validity of your assessment. Therefore, we urge our readers to go beyond our reviews.

9

How to Evaluate a Test

Chapter Goals

1 Understand the considerations in selecting a test to review.

2 Understand that reviewing a test requires an analysis of the test's purpose, content and assessment procedures, scores and norms, and reliability and validity in order to reach a summative evaluation.

1 Selecting a Test to Review

THE FIRST STEP IN EVALUATING A TEST IS TO CHOOSE A TEST TO EVALUATE. UNLESS we know the specific test we want to evaluate, our first task is to find a test to use. It is usually necessary to conduct a pre-review of the available tests in the domain of interest (for example, individually administered reading tests). Current publisher's catalogs or a reference work [for example, *Tests, Sixth Edition—A Comprehensive Reference for Assessments in Psychology, Education, and Business* (Maddox, 2008)] can generally help us hone in on a few tests for further review.[1]

In this honing-in phase, we concentrate on five questions that can be answered with information in a test catalog or reference text:

1. What is the domain we want to test? Usually, we can find suitable tests by simply reading test names.

2. Are we qualified to administer the test? Some tests require special training to administer or specific licenses or credentials to purchase.

3. Can the test be used appropriately with students of the age or grade in which we are interested?

4. Can the test be administered to groups or must it be individually administered? If we are interested in testing one student or a group of students, a group administered test can be used appropriately. However, if we are going to be testing groups of students, an individually administered test cannot be given; we must use a group test.

5. How old is the test? Generally, tests that were published 15 or more years ago are dated and should not be used unless absolutely necessary (for example, it is the only test available to assess a specific domain or the newer tests lack adequate norms, reliability, or validity). Also, it is also a good idea to contact the publisher to make sure that you are considering the most recent version of a test. It is a waste of time to evaluate a test that is not the latest edition or one that will be replaced soon by a newer version.

The next step is to acquire all of the relevant materials. Usually, this means contacting a test publisher and obtaining a specimen kit and any supplementary manuals that are available. Sometimes publishers will give or lend specimen kits; sometimes they must be purchased. Tests are not just sold by the company that owns the copyright; the same test kit may be sold by several publishers. Usually, the company that owns the copyright on a test is more willing to provide a specimen kit.

The last step in preparing to evaluate a test is to prepare the work area. For most of us, test materials are not spellbinding. Thus, the workspace in which the evaluation is conducted should not be conducive to nodding off. It is also a good idea to have a copy of *Standards for Educational and Psychological Testing* developed by the American Educational Research Association (AERA), American Psychological Association, and the National Council on Measurement in Education (1999). The standards provide guidelines about the kinds of evidence that should be used to evaluate a test's usefulness.

---

[1]It is cumbersome and time-consuming, but one can visit the websites of specific publishers (such as Harcourt) to find out what tests they have in a domain of interest.

2 How Do We Review a Test?

Test users must determine if a test will result in accurate and appropriate inferences about the specific students who will be assessed. This and other books can only evaluate tests in terms of their general usefulness. There are so many idiosyncratic student characteristics and life circumstances that it is impossible to consider a test's usefulness with all possible combinations of characteristics and circumstances in a general assessment text.

In evaluating the general accuracy and appropriateness of inferences drawn from students' test performances, we rely on *Standards for Educational and Psychological Testing* (American Educational Research Association, American Psychological Association, and the National Council on Measurement in Education, 1999). However, our examination goes beyond checking to determine if specific information relating to important standards is provided; we also consider the quality of the evidence presented. Evaluating the evidence presented in test materials requires a *"prove or show me"* mind-set. Test authors must demonstrate to potential users that their tests provide accurate educational and psychological information that can be properly used to draw inferences about students. One should not rely on test authors to admit that their test was poorly normed because there was no money to pay testers or their test was unreliable because they developed too few test items. One should expect that test authors will tend to put the best face on their tests.

Our first task is to locate the evidence presented by the author. Often, we find neatly organized test manuals that have useful chapter titles, subsections, and indexes so that we can readily find the sections we seek (for example, reliability). Even when a test manual is organized carefully, we often must extract the evidence we are seeking from large tables or appendices.

When test materials are not well organized or use idiosyncratic terminology, locating the evidence is more difficult. In such instances, we need to assemble all materials. (Because we often need to have all of them open at once, we will need a large workspace). Then we begin reading and making notes on the topics of interest, using different sheets of paper for the various topics of interest: purpose, content, testing procedures, scores, norms, reliability, and validity. It does not matter where one starts; however, validity and usefulness of inferences based on test scores are better left for last.

Test Purposes

Our search begins by finding the uses that the author recommends for a test. For example, the authors of the *Gray Oral Reading Test* (Wiederholt & Bryant, 2001, p. 4) state that their test is intended to (1) help identify students who are significantly below their peers in oral reading proficiency, (2) aid in determining particular kinds of reading strengths and weaknesses, (3) document students' progress in reading as a consequence of special intervention programs, and (4) be used in research of the abilities of school children. Thus, in evaluating the Gray Oral or any other test, we look for evidence that the test can be used effectively for the purposes intended by the test authors.

Test Content and Assessment Procedures

r a definition of the domain being assessed. The adequacy and
t interpretations depend on the rigor with which the purposes of
domain represented by the test have been defined and explained
99, p. 43).

anuals contain extensive descriptions of the domains they assess.
herely name the domains, and those names can imply a far broader
the test content actually provides. For example, the Wide Range
t 3 claims to measure reading. However, cursory examination of
reveals that the test only assesses letter recognition, letter naming,
ls in isolation. It does not assess accuracy and fluency of reading
rse (for example, prose); it does not assess comprehension.

mine testing procedures. Some tests use very tight testing proce-
pecifies exactly how test materials are to be presented, how test
be asked, if and when questions can be restated or rephrased, and
students can be asked to explain or elaborate on their answers.
loose testing procedures—that is, flexible directions and pro-
r case, the directions and procedures should contain sufficient
st takers can respond to a task in the manner that the author
A et al., 1999, p. 47). When test authors provide adaptations and
ns for students who lack the enabling skills to take the test in
ner, the author should provide evidence that the adaptations and
ns produce scores with the same meaning as those produced by
onaccommodated procedures. Generally, the more flexible the
directions, the more valid the test results will be for students with
ies. For example, the Scales of Independent Behavior–Revised can
d to any respondent who is thoroughly familiar with the person

ecessary to examine how test content is tested. Specifically, we look
at the test's content and scoring procedures represent the defined
A et al., 1999, p. 45). Evidence may include any of the following,
nbination:

is of tested content with some external standard. For example,
l Council of Teachers of Mathematics has explicated extensive
r what and how mathematical knowledge should be tested.

is of tested content with the content tested by other accepted tests.

▨ Expert opinion.

▨ Reasoned rationale for the inclusion and exclusion of test content as well as
assessment procedures.

Handwritten note (left margin, top):
- Find the definition of the domain being assessed
- Examine how test content is tested.

Handwritten note (left margin, bottom):
Generally, the more flexible the materials and directions, the more valid the test results will be for students with severe disabilities.

 Scores

First, we consider the types of derived scores available on a test. This should be
the most straightforward aspect of gathering and evaluating evidence about a test.
Information about the types of scores might be found in several places: in a section
on scoring the test, in a description of the norms, in a separate section on scores,
in a section on interpreting scores, on the scoring form, or in norm tables.

Next, we must consider if the types of scores lead to correct inferences about students. For example, norm-referenced scores lead to inferences about a student's relative standing on the skills or abilities tested. Such scores are appropriate when a student is being compared to other students, for example, when trying to determine if a student is lagging behind peers significantly. Such scores are not appropriate when trying to determine if a student has acquired specific information (for example, knows the meaning of various traffic signs) or skills (for example, can read fluently material at grade level). On the other hand, knowing that a student can perform accurately and fluently with grade level material provides no information about how that performance compares to the performances of other similarly situated students.[2]

If test authors use unique kinds of scores (or even scores that they create), it is their responsibility to define the scores. For example, the authors of the Woodcock–Johnson Psychoeducational Battery created a "W-Score" as one unit of analysis. They define the score and give examples of how to use it. We always look to see if the explanation of scores is clear, if they assume a great deal of technical knowledge that typical users cannot be expected to have (such as teacher knowledge of Rasch[3] item calibrating procedures), or if the derivation and use of scores are clear.

Norms

Whenever a student's score is interpreted by comparing it to scores earned by a reference population (that is, scores earned by other test takers who comprise the normative sample), the reference population must be clearly and carefully described (AERA et al., 1999, p. 51). For example, whenever a student's performance is converted to a percentile or some other derived score, it is essential that those students who make up the normative sample be of sufficient number and relevant characteristics.

In evaluating a test's norms, we must first determine the groups to which students' performances are actually compared.

Most often, a student's score is never intended to be compared to the scores of all of the students in the normative sample. Rather, a student's score is usually compared to the scores of same-age (or same-grade) students; sometimes they are compared to same-age (or -grade) and same-sex students. To ascertain to whom a student's score is compared, we usually need only inspect a manual's conversion tables or read their description in the manual.

A word of caution is warranted. In developing test norms, several thousand students may actually be tested, but not all of those students' scores may be used. Scores might be dropped for any one of several reasons:

■ Demographic data are missing (for example, a student's gender or age might not be noted).

■ A student failed to complete the test or an examiner inadvertently failed to administer all items.

---

[2]We repeat the warning that grade equivalents do not indicate the level of materials at which a student is instructional. A grade equivalent of 3.0 does not indicate that a student is accurate or fluent in 3.0 materials. More likely, 3.0 materials are far too difficult for a person with a grade equivalent of 3.0.
[3]More information about Rasch scaling and item response theory is available for download on the student website.

d to conform to criteria for inclusion in the norm group (for
she may be too old or too young).

an outlier (for example, a fifth grader may correctly answer
ions that could be given to an adult).

ber of students initially tested will not be the same as the num-
the norm group.[4]

are based on far more that just the age (or grade) and gender
s must be generally representative of all students of that age
e would expect students from major racial and ethnic groups
Americans, African Americans, Asian Americans, and Hispanic
ncluded. We would also expect students from throughout the
ll as students from urban, suburban, and rural communities to
y, we would expect students from all socioeconomic classes to
over, we would expect that the proportions of students from
s would be approximately the same as the proportions found
in the general population. Therefore, we look for a systematic comparison of the
proportion of students with each characteristic to the general population for each
separate norm group. For example, when the score of a 9-year-old girl is compared
to those of 9-year-old girls in general, we look for evidence that the norm group
of 9-year-old girls (1) consists of the correct proportions of Caucasian Americans,
African Americans, and Asian Americans, (2) contains the correct proportion of
Hispanic students, (3) contains the correct proportion of students from each region
of the country and each type of community, and so forth. Because some authors
do not use weighting procedures, we do not expect perfect congruence with the
population proportions. However, when the majority group's proportion differs
by 5 or more percent from its proportion in the general population, we believe the
norms may have problems. (We recognize that this is an arbitrary criterion; but it
seems generally reasonable to us.)

Reliability

For every score that is recommended for interpretation, a test author must provide
evidence of reliability. First, every score means all domain and norm comparisons
scores. Domain scores are scores for each area or subarea that can be interpreted
appropriately. For example, an author of an achievement test might recommend
interpreting scores for reading, written language, and mathematics; an author
might recommend interpreting scores for oral reading and reading comprehension, whereas another author might use oral reading and reading comprehension
as intermediate calculations that should not be interpreted. Next, norm comparison means each normative group to which a person's score could be compared
(for example, a reading score for third-grade girls, for second-grade boys, or for
fifth graders). Thus, if an author provides whole year norms for students (boys
and girls combined) in the first through third grades in reading and mathematics, there should be reliability information for 6 scores—that is, 3 (grades) multiplied by 2 (subject matter areas). If there were whole year norms for students

---

[4]The difference between the number of students tested and the number of students actually used in the
norms is of relevance only when a number of students are dropped and the validity of the norming
process is therefore called into question.

Handwritten margin note:

—When the majority group's proportion differs by 5% or more from the proportion in the gen. population, there is a norm problem.

in the first through the twelfth grades in three subject matter areas, there would be 36 recommended scores—that is, 12 grades multiplied by 3 subject matter areas. In practice, it is not unusual to see reliability information for 100 or more domain-by-age (or grade) scores.[5]

As we have already learned, reliability is not a unitary concept. It refers to the consistency with which a test samples items from a domain (that is, item reliability), to the stability of scores over time, and to the consistency that testers score responses. Information about a test's item reliability as well as its stability estimates must be presented; these indices are necessary for all tests. Information about interscorer reliability is only required when scoring is difficult or not highly objective. Thus, we expect to see estimates of item reliability and stability (and perhaps interscorer agreement) for each domain or subdomain by norm–group combination. If there are normative comparisons for reading and mathematics for students in the first through third grades, and item reliability and stability were estimated, there would be 12 reliability estimates: 6 estimates of item reliability for reading and mathematics at each grade and 6 estimates of stability for reading and mathematics at each grade.

Given modern computer technology, there is really no excuse for failing to provide all estimates of internal consistency. Collecting evidence of a test's stability is far more expensive and time-consuming. Thus, we often find incomplete stability data. This can occur in a couple of ways. One way is for authors to report an average stability by using standard scores from a sample that represents the entire age or grade range of the test.[6] Although this procedure gives an idea of the test's stability in general, it provides no information about the stability of scores at a particular age or grade. Another way authors incompletely report stability data is to provide data for selected ages (or age ranges) that span a test's age range. For example, if a test was intended for students in kindergarten through sixth grade, an author might report stability for first, third, and fifth grades.

It is not enough, however, for a test merely to contain the necessary reliability estimates. Every reliability estimate should be sufficient for every purpose for which the test was intended. Thus, tests (or subtests) used in making important educational decisions for students should have reliability estimates of .90 or higher. Also, each test (and subtest) must have sufficient reliability for each age or grade at which it is used. For example, if a reading test was highly reliable for all grades except second grade, it would not be suitable for use with second graders.

Finally, when test scoring is subjective, evidence of interscorer agreement must be provided. Failure to report this type of evidence severely limits the utility of a test.

Validity

The evaluation of a test's general validity can be the most complicated aspect of test evaluation. Strictly speaking, a test found lacking in its content, procedures, scores, norms, or reliability cannot yield valid inferences. Regardless of the domains

---

[5]Note that information about reliability coefficients applies to any type of score (for example, standard scores, raw scores, and so forth). Information about standard errors of measurement is specific to each type of score.

[6]Using raw scores would overestimate the test's stability if raw scores were correlated with age or grade.

they assess, all tests should present convincing evidence of general validity. General validity refers to evidence that a test measures what its authors claim it measures. Thus, we would expect some evidence for content validity, criterion-related validity, and construct validity.

However, we expect more. Test authors should also present evidence that their test leads to valid inferences for each recommended purpose of the test. For example, if test authors claim their test can be used to identify students with learning disabilities, we would expect to see evidence that use of the test leads to correct inferences about the presence of a disability. When these inferences rely on the use of cutoff scores, there should be evidence that a specific cutoff score is valid. Similarly, if test authors claim their test is useful in planning instruction, evidence is needed. Evidence for a standardized test's utility in planning instruction would consist of data showing how a test score or profile can be used to find instructional starting points—and the accuracy of those starting points.

Making a Summative Evaluation

In reaching an overall evaluation of a test, it is a good idea to remember that it is the test authors' responsibility to convince potential test users of the usefulness of their test. However, once you use a test, you—not the test author—become responsible for test-based inferences.

Test-based inferences can only be correct when a test is properly normed, yields reliable scores, and has evidence for its general validity. If evidence for any one of these components is lacking or insufficient (for example, the norms are inadequate or the scores are unreliable), then the inferences cannot be trusted. Having found that a test is generally useful, it is still necessary to determine if it is appropriately used with the specific students you intend to test. Of course, a test that is not generally useful will not be useful with a specific student.

CHAPTER COMPREHENSION QUESTIONS

Write your answers to each of the following questions, and then compare your responses to the text or the study guide.

1. What are five questions that you should ask when choosing a test for careful review?

2. What kinds of evidence should test authors provide to support the uses they recommend for their test?

3. What kinds of evidence should test authors provide to support the interpretations that they recommend for their test?

10

Assessment of Academic Achievement with Multiple-Skill Devices

Chapter Goals

1 Know factors to consider in selecting an achievement test.

2 Know the categories of achievement tests: group versus individual, norm referenced versus standards referenced, multiple skill versus single skill, and diagnostic versus survey.

3 Know the reasons why we assess academic achievement.

4 Be able to describe and compare representative achievement tests.

5 Know major dilemmas in the current practice of achievement testing.

6 Know how to get the most out of an achievement test.

Key Terms

achievement

attainment

norm referenced

standards
    referenced

diagnostic achievement
    test

instructional match

normative update

Stanford Achievement
    Test (SESAT, SAT, TASK)

TerraNova

Wechsler Individual
    Achievement Test

Peabody Individual
    Achievement Test

Wide Range Achievement
    Test

Diagnostic
    Achievement Battery

ACHIEVEMENT TESTS ARE THE MOST FREQUENTLY USED TESTS IN EDUCATIONAL settings. Multiple-skill achievement tests evaluate knowledge and understanding in several curricular areas, such as reading, science, and math. These tests are intended to assess the extent to which students have profited from schooling and other life experiences, compared with other students of the same age or grade. Consequently, most achievement tests are norm referenced, although some are standards-referenced measures. Norm-referenced and standards-referenced achievement tests are designed in consultation with subject matter experts and are believed to reflect national curricula and national curricular trends in general.

Achievement tests can be classified along several dimensions; perhaps the most important one describes their specificity and density of content. *Diagnostic achievement tests* have dense content; they have many more items to assess specific skills and concepts and allow finer analyses to pinpoint specific strengths and weaknesses in academic development. Tests with fewer items per skill allow comparisons among test takers but do not have enough items to pinpoint students' strengths and weaknesses. These tests may still be useful for estimating a student's current general level of functioning in comparison with other students, and they estimate the extent to which an individual has acquired the skills and concepts that other students of the same age or grade have acquired.

Another important dimension is the number of students who can be tested at once. Achievement tests are designed to be given to groups of students or to individual students. Generally, group tests require students to read and either write or mark answers; individually administered tests may require an examiner to read questions to a student and may allow students to respond orally. The primary advantage of individually administered tests is that they afford examiners the opportunity to observe students working and solving problems. Therefore, examiners can glean valuable qualitative information in addition to the quantitative information that scores provide. Finally, a group test may be appropriately given to one student at a time, but individual tests should not be given to a group of students.

Table 10.1 shows the different categories of achievement tests. The Stanford Achievement Test (SAT), for example, is both a norm-referenced and a standards-referenced (objective-referenced), group-administered screening test that samples skill development in many content areas. The Stanford Diagnostic Reading Test (SDRT), detailed in Chapter 11, is both a norm-referenced, group-administered test and a standards-referenced, individually administered diagnostic test that samples skill development strengths and weaknesses in the single skill of reading. The SDRT is intended to provide a classroom teacher with a more detailed analysis of students' strengths and weaknesses in reading, which may be of assistance in program planning and evaluation.

The most obvious advantage of multiple-skill achievement tests is that they can provide teachers or administrators with data showing the extent to which their pupils have acquired information and skills. By using group-administered, multiple-skill batteries, teachers and administrators can obtain a considerable amount of information in a relatively short time. They are especially useful in comparing classrooms, schools, districts, or individual students within those settings.

1 Considerations for Selecting a Test

In selecting a multiple-skill achievement test, teachers must consider four factors: content validity, stimulus–response modes, the standards used in his or her state, and relevant norms. First, teachers must evaluate evidence for content validity, the most important kind of validity for achievement tests. Many multiple-skill tests have general content validity—the tests measure important concepts and skills that are generally part of most curricula. This validity makes their content suitable for assessing general attainment.[1] However, if a test is to be used to assess the extent to which students have profited from school instruction—that is, to measure student achievement—more than general content validity is required: The test must match the instruction provided. Tests that do not match instruction lack content validity, and decisions based on such tests should be restricted. When making decisions about content validity for students with disabilities, educators must consider the extent to which the student has had an opportunity to learn the content of the test. Many students with disabilities are assigned to a curriculum (often a functional curriculum) that differs from the curriculum to which non-disabled students are exposed. These students are often assessed using the same test that others take, but they are provided accommodations to compensate for their disability (see Chapter 5). Many students with severe cognitive impairments are given alternate assessments, and their performance is evaluated relative to modified achievement standards or alternate achievement standards. We discuss alternate assessment and modified assessment practices in Chapter 22.

Second, educators who use achievement tests for students with disabilities need to consider whether the stimulus–response modes of subtests may be exceptionally difficult for students with physical or motor problems. Tests that are timed may be inappropriately difficult for students whose reading or motor difficulties cause them to take more time on specific tasks. (Many of these issues were described in greater detail in Chapter 5.)

---

[1]Recall the previous discussion on the distinction between attainment and achievement. Achievement generally refers to content that has been learned as a product of schooling. Attainment is a broader term referring to what individuals have learned as a result of both schooling and other life experiences.

Third, educators must consider the state education standards for the state in which they work. In doing so, they should examine the extent to which the achievement test they select measures the content of their state standards.

Fourth, educational professionals must evaluate the adequacy of each test's norms by asking whether the normative group is composed of the kinds of individuals with which they wish to compare their students. If a test is used to estimate general attainment, a representative sample of students from throughout the nation is preferred. However, if a test is used to estimate achievement in a school system, local norms are probably better. Finally, teachers should examine the extent to which a total test and its components have the reliability necessary for making decisions about what students have learned.

2 Categories of Achievement Tests

Achievement tests are the most common kinds of tests administered in school. Table 10.1 provides a list of commonly used tests and indicates the type of each test. The Stanford Achievement Test (SAT 10), for example, is both a norm-referenced

TABLE 10.1							Commonly Used Achievement Tests
Test	**Author**	**Publisher**	**Year**	**Ages/ Grades**	**Administered**	**NRT/ CRT**	**Subtests**
Metropolitan Achievement Tests (survey battery)		Pearson	2002	Grades 1–10 and 11/12	Group	NRT	Sounds and Print, Reading Vocabulary, Reading Comprehension, Open-Ended Reading, Mathematics, Mathematics Concepts and Problem Solving, Mathematics Computation, Open-Ended Mathematics, Language, Spelling, Open-Ended Writing, Science, Social Studies
Stanford Achievement Test Series		Pearson	2004	Grades K–12	Group	NRT and CRT	Sounds and Letters, Word Study Skills, Word Reading, Sentence Reading, Reading Vocabulary, Reading Comprehension, Mathematics, Mathematics Problem Solving, Mathematics Procedures, Language, Spelling, Listening to Words and Stories, Listening, Environment, Science, Social Science

continued on the next page

TABLE 10.1		Commonly Used Achievement Tests, *continued*					
Test	**Author**	**Publisher**	**Year**	**Ages/ Grades**	**Administered**	**NRT/ CRT**	**Subtests**
TerraNova 3		CTB/ McGraw-Hill	2008	Grades K–12	Group	NRT	Reading, Language, Mathematics, Science, Social Studies
Kaufman Test of Educational Achievement-II	Kaufman & Kaufman	Pearson	1998	Grades 1–12	Individual	NRT	Reading, Decoding, Reading Comprehension, Mathematics Application, Mathematics Computation, Spelling
Peabody Individual Achievement Test-Revised-Normative update	Dunn & Markwardt	Pearson	1998	Grades K–12	Individual	NRT	Mathematics, Reading Recognition, Reading Comprehension, Spelling, General Information, Written Expression
Wide Range Achievement Test–4	Wilkinson & Robertson	Pro-Ed	2007	Ages 5–75	Individual	NRT	Word Reading, Sentence Comprehension, Spelling, Math Computation
Woodcock–Johnson Psychoeducational Battery III (reviewed in Chapter 14)	Woodcock, McGrew, Mather	Riverside	2001	Ages 2–90+	Individual	NRT	Story Recall, Picture Vocabulary, Understanding Directions, Oral Comprehension, Letter–Word Identification, Word Attack, Passage Comprehension, Reading Vocabulary, Calculation, Math Fluency, Applied Problems, Quantitative Concepts, Writing Samples, Writing Fluency
Kaufman Assessment Battery for Children-2 (reviewed on the website under Chapter 14)	Kaufman & Kaufman	Pearson	1983	Grades 1–12	Individual	NRT	Letter & Word Recognition, Reading Comprehension, Phonological Awareness, Nonsense Word Decoding, Word Recognition Fluency, Decoding Fluency, Associational Fluency, Naming Facility, Math Concepts & Applications, Math Computation, Written Expression, Spelling, Listening Comprehension, Oral Expression

Test	Author	Publisher	Year	Ages/ Grades	Administered	NRT/ CRT	Subtests
Wechsler Individual Achievement Test–II	Wechsler	Pearson	2001	Grades pre-K–12	Individual	NRT	Word Reading, Reading Comprehension, Pseudoword Decoding, Numerical Operations, Math Reasoning, Spelling, Written Expression, Listening Comprehension, Oral Expression
Iowa Tests of Basic Skills		Riverside	2001	Grades K–8	Group	CRT	Vocabulary, Reading/Reading Comprehension, Listening, Language, Mathematics, Social Studies, Science, Sources of Information
Metropolitan Achievement Tests (instructional battery)		Pearson	2002	Grades K–12	Group	CRT	Sounds and Print, Reading Vocabulary, Reading Comprehension, Open–Ended Reading, Mathematics, Mathematics Concepts and Problem Solving, Mathematics Computation, Open–Ended Mathematics, Language, Spelling, Open-Ended Writing, Science, Social Studies
Stanford Achievement Test Series		Pearson	2004	Grades K–12	Group	CRT	Sounds and Letters, Word Study Skills, Word Reading, Sentence Reading, Reading Vocabulary, Reading Comprehension, Mathematics, Mathematics Problem Solving, Mathematics Procedures, Language, Spelling, Listening to Words and Stories, Listening, Environment, Science, Social Studies
Diagnostic Achievement Battery–3	Newcomer	Pro-Ed	2001	Ages 6–14	Individual	NRT	Story Comprehension, Capitalization, Characteristics, Punctuation, Synonyms, Spelling, Grammatic Completion, Contextual Language, Alphabet/Word Knowledge, Math Reasoning, Reading Comprehension, Math Calculation, Story Construction, Phonemic Analysis

and a criterion-referenced, group-administered screening test that samples skill development in many content areas. The most obvious advantage of multiple-skill achievement tests is that they can provide teachers with data showing the extent to which their pupils have acquired information and skills. By using group-administered, multiple-skill batteries, teachers can obtain a considerable amount of information in a relatively short time.

3 Why Do We Assess Academic Achievement?

The term *screening device* reflects the major purpose of achievement tests. These tests are used most often to screen students to identify those who demonstrate low-level, average, or high-level attainment in comparison with their peers. Achievement tests provide a global estimate of academic skill development and may be used to identify individual students for whom educational intervention is necessary, either in the form of remediation (for those who demonstrate relatively low-level skill development) or in the form of academic enrichment (for those who exhibit exceptionally high-level skill development). However, screening tests have limited behavior samples and lower requirements for reliability. Therefore, students who are identified with screening tests should be further assessed with diagnostic tests to verify their need for educational intervention.

Although multiple-skill, group-administered achievement tests are usually considered to be screening devices, they are occasionally used in eligibility decisions. In principle, such a use is generally inappropriate, although it may be justifiable and even desirable when the group tests (for example, the Stanford Achievement Test Series or the Metropolitan Achievement Tests) contain behavior samples that are more complete than those contained in some individually administered tests of achievement used for placement (such as the Wide Range Achievement Test 4 [WRAT4]). Use of an achievement test with a better behavior sample is desirable if the tester goes beyond the scores earned to examine performance on specific test items.

Multiple-skill achievement tests may also be used for progress evaluation. Most school districts have routine testing programs at various grade levels to evaluate the extent to which pupils in their schools are progressing in comparison with state standards. Scores on achievement tests provide communities, school boards, and parents with an index of the quality of schooling. Schools and the teachers within those schools are often subject to question when pupils fail to demonstrate expected progress.

Finally, achievement tests are used to evaluate the relative effectiveness of alternative curricula. For instance, Brown School may choose to use the Read Well Reading Series in third grade, whereas Green School decides to use the Open Court Reading Program. If school personnel can assume that children were at relatively comparable reading levels when they entered the third grade, then achievement tests may be administered at the end of the year to ascertain the relative effectiveness of the Read Well and the Open Court programs. Educators must, of course, avoid many assumptions in such evaluations (for example, that the quality of individual teachers and the instructional environment are comparable in the two schools) and many research pitfalls if comparative evaluation is to have meaning.

SPECIFIC TESTS OF ACADEMIC ACHIEVEMENT

The remainder of this chapter addresses specific multiple-skill devices and examines two popular group-administered, multiple-skill batteries (the Stanford Achievement Test Series and TerraNova 3); one individually administered, multiple-skill battery (the Peabody Individual Achievement Test–Revised–Normative Update [PIAT-R-NU]); and one individually administered, norm-referenced measure that is co-normed with intelligence tests (the Wechsler Individual Achievement Test–Second Edition [WIAT-II]); and one individually administered, norm-referenced, multiple-skill measure (the Diagnostic Achievement Battery–Third Edition [DAB-3]). Later chapters discuss both screening and diagnostic tests that are devoted to specific content areas, such as reading and mathematics. In Chapter 14, we review the Achievement Battery of the Woodcock–Johnson Psychoeducational Battery–IIINU.

Stanford Achievement Test Series (SESAT, SAT, and TASK)

Three separate measures are included in the Stanford Achievement Test Series, Tenth Edition (SAT-10; Harcourt Assessment, 2004), which is a test series that samples skill development in several different academic areas. The series includes the following: the Stanford Early School Achievement Test (SESAT), the Stanford Achievement Test (SAT), and the Test of Academic Skills (TASK). The SESAT has two levels and is intended for use in the assessment of kindergarteners and first graders. There are eight levels of the SAT, seven of which are typically administered to first through seventh graders and one that is administered to eighth and ninth graders; these eight levels are arranged according to primary, intermediate, and advanced categories. The TASK is intended for students in the ninth through twelfth grades.

All levels of the test are group administered. The test is both norm referenced and criterion referenced, and all items are presented in a multiple-choice format. The grades at which each subtest is administered, as

well the number of items and administration time associated with each subtest, are listed in Table 10.2. Although the extended version of the test is the focus of this review, an abbreviated version of the test is available that consists of a subset of items from the full-length test. Total administration time for the full-length test typically ranges from 2 hours, 15 minutes to 5 hours, 30 minutes. Administration time for the abbreviated format ranges from 1 hour, 41 minutes to 3 hours, 54 minutes.

Subtests

This section describes the subtests of the Stanford series and the associated behaviors that are sampled.

Sounds and Letters. This subtest, included only in SESAT 1 and 2, assesses the following early reading skills: matching two words that begin or end with the same sound, recognizing letters, and matching letters to sounds.

Word Reading. This subtest, available only at the SESAT and Primary 1 levels, measures students' abilities to recognize words by identifying the printed word for a given illustration or a spoken word.

Sentence Reading. This subtest, used at the SESAT 2 and Primary 1 levels, assesses students' abilities to comprehend single, simple sentences.

Word Study Skills. This subtest, used in the Primary 1 through Intermediate 1 levels, measures students' skills in decoding words and identifying relationships between sounds and spellings.

Reading Vocabulary. This subtest assesses a student's vocabulary knowledge and acquisition strategies. Items focus on measuring student knowledge of synonyms (for example, general word knowledge), multiple-meaning words (defined based on the context), and using context clues (students must rely on other parts of the sentence in order to define an unknown word).

TABLE 10.2 Subtests Included at Various Levels of the SAT-10

Test Levels	S (K.0–K.5)	S2 (K.5–1.5)	P1 (1.5–2.5)	P2 (2.5–3.5)	P3 (3.5–4.5)	I1 (4.5–5.5)	I2 (5.5–6.5)	I3 (6.5–7.5)	A1 (7.5–8.5)	A2 (8.5–9.9)	T1 (9.0–9.9)	T2 (10.0–10.9)	T3 (11.0–12.9)
Sounds and Letters	X	X											
Word Study Skills			X	X	X	X							
Word Reading	X	X	X										
Sentence Reading		X	X										
Reading Vocabulary				X	X	X	X	X	X	X	X	X	X
Reading Comprehension			X	X	X	X	X	X	X	X	X	X	X
Mathematics	X	X									X	X	X
Mathematics Problem Solving			X	X	X	X	X	X	X	X			
Mathematics Procedures			X	X	X	X	X	X	X	X			
Language			X	X	X	X	X	X	X	X	X	X	X
Spelling			X	X	X	X	X	X	X	X	X	X	X
Listening to Words and Stories	X	X											
Listening			X	X	X	X	X	X	X	X			
Environment	X	X	X	X									
Science					X	X	X	X	X	X	X	X	X
Social Science					X	X	X	X	X	X	X	X	X
Testing Time	2 h, 15 min	2 h, 50 min	5 h, 25 min	4 h, 55 min	5 h, 30 min	5 h, 30 min	5 h, 10 min	5 h, 10 min	5 h, 10 min	5 h, 10 min	3 h, 50 min	3 h, 50 min	3 h, 50 min

Reading Comprehension. At the Primary 1 level, this subtest assesses students' abilities to identify a picture described by a two-sentence story that is read, complete sentences in short reading passages using the Cloze format, and answer more general questions about a passage. At the Primary 2 level and beyond, students read textual, functional, or recreational passages. These passages are followed by multiple-choice test items that assess important reading processes such as initial understanding, interpretation, critical analysis, and the use of reading strategies.

Mathematics. The Primary 1 through Advanced 2 levels include two mathematics subtests: Mathematics Problem Solving and Mathematics Procedures. The single subtest Mathematics is used at the SESAT and TASK levels. The Mathematics and Mathematics Problem-Solving Test both assess mathematical problem-solving processes. Calculators are allowed for some levels. Mathematics Procedures focuses on the application of math computation procedures; calculators are not allowed for this subtest. The math subtests were developed in alignment with the National Council of Teachers of Mathematics standards for school mathematics (NCTM, 2000).

Language. This subtest is available in two formats: Traditional Language and Comprehensive Language. Traditional Language assesses students' abilities in mechanics and expression. Comprehensive Language assesses proficiency "through techniques that support actual instruction including prewriting, composing, and editing processes" (Harcourt Assessment, 2004, p. 65).

Spelling. In this subtest, students are presented with a sentence in which three words are underlined. Students must decide which word is misspelled. At higher levels, students are presented with a fourth "no mistake" option.

Environment. This is a teacher-dictated subtest that measures kindergarten through second grade student understanding of natural and social science concepts.

Science. This subtest measures students' understanding of "life sciences, physical sciences, Earth and space sciences, and the nature of science" (Harcourt Assessment, 2004, p. 66), with a focus on student knowledge of unifying themes in science rather than specific vocabulary. Test items assess students' processing of science information and their science inquiry skills. In developing this subtest, the authors aligned item content with the standards and skills emphasized in the National Science Education Standards, *Benchmarks for Science Literacy*, and *Science for All Americans* (American Association for the Advancement of Science, 1987, 1993).

Social Science. This subtest measures students' skill development in history, geography, political science, and economics, as well as students' abilities to interpret data presented through maps, charts, or political cartoons. The authors state that this subtest "primarily measures students' thinking skills" (Harcourt Assessment, 2004, p. 68), requiring students to use both acquired knowledge and processing skills in order to interpret associated data.

Listening. This subtest is used at the SESAT 1 through Advanced levels and is composed of both a listening vocabulary and listening comprehension section. In the listening vocabulary section, a sentence is read to the class and students must answer a question about the meaning of one of the words in the sentence. In the listening comprehension section, literary, informational, and functional passages are read to students. Older students (grade 3 and higher) are encouraged to take notes as the tester reads the material. This section measures students' initial understanding as well as their ability to interpret and analyze the material.

Special Editions

There are three special editions of the Stanford Achievement Test. The Braille edition can be used to assess blind or partially sighted students. Harcourt also provides a large-print edition (with content identical to the regular edition but containing adjusted graphics) for students who are visually impaired. There is also an edition for assessing students who are deaf and hearing impaired. This edition includes screening tests and special norms for students who are deaf and hearing impaired that were gathered by the Gallaudet Research Institute and the Harcourt Educational Measurement Research Group.

The *Technical Data Report* manual provides additional information on the accommodations that are considered "standard" and "nonstandard" for the test.

Scores

A variety of transformed scores are obtained for the Stanford series: stanines, grade-equivalent scores, percentiles, and various standard scores. The tests may be scored by hand or submitted to the publisher for machine scoring. When protocols are submitted to the publisher's scoring service, the publisher can provide record sheets for individual students, forms for reporting test results to parents, item analyses, class profiles, profiles comparing individual achievement with individual capability, analyses of each student's attainment of specific objectives, local norms, and so forth.

Performance scores can also be obtained. Performance standards were developed through the expert judgment of national panels of educators in each content area. Performance is scored as Below Basic, Basic, Proficient, and Advanced. These standards have been linked to the performance standards developed for the SAT 9.

Norms

The 10th edition of the Stanford Achievement Test Series was standardized simultaneously with the OLSAT 8 in both the spring and the fall of 2002. Separate norms are thus provided for schools in which students must be tested at these varying times of the year. Standardizing the series along with the OLSAT 8 enabled the authors to account for the ability levels of the students in the standardization population and also to develop a set of tables for comparison of ability to achievement.

Sample selection was based on several variables, including socioeconomic status, community type (urban, suburban, or rural), public/nonpublic school status, and ethnicity. Students from all but two states and the District of Columbia were included. Student scores were weighted to best match the aforementioned demographic characteristics of the U.S. population. For the most part, the fall and spring standardization samples appear to adequately represent characteristics of the U.S. population, although there are a few examples of over- or underrepresentation within a particular standardization sample (for example, underrepresentation of students from the Northeast and from urban areas in the fall standardization sample). Approximately 250,000 students participated in the spring standardization, and 110,000 students participated in the fall standardization.

Cross-tabulations are not shown, so we do not know, for example, the number of eighth graders from urban areas.

Reliability

Reliability data for the SESAT, SAT, and TASK consist of KR-20 internal-consistency coefficients and alternate-forms reliability coefficients for each level of the test according to the fall and spring standardization data separately. KR-20 coefficients for subtests from the full-length test (Forms A and B) ranged from .69 to .97, with only 25 of the more than 400 coefficients below .80. KR-20 coefficients for the abbreviated test (Forms A and B) ranged from .59 to .96. Alternate-forms reliability estimates (Forms A and B) ranged from .63 to 93.

Extensive tables listing reliability coefficients and standard errors of measurement are included in the technical manual. With only a few exceptions, the scores for subtests are reliable enough for group decision making and reporting.

Validity

The validity evidence provided for the Stanford series rests primarily on item development procedures. In developing the Stanford 10 items, the authors reviewed recent editions of textbooks, analyzed current curricula and instructional standards, and consulted professional organizations. Originally, pools of new test items were written by trained writers experienced in the different content areas. These items were then submitted to a group of content experts to establish content accuracy and alignment to standards, levels, and processes. Measurement experts examined and edited the items, and the items were reviewed by general editors for writing clarity.

Following this process, an item tryout program was conducted in order to choose items for the final test. Of interest during the item tryout were issues relating to item format, question difficulty, item sensitivity, progressive difficulty of items, and test length. Teachers in tryout samples provided feedback on the clarity of the item layout, appropriateness, and artwork. Following the tryout program, test items were reviewed for bias by a culturally diverse panel of prominent members in the educational community. Furthermore, all items were analyzed using Mantel–Haenszel procedures to determine differential item functioning between majority and minority groups. Data from the item tryout were also analyzed using traditional item-analysis and Rasch model techniques to inform final decisions about item inclusion. Information on correlations with the SAT 9 was provided, and correlations were generally in the .60 to .90 range for corresponding subtests and total scores. Correlations with the OLSAT 8 were generally much lower, as expected.

Summary

The Stanford Achievement Test Series is composed of the SESAT, SAT, and TASK. The tests provide a comprehensive continuous assessment of skill development in a variety of areas. Standardization, reliability, and validity are adequate for screening purposes.

TerraNova, Third Edition

The TerraNova, Third Edition (TN3; CTB/McGraw-Hill, 2008) is a norm-referenced, group-administered assessment system designed to measure educational concepts, processes, and skills of students in grades K–12. The TN3 was developed to measure student achievement in multiple content areas (reading, math, science, social studies, and language). The test is also designed to measure student progress in multiple ways, provide information relevant to instructional planning, reflect current curricula and national standards, and engage/motivate students so they do their best work.

The TN3 measures multiple content areas and uses multiple types of response formats (selected response, constructed response, and extended response). The test contains 12 overlapping levels (10–21/22) and is available in three interrelated editions: the TN3 survey, complete battery, and multiple assessments. Table 10.3 lists the grade levels for which each level of the test is appropriate. A locator test is available for teachers to administer and then match students at specific grades with a level of the test. This enables teachers to use multiple levels of the test within a grade, matched to their students who differ in skill level.

TABLE 10.3	Grade Ranges for Specific Levels of the TerraNova 3
TerraNova Level	**Grade Range**
10	K.6–1.6
11	1.6–2.6
12	2.0–3.2
13	2.6–4.2
14	3.6–5.2
15	4.6–6.2
16	5.6–7.2
17	6.6–8.2
18	7.6–9.2
19	8.6–10.2
20	9.6–11.2
21/22	10.6–12.9

SOURCE: From *Preliminary Technical Manual for the Terra NOVA™, Third Edition*, p. 4, published by CTB/McGraw-Hill LLC. Copyright © 2004 by CTB/McGraw-Hill LLC. Reproduced with permission of The McGraw-Hill Companies, Inc.

The three editions focus on five main content areas: reading, mathematics, science, social studies, and language. Furthermore, users of the TN3 can use the TerraNova, Second Edition Plus (TN2+) to measure five additional areas: word analysis, vocabulary, language mechanics, spelling, and mathematics computation. The content areas and test items of the TN3 were developed in conjunction with a comprehensive review of state, district, and diocese content standards in order to determine and assess common education goals.

Subtests

Reading. This section contains two significant changes from previous TerraNova editions. First, reading is now a separate subtest no longer included in language. Second, phonics and phonemic awareness in the K–2 level tests are now located in the reading test scales. Reading comprehension items focus on the central meaning of the passage rather than surface details.

The progression of items in this section was designed as a continuum to reflect the reading process by moving from initial understanding to generalization of concepts to other contexts. The multiple assessment edition includes open-ended items that involve comparing information across texts and extending meaning beyond the assessment.

Language. This section includes items that assess usage issues such as verb tense, subject–verb agreement, pronoun agreement, and modifiers. Students are also evaluated on sentence formation, sentence combining, and paragraph writing skills. Students are required to use critical thinking skills to make decisions about conveying meaning.

Mathematics. In the TN3, emphasis is on sampling a balance of skills, concepts, knowledge, and problem solving rather than on procedural/computational processes. The TN3 math section includes nonroutine problem-solving items in every test objective. The math section also includes a balance among numeration, number theory, data interpretation, pre-algebra, measurement, and geometry. Students are required to use calculators and rulers during the assessment.

Science. The science battery focuses on core concepts. Test items are based on recent national science standards and are grouped into life, physical, and earth/space science. In the upper levels of the test, items assessing the history and nature of science are included. The test also extends these subject areas by relating science to technology and society. Furthermore, the test includes a separate objective that assesses student scientific inquiry skills. These items measure skills independent of content-specific knowledge.

Social Studies. This test aims to determine how well students understand the relationships between social studies disciplines. The test was designed based on state and national standards. Student ability to synthesize information and make interdisciplinary connections is also assessed.

The TN3 survey edition is designed to give educators norm- and curriculum-referenced information from a short testing period. The survey edition is available for levels 12 through 21/22 and, like the other editions of the TN3, tests students on all content areas.

Developers suggest using the survey edition when testing time is at a premium. However, if educators need a larger array of diagnostic information, then the developers suggest using the TN3 complete battery. The TN3 complete battery combines the items of the TN3 survey edition with additional selected response items. The complete battery edition is available for levels 10 through 21/22 and tests on all of the content areas included in the survey edition. This edition of the TN3 also reduces measurement error due to its increased length.

The TN3 multiple assessments edition assesses students in the same five content areas. It is available for levels 11 through 21/22 (except language, which is not available for levels 11 and 12). In each of the content areas, the test items from the survey edition are combined with constructed response items. During these items, students produce short and extended responses that are scored by readers according to TN3 scoring guides. The developers report that the addition of the constructed response information significantly extends the range of the competencies covered.

All three of the TN3 editions can be conjoined with the TN2+ in order to test five additional content areas. The TN2+ assessments are available from level 11 to level 21/22. This additional battery of assessments adds supplemental tests in word analysis, vocabulary, language mechanics, spelling, and mathematics computation.

Much of the development of the TN3 reflects the philosophy of the National Assessment of Educational Progress (for example, the TN3 reading passage types generally match the National Assessment of Educational Progress passage types). In order to develop the content of the TN3, developers conducted a comprehensive review of state, district, and diocese content standards and curriculum frameworks. Along with this review, the developers also carefully examined content of recent textbooks, instructional programs, and national standards publications.

Scores

The TN3 yields multiple types of scores, including objective-, norm-, and curriculum-referenced scores. In the complete battery edition, every item contributes to a scale score that is used to report a student's norm-referenced information.

In all three editions of the TN3, each student's score in a content area is totaled and labeled as a composite. The reading composite is the average of the TN3 reading and TN2+ vocabulary; the language composite is the average of the TN3 language and TN2+, language mechanics; and the math composite is the average of the TN3 math and TN2+ math computation. The TN3 also yields total scores that are obtained by taking the averages of the three composite scores.

Student performance can also be described using a standards-referenced approach. TN3 will allow educators to measure progress by monitoring how many students are progressing through specific performance levels. The developers were in the process of identifying specific cut scores for performance levels at the time this book went to press.

Norms

Norming of the TN3 occurred in three phases: fall, winter, and spring. Developers estimate that more than 210,000 students, grades K–12, participated in the fall and spring standardizations. The winter standardization included approximately 8,000 students. The students were identified using a stratified random sampling procedure in order to represent the nation's school population. Schools were stratified by region (east, west, south, and middle continent states), community type, socioeconomic status, and public/private/parochial classification. Developers asked schools to test all students who were included in regular testing. They also included students who required special testing accommodations as specified by their individualized education program.

Reliability

During the fall standardization period, internal-consistency coefficients ranged from .77 to .90 for survey battery subtests, .80 to .92 for complete battery subtests, and .84 to .93 for the multiple assessment battery subtests. Reliabilities of the winter and spring administrations are yet to be computed. The TerraNova has sufficient reliability to be used for screening purposes, but reliabilities are not high enough (they should exceed .90) to be used to make eligibility decisions.

Validity

Content-related validity of the TN3 is evidenced by a correspondence between test content and instructional content. To ensure that the TN3 had high content-related validity, the developers used a comprehensive curriculum review to determine current educational goals and designed the test items to assess these goals. Also, developers examined differential item functioning in order to minimize ethnic and gender bias in the TN3.

The criterion-related validity has not been established for the TN3. The developers report that performance on the TN3 will be examined according to the performance on other, similar assessments such as InView. These intercorrelations will be reported in a later TN3 manual.

Peabody Individual Achievement Test–Revised–Normative Update

The most recent edition of the Peabody Individual Achievement Test (PIAT; Markwardt, 1998) is not a new edition of the test but a normative update of the 1989 edition of the PIAT-R. The test is an individually administered, norm-referenced instrument designed to provide a wide-ranging screening measure of academic achievement in six content areas. It can be used with students in kindergarten through twelfth grade. PIAT-R test materials are contained in four easel kits, one for each volume of the test. Easel kit volumes present stimulus materials to the student at eye level; the examiner's instructions are placed on the reverse side. The student can see one side of the response plate, whereas the examiner can see both sides. The test is recommended by the author for use in individual evaluation, guidance, admissions and transfers, grouping of students, progress evaluation, and personnel selection.

The original PIAT (Dunn & Markwardt, 1970) included five subtests. The PIAT-R added a written expression subtest. The 1989 edition updated the content of the test. The 1998 edition is identical to the 1989 edition. Behaviors sampled by the six subtests of the PIAT-R-NU follow.

Subtests

Mathematics. This subtest contains 100 multiple-choice items, ranging from items that assess such early skills as matching, discriminating, and recognizing numerals to items that assess advanced concepts in geometry and trigonometry. The test is a measure of the student's knowledge and application of math concepts and facts.

Reading Recognition. This subtest contains 100 items, ranging in difficulty from preschool level through high school level. Items assess skill development in matching letters, naming capital and lowercase letters, and recognizing words in isolation.

Reading Comprehension. This subtest contains 81 multiple-choice items assessing skill development in understanding what is read. After reading a sentence, the student must indicate comprehension by choosing the correct picture out of a group of four.

Spelling. This subtest consists of 100 items sampling behaviors from kindergarten level through high school level. Initial items assess the student's ability to distinguish a printed letter of the alphabet from pictured objects and to associate letter symbols with speech sounds. More difficult items assess the student's ability to identify, from a response bank of four words, the correct spelling of a word read aloud by the examiner.

General Information. This subtest consists of 100 questions presented orally, which the student must answer orally. Items assess the extent to which the student has learned facts in social studies, science, sports, and the fine arts.

Written Expression. This subtest assesses written-language skills at two levels. Level I, appropriate for students in kindergarten and first grade, is a measure of prewriting skills, such as skill in copying and writing letters, words, and sentences from dictation. At Level II, the student writes a story in response to a picture prompt.

Scores

All but one of the PIAT-R subtests are scored in the same way: The student's response to each item is rated pass–fail. On these five subtests, raw scores are converted to grade and age equivalents, grade- and age-based standard scores, percentile ranks, normal-curve equivalents, and stanines. The Written Expression subtest is scored differently from the other subtests. The examiner uses a set of scoring criteria included in an

appendix in the test manual. At Level I, the examiner scores the student's writing of his or her name and then scores 18 items pass–fail. For the more difficult items at Level I, the student must earn a specified number of subcredits to pass the item. Methods for assigning subcredits are specified clearly in the manual. At Level II, the student generates a free response, and the assessor examines the response for certain specified characteristics. For example, the student is given credit for each letter correctly capitalized, each correct punctuation, and the absence of inappropriate words. Scores earned on the Written Expression subtest include grade-based stanines and developmental scaled scores (with mean = 8 and standard deviation = 3).

Three composite scores are used to summarize student performance on the PIAT-R: total reading, total test, and written language. Total reading is described as an overall measure of "reading ability" and is obtained by combining scores on Reading Recognition and Reading Comprehension. The total test score is obtained by combining performance on the General Information, Reading Recognition, Reading Comprehension, Mathematics, and Spelling subtests. A third composite score, the written-language composite score, is optional and is obtained by combining performance on the Spelling and Written Expression subtests.

Norms

The 1989 edition of the PIAT-R was standardized on 1,563 students in kindergarten through grade 12. The 1998 normative update was completed in conjunction with normative updating of the Kaufman Test of Educational Achievement, the Key Math–Revised, and the Woodcock Reading Mastery Tests–Revised. The sample for the normative updates was 3,184 students in kindergarten through grade 12. A stratified multistage sampling procedure was used to ensure selection of a nationally representative group at each grade level. Students in the norm group did not all take each of the five tests. Rather, one-fifth of the students took each test, along with portions of each of the other tests. Thus, the norm groups for the brief and comprehensive forms consist of approximately 600 students. There are as few as 91 students at 3-year age ranges. Because multiple measures were given to each student, the authors could use linking and equating to increase the size of the norm sample.

Approximately 10 years separate the data-collection periods for the original PIAT norms and the updated norms. Changes during that time in curriculum and educational practice, in population demographics, and in the general cultural environment may have affected levels of academic achievement.

Reliability

All data on the reliability of the PIAT-R-NU are for the original PIAT-R. The performance of students on the two measures has changed, and so the authors should have conducted a few reliability studies on students in the late 1990s. Generalizations from the reliability of the original PIAT-R to reliability of the PIAT-R-NU are suspect.

Validity

All data on validity of the PIAT-R-NU are for the original PIAT-R. The performance of students on the two measures has changed, and so the authors should have conducted a few validity studies on students in the late 1990s. Generalizations from the validity of the original PIAT-R to validity of PIAT-R-NU are suspect. This is especially true for measures of validity based on relations with external measures where the measures (for example, the Wide Range Achievement Test or the Peabody Picture Vocabulary Test) have been revised.

Summary

The PIAT-R is an individually administered achievement test that was renormed in 1998. Reliability and validity information is based on studies of the 1989 edition of the test. As with any achievement test, the most crucial concern is content validity. Users must be sensitive to the correspondence of the content of the PIAT-R to a student's curriculum. The test is essentially a 1970 test that was revised and renormed in 1989 and then renormed again in 1998. Data on reliability and validity are based on the earlier version of the scale, which of course has gone unchanged. The practice of updating norms without gathering data on continued technical adequacy is dubious.

Wide Range Achievement Test–4

The Wide Range Achievement Test–4 (WRAT4; Wilkinson & Robertson, 2007) is an individually administered norm-referenced test designed to measure word recognition, spelling, and math computation skills in individuals 5 to 94 years of age. The test takes approximately 15 to 25 minutes to administer to students ages 5 to 7 years and approximately 35 to 45 minutes for older students. There are two alternate forms of the WRAT4. The test contains four subtests.

Subtests

Word Reading. The student is required to name letters and read words.

Sentence Comprehension. The student is shown sentences and is to indicate understanding of the sentences by filling in missing words.

Spelling. The examiner dictates words and the student must write these down, earning credit for each word spelled correctly.

Math Computation. The student is required to solve basic computation problems through counting, identifying numbers, solving simple oral problems, and calculating written math problems.

Scores

The raw scores that students earn on the WRAT4 can be converted to standard scores, confidence intervals (85, 90, and 95%), percentiles, grade equivalents, normal curve equivalents, and stanines. Separate scores are available for each subtest and for a reading composite (made up of Word Recognition and Sentence Comprehension).

Norms

The WRAT4 was standardized on a national sample of more than 3,000 individuals ages 5 to 94 years. The sample was stratified on the basis of age, gender, ethnicity, geographic region, and parental education. Although tables in the manual report the relationship between the standardization sample and the composition of the U.S. population, cross-tabs (indicating, for example, the number of boys of each ethnicity from each geographic region) are not provided.

Reliability

Two kinds of reliability information are provided for the WRAT4: internal consistency and alternate-form reliability. Internal consistency coefficients range from .81 to .99, with median internal consistency coefficients ranging from .87 to .96. Alternate-form reliabilities range from .78 to .89 for an age-based sample and from .86 to .90 for a grade-based sample. The reliabilities of the Math Computation subtest are noticeably lower than those for other subtests. Test–retest reliabilities are sufficient, again with the exception of the Math Computation subtest. With the exception of the Math Computation subtest, the test is reliable enough for use in making screening decisions.

Validity

The WRAT4 is a screening test that covers a broad range of behaviors, so there are few items of each specific type. This results in a relatively limited behavior sample. The authors provide evidence of validity by demonstrating that test scores increase with age, that intercorrelations among the various subtests are as theoretically would be expected, and that correlations are high among performance on WRAT4 and previous versions of the test. Validity is also demonstrated by high correlations among subtests of the WRAT4 and comparable samples of behavior from the WIAT-II, Kaufman Test of Educational Achievement–II (KTEA-II), and the Woodcock–Johnson III Tests of Achievement (note: not the new normative update for this test). WRAT4 is valid for screening purposes.

Wechsler Individual Achievement Test–Second Edition

The WIAT-II (Psychological Corporation, 2001) is an individually administered, norm-referenced achievement test designed to be used with students in grades pre-K through 12 who are between the ages of 4 and 19 years. A supplemental manual is available that provides norms for adults through 85 years of age. The first edition (WIAT) was co-normed with the Wechsler series of intelligence tests: the Wechsler Preschool and Primary Scale on Intelligence–Revised (WPPSI-R), the WISC-III, and the WAIS-R. The WIAT-II was linked to the WPPSI-R, WISC-III, and WAIS-III through a sample of 1,069 individuals who took the WIAT-II and the age-appropriate intelligence test. The authors contend that this linking of ability and achievement tests provides more reliable estimates of a student's aptitude–achievement discrepancy.

The test's authors created subtests that parallel and, they argue, comprehensively cover the seven areas of learning disability specified in Public Law 94-142: basic reading skills, reading comprehension, mathematics reasoning, mathematics calculation, listening comprehension, oral expression, and written expression. These seven domains, in addition to spelling and pseudoword (a combination of letters that can be pronounced but is not an English word) decoding, compose the nine subtests of the WIAT-II. The WIAT-II can be completed in approximately 45 minutes for very young children (pre-K and kindergarten), 90 minutes for grades 1 through 6, and 1 to 2 hours for grades 7 through 16. The behaviors sampled by the WIAT-II subtests are described in Table 10.4.

Scores

Eight types of scores—standard, percentile rank, age equivalent, grade equivalent, normal-curve equivalent, stanine, quartile, and decile—can be derived from each of the subtests and five composites. The mathematics, oral language, and written language composites are each based on two subtests; the reading composite is based on three subtests. The total composite is based on all the subtests. The standard score, which has a mean of 100 and a standard deviation of 15, can be computed by age or grade. Quartile scores represent corresponding quarters of the distribution; decile scores represent corresponding tenths of the distribution (that is, a decile score of 1 represents the first tenth, or the bottom 10 percent, of the distribution). Ability–achievement discrepancy scores based on the WIAT-II standard scores and one of the three Wechsler ability tests (WPPSI-R, WISC-III, or WAIS-III) are also provided. The test authors provide two methods of computing discrepancy scores—simple difference and predicted achievement—and provide information regarding the limitations of each approach.

Norms

The WIAT-II was standardized on 3,600 children for the grade-based sample (K–12) and on 2,950 children for the age-based sample (ages 4 to 19 years); 2,171 students were included in both samples. A sample of 1,069 children was used to link the WIAT-II with the WPPSI-R, the WISC-III, and the WAIS-III. The information collected from the linking studies was used to develop the ability–achievement discrepancy statistics.

TABLE 10.4		Description of the WIAT-II Composites and Subtests

Composite	Subtest	Description
Reading	Word Reading	Assess prereading (phonological awareness) and decoding skills ▪ Name the letters of the alphabet ▪ Identify and generate rhyming words ▪ Identify the beginning and ending sounds of words ▪ Match sounds with letters and letter blends ▪ Read aloud from a graded word list
	Reading Comprehension	Reflect reading instruction in the classroom ▪ Match a written word with its representative picture ▪ Read passages and answer content questions ▪ Read short sentences aloud, and respond to comprehension questions
	Pseudoword Decoding	Assess the ability to apply phonetic decoding skills ▪ Read aloud a list of nonsense words designed to mimic the phonetic structure of words in the English language
Mathematics	Numerical Operations	Evaluate the ability to identify and write numbers ▪ Count using 1:1 correspondence ▪ Solve written calculation problems ▪ Solve simple equations involving all basic operations (addition, subtraction, multiplication, and division)
	Math Reasoning	Assess the ability to reason mathematically ▪ Count ▪ Identify geometric shapes ▪ Solve single- and multistep word problems ▪ Interpret graphs ▪ Identify mathematical patterns ▪ Solve problems related to statistics and probability
Written Language	Spelling	Evaluate the ability to spell ▪ Write dictated letters, letter blends, and words
	Written Expression	Measure the examinee's writing skills at all levels of language ▪ Write the alphabet (timed) ▪ Demonstrate written word fluency ▪ Combine and generate sentences ▪ Produce a rough draft paragraph (grades 3–8) or a persuasive essay (grades 7–college senior)
Oral Language	Listening Comprehension	Measure the ability to listen for details ▪ Select the picture that matches a word or sentence ▪ Generate a word that matches a picture and oral description
	Oral Expression	Reflect a broad range of oral language activities ▪ Demonstrate verbal word fluency ▪ Repeat sentences verbatim ▪ Generate stories from visual clues ▪ Generate directions from visual or verbal clues

The sample selection was based on 1998 U.S. census data. The sample was randomly selected and stratified by age, grade, gender, race/ethnicity, geographic region, and parent education. Economic status was not used as a stratification variable. Demographic information on race/ethnicity, gender, geographic region, and parent education is disaggregated by age and grade. Cross-tabulations of parent education level by ethnicity are also provided.

Reliability

Three forms of reliability data were calculated for the WIAT-II. Split-half reliability coefficients based on age and grade subtest scores generally exceed .80. Numerical Operations, Written Expression, Listening Comprehension, and Oral Expression fall below .80 for certain ages and grades. The split-half coefficients for the four composites are all greater than .80, with two of the four composites exceeding .90 at all age and grade levels (Reading and Written Expression). A sample of 297 students ages 6 to 19 years was selected to determine the test–retest reliability of the WIAT-II. The subtest reliabilities are all above .80; coefficients are provided according to three age groups (6 to 9 years, 10 to 12 years, and 13 to 19 years). Interrater agreement was calculated among 2,180 examinee responses for three subtests that require subjective scoring. The correlation between raters for Reading Comprehension ranges from .94 to .98. The interrater agreement for Oral Expression ranges from .91 to .99. The interrater agreement for Written Expression ranges from .71 to .94.

Validity

The WIAT-II has evidence for validity based on test content, internal structure, and relations with other measures. Expert judgment and empirical item analyses were used to establish the content validity of the instrument. Experts analyzed the extent to which the items measured specific curriculum objectives. Empirical item analyses were used to eliminate poorly constructed items in order to prevent bias. The validity based on internal structure of the WIAT-II was documented through analysis of subtest intercorrelations, correlations with ability measures, and expected developmental differences across age and grade groups.

Several forms of support for validity based on relations with external criteria are provided. There are many moderate correlations between WIAT-II subtests and subtests from the Wide Range Achievement Test–Third Edition, the Differential Ability Scales, and the Peabody Picture Vocabulary Test–Third Edition. The WIAT-II also correlated as would be expected with subtests of several group-administered achievement tests, including the Stanford Achievement Test–Ninth Edition and the Metropolitan Achievement Tests–Eighth Edition. The correlation between the WIAT-II and school grades was generally low, but this is no different from what would be expected, given the low reliability of school grades.

Summary

The WIAT-II is an individually administered achievement test that is linked to the Wechsler series of intelligence tests. The subtests are designed to measure the seven areas of learning disability defined in Public Law 94–142. The test has an adequate standardization sample and appears to be reliable and valid. Two methods and statistical tables for computing ability–achievement discrepancies are provided, along with a description of the limitations of each method.

Diagnostic Achievement Battery–Third Edition

The Diagnostic Achievement Battery–Third Edition (DAB-3; Newcomer, 2001) is an individually administered measure of children's skills in listening, speaking, reading, writing, and mathematics. Although the test is called "diagnostic," it is essentially similar to the PIAT-R, WRAT3, and KTEA. Test givers use this test not to "diagnose" skill strengths and weaknesses in individual content areas but, rather, to obtain profile scores across areas. The test is designed to meet four purposes: (1) to identify students who are significantly below their peers in spoken language (listening and speaking), written language (reading and writing), and mathematics; (2) to ascertain an individual student's skill-development strengths and weaknesses; (3) to document intervention progress for individual students; and (4) to conduct research. The test is designed to be administered to children between the ages of

6 and 14 years. Updated norms, reliability and validity studies, minor changes among subtests, and an added optional subtest (Phonemic Analysis) represent modifications present in this latest edition of the DAB.

The DAB-3 is based on a specific conceptual model of academic achievement (Figure 10.1). Subtests are divided into five areas: Listening (Story Comprehension, Characteristics, and Phonemic Analysis), Speaking (Synonyms and Grammatic Completion), Reading (Reading Comprehension and Alphabet/Word Knowledge), Writing (Capitalization, Punctuation, Spelling, Writing: Contextual Language, and Writing: Story Construction), and Mathematics (Math Calculation and Math Reasoning). Behaviors sampled by the subtests follow.

Subtests

Story Comprehension. The student must listen to the examiner read stories and then answer oral questions about the stories.

Characteristics. After listening to the examiner read brief statements, the student must indicate whether the statements are true or false.

Phonemic Analysis. The optional subtest requires the student to segment words into phonemic units.

Grammatic Completion. The student must supply missing words or phrases in sentences read by the examiner.

Synonyms. The student must provide synonyms for words read by the examiner.

Reading Comprehension. The student must read short stories and then answer questions presented by the examiner.

Alphabet/Word Knowledge. The student must identify letters or words.

Capitalization. The student must indicate appropriate placement of capital letters in a set of 28 sentences.

Punctuation. The student must indicate appropriate punctuation in a set of 28 sentences.

Spelling. The student must write and spell correctly 27 dictated words.

Writing: Contextual Language and Writing: Story Construction. The student must write a story in response to three pictures that represent a modified version of the classic fable *The Tortoise and the Hare*. The story quality is evaluated according to 14 aspects of contextual language and 11 aspects of story construction.

Math Calculation. The student must solve 36 written calculation problems.

Math Reasoning. The student is presented with mathematical information in the form of pictures (for a

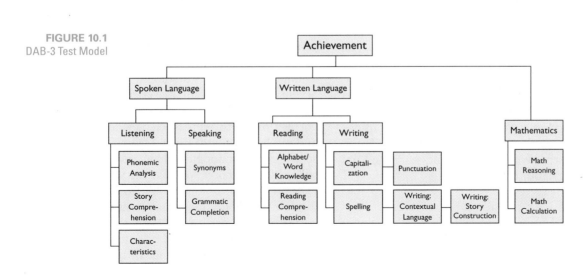

FIGURE 10.1
DAB-3 Test Model

young child) or statements presented orally and must use the information to solve math problems.

There are no set time limits for the DAB-3. Testing time typically ranges from 90 to 120 minutes. Most subtests are administered individually; however, the Punctuation, Spelling, Writing: Contextual Language, Writing: Story Construction, and Math Calculation subtests may be group administered.

Scores

Raw scores, percentile ranks, standard scores, and age/grade–equivalent scores can be calculated for each subtest. Standard scores for corresponding subtests are added and converted into a quotient (similar to a standard score) and percentile rank for each of the eight composites (Listening, Speaking, Reading, Writing, Mathematics, Spoken Language, Written Language, and Total Achievement) using tables in the back of the examiner's manual. DAB-3 results can be compared to results from other standardized tests using formulas provided in the manual. Information is also provided for conducting discrepancy analyses among the subtests and composites.

Norms

The DAB-3 norm sample consists of 1,094 individuals from 16 states (ages 6 years, 0 months to 14 years, 11 months) who were tested between 1997 and 2000. Comparisons between the sample and the school-age population (U.S. Bureau of the Census, 1997) are provided for geographic area, gender, race, residence (urban versus rural), ethnicity, family income, parental education, and disability status. Stratifications are provided by age for each of these variables, with the exceptions of residence and disability status. No further cross-tabulations are provided in the manual, which makes it difficult to determine whether comparisons are appropriate (for example, all of the low-income students may be from the South and not representative of low-income students from throughout the nation).

Reliability

Coefficient alphas for each subtest and composite according to age are provided by the author as a measure of internal-consistency reliability. Of the 126 subtest coefficient alphas, 102 meet or exceed .80. Subtests having several lower coefficient alphas include Synonyms, Punctuation, and Math Reasoning. Among the composite scores, all have alpha coefficients that exceed .80, with the Listening, Spoken Language, and Written Language coefficients exceeding .90. The Total Achievement coefficients range from .98 to .99. Coefficient alphas are also provided for gender and ethnicity groups, as well as for students with learning disabilities. These reliabilities all meet or exceed .80, except those for Punctuation, Writing: Contextual Language, and Math Reasoning among students with learning disabilities, as well as Writing: Contextual Language among African American students. Test–retest was determined using a sample of 65 elementary and middle school students from Pennsylvania tested twice with an intervening 2-week period. Results indicated adequate test–retest reliability (greater than .80) for all subtests except for Writing: Contextual Language and Writing: Story Construction.

Validity

Various measures of DAB-3 validity based on test content and internal structure are described in the examiner's manual. Rationale is provided for including the specific subtest content in the DAB-3, and comparisons are made between the content of the DAB-3 and other widely used achievement tests. Relatively few items were identified as being moderately to severely biased for different ethnic groups, and none were identified as being gender biased. Evidence of validity based on relations with other measures is provided by correlating scores for the DAB-3 and the Stanford Achievement Test–Ninth Edition among a limited sample of 70 students from Pennsylvania. Seventy-five percent of the coefficients were in the "high" range (.60 to .80). Corresponding composite correlation coefficients (such as reading with reading and math with math) ranged from .52 to .80. Higher scores were obtained by older students than younger students, and scores for students who were expected to score lower or higher due to having a learning disability or being identified as gifted demonstrated corresponding performance on the DAB-3. Finally, evidence for validity based on internal structure was provided by demonstrating through confirmatory factor analyses an appropriate fit to both a one-factor and a five-factor model (corresponding to the Total Achievement and five composite scores). However, the Speaking and Listening factors were highly inter-correlated and therefore were considered to more accurately constitute one factor. No data are presented to demonstrate that DAB-3 scores are useful for identifying children with academic difficulties or for monitoring intervention effects.

Summary

The DAB-3 is an individually administered test of a variety of academic areas. The test has been slightly modified from the previous edition and has an updated norm sample and adequate reliability information. Limited stratification among the norm sample is evident; however, the manual displays considerable evidence of test validity.

4 Getting the Most Out of an Achievement Test

The achievement tests described in this chapter provide the teacher with global scores in areas such as word meaning and work-study skills. Although global scores can help in screening children, they generally lack the specificity to help in planning individualized instructional programs. The fact that Emily earned a standard score of 85 on the Mathematics Computation subtest of the ITBS does not tell us what math skills Emily has. In addition, a teacher cannot rely on test names as an indication of what is measured by a specific test. For example, a reading score of 115 on the WRAT3 tells a teacher nothing about reading comprehension or rate of oral reading.

A teacher must look at any screening test (or any test, for that matter) in terms of the behaviors sampled by that test. Here is a case in point. Suppose Richard

Dilemmas in Current Practice

Problem

Two limitations affect the use of achievement tests as screening devices: the match of the test to the content of the curriculum, and the fact that the tests are group administered. Unless the content assessed by an achievement test reflects the content of the curriculum, the results are meaningless. Students will not have had a formal opportunity to learn the material tested. When students are tested on material they have not been taught, or tested in ways other than those by which they are taught, the test results will not reflect their actual skills. Jenkins and Pany (1978) compared the contents of four reading achievement tests with the contents of five commercial reading series at grades 1 and 2. Their major concern was the extent to which students might earn different scores on different tests of reading achievement simply as a function of the degree of overlap in content between tests and curricula. Jenkins and Pany calculated the grade scores that would be earned by students who had mastered the words taught in the respective curricula and who had

correctly read those words on the four tests. Grade scores are shown in Table 10.5. It is clear that different curricula result in different performances on different tests.

Authors' Viewpoint

The data produced by Jenkins and Pany are now more than 30 years old. Yet the table is still the best visual illustration of test curriculum overlap. Shapiro and Derr (1987) showed that the degree of overlap between what is taught and what is tested varied considerably across tests and curricula. Also, Good and Salvia (1988) demonstrated significant differences in test performance for the same students on different reading tests. They indicate the significance of the test curriculum overlap issue, stating,

Curriculum bias is undesirable because it severely limits the interpretation of a student's test score. For example, it is unclear whether a student's reading score of 78 reflects deficient reading skills or the selection of a test with poor content validity for the pupil's curriculum. (p. 56)

| TABLE 10.5 | | Grade-Equivalent Scores Obtained by Matching Specific Reading Test Words to Standardized Reading Test Words | | | |

Curriculum	PIAT	MAT		SDRT	WRAT
		Word Knowledge	Word Analysis		
Bank Street Reading Series					
Grade 1	1.5	1.0	1.1	1.8	2.0
Grade 2	2.8	2.5	1.2	2.9	2.7
Keys to Reading					
Grade 1	2.0	1.4	1.2	2.2	2.2
Grade 2	3.3	1.9	1.0	3.0	3.0
Reading 360					
Grade 1	1.5	1.0	1.0	1.4	1.7
Grade 2	2.2	2.1	1.0	2.7	2.3
SRA Reading Program					
Grade 1	1.5	1.2	1.3	1.0	2.1
Grade 2	3.1	2.5	1.4	2.9	3.5
Sullivan Associates Programmed Reading					
Grade 1	1.8	1.4	1.2	1.1	2.0
Grade 2	2.2	2.4	1.1	2.5	2.5

SOURCE: From "Standardized Achievement Tests: How Useful for Special Education?" by J. Jenkins & D. Pany, *Exceptional Children*, 44 (1978), 450. Copyright 1978 by The Council for Exceptional Children. Reprinted with permission.

earned a standard score of 70 on a spelling subtest. What do we know about Richard? We know that Richard earned enough raw score points to place him two standard deviations below the mean of students in his grade. That is all we know without going beyond the score and examining the kinds of behaviors sampled by the test. The test title tells us only that the test measures skill development in spelling. However, we still do not know what Richard did to earn a score of 70.

First, we need to ask, "What is the nature of the behaviors sampled by the test?" Spelling tests can be of several kinds. Richard may have been asked to write a word read by his teacher, as is the case in the Spelling subtest of the WRAT3. Such a behavior sampling demands that he recall the correct spelling of a word and actually produce that correct spelling in writing. On the other hand, Richard's score of 70 may have been earned on a spelling test that asked him just to recognize the correct spelling of a word. For example, the Spelling subtest of the PIAT-R presents the student with four alternative spellings of a word (for example, "empti," "empty," "impty," and "emity"), and the teacher asks a child to point to the word "empty." Such an item demands recognition and pointing, rather than recall and production. Thus, we need to look first at the nature of the behaviors sampled by the test.

Second, we must look at the specific items a student passes or fails. This requires going back to the original test protocol to analyze the specific nature of skill development in a given area. We need to ask, "What kinds of items did the child fail?" and then look for consistent patterns among the failures. In trying to identify the nature of spelling errors, we need to know, "Does the student consistently demonstrate errors in spelling words with long vowels? With silent *e*'s? With specific consonant blends?" and so on. The search is for specific patterns of errors, and we try to ascertain the student's relative degree of consistency in making certain errors. Of course, finding error patterns requires that the test content be sufficiently dense to allow a student to make the same error at least two times.

Similar procedures are followed with any screening device. Obviously, the information achieved is not nearly as specific as the information obtained from diagnostic tests. Administration of an achievement test that is a screening test gives the classroom teacher a general idea of where to start with any additional diagnostic assessment.

5 Summary

Screening devices used for assessing academic achievement provide a global picture of a student's skill development in academic content areas. Screening tests must be selected on the basis of the kinds of behavior each test samples, the adequacy of its norms, its reliability, and its validity. When selecting an achievement test or when evaluating the results of a student's performance on an achievement test, the classroom teacher needs to take into careful consideration not only the technical characteristics of the test but also the extent to which the behaviors sampled represent the goals and objectives of the student's curriculum. The teacher can adapt certain techniques for administering group tests and for getting the most mileage out of the results of group tests.

CHAPTER COMPREHENSION QUESTIONS

Write your answers to each of the following questions, and then compare your responses to the text or the study guide.

1. Identify at least four important considerations in selecting a specific achievement test for use with the third graders in your local school system.

2. Describe the major advantages and disadvantages of using group-administered, multiple-skill achievement tests.

3. A new student is assessed in September using the WRAT4. Her achievement test scores (using the PIAT-3NU) are forwarded from her previous school and place her in the 90th percentile overall. However, the latest assessment places her only in the 77th percentile. Give three possible explanations for this discrepancy.

4. Ms. Epstein decides to assess the achievement of her fifth-grade pupils. She believes that they are unusually "slow" learners and estimates that, in general, they are functioning on approximately a third-grade level. She decides to use Primary Level III of the SAT. What difficulties will she face?

5. Mr. Fitzpatrick has used the results of a group-administered achievement test to make a placement decision concerning John. What facts about group-administered achievement tests has Mr. Fitzpatrick failed to attend to? Under what conditions could he use an achievement test designed to be administered to a group?

11 Using Diagnostic Reading Measures

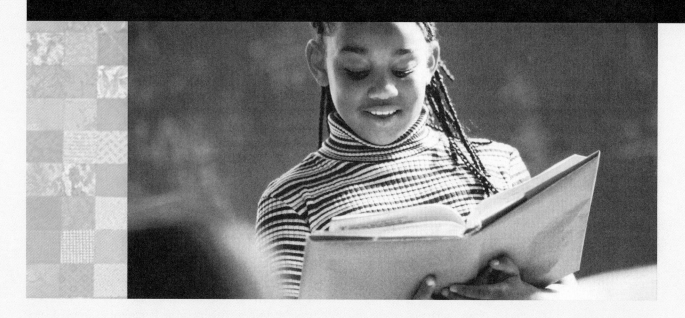

Chapter Goals

1 Know why we assess reading.

2 Understand the ways in which reading is taught.

3 Know the areas assessed by diagnostic reading tests, including oral reading, comprehension, word-attack, reading recognition, and reading-related behaviors.

4 Be familiar with three reading tests.

5 Be familiar with some of the current dilemmas we face in using reading measures.

Key Terms

oral reading

word-attack skills

rate of reading

word recognition skills

oral reading errors

literal comprehension

inferential comprehension

critical comprehension

affective comprehension

lexical comprehension

1 Why Do We Assess Reading?

READING IS ONE OF THE MOST FUNDAMENTAL SKILLS THAT STUDENTS LEARN. FOR poor readers, life in school is likely to be difficult even with appropriate curricular and testing accommodations and adaptations, and life after school is likely to have constrained opportunities and less personal independence and satisfaction. Moreover, students who have not learned to read fluently by the end of third grade are unlikely ever to read fluently (Adams, 1990). For these reasons, students' development of reading skills is closely monitored in order to identify those with problems early enough to enable remediation.

Diagnostic tests are used primarily to improve two educational decisions. First, they are administered to children who are experiencing difficulty in learning to read. In this case, tests identify a student's strengths and weaknesses so that educators can plan appropriate interventions. Second, they are given to ascertain a student's initial or continuing eligibility for special services. Tests given for this purpose are used to compare a student's achievement with the achievement of other students. Diagnostic reading tests may also be administered to evaluate the effects of instruction. However, this use of diagnostic reading tests is generally unwise. Individually administered tests are an inefficient way to evaluate instructional effectiveness for large groups of students; group survey tests are generally more appropriate for this purpose. Diagnostic tests are generally too insensitive to identify small but important gains by individual students. Teachers should monitor students' daily or weekly progress with direct performance measures (such as having a student read aloud currently used materials to ascertain accuracy [percentage correct] and fluency [rate of correct words per minute]).

2 The Ways in Which Reading Is Taught

For approximately 150 years, educators have been divided (sometimes acrimoniously) over the issue of teaching the language code (letters and sounds). Some educators favor a "look–say" (or whole-word) approach, in which students learn whole words and practice them by reading appropriate stories and other passages. Proponents of this approach stress the meaning of the words and usually believe that students learn the code incidentally (or with a little coaching). Finally, proponents of this approach offer the opinion (contradicted by empirical research) that drilling children in letters and sounds destroys their motivation to read. Other educators favor systematically teaching the language code: how letters represent sounds and how sounds and letters are combined to form words—both spoken and written. Proponents of this approach argue that specifically and systematically teaching phonics produces more skillful readers more easily; they also argue that reading failure destroys motivation to read.

For the first 100 years or so of the debate, observations of reading were too crude to indicate more than that the reader looked at print and said the printed words (or answered questions about the content conveyed by those printed words). Consequently, theoreticians speculated about the processes occurring inside the reader, and the speculations of advocates of whole-word instruction dominated the debate until the 1950s. Thereafter, phonics instruction (systematically teaching beginning readers the relationships among the alphabetic code, phonemes, and words) increasingly became part of prereading and reading instruction. Some of that increased emphasis on phonics may be attributable to *Why Johnny Can't Read* (Flesch, 1955), a book vigorously advocating phonics instruction; more important, the growing body of empirical evidence increasingly showed phonics instruction's effectiveness. By 1967, there was substantial evidence that systematic instruction in phonics produced better readers and that the effect of phonics instruction was greater for children of low ability or from disadvantaged backgrounds. With phonics instruction, beginning readers had better word recognition, better reading comprehension, and better reading vocabulary (Bond & Dykstra, 1967; Chall, 1967). Subsequent empirical evidence leads to the same conclusions (Rayner, Foorman, Perfetti, Pesetsky, & Seidenberg, 2001; National Institute of Child Health and Human Development, 2000a, 2000b; Adams, 1990; Foorman, Francis, Fletcher, Schatschneider, & Mehta, 1998; Pflaum, Walberg, Karegianes, & Rasher, 1980; Stanovich, 1986).

While some scholars were demonstrating the efficacy of phonics instruction, others began unraveling the ways in which beginners learn to read. Today, that process is much clearer than it was even in the 1970s. Armbruster and Osborn (2001) have provided an excellent summary of the processes involved in early reading. First, beginning readers must understand how words are made up of sounds before they need to read. This process, called "phonemic awareness," is the ability to recognize and manipulate phonemes, which are the spoken sounds that affect the meaning of a communication. Phonemic awareness can be taught if it has not already developed before reading instruction begins. Second, beginning readers must associate graphemes (alphabet letters) with phonemes. Beginning readers learn these associations best through explicit phonics instruction. Third, beginning readers must read fluently in order to comprehend what they are reading.

After students become fluent decoders, they read more difficult material. This material often contains advanced vocabulary that students must learn. It contains more complex sentence structure, more condensed and abstract ideas, and perhaps less literal and more inferential meaning. Finally, more difficult material frequently requires that readers read with the purpose of understanding what they are reading.

While learning more about how students begin to read, scholars also learned that some long-held beliefs were not valid. For example, it is incorrect to say that poor readers read letter by letter, but skilled readers read entire words and phrases as a unit. Actually, skilled readers read letter by letter and word by word, but they do it so quickly that they appear to be reading words and phrases (see, for example, Snow, Burns, & Griffin, 1998). It is also incorrect to say that good readers rely heavily on context cues to identify words (Share & Stanovich, 1995). Good readers do use context cues to verify their decoding accuracy. Poor readers rely on them heavily, however, probably because they lack skill in more appropriate word-attack skills (see, for example, Briggs & Underwood, 1984).

Scenario in Assessment

Lloyd

The Springfield School District uses a child-centered whole-language approach to teaching reading. Near the end of the school year, the district screened all first-grade students to identify students who would require supplementary services in reading the following year. Lloyd earned a score that was at the seventh percentile on the district's norms, and the district notified his parents that he would be receiving additional help the next year so that he could improve his skills. Lloyd's parents were upset by the news because until the notification they thought that Lloyd was progressing well in all school subjects.

The parents requested a meeting with Lloyd's teacher, who also invited the reading specialist. At that meeting, the reading specialist told the parents that a fairly large percentage of first graders were in the same predicament as Lloyd but not to worry because many students matured into readers. She said that Lloyd only needed time. She urged the parents to let Lloyd enjoy his summer, and the district would retest him at the beginning of the second grade to determine if he still needed the extra help.

Lloyd's parents ignored the district's advice and enrolled him in a reading course at a local tutoring program. Lloyd was first tested to identify the exact nature of his problem. The test results indicated that he had excellent phonemic awareness, could print and name all upper- and lowercase letters, knew all the consonant sounds, knew the sounds of all long vowels, did not know any of the short vowel sounds, could not sound blend, and had a sight vocabulary of approximately 50 words. Lloyd's tutor taught him the short vowel sounds rather quickly. However, he had trouble with sound blending until his tutor used his interest and skill in math to explain the principles. She wrote: c + a + t = cat, and then said each of the three sounds and "cat." As she explained to Lloyd's parents, it was like a light going on in his head. He got it. The tutor spent a few more sessions using phonics to help Lloyd increase his sight vocabulary.

In September, the district retested Lloyd as it had promised. The district sent home a form letter in which it explained that Lloyd was now at the 99th percentile in reading and no longer needed supplementary services. At the bottom was a hand-written note from the reading specialist: "Lloyd just needed a little time to become a reader. We're so glad you let him just enjoy his summer!"

Epigram Lloyd did enjoy his summer as well as the second grade. Also, he won an award as the best second-grade reader in the district.

Today, despite clear evidence indicating the essential role of phonics in reading and strong indications of the superiority of reading programs with direct instruction in phonics (Foorman et al., 1998), some professionals continue to reject phonics instruction. Perhaps this may explain why most students who are referred for psychological assessment are referred because of reading problems and why most of these students have problems changing the symbols (that is, alphabet letters) into sounds and words. The obvious connection between phonics instruction and beginning reading has not escaped the notice of many parents, however. They have become eager consumers of educational materials (such as "Hooked on Phonics" and "The Phonics Game") and private tutoring (for example, instruction at a Sylvan Learning Center).

Educators' views of how students learn to read and how students should be taught will determine their beliefs about reading assessment. Thus, diagnostic testing in reading is caught between the opposing camps. If the test includes an assessment of the skills needed to decode text, it is attacked by those who reject analytic approaches to reading. If the test does not include an assessment of decoding skills, it is attacked by those who know the importance of those skills in beginning reading.

3 Skills Assessed by Diagnostic Reading Tests

Reading is a complex process that changes as readers develop. Beginning readers rely heavily on a complex set of decoding skills that can be assessed holistically by having a student read orally and assessing his or her accuracy and fluency. Decoding skills may also be measured analytically by having students apply these skills in isolation (for example, using phonics to read nonsense words). Once fluency in decoding has been attained, readers are expected to go beyond the comprehension of simple language and simple ideas to the process of understanding and evaluating what is written. Advanced readers rely on different skills (that is, linguistic competence and abstract reasoning) and different facts (that is, vocabulary, prior knowledge and experience, and beliefs). Comprehension may be assessed by having a student read a passage that deals with an esoteric topic and is filled with abstract concepts and difficult vocabulary; moreover, the sentences in that passage may have complicated grammar with minimal redundancy.

Oral Reading

A number of tests and subtests are designed to assess the accuracy and/or fluency of a student's oral reading. Oral reading tests consist of a series of graded paragraphs that are read sequentially by a student. The examiner notes reading errors and behaviors that characterize the student's oral reading.

Rate of Reading

Good readers are fluent; they recognize words quickly (without having to rely on phonetic analysis) and are in a good position to construct meaning of sentences and paragraphs. Readers who are not fluent have problems comprehending what they read, and the problems become more severe as the complexity of the reading material increases. Indeed, reading fluency is an excellent general indicator of reading achievement. Consequently, increasingly more states are including reading fluency as part of their comprehensive reading assessment systems.

Nonetheless, many commercially available reading tests do not assess reading fluency. However, there are some exceptions. Two levels of the Stanford Diagnostic Reading Test have subtests to assess rate of reading. Tests such as the Gray Oral Reading Test–4 (GORT-4) are timed. A pupil who reads a passage on the GORT-4 slowly but makes no errors in reading may earn a lower score than a rapid reader who makes one or two errors in reading.

Oral Reading Errors

Oral reading requires that students say the word that is printed on the page correctly. However, all errors made by a student are not equal. Some errors are relatively unimportant to the extent that they do not affect the student's comprehension of the material. Other errors are ignored. Examiners may note characteristics of a student's oral reading that are not counted as errors. Self-corrections are not counted as errors. Disregarded punctuation marks (for example, failing to pause for a comma or to inflect vocally to indicate a question mark) are not counted as errors. Repetitions and hesitations due to speech handicaps (for example, stuttering or stammering) are not counted as errors. Dialectic accents are not counted as mispronunciations.[1]

The following types of errors count against the student:

Teacher Pronunciation or Aid If a student either hesitates for a time without making an audible effort to pronounce a word or appears to be attempting for 10 seconds to pronounce the word, the examiner pronounces the word and records an error.

Hesitation The student hesitates for 2 or more seconds before pronouncing a word.

Gross Mispronunciation of a Word A gross mispronunciation is recorded when the pupil's pronunciation of a word bears so little resemblance to the proper pronunciation that the examiner must be looking at the word to recognize it. An example of gross mispronunciation is reading "encounter" as "actors."

Partial Mispronunciation of a Word A partial mispronunciation can be one of several different kinds of errors. The examiner may have to pronounce part of a word for the student (an aid); the student may phonetically mispronounce specific letters (for example, by reading "red" as "reed"); or the student may omit part of a word, insert elements of words, or make errors in syllabication, accent, or inversion.

Omission of a Word or Group of Words Omissions consist of skipping individual words or groups of words.

Insertion of a Word or Group of Words Insertions consist of the student's putting one or more words into the sentence being read. The student may, for example, read "the dog" as "the mean dog."

Substitution of One Meaningful Word for Another Substitutions consist of the replacement of one or more words in the passage by one or more different meaningful words. The student might read "dense" as "depress." Students often replace entire sequences of words with others, as illustrated by the replacement of "he is his own mechanic" with "he sat on his own machine." Some oral reading tests require that examiners record the specific kind of substitution error. Substitutions are classified as meaning similarity (the words have similar meanings), function similarity (the two words have syntactically similar functions), graphic/phoneme similarity (the words look or sound alike), or a combination of the preceding.

Repetition Repetition occurs when students repeat words or groups of words while attempting to read sentences or paragraphs. In some cases, if a student repeats a group of words to correct an error, the original error is not recorded, but a repetition error is. In other cases, such behaviors are recorded simply as spontaneous self-corrections.

---

[1]Other characteristics of a student's oral reading are problematic (although not errors): poor posture, inappropriate head movement, finger pointing, loss of place, lack of expression (for example, word-by-word reading, lack of phrasing, or monotone voice), and strained voice.

Inversion, or Changing of Word Order Errors of inversion are recorded when the child changes the order of words appearing in a sentence; for example, "house the" is an inversion.

Assessment of Reading Comprehension

Diagnostic tests assess five different types of reading comprehension:

1. *Literal comprehension* entails understanding the information that is explicit in the reading material.
2. *Inferential comprehension* means interpreting, synthesizing, or extending the information that is explicit in the reading material.
3. *Critical comprehension* requires analyzing, evaluating, and making judgments about the material read.
4. *Affective comprehension* involves a reader's personal and emotional responses to the reading material.
5. *Lexical comprehension* means knowing the meaning of key vocabulary words.

In our opinion, the best way to assess reading comprehension is to give readers access to the material and have them restate or paraphrase what they have read.

Poor comprehension has many causes. The most common is poor decoding, which affects comprehension in two ways. First, if a student cannot convert the symbols to words, he or she cannot comprehend the message conveyed by those words. The second issue is more subtle. If a student expends all of his or her mental resources on sounding out the words, he or she will have no resources left to process their meaning. For that reason, increasing reading fluency frequently eliminates problems in comprehension.

Another problem is that students may not know how to read for comprehension (Taylor, Harris, Pearson, & Garcia, 1995). They may not actively focus on the meaning of what they read or know how to monitor their comprehension (for example, by asking themselves questions about what they have read or whether they understand what they have read). Students may not know how to foster comprehension (for example, by summarizing material, determining the main ideas and supporting facts, and integrating material with previous knowledge). Finally, individual characteristics can interact with the assessment of reading comprehension. For example, in an assessment of literal comprehension, a reader's memory capacity can affect comprehension scores unless the reader has access to the passage while answering questions about it or retelling its gist. Inferential comprehension depends on more than reading; it also depends on a reader's ability to see relationships (a defining element of intelligence) and on background information and experiences.

Assessment of Word-Attack Skills

Word-attack, or word analysis, skills are those used to derive the pronunciation or meaning of a word through phonic analysis, structural analysis, or context cues. Phonic analysis is the use of letter–sound correspondences and sound blending to identify words. Structural analysis is a process of breaking words into morphemes, or meaningful units. Words contain free morphemes (such as *farm*, *book*, and *land*) and bound morphemes (such as *-ed*, *-s*, and *-er*).

Because lack of word-attack skills is the principal reason why students have trouble reading, a variety of subtests of commonly used diagnostic reading tests specifically assess these skills. Subtests that assess word-attack skills range from such basic assessments as analysis of skill in associating letters with sounds to tests of syllabication and blending. Generally, for subtests that assess skill in associating letters with sounds, the examiner reads a word aloud and the student must identify the consonant–vowel–consonant cluster or digraph that has the same sound as the beginning, middle, or ending letters of the word. Syllabication subtests present polysyllabic words, and the student must either divide the word orally into syllables or circle specific syllables.

Blending subtests, on the other hand, are of three types. In the first method, the examiner may read syllables out loud (for example, "wa-ter-mel-on") and ask the student to pronounce the word. In the second type of subtest, the student may be asked to read word parts and to pronounce whole words. In the third method, the student may be presented with alternative beginning, middle, and ending sounds and asked to produce a word. Figure 11.1 illustrates the third method, used with the Stanford Diagnostic Reading Test 4.

Assessment of Word Recognition Skills

Subtests of diagnostic reading tests that assess a pupil's word recognition skills are designed to ascertain what many educators call "sight vocabulary." A student learns the correct pronunciation of letters and words through a variety of experiences. The more a student is exposed to specific words and the more familiar those words become to the student, the more readily he or she recognizes those words and is able to pronounce them correctly. Well-known words require very little reliance on word-attack skills. Most readers of this book immediately recognize the word *hemorrhage* and do not have to employ phonetic skills to pronounce it. On the other hand, a word such as *nephrocystanastomosis* is not a part of the sight vocabulary for most of us. Such words slow us down; we must use phonetics to analyze them.

Word recognition subtests form a major part of most diagnostic reading tests. Some tests use paper tachistoscopes to expose words for brief periods of time (usually one-half second). Students who recognize many words are said to have good sight vocabularies or good word recognition skills. Other subtests assess letter recognition, recognition of words in isolation, and recognition of words in context.

Assessment of Other Reading and Reading-Related Behaviors

A variety of subtests that fit none of the aforementioned categories are included in diagnostic reading tests as either major or supplementary subtests. Examples of such tests include oral vocabulary, spelling, handwriting, and auditory discrimination. In most cases, such subtests are included simply to provide the examiner with additional diagnostic information.

FIGURE 11.1
An Item That Assesses
Blending Skill

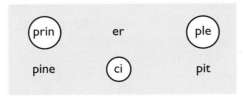

SPECIFIC DIAGNOSTIC READING TESTS

In Table 11.1, we provide basic information about several commonly used diagnostic reading tests. Then we provide a detailed review of the Dynamic Indicators of Basic Early Literacy Skills, Sixth Edition (DIBELS); the Group Reading Assessment and Diagnostic Evaluation (GRADE); and the Test of Phonological Awareness–Second Edition: Plus.

Group Reading Assessment and Diagnostic Evaluation (GRADE)

The Group Reading Assessment and Diagnostic Evaluation (GRADE; Williams, 2001) is a norm-referenced test of reading achievement that can be administered individually or in a group. It is designed to be used for students between the ages of 4 years (preschool) and 18 years (twelfth grade). There are 11 test levels, each with two forms (A and B). These include separate levels across each grade for prekindergarten through sixth grade, a middle school level (M), and two high school levels (H and A). Although the test is untimed, the author estimates that older students should be able to complete the assessment in 1 hour, whereas younger children may require up to 90 minutes. The manual provides both fall and spring norms to help in tracking progress over a school year. The following five test applications are discussed by the author: (1) placement and planning, (2) understanding the reading skills of students, (3) testing on level and out of level (which may allow more appropriate information on a child's strengths and weaknesses to be obtained among children at the margins), (4) monitoring growth, and (5) research.

Subtests

Five components of reading are assessed: prereading, reading readiness, vocabulary, comprehension, and oral language. Different subtests are used to assess these components at different levels.

Prereading Component

Picture Matching. For each of the 10 items in this subtest, a student must mark the one picture in the four-picture array that is the same as the stimulus picture.

Picture Differences. For each of the eight items in this subtest, a student must mark the one picture in the four-picture array that is different from the other pictures.

Verbal Concepts. For each of the 10 items in this subtest, a student must mark the one picture in the four-picture array that is described by the examiner. For each of the 10 items in this subtest, a student must mark the one picture in the four-picture array that does not belong with the other pictures.

Reading Readiness

Sound Matching. For each of the 12 items in this subtest, a student must mark the one picture in the four-picture array that has the same beginning (or ending) sound as a stimulus word. Students are told what words the pictures represent.

Rhyming. For each of the 14 items in this subtest, a student must mark the one picture in the four-picture array that rhymes with a stimulus word. Students are again told what words the pictures represent.

Print Awareness. For each of the four items in this subtest, a student must mark the one picture in the four-picture array that has the following print elements: letters, words, sentences, capital letters, and punctuation.

Letter Recognition. For each of the 11 items in this subtest, a student is given a five-letter array and must mark the capital or lowercase letter read by the examiner.

TABLE 11.1 Commonly Used Diagnostic Reading Tests

Test	Author	Publisher	Year	Ages/Grades	Individual/Group	NRT/SRT/CRT	Subtests
Comprehensive Test of Phonological Processing	Wagner, Torgesen, & Rashotte	Pro-Ed	1999	Ages 5–25	Individual	NRT	Elision, Blending Words, Sound Matching, Blending Non Words, Segmenting Non Words, Memory for Digit, Non Word Repetition, Rapid Color Naming, Rapid Object Naming, Rapid Digit Naming, Rapid Letter Naming, Phoneme Reversal, Segmenting Words. Composites: Phonological Awareness, Phonological Memory, Rapid Naming
Dynamic Indicators of Basic Early Literacy Skills–6	Good & Kaminski	University of Oregon	No date	Grades K–6	Individual	NRT Norms are local	Subtests vary by grade: Initial Sound Fluency, Letter Naming Fluency, Phoneme Segmentation Fluency, Nonsense Word Fluency, Oral Reading Fluency, Retell Fluency
Gray Oral Reading Test–4 (GORT-4)	Wiederholt & Bryant	Pro-Ed	2001	Ages 6-0–18-11	Individual	NRT	Rate, Accuracy, Fluency, Comprehension
Group Reading Assessment and Diagnostic Evaluation	Williams	Pearson	2001	Ages 4–18 Grades pre-K–12	Individual or group	NRT	Picture Matching, Picture Differences, Verbal Concepts, Matching, Rhyming, Print Awareness, Letter Recognition, Same and Different Words, Phoneme–Grapheme Correspondence, Word Reading, Word Meaning, Vocabulary, Sentence Comprehension, Passage Comprehension, Listening Comprehension. Composites: Pre-Reading, Reading Readiness, Vocabulary, Comprehension, Oral Language
Standardized Test for the Assessment of Reading (STAR Reading; reviewed in Chapter 19)	Advantage Learning Systems	Advantage Learning Systems	1997	Grades K–12	Individual	NRT	None

continued on the next page

TABLE 11.1	Commonly Used Diagnostic Reading Tests, *continued*						
Test	**Author**	**Publisher**	**Year**	**Ages/ Grades**	**Individual/ Group**	**NRT/SRT/ CRT**	**Subtests**
Stanford Diagnostic Reading Test–4	Karlsen & Gardner	Pearson	1996	Grades 1-5-13	Group or individual	NRT	Sounds, Letters, Words, Pictures, Stories
STAR Early Literacy (reviewed on website under Chapter 19)	Renaissance Learning	Renaissance Learning	2001	Ages 3-9	Individual	NRT	General Readiness, Phonemic Awareness, Phonics, Graphophonemic Knowledge, Structural Analysis, Vocabulary, Reading and Listening Comprehension
Test of Early Reading Ability–Third Edition (TERA-3; reviewed on website under Chapter 18)	Reid, Hresko, & Hammill	Pearson	2001	Ages 3-6 to 8-6	Individual	NRT	Alphabet, Conventions, Meaning
The Test of Phonological Awareness–2 Plus	Torgesen & Bryant	Pro-Ed	2004	Age 5–8	Group or individual	NRT	Phonological Awareness, Letter Sounds
Test of Reading Comprehension–4	Brown, Wiederholt & Brown	Pro-Ed	2008	Age 7-0–17-11	Group or individual	NRT	Relational Vocabulary, Sentence Completion, Paragraph Construction, Text Comprehension, Contextual Fluency
Test of Silent Word Reading Fluency	Mather, Hammill, Allen, & Roberts	Pro-Ed	2004	Age 6-6–17-11	Group or individual	NRT	None
Woodcock Diagnostic Reading Battery 3	Woodcock, Mather, & Schrank	Riverside	2004	Ages 2–80+ Grades K–16.9	Individual	NRT	Basic Reading Skills, Reading Comprehension, Phonics Knowledge, Phonemic Awareness, Oral Language Comprehension. Composite: Total Reading
Woodcock Reading Mastery Test–Revised, Normative Update	Woodcock	Pearson	1998	Kindergarten–75 years	Individual	NRT	Visual-Auditory Learning, Letter Identification, Word Identification, Word Attack, Word Comprehension, Passage Comprehension

Same and Different Words. For each of the nine items in this subtest, a student must mark the one word in the four-word array that is either the same as or different from the stimulus word.

Phoneme–Grapheme Correspondence. For each of the 16 items in this subtest, a student must mark the one letter in the four-word array that is the same as the beginning (or ending) sound of a word read by the examiner.

Vocabulary

Word Reading. The subtest contains 10 to 30 items, depending on the level. For each item in this subtest, a student is given a four-word array and must mark the word read by the examiner.

Word Meaning. For each of the 27 items in this subtest, a student must mark the one picture in the four-picture array that represents a written stimulus word.

Vocabulary. This subtest contains 30 to 40 items, depending on the test level. Students are presented a short written phrase or sentence that has one word bolded. A student must mark the one word in the four- or five-word array that has the same meaning as the bolded word.

Comprehension

Sentence Comprehension. For each of the 19 Cloze items in this subtest, a student must choose the one word in the four- or five-word array that best fits in the blank.

Passage Comprehension. The number of reading passages and items for this subtest varies by test level. A student must read a passage and answer several multiple-choice questions about the passage. Questions are of four types: questioning, clarifying, summarizing, and predicting.

Oral Language

Listening Comprehension. In this 17- or 18-item subtest, the test administrator reads aloud a sentence. A student must choose which of four pictures represents what was read. Items require students to comprehend basic words, understand grammar structure, make inferences, understand idioms, and comprehend other nonliteral statements.

Scores

Subtest raw scores can be converted into stanines. Depending on the level administered, certain subtest raw scores can be added to produce composite scores. Similarly, each level has a different set of subtest raw scores that are added in computing the total test raw score. Composite and total test raw scores can be converted to unweighted standard scores (mean of 100 and standard deviation of 15), stanines, percentiles, normal-curve equivalents, grade equivalents, and growth scale values.[2] Conversion tables provide both fall and spring normative scores. For students who are very skilled or very unskilled readers in comparison to their same-grade peers, out-of-level tests may be administered. Appropriate normative tables are available for some out-of-level tests in the teacher's scoring and interpretative manuals. Other out-of-level normative scores are reported only in the scoring and reporting software.

Norms

The GRADE standardization sample included 16,408 students in the spring sample and 17,024 in the fall sample. Numbers of students tested in each grade ranged from 808 (seventh grade, spring) to 2,995 (kindergarten, spring). Gender characteristics of the sample were presented by grade level, and roughly equal numbers of males and females were represented in each grade and season level (fall and spring). Geographic region characteristics were presented without disaggregating results by grade and were compared to the population data as reported by the U.S. Census Bureau (1998). Southern states were slightly overrepresented, whereas western states were slightly underrepresented in both the fall and the spring norm samples. Information on community type was also presented for the entire fall and spring

---

[2]Because growth scale values include all levels on the same scale, these scores make it possible to track a student's reading growth when the student has been given different GRADE levels throughout the years. It is important to note, however, that particular skills measured on the test vary from level to level, so growth scale values may not represent the same skills at different years.

norm samples; the samples are appropriately representative of urban, suburban, and rural communities. Information on students receiving free lunch was also provided. Information on race was also compared to the percentages reported by the U.S. Census Bureau (1998) and appeared to be representative of the population. It is important to note, again, that this information was not reported by grade level. Finally, the authors report that special education students were included in the sample but do not provide the number included.

Reliability

Total test coefficient alphas were calculated as measures of internal consistency for each form of the test, for each season of administration (fall and spring). These ranged from .89 to .98. Coefficient alphas were also computed for various subtests and subtest combinations (for example, Picture Matching and Picture Differences were combined into a Visual Skills category at the preschool and kindergarten levels). These were calculated for each GRADE level, form, and season of administration; several reliabilities were calculated for out-of-level tests (for example, separate alpha coefficients were computed for preschoolers and kindergartners taking the kindergarten-level test). These subtest–subtest combination coefficients ranged from .45 (Listening Comprehension, Form B, eleventh grade, spring administration) to .97 (Listening Comprehension, Form A, preschool, fall administration). Of the 350 coefficients calculated, 99 met or exceeded .90. The Comprehension Composite was found to be the most reliable composite score across levels. Listening Comprehension had consistently low coefficients from the first grade level to the highest level (Level A); thus, these are not included in calculating the total test raw scores for these levels. Alternate-forms reliability was determined across a sample of 696 students (students were included at each grade level). Average time between testing ranged from 8 to 32.2 days. Correlation coefficients ranged from .81 (eleventh grade) to .94 (preschool and third grade). Test–retest reliability was determined from a sample of 816 students. The average interval between testing ranged from 3.5 days (eighth-grade students taking Form A of Level M) to 42 days (fifth-grade students taking Form A of Level 5). Test–retest correlation coefficients ranged from .77 (fifth-grade

students taking Form A of Level 5) to .98 (fourth-grade students taking Form A of Level 4). Reliability data were not provided on growth scale values.

Validity

The author presents three types of validity: content, criterion-related, and construct validity. A rationale is provided for why particular item formats and subtests were included at particular ages and what skills each subtest is intended to measure. Also, a comprehensive item tryout was conducted on a sample of children throughout the nation. Information from this tryout informed item revision procedures. Statistical tests and qualitative investigations of item bias were also conducted during the tryout. Finally, teachers were surveyed, and this information was used in modifying content and administration procedures (although specific information on this survey is not provided). Criterion-related validity provided by the author included correlations of the GRADE total test standard score with five other measures of reading achievement: the total reading standard score of the Iowa Test of Basic Skills, the California Achievement Test total reading score, the Gates–MacGinitie Reading Tests total score, the Peabody Individual Achievement Test–Revised (PIAT-R) scores (General Information, Reading Recognition, Reading Comprehension, and Total Reading subtests), and the TerraNova. Each of these correlation studies was conducted with somewhat limited samples of elementary and middle school students. Coefficients ranged from .61 (GRADE total test score correlated with PIAT-R General Information among 30 fifth-grade students) to .90 (GRADE total test score correlated with Gates total reading score for 177 first-, second-, and sixth-grade students). Finally, construct validity was addressed by showing that the GRADE scores were correlated with age. Also, scores for students with dyslexia ($N = 242$) and learning disabilities in reading ($N = 191$) were compared with scores for students included in the standardization sample that were matched on GRADE level, form taken, gender, and race/ethnicity but who were not receiving special education services. As a group, students with dyslexia performed significantly below the matched control group. Similarly, students with learning disabilities in reading performed significantly below the matched control group.

Summary

The GRADE is a standardized, norm-referenced test of reading achievement that can be group administered. It can be used with children of a variety of ages (4 to 18 years) and provides a "growth scale value" score that can be used to track growth in reading achievement over several years. Different subtests and skills are tested, depending on the grade level tested; 11 forms corresponding to 11 GRADE levels are included. Although the norm sample is large, certain demographic information on the students in the sample is not provided, and in some cases, groups of students are over- or underrepresented. Total test score reliability data are strong. However, other subtest–subtest composite reliability data do not support the use of these particular scores for decision-making purposes, although the validity data provided in the manual suggest that this test is a useful measure of reading skills.

Dynamic Indicators of Basic Early Literacy Skills, Sixth Edition (DIBELS)

The Dynamic Indicators of Basic Early Literacy Skills, Sixth Edition (DIBELS; Good & Kaminski, undated), is intended to screen and monitor progress in beginning reading three times each year, beginning in kindergarten and continuing through third grade. The DIBELS consists of seven individually administered tests assessing phonological awareness, alphabetic understanding, and fluency with connected text. The DIBELS has English and Spanish versions, is available on the Internet (at http://dibels.uoregon.edu), and materials can be downloaded without charge.

There are two measures of phonological awareness. Initial Sounds Fluency[3] assesses the skill of preschoolers through mid-kindergartners in identifying and producing the initial sound of a given word. Students must select from an array of pictures named by the examiner the one picture that begins with a specific sound. Then students are asked to give the beginning sound of the previously named pictures.

Phonemic Segmentation Fluency[4] assesses the skill of mid-kindergartners through students at the end of first grade in segmenting words into phonemes. Students must produce the individual phonemes of words read by the examiner. In this task, examiners orally present words consisting of three or four phonemes, and students must verbally produce the individual phonemes that comprise the word.

There are two measures of alphabetic understanding. Letter Naming Fluency[5] assesses the skill of beginning kindergartners through beginning first graders in naming upper- and lowercase letters in 1 minute. Nonsense Word Fluency[6] assesses the knowledge of mid-kindergartners through students at the end of first grade of letter–sound correspondences as well as their ability to blend letters using their most common sound to form nonsense words.

Fluency is measured by three tests. Oral Reading Fluency[7] assesses the skill of students from the mid-first grade through the end of second grade in reading aloud connected text in grade-level material for 1 minute. Retell Fluency is administered to check reading comprehension. Students retell everything they can remember from the Oral Reading Fluency passage, and the number of words used in the student's retell is tabulated. Word Use Fluency assesses the ability of students from the beginning of kindergarten through third grade to correctly use specific words in sentences.

Scores

Except for Word Use Fluency, which uses the number correct, student performances are converted to the number of correct responses per minute. Subtest scores are converted by grade placement to three ranges: students who are at risk for achieving early literacy benchmarks, at some risk for achieving those goals, and at low risk of achieving those goals.

Norms

DIBELS tests are designed to provide local normative comparisons. As a result, the normative, or compari-

---

[3]Developed by Roland H. Good III, Deborah Laimon, Ruth A. Kaminski, and Sylvia Smith.

[4]Developed by Roland H. Good III, Ruth Kaminski, and Sylvia Smith.
[5]Developed by Ruth A. Kaminski and Roland H. Good III.
[6]Developed by Roland H. Good III and Ruth A. Kaminski.
[7]Developed by Roland H. Good III, Ruth A. Kaminski, and Sheila Dill.

son, sample is representative because it is the group to which scores are compared; the comparisons are current because the local districts provide the normative information.

Reliability

Alternate-form methods must be used to estimate the item sample reliability of timed tests. However, when there are weeks between administrations of the forms, error associated with time is added to error associated with item sampling. This appears to be the case for DIBELS tests. Combined item-stability estimates range from .72 for Initial Sounds Fluency to .94 for Oral Reading Fluency. When multiple tests (three seems to be sufficient) are given, estimated reliability exceeds .90. No estimates of item-sample reliability are presented for Retell Fluency or Word Use Fluency.

Validity

The DIBELS's general validity rests on the content- and criterion-related validity. The content is directly based on current empirical research that stresses the importance of fluency in basic skill areas: phonemic awareness, alphabetic principle, and reading fluency. Fluency on each subtest is well documented in the research literature as essential to success in learning to read. Benchmark goals and timelines are based on research reviews.

In addition, numerous studies indicate that each subtest correlates well with established reading measures. For example, Letter Naming Fluency correlates .70 with the Readiness Cluster and .65 with the Reading Cluster of the Woodcock–Johnson Psychoeducational Battery–Revised; it correlates .77 with the Metropolitan Readiness Test. Oral Reading Fluency correlates .36 with the Reading Cluster of the Woodcock–Johnson. Phonemic Segmentation Fluency correlates .54 with Woodcock–Johnson Readiness Cluster and .65 with the Metropolitan Readiness Test. Correlations between Nonsense Word Fluency and the Woodcock–Johnson Readiness cluster range from .36 to .59, depending on the student's grade; the correlation with Total Reading Cluster is .66. Oral Reading Fluency correlations with various reading measures range from .52 to .91.

Summary

The DIBELS consists of seven individually administered tests assessing phonological awareness, alphabetic understanding, and fluency. Single tests are generally sufficient for screening purposes; however, three or four tests must be administered for there to be sufficient reliability to make important educational decisions regarding individual students. Evidence for content validity is excellent, and criterion-related validity is good.

The Test of Phonological Awareness, Second Edition: Plus (TOPA 2+)

The Test of Phonological Awareness, Second Edition: Plus (TOPA 2+; Torgesen & Bryant, 2004) is a norm-referenced device intended to identify students who need supplemental services in phonemic awareness and letter–sound correspondence. The TOPA 2+ can be administered individually or to groups of students between the ages of 5 and 8 years to assess phonological awareness and letter–sound correspondences.

Two forms are available: the Kindergarten form and the Early Elementary form for students in first or second grades. The Kindergarten form has two subtests. The first, Phonological Awareness, has two parts, each consisting of 10 items. In the first part, students must select from a three-choice array the word that begins with the same sound as the stimulus word read by the examiner. In the second part, students must select from a three-choice array the word that begins with a different sound. The second subtest, Letter Sounds, consists of 15 items requiring students to mark the letter in a letter array that corresponds to a specific phoneme. The Early Elementary form also has two subtests. The first, Phonological Awareness, also has two parts, each consisting of 10 items. In the first part, students must select from a three-choice array the word that ends with the same sound as the stimulus word read by the examiner. In the second part, students must select from a three-choice array the word that ends with a different sound. The second subtest, Letter Sounds, requires students to spell 18 nonsense words that vary in length from two to five phonemes.

Scores

The number correct on each subtest is summed, and sums can be converted to percentiles and a variety of standard scores.

Norms

Separate norms for the Kindergarten form are in four 6-month age intervals (that is, 5-0 through 5-5, 5-6 through 5-11, 6-0 through 6-5, and 6-6 through 6-11). Separate norms for the Early Elementary form are in 12-month age groups (that is, 6-0 through 6-11, 7-0 through 7-11, and 8-0 through 8-11).

The TOPA 2+ was standardized on a total of 2,085 students, 1,035 of whom were in the Kindergarten form and the remaining 1,050 of whom were in the Early Elementary form. Norms for each form at each age are representative of the U.S. population in 2001 in terms of geographic regions, gender, race, ethnicity, and family income. Parents without a college education are slightly underrepresented.

Reliability

Coefficient alpha was calculated for each subtest at each age. For the Kindergarten form, only Letter Sounds for 6-year-olds fell below .90; that subtest reliability was .88. For the Early Elementary form, all alphas were between .80 and .87. In addition, alphas were calculated separately for males and females, whites, blacks, Hispanics, and students with language or learning disabilities. These alphas ranged from .82 to .91.

Test–retest correlations were used to estimate stabilities. For the Kindergarten form, 51 students were retested within approximately a 2-week interval. Stability for Phonological Awareness was .87, and stability for Letter Sounds was .85. For the Early Elementary form, 88 students were retested within approximately a 2-week interval. Stability for Phonological Awareness was .81, and stability for Letter Sounds was .84.

Finally, interscorer agreement was evaluated by having two trained examiners each score 50 tests. On the Kindergarten form, interscorer agreement for Phonological Awareness was .98 and for Letter Sounds was .99. On the Early Elementary form, interscorer agreement for Phonological Awareness was .98 and for Letter Sounds was .98.

Overall, care should be taken when interpreting the results of the TOPA 2+. The internal consistency is sufficient for screening and in some cases for use in making important educational decisions for students.

Validity

Evidence for the general validity of the TOPA 2+ comes from several sources. First, the contents of scales were carefully developed to represent phonemic awareness and knowledge of letter–sound correspondence. For example, the words in the Phonological Awareness subscales come from the 2,500 most frequently used words in first graders' oral language, and all consonant phonemes had a median age of customary articulation no later than 3.5 years of age. Next, the TOPA 2+ correlates well with another scale measuring similar skills and abilities (Dynamic Indicators of Basic Early Literacy Skills) and with teacher judgments of students' reading abilities. Evidence for differentiated validity comes from the scales' ability to distinguish students with language and learning disabilities from those without such problems. Other indices of validity include the absence of bias against males or females, whites, African Americans, and Hispanics.

Summary

The TOPA 2+ assesses phonemic awareness using beginning and ending sounds and letter–sound correspondence at the kindergarten and early elementary levels. The norms appear representative and are well described. Coefficient alpha for phonemic awareness is generally good for kindergartners but only suitable for screening students in the early elementary grades and for letter–sound correspondence for all students. Stability was estimated in the .80s, but interscorer agreement was excellent. Overall, care should be taken when interpreting the results of the TOPA 2+. Evidence for validity is adequate.

Dilemmas in Current Practice

There are four major problems in the diagnostic assessment of reading strengths and weaknesses. The first is the problem of curriculum match. Students enrolled in different reading curricula have different opportunities to learn specific skills. Reading series differ in the skills that are taught, in the emphasis placed on different skills, in the sequence in which skills are taught, and in the time at which skills are taught. Tests differ in the skills they assess. Thus, it can be expected that pupils studying different curricula will perform differently on the same reading test. It can also be expected that pupils studying the same curriculum will perform differently on different reading tests. Diagnostic personnel must be very careful to examine the match between skills taught in the students' curriculum and skills tested. Most teachers' manuals for reading series include a listing of the skills taught at each level in the series. Many authors of diagnostic reading tests now include in test manuals a list of the objectives measured by the test. At the very least, assessors should carefully examine the extent to which the test measures what has been taught. Ideally, assessors would select specific parts of tests to measure exactly what has been taught. To the extent that there is a difference between what has been taught and what is tested, the test is not a valid measure.

The second problem is also a test–curriculum match problem. Most reading instruction now takes place in general education classrooms, using the content of typical reading textbooks. This is true for developmental reading instruction, remedial reading instruction, and the teaching of reading to students with disabilities. Most diagnostic reading tests measure student skill-development competence in isolation. Also, they do not include assessments of the comprehension strategies, such as the metacognitive strategies that are now part of reading instruction.

A third problem is the selection of tests that are appropriate for making different kinds of educational decisions. We noted that there are different types of diagnostic reading tests. In making classification decisions, educators must administer tests individually. They may either use an individually administered test or give a group test to one individual. For making instructional planning decisions, the most precise and helpful information will be obtained by giving individually administered criterion-referenced measures. Educators can, of course, systematically analyze pupil performance on a norm-referenced test, but the approach is difficult and time-consuming. It may also be futile because norm-referenced tests usually do not contain enough items on which to base a diagnosis. When evaluating individual pupil progress, assessors must consider carefully the kinds of comparisons they want to make. If they want to compare pupils with same-age peers, norm-referenced measures are useful. If, on the other hand, they want to know the extent to which individual pupils are mastering curriculum objectives, criterion-referenced measures are the tests of choice.

The fourth problem is one of generalization. Assessors are faced with the difficult task of describing or predicting pupil performance in reading. Yet reading itself is difficult to describe, being a complex behavior composed of numerous subskills. Those who engage in reading diagnosis will do well to describe pupil performance in terms of specific skills or subskills (such as recognition of words in isolation, listening comprehension, and specific word-attack skills). They should also limit their predictions to making statements about probable performance of specific reading behaviors, not probable performance in reading.

CHAPTER COMPREHENSION QUESTIONS

Write your answers to each of the following questions, and then compare your responses to the text or the study guide.

1. Why is reading important to assess?

2. Explain the two approaches traditionally used to teach reading.

3. Explain what is assessed in oral reading, word attack, reading recognition, and reading comprehension.

4. Explain two potential problems in diagnostic testing of reading.

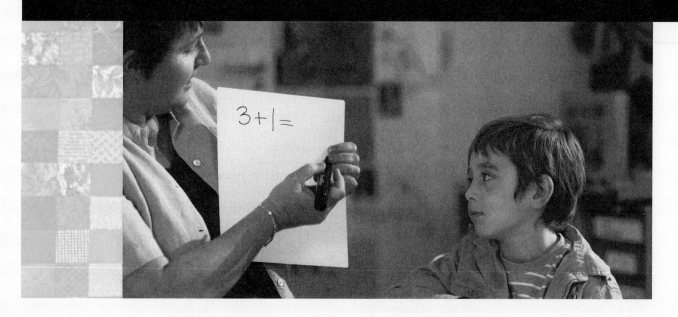

12

Using Diagnostic Mathematics Measures

Chapter Goals

1 Know why we administer and use diagnostic math tests.

2 Understand the content and processes sampled by diagnostic mathematics tests.

3 Understand the distinction between assessment of mathematics content and assessment of mathematics process.

4 Understand the kinds of behaviors sampled by two commonly used diagnostic mathematics tests: G•MADE and KeyMath-3 DA.

5 Understand three major dilemmas in diagnostic testing in mathematics: (a) curriculum match, (b) selecting the correct tests for making specific decisions, and (c) adequate and sufficient behavior sampling.

Key Terms

NCTM standards

content standards

process standards

focal points

computer adaptive math
   tests

curriculum match

G•MADE

KeyMath-3 DA

STAR Math

DIAGNOSTIC TESTING IN MATHEMATICS IS DESIGNED TO IDENTIFY SPECIFIC strengths and weaknesses in skill development. We have seen that all major achievement tests designed to assess multiple skills include subtests that measure mathematics competence. These tests are necessarily global and attempt to assess a wide range of skills. However, in most cases these multiple skills tests include only a small number of items assessing specific math skills and the sample of math behaviors is insufficient for diagnostic purposes. Diagnostic testing in mathematics is more specific, providing more depth and a detailed assessment of skill development within specific areas.

There are fewer diagnostic math tests than diagnostic reading tests, but math assessment is more clear-cut. Because the successful performance of some mathematical operations clearly depends on the successful performance of other operations (for example, multiplication depends on addition), it is easier to sequence skill development and assessment in math than in reading. Diagnostic math tests generally sample similar behaviors. They sample various mathematical contents, concepts, and operations, as well as applications of mathematical facts and principles. Some now also include assessment of students' attitudes toward math.

1   Why Do We Assess Mathematics?

There are several reasons to assess mathematics skills. First, diagnostic math tests are intended to provide sufficiently detailed information so that teachers and intervention-assistance teams can ascertain a student's mastery of specific math skills and plan individualized math instruction. Second, some diagnostic math tests provide teachers with specific information on the kinds of items students in their classes pass and fail. This gives them information about the extent to which the curriculum and instruction in their class are working, and it provides opportunities to modify curricula. Third, all public school programs teach math facts and concepts. Teachers need to know whether pupils have mastered those facts and concepts. Finally, diagnostic math tests are occasionally used to make exceptionality and eligibility decisions. Individually administered tests are usually required for eligibility and placement decisions. Therefore, diagnostic math tests are often used to establish special learning needs and eligibility for programs for children with learning disabilities in mathematics.

2 Behaviors Sampled by Diagnostic Mathematics Tests

The National Council of Teachers of Mathematics (NCTM) has specified a set of standards for learning and teaching in mathematics. The most recent specification of those standards was in a document titled *Principles and Standards for School Mathematics* issued in 2000.[1] The NCTM specified five content standards and five process standards. Diagnostic math tests now typically assess knowledge and skill in some subset of those 10 standards, or they specify how what they assess relates to the NCTM standards. The standards are listed in Table 12.1, and for each of the standards we list the kinds of behaviors or skills identified by NCTM as important.

Some math tests include survey questions asking students about their attitudes toward math. Students are asked the extent to which they enjoy math, the extent to which their friends like math more than they do, and so on.

| TABLE 12.1 | NCTM Standards for Learning and Teaching in Mathematics |

Content Standards

Number and Operations Instructional programs from prekindergarten through grade 12 should enable all students to

- understand numbers, ways of representing numbers, relationships among numbers, and number systems;
- understand meanings of operations and how they relate to one another; and
- compute fluently and make reasonable estimates.

Algebra Instructional programs from prekindergarten through grade 12 should enable all students to

- understand patterns, relations, and functions;
- represent and analyze mathematical situations and structures using algebraic symbols;
- use mathematical models to represent and understand quantitative relationships; and
- analyze change in various contexts.

Geometry Instructional programs from prekindergarten through grade 12 should enable all students to

- analyze characteristics and properties of two- and three-dimensional geometric shapes and develop mathematical arguments about geometric relationships;
- specify locations and describe spatial relationships using coordinate geometry and other representational systems;
- apply transformations and use symmetry to analyze mathematical situations; and
- use visualization, spatial reasoning, and geometric modeling to solve problems.

---

continued on the next page

[1] In 2006, NCTM published *Curriculum Focal Points for Prekindergarten Through Grade 8 Mathematics*. Focal Points are a small number of mathematical topics that should be focused on at each grade level and serve as areas teachers should focus on. Currently, state and district math standards are not reflective of the Focal Points but probably will be in the near future. Therefore, practitioners must consider alignment of diagnostic math tests to the current standards and also the Focal Points. (Keep abreast of changes by visiting www.nctm.org/standards/default.aspx?id=58.)

| TABLE 12.1 | NCTM Standards for Learning and Teaching in Mathematics, *continued* |

Measurement Instructional programs from prekindergarten through grade 12 should enable all students to

- ▦ understand measurable attributes of objects and the units, systems, and processes of measurement; and
- ▦ apply appropriate techniques, tools, and formulas to determine measurements.

Data Analysis and Probability Instructional programs from prekindergarten through grade 12 should enable all students to

- ▦ formulate questions that can be addressed with data and collect, organize, and display relevant data to answer them;
- ▦ select and use appropriate statistical methods to analyze data;
- ▦ develop and evaluate inferences and predictions that are based on data; and
- ▦ understand and apply basic concepts of probability.

Process Standards

Problem Solving Instructional programs from prekindergarten through grade 12 should enable all students to

- ▦ build new mathematical knowledge through problem solving;
- ▦ solve problems that arise in mathematics and in other contexts;
- ▦ apply and adapt a variety of appropriate strategies to solve problems; and
- ▦ monitor and reflect on the process of mathematical problem solving.

Reasoning and Proof Instructional programs from prekindergarten through grade 12 should enable all students to

- ▦ recognize reasoning and proof as fundamental aspects of mathematics;
- ▦ make and investigate mathematical conjectures;
- ▦ develop and evaluate mathematical arguments and proofs; and
- ▦ select and use various types of reasoning and methods of proof.

Communication Instructional programs from prekindergarten through grade 12 should enable all students to

- ▦ organize and consolidate their mathematical thinking through communication;
- ▦ communicate their mathematical thinking coherently and clearly to peers, teachers, and others;
- ▦ analyze and evaluate the mathematical thinking and strategies of others; and
- ▦ use the language of mathematics to express mathematical ideas precisely.

Connections Instructional programs from prekindergarten through grade 12 should enable all students to

- ▦ recognize and use connections among mathematical ideas;
- ▦ understand how mathematical ideas interconnect and build on one another to produce a coherent whole; and
- ▦ recognize and apply mathematics in contexts outside of mathematics.

Representation Instructional programs from prekindergarten through grade 12 should enable all students to

- ▦ create and use representations to organize, record, and communicate mathematical ideas;
- ▦ select, apply, and translate among mathematical representations to solve problems; and
- ▦ use representations to model and interpret physical, social, and mathematical phenomena

SOURCE: Reprinted with permission from *Principles & Standards for School Mathematics,* copyright 2000–2004 by the National Council of Teachers of Mathematics (NCTM). All rights reserved. Standards are listed with the permission of the NCTM. NCTM does not endorse the content or validity of these alignments.

SPECIFIC DIAGNOSTIC MATHEMATICS TESTS

Commonly used diagnostic mathematics tests are listed in Table 12.2. Two of the tests (Group Mathematics Assessment and Diagnostic Evaluation [G•MADE] and KeyMath-3 Diagnostic Assessment [KeyMath-3 DA]) are reviewed in detail in this chapter. Detailed reviews of the others are provided at the website for this textbook.

Group Mathematics Assessment and Diagnostic Evaluation (G•MADE)

The Group Mathematics Assessment and Diagnostic Evaluation (G•MADE; (Williams, 2004) is a group-administered, norm-referenced, standards-based test for assessing the math skills of students in grades K–12. It is norm referenced in that it is standardized on a nationally representative group. It is standards based in that the content assessed is based on the standards of NCTM.

G•MADE is a diagnostic test designed to identify specific math skill development strengths and weaknesses, and the test is designed to lead to teaching strategies. The test provides information about math skills and error patterns of each student, using the efficiencies of group administration. Test materials include a CD that provides a cross-reference between specific math skills and math teaching resources. Teaching resources are also available in print.

There are nine levels, each with two parallel forms. Eight of the nine levels have three subtests (the lowest level has two). The three subtests are Concepts and Communication, Operations and Computation, and Process and Applications. The items in each subtest fit the content of the following categories: numeration, quantity, geometry, measurement, time/sequence, money, comparison, statistics, and algebra. Diagnosis of skill development strengths and needs is fairly broad. For example, teachers learn that an individual student has difficulty with concepts and communication in the area of geometry.

Subtests

Concepts and Communication. This subtest measures students' knowledge of the language, vocabulary, and representations of math. A symbol, word, or short phrase is presented with four choices (pictures, symbols, or numbers). It is permissible for teachers to read words to students, but they may not define or explain the words. Figure 12.1 is a representation of the kinds of items used to measure concepts and communication skills.

Operations and Computation. This subtest measures student's skills in using the basic operations of addition, subtraction, multiplication, and division. This subtest is not included at Level R (the readiness level and lowest level of the test). There are 24 items on this subtest at each level, and each consists of an incomplete equation with four answer choices. An example is shown in Figure 12.2.

Process and Applications. This subtest measures students' skill in taking the language and concepts of math and applying the appropriate operations and computations to solve a word problem. Each item consists of a short passage of one or more sentences and four response choices. An example is shown in Figure 12.3. At lower levels of the test, the problems are one-step problems, whereas at higher levels they require application of multiple steps.

The G•MADE levels each contain items that are on grade level, items that are somewhat above, and items that are below level. Each level can be administered on grade level or can be given out of level (matched to the ability level of the student). Teachers can choose to administer a lower or higher level of the test.

Scores

Raw scores for the G•MADE can be converted to standard scores (with a mean of 100 and a standard deviation of 15) using fall or spring norms. Grade scores, stanines, percentiles, and normal curve equivalents are

TABLE 12.2	Commonly Used Diagnostic Mathematics Tests						
Test	**Author**	**Publisher**	**Year**	**Ages/ Grades**	**Individual/ Group**	**NRT/SRT/ CAT**	**Subtests**
KeyMath-3 DA	Connolly	Pearson	2007	Ages 4-6 to 21	Individual	NRT	Numeration, Algebra, Geometry, Measurement, Data Analysis and Probability, Mental Computation and Estimation, Addition and Subtraction, Multiplication and Division, Foundations of Problem Solving, Applied Problem Solving Composite scores: Basic Concepts (conceptual knowledge), Operations (computational skills), Applications (problem solving)
Comprehensive Mathematical Abilities Test (CMAT)	Hresko, Schlieve, Heron, Swain, & Sherbenou	Pro-Ed	2003	Ages 7-0 to 18-11	Individual	NRT	Core subtests: Addition; Subtraction; Multiplication; Division; Problem Solving; Charts, Tables & Graphs Supplemental subtests: Algebra, Geometry, Rational Numbers, Time, Money, Measurement Core composites: General Mathematics, Basic Calculations, Mathematical Reasoning Supplemental composites: Advanced Calculations, Practical Applications Global Composite: Global Mathematical Ability
Group Mathematics Assessment and Diagnostic Evaluation (G•MADE)	Williams	Pearson	2004	Grades K–12	Group	NRT and SRT	Concepts and Communication, Operations and Computation, Process and Applications In each subtest, the following content is assessed: numeration, quantity, geometry, measurement, time/sequence, money, comparison, statistics, and algebra.
Stanford Diagnostic Mathematics Test (SDMT4)	Harcourt Brace Educational Measurement	Pearson	1996	Grades 1.5–13	Group	NRT	Concepts and Applications, Computation
Test of Early Mathematics Abilities (reviewed on website under Chapter 18)	Ginsburg & Baroody	Pro-Ed	2003	Ages 3-0 to 8-11	Individual	NRT	Formal Mathematical Thinking, Informal Mathematical Thinking
STAR Math (reviewed in Chapter 19)	Renaissance Learning	Renaissance Learning	1998	Grades 3-12	Individual	CAT	No subtests for this computer adaptive test

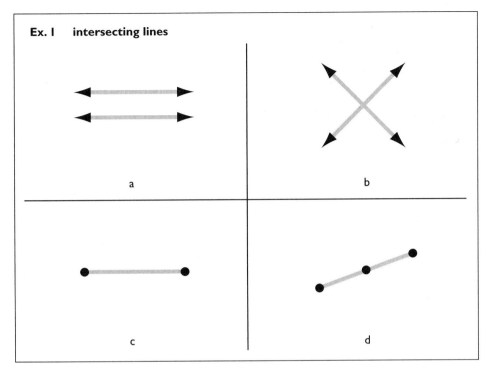

FIGURE 12.1
Concepts and Communication Example from Levels M and H

Ex. I   943
                    −812

Work Area

                              a   136

                              b   132

                              c   135

                              d   131

FIGURE 12.2
Operations and Computation Example

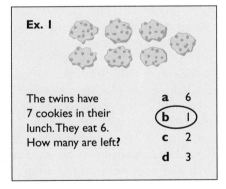

FIGURE 12.3
Process and Applications Example

also available. Growth Scale Values are provided for the purpose of tracking growth in math skills for students who are given different levels of the test over the years. G•MADE can be used to track growth over the course of a year or from year to year.

The publisher provides diagnostic worksheets that consist of cross-tabulations of the subtests with the content areas. The worksheets are used to identify areas in which individual students or whole classes did or did not demonstrate skills. The worksheets are used to prepare reports identifying specific areas of need. For example, the objective assessed by item 28 in Level 1, Form B is skill in solving a one-step sequence problem that requires the ability to recognize a pattern. When reporting on performance on this item, the teacher might report that "Joe did not solve one-step sequence problems that require the ability to recognize a pattern." He might also indicate that "two-thirds of the class did not solve one-step problems that require the ability to recognize a pattern."

Norms

There were two phases to standardization of the G•MADE. First, a study of bias by gender, race/ethnicity, and region was conducted on more than 10,000 students during a national tryout. In addition, the test was reviewed by a panel of educators who represented minority perspectives, and items they identified as apparently biased were modified or removed.

During the fall of 2002, G•MADE was standardized on a nationwide sample of students at 72 sites. In spring 2003, the sampling was repeated at 71 sites. Approximately 1,000 students per level per grade participated in the standardization (a total of nearly 28,000 students). The sample was selected based on geographic region, community type (rural, and so on), and socioeconomic status (percentage of students on free and reduced-price lunch). Students with disabilities were included in the standardization if they attended regular education classes all or part of the day. Fall and spring grade-based and age-based norms are provided for each level of the G•MADE. Norms that allow for out-of-level testing are available in a G•MADE Out-of-Level Norms Supplement and through the scoring and reporting software. Templates are available for hand scoring, or the test can be scored and reported by computer.

Reliability

Data on internal consistency and stability over time are presented in the G•MADE manual. Internal consistency reliabilities were computed for each G•MADE subtest and the total test score for each level and form using the split-half method. All reliabilities exceed .74, with more than 90 percent exceeding .80. The only

low reliabilities are at seventh grade for Concepts and Communications and for Process and Applications at all grades beyond grade 4. Thus, the only really questionable subtest is Process and Applications beyond grade 4. Internal consistency reliability coefficients are above .90 for the total score at all levels of the test.

Alternate-form reliability was established on a sample of 651 students, and all reliabilities exceeded .80. Stability of the test was established by giving it twice to a sample of 761 students. The test–retest reliability coefficients for this group of students exceeded .80, with the exception only of .78 for Level 4, Form A. Overall, there is good support for the reliability of the grade. Internal consistency and stability are sufficient for using the test to make decisions about individuals. The two forms of the test are comparable.

Validity

The content of the G•MADE is based on the NCTM Math Standards, though the test was developed following a year-long research study of state standards, curriculum benchmarks, the score and sequence plans of commonly used math textbooks, and review of research on best practices for teaching math concepts and skills. The author provides a strong argument for the validity of the content of the G•MADE.

Several studies support the criterion-related validity of the test. Correlations with subtests of the Iowa Tests of Basic Skills (ITBS), the TerraNova, and the Iowa Tests of Educational Development are reported. Surprisingly, correlations between G•MADE subtests and reading subtests of the ITBS are as high as they are between G•MADE subtests and math subtests of the G•MADE. This was not the case for correlations with the TerraNova, in which those with the math subtests exceeded by far correlations with the reading subtests. In a comparison of performance on KeyMath and the G•MADE, all correlations were in excess of .80. The two tests measure highly comparable skills.

Summary

The G•MADE is a group-administered, norm-referenced, standards-based and diagnostic measure of student skill development in three separate areas. There is good evidence for the content validity of the test, and the test was appropriately and adequately standardized. Evidence for reliability and validity of the G•MADE is good. The lone exception to this is the finding that performance on the test is as highly correlated with the reading subtests of some other criterion measures as it is with the math subtests of those measures.

KeyMath-3 Diagnostic Assessment (KeyMath-3 DA)

KeyMath-3 Diagnostic Assessment (KeyMath-3 DA; Connolly, 2007) is the third revision of the test originally published in 1971. Over the three editions of the test, a number of "normative updates" have been published. KeyMath-3 DA is an untimed, individually administered, norm-referenced test designed to provide a comprehensive assessment of essential math concepts and skills in individuals aged 4 years, 6 months through 21 years. The test takes 30 to 40 minutes for students in the lower elementary grades and 75 to 90 minutes for older students. Four uses are suggested for the test: (1) assess math proficiency by providing comprehensive coverage of the concepts and skills taught in regular math instruction, (2) assess student progress in math, (3) support instructional planning, and (4) support educational placement decisions. The author designed this revision of the test to reflect the NCTM content and process standards described previously in this chapter.

KeyMath-3 DA includes a manual, two freestanding easels for either Form A or Form B, and 25 record forms with detachable Written Computation Examinee Booklets. Two ancillary products are available for KeyMath-3 DA: an ASSIST Scoring and Reporting Software program and a KeyMath-3 Essential Resources instructional program. There are two parallel forms (A and B) of the test, and each has 372 items divided into the following subtests: Numeration, Algebra, Geometry, Measurement, Data Analysis and Probability, Mental Computation and Estimation, Addition and Subtraction, Multiplication and Division, Foundations of Problem Solving, and Applied Problem Solving.

Scores

The test can be hand scored or scored by using the KeyMath-3 DA ASSIST Scoring and Reporting Software. Users can obtain three indices of relative standing (scale scores, standard scores, and percentile ranks) and three developmental scores (grade and age equivalents and growth scale values). Users also obtain three composite scores: Basic Concepts (conceptual knowledge), Operations (computational skills), and Application (problem solving). In addition, tools are available to help users analyze students' functional range in math, and they provide an analysis of students' performance specific to focus items and behavioral objectives. The scoring software can be used to create progress reports across multiple administrations of the test, produce a narrative summary report, export derived scores to Excel spreadsheets for statistical analysis, and generate reports for parents.

Norms

KeyMath-3 DA was standardized on 3,630 individuals ages 4 years, 6 months to 21 years. The test was standardized by contacting examiners and having them get permission to assess students, sending the permissions to the publisher, and then randomly selecting students to participate in the norming. The sample closely approximates the distributions reported in the 2004 census, and cross-tabs (i.e., how many males were from the Northeast) are reported in the manual. In addition, the test was standardized on representative proportions of students with specific learning disability, speech/language impairment, intellectual disability, emotional/behavioral disturbance, and developmental delays. The test appears adequately standardized.

Reliability

The author reports data on internal consistency, alternate-form, and test–retest reliability. Internal consistency reliabilities for students in kindergarten and first grade are low. At other ages, internal consistency reliability coefficients generally exceed .80. Internal consistency coefficients for the composite scores exceed .90 except in grades K–2. Alternate-form reliabilities exceed .80 with the exception of the reliabilities for different forms of the Geometry and the Data Analysis and Probability subtests. Adjusted test–retest reliabilities based on the performance of 103 students (approximately half on each form) in grades K–12 generally exceed .80 with the exception of the Foundations of Problem Solving subtest (.70) and the Geometry subtest (.78). The reliability of all subtests and composites is adequate for screening purposes and good for diagnostic purposes.

Validity

The authors report extensive validity information in the manual. All validity data are for composite scores. KeyMath-3 DA composites correlate very highly with scores on the KeyMath-Revised normative update and math scores on the Kaufman Test of Educational Achievement (with the exception of the Applications and Mathematics Composite), ITBS, Measures of Academic Progress, and the G•MADE (with the exception of the operations composite [.63]). Evidence for content validity is good based on alignment with state and NCTM standards. The authors provide data on how representatives of special populations perform relative to the general population, and scores are within expected ranges.

Summary

KeyMath-3 DA is a norm-referenced, individually administered comprehensive assessment of skills and problem solving in math appropriate for use with students 4–6 to 21 years of age. The test is adequately standardized, and there is good evidence for reliability and validity. Comparative data are provided on the performance of students with disabilities.

Dilemmas in Current Practice

There are three major problems in the diagnostic assessment of math skills.

The first problem is the recurring issue of curriculum match. There is considerable variation in math curricula. This variation means that diagnostic math tests will not be equally representative of all curricula or even appropriate for some commonly used ones. As a result, great care must be exercised in using diagnostic math tests to make various educational decisions. Assessment personnel must be extremely careful to note the match between test content and school curriculum. This should involve far more than a quick inspection of test items by someone unfamiliar with the specific classroom curriculum. For example, a professional could inspect the teacher's manual to ensure that the teacher assesses only material that has been taught and that there is reasonable correspondence between the relative emphasis placed on teaching the material and testing the material. To do this, the professional might have to develop a table of specifications for the math curriculum and compare test items with that table. However, once a table of specifications has been developed for the curriculum, a better procedure would be to select items from a standards-referenced system to fit the cells in the table exactly.

The second problem is selecting an appropriate test for the type of decision to be made. School personnel are usually required to use individually administered norm-referenced devices in eligibility decisions. Decisions about a pupil's eligibility for special services, however, need not be based on detailed information about the pupil's strengths and weaknesses, as provided by diagnostic tests; diagnosticians are interested in a pupil's relative standing. In our opinion, the best mathematical achievement survey tests are subtests of group-administered tests. A practical solution is not to use a diagnostic math test for eligibility decisions but to administer individually a subtest from one of the better group-administered achievement tests.

The third problem is that most of the diagnostic tests in mathematics do not test a sufficiently detailed sample of facts and concepts. Consequently, assessors must generalize from a student's performance on the items tested to his or her performance on the items that are not tested. The reliabilities of the subtests of diagnostic math tests are often not high enough for educators to make such a generalization with any great degree of confidence. As a result, these tests are not very useful in assessing readiness or strengths and weaknesses in order to plan instructional programs. We believe that the preferred practice in diagnostic testing in mathematics is for teachers to develop curriculum-based achievement tests that exactly parallel the curriculum being taught.

CHAPTER COMPREHENSION QUESTIONS

Write your answers to each of the following questions, and then compare your responses to the text or the study guide.

1. Why do we administer and use diagnostic math tests?

2. Provide two examples each of content and processes sampled by diagnostic mathematics tests.

3. What is the distinction between assessment of mathematics content and assessment of mathematics process?

4. Identify two differences in the kinds of behaviors sampled by two commonly used diagnostic mathematics tests: G•MADE and KeyMath-3 DA.

5. Briefly describe three major dilemmas in diagnostic testing in mathematics:

   a. Curriculum match

   b. Selecting the correct tests for making specific decisions

   c. Adequate and sufficient behavior sampling

6. How can educational professionals overcome the problem of curriculum match in the diagnostic assessment of mathematical competence?

RESOURCE FOR FURTHER INVESTIGATION

NATIONAL COUNCIL OF TEACHERS OF MATHEMATWICS (NCTM)
http://www.nctm.org
This website is designed for teachers of mathematics and contains information and resources related to the subject of math.

13 Using Measures of Oral and Written Language

Chapter Goals

1 Know why we assess oral and written language.

2 Understand various behaviors and skills associated with language.

3 Understand how cultural background may influence language assessment.

4 Know methods for eliciting oral language samples.

5 Be familiar with two language tests.

6 Be familiar with some of the current dilemmas we face in using language measures.

Key Terms

morphology

pragmatics

semantics

supralinguistic functioning

syntax

phonology

Scenario in Assessment

Jill

Jill's fifth-grade teacher and parent expressed concerns to the Teacher Assistance Team at Brownville Elementary School. According to the teacher and parent, Jill was demonstrating all the classic signs of a student with a central auditory processing disorder (CAPD). Her behavior in the classroom was characterized as often off task, and she had difficulty attending to tasks and following oral directions, was easily distracted by noise, made frequent requests for repetition of information, daydreamed, often appeared not to be listening, and had poor memory skills. The teacher and parent completed checklists indicating concerns with central auditory processing. At the recommendation of the Teacher Assistance Team, Jill was taken to her family doctor to address concerns related to attention challenges and to rule these out as a possible reason for classroom performance issues. A trial of medication for attention deficit disorder was completed and Jill showed remarkable improvements in attention and focus but continued to struggle with what appeared to be listening and comprehension components of classroom activities. The speech–language pathologist was brought in to assess Jill's language skills as well as make recommendations about audiological assessment for CAPD.

Jill completed the Clinical Evaluation of Language Fundamentals test. The results were surprising: Her receptive language standard score was 91 and expressive language standard score was 76. This child did not have a CAPD but, rather, expressive language impairment. She could understand and process what was taking place and being asked of her, but she could not organize or formulate the response. The speech language pathologist recommended extensive language therapy to address expressive language and the results have been amazing. Language testing is a vital component of assessing what disabilities are and are not present.

THE ASSESSMENT OF LANGUAGE COMPETENCE SHOULD INCLUDE EVALUATION OF a student's ability to process, both in comprehension and in expression, language in a spoken or written format. There are four major communication processes: oral comprehension (listening and comprehending speech), written comprehension (reading), oral expression (speaking), and written expression (writing). These are illustrated in Figure 13.1.

In assessing language skills, it is important to break language down into processes and measure each one because each process makes different demands on the person's ability to communicate. Performance in one area does not always predict performance in the others. For example, a child who has normal comprehension does not necessarily have normal production skills. Also, a child with relatively normal expressive skills may have problems with receptive language. Therefore, a complete language assessment will include examination of both oral and written reception (comprehension) and expression (production).

FIGURE 13.1
The Four Major
Communication Processes

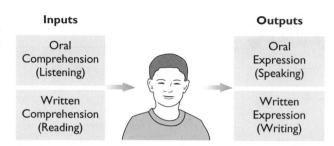

1 Terminology

Educators, psychologists, linguists, and speech–language pathologists often have different perspectives on which skills make up language. These different views have resulted in the development of a plethora of language assessment tests, each with an apparently unique method of assessing language. The terminology used to describe the behaviors and skills assessed can be confusing as well. Terms such as *morphology*, *semantics*, *syntax*, and *supralinguistic functioning* are used, and sometimes different test authors use different terms to mean the same thing. One author's vocabulary subtest is another's measure of "lexical semantics."

We define *language* as a code for conveying ideas—a code that includes phonology, semantics, morphology, syntax, and pragmatics. These terms are defined as follows:

Phonology: the hearing and production of speech sounds. The term *articulation* is considered a synonym for phonology.

Semantics: the study of word meanings. In assessment, this term is generally used to refer to the derivation of meaning from single words. The term *vocabulary* is often used interchangeably with semantics.

Morphology: the use of affixes (prefixes and suffixes) to change the meaning of words used in sentences. Morphology also includes verb tense ("John *is* going" versus "John *was* going").

Syntax: the use of word order to convey meaning. Typically there are rules for arranging words into sentences. In language assessment, the word *grammar* is often used to refer to a combination of morphology and syntax.

Pragmatics: the social context in which a sentence occurs. Context influences both the way a message is expressed and the way it is interpreted. For example, the sentence, "Can you close the door?" can have different meanings to a student sitting closest to an open door in a classroom and a student undergoing physical therapy to rehabilitate motor skills. According to Carrow-Woolfolk (1995), contexts that influence language comprehension and production include

- social variables, such as the setting and the age, roles, relationships, and number of participants in a discourse;
- linguistic variables produced by the type of discourse (which might be a conversation, narrative, lecture, or text); and
- the intention, motivation, knowledge, and style of the sender.

TABLE 13.1	Language Subskills for Each Channel of Communication	
	Channel of Communication	
Language Component	**Reception (Comprehension)**	**Expression (Production)**
Phonology	Hearing and discriminating speech sounds	Articulating speech sounds
Morphology and syntax	Understanding the grammatical structure of language	Using the grammatical structure of language
Semantics	Understanding vocabulary, meaning, and concepts	Using vocabulary, meaning, and concepts
Pragmatics and supralinguistics	Understanding a speaker's or writer's intentions	Using awareness of social aspects of language
Ultimate language skill	Understanding spoken or written language	Speaking or writing

Supralinguistics: a second order of analysis required to understand the meaning of words or sentences. For example, much language must be interpreted in a nonliteral way (sarcasm, indirect requests, and figurative language). Dad may say that the lawn looks like a hay field, when he is actually implying that he wants his child to cut the grass. Mom may say that the weather is "great," when she really means that she is tired of all the cloudy and rainy weather.

Throughout this chapter, we use "comprehension" as a synonym for receptive language and "production" as a synonym for expressive language. Table 13.1 defines each of the basic language components for receptive and expressive modalities.

2 Why Assess Oral and Written Language?

There are two primary reasons for assessing language abilities. First, well-developed language abilities are desirable in and of themselves. The ability to converse and to express thoughts and feelings is a goal of most individuals. Those who have difficulties with various aspects of language are often eligible for special services from speech–language specialists or from special educators. Second, various language processes and skills are believed to underlie subsequent development. Students who experience language difficulties have also been shown to experience behavior disorders, learning disabilities, and reading disorders.

Written language and spelling are regularly taught in school, and these areas are singled out for assessment in the Individuals with Disabilities Education Act. Written and oral language tests are administered for purposes of screening, instructional planning and modification, eligibility, and progress monitoring.

Considerations in Assessing Oral Language

Those who assess oral language must necessarily give consideration to cultural diversity and the developmental status of those they assess.

Cultural Diversity

Cultural background must be considered in assessing oral language competence. Although most children in the United States learn English, the form of English they learn depends on where they were born, who their parents are, and so on. For example, in central Pennsylvania, a child might say, "My hands need washed" instead of the standard "My hands need to be washed." In New York City, a child learning Black English might say "birfday" instead of "birthday" or "He be running" instead of "He is running." These and other culturally determined alternative constructions and pronunciations are not incorrect or inferior; they are just different. Indeed, they are appropriate within the child's surrounding community. Children should be viewed as having a language disorder only if they exhibit disordered production of their own primary language or dialect.

Cultural background is particularly important when the language assessment devices that are currently available are considered. Ideally, a child should be compared with others in the same language community. There should be separate norms for each language community, including Standard American English. Unfortunately, the norm samples of most language tests are heterogeneous, and scores on these tests may not be valid indicators of a child's language ability. Consider Plate 25 of the original Peabody Picture Vocabulary Test. This plate contained four pictures, and the examiner said, "Show me the wiener." There are many places in this country where the only word for that item is *hot dog* or *frankfurter*. Yet, because the test was standardized using *wiener*, the examiner was required to use that term. If a child had never heard "wiener," he or she was penalized and received a lower score, even though the error was cultural and not indicative of a semantic or intellectual deficiency. If there are a number of such items on a language test, the child's score can hardly be considered a valid indicator of language ability.

Developmental Considerations

Age is a major consideration in assessment of the child's language. Language acquisition is developmental; some sounds, linguistic structures, and even semantic elements are correctly produced at an earlier age than others. Thus, it is not unusual or indicative of language disorder for a 2-year-old child to say, "Kitty house" for "The cat is in the house," although the same phrase would be an indication of a disorder in a 3-year-old. It is important to be aware of developmental norms for language acquisition and to use those norms when making judgments about a child's language competence.

Considerations in Assessing Written Language

There are two major components of written language: content and form. The content of written expression is the product of considerable intellectual and linguistic activity: formulating, elaborating, sequencing, and then clarifying and revising ideas; choosing the precise word to convey meaning; and so forth. Moreover, much of what we consider to be content is the result of a creative endeavor. Our ability to use words to excite, to depict vividly, to imply, and to describe complex ideas is far more involved than simply putting symbols on paper.

The form of written language is far more mechanistic than its content. For writer and reader to communicate, three sets of conventions or rules are used: penmanship, spelling, and style rules. The most fundamental rules deal with *penmanship*, the formation of individual letters and letter sequences that make up words. Although letter formation tends to become more individualistic with age, there are a limited number of ways, for example, that the letter *A* can be written and still be recognized as an *A*. Moreover, there are conventions about the relative spacing of letters between and within words.

Spelling is also rule governed. Although American English is more irregular phonetically than other languages, it remains largely regular, and students should be able to spell most words by applying a few phonetic rules. For example, we have known since the mid-1960s that approximately 80 percent of all consonants have a single spelling (Hanna, Hanna, Hodges, & Rudoff, 1966). Short vowels are the major source of difficulty for most writers. The third set of conventions involves style. *Style* is a catchall term for rule-governed writing, which includes grammar (such as parts of speech, pronoun use, agreement, and verb voice and mood) and mechanics (such as punctuation, capitalization, abbreviations, and referencing).

The conventions of written language are tested on many standardized achievement tests. However, the spelling words that students are to learn vary considerably from curriculum to curriculum. For example, Ames (1965) examined seven spelling series and found that they introduced an average of 3,200 words between the second and eighth grades. However, only approximately 1,300 words were common to all the series; approximately 1,700 words were taught in only one series. Moreover, those words that were taught in several series varied considerably in their grade placement, sometimes by as many as five grades.

Capitalization and punctuation are also assessed on the current forms of several achievement batteries. Again, standardized tests are not well suited to measuring achievement in these areas because the grade level at which these skills are taught varies so much from one curriculum to another. To be valid, the measurement of achievement in these areas must be closely tied to the curriculum being taught. For example, pupils may learn in kindergarten, first grade, second grade, or later that a sentence always begins with a capital letter. They may learn in the sixth grade or several grades earlier that commercial brand names are capitalized. Students may be taught in the second or third grade that the apostrophe in "it's" makes the word a contraction of "it is" or may still be studying "it's" in high school. Finally, in assessing word usage, organization, and penmanship, we must take into account the emphasis that individual teachers place on these components of written language and when and how students are taught.

The more usual way to assess written language is to evaluate a student's written work and to develop vocabulary and spelling tests, as well as written expression rubrics, that parallel the curriculum. In this way, teachers can be sure that they are measuring precisely what has been taught. Most teacher's editions of language arts textbook series contain scope-and-sequence charts that specify fairly clearly the objectives that are taught in each unit. From these charts, teachers can develop appropriate criterion-referenced and curriculum-based assessments. There are also some rubrics available in the research literature that may be used by teachers to guide their instruction toward important components of writing content (Tindal & Hasbrouck, 1991).

Scenario in Assessment

Jose

In the Fairfield School District, students are encouraged to use inventive spelling from kindergarten to second grade. In other words, they are encouraged to come up with their own spelling for words that they do not yet know how to spell. When completing independent writing assignments, Fairfield teachers simply encourage students to focus on getting their thoughts on paper. Although spelling is taught in Fairfield, it is not expected that students know how to correctly spell the words that they choose to use in their independent writing assignments. Students are provided feedback on the quality of description and organization evident in their writing. As long as the spelling makes sense, they are not corrected.

In the Lakewood School District, just to the north of Fairfield, the focus of writing instruction and feedback is on the form of writing (that is, handwriting, spelling, punctuation, and so on). Students are encouraged to use those words that have been taught as weekly spelling words in their weekly independent writing assignments. Teachers spend a substantial amount of time teaching letter formation, word spacing, capitalization, and spelling during writing instruction. Students' grades on their independent writing assignments are based on the percentage of words spelled correctly.

Jose is a first grader who just moved into the Lakewood School District after attending Fairfield for kindergarten and part of first grade. His new teacher is appalled when Jose turns in the following independent writing assignment:

Mi trip to flourda

I went to flourda on brake and it was rely wrm and i wint swemmin in a pul. I jummd of a dyving bord and mad a big splaz that mad evrywon wet. I wood like to go thare agin neckst yeer.

The teacher views this writing sample to be far below the quality of Meika's writing assignment, which is much shorter but includes correct spelling and capitalization. Meika's writing sample is as follows:

My Winter Break

I had fun with my sister. We played games. We watched T.V.

The teacher is very concerned that Jose will not be successful in her class and requests the assistance of the school psychologist to help determine whether he may have a writing disability and need additional services. Although Jose performs similarly to Meika on a standardized measure of written language in which scores are based on both spelling achievement and total words written, greater differences in their achievement are evident when applying the different writing standards associated with the two different districts. In Fairfield, where total words written in 3 minutes is the measure used, he scored at the 85th percentile. In Lakewood, where total words spelled correctly in 3 minutes is the measure used, he scored at the 9th percentile.

Instead of considering a full-blown special education evaluation, the school psychologist recommends that Jose be specifically instructed to use only the words he knows how to spell in his independent writing. As Jose receives more consistent feedback on his mechanics, he begins to increase his performance according to his new school district's standards and eventually is performing above average according to both total words written and words spelled correctly on the 3-minute writing task.

The message here is that measures of student achievement should be aligned with instruction. For students who have not had exposure to the associated instruction, it is important to be patient and provide opportunities to learn accordingly.

3 Observing Language Behavior

There has been some disagreement among language professionals about the most valid method of evaluating a child's language performance, especially in the expressive channel of communication. There are three procedures used to gather a sample of a child's language behavior: spontaneous, imitative, and elicited.

Spontaneous Language

One school of thought holds that the only valid measure of a child's language abilities is one that studies the language the child produces spontaneously (for example, see Miller, 1981). Using this approach, the examiner records 50 to 100 consecutive utterances produced as the child is talking to an adult or playing with toys. With older children, conversations or storytelling tasks are often used. The child's utterances are then analyzed in terms of phonology, semantics, morphology, syntax, and pragmatics in order to provide information about the child's conversational abilities. Because the construct of pragmatics has been developed only recently, there are few standard assessment instruments available to sample this domain. Therefore, spontaneous language-sampling procedures are widely used to evaluate pragmatic abilities (see Prutting & Kirshner, 1987). Although analysis of a child's spontaneous language production is not the purpose of any standard oral language assessment instruments, some interest has been shown in standard assessment of handwriting and spelling skills in an uncontrived, spontaneous situation (for example, the revised *Test of Written Language* by Hammill and Larsen, 2008).

Imitation

Imitation tasks require a child to repeat directly the word, phrase, or sentence produced by the examiner. It might seem that such tasks bear little relation to spontaneous performance, but evidence suggests that such tasks are valid predictors of spontaneous production. In fact, many investigators have demonstrated that children's imitative language is essentially the same in content and structure as their spontaneous language (R. Brown & Bellugi, 1964; Ervin, 1964; Slobin & Welsh, 1973). Evidently, children translate adult sentences into their own language system and then repeat the sentences using their own language rules. A young child might imitate "The boy is running and jumping" as "Boy run and jump." Imitation thus seems to be a valuable tool for providing information about a child's language abilities. We note one caution, however: Features of a child's language systems can be obtained using imitation only if the stimulus sentences are long enough to tax the child's memory, because a child will imitate any sentence perfectly if the length of that sentence is within the child's memory capacity (Slobin & Welsh, 1973).

The use of imitation does not preclude the need for spontaneous sampling because the examiner also needs information derived from direct observation of conversational skills. Rather, imitation tasks should be used to augment the information obtained from the spontaneous sample because such tasks can be used to elicit forms that the child did not attempt in the conversations. Standardized imitation tasks are widely used in oral language assessment instruments (such as the Test of Language Development–P:4 and I:4). Assessment devices that use imitation usually contain a number of grammatically loaded words, phrases, or sentences that children are asked to imitate. The examiner records and transcribes the children's responses and then analyzes their phonology, morphology, and syntax. (Semantics and pragmatics are rarely assessed using an imitative mode.) Finally, imitation generally is used only in assessing expressive oral language.

Elicited Language

Using a picture stimulus to elicit language involves no imitation on the part of the child, but the procedure cannot be classified as totally spontaneous. In this type of task, the child is presented with a picture or pictures of objects or action scenes and is asked to do one of the following: (1) point to the correct object (a receptive vocabulary task), (2) point to the action picture that best describes a sentence (receptive language, including vocabulary), (3) name the picture (expressive vocabulary), or (4) describe the picture (expressive language, including vocabulary). Although only stimulus pictures are described in this section, some tests use concrete objects rather than pictures to elicit language responses.

Advantages and Disadvantages of Each Procedure

There are advantages and disadvantages to all three methods of language observation (spontaneous, imitative, and elicited). The use of spontaneous language samples has two major advantages. First, a child's spontaneous language is undoubtedly the best and most natural indicator of everyday language performance. Second, the informality of the procedure often allows the examiner to assess children quite easily, without the difficulties sometimes associated with a formal testing atmosphere.

The disadvantages associated with this procedure relate to the nonstandardized nature of the data collection. Although some aspects of language sampling are stable across a variety of parameters, this procedure shows much wider variability than is seen with other standardized assessments. In addition, language sampling requires detailed analyses across language domains; such analyses are more time-consuming than administering a standardized instrument. Finally, because the examiner does not directly control the selection of target words and phrases, he or she may have difficulty understanding a young child, or there may be several different interpretations of what a child intended to say. Moreover, the child may have avoided, or may not have had an opportunity to attempt, a particular structure that is of interest to the examiner.

The use of imitation overcomes many of the disadvantages inherent in the spontaneous approach. An imitation task will often assess many different language elements and provide a representative view of a child's language system.

Also, because of the structure of the test, the examiner knows at all times what elements of language are being assessed. Thus, even the language abilities of a child with a severe language disorder (especially a severe phonological disorder) can be quantified. Finally, imitation devices can be administered much more quickly than can spontaneous language samples.

Unfortunately, the advantages of the spontaneous approach become the disadvantages of the imitative method. First, a child's auditory memory may have some effect on the results. For example, an echolalic child may score well on an imitative test without demonstrating productive knowledge of the language structures being imitated. Second, a child may repeat part of a sentence exactly because the utterance is too simple or short to place a load on the child's memory. Therefore, accurate production is not necessarily evidence that the child uses the structure spontaneously. However, inaccurate productions often do reflect a child's lack of mastery of the structure. Thus, test givers should draw conclusions only about a child's errors from an imitative test. A third disadvantage of imitative tests is that they are often quite boring to the child. Not all children will sit still for the time required to repeat 50 to 100 sentences without any other stimulation, such as pictures or toys.

The use of pictures to elicit language production is an attempt to overcome the disadvantages of both imitation and spontaneous language. Pictures are easy to administer, are interesting to children, and require minimal administration time. They can be structured to test desired language elements and yet retain some of the impromptu nature of spontaneous language samples because children have to formulate the language on their own. Because there is no time limit, results do not depend on the child's word-retention skills. Despite these advantages, a major disadvantage limits the usefulness of picture stimuli in language assessment: It is difficult to create pictures guaranteed to elicit specific language elements. Although it is probably easiest to create pictures for object identification, difficulties arise even in this area. Thus, the disadvantage seen in spontaneous sampling is evident with picture stimuli as well—the child may not produce or attempt to produce the desired language structure.

In summary, all three methods of language observation have advantages and disadvantages. The examiner must decide which elements of language should be tested, which methods of observation are most appropriate for assessing those elements, and which assessment devices satisfy these needs. It should not be surprising that more than one test is often necessary to assess all components of language (phonology, semantics, morphology, syntax, and pragmatics), both receptively and expressively. As noted, standardized instruments should be supplemented with measures of conversational abilities within any oral language assessment. In addition, the different language domains are often best assessed by different procedures. For example, picture stimuli are particularly well suited for assessment of phonological abilities because the examiner should know the intended production. Similarly, imitation tasks are often employed to assess morphological abilities because the child having difficulty with this component will often delete suffixes and prefixes during imitation. Finally, because assessment of pragmatics involves determining the child's conversational use of language, this domain should be assessed with spontaneous production.

SPECIFIC ORAL AND WRITTEN LANGUAGE TESTS

Table 13.2 provides characteristics of several commonly administered tests of oral and written language. Reviews of four of these tests (that is, the Test of Written Language–Fourth Edition, the Test of Language Development: Primary–Fourth Edition, the Test of Language Development: Intermediate–Fourth Edition, and the Oral and Written Language Scales) are provided in the following section. Reviews for the remaining tests represented in the table are available on the website for this book.

Test of Written Language–Fourth Edition (TOWL-4)

The Test of Written Language–4 (TOWL-4; Hammill & Larsen, 2008) is a norm-referenced device designed to assess the written language competence of students between the ages of 9-0 and 17-11. Although the TOWL-4 was designed to be individually administered, the authors provide a series of modifications to allow group administration, with follow-up testing of individual students to ensure valid testing. The recommended uses of the TOWL-4 include identifying students who have substantial difficulty in writing, determining strengths and weaknesses of individual students, documenting student progress, and conducting research. Two alternative forms (A and B) are available.

The TOWL-4 uses two writing formats (contrived and spontaneous) to evaluate written language. In a contrived format, students' linguistic options are purposely constrained to force the students to use specific words or conventions. The TOWL-4 uses these two formats to assess three components of written language (conventional, linguistic, and cognitive). The conventional component deals with using widely accepted rules in punctuation and spelling. The linguistic component deals with syntactic and semantic structures. The cognitive component deals with producing "logical, coherent, and contextual written material" (Hammill & Larsen, 2008, p. 25).

Subtests

The first five subtests, eliciting writing in contrived contexts, are briefly described here.

Vocabulary. This area is assessed by having a student write correct sentences containing stimulus words.

Spelling. The TOWL-4 assesses spelling by having a student write sentences from dictation.

Punctuation. Competence in this aspect of writing is assessed by evaluating the punctuation and capitalization in sentences written by a student from dictation.

Logical Sentences. Competence in this area is assessed by having a student rewrite illogical sentences so that they make sense.

Sentence Combining. The TOWL-4 requires a student to write one grammatically correct sentence based on the information in several short sentences.

The last two subtests elicit more spontaneous, contextual writing by the student in response to a picture used as a story starter. After the story has been written (and the other five subtests administered), the story is scored on two dimensions. Each dimension is treated as a subtest. Following are brief descriptions of these subtests:

Contextual Conventions. A student's ability to use appropriate grammatical rules and conventions of mechanics (such as punctuation and spelling) in context is assessed using the student's story.

Story Composition. As described by Hammill and Larsen (2008, p. 29), this subtest evaluates a student's story on the basis of the "quality of its composition (e.g., vocabulary, plot, prose, development of characters, and interest to the reader)."

TABLE 13.2 Commonly Used Diagnostic Language Tests

Test	Author	Publisher	Year	Ages/Grades	Individual/ Group	NRT/SRT/ CRT	Subtests
Comprehensive Assessment of Spoken Language (CASL)	Carrow-Woolfolk	Pro-Ed	1999	Ages 3–21 years	Individual	NRT	Comprehension of Basic Concepts, Synonyms, Antonyms, Sentence Completion, Idiomatic Language, Syntax Construction, Paragraph Comprehension of Syntax, Grammatic Morphemes, Sentence Comprehension of Syntax, Grammaticality Judgment, Nonliteral Language Test, Meaning from Context, Inference Test, Ambiguous Sentences Test, Pragmatic Judgment
Comprehensive Receptive and Expressive Vocabulary Test– Second Edition (CREVT-2)	Wallace & Hammill	Pro-Ed	2002	Ages 4-0 to 89-11 years	Individual	NRT	Receptive Vocabulary, Expressive Vocabulary
Goldman–Fristoe Test of Articulation, Second Edition (GFTA-2)	Goldman & Fristoe	Pearson	2000	Ages 2-0 to 21-11 years	Individual	NRT	Sounds-in-Words, Sounds-in-Sentences, Stimulability
Illinois Test of Psycholinguistic Abilities-3 (ITPA-3)	Hammill, Mather, & Roberts	Pro-Ed	2001	Ages 5-0 to 12-11 years	Individual	NRT	Spoken Analogies, Spoken Vocabulary, Morphological Closure, Syntactic Sentences, Sound Deletion, Rhyming Sequences, Sentence Sequencing, Written Vocabulary, Sight Decoding, Sound Decoding, Sight Spelling, Sound Spelling
Oral and Written Language Scales	Carrow-Woolfolk	Pearson	1995	Ages 3–21 years	Individual	NRT	Listening Comprehension, Oral Expression, Written Expression

continued on the next page

TABLE 13.2   Commonly Used Diagnostic Language Tests, *continued*

Test	Author	Publisher	Year	Ages/Grades	Individual/ Group	NRT/SRT/ CRT	Subtests
Test for Auditory Comprehension of Language, Third Edition (TACL-3)	Carrow-Woolfolk	Pro-Ed	1999	Ages 3-0 to 9-11 years	Individual	NRT	Vocabulary, Grammatical Morphemes, Elaborated Phrases and Sentences
Test of Language Development: Intermediate–Fourth Edition (TOLD-I:4)	Hammill & Newcomer	Pro-Ed	2008	Ages 8-0 to 17-11 years	Individual	NRT	Sentence Combining, Picture Vocabulary, Word Ordering, Relational Vocabulary, Morphological Comprehension, Multiple Meanings
Test of Language Development: Primary–Fourth Edition (TOLD-P:4)	Newcomer & Hammill	Pro-Ed	2008	Ages 4-0 to 8-11 years	Individual	NRT	Picture Vocabulary, Relational Vocabulary, Oral Vocabulary, Syntactic Understanding, Sentence Imitation, Morphological Completion, Word Discrimination, Word Analysis, Word Articulation
Test of Written Language–Fourth Edition (TOWL-4)	Hammill & Larsen	Pro-Ed	2008	Ages 9–17 years	Individual, can be administered to a group	NRT	Vocabulary, Spelling, Punctuation, Logical Sentences, Sentence Combining, Contextual Conventions, Story Composition
Test of Written Spelling–Fourth Edition (TWS-4)	Larsen, Hammill, & Moats	Pro-Ed	1999	Ages 6-0 to 18-11 years	Individual, can be administered to a group	NRT	No separate subtests

Scores

Raw scores for each subtest can be converted to percentiles or standard scores. The standard scores have a mean of 10 and a standard deviation of 3. Various combinations of subtests result in three composites: contrived writing (Vocabulary, Spelling, Punctuation, Logical Sentences, and Sentence Combining), spontaneous writing (Contextual Conventions and Story Composition), and overall writing (all subtests). Subtest standard scores can be summed and converted to standard scores (that is, "index scores") and percentiles for each composite. The composite index scores have a mean of 100 and a standard deviation of 15. Both age and grade equivalents are available; however, the authors appropriately warn against reporting these scores.

Norms

Two different sampling techniques were used to establish norms for the TOWL-4. First, sites in each of the four geographic regions of the United States were selected, and 977 students were tested. Second, an additional 1,229 students were tested by volunteers who had previously purchased materials from the publisher. The total sample is distributed such that there are at least 200 students represented at each age level; however, at some age levels there are very few students represented in either the fall or the spring sample. The total sample varies no more than 5 percent from information provided by the U.S. Census Bureau for the 2005 school-age population on various demographic variables (that is, gender, geographic region, ethnicity, family income, educational attainment of parents, and disability), with the exception that those with a very high household income are overrepresented (that is, 35 percent of the sample has a household income of more than $75,000, whereas just 27 percent of the population has this level of household income). The authors also present data for three age ranges (that is, 9 to 11, 12 to 14, and 15 to 17), showing that each age range also approximates information on the nationwide school-age population for 2005. However, the comparisons of interest (that is, the degree to which each normative group approximates the census) are absent.

Reliability

Three types of reliability are discussed in the TOWL-4 manual: internal consistencies (both coefficient alpha and alternate-form reliability), stability, and inter scorer agreement.

Two procedures were used to estimate the internal consistency of the TOWL-4. First, a series of coefficient alphas was computed. Using the entire normative sample, coefficient alpha was used to estimate the internal consistency of each score (age and grade) and composite on each form at each age. Of the 238 alphas reported, 85 are in the .90s, 80 are in the .80s, 62 are in the .70s, 10 are in the .60s, and 1 is below .60. Alphas are consistently higher on the Vocabulary, Punctuation, and Spelling subtests and lowest on the Logical Sentences and Story Composition subtests. As is typical, coefficient alpha was substantially higher for the composites. For Contrived Writing and Overall Writing, all coefficients equaled or exceeded .95. For Spontaneous Writing, they were substantially lower, with all in the .70s and .80s. Thus, two of the composites are sufficiently reliable for making important educational decisions about students.

The authors are to be commended for also reporting subtest internal consistencies for several demographic subgroups (that is, males and females, Caucasian Americans, African Americans, Hispanic Americans, and Asian Americans), as well as students with disabilities (that is, learning disabled, speech impaired, and attention deficit hyperactive). The obtained coefficients for the various demographic subgroups are comparable to those for the entire normative sample.

Second, alternate-form reliability was also computed for each subtest and each composite at each age and grade, using the entire normative sample. These coefficients were distributed in approximately the same way as were the alphas.

The 2-week stability of each subtest and each composite on both forms was estimated with 84 students ranging in age from 9 to 17 years; results were examined according to two age and grade ranges. Of the 80 associated coefficients, 30 coefficients equaled or exceeded .90, 34 were in the .80s, 15 were in the .70s, and 1 was in the .60s. These followed the pattern of other reliability indices, with higher coefficients identified for the contrived writing and overall writing composites than for the spontaneous writing composite.

To estimate interscorer agreement, 41 TOWL-4 protocols were selected at random and scored. The correlations between scorers were remarkably consistent. Of the 40 coefficients associated with subtest and composite scoring agreement, 36 were in the .90s, 2 were in the .80s, and 2 were in the .70s. The scoring of written language samples is quite difficult, and unacceptably low levels of interscorer agreement appear to be the rule rather than the exception. It appears that the scoring criteria contained in the TOWL-4 manual are sufficiently precise and clear to allow for consistent scoring. The only subtest with interscorer reliability below .90 was Story Composition.

Validity

Support for content validity comes from the way in which the test was developed, the many dimensions of written language assessed, and the methods by which competence in written language is assessed. The evidence for criterion-related validity comes from a study in which three measures—the Written Language Observation Scale (Hammill & Larsen, 2009), the Reading Observation Scale (Hammill & Larsen, 2009), and the Test of Reading Comprehension–Fourth Edition (TORC-4; Brown, Wiederholt, & Hammill, 2009)—were correlated with each score on the TOWL-4. Correlations ranging from .34 (Story Composition correlated with the Written Language Observation Scale) to .80 (Spelling correlated with the TORC-4) provide somewhat limited support for the TOWL-4's validity; teacher ratings for reading correlated as well as or better than those for writing. The authors also conducted positive predictive analyses using these data on the three literacy measures. Based on the results, which indicate levels of sensitivity and specificity exist meeting the .70 threshold, the authors suggest that the TOWL-4 can be used to identify those students who have literacy difficulties.

Construct validity is considered at some length in the TOWL-4 manual. First, the authors present evidence to show that TOWL-4 scores increase with age and grade. The correlations with age are substantially stronger for students between the ages of 9 and 12 years than for students 13 to 17 years old, for whom correlations are small. Second, in examining the subtest intercorrelations and conducting a factor analysis, the TOWL-4 appears to assess a single factor for the sample as a whole. Thus, although individual subtests (or the contrived and spontaneous composites) may be of interest, they are not independent of the other skills measured on the test. Third, scores on the TOWL-4 for students with learning disabilities and

speech/language impairments, who are anticipated to struggle in the area of written language, were generally lower than those for other subgroups. However, it is important to note that score differences for these exceptionality groups tended to be no more than one standard deviation below the average.

The authors were careful to examine the possibility of racial or ethnic bias in their assessment tool. They conducted reliability analyses separately by gender, race/ethnicity, and exceptionality grouping. They also conducted an analysis of differential item functioning in which they examined whether item characteristics varied by gender and ethnicity, which would suggest the possibility of item bias. Although two items were identified with differences in item characteristics across groups, these represented less than 5 percent of the test items.

Summary

The TOWL-4 is designed to assess written language competence of students aged 9-0 to 17-11. Contrived and spontaneous formats are used to evaluate the conventional, linguistic, and cognitive components of written language. The content and structure of the TOWL-4 appear appropriate.

Although the TOWL-4's norms appear representative in general, the fall and spring samples tend to be uneven by age group, with some of these seasonal samples including very few students at certain grade levels. Interscorer reliability is quite good for this type of test. The internal consistencies of one composite (that is, Contrived Writing) and the total composite are high enough for use in making individual decisions; the stabilities of subtests and the remaining composite (that is, Spontaneous Writing) are lower.

Although the test's content appears appropriate and well conceived, the validity of the inferences to be drawn from the scores is unclear. Specifically, group means are the only data to suggest that the TOWL-4 is useful in identifying students with disabilities or in determining strengths and weaknesses of individual students. Students with learning disabilities and speech/language disorders earn TOWL-4 subtest scores that are only 1 standard deviation (or less) below the mean; they earn composite scores that are no more than 1.2 standard deviations below the mean. However, because we do not know whether these students had disabilities in written language, their scores tell us little about the TOWL-4's ability to identify students with specific written language needs. Although positive predictive analyses were conducted to determine whether the TOWL-4 could identify students with literacy difficulties, these similarly do not provide evidence that the test is particularly helpful in identifying specific written language difficulties. Given that the TOWL-4 has only two forms and relatively low stability, its usefulness in evaluating pupil progress is also limited.

Test of Language Development: Primary–Fourth Edition

The Test of Language Development: Primary–Fourth Edition (TOLD-P:4; Newcomer & Hammill, 2008) is a norm-referenced, nontimed, individually administered test designed to (1) identify children who are significantly below their peers in oral language proficiency, (2) determine a child's specific strengths and weaknesses in oral language skills, (3) document progress in remedial programs, and (4) measure oral language in research studies (Newcomer & Hammill, 2008). The TOLD-P:4 is intended to be used with children ages 4-0 to 8-11 years. Although the test is not timed, the average student is able to complete the core subtests in 35 to 50 minutes and the supplemental tests in an additional 30 minutes.

Subtests

The TOLD-P:4 consists of nine subtests, each measuring different components of oral language. Six of the subtests are considered core subtests and their scores are combined to form composite scores. The composite scores cover the main areas of language: semantics and grammar; listening, organizing, and speaking; and overall language ability. The subtests measuring phonology are excluded from the composite scores in order to create a clear separation between speech competence and language competence, making it easier to determine specific disorders. Descriptions of the individual subtests are as follows:

Picture Vocabulary. This subtest assesses a child's ability to understand the meaning of spoken English words (semantics and listening).

Relational Vocabulary. This subtest assesses a child's understanding and ability to orally express the relationships between two words spoken by the examiner (semantics and organizing).

Oral Vocabulary. This subtest assesses a child's ability to give oral directions to common English words that are spoken by the examiner (semantics and speaking).

Syntactic Understanding. This subtest assesses a child's ability to understand the meaning of sentences (grammar and listening).

Sentence Imitation. This subtest assesses a child's ability to imitate English sentences (grammar and organizing).

Morphological Completion. This subtest assesses a child's ability to recognize, understand, and use common English morphological forms (grammar and speaking).

Word Discrimination. This subtest assesses a child's ability to recognize the differences in speech sounds (phonology and listening).

Word Analysis. This subtest assesses a child's ability to segment words into smaller phonemic units (phonology and organizing)

Word Articulation. This subtest assesses a child's ability to produce various English speech sounds (phonology and speaking).

Scores

The TOLD-P:4 generates four types of normative scores: age equivalents, percentile ranks, scaled scores, and composite indexes. The subtests of the TOLD-P:4 are designed on a two-dimensional model of linguistic features and linguistic systems. The subtests can be combined into the following six composites:

1. Listening (Picture Vocabulary and Syntactic Understanding)

2. Organizing (Relational Vocabulary and Sentence Imitation)

3. Speaking (Oral Vocabulary and Morphological Completion)

4. Grammar (Syntactic Understanding, Sentence Imitation, and Morphological Completion)

5. Semantics (Picture Vocabulary, Relational Vocabulary, and Oral Vocabulary)

6. Spoken Language (Picture Vocabulary, Relational Vocabulary, Oral Vocabulary, Syntactic Understanding, Sentence Imitation, and Morphological Completion). This is a measure of the overall language ability.

Norms

The TOLD-P:4 was standardized in 2006 and 2007 on a demographic representative sample of 1,108 children from four regions of the United States. The norm sample was stratified on the basis of gender, age, race, geographic region, Hispanic status, exceptionality status (disability area), family income, and parental education level. The examiner's manual contains charts indicating the breakdown of the norm sample according to the 2007 census. Some cross-tabs (for example, the number of students in each specific racial/ethnic group from each region) are provided, and there is good correspondence between census and norm sample data.

Reliability

To determine test reliability, the TOLD-P:4 uses three types of correlation coefficients—coefficient alpha, test–retest, and scorer difference—to measure three types of error (content, time, and scorer). Coefficient alphas were calculated for each subtest and composite scores. The coefficients for the subtests exceeded .80, and seven of the nine subtest coefficients exceeded .90. The composite scores averaged coefficients greater than .90. Test–retest reliability was completed using two groups of students ages 4 to 6 years and ages 7 to 8 years; time between assessments was 1 or 2 weeks. With the exception of one subtest, the reliability coefficients for the subtests for both groups were greater than .80. The coefficients for the composites, with the exception of one, exceeded .90. Results indicate that TOLD-P:4 scores show little time sampling error. The scoring differences were calculated and all coefficients exceeded .90. The TOLD-P:4 appears to meet and often exceed the standards for reliability.

Validity

The examiner's manual includes extensive information on the validity of the TOLD-P:4, including various studies validating content—description validity, criterion prediction validity, and construct identification validity. The authors describe their theory of oral language development, indicate why they selected specific subtest measures, and provide a rationale for how each subtest matches their theory. The arguments are convincing. Evidence for criterion validity is based on correlations with scores on three other oral language measures: the Pragmatic Language Observation Scale, TOLD-I:4, and the WISC-IV Verbal Composite. Correlations were moderate, as would be expected, and comparable means and standard deviations were earned on the various measures.

Evidence for construct validity is based on testing hypotheses derived from theory, for example, "Because the TOLD-4:P subtests and composites are supposed to measure aspects of language, the test results should differentiate between groups of people known to be normal in language and those known to be poor in language" (Newcomer & Hammill, 2008, p. 60). Overall, there is good evidence for the validity of the TOLD-P:4.

Summary

The TOLD-P:4 is an individually administered, nontimed, norm-referenced test used to evaluate the spoken language abilities of children ages 4 years to 8 years 11 months. The test contains nine subtests and yields subtest standard scores as well as composite scores. The TOLD-P:4 contains new normative data obtained from a demographic representation of the 2005 U.S. population, an expanded study on bias items, an increased number of validity studies, and an updated and easy to use examiner's manual. The TOLD-P:4 appears to meet and often exceed the standards for reliability. There is extensive information on content description validity, criterion prediction validity, and construct identification validity. The test seems appropriate to identify students' oral language strengths and weaknesses, identify those who are below their peers in oral language skills, and document progress in intervention programs.

Test of Language Development: Intermediate–Fourth Edition

The Test of Language Development: Intermediate–Fourth Edition (TOLD-I:4; Hammill & Newcomer, 2008) is a norm-referenced, nontimed, individually administered test designed to (1) identify students who are significantly below their peers in oral language proficiency, (2) determine students' specific strengths and weaknesses in oral language skills, (3) document their progress in remedial programs, and (4) measure oral language in research studies (Newcomer & Hammill, 2008). The TOLD-I:4 is intended to be used with students ages 8-0 to 17-11 years. Although the test is not timed, the average student is able to complete the entire test in 35 to 50 minutes.

Subtests

The TOLD-I:4 consists of six subtests, each measuring different components of semantics or grammar. The six scores students earn are converted to standard scores for each subtest, and the standard scores for subtests are combined to form composite scores. The composite scores cover the main areas of language: semantics and grammar; listening, organizing, and speaking; and overall language ability. Descriptions of the individual subtests are as follows:

Sentence Combining. The student is asked to create a compound sentence from two or more simple sentences presented verbally by the examiner (grammar and speaking).

Picture Vocabulary. Given a set of six pictures, the pupil is to identify, by pointing, the picture that represents the two-word stimulus.

Word Ordering. Given a randomly ordered word set, the student is to generate a complete, grammatically correct sentence (grammar and organizing).

Relational Vocabulary. Given three words from the examiner, the student must state how they are alike (semantics and organizing).

Morphological Comprehension. Given verbal sentences from the examiner, the student must identify grammatically correct and incorrect sentences (grammar and listening).

Multiple Meanings. Given a word from the examiner, the pupil is asked to generate as many different meanings for that word as he or she is able to (semantics and speaking).

Scores

The TOLD-I:4 yields four types of normative scores: age equivalents, percentile ranks, subtest standard (scaled) scores, and composite scores. The subtests of the TOLD-I:4 are designed on a two-dimensional model of linguistic features and linguistic systems. The subtests can be combined into the following six composite scores:

1. Listening (Picture Vocabulary and Morphological Comprehension)
2. Organizing (Word Ordering and Relational Vocabulary)
3. Speaking (Sentence Combining and Multiple Meanings)
4. Grammar (Sentence Combining, Word Ordering, and Morphological Comprehension)
5. Semantics (Picture Vocabulary, Relational Vocabulary, and Multiple Meanings)
6. Spoken Language (Sentence Combining, Picture Vocabulary, Word Ordering, Relational Vocabulary, Morphological Comprehension, and Multiple Meanings)

Norms

The TOLD-I:4 was standardized during 2006 and 2007 on a demographic representative sample of 1,097 students from four regions of the United States. The norm sample was gathered on the basis of gender, age, race, geographic region, Hispanic status, exceptionality status (disability area), family income, and parental education level. The manual contains charts indicating the breakdown of the norm sample according to the 2005 census. Some cross-tabs (number of males sampled from each geographic region) are provided and are further indicative of the representativeness of the sample.

Reliability

The TOLD-I:4 uses coefficient alpha, test–retest, and scorer differences to measure three different types of test error: content, time, and scorer. Coefficient alphas were calculated for each subtest at 10 age intervals; in all subtests, the average coefficient alphas exceed .90. The composite scores average a coefficient of .90 or greater. Test–retest reliability was completed using two groups of students, ages 8 to 12 years and ages 13 to 17 years; time between assessments was no more than 2 weeks. The reliability coefficients for all subtests were at or above .80 and for all composite scores were above .90. The coefficients for interscorer agreement all exceeded .90. The TOLD-I:4 appears to meet and often exceed the standards for reliability necessary for making screening and diagnostic decisions.

Validity

The examiner's manual included extensive information on the validity of the TOLD-I:4, including studies validating the content validity, criterion prediction validity, and construct validity. The authors provide an extensive rationale for selecting each of the subtests and for their method of measuring language skills. The arguments seem solid and are convincing. Criterion predictive validity was established by correlating performance on TOLD-I:4 subtests and composites with performance on eight other measures of spoken language, using a different sample of students for each comparison. There is good evidence for criterion predictive validity.

Evidence for construct validity is based on examination of the extent to which hypotheses based on theoretical analysis are supported; for example, "Because oral language ability is known to be related to literacy, the TOLD-4:I should correlate highly with tests of reading and writing." (Hammill & Newcomer, 2008, p. 56). There is good evidence for the construct validity of the test.

Summary

The TOLD-I:4 is an individually administered, non-timed, norm-referenced test used to evaluate the spoken language abilities of students ages 8 years 0 months to 17 years 11 months. The test contains six subtests and yields standard scores, composite scores, and an overall spoken language score. The TOLD-I:4 contains new normative data obtained from a demographic representation of the 2005 U.S. population, the floor effect has been eliminated, an expanded study of test bias is provided, and many validity studies have been completed and included in the manual. Also, it contains a new composite (Organizing) and a Multiple Meanings subtest. The General and Multiple Meanings subtests have been renamed to better represent what they assess; the new names are Relational Vocabulary and Morphological Comprehension. The age range has been extended to include students ages 13-0 to 17-11 years, and an updated, easy to use examiner's manual is included. The TOLD-I:4 appears to meet and often exceed reliability standards for making screening or diagnostic decisions. The manual contains extensive information on validity, and the evidence supports the validity of the scale. The test appears appropriate to identify students' oral language strengths and weaknesses, identify those who are below their peers in oral language functioning, and document progress in intervention programs.

Oral and Written Language Scales (OWLS)

The Oral and Written Language Scales (OWLS; Carrow-Woolfolk, 1995) are an individually administered assessment of receptive and expressive language for children and young adults ages 3 through 21 years. The test includes three scales: Listening Comprehension, Oral Expression, and Written Expression. Test results are used to determine broad levels of language skills and specific performance in listening, speaking, and writing. The scales are described here.

Subtests

Listening Comprehension. This scale is designed to measure understanding of spoken language. It consists of 111 items. The examiner reads aloud a verbal stimulus, and the student has to identify which of four pictures is the best response to the stimulus. The scale takes 5 to 15 minutes to administer.

Oral Expression. This scale is a measure of understanding and use of spoken language. It consists of 96 items. The examiner reads aloud a verbal stimulus and shows a picture. The student responds orally by answering a question, completing a sentence, or generating one or more sentences. The scale takes 10 to 25 minutes to administer.

Written Expression. This scale is an assessment of written language for students 5 to 21 years of age. It is designed to measure ability to use conventions (spelling, punctuation, and so on), use syntactical forms (modifiers, phrases, sentence structures, and so on), and communicate meaningfully (with appropriate content, coherence, organization, and so on). The student responds to direct writing prompts provided by the examiner.

The OWLS is designed to be used in identification of students with language difficulties and disorders, in intervention planning, and in monitoring student progress.

Norms

The OWLS standardization sample consisted of 1,985 students chosen to match the U.S. census data from the 1991 Current Population Survey. The sample was stratified within age group by gender, race, geographic region, and socioeconomic status. Tables in the manual show the comparison of the sample to the U.S. population. Cross-tabulations are shown only for age and not for other variables. The 14- to 21-year-old age group is overrepresented by students in the North Central region and underrepresented by students in the West.

Scores

The OWLS produces raw scores, which may be transformed to standard scores with a mean of 100 and a standard deviation of 15. In addition, test age equivalents, normal-curve equivalents, percentiles, and stanines can be obtained. Scores are obtained for each subtest, for an oral language composite, and for a written language composite.

Reliability

Internal consistency reliability was calculated using students in the standardization. Reliability coefficients range from .75 to .89 for Listening Comprehension, from .76 to .91 for Oral Expression, and from .87 to .94 for the oral composite. They range from .77 to .89 for Written Expression. Test–retest reliabilities were computed on a small sample of students who are not described. The coefficients range from .58 to .85 for the oral subtests and composite and from .66 to .83 for the Written Expression subtest. Reliabilities are sufficient to use this measure as a screening device. They are not sufficient to use it in making important decisions about individual students. This latter, of course, is the use the authors suggest for the test.

Validity

The authors report the results of a set of external validity studies, each consisting of a comparison of performance on the OWLS to performance on other measures. Sample sizes were small, but correlations were in the expected range. The Written Expression subtest was compared to the Kaufman Test of Educational Achievement, the Peabody Individual Achievement Test–Revised, the Woodcock Reading Mastery Test, and the Peabody Picture Vocabulary Test. Student performance on the Oral Expression and Listening Comprehension subtests was compared to performance on the Test for Auditory Comprehension of Language–Revised, the Peabody Picture Vocabulary Test, the Clinical Evaluation of Language Fundamentals–Revised, and the Kaufman Assessment Battery for Children.

Summary

The OWLS is a language test combining assessment of oral and written language. The test was standardized on the same population, so comparisons of student performance on oral and written measures are enhanced. The manual includes data showing that the standardization sample is generally representative of the U.S. population. Reliability coefficients are too low to permit use of this measure in making important decisions for individuals. Evidence for validity is good, although it is based on a set of studies with limited numbers of students.

Dilemmas in Current Practice

Oral Language Issues

Three issues are particularly troublesome in the assessment of oral language: (1) ensuring that the elicited language assessment is a true reflection of the child's general spontaneous language capacity; (2) using the results of standardized tests to generate effective therapy; and (3) adapting assessment to individuals who do not match the characteristics of the standardization sample. All these dilemmas stem from the limited nature of the standardized tests and must be addressed in practice.

From a practical standpoint, the clinician must use standardized tests to identify a child with a language impairment. However, as noted previously in this chapter, such instruments may not directly measure a child's true language abilities. Thus, the clinician must supplement the standard tests with nonstandard spontaneous language sampling. In addition, if possible, the child should be observed in a number of settings outside the formal testing situation. After the spontaneous samples have been gathered, the results of these analyses should be compared with the performance on the standardized tests.

Selection of targets for intervention is one of the more difficult tasks facing the clinician. Many standardized tests that are useful for identifying language disorders in children may not lend themselves to determining efficient treatment. The clinician must evaluate the results of both the standard and the nonstandard assessment procedures and decide which language skills are most important to the child. Although it is tempting simply to train the child to perform better on a particular test (hence boosting performance on that instrument), the clinician must bear in mind that such tasks are often metalinguistic in nature and will not ultimately result in generalized language skills. Rather, the focus of treatment should be on those language behaviors and structures that are needed for improved language competence in the home and in the classroom.

Authors' Viewpoint

In today's language assessment environment, with a plethora of multicultural and socioeconomic variation within caseloads, a clinician is bound to encounter many children who differ in one or more respects from the normative sample of a particular test. Indeed, clinicians are likely to see children who do not match the normative sample of any standardized test. When this occurs, the clinician must interpret the scores derived from these tests conservatively. Information from nonstandard assessment becomes even more important, and the clinician should obtain reports from parents, teachers, and peers regarding their impressions of the child's language competence. The clinician should also determine whether local norms have been developed for the standard and nonstandard assessment procedures. As previously noted, it is inappropriate to treat multicultural language differences as if they were language disorders. However, the clinician performing an assessment must judge whether the child's language is disordered within his or her language community and what impact such disorders may have on classroom performance and communication skills generally.

Written Language Issues

There are two serious problems in the assessment of written language.

Problem 1

The first problem involves assessing the content of written expression. The content of written language is usually scored holistically and subjectively. Holistic evaluations tend to be unreliable. When content on the same topic and of the same genre (such as narratives) is scored, interscorer agreement varies from the .50 to .65 range (as in Breland, 1983; Breland, Camp, Jones, Morris, & Rock, 1987) to the .75 to .90 range immediately following intensive training (such as Educational Testing Service, 1990). Consistent scoring is even more difficult when topics and genres vary. Interscorer agreement can decrease to a range of .35 to .45 when the writing tasks vary (as in Breland, 1983; Breland et al., 1987). Subjective scoring and decision making are susceptible to the biasing effects associated with racial, ethnic, social class, gender, and disability stereotypes.

Authors' Viewpoint

We believe the best alternative to holistic and subjective scoring schemes is to use a measure of writing fluency as an indicator of content generation. Two options have received some support in the research literature: (1) the number of words written (Shinn, Tindall, & Stein, 1988) and (2) the percentage of correctly written words (Isaacson, 1988).

Problem 2

The second problem is in identifying a match between what is taught in the school curriculum and what is tested. The great variation in the time at which various skills and facts are taught renders a general test of achievement inappropriate. This dilemma also attends diagnostic assessment of written language. Commercially prepared tests have doubtful validity for planning individual programs and evaluating the progress of individual pupils.

Authors' Viewpoint

We recommend that teachers and diagnosticians construct criterion-referenced achievement tests that closely parallel the curricula followed by the students being tested.

In cases in which normative data are required, there are three choices. Diagnosticians can (1) select the devices that most closely parallel the curriculum, (2) develop local norms, or (3) select individual students for comparative purposes. Care should be exercised in selecting methods of assessing language skills. For example, it is probably better to test pupils in ways that are familiar to them. Thus, if the teacher's weekly spelling test is from dictation, then spelling tests using dictation are probably preferable to tests requiring the students to identify incorrectly spelled words.

CHAPTER COMPREHENSION QUESTIONS

Write your answers to each of the following questions, and then compare your responses to the text or the study guide.

1. Describe five processes associated with communication.

2. Explain how cultural background may play a role in determining appropriate language expectations.

3. Identify and describe the three techniques for obtaining a sample of a child's language.

4. What are the two major components of written language, and how might they be assessed?

5. What are some of the dilemmas associated with assessment of oral and written language?

Chapter Goals

1 Understand how student characteristics, particularly acculturation, can affect student performance on intelligence tests.

2 Understand behaviors commonly sampled on intelligence tests.

3 Know the historical and theoretical foundation for the development of intelligence tests.

4 Know the factors that are commonly interpreted using intelligence tests.

5 Understand a recent advancement in intelligence testing— the assessment of processing deficits.

6 Know the various types of intelligence tests (that is, nonverbal and group administered).

7 Understand three commonly used measures of intelligence (WISC-IV, WJ-III NU, and PPVT-IV)

Key Terms

Thurstone

Cattell–Horn–
    Carroll theory

acculturation

processing deficits

nonverbal tests

intelligence factors

Wechsler Intelligence Scale
    for Children–IV
    (WISC-IV)

Woodcock–Johnson III
    Normative Update
    (WJ-III NU)

Peabody Picture Vocabulary
    Test–IV (PPVT-IV)

NO OTHER AREA OF ASSESSMENT HAS GENERATED AS MUCH ATTENTION, controversy, and debate as the testing of what we call "intelligence." For centuries, philosophers, psychologists, educators, and laypeople have debated the meaning of intelligence. Numerous definitions of the term *intelligence* have been proposed, with each definition serving as a stimulus for counterdefinitions and counterproposals. Several theories have been advanced to describe and explain intelligence and its development. Some theorists argue that intelligence is a general ability that enables people to do many different things, whereas other theorists contend that there are multiple intelligences and that people are better at some things than others. Some argue that, for the most part, intelligence is genetically determined (hereditary), inborn, and something you get from your parents. Others contend that intelligence is, for the most part, learned—that it is acquired through experience. Most theorists today recognize the importance of both heredity and experience, including the impact of parental education, parental experience, maternal nutrition, maternal substance abuse, and many other factors. However, most theorists take positions on the relative importance of these factors.

Both the interpretation of group differences in performance on intelligence tests and the practice of testing the intelligence of schoolchildren have been topics of recurrent controversy and debate. In some instances, the courts have acted to curtail or halt intelligence assessment in the public schools; in other cases, the courts have defined what composes intelligence assessment. Debate and controversy have flourished about whether intelligence tests should be given, what they measure, and how different levels of performance attained by different populations are to be explained.

During the past 25 years, there has been a significant decline in the use of intelligence tests in schools as a result of several factors. Teachers and related services personnel have found that knowing the score a student earns on an intelligence test (IQ or mental age) has not been especially helpful in making decisions about specific instructional interventions or teaching approaches to use. It has only provided them with general information about how rapidly to pace instruction. Also, it is argued that scores on intelligence tests too often are used to set low expectations for students, resulting in diminished effort to teach students who earn low scores. This has been the case especially with students who were labeled mentally retarded on the basis of low scores on intelligence tests. In cases in which specific groups of students (such as African American or Hispanic students) have earned lower scores on tests and this has resulted in disproportionate placement of these groups of students in special education or diminished expectations for performance, the courts have found intelligence tests discriminatory and mandated an end to their use.

No one has seen a specific thing called "intelligence." Rather, we observe differences in the ways peop[...] [...]r in a variety of situations or dif[...] [...]timuli; then we attribute those di[...] [...] In this sense, intelligence is an i[...] [...]xplain differences in present beh[...]

We have repeatedly s[...] [...] tests, assess samples of behavio[...] [...]n any given test is viewed and [...] those tests—simply sample beh[...] [...]plings are used to assess intellige[...] [...]reflect a test author's conceptio[...] [...]ned in different ways by differe[...] [...]gence. In this chapter, we revie[...] [...] tests, with emphasis on the psy[...] [...]nction of pupil characteristics. V[...] [...] theorists and test authors hav[...]

In evaluating the pe[...] [...]achers, administrators, counselors, and diagnostic specialists must go beyond test names and scores to examine the kinds of behaviors sampled on the test. They must be willing to question the ways in which test stimuli are presented, to question the response requirements, and to evaluate the psychological demands placed on the individual.

> *[handwritten note:]* Acculturation: An individual's particular set of background experiences and opportunities to learn in both formal & informal educational settings

1 The Effect of Pupil Characteristics on Assessment of Intelligence

Acculturation is the most important characteristic to consider in evaluating performance on intelligence tests. Acculturation refers to an individual's particular set of background experiences and opportunities to learn in both formal and informal educational settings. This, in turn, depends on the person's culture, the experiences available in the person's environment, and the length of time the person has had to assimilate those experiences. The culture in which an individual lives and the length of time the person has lived in that culture may influence the psychological demands presented by a test item. Simply knowing the kind of behavior sampled by a test is not enough because the same test item may create different psychological demands for people undergoing different experiences and acculturation.

Suppose, for example, that we assess intelligence by asking children to tell how hail and sleet are alike. Children may fail the item for very different reasons. Consider Juan (a student who recently moved to the United States from Mexico) and Marcie (a student from Michigan). Juan does not know what hail and sleet are, so he stands little chance of telling how hail and sleet are alike; he will fail the item simply because he does not know the meanings of the words. Marcie may know what hail is and what sleet is, but she fails the item because she is unable to integrate these two words into a conceptual category (precipitation). The psychological demand of the item changes as a function of the children's knowledge. For the child who has not learned the meanings of the words, the item assesses vocabulary. For the child who knows the meanings of the words, the item is a generalization task.

In considering how individuals perform on intelligence tests, we need to know how acculturation affects test performance. Items on intelligence tests range along a continuum from items that sample fundamental psychological behaviors that are relatively unaffected by the test taker's learning history to items that sample primarily learned behavior. To determine exactly what is being assessed, we need to know the essential background of the student. Consider the following item:

> Jeff went walking in the forest. He saw a porcupine that he tried to take home for a pet. It got away from him, but when he got home, his father took him to the doctor. Why?

For a student who knows what a porcupine is, that a porcupine has quills, and that quills are sharp, the item can assess comprehension, abstract reasoning, and problem-solving skill. The student who does not know any of this information may very well fail the item. In this case, failure is due not to an inability to comprehend or solve the problem but to a deficiency in background experience.

Similarly, ...could ask a child to identify the seasons of the year. The experi- ...children's environments are reflected in the way they respond ...dren from central Illinois, who experience four discernibly dif- ...onditions, may well respond "summer, fall, winter, and spring." ...ntral Pennsylvania, who also experience four discernibly differ- ...itions but who live in an environment in which hunting is preva- ...nd "buck season, doe season, small game and fishing." Within ...both responses are logical and appropriate; only one is scored

...elligence tests also sample different behaviors as a function of ...ld assessed. Age and acculturation are positively related: Older ...al have had more opportunities to acquire the skills and cul- ...assessed by intelligence tests. The performances of 5-year-old ...tem requiring them to tell how a cardinal, a blue jay, and a ...e are almost entirely a function of their knowledge of the word ...college students know the meanings of the three words; for ...sesses primarily their ability to identify similarities and to inte- ...objects into a conceptual category. As children get older, they have increasing opportunities to acquire the elements of the collective intelligence of a culture.

The interaction between acculturation and the behavior sampled determines the psychological demands of an intelligence test item. For this reason, it is impossible to define exactly what any one intelligence test would assess for any one student. Identical test items place different psychological demands on different children. Thirteen kinds of behaviors sampled by intelligence tests are described later in this chapter. These types of behavior will vary in their psychological demands based on the test taker's experience and acculturation. Given the great number of potential questions that could be asked for each type of question as well as the number of combinations of question types, the number of questions is practically infinite.

Used appropriately, intelligence tests can provide information that can lead to the enhancement of both individual opportunity and protection of the rights of students. Used inappropriately, they can restrict opportunity and rights.

Given the examples of possible misuses of intelligence test, how does a psychologist determine if the intelligence test being used is appropriate for the student?

The Importance of Acculturation

Xong was born in Laos and eventually she and her family were moved to a refugee camp in the Philippines. When she was 10 years old, Xong left the Philippines with her mother and sister as part of a group brought to the United States by the Lutheran Church. She moved to a suburb of Minneapolis, and Xong was enrolled immediately in an elementary school. Due to her age and size, she was placed in the third grade. There were no other Laotian children in the school; Xong and her sister were not presented with a bilingual or English language learner program option but were placed in classrooms with English-speaking teachers and students. As the year went by, Xong's teacher became increasingly alarmed at the child's lack of progress in picking up English and academic skills. Xong's younger sister was becoming quite chatty. She could count, identify letters, and write her first name. A referral was made to the child study team. The consensus of the group was that Xong was developmentally delayed and performing substantially less well than school personnel had hoped—certainly if one compared her progress to that shown by her sister. Psychological testing seemed in order to confirm the group's suspicions. Due process procedures were followed. An interpreter discussed parental rights with Xong's mother and had her sign for permission to assess.

During the assessment process, the psychologist felt challenged in attempting to do a good assessment. She tried using an interpreter, but verbal items were outside of Xong's cultural experience. She tried using nonverbal subtests, but they still were not culturally appropriate. The psychologist administered the Nebraska Test of Learning Aptitude, a test that is given to deaf students and requires only pantomime directions. This test was used more to gain qualitative insight into Xong's performance; actual scores were not meaningful because the test is normed on deaf students. The psychologist also administered the Leiter International Performance Scale, a test requiring no verbal directions or response, and Xong earned a score in the mildly deficient range. An adaptive behavior scale was administered—both the teacher and the parent versions. Then, although not totally comfortable with the test results, the psychologist assembled the multidisciplinary individualized educational program (IEP) team.

Although the IEP conference complied with all state and federal guidelines and appropriate procedures were followed (that is, an interpreter was present, introductions were made, and assessment data were shared), the school psychologist remained somewhat concerned that slow English language development rather than true intellectual deficits was contributing to Xong's academic difficulties. Nevertheless, the team agreed (and enough data were present) to consider Xong as showing signs of mental retardation. Acceptable levels of performance, goals, and short-term objectives were agreed upon. Program recommendations were made and forms signed. As a result of the meeting, Xong was placed in a class with fewer students. She was not aware of the fact that it was a class for students who are mentally retarded. She did realize that less was expected of her as a student.

If Xong had participated in a program designed to foster English language development, and data had been collected on her response to this programming, the team may have been in a better position to know whether her delays were based on the need for greater emphasis on her English or true intellectual deficits. They may have also identified what types of support would be needed for her to make academic progress.

2 Behaviors Sampled by Intelligence Tests

Regardless of the interpretation of measured intelligence, it is a fact that intelligence tests simply sample behaviors. This section describes the kinds of behaviors sampled, including discrimination, generalization, motor behavior, general knowledge, vocabulary, induction, comprehension, sequencing, detail recognition, analogical reasoning, pattern completion, abstract reasoning, and memory.

Discrimination

Intelligence test items that sample skill in discrimination usually present a variety of stimuli and ask the student to find the one that differs from all the others. Figure 14.1 illustrates items assessing discrimination: Items a and b assess discrimination of figures, items c and d assess symbolic discrimination, and items e and f assess semantic discrimination. In each case, the student must identify the item that differs from the others.

Generalization

Items assessing generalization present a stimulus and ask the student to identify which of several response possibilities goes with the stimulus. Figure 14.2 illustrates several items assessing generalization. In each case, the student is given a stimulus element and is required to identify the one that is like it or that goes with it.

FIGURE 14.1
Items That Assess Figural, Symbolic, and Semantic Discrimination

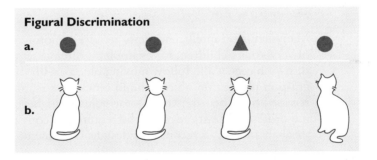

FIGURE 14.2
Items That Assess Figural,
Symbolic, and Semantic
Generalization

Figural Generalization

a.

b.

Symbolic Generalization

c.	J	H	8	6	9
d.	81	21	23	26	25

Semantic Generalization

e.	tree	car	man	horse	walk
f.	salvia	flashlight	frog	tulip	banana

Motor Behavior

Many items on intelligence tests require a motor response. The intellectual level of very young children, for example, is often assessed by items requiring them to throw objects, walk, follow moving objects with their eyes, demonstrate a pincer grasp in picking up objects, build block towers, and place geometric forms in a recessed-form board. Most motor items at higher age levels are actually visual–motor items. The student may be required to copy geometric designs, trace paths through a maze, or reconstruct designs from memory.

General Knowledge

Items on intelligence tests sometimes require a student to answer specific factual questions, such as "In what direction would you travel if you were to go from Poland to Argentina?" and "What is the cube root of 8?" Essentially, such items are like the kinds of items in achievement tests; they assess primarily what has been learned.

Vocabulary

Many different kinds of test items are used to assess vocabulary. In some cases, the student must name pictures, and in others he or she must point to objects in response to words read by the examiner. Some vocabulary items require the student to produce oral definitions of words, whereas others call for reading a definition and selecting one of several words to match the definition.

Induction

Induction items present a series of examples and require the student to induce a governing principle. For example, the student is given a magnet and several different cloth, wooden, and metal objects and is asked to try to pick up the objects with the magnet. After several trials, the student is asked to state a rule or principle about the kinds of objects that magnets can pick up.

Comprehension

There are three kinds of items used to assess comprehension: items related to directions, to printed material, and to societal customs and mores. In some instances, the examiner presents a specific situation and asks what actions the student would take (for example, "What would you do if you saw a train approaching a washed-out bridge?"). In other cases, the examiner reads paragraphs to a student and then asks specific questions about the content of the paragraphs. In still other instances, the student is asked questions about social mores, such as "Why should we keep promises?"

Sequencing

Items assessing sequencing consist of a series of stimuli that have a progressive relationship among them. The student must identify a response that continues the relationship. Four sequencing items are illustrated in Figure 14.3.

Detail Recognition

In general, not many tests or test items assess detail recognition. Those that do evaluate the completeness and detail with which a student solves problems. For instance, items may require a student to count the blocks in pictured piles of blocks in which some of the blocks are not directly visible, to copy geometric designs, or to identify missing parts in pictures. To do so correctly, the student must attend to detail in the stimulus drawings and must reflect this attention to detail in making responses.

Analogical Reasoning

"A is to B as C is to _____" is the usual form for analogies. Element A is related to element B. The student must identify the response having the same relationship to element C as B has to A. Figure 14.4 illustrates several different analogy items.

FIGURE 14.3
Items That Assess
Sequencing Skill

FIGURE 14.4
Analogy Items

Pattern Completion

Some tests and test items require a student to select from several possibilities the missing part of a pattern or matrix. Figures 14.5 and 14.6 illustrate two different completion items. The item in Figure 14.5 requires identification of a missing part in a pattern. The item in Figure 14.6 calls for identification of the response that completes the matrix by continuing both the triangle, circle, rectangle sequence and the solid, striped, and clear sequence.

Abstract Reasoning

A variety of items on intelligence tests sample abstract reasoning ability. The Stanford–Binet Intelligence Scale, for example, presents absurd verbal statements and pictures and asks the student to identify the absurdity. In the Stanford–Binet and other scales, arithmetic reasoning problems are often thought to assess abstract reasoning.

FIGURE 14.5
A Pattern Completion Item

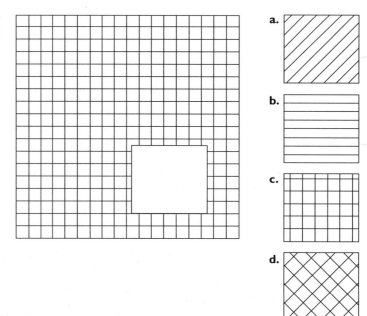

FIGURE 14.6
A Matrix Completion Item

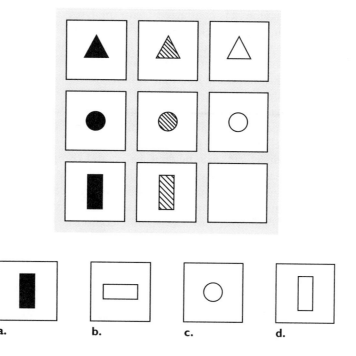

Memory

Several different kinds of tasks assess memory: repetition of sequences of digits presented orally, reproduction of geometric designs from memory, verbatim repetition of sentences, and reconstruction of the essential meaning of paragraphs or stories. Simply saying that an item assesses memory is too simplistic. We need to ask: Memory for what? The psychological demand of a memory task changes in relation to both the method of assessment and the meaningfulness of the material to be recalled.

3 Factors Underlying Intelligence Test Behaviors

Early in the study of intelligence, it became apparent that the behaviors used to assess intelligence were highly related to one another. Charles Spearman, an early twentieth-century psychologist, demonstrated that a single statistical factor could explain the high degree of intercorrelation among the behaviors. He named this single factor *general intelligence* (*g*). Although he noted that performance on different tasks was influenced by other specific intelligence factors, he argued that knowing a person's level of *g* could greatly improve predictions of performance on a variety of tasks. Today, nearly every intelligence test allows for the calculation of an overall test score that is frequently considered indicative of an individual's level of *g* in comparison to same-age peers.

Later, it became clear that different factor structures would emerge depending on the variables analyzed and the statistical procedures used. Thurstone (1941) proposed an alternative interpretation of the correlations among intelligence test behaviors. He conducted factor analyses of several tests of intelligence and perception, and he concluded that there exist seven different intelligences that he called "primary mental abilities": verbal comprehension, word fluency, number, space, associative memory, perceptual speed, and reasoning. Although Thurstone recognized that these different abilities were often positively correlated, he emphasized multiplicity rather than unity within the construct of intelligence. This approach to interpreting intellectual performance was further expanded by Raymond Cattell and associates. Cattell suggested the existence of two primary intelligence factors: fluid intelligence and crystallized intelligence. *Fluid intelligence* refers to the efficiency with which an individual learns and completes various tasks. This type of intelligence increases as a person ages until early adulthood and then decreases somewhat steadily over time. *Crystallized intelligence* represents the knowledge and skill one acquires over time and increases steadily throughout one's life. Several current tests of intelligence provide separate composite scores for behaviors that are representative of fluid and crystallized intelligence. The fluid intelligence score might represent performance on tasks such as memorizing and later recalling names of symbols or recalling unrelated words presented in a particular sequence. A crystallized intelligence score might represent performance on items that measure vocabulary or general knowledge. James Horn and John Carroll expanded on this theory to include additional intelligence factors, now called the Cattell–Horn–Carroll (CHC) theory. These factors include general memory and learning, broad visual perception, broad auditory perception, broad retrieval ability, broad cognitive speediness, and decision/reaction time/speed. This is the theory on which the Woodcock–Johnson III Tests of Cognitive Abilities is based.

4 Commonly Interpreted Factors on Intelligence Tests

Educational professionals will encounter many different terms that describe various intelligence test factors, clusters, indexes, and processes. We describe several common (and overlapping) terms in Table 14.1.

5 Assessment of Processing Deficits

People have become increasingly intrigued with the possibility of identifying specific cognitive processing deficits that contribute to a student's academic difficulties. Some current conceptualizations of learning disabilities include cognitive processing deficits as a defining characteristic. Test developers have begun to develop specific tests that are intended to measure particular weaknesses that students might have in processing information. For instance, there is now a supplemental instrument to the Wechsler Intelligence Scale for Children–IV (WISC-IV) called the WISC-IV Integrated. This supplemental material, which includes a variety of additional subtests that allow for the comparison of student performance across a variety of conditions, is intended to facilitate the identification of specific processing deficits. The Woodcock–Johnson III Tests of Cognitive Abilities includes a related vehicle for test score interpretation, whereby one can analyze student performance according to an information processing model.

| TABLE 14.1 | | Common Intelligence Test Terms, Associated Theorists and Tests, and Examples of Associated Behaviors Sampled | | | | |

Term	Definition	Theorists[a]	Tests	Example of a Behavior Sampled	Source of Information Obtained
Attention	Alertness	Das, Naglieri	CAS, WJ-III	When given a target figure and many distracting stimuli, the individual must quickly select those that are identical to the target figure.	www.riverpub .com/products/ cas/cas_pass .html
Auditory perception/ processing	Ability to analyze, manipulate, and discriminate sounds	Cattell, Horn, Carroll	WJ-III	When given a set of pictures and listening to a recording in which a spoken word is presented along with noise distractions, the individual must select the picture that goes with the spoken word.	*WJ-III Examiner's Manual*
Cognitive efficiency/ speediness	Ability to process information quickly and automatically	Carroll	WJ-III	When given several figures, the individual must quickly select the two that are most alike.	*WJ-III Examiner's Manual*
Cognitive fluency	Speed in completing cognitive tasks		WJ-III	When given a set of pictures, the individual must quickly say the names of the pictures.	*WJ-III Examiner's Manual*
Comprehension knowledge	Term used on the WJ-III to describe crystallized intelligence	Cattell, Horn, Carroll	WJ-III	When shown various pictures, the individual must provide the names for the pictures.	*WJ-III Examiner's Manual*
Executive processing	Use of higher level thinking strategies to organize thought and behavior		WJ-III	When given a maze to complete, the individual must complete the maze correctly without mistakes on the first try.	*WJ-III Examiner's Manual*
Fluid reasoning/ intelligence	Efficiency with which an individual learns and completes various tasks	Cattell, Horn, Carroll	WJ-III	When given a set of simple relationships or rules among symbols, the individual must apply the rules to correctly identify missing links within increasingly complicated patterns.	*WJ-III Examiner's Manual*
Long-term retrieval/delayed recall	Ability to store and easily recall information at a much later point in time	Cattell, Horn, Carroll	WJ-III	Two days after an individual was taught the words associated with certain symbols, the symbol is presented and the individual must recall the associated words.	*WJ-III Examiner's Manual*

continued on the next page

TABLE 14.1   Common Intelligence Test Terms, Associated Theorists and Tests, and Examples of Associated Behaviors Sampled, *continued*

Term	Definition	Theorists[a]	Tests	Example of a Behavior Sampled	Source of Information Obtained
Perceptual reasoning	Ability to identify and form patterns		WISC-IV	When given a pattern and various colored blocks, the individual must form the blocks in the shape of the given pattern.	*WISC-IV Technical and Interpretive Manual*
Planning	Ability to identify effective strategies to reach a particular goal	Das, Naglieri	CAS	When given multiple numbers, the individual must select the two that are the same.	http://www.riverpub.com/products/cas/cas_pass.html
Processing speed	Ability to quickly complete tasks that require limited complex thought	Cattell, Horn, Carroll	WJ-III, WISC-IV	The individual is presented with a key for converting numbers to symbols and must quickly write down the associated symbols for numbers that are presented.	*WISC-IV Technical and Interpretive Manual*
Quantitative knowledge	Mathematical knowledge and achievement	Cattell, Horn	WJ-III	The individual must answer math word problems correctly.	*WJ-III Examiner's Manual*
Short-term memory or working memory	Ability to quickly store and then immediately retrieve information within a short period of time	Cattell, Horn	WISC-IV, WJ-III	The examiner says several numbers, and the individual must repeat them accurately and in the same order.	*WISC-IV Technical and Interpretive Manual*
Simultaneous processing	Extent to which one can integrate pieces of information into a complete pattern	Das, Naglieri	CAS	When asked a question verbally and presented with figures, the individual must pick the figure that answers the question.	http://www.riverpub.com/products/cas/cas_pass.html
Speed of lexical access	Fluency with which one can recall pronunciations of words, word parts, and letters	Carroll	WJ-III	When given many pictures, the individual must say the picture names as quickly as possible.	*WJ-III Examiner's Manual*
Successive processing	Extent to which one can recall things presented in a particular order	Das, Naglieri	CAS	When given a set of words, the individual must repeat them back in the same order.	http://www.riverpub.com/products/cas/cas_pass.html
Thinking ability	Composite cluster within the WJ-III that is composed of performance on several less automatic cognitive tasks		WJ-III	This includes tasks associated with long-term retrieval, visual–spatial thinking, auditory processing, and fluid reasoning (see task examples for these terms in this table).	*WJ-III Technical Manual*

Term	Definition	Theorists[a]	Tests	Example of a Behavior Sampled	Source of Information Obtained
Verbal ability	Composite cluster within the WJ-III that is composed of language tasks		WJ-III	This includes tasks associated with comprehension/ knowledge (see task example for this term above).	*WJ-III Technical Manual*
Verbal comprehension	"Verbal abilities utilizing reasoning, comprehension, and conceptualization" (p. 6)		WISC-IV	The individual must verbally express how two things are similar.	*WISC-IV Technical and Interpretive Manual*
Visual perception/ processing	Integrating and interpreting visual information	Cattell, Horn, Carroll	†	When presented only part of an image, the individual must identify what the entire image is.	*WJ-III Examiner's Manual*
Visual–spatial thinking	Ability to store and manipulate visual images in one's mind		WJ-III	A picture is briefly shown and removed; the individual must then select the originally shown picture from a set of additional pictures.	*WJ-III Technical Manual*

[a]There are often many theorists, researchers, and tests associated with a given intelligence term; we provide here just one or two individuals who were key in defining these terms and tests that involve measurement of behaviors associated with these terms.
†No test we reviewed specifically includes this as an index or factor, but it is a factor in CHC theory and is associated with many tasks included on intelligence tests.
CAS, Cognitive Assessment System; WISC-IV, Wechsler Intelligence Scale for Children–IV; WJ-III, Woodcock–Johnson III.

6 Types of Intelligence Tests

Depending on what types of decisions are being made, as well as the specific characteristics of the student, different types of intelligence tests might be selected for administration. We describe three different types in the following sections.

Individual Tests

Individually administered intelligence tests are most frequently used for making exceptionality, eligibility, and educational placement decisions. State special education eligibility guidelines and criteria typically specify that the collection of data about intellectual functioning must be included in the decision-making process for eligibility and placement decisions, and that these data must come from individual intellectual evaluation by a certified school psychologist.

Group Tests

Group-administered intelligence tests are used for one of two purposes: as screening devices for individual students or as sources of descriptive information about groups of students. Most often, they are administered as screening devices to identify those students who differ enough from average to warrant further

When a student, new to the States and an ELL student and for some reason they need an intelligence test. B their a certain amount of time that needs to laps from them starting schal or is it better to test right away?

...ses, the tests' merit is that teachers can administer them [larg]e numbers of students. The tests suffer from the same lim[i]t: They can be made to yield qualitative information only [...] require students to sit still for approximately 20 minutes, [...]nd, often, to read. During the past 25 years, it has become [...]r school districts to eliminate the practice of group intel[...] [a]dministrators are asked why they are doing so, they cite [...]e of knowing about students' capability, as opposed to [...subj]ect matter skills (such as for reading and math) that stu[...] (2) the difficulty teachers experience in trying to use the [...]nal purposes; and (3) the cost of a schoolwide intellectual

[...] Tests

[...] tests are among the most widely used tests for assessment of intelligence, particularly when there are questions about the intelligence of a child who is not proficient in English or who is deaf. Some nonverbal tests are designed to measure intelligence broadly; others are called "picture–vocabulary tests." The latter are not measures of intelligence per se; rather, they measure only one aspect of intelligence—receptive vocabulary. In picture–vocabulary tests, pictures are presented to the test taker, who is asked to identify those pictures that correspond to words read by the examiner. Some authors of picture–vocabulary measures state that the tests measure receptive vocabulary; others equate receptive vocabulary with intelligence and claim that their tests assess intelligence. Because the tests measure only one aspect of intelligence, they should not be used to make eligibility decisions.

ASSESSMENT OF INTELLIGENCE: COMMONLY USED TESTS

In this section, we provide information on some of the most commonly used intelligence tests. Table 14.2 provides information on other intelligence tests that you may come across in educational settings; more extensive reviews of these tests are available on the website. Following the table, we also provide more detailed reviews of several intelligence tests, with special reference to the kinds of behaviors they sample and to their technical adequacy. Although some individual intelligence tests may be appropriately administered by teachers, counselors, or other specialists, the intelligence tests on which school personnel rely most heavily must be given by psychologists.

Wechsler Intelligence Scale for Children–IV

The Wechsler Intelligence Scale for Children–IV (WISC-IV; Wechsler, 2003)[1] is the latest version of the WISC and is designed to assess the cognitive ability

[1]The WISC-IV is also available as the WISC-IV Integrated (Kaplan, Fein, Kramer, Morris, Delis, & Maerlender, 2004). The WISC-IV Integrated is composed of the core and supplemental subtests of the WISC-IV plus 16 additional process-oriented subtests. The WISC-IV Integrated is a clinical instrument that, in our opinion, has limited application to school settings. The process-oriented subtests of the WISC-IV Integrated do not have sufficient reliability to be used to make decisions in school settings. The 16 process-oriented subtests are in addition to the core and supplemental subtests, and they can not be substituted for core or supplemental subtests.

TABLE 14.2				Commonly Used Intelligence Tests			
Test	**Author**	**Publisher**	**Year**	**Ages/ Grades**	**Individual/ Group**	**NRT/ SRT/ CRT**	**Subtests**
Cognitive Abilities Test (CogAT)	Lohman & Hagan	Riverside	2001	Grades K–12	Group	NRT	Oral Vocabulary, Verbal Reasoning, Quantitative Concepts, Relational Concepts, Matrices, Figure Classification, Sentence Completion, Verbal Classification, Verbal Analogies, Quantitative Relations, Number Series, Equation Building, Figure Classification, Figure Analogies, Figure Analysis
Cognitive Assessment System	Das & Naglieri	Riverside	1997	Ages 5 to 17-11 years	Individual	NRT	Matching Numbers, Planned Codes, Planned Connections, Nonverbal Matrices, Verbal–Spatial Relations, Figure Memory, Expressive Attention, Number Detection, Receptive Attention, Word Series, Sentence Repetition, Speech Rate, Sentence Questions
Comprehensive Test of Nonverbal Intelligence (C-TONI)	Hammill, Pearson, & Wiederholt	Pro-Ed	1997	Ages 6 to 18-11 years	Individual	NRT	Pictorial Analogies, Geometric Analogies, Pictorial Categories, Geometric Categories, Pictorial Sequences, Geometric Sequences
Detroit Tests of Learning Aptitude, Fourth Edition (DTLA-4)	Hammill	Pro-Ed	1998	Ages 6 to 17-11 years	Individual	NRT	Word Opposites, Design Sequences, Sentence Imitation, Reversed Letters, Story Construction, Design Reproduction, Basic Information, Symbolic Relations, Word Sequences, Story Sequences
Kaufman Assessment Battery for Children, Second Edition (KABC-2)	Kaufman & Kaufman	Pearson	2004	Ages 3-18 years	Individual	NRT	Triangles, Face Recognition, Pattern Reasoning, Block Counting, Story Completion, Conceptual Thinking, Rover, Gestalt Closure, Word Order, Number Recall, Hand Movements, Atlantis, Atlantis-Delayed, Rebus, Rebus-Delayed, Riddles, Expressive Vocabulary, Verbal Knowledge
Leiter International Performance Scale–Revised	Roid & Miller	Stoelting	1997	Ages 2 to 20-11 years	Individual	NRT	Classification, Sequencing, Repeated Patterns, Design Analogies, Matching, Figure-Ground, Form Completion, Picture Context, Paper Folding, Figure Rotation, Immediate Recognition, Delayed Recognition, Associated Pairs, Delayed Pairs, Forward Memory, Reversed Memory, Spatial Memory, Visual Coding, Attention Sustained, Attention Divided

continued on the next page

TABLE 14.2							

Commonly Used Intelligence Tests, *continued*

Test	Author	Publisher	Year	Ages/ Grades	Individual/ Group	NRT/ SRT/ CRT	Subtests
Otis–Lennon School Ability Test, Eighth Edition (OLSAT-8)	Harcourt Educational Measurement	Pearson	2003	Grades K–12	Group	NRT	Verbal Comprehension, Verbal Reasoning, Pictorial Reasoning, Figural Reasoning, Quantitative Reasoning
Peabody Picture Vocabulary Test–IV	Dunn & Dunn	Pearson	2007	Ages 2-6 to 90+ years	Individual	NRT	Not applicable
Test of Nonverbal Intelligence–3	Brown, Sherbenou, & Johnsen	Pro-Ed	1997	Ages 5 to 85-11 years	Individual	NRT	Matching, Analogies, Classification, Intersections, Progressions
Stanford–Binet Intelligence Scale, Fifth Edition	Roid	Riverside	2003	Ages 2-85+ years	Individual	NRT	Object Series/Matrices, Early Reasoning, Verbal Absurdities, Verbal Analogies, Procedural Knowledge, Picture Absurdities, Vocabulary, Quantitative Reasoning, Form Board, Form Patterns, Position and Direction, Delayed Response, Block Span, Memory for Sentences, Last Word
Universal Nonverbal Intelligence Test (UNIT)	Bracken & McCallem	Riverside	1996	Ages 5 to 17-11 years	Individual	NRT	Symbolic Memory, Object Memory, Analogic Reasoning, Spatial Memory, Cube Design, Mazes
Wechsler Intelligence Scale for Children–IV (WISC-IV)	Wechsler	Pearson	2003	Ages 6 to 16-11 years	Individual	NRT	Similarities, Vocabulary, Comprehension, Information, Word Reasoning, Block Design, Picture Concepts, Matrix Reasoning, Picture Completion, Digit Span, Letter–Number Sequencing, Arithmetic, Coding, Symbol Search, Cancellation
Wechsler Preschool and Primary Scale of Intelligence–III (WPPSI-III)	Wechsler	Pearson	2002	Ages 2-6 to 7-3 years	Individual	NRT	Information, Vocabulary, Word Reasoning, Receptive Vocabulary, Picture Naming, Comprehension, Similarities, Block Design, Object Assembly, Matrix Reasoning, Picture Concepts, Picture Completion, Coding, Symbol Search

Test	Author	Publisher	Year	Ages/ Grades	Individual/ Group	NRT/ SRT/ CRT	Subtests
Woodcock–Johnson III Tests of Cognitive Abilities (WJ-III)	Woodcock, McGrew, & Mather	Riverside	2001	Ages 2–90+ years	Individual	NRT	Verbal Comprehension, Visual–Auditory Learning, Visual–Auditory Learning–Delayed, Spatial Relations, Sound Blending, Incomplete Words, Concept Formation, Visual Matching, Numbers Reversed, Auditory Working Memory, General Information, Retrieval Fluency, Picture Recognition, Planning, Auditory Attention, Analysis-Synthesis, Planning, Decision Speed, Rapid Picture Naming, Pair Cancellation, Memory for Words

and problem-solving processes of individuals ranging in age from 6 years 0 months to 16 years 11 months.

Developed by David Wechsler in 1949, the WISC adapted the 11 subtests found in the original Wechsler Scale, the Wechsler–Bellevue Intelligence Scale (1939), for use with children, and added the Mazes subtest. In 1974, the Wechsler Intelligence Scale for Children–Revised (WISC-R) was developed. This revision retained the 12 subtests found in the original WISC but altered the age range from 5 to 15 years to 6 to 16 years. The Wechsler Intelligence Scale for Children–III (WISC-III) was developed in 1991. This scale retained the 12 subtests and added a new subtest, Symbol Search. Previous editions of the WISC provided verbal IQ, performance IQ, and full-scale IQ scores. The WISC-III maintained this tradition but introduced four new index scores: Verbal Comprehension Index (VCI), Perceptual Organization Index (POI), Freedom from Distractibility Index (FDI), and Processing Speed Index (PSI).

The WISC-IV provides a new scoring framework while maintaining the theory of intelligence underlying the previous scales. This theory was summarized by Wechsler when he stated that "intelligence is the overall capacity of an individual to understand and cope with the world around him" (Wechsler, 1974, p. 5). The definition is consistent with his original one,

in which he stated that intelligence is "the capacity of the individual to act purposefully, to think rationally, and to deal effectively with his or her environment" (Wechsler, 1974, p. 3).

Based on the premise that intelligence is both global (characterizing an individual's behavior as a whole) and specific (composed of distinct elements) (Wechsler, 2004, p. 2), the WISC-IV measures overall global intelligence, as well as discrete domains of cognitive functioning.

The WISC-IV presents a new scoring framework. Unlike its predecessors, it does not provide verbal and performance IQ scores. However, it maintains both the full-scale IQ (FSIQ) as a measure of general intellectual functioning and the four index scores as measures of specific cognitive domains. The WISC-IV developed new terminology for the four index scores in order to more accurately reflect the cognitive abilities measured by the subtest composition of each index. The four indexes are the VCI, the Perceptual Reasoning Index (PRI), the Working Memory Index (WMI), and the PSI. A description of the subtests that comprise each index is provided next. Subtests can be categorized as either core or supplemental. Core subtests provide composite scores. Supplemental subtests (indicated by a "*") provide additional clinical information and can be used as substitutes for core subtests. Those familiar with the WISC-III will note that in the WISC-IV revisions, 3 subtests have been dropped, 10 subtests have been retained, and 5 subtests have been added (indicated with an asterisk).

Subtests

Verbal Comprehension Subtests

Similarities. This subtest requires identification of similarities or commonalities in superficially unrelated verbal stimuli.

Vocabulary. Items on this subtest assess ability to define words. Beginning items require individuals to name picture objects. Later items require individuals to verbally define words that are read aloud by the examiner.

Comprehension. This subtest assesses ability to comprehend verbal directions or to understand specific customs and mores. The examinee is asked questions such as "Why is it important to wear boots after a large snowfall?"

Information. This subtest assesses ability to answer specific factual questions. The content is learned; it consists of information that a person is expected to have acquired in both formal and informal educational settings. The examinee is asked questions such as "Which fast-food franchise is represented by the symbol of golden arches?"

Word Reasoning*. In this subtest, individuals are presented with a clue or a series of clues and must identify the common concept that each clue or group of clues describes. It is thought to measure comprehension, identification of analogies, generalization, and verbal abstraction. A sample item for this scale is "This has a long handle and is used with water to clean the floor" (mop). When partially correct responses are given, additional clues are provided.

Perceptual Reasoning Subtests

Block Design. In this subtest, individuals are given a specified amount of time to manipulate blocks in order to reproduce a stimulus design that is presented visually.

Picture Concepts*. In this subtest, an individual is shown two or three rows of pictures and must choose one picture from each row in order to form a group that shares a common characteristic. For example, an individual would choose the picture of the horse in row 1 and the picture of the mouse in row 2 because they are both animals. This is basically a picture classification task.

Matrix Reasoning*. In this subtest, children must select the missing portion of an incomplete matrix given five response options. Matrices range from 2×2 to 3×3. The last item differs from this general form, requiring individuals to identify the fifth square in a row of six.

Picture Completion. This subtest assesses the ability to identify missing parts in pictures within a specified time limit.

Working Memory Subtests

Digit Span. This subtest assesses immediate recall of orally presented digits. In Digit Span Forward, children repeat numbers in the same order that they were presented aloud by the examiner. In Digit Span Backward, children repeat numbers in the reverse of the order that they were presented by the examiner.

Letter–Number Sequencing*. This subtest assesses an individual's ability to recall and mentally manipulate a series of numbers and letters that are orally presented to them. After hearing a random sequence of numbers and letters, individuals must first repeat the numbers in ascending order and then repeat the letters in alphabetical order.

Arithmetic. This subtest assesses ability to solve problems requiring the application of arithmetic operations. In this subtest, children must mentally solve problems presented orally within a specified time limit.

Processing Speed Subtests

Coding. This subtest assesses the ability to associate symbols with either geometric shapes or numbers and to copy these symbols onto paper within a specified time limit.

Symbol Search. This subtest consists of a series of paired groups of symbols, with each pair including a target group and a search group. The child scans the two groups and indicates whether the target symbols appear in the search group within a specified time limit.

Cancellation*. In this subtest, individuals are presented with first a random and then a structured arrangement of pictures. For both arrangements, individuals must mark the target pictures within the specified time limit.

Scores

Subtest raw scores obtained on the WISC-IV are transformed to scaled scores with a mean of 10 and a standard deviation of 3. The scaled scores for 3 Verbal Comprehension subtests, 3 Perceptual Reasoning subtests, 2 Working Memory subtests, 2 Processing Speed subtests, and all 10 subtests are added and then transformed to obtain the composite VCI, PRI, WMI, PSI, and FSIQ scores, respectively. IQs for Wechsler scales are deviation IQs with a mean of 100 and a standard deviation of 15. Tables are provided for converting the subtest scaled scores and composite scores to percentile ranks and confidence intervals. Raw scores may also be transformed to test ages that represent the average performance on each of the subtests by individuals of specific ages. Seven process scores can also be derived. Process scores are "designed to provide more detailed information on the cognitive abilities that contribute to a child's subtest performance" (Wechsler, 2004, p. 107). The WISC-IV provides for subtest, index, and process score discrepancy comparisons. Tables provide the difference scores needed in order to be considered statistically significant at the .15 and .05 confidence level for each age group, and they also provide information on the percentage of children in the standardization sample who obtained the same or a greater discrepancy between scores.

The WISC-IV employs a differential scoring system for some of the subtests. Responses for the Digit Span, Picture Concepts, Letter–Number Sequencing, Matrix Reasoning, Picture Completion, Information, and Word Reasoning subtests are scored pass–fail. A weighted scoring system is used for the Similarities, Vocabulary, and Comprehension subtests. Incorrect responses receive a score of 0, lower level or lower quality responses are assigned a score of 1, and more abstract responses are assigned a score of 2. The remainder of the subtests are timed. Individuals who complete the tasks in shorter periods of time receive more credit. These differential weightings of responses must be given special consideration, especially when the timed tests are used with children who demonstrate motor impairments that interfere with the speed of response.

Norms

The WISC-IV was standardized on 2,200 children ages 6-0 to 16-11 years. This age range was divided into 11 whole-year groups (for example, 6-0 to 6-11). All groups had 200 participants. The standardization group was stratified on the basis of age, sex, race/ethnicity (whites, African Americans, Hispanics, Asians, and others), parent education level (based on number of years and degree held), and geographic region (Northeast, South, Midwest, and West), according to 2000 U.S. census information. A representative sample of children from the special group studies (such as children with learning disorders, children identified as gifted, children with attention deficit hyperactivity disorder, and so on) conducted during the national tryout was included in the normative sample (approximately 5.7 percent) in order to accurately represent the population of children enrolled in school. Extensive tables in the manual are used to compare sample data with census data. These tables are stratified across the following characteristics: (1) age, race/ethnicity, and parent education level; (2) age, sex, and parent education level; (3) age, sex, and race/ethnicity; and (4) age, race/ethnicity, and geographic region. Overall, the samples appear representative of the U.S. population of children across the stratified variables.

Reliability

Because the Coding, Symbol Search, and Cancellation subtests are timed, reliability estimates for these subtests are based on test–retest coefficients. However, split-half reliability coefficient alphas corrected by the Spearman–Brown formula are reported for all the remaining subtest and composite scores. Moreover, standard errors of measurement (SEMs) are reported for all scores. Scores are reported for each age group and as an average across all age groups. As would be expected, subtest reliabilities (overall averages range from .79 to .90; age levels range from .72 to .94) are lower than index reliabilities (overall averages range from .88 to .94; age levels range from .81 to .95). Reliabilities for the full-scale IQ are excellent, with age-level coefficient alphas ranging from .96 to .97.

Test–retest stability data were collected on a sample of 243 children. These data were calculated for five age groups (6 to 7, 8 to 9, 10 to 11, 12 to 13, and 14 to 16) using Pearson's product–moment correlation. Scores for the overall sample were calculated using Fisher's z-transformation. Stability coefficients[2] are provided for each subtest, process, index, and IQ. Stability coefficients for the FSIQ among these five groups ranged from .91 to .96. Process stabilities ranged from .64 to .83. Index stabilities ranged from .84 (Working Memory, ages 8 to 9) to .95 (Verbal Comprehension, ages 14 to 16), and subtest stability correlations ranged from .71 (Picture Concepts, ages 6 to 7; Cancellation, ages 8 to 9) to .95 (Vocabulary, ages 14 to 16).

The full-scale IQ and index scores are reliable enough to be used to make important educational decisions. The subtests and process indicators are not sufficiently reliable to be used in making these important decisions.

Validity

The authors present evidence for validity based on four areas: test content, response processes, internal structure, and relationship to other variables. In terms of test content, they emphasize the extensive revision process, based on comprehensive literature and expert reviews, which was used to select items and subtests that would adequately sample the domains of intellectual functioning they sought to measure.

Evidence for appropriate response processes (child's cognitive process during subtest task) is based on (1) prior research that supports retained subtests and (2) literature reviews, expert opinion, and empirical examinations that support the new subtests. Furthermore, during development, the authors

engaged in empirical (for instance, response frequencies conducted to identify incorrect answers that occurred frequently) and qualitative (for instance, directly questioned students regarding their use of problem-solving strategies) examination of response processes and made adjustments accordingly.

In terms of internal structure, evidence of convergent and discriminant validity is provided based on the correlations between subtests using Fisher's z-transformation. All subtests were found to significantly correlate with one another, as would be expected considering that they all presumably measure g (general intelligence). Moreover, subtests that contribute to the same index score (VC, PR, WM, or PS) were generally found to highly correlate with one another.

Further evidence of internal structure is presented through both exploratory and confirmatory factor analysis. Exploratory factor analysis was conducted on two samples. Support for the four-factor structure and the stability of index scores across samples was found in cross-validation analysis. Moreover, confirmatory factor analysis using structural equation modeling and three goodness-of-fit measures confirmed that the four-factor model provided the best fit for the data.

In terms of relationships with other variables, evidence is provided based on correlations between WISC-IV and other Wechsler measures. The WISC-IV FSIQ score was correlated with the full-scale IQ or achievement measures from other Wechsler scales. The correlations are as follows: WISC-III, $r = .89$; WPPSI-III, $r = .89$; Wechsler Adult Intelligence Scale–III (WAIS-III), $r = .89$; Wechsler Abbreviated Scale of Intelligence (WASI), $r = .83$ (with FSIQ-4 measure) and $r = .86$ (with FSIQ-2 measure); and Wechsler Individual Achievement Test–II (WIAT-II), $r = .87$. Correlations were made with a set of specific intellectual measures, such as the Children's Memory Scale (CMS), Gifted Rating Scale–School Form (GRS-S), Bar On Emotional Quotient Inventory: Youth Edition (Bar On EQ), Adaptive Behavior Assessment System–II–Parent Form (ABAS-II-P), and Adaptive Behavior Assessment System–II–Teacher Form (ABAS-II-T). Correlations were very low (ranging from −.01 to .72). There is no evidence of the predictive validity of the WISC-IV.

The authors conclude by presenting special group studies that they conducted during standardization in order to examine the clinical utility of the WISC-IV. They note the following four limitations to

---

[2]Stability coefficients provided are based on corrected correlations.

these studies: (1) Random selection was not used, (2) diagnoses might have been based on different criteria due to the various clinical settings from which participants were selected, (3) small sample sizes that covered only a portion of the WISC-IV age range were used, and (4) only group performance is reported. The authors caution that these studies provide examples but are not fully representative of the diagnostic categories. The studies were conducted on children identified as intellectually gifted and children with mild to moderate mental retardation, learning disorders, learning disorders and attention deficit hyperactivity disorder (ADHD), ADHD, expressive language disorder, mixed receptive–expressive language disorder, traumatic brain injury, autistic disorder, Asperger's syndrome, and motor impairment.

Summary

The WISC-IV is a widely used individually administered intelligence test that assesses individuals ranging in age from 6 years 0 months to 16 years 11 months. Evidence for the reliability of the scales is good. Reliabilities are much lower for subtests, so subtest scores should not be used in making placement or instructional planning decisions. Evidence for validity, as presented in the manual, is based on four areas: test content, response processes, internal structure, and relationship to other variables. Evidence for validity is limited.

The WISC-IV is of limited usefulness in making educational decisions. The WISC-IV Integrated adds 16 process-oriented subtests to explain poor performance on WISC-IV subtests that have limited reliability. The process-oriented subtests are even less reliable than the WISC-IV core and supplemental subtests. Those who use the WISC-IV in educational settings would do well not to go beyond using the full-scale and four domain scores in making decisions about students.

Woodcock–Johnson–III Normative Update: Tests of Cognitive Abilities and Tests of Achievement

The third edition of the Woodcock–Johnson Psychoeducational Battery (WJ-III) was developed in 2001 (Woodcock, McGrew, & Mather, 2001), and a normative update of the test (WJ-III NU) was conducted in 2007 (Woodcock, Schrank, McGrew, & Mather, 2007). The WJ-III is an individually administered, norm-referenced assessment system for the measurement of general intellectual ability, specific cognitive abilities, scholastic aptitudes, oral language, and achievement. The battery is intended for use from preschool to geriatric ages. The complete set of WJ-III test materials includes four easels for presenting the stimulus items: One for the standard battery cognitive tests, one for the extended battery cognitive tests, one for the standard achievement battery, and one for the extended achievement battery. Other materials include examiner's manuals for the cognitive and achievement tests, one technical manual, test records, and subject response booklets.

The WJ-III contains several modifications to the previous version of the battery (that is, WJ-R). The Tests of Cognitive Abilities (WJ-III-COG) were revised to reflect more current theory and research on intelligence, and several clusters have been added to the battery. New clusters were added to the Tests of Achievement (WJ-III-ACH) to assess several specific types of learning disabilities. Finally, a new procedure was added to ascertain intraindividual differences. The procedure allows professionals to compute discrepancies between cognitive and achievement scores within any specific domain. In 2007, normative calculation procedures were changed to more adequately represent the population according to updated 2005 census statistics, and associated materials were published as the WJ-III NU. These changes are described in the associated sections (that is, Norms, Reliability, and Validity) of this review.

WJ-III Tests of Cognitive Abilities

The 20 subtests of WJ-III-COG are based on the CHC theory of cognitive abilities. General Intellectual Ability is intended to represent the common ability underlying all intellectual performance. A Brief Intellectual Ability score is also available for screening purposes.

The primary interpretive scores on the WJ-III-COG are based on the broad cognitive clusters. Examiners are urged to note significant score differences among the tests comprising each broad ability to learn how the narrow abilities contribute. The broad and narrow abilities measured by the WJ-III-COG are presented in Table 14.3.

TABLE 14.3	Broad and Narrow Abilities Measured by the WJ-III Tests of Cognitive Abilities		
	WJ-III Tests of Cognitive Abilities		
Broad CHC Factor	**Standard Battery Test**		**Extended Battery Test**
	Primary Narrow Abilities Measured		*Primary Narrow Abilities Measured*
Comprehension–Knowledge (Gc)	Test 1:	Verbal Comprehension *Lexical knowledge* *Language development*	Test 11: General Information *General (verbal) information*
Long-Term Retrieval (Glr)	Test 2:	Visual–Auditory Learning *Associative memory*	Test 12: Retrieval Fluency *Ideational fluency*
	Test 10:	Visual–Auditory Learning–Delayed *Associative memory*	
Visual–Spatial Thinking (Gv)	Test 3:	Spatial Relations *Visualization* *Spatial relations*	Test 13: Picture Recognition *Visual memory*
			Test 19: Planning *Deductive reasoning* *Spatial scanning*
Auditory Processing (Ga)	Test 4:	Sound Blending *Phonetic coding: synthesis*	Test 14: Auditory Attention *Speech–sound discrimination* *Resistance to auditory stimulus distortion*
	Test 8:	Incomplete Words *Phonetic coding: analysis*	
Fluid Reasoning (Gf)	Test 5:	Concept Formation *Induction*	Test 15: Analysis–Synthesis *Sequential reasoning*
			Test 19: Planning *Deductive reasoning* *Spatial scanning*
Processing Speed (Gs)	Test 6:	Visual Matching *Perceptual speed*	Test 16: Decision Speed *Semantic processing speed*
			Test 18: Rapid Picture Naming *Naming facility*
			Test 20: Pair Cancellation *Attention and concentration*
Short-Term Memory (Gsm)	Test 7:	Numbers Reversed *Working memory*	Test 17: Memory for Words *Memory span*
	Test 9:	Auditory Working Memory *Working memory*	

SOURCE: Copyright © 2007 by The Riverside Publishing Company. Table 2.2 "Broad and Narrow Abilities Measured by the WJ-III Tests of Cognitive Abilities" from the Woodcock-Johnson® III Normative Update (WJ III® NU) reproduced with permission of the publisher. All rights reserved.

The standard WJ-III-COG subtests shown in Table 14.3 can be combined to create additional clusters: Verbal Ability, Thinking Ability, Cognitive Efficiency, Phonemic Awareness, and Working Memory. If the supplemental subtests are also administered, additional clusters can be created: Broad Attention, Cognitive Fluency, and Executive Processes.

Comprehension–Knowledge (Gc) assesses a person's acquired knowledge, the ability to communicate one's knowledge (especially verbally), and the ability to reason using two subtests: Verbal Comprehension (measuring lexical knowledge and language development) and General Information.

Long-Term Retrieval (Glr) assesses a person's ability to retrieve information from memory fluently. Two subtests are included: *Visual–Auditory Learning* (measuring associative memory) and *Retrieval Fluency* (measuring ideational fluency).

Visual–Spatial Thinking (Gv) assesses a person's ability to think with visual patterns with two subtests: *Spatial Relations* (measuring visualization) and *Picture Recognition* (a visual memory task).

Auditory Processing (Ga) assesses a person's ability to analyze, synthesize, and discriminate speech and other auditory stimuli with two subtests: *Sound Blending* and *Auditory Attention* (measuring one's understanding of distorted or masked speech).

Fluid Reasoning (Gf) assesses a person's ability to reason and solve problems using unfamiliar information or novel procedures. The *Gf* cluster includes two subtests: *Concept Formation* (assessing induction) and *Analysis–Synthesis* (assessing sequential reasoning).

Processing Speed (Gs) assesses a person's ability to perform automatic cognitive tasks. Two subtests are included: *Visual Matching* (a measure of perceptual speed) and *Decision Speed* (a measure of semantic processing speed).

Short-Term Memory (Gsm) is assessed by two subtests: *Numbers Reversed* and *Memory for Words*.

WJ-III Tests of Achievement

Several new subtests have been added to the WJ-III-ACH. As shown in Table 14.4, the WJ-III-ACH now contains 22 tests that can be combined to form several clusters. The subtests and clusters from the standard battery can be combined to form scores for broad areas in reading, mathematics, and writing.

The Oral Expression cluster assesses linguistic competency and semantic expression with two subtests: *Story Recall* (measuring listening skills) and *Picture Vocabulary*.

The Listening Comprehension cluster assesses listening comprehension with two subtests: *Understanding Directions* and *Oral Comprehension*.

The Basic Reading Skills cluster assesses sight vocabulary and phonological awareness with two subtests: *Letter–Word Identification* and *Word Attack* (measuring one's skill in applying phonic and structural analysis skills to nonwords).

The Reading Comprehension cluster assesses reading comprehension and reasoning with two subtests: *Passage Comprehension* and *Reading Vocabulary*.

The Phoneme/Grapheme Knowledge cluster assesses knowledge of sound/symbol relationships.

The Math Calculation Skills cluster assesses computational skills and automaticity with basic math facts using two subtests: *Calculation* and *Math Fluency*.

The Math Reasoning cluster assesses mathematical problem solving and vocabulary with two subtests: *Applied Problems* (measuring skill in solving word problems) and *Quantitative Concepts* (measuring mathematical knowledge and reasoning).

The Written Expression cluster assesses writing skills and fluency with two subtests: *Writing Samples* and *Writing Fluency*.

Scores

The WJ-III NU must be scored by a computer program—a change that eliminates complex hand-scoring

TABLE 14.4	Broad and Narrow Abilities Measured by the WJ-III Tests of Achievement

	WJ-III Tests of Achievement	
Broad CHC Factor	**Standard Battery Test**	**Extended Battery Test**
	Primary Narrow Abilities Measured	*Primary Narrow Abilities Measured*
Reading–Writing (Grw)	Test 1: Letter–Word Identification *Reading decoding*	Test 13: Word Attack *Reading decoding* *Phonetic coding: analysis and synthesis*
	Test 2: Reading Fluency *Reading speed*	Test 17: Reading Vocabulary *Language development/ comprehension*
	Test 9: Passage Comprehension *Reading comprehension* *Lexical knowledge*	Test 16 Editing *Language development* *English usage*
	Test 7: Spelling *Spelling*	Test 22: Punctuation and Capitalization *English usage*
	Test 8: Writing Fluency *Writing ability*	
	Test 11: Writing Samples *Writing ability*	
Mathematics (Gq)	Test 5: Calculation *Mathematics achievement*	Test 18: Quantitative Concepts *Knowledge of mathematics* *Quantitative reasoning*
	Test 6: Math Fluency *Mathematics achievement* *Numerical facility*	
	Test 10: Applied Problems *Quantitative reasoning* *Mathematics achievement* *Knowledge of mathematics*	
Comprehension Knowledge (Gc)	Test 3: Story Recall *Language development* *Listening ability*	Test 14: Picture Vocabulary *Language development* *Lexical knowledge*
	Test 4: Understanding Directions *Listening ability* *Language development*	Test 15: Oral Comprehension *Listening ability*
		Test 19: Academic Knowledge *General information* *Science information* *Cultural information* *Geography achievement*

Broad CHC Factor	WJ-III Tests of Achievement			
	Standard Battery Test		Extended Battery Test	
	Primary Narrow Abilities Measured		*Primary Narrow Abilities Measured*	
Auditory Processing (Ga)			Test 13:	Word Attack *Reading decoding* *Phonetic coding: analysis and synthesis*
			Test 20:	Spelling of Sounds *Spelling* *Phonetic coding: analysis*
			Test 21:	Sound Awareness *Phonetic coding: analysis* *Phonetic coding: synthesis*
Long-Term Retrieval (Glr)	Test 12:	Story Recall–Delayed *Meaningful memory*		

SOURCE: Copyright © 2007 by The Riverside Publishing Company. Table 2.2 "Broad and Narrow Abilities Measured by the WJ-III Tests of Cognitive Abilities" from the Woodcock-Johnson® III Normative Update (WJ III® NU) reproduced with permission of the publisher. All rights reserved.

procedures. Age norms (age 2 to 90+ years) and grade norms (from kindergarten to first-year graduate school) are included. Although WJ-III age and grade equivalents are not extrapolated, they still imply a false standard and promote typological thinking. (See Chapter 3 for a discussion of these issues.) A variety of other derived scores are also available: percentile ranks, standard scores, and Relative Proficiency Indexes. Scores can also be reported in 68 percent, 90 percent, or 95 percent confidence bands around the standard score. Discrepancy scores (predicted differences) are also available. Finally, each Test Record contains a seven-category Test Session Observation Checklist to rate a student's conversational proficiency, cooperation, activity, attention and concentration, self-confidence, care in responding, and response to difficult tasks.

Norms

WJ-III NU calculations are based on the performances of 8,782 individuals living in more than 100 geographically and economically diverse communities in the United States. Individuals were randomly selected within a stratified sampling design that controlled for 10 specific community and individual variables. The preschool sample includes 1,153 children from 2 to 5 years of age (not enrolled in kindergarten). The K–12 sample is composed of 4,740 students. The college/university sample is based on 1,162 students. The adult sample includes 2,889 individuals. An oversampling plan was employed to ensure that the resultant norms would match, as closely as possible, the statistics from the U.S. Department of Commerce, Bureau of the Census.

Reliability

The *WJ-III Normative Update Technical Manual* contains extensive information on the reliability of the WJ-III. The precision of each test and cluster score is reported in terms of the SEM. SEMs are provided for the *W* and standard scores at each age level. The precision with which relative standing in a group can be indicated (rather than the precision of the underlying scores) is reported for each test and cluster by the reliability coefficient. Odd–even correlations, corrected by the Spearman–Brown formulas, were used to estimate reliability for each untimed test.

Some human traits are more stable than others; consequently, some WJ-III tests that precisely measure important, but less stable, human traits show reliabilities in the .80s. However, in the WJ-III, individual tests are combined to provide clusters for educational decision making. Although cluster reliabilities for some age groups are less than .90, all median reliabilities (across age groups) for the standard broad cognitive and achievement clusters exceed .90.

Validity

Careful item selection is consistent with claims for the content validity of both the Tests of Cognitive Ability and the Tests of Achievement. All items retained had to fit the Rasch measurement model as well as other criteria, including bias and sensitivity.

The evidence for validity based on internal structure comes from studies using a broad age range of individuals.

Factor-analytic studies support the presence of seven CHC factors of cognitive ability and several domains of academic achievement. To augment evidence of validity based on internal structure, the authors examined the intercorrelations among tests within each battery. As expected, tests assessing the same broad cognitive ability or achievement area usually correlated more highly with each other than with tests assessing different cognitive abilities or areas of achievement.

For the Tests of Cognitive Ability, evidence of validity based on relations with other measures is provided. Scores were compared with performances on other intellectual measures appropriate for individuals at the ages tested. The criterion measures included the WISC-III, the Differential Ability Scale, the Universal Nonverbal Intelligence Test, and the Leiter International Performance Scale–Revised. The correlations between the WJ-III General Intellectual Ability score and the WISC-III Full-Scale IQ range from .69 to .73.

For the Tests of Achievement, scores were compared with other appropriate achievement measures (for example, the Wechsler Individual Achievement Tests, Kaufman Tests of Educational Achievement, and Wide Range Achievement Test–III). The pattern and magnitude of correlations suggest that the WJ-III-ACH is measuring skills similar to those measured by other achievement tests.

Summary

The WJ-III NU consists of two batteries—the WJ-III Tests of Cognitive Abilities and the WJ-III Tests of Achievement. These batteries provide a comprehensive system for measuring general intellectual ability, specific cognitive abilities, scholastic aptitude, oral language, and achievement over a broad age range. There are 20 cognitive tests and 22 achievement tests. A variety of scores are available for the tests and are combined to form clusters for interpretive purposes. A wide variety of derived scores are available. The WJ-III NU's norms, reliability, and validity appear adequate.

Peabody Picture Vocabulary Test–Fourth Edition (PPVT-4)

The Peabody Picture Vocabulary Test–4 (PPVT-4; Dunn & Dunn, 2007) is an individually administered, norm-referenced, nontimed test assessing the receptive (hearing) vocabulary of children and adults. The authors identify additional uses for the test results: "It is useful (perhaps as part of a broader assessment) when evaluating language competence, selecting the level and content of instruction, and measuring learning. In individuals whose primary language is English, vocabulary correlates highly with general verbal ability" (Dunn & Dunn, 2007, p. 1). The assessment of vocabulary can also be useful when evaluating the effects of injury or disease and is a key component of reading comprehension.

The PPVT-4 is a revised version of the PPVT, PPVT-R, and PPVT III, which were written and revised in 1959, 1981 and 1997, respectively. The new version contains many of the features of its predecessors, such as individual administration, efficient scoring, and the fact that it is untimed. The test continues to offer two parallel forms, broad samples of stimulus words, and it can be used to assess a wide range of examinees. The PPVT-4 has a streamlined administration and contains larger, full-color pictures; new stimulus words; expanded interpretive options to analyze items by parts of speech; a new growth scale value scale for measuring change; and a report to parents and letter to parents (available in Spanish and

English). Other conveniences include a carrying tote and optional computerized scoring.

The PPVT-4 is administered using an easel. The examinee is shown a series of plates, each containing a set of four colored pictures. The examiner states a word and the examinee selects the picture that best represents the stimulus word. The PPVT-4 is an untimed power test, usually finished in 20 minutes or less. It consists of stimuli sets of 12 and examinees are tested at their ability or age level; therefore, test items that are either too difficult or too easy are not administered. The authors provide recommended starting points by age.

Scores

Examinees earn a raw score based on the number of pictures correctly identified between basal and ceiling items. A basal is defined as the lowest set administered that contains one or no errors. A ceiling is defined as the highest set administered that contains eight or more error responses. Once a ceiling is established, testing is discontinued. The raw score is determined by subtracting the total number of errors from the ceiling item. The PPVT-4 has two types of normative scores: deviation (standard scores, percentiles, normal curve equivalents, and stanines) and developmental (age equivalent and grade equivalent). The test also produces a nonnormative score called a growth scale value that measures change in PPVT-4 performance over time. It is a nonnormative score because it does not involve comparison with a norm group.

Norms

Two national tryouts were conducted in 2004 and 2005 to determine stimulus items for the test. Both classical and Rasch item analysis methods were applied to determine item difficulty, discrimination, bias, distracter performance, reliability, and the range of raw score by age. Some items from the previous versions of the PPVT were maintained in the development of the PPVT-4. The PPVT-4 contains two parallel forms with a total of 456 items, 340 of which were adapted from the third edition and 116 were created for this edition.

The PPVT-4 was standardized on a representative national sample of 3,540 people ages 2 years 6 months to 90 years or older (for age norms) and a subsample of 2,003 individuals from kindergarten

through grade 12 (for grade norms). The goal was to have approximately 100 to 200 cases in each age group, with the exception of the oldest two age groups, for which the target was 60. Due to rapid vocabulary growth in young children, the samples were divided into 6-month age intervals at ages 2 years 6 months through 6 years. Whole-year intervals were used for ages 7 through 14 years. The adult age groups use multiyear age intervals. The manual includes a table showing the number of individuals at each age level included in the standardization.

The standardization sample for the PPVT-4 was composed of more than 450 examiners tested at 320 sites in four geographical areas of the United States. Background information, including birth date, sex, race/ethnicity, number of years of education completed, school enrollment status, special education status, and English language proficiency, was gathered either from the examinee (those older than 18 years) or from parents for children 17 years old or younger. All potential examinee information was entered, a stratified random sampling was made from the pool, and testing assignments for each site were determined. More cases were collected than planned, allowing the opportunity to choose final age and grade samples that closely matched the U.S. population characteristics. The test appears to adequately represent the population at each age and grade level.

Reliability

There are multiple kinds of reliability reported for the PPVT-4. The manual contains detailed information on reliability data. The PPVT-4 reports split-half reliability and coefficient alpha as indicators of internal consistency reliability; also included are alternate-form reliability and test–retest reliability. The split-half reliabilities average .94 or .95 for each form across the entire age and grade ranges. Coefficient alpha is also consistently high across all ages and grades, averaging .97 for Form A and .96 for Form B. During the standardization, a total of 508 examinees took both Form A and Form B (most during the same testing session, but some as many as 7 days apart). The alternate-form reliability is very high, falling between .87 and .93 with a mean of .89. The average test–retest correlation, reported on 349 examinees retested with the same form an average of 4 weeks after initial trial, is .93. The information on reliability indicates that the PPVT-4 scores are very precise and users can depend on consistent scores from the PPVT-4.

Validity

The manual discusses in detail validity information. Five studies were conducted comparing the PPVT-4 with the Expressive Vocabulary Test, second edition; the Comprehensive Assessment of Spoken Language; the Clinical Evaluation of Language Fundamentals, fourth edition; the PPVT-III; and the Group Reading Assessment and Diagnostic Evaluation. The PPVT-4 scores correlate highly with those of the previously mentioned assessments. Note that slightly lower correlations were found on assessments that measured broader areas of language than primarily vocabulary.

The authors provide data on how representatives of special populations (speech and language impairment, hearing impairment, specific learning disability, mental retardation, giftedness, emotional/behavioral disturbances, and ADHD) perform in relation to the general population. The results indicate the value of the PPVT-4 in assessing special populations.

Summary

The PPVT-4 is an individually administered, norm-referenced, nontimed test assessing the receptive vocabulary of children and adults. The test is adequately standardized, and there is good evidence for reliability and validity. Data are also included on the testing and performance of students with disabilities.

Dilemmas in Current Practice

The practice of assessing children's intelligence is currently marked by controversy. Intelligence tests simply assess samples of behavior, and different intelligence tests sample different behaviors. For that reason, it is wrong to speak of a person's IQ. Instead, we can refer only to a person's IQ on a specific test. An IQ on the Stanford–Binet Intelligence Scale is not derived from the same samples of behavior as an IQ on any other intelligence test. Because the behavior samples are different for different tests, educators and others must always ask, "IQ on what test?"

This should also be considered when interpreting factor scores for different intelligence tests. Just as the measurement of overall intelligence varies across tests, factor structures and the behaviors that comprise factors differ across tests. Although authors of intelligence tests may include similar factor names, these factors may represent different behaviors across different tests. It is helpful to understand that, for the most part, the particular kinds of items and subtests found on an intelligence test are a matter of the way in which a test author defines intelligence and thinks about the kinds of behaviors that represent it.

When interpreting intelligence test scores, it is best to avoid making judgments that involve a high level of inference (judgments that suggest that the score represents much more than the specific behaviors sampled). Always remember that these factor, index, and cluster scores represent merely student performance on certain sampled behaviors and that the quality of measurement can be affected by a host of unique student characteristics that need to be taken into consideration.

Authors' Viewpoint

Interpreting a student's performance on intelligence tests must be done with great caution. First, it is important to note that factor scores tend to be less reliable than total scores because they have fewer items. Second, the same test may make different psychological demands on various test takers, depending on their ages and acculturation. Test results mean different things for different students. It is imperative that we be especially aware of the relationship between a person's acculturation and the acculturation of the norm group with which that person is compared.

We think it is also important to note that many of the behaviors sampled on intelligence tests are more indicative of actual achievement than ability to achieve. For instance, quantitative reasoning (a factor commonly included in intelligence tests) typically involves measuring a student's math knowledge and skill. Students who have had more opportunities to learn and achieve are likely to perform better on intelligence tests than those who have had less exposure to information, even if they both have the same overall potential to learn. Intelligence tests, as they are currently available, are by no means a pure representation of a student's ability to learn.

CHAPTER COMPREHENSION QUESTIONS

Write your answers to each of the following questions, and then compare your responses to the text or the study guide.

1. Explain the possible impact of acculturation on intelligence test performance.

2. Describe four behaviors that are commonly sampled on intelligence tests.

3. Describe the theoretical contributions of three individuals to the development of intelligence tests.

4. Describe four commonly interpreted factors in intelligence testing.

5. What are processing deficits, and what tests are currently being used to assess them?

6. What are three types of intelligence testing, and for what purposes might you use each of them?

7. Compare and contrast three commonly used tests of intelligence.

Using Measures of Perceptual and Perceptual–Motor Skills

Chapter Goals

1 Identify three reasons why educational personnel assess perceptual–motor skills.

2 Identify two technical difficulties in using perceptual–motor tests.

Key Terms

perception

perceptual–motor skills

visual discrimination

visual–motor integration

process deficits

BVMGT-2

Koppitz-2

Beery VMI

Kenneth

Kenneth is an 8-year-old second grader with noticeable motor difficulties and considerable difficulty acquiring basic reading skills. At age 6 years, his teacher referred him for a psychological evaluation and the individualized educational program (IEP) team identified him as a student with development disabilities in visual–motor development and early reading skills. The IEP team thought that it would be better to work on development of skills that were believed to underlie reading difficulties before engaging in intensive reading instruction. The team recommended an adaptive physical education program and visual–motor services in a special education resource room. The resource teacher worked with Kenneth on tracing patterns, reproduction of designs, rhythm tapping, tracing paths through mazes, and figural discrimination and generalization skills (finding which of several shapes differed from the others and finding shapes that were alike). In adaptive physical education, the focus was on balance (balancing on his toes and walking on a balance beam) and locomotor skills such as jumping in place with both feet together, hopping, skipping, marching in place, and swinging his arms when walking. Kenneth also participated in "object control" activities such as throwing a softball underhand, dribbling a basketball, and catching a softball.

For all of first grade, Kenneth participated in the perceptual and motor training. The IEP team met to draft an IEP for the second grade. The team noted Kenneth was better in directionality, rhythm, and throwing; his printing and fine motor skills had shown good improvement. He still had difficulty in balance and tasks requiring alternating left-to-right movements. He had made little progress in reading. Kenneth's special education teacher questioned if the time spent focusing on development of visual and motor skills might better have been spent teaching him to read.

PERCEPTION IS THE PROCESS OF ACQUIRING, INTERPRETING, AND ORGANIZING sensory information. Experience, learning, cognitive ability, and personality all influence how one interprets and organizes that sensory information. Perceptual–motor skills refer to the production of motor behavior that is dependent on sensory information.

Educators and psychologists recognize that adequate perception and perceptual–motor skills are important in and of themselves. Thus, perception and perceptual–motor tasks are regularly incorporated in tests of intelligence. For example, the Perceptual Organization portion of the Wechsler Intelligence Scale for Children–IV requires visual discrimination, attention to visual detail, sequencing, spatial and nonverbal problem solving, part-to-whole relationships, visual motor coordination, and concentration. Many perceptual and perceptual–motor skills (especially those involving vision, audition, and proprioception) are necessary for school success. For example, the ability to coordinate visual information with motor performance is essential in writing and drawing.

Psychologists have long been interested in perceptual distortions and perceptual–motor difficulties for at least two reasons. First, various groups of individuals with disabilities demonstrate distorted perceptions. Some individuals with diagnosed psychoses show distortions in visual, auditory, and olfactory perceptions. Many individuals known to have sustained brain damage have great difficulty writing and copying, regularly reverse letters and other symbols, have distortions in figure-ground perception, and show deficits in attention and focus. Moreover, some educators and psychologists believe that learning and behavior invariably build on and evolve out of early perceptual–motor integration, and any failures in early learning will adversely affect later learning. Thus, some professionals in the 1960s and 1980s sought to remediate learning disabilities by first remediating perceptual–motor problems (Barsch, 1966; Doman et al., 1967; Kephart, 1971), visual–perceptual problems (Frostig, 1968), psycholinguistic problems (Kirk & Kirk, 1971), or sensory integration (Johnson & Myklebust, 1967; Ayers, 1981). Although many of these approaches were recognized as lacking merit (see, for example, Ysseldyke & Salvia, 1974) and have subsequently been abandoned because of a lack of evidence of their efficacy, some (such as sensory integration) persist today. Recently, professional interest in process deficits and learning disabilities has increased and has resulted in much better assessment procedures.

1 Why Do We Assess Perceptual–Motor Skills?

Perceptual and perceptual–motor skills are assessed for four reasons. In the schools, these tests are used to screen students who may need instruction to remediate or ameliorate visual or auditory perceptual problems before they interfere with school learning. Second, they are used to assess perceptual and perceptual–motor problems in students who are already experiencing school learning problems. If such students also demonstrate poor perceptual–motor performance, they may also receive special instruction aimed at improving their perceptual abilities. Third, perceptual–motor tests are often used in assessments to determine a student's eligibility for special education. Students thought to be learning disabled are often given these tests to ascertain whether perceptual problems coexist with learning problems. Moreover, in some states, there is a specific category of "perceptually handicapped"; tests of perceptual–motor skills would likely be used in eligibility decisions for this category. Finally, perceptual–motor tests are often used by clinical psychologists as an adjunct in the diagnosis of brain injury or emotional disturbance.

SPECIFIC TESTS OF PERCEPTUAL AND PERCEPTUAL–MOTOR SKILLS

In Table 15.1, we provide a list of commonly used perceptual and perceptual–motor tests. In the sections that follow, we review the Bender Family of Tests with the Koppitz scoring system, and the Developmental Test of Visual–Motor Integration (Beery VMI). The other tests shown in the table are reviewed on the website for this text.

The Bender Visual–Motor Gestalt Test Family

Among the perceptual–motor tests used in schools are two tests that are derived from early work begun on assessment of visual–motor skills by Lauretta Bender

TABLE 15.1		Common Perceptual and Perceptual–Motor Tests					
Test	**Author**	**Publisher**	**Year**	**Ages**	**Administration**	**NRT/SRT/CRT**	**Subtests**
Developmental Test of Visual Perception, 2nd Edition	Hammill, Pearson & Voress	Pearson	1993	4–10 years	Individual	NRT	Eye–Hand Coordination, Position in Space, Copying, Figure-Ground, Spatial Relations, Visual Closure, Visual–Motor Speed, Form Constancy
Bender Visual Motor Gestalt Test–2	Brannigan & Decker	Pearson	2003	4–85 years	Individual	NRT	Copying Designs, Recalling Designs, Motor Test, Perception Test
Koppitz-2 Scoring System	Reynolds	Pro-Ed	2007	4–85 years	Individual	NRT	
Developmental Test of Visual–Motor Integration (Beery VMI)	Beery Buktenia, & Beery	Pro-Ed	2004	2 years to adult	Individual	NRT	
Test of Visual–Motor Integration	Hammill, Pearson & Voress	Pro-Ed	1996	4–17 years	Individual	NRT	

in 1938. Bender built a test, the Bender Visual–Motor Gestalt Test (BVMGT), consisting of 9 geometric designs (for example, a circle) that examinees were asked to copy. The examinees' reproductions of the designs were scored for accuracy. In 1963, Elizabeth Koppitz developed a 30-item method of scoring the BVMGT, scoring each design on as many as four criteria. The Koppitz developmental Bender scoring system was widely used in school and clinical settings between the mid-1960s and the early 2000s. In 2003, Brannigan and Decker revised the original BVMGT to produce the BVMGT-2, adding 7 new designs and using a holistic scoring system (described in detail later) to score examinees' reproductions of the designs. In 2007, Reynolds obtained rights to the original Koppitz developmental scoring system, used the system to score the 16 designs that are a part of the BVMGT-2, and produced the Koppitz Developmental Scoring System for the Bender Gestalt Test, second edition (Koppitz-2). In

the following sections, we review the BVMGT-2 and the Koppitz-2.

Bender Visual–Motor Gestalt Test, Second Edition

The second edition of the Bender Visual Motor Gestalt Test (BVMGT-2; Brannigan & Decker, 2003) is a norm-referenced, individually administered test intended to assess the visual–motor integration skills of individuals ages 4 years to older than 85 years. The BVMGT-2 consists of a copying test and three supplementary subtests. The copying test requires test takers to reproduce designs presented individually on stimulus cards that remain in view. There are two sets of designs, with 13 designs for children younger than 8 years of age and 12 designs for test takers

8 years of age or older. The two sets have 8 designs that are common to both sets. The test is untimed. The three supplementary tests are a design recall subtest, a motor subtest, and a perception subtest.

Recalling Designs. After the designs and the stimulus materials have been copied and removed from sight, test takers are asked to draw as many of the designs as they can remember. The subtest is untimed.

Motor Test. This test consists of four test items, and each item contains three figures. Test takers are required to connect dots in each figure without lifting their pencil, erasing, or tilting their paper. Four minutes are allowed to complete the subtest.

Perception Test. This test consists of 10 items that require a test taker to match a design in a multiple-choice array to a stimulus design. Four minutes are allowed to complete the task.

Scores

Each copied and recalled design is scored holistically on a 5-point scale: 0 = no resemblance to the stimulus; 1 = slight or vague resemblance to the stimulus; 2 = some or moderate resemblance to the stimulus; 3 = strong or close resemblance to the stimulus; and 4 = nearly perfect. Examples of each score are presented for each design in the test manual. Each figure on the motor subtest and each item on the perception subtest are scored pass or fail. Raw scores from the copying and recall subtests can be converted to standard scores (mean = 100; standard deviation = 15) and percentiles; 90 percent and 95 percent confidence intervals are available for standard scores. Percentiles are available for the motor and perception subtests.

Norms

The normative sample consists of 4,000 individuals ages 4 years to older than 85 years. Individuals with limited English proficiency, severe sensory or communication deficits, traumatic brain injury, and severe behavioral or emotional disorders were excluded from the normative sample. Students placed in special education for more than 50 percent of the school day were also excluded from the normative sample. Approximately 5 percent of the school-age population was included in regular education classrooms. Thus,

the normative sample systematically underrepresents the proportion of students with disabilities, the population with whom the BVMGT-2 is intended to be used. For students of preschool and school age, the norms appear generally representative in terms of race/ethnicity, educational level of parents, and geographical region for each age group.

Reliability

Corrected split-half correlations were used to estimate the internal consistency of the copying test. Of the 14 coefficients for students between 4 and 20 years of age, only 4 were less than .90, and they were in the .80s. Thus, the BVMGT-2 usually has sufficient reliability for use in making important education decisions.

Stability of the copying and recall tests was estimated by test–retest using the standard scores of 213 individuals in four age groups. There were 39 students in the 5- to 7-year-old group and 62 students in the 8- to 17-year-old group. The obtained correlation for the younger group was .77, and the correlation for the older group was .76. Thus, the BVMGT-2 is insufficiently stable to use in making important education decisions.

Interscorer agreement was assessed in two ways. Five experienced scorers scored 30 protocols independently. Correlations among scorers for copied designs ranged from .83 to .94; correlations for recalled designs were adequate, ranging from .94 to .97. The agreement between the scoring of 60 protocols by one experienced and one inexperienced scorer was also examined. The correlation for copied designs was .85, whereas the correlation for recalled designs was .92. Thus, the scoring of copied designs may not consistently have sufficient reliability for use in making important educational decisions on behalf of students.

No reliability data of any kind are presented for the motor or perception subtests.

Validity

Evidence for the internal validity of the copying test of the BVMGT-2 comes from three sources. First, the items were carefully developed to assess the ability to reproduce designs. Second, factor analysis of test items using the normative sample suggests that a single factor underlies copying test performance. Third, copying test performance varies with age in expected ways: It increases sharply at approximately age 7 years and continues to increase, although less rapidly, until approximately age 15 years, when it plateaus until approximately age 40 years, after which it begins to decline. No evidence of content validity is presented for the recall, motor, or perception subtests.

Criterion-related validity was examined by studying the relationship between the BVMGT-2 and the Beery–Buktenica Developmental Test of Visual–Motor Integration (DTVMI) with 75 individuals between the ages of 4 and 17 years. The obtained correlation between the copying score on the BVMGT-2 and the DTVMI was .55, whereas the obtained correlation between the recall score and the DTVMI was .32.

Other studies examined the relationship between copying and recall on the BVMGT-2 and academic achievement. Obtained correlations with the Woodcock–Johnson Psychoeducational Battery, Achievement Battery–III for the copying test ranged from .22 (with Basic Reading) to .43 (with Math Reasoning), and obtained correlations for the recall subtest ranged from .21 (with Basic Reading) to .38 (with Broad Math). Obtained correlations with the Wechsler Individual Achievement Test–II for the copying test ranged from .18 (with Oral Language) to .42 (with Written Language), and the obtained correlations for the recall subtest ranged from .18 (with Written Language) to .32 (with Math). The relationship between performance on this test and academic achievement is very low.

The relationship between BVMGT-2 scores and IQs was also examined. In one study, the Stanford–Binet Intelligence Scale, Fifth Edition, was used as the criterion measure. Obtained correlations for the copying test ranged from .47 with verbal IQ to .51 with nonverbal IQ; obtained correlations for the recall subtest ranged from .44 with verbal IQ to .47 with nonverbal IQ. In another study, copying and recall scores were correlated with IQs from the Wechsler Intelligence Scale for Children–III. Obtained correlations for the copying test ranged from .31 with Verbal IQ to .62 with Performance IQ; obtained correlations for the recall subtest ranged from .16 with VIQ to .32 with PIQ. A third study with the Wechsler Adult Intelligence Scale–III had similar findings.

Finally, evidence is presented for differential performance by groups of individuals with disabilities. The means of individuals with mental retardation, learning disabilities in reading, learning disabilities in math, learning disabilities in written language, autism, and attention deficit hyperactivity disorder are all significantly lower than those of nondisabled individuals on both the copying and the recall tests. Gifted students earn significantly higher scores on the copying and recall tests.

No evidence of validity is presented for motor or perception subtests.

Summary

The BVMGT-2 is a norm-referenced, individually administered test intended to assess an individual's ability to copy and recall geometric designs as well as to connect dots and perform match-to-sample tasks with such designs. The norms for school-age people appear generally representative, although they exclude some of the very individuals with whom the test is intended to be used. No reliability data of any kind are presented for the motor or perception subtests. The copying test appears generally to have adequate internal consistency, but there is no information about the internal consistency of the recall subtest. The copying and recall tests have poor stability and may have inadequate interscorer agreement. Evidence for the content validity of the copying test is adequate, but the correlations to establish criterion-related validity are too low to be compelling. Although the copying and recall tests of the BVMGT-2 can discriminate groups of individuals known to have disabilities, no evidence is presented regarding these tests' accuracy in categorizing undiagnosed individuals. Reliability and validity evidence for the motor and perception subtests is absent; these subtests should not be used in educational decision making and are of unknown value in clinical situations.

Koppitz-2 Scoring System for the BVMGT-2

The Koppitz developmental scoring system for the BVMGT, developed in 1963, received widespread application in school and clinic settings. Once the BVMGT was revised as the BVMGT-2 and PRO-ED received the rights to the original Koppitz scoring system, it was only a matter of time until the author (Reynolds, 2007) developed the Koppitz-2 as a scoring system for the BVMGT-2.

The Koppitz scoring system is applied to the same 16 cards given for the BVMGT-2. The cards can be obtained as part of the Koppitz-2, or the Koppitz materials may be ordered separately by those who already have the BVMGT-2 stimulus cards. Additional materials included with the Koppitz-2 are two record forms (one for ages 5 to 7 years and the other for individuals older than 8 years), a supplemental emotional indicators record form, a scoring template, and an examiner's manual that includes detailed instructions for scoring.

The Koppitz-2 developmental scoring system has 45 items as opposed to the 30 items that were part of the original Koppitz system. Examinees copy the BVMGT-2 designs and then a standardized set of rules is applied to score their performance. There are as many as 5 items for each design. The author states that the Koppitz-2 scoring system is designed to document the presence and degree of visual–motor difficulties, identify candidates for referral, assess effectiveness of intervention programs, research, and assist in differential diagnosis of various neuropsychological and psychological conditions.

Scores

Raw scores earned using the Koppitz-2 scoring system are converted to scaled scores with a mean of 100 and a standard deviation of 15. Descriptive ratings of performance (for example, average and below average) are assigned. Scaled scores can be converted to T scores, Z scores, normal curve equivalents, stanines, and age equivalents. Time to complete the drawings is also recorded. The author states that a short completion time may reflect impulsive responding and problems with impulse control and planning ability.

Norms

The standardization sample for the Koppitz-2 scoring system is identical to that for the BVMGT-2.

Reliability

Data on internal consistency are reported in the manual separately for each age range. Coefficients range from .77 to .91, with all but one coefficient greater than .80. Reliabilities are also shown for subgroups such as racial/ethnic groups and disability groups. Test–retest reliabilities are reported on 202

individuals ages 5 to 85 years, and they range from .75 to .84. The test is reliable for screening purposes but not for diagnostic purposes. Interscorer reliabilities average .91 for ages 5 to 7 years and .93 for those older than 8 years.

Validity

The author presents theory-based, logic-based, and empirically based evidence for the validity of the Koppitz-2 scoring system. The theory-based argument is relatively weak, consisting primarily of the contention that the test is valid because scores increase with age. As empirical evidence for validity of the Koppitz-2 scoring system, the test is compared to measures of intelligence, academic achievement, other visual–motor tests, and clinical and academic status. It is argued that the fact that the application of the scoring system to the BVMGT-2 shows that correlations with verbal measures (average .34) are half what they are with nonverbal measures (.63) is evidence for validity of the scoring system. In describing the relationship of scores earned on the Koppitz-2 system with other perceptual–motor measures, the author reports moderate correlations with an old version of the Beery VMI with only 45 examinees. The author states that demonstration of validity is a work in progress.

Summary

The Koppitz-2 is a revision of a 1963 Koppitz system of scoring, the BVMGT. The Koppitz-2 scoring system is applied to the BVMGT-2 as an alternative way to score that test. There is no comparison of results obtained when the two systems are compared, reliability is adequate for screening purposes, and evidence for validity is very limited.

Developmental Test of Visual–Motor Integration (Beery VMI)

The Developmental Test of Visual–Motor Integration (Beery VMI; Beery, Buktenia, & Beery, 2004) is a set of geometric forms to be copied on paper using a pencil. The authors contend that the set of forms is arranged in a developmental sequence from easy to more difficult. The Beery VMI is designed to assess the extent to which individuals can integrate their visual and motor abilities. The authors state that the primary purpose of the Beery VMI is to "help identify, through early screening, significant difficulties that some children have integrating, or coordinating their visual–perceptual and motor (finger and hand movement) abilities" (p. 9). The authors define visual–motor integration as the degree to which visual perception and finger–hand movements are well coordinated (p. 12). They indicate that if a child performs poorly on the Beery VMI, it could be because he or she has adequate visual–perceptual and motor coordination abilities but has not yet learned to integrate, or coordinate, these two domains. Two supplemental tests, the Beery VMI Visual Perception Test and the Beery VMI Motor Coordination Test, are provided to enable users to attempt to sort out the relative contribution of visual and motor difficulties to poor performance on measures of visual–motor integration.

There are two versions of the Beery VMI. The full Beery VMI is intended for use with individuals from age 2 years to adults. It contains all 30 VMI forms, including the initial 3 that are both imitated and copied directly. The short Beery VMI contains 21 items and is intended for use with children ages 2 to 7 years. Items for the supplemental tests are identical to items for the full VMI. The VMI may be administered individually or to groups. The test can be administered and scored by a classroom teacher and usually takes approximately 15 minutes. Scoring is relatively easy because the designs are scored pass–fail, and individual protocols can be scored in a few minutes.

Scores

The manual for the Beery VMI includes two pages of scoring information for each of the 30 designs. The child's reproduction of each design is scored pass–fail, and criteria for successful performance are clearly articulated. A raw score for the total test is obtained by adding the number of reproductions copied correctly before the test taker has three consecutive failures. Normative tables provided in the manual allow the examiner to convert the total raw score to a developmental age equivalent, grade equivalent, standard score, scaled score, stanine, or percentile.

Norms

The Beery VMI has been standardized in the United States five times since its initial development in 1967.

The test was originally standardized on 1,030 children in rural, urban, and suburban Illinois. In 1981, the test was cross-validated with samples of children "from various ethnic and income groups in California" (Beery, 1982, p. 10). In 1988, the test was again cross-validated with an unspecified group of students "from several Eastern, Northern and Southern states" (Beery, 1989, p. 10). The 1988 norm sample is not representative of the U.S. population with respect to ethnicity and residence of the students. The Beery VMI and its supplemental tests were normed in 2003 on 2,512 children 2 to 18 years of age selected from five major areas of the United States. The sample was selected by contacting school psychologists and learning disabilities specialists chosen at random from membership lists of major professional organizations. Those who indicated a willingness to participate tested the subjects. A total of 23 child care, preschool, private, and public schools participated. Although the norms collectively were representative of the U.S. population, cross-tabulations are shown only for age by gender, ethnicity, socioeconomic status, and geographic region. Thus, we do not know whether, for example, all the African American students were from middle-socioeconomic status families, from the East, and so on.

Reliability

The authors report the results of studies of internal consistency on an unspecified sample of individuals. Internal consistency ranges from .76 to .91, with an average of .85. Interscorer reliability is .92 for the Beery VMI, .98 for the Beery visual supplement, and .93 for the motor supplement. Test–retest reliability was assessed by administering the Beery VMI to 122 children between the ages of 6 and 10 years in general education public school classrooms. The sample is not further defined. Test–retest reliability is .87 for the Beery VMI, .84 for the visual supplement, and .83 for the motor supplement. The Beery VMI has adequate reliability for screening purposes.

Validity

The authors contend that the Beery VMI has good content validity because of the way in which the items were selected. Evidence for validity based on internal structure comes from comparing results of performance on the Beery VMI to performance results on the copying subtest of the Developmental Test of Visual Perception–2 and the drawing subtest of the Wide Range Assessment of Visual–Motor Abilities. The sample is described only as 122 students attending public schools. Correlations were moderate.

The authors provide evidence for validity based on internal structure by (1) generating a set of hypotheses about what performance on the test would look like if it were measuring what is intended and (2) providing answers to the hypotheses. They show that the abilities measured by the Beery VMI are developmental; that they are related to one another; and that the supplements measure a part, but not the whole, of the abilities measured by the Beery VMI. They also show that performance on the Beery VMI is related more closely to nonverbal than to verbal aspects of intelligence, that performance on the test correlates moderately with performance on academic achievement tests, and that test performance is related to disabling conditions.

Summary

The Beery VMI is designed to assess the integration of visual and motor skills by asking a child to copy geometric designs. As is the case with other such tests, the behavior sampling is limited, although the 30 items on the VMI certainly provide a larger sample of behavior than is provided by the 9 items on the BVMGT. The VMI has relatively high reliability and validity in comparison with other measures of perceptual–motor skills.

Dilemmas in Current Practice

The assessment of perceptual–motor skills or visual–motor integration is a difficult undertaking. Without an adequate definition of perceptual and perceptual–motor skills and with few technically adequate tests to rely on, the assessor is in a bind. Usually, the best way to cope with these problems is not to test. If assessments cannot be done properly or are not educationally necessary, they should not be conducted. Assessment of perceptual and perceptual–motor skills usually falls into this category. We encourage those who are concerned about development of these skills to engage in direct systematic observation in the natural environment in which these skills actually occur. After all, when students cannot print legibly, we do not need to know that they have difficulty copying geometric designs.

Authors' Viewpoint

It is important to realize that when test authors write about perceptual–motor skills, they are talking only about a very small subset of those skills—visual perception and fine hand movements. These tests do not address auditory or proprioceptive perception, and they do not address gross motor skills or fine motor skills other than manual ones. It is also important to recognize that much of the theoretical importance of perceptual–motor assessment is not well founded. First, the specific mechanisms by which perceptual–motor development affects reading are seldom specified and never validated. Thus, theorists may opine that perceptual–motor skills are necessary for reading, but they do not specify what those skills are and how they affect reading. Other than focusing on print material and turning pages, the motor component of reading is unclear. Second, it is based on an incorrect interpretation of the correlation between achievement and perceptual–motor skills. For example, it is well established that poor readers also tend to have poorly developed perceptual–motor skills. However, it is not poor perceptual–motor skills that cause poor reading. Rather, it is poor reading that causes poor perceptual–motor skills. Perceptual–motor skills improve with practice, and learning academics provides that practice. Thus, good readers of material written in English typically develop good left-to-right tracking because they practice tracking from left to right as they read.

The practice of perceptual–motor assessment is linked directly to perceptual–motor training or remediation. There is an appalling lack of empirical evidence to support the claim that specific perceptual–motor training facilitates the acquisition of academic skills or improves the chances of academic success. In fact, major professional associations and insurance companies have taken strong stands against the practice of perceptual–motor assessment and training (see the box for material published on the Cigna Insurance Company website). Perceptual–motor training will improve perceptual–motor functioning. When the purpose of perceptual–motor assessment is to identify specific important perceptual and motor behaviors that children have not yet mastered, some of the devices reviewed in this chapter may provide useful information; performance on individual items will indicate the extent to which specific skills (for example, walking along a straight line) have been mastered. There is no support for the use of perceptual–motor tests in planning programs designed to facilitate academic learning or to remediate academic difficulties.

The American Association for Pediatric Ophthalmology and Strabismus (AAPOS), in "Learning Disabilities: Information for Parents" (2005), states, "There is no scientific evidence to suggest that any ophthalmologic manipulation or therapy including vision training, orthoptic exercises, visual perceptual training, or colored spectacle lenses will improve academic performance in children with learning disabilities."

The Committee on Children with Disabilities of the American Academy of Pediatrics, the American Academy of Ophthalmology (AAO), and AAPOS statement, "Learning Disabilities, Dyslexia, and Vision: A Subject Review" (1998), states, "No scientific evidence supports claims that the academic abilities of children with learning disabilities can be improved with treatments that are based on (1) visual training, including muscle exercises, ocular pursuit, tracking exercises, or 'training' glasses (with or without bifocals or prisms), (2) neurologic organizational training (laterality training, crawling, balance board, perceptual training), or (3) colored lenses. These more controversial methods of treatment may give parents and teachers a false sense of security that a child's reading difficulties are being addressed, which may delay proper instruction or

remediation. The expense of these methods is unwarranted, and they cannot be substituted for appropriate educational measures."

The AAO (2001) states, "It seems intuitive that oculomotor abilities and visual perception play a role in learning skills such as reading and writing. However, several studies in the literature demonstrate that eye movements and visual perception are not critical factors in the reading impairment found in dyslexia, but that brain processing of language plays a greater role."

Summary

Visual perceptual training has been proposed as a treatment for learning disabilities or disorders. Visual perceptual training is considered behavioral training and educational/training in nature. Evidence in the published, peer-reviewed scientific literature does not indicate that visual perceptual therapy is a treatment for any type of learning disability or disorder. The available evidence does not support the conclusion that visual perceptual training will improve learning skills or treat the underlying cause of the learning disability.

Source: www.cigna.com.

CHAPTER COMPREHENSION QUESTIONS

Write your answers to each of the following questions, and then compare your responses to the text or the study guide.

1. Identify three reasons why educational personnel administer perceptual–motor tests.

2. Identify two technical difficulties in using perceptual–motor tests.

3. Assume that you have to assess a student's perceptual–motor skills. How would you go about doing this in a way that would be appropriate?

4. Homer, age 6-3, takes two visual–perceptual–motor tests, the BVMGT-2 and the DTVMI. On the BVMGT-2, he earns a developmental age of 5-6, and on the DTVMI he earns a developmental age of 7-4. Give two different explanations for the discrepancy between the scores.

5. Performance on the BVMGT–2 is used as a criterion in the differential identification of children as brain injured, perceptually handicapped, or emotionally disturbed. Why must the examiner use caution in interpreting and using test results for these purposes?

16 Using Measures of Social and Emotional Behavior

Chapter Goals

1 Know several methods for assessing social–emotional functioning.

2 Know two reasons for assessing social–emotional functioning.

3 Understand the components of a functional behavioral assessment.

4 Be familiar with some commonly used scales for assessing social–emotional functioning.

Key Terms	internalizing problems	peer-acceptance nomination scales	functional behavioral assessment
	externalizing problems	sociometric ranking	Behavior Assessment System for Children, Second Edition (BASC-2)
	acquisition deficit	Systematic Screening for Behavior Disorders	
	performance deficit		
	multiple gating		

SOCIAL AND EMOTIONAL FUNCTIONING OFTEN PLAYS AN IMPORTANT ROLE IN THE development of student academic skills. When students either lack or fail to demonstrate a certain repertoire of expected behavioral, coping, and social skills, their academic learning can be hindered. The reverse is also true: School experiences can impact student social–emotional well-being and related behaviors. To be successful in school, students frequently need to engage in certain positive social behaviors, such as turn taking and responding appropriately to criticism. Other behaviors, such as name calling and uttering self-deprecating remarks, may cause concern and can denote underlying social and emotional problems. In Chapter 6, we noted that teachers, psychologists, and other diagnosticians systematically observe a variety of student behaviors. In this chapter, we discuss additional methods and considerations for the assessment of behaviors variously called social, emotional, and problem behaviors.

The appropriateness of social and emotional behavior is somewhat dependent on societal expectations, which may vary according to the age of a child, the setting in which the behavior occurs, the frequency or duration of the behavior, and the intensity of the behavior. For example, it is not uncommon for preschool students to cry in front of other children when their parents send them off on the first day of school. However, the same behavior would be considered atypical if exhibited by an eleventh grader. It would be even more problematic if the eleventh grader cried every day in front of her peers at school. Some behaviors are of concern even when they occur infrequently, if they are very intense. For example, setting fire to an animal is significant even if it occurs rarely—only every year or so.

Although some social and emotional problems that students experience are clearly apparent, others may be much less easily observed, even though they have a similar negative impact on overall student functioning. Externalizing problems, particularly those that contribute to disruption in classroom routines, are typically quite easily detected. Excessive shouting, hitting or pushing of classmates, and talking back to the teacher are behaviors that are not easily overlooked. Internalizing problems, such as anxiety and depression, are often less readily identified. These problems might be manifested in the form of social isolation, excessive fatigue, or self-destructive behavior. In assessing both externalizing and internalizing problems, it can be helpful to identify both behavioral excesses (for instance, out-of-seat behavior or interrupting) and deficits (such as sharing, positive self-talk, and other coping skills) that can then become targets for intervention.

Sometimes students fail to behave in expected ways because they do not have the requisite coping or social skills; in other cases, students may actually have the necessary skills but fail to demonstrate them under certain conditions.

Bandura (1969) points to the importance of distinguishing between such acquisition and performance deficits in the assessment of social behavior. If students never demonstrate certain expected social behaviors, they may need to be instructed how to do so, or it may be necessary for someone to more frequently model the expected behavior for them. If the behavior is expected to be demonstrated across all contexts and is restricted to one or few contexts, there may be discriminative stimuli unique to the few environments that occasion the behavior, or there may be specific contingencies in those environments that increase or at least maintain the behavior. An analysis of associated environmental variables can help determine how best to intervene. When problematic behavior is generalized across a variety of settings, it can be particularly difficult to modify and may have multiple determinants, including biological underpinnings.

1 Ways of Assessing Problem Behavior

Four methods are commonly used, singly or in combination, to gather information about social and emotional functioning: observational procedures, interview techniques, situational measures, and rating scales. Direct observation of social and emotional behavior is often preferred, given that the results using this method are generally quite accurate. However, obtaining useful observational data across multiple settings can be time-consuming, particularly when the behavior is very limited in frequency or duration. Furthermore, internalizing problems can go undetected unless specific questions are posited, given that the associated behaviors may be less readily detected. The use of rating scales and interviews can often allow for more efficient collection of data across multiple settings and informants, which is particularly important in the assessment of social and emotional behavior. Observational procedures were discussed in Chapter 6; the remaining methods are described in the following sections.

Interview Techniques

Interviews are most often used by experienced professionals to gain information about the perspectives of various knowledgeable individuals, as well as to gain further insight into a student's overall patterns of thinking and behaving. Martin (1988) maintains that self-reports of "aspirations, anxieties, feelings of self-worth, attributions about the causes of behavior, and attitudes about school are [important] regardless of the theoretical orientation of the psychologist" (p. 230). There are many variations on the interview method—most distinctions are made along a continuum from structured to unstructured or from formal to informal. Regardless of the format, Merrell (1994) suggests that most interviews probe for information in one or more of the following areas of functioning and development: medical/developmental history, social–emotional functioning, educational progress, and community involvement. Increasingly, the family as a unit (or individual family members) is the focus of interviews that seek to identify salient home environment factors that may be having an impact on the student (Broderick, 1993).

Situational Measures

Situational measures of social–emotional behavior can include nearly any reasonable activity (D. K. Walker, 1973), but two well-known methods are peer-acceptance nomination scales and sociometric ranking techniques. Both types of measures provide an indication of an individual's social status and may help describe the attitude of a particular group (such as the class) toward the target student. Peer nomination techniques require that students identify other students whom they prefer on some set of criteria (such as students they would like to have as study partners). From these measurements, sociograms, pictorial representations of the results, can be created. Overall, sociometric techniques provide a contemporary point of reference for comparisons of a student's status among members of a specified group.

Rating Scales

There are several types of rating scales; generally a parent, teacher, peer, or "significant other" in a student's environment must rate the extent to which that student demonstrates certain desirable or undesirable behaviors. Raters are often asked to determine the presence or absence of a particular behavior and may be asked to quantify the amount, intensity, or frequency of the behavior. Rating scales are popular because they are easy to administer and useful in providing basic information about a student's level of functioning. They bring structure to an assessment or evaluation and can be used in almost any environment to gather data from almost any source. The important concept to remember is that rating scales provide an index of someone's perception of a student's behavior. Different raters will probably have different perceptions of the same student's behavior and are likely to provide different ratings of the student; each is likely to have different views of acceptable and unacceptable expectations or standards. Self-report is also often a part of rating scale systems. Gresham and Elliott (1990) point out that rating scales are inexact and should be supplemented by other data collection methods.

One procedure that has been developed to incorporate multiple methods in the assessment of social and emotional behavior is multiple gating (Walker & Severson, 1992). This procedure is evident in the Systematic Screening for Behavior Disorders, which involves the systematic screening of all students using brief rating scales. Screening is followed by the use of more extensive rating scales, interviews, and observations for those students who are identified as likely to have social–emotional problems. Multiple gating may help limit the number of undetected problems, as well as target time-consuming assessment methods toward the most severe problems.

2 Why Do We Assess Problem Behavior?

There are two major reasons for assessing problem behavior: (1) identification and classification and (2) intervention. First, some disabilities are defined, in part, by inappropriate behavior. For example, the regulations for implementing the Individuals with Disabilities Education Act (IDEA) describe in general terms the types of inappropriate behavior that are indicative of emotional disturbance and autism. Thus, to classify a pupil as having a disability and in need of special education, educators need to assess social and emotional behavior.

Second, assessment of problem behavior may lead to appropriate intervention. For students whose disabilities are defined by behavior problems, the need for intervention is obvious. However, the development and demonstration of social and coping skills, and the reduction of problem behavior, are worthwhile goals for any student. Both during and after intervention, behaviors are monitored and assessed to learn whether the treatment has been successful and the desired behavior has generalized.

3 Functional Behavioral Assessment and Analysis

One assessment strategy that has become more commonly used to address problem behavior is functional behavioral assessment (FBA). An FBA represents a set of assessment procedures used to identify the function of a student's problematic behavior, as well as the various conditions under which it tends to occur. Those who conduct FBAs may use a variety of different assessment methods and tools (for example, interviews, observations, and rating scales), depending on the nature of the student's behavioral difficulties. Once an FBA has been conducted, a behavior intervention plan can be developed that has a high likelihood of reducing the problem behavior. According to IDEA 2004, an FBA must be conducted for any student undergoing special education eligibility evaluation in which problem behavior is of concern. An FBA must also be conducted (or reviewed) following a manifestation determination review[1] in which the associated suspensions from school were determined to be due to the child's disability. FBAs are to be conducted by those who have been appropriately trained.

Steps for Completing a Functional Behavior Assessment

Although a variety of different tools and measures might be used to conduct an FBA, certain steps are essential to the process. These include the following:

Defining the behavior. Although a student may display a variety of
   problematic behaviors, for the purpose of conducting a functional
   behavioral assessment, it is important to narrow in on just one or two of
   the most problematic behaviors. For example, although Annie may exhibit a
   variety of problematic behaviors, including excessive crying, self-mutilation
   (that is, repeatedly banging her head against her desk until she develops
   bruises), and noncompliance with teacher directions, a support team may
   decide to focus on her self-mutilation behavior, given that it is particularly
   intense and harmful to her body. It is important to define the behavior such
   that it is observable, measurable, and specific (see Chapter 6 for ways in
   which behaviors can be measured). A review of records, interviews with

---

[1]A manifestation determination review must be conducted when a student receiving special education services has been the recipient of disciplinary action that constitutes a change of placement for more than 10 days within a school year.

teachers and caregivers, and direct observations may help in defining the behavior of concern.

Identifying the conditions under which behavior is manifested. Once the behavior has been carefully defined, it is necessary to identify any patterns associated with occurrences of the behavior. In doing so, it is important to identify the following:

- Antecedents: These represent events that occur immediately before the problem behavior. They may include such things as being asked to complete a particular task, having a particularly disliked person enter the room, or receiving a bad grade.

- Setting events: These represent events that make it such that the student is particularly sensitive to the antecedents and consequences associated with the problem behavior. For example, a setting event might include not having gotten enough sleep the night before school, such that the student is particularly sensitive to a teacher's request for her to finish work quickly and subsequently acts out in response to the teacher's request.

- Consequences: These represent what happens as a result of the behavior. For example, the consequence for a student tearing up a paper that he or she does not want to work on may be that the student does not have to complete the difficult task presented on the paper. Or, if a student hits another student in the arm, the consequence may be that he is sent to the office, and his parents are called to pick him up and take him home.

Developing a hypothesis about the function of the behavior. Using information that is collected about antecedents, setting events, and consequences through record review, interview, and observation, one can begin to develop hypotheses about the function of the behavior. In Chapter 6, we described several different functions of behavior, including (1) social attention/communication; (2) access to tangibles or preferred activities; (3) escape, delay, reduction, or avoidance of aversive tasks or activities; (4) escape or avoidance of other individuals; and (5) internal stimulation (Carr, 1994).

Testing the hypothesized function of the behavior. Although this step is typically considered part of a functional behavioral *analysis* (as opposed to a functional behavioral *assessment*), it is important to verify that your hypothesis about the function of the behavior is correct. Otherwise, the associated intervention plan may not work. By manipulating the antecedents and consequences, one can determine whether the function is correct. For example, if it is assumed that escape from difficult tasks is a function of the student's problematic behavior of tearing up assignments, one could provide tasks that the student finds easy, and enjoys, and examine whether he or she tears up the paper. If not, this would provide evidence that the function of the behavior may be to escape from a difficult task.

Developing a behavioral intervention plan. Although this comes after the actual FBA, it is important to know how to use the assessment data that

Scenario in Assessment

Joseph

Joseph was a kindergarten student who, within the first 3 weeks of school, had been sent to the office more than 15 times for his inappropriate behavior, which included hitting and shouting at his peers. Joseph's teacher used a time-out procedure to discipline students in her classroom, and Joseph frequently received multiple time-outs in a single morning, at which point the teacher would decide that he needed to receive a more substantial consequence, which typically included being sent to the principal's office.

After a very brief consultation with one of the school's special education teachers and another kindergarten teacher, Joseph's teacher decided to keep track of the antecedents and consequences associated with his behavior for a few days using the following recording device. This is what Joseph's teacher recorded:

Antecedents	Behavior	Consequence
Morning large group time, students sitting on the floor while the teacher was pointing to the calendar	Hit the peer sitting next to him in the arm	Reprimanded, sent to the time-out corner
Morning group time, while the teacher was reading a story	Kicked the peer sitting next to him	Reprimanded, sent to the time-out corner
Afternoon group time, while watching a video	Shouted "I hate this; I hate this video!"	Peers laugh, Joseph is reprimanded, and sent to the office
Morning group time, when a student was describing the weather	Kicked the peer sitting next to him	Reprimanded, sent to the time-out corner
Morning group time, when the teacher was asking questions about the story that was just read	Hit the peer sitting next to him	Reprimanded, sent to the office

Joseph's teacher brought this information to the other two teachers and sought their guidance. Based on the information, they thought that Joseph's behavior served an attention function. Joseph seemed to get quite a bit of negative attention from his teacher and peers following his behavior; he also likely got some attention from the principal when he was sent to her office. They suggested that Joseph be provided with more attention when he was behaving appropriately; they also suggested developing a very brief signal (rather than using words) to send him to the time-out area when he behaved inappropriately. This way the teacher would not have to verbally reprimand and call attention to his inappropriate behavior.

Unfortunately, this did not seem to help decrease Joseph's behavior. In fact, in the next month it escalated. The other teachers suggested that they bring this to the attention of the district behavior consultant. After analyzing the data that had been collected and asking a few questions, the consultant decided to observe Joseph in the classroom environment. She made a couple of interesting observations that were pertinent to the situation: (1) The area where the teacher held group time was very crowded,

(2) Joseph tended to engage in the problem behavior toward the end of group times, and (3) he had a very difficult time sitting still during group time. This led her to believe that the function of the behavior was to escape from having to do something he had not yet developed the skill to do (that is, sit and listen for long periods of time). If this was the case, the teacher's consequence of time-out would only serve to reinforce the problem behavior. The consultant suggested developing an intervention that involved changing the space available for the group activities such that there was more of it, teaching Joseph how to appropriately signal when he needed a break from activities, reinforcing him for appropriately asking for a break, and eventually increasing the amount of time that he was expected to stay in the group prior to being able to take a break. Using this intervention plan, Joseph's behavioral problems decreased dramatically.

Conclusion: Make sure you appropriately identify the function of a problem behavior; without this, the intervention is not likely to work.

are collected to inform the development of an intervention plan. Ideally, a behavior intervention plan will involve the following:

- Identifying, teaching, and reinforcing a replacement behavior. As part of the behavior intervention plan, the support team needs to identify a behavior that the student can use to address the identified function in an appropriate manner. For example, if the function of a problematic behavior (such as tearing up work) is escape from a difficult task, the student might be taught how to request a break from the difficult task, such that the same function (escape) would be met when the student engaged in a more appropriate behavior. Although some might initially think that teaching replacement behaviors (that is, to ask for a break and have it granted) results in a lowering of standards, it is important to highlight that having the student ask for a break is certainly more socially appropriate behavior than tearing up an assignment, and it is a step in the right direction. In order to ensure that the student makes use of newly taught replacement behaviors, the intervention plan might include a reward for when the student initially makes appropriate use of the replacement behavior.

- Appropriately addressing setting events, antecedents, and consequences. Behavior intervention plans may include an alteration of the conditions surrounding antecedents and/or a change in consequences. For example, if escape from difficult items presented on a worksheet is the function of a behavior, and the antecedent is presentation of those difficult items, the teacher might set up a task to begin with a few very easy tasks, followed by a medium task, some more easy tasks, and perhaps one difficult task toward the end. If peer attention is the function of a behavior, the teacher might train the entire class how to ignore the target student's problematic behavior.

Once a behavior intervention plan is developed, it is important to also create a method for measuring implementation integrity as well as a monitoring strategy to determine whether the behavioral intervention plan is appropriately addressing the student's problem behavior.

SPECIFIC RATING SCALES OF SOCIAL–EMOTIONAL BEHAVIOR

In the following sections, we provide information on several commonly used scales of social–emotional behavior. We provide a full review of the Behavior Assessment System for Children, Second Edition; full reviews for each of the scales listed in the table are provided on our website.

TABLE 16.1		Commonly Used Scales for Measuring Social–Emotional Functioning and Problem Behavior					
Test	**Author**	**Publisher**	**Year**	**Ages/ Grades**	**Individual/ Group**	**Norm vs. Criterion**	**Sections or Subscales**
Achenbach System of Empirically Based Assessment (ASEBA)							
Caregiver–Teacher Report Form (C-TRF)—1.5–5	Achenbach & Rescorla	Research Center for Children, Youth, & Families, University of Vermont	2000	Ages 1–5 to 5 years	Individual	Norm	Internalizing (Emotionally Reactive, Anxious/Depressed, Somatic Complaints, Withdrawn), Externalizing (Attention Problems, Aggressive Behavior)
Child Behavior Checklist (CBCL)—1.5–5	Achenbach & Rescorla	Research Center for Children, Youth, & Families, University of Vermont	2000	Ages 1–5 to 5 years	Individual	Norm	Internalizing (Emotionally Reactive, Anxious/Depressed, Somatic Complaints, Withdrawn), Externalizing (Attention Problems, Aggressive Behavior, Sleep Problems)
Child Behavior Checklist (CBCL)—6–18	Achenbach & Rescorla	Research Center for Children, Youth, & Families, University of Vermont	2001	Ages 6–18 years	Individual	Norm	Activities, Social, School, Internalizing (Anxious/ Depressed, Withdrawn/ Depressed, Somatic Complaints), Externalizing (Rule-Breaking Behavior, Aggressive Behavior, Social Problems, Thought Problems, Attention Problems)
Direct Observation Form (DOF)	Achenbach	Research Center for Children, Youth, & Families, University of Vermont	1986	None specified	Individual	Norm	On Task, Internalizing (Withdrawn/Inattentive, Nervous/Obsessive, Depressed), Externalizing (Hyperactive, Attention Demanding, Aggressive)

Test	Author	Publisher	Year	Ages/ Grades	Individual/ Group	Norm vs. Criterion	Sections or Subscales
Teacher's Report Form (TRF)	Achenbach & Rescorla	Research Center for Children, Youth, & Families, University of Vermont	2001	Ages 6–18 years	Individual	Norm	Academic Performance, Working Hard, Behaving Appropriately, Learning, Happy, Internalizing (Anxious/Depressed, Withdrawn/Depressed, Somatic Complaints), Externalizing (Rule-Breaking Behavior, Aggressive Behavior, Social Problems, Thought Problems, Attention Problems)
Youth Self Report (YSF)	Achenbach & Rescorla	Research Center for Children, Youth, & Families, University of Vermont	2001	Ages 11–18 years	Individual	Norm	Activities, Social, Internalizing, (Anxious/Depressed, Withdrawn/Depressed, Somatic Complaints), Externalizing (Rule-Breaking Behavior, Aggressive Behavior, Social Problems, Thought Problems, Attention Problems)
Other Measures							
Asperger Syndrome Diagnostic Scale (ASDS)	Myles, Bock, & Simpson	Pro-Ed	2001	Ages 5–18 years	Individual	Norm	Language, Social Skills, Maladaptive Behavior, Cognition, Sensorimotor Development
Behavioral and Emotional Rating Scale, 2nd Edition (BERS-2)	Epstein	Pro-Ed	2004	Ages 5–18 years	Individual	Norm	Interpersonal Strength, Family Involvement, Intrapersonal Strength, School Functioning, Affective Strength, Career Strength
Behavior Assessment System for Children, Second Edition (BASC-2)	Reynolds & Kamphaus	Pearson	2004	Ages 2–25 years	Individual	Norm	Teacher Rating Scale: Externalizing Problems, Internalizing Problems, School Problems. Parent Rating Scale: Externalizing Problems, Internalizing Problems, Activities of Daily Living. Self-Report of Personality: Inattention/Hyperactivity, Internalizing Problems, Personal Adjustment, School Problems

continued on the next page

| TABLE 16.1 | | | | | | | Commonly Used Scales for Measuring Social–Emotional Functioning and Problem Behavior, *continued* |

Test	Author	Publisher	Year	Ages/ Grades	Individual/ Group	Norm vs. Criterion	Sections or Subscales
Behavior Rating Profile, Second Edition	L. Brown & Hammill	Pro-Ed	1990	Ages 6-5 to 18-5 years	Individual	Norm	Includes three student rating scales (peers, home, school), a parent rating scale, a teacher rating scale, and a sociogram
Early Childhood Behavior Scale (reviewed on website under Chapter 18)	S. B. McCarney	Hawthorne	1992	Ages 36–72 months	Individual	Norm	Academic Progress, Social Relationships, Personal Adjustment
Gilliam Asperger's Disorder Scale (GADS)	Gilliam	Pro-Ed	2001	Ages 3–22 years	Individual	Norm	Social Interaction, Restricted Patterns of Behavior, Cognitive Patterns, Pragmatic Skills
Gilliam Autism Rating Scale– 2nd edition	Gilliam	Pro-Ed	2006	Ages 3–22 years	Individual	Norm	Stereotyped Behaviors, Communication Behaviors, Social Interaction Behaviors
Systematic Screening for Behavior Disorders	H. M. Walker & Severson	Sopris–West	1992	Grades 1–6	Individual	Norm	Adaptive Behavior, Maladaptive Behavior, Academic Engaged Time, Peer Social Behavior
Temperament and Atypical Behavior Scale (TABS)	Neisworth, Bagnato, Salvia, & Hunt	Brookes	1999	Ages 11–71 months	Individual	Norm	Detached, Hypersensitive/ Active, Underactive, Dysregulated
Walker– McConnell Scale of Social Competence and School Adjustment, Elementary Version	H. M. Walker & McConnell	Wadsworth	1988	Grades K–6	Individual	Norm	Teacher Preferred Behavior, Peer Preferred Behavior, School Adjustment Behavior

*[Handwritten note: BASC-2 has 5 measures of behavior
1) Teacher Rating Scale (TRS)
2) Parent Rating Scale (PRS)
3) Self-Report of Personality (SRP)
4) Structured Developmental History (SDH)
5) Student Observation ~~History~~ System (SOS)]*

Behavior Assessment System for Children, Second Edition (BASC-2)

The Behavior Assessment System for Children, Second Edition (BASC-2; Reynolds & Kamphaus, 2004) is a "multimethod, multidimensional system used to evaluate the behavior and self-perceptions of children and young infants aged 2 through 25 years" (p. 1). This comprehensive assessment system is designed to assess numerous aspects of an individual's adaptive and maladaptive behavior. The BASC-2 is composed of five main measures of behavior: (1) Teacher Rating Scale (TRS), (2) Parent Rating Scale (PRS), (3) Self-Report of Personality (SRP), (4) Structured Developmental History (SDH), and (5) Student Observation System (SOS).

The test authors indicate that the BASC-2 can be used for clinical diagnosis, educational classification, and program evaluation. They indicate that it can facilitate treatment planning and describe how it may be used in forensic evaluation and research, as well as in making manifestation determination decisions.

Behaviors Sampled

The Teacher Rating Scale (TRS) is a comprehensive measure of both adaptive and problem behaviors that children exhibit in school and caregiving settings. Three different forms are available—preschool (2 to 5 years), child (6 to 11 years), and adolescent (12 to 21 years)—with the behavior items specifically tailored for each age range. Teachers, school personnel, or caregivers rate children on a list of behavioral descriptions using a 4-point scale of frequency ("never," "sometimes," "often," or "almost always"). Estimated time to complete the TRS is 10 to 15 minutes. The TRS for preschool is composed of 100 items; the TRS for children, 139 items; and the TRS for adolescents, 139 items. Items consist of ratings of behaviors similar to the following: "Has the flu," "Displays fear in new settings," "Speeds through assignments without careful thought," and "Works well with others."

The Parent Rating Scale (PRS) is a comprehensive measure of a child's adaptive and problem behavior exhibited in community and home settings. The PRS uses the same 4-point rating scale as the TRS. In addition, three forms are provided by age groups, as defined previously. Estimated time to complete this measure is 10 to 20 minutes.

The Self-Report of Personality (SRP) contains short statements that a student is expected to mark as either true or false or to provide a rating ranging from "never" to "almost always." Three forms are available by age/schooling level: child (8 to 11 years), adolescent (12 to 21 years), and young adult/college (for 18- to 25-year-old students in a postsecondary educational setting). Estimated administration time is 20 to 30 minutes. Spanish translations of the PRS and SRP are available.

The Structured Developmental History (SDH) is a broad-based developmental history instrument developed to obtain information on the following areas: social, psychological, developmental, educational, and medical history. The SDH may be used either as an interview format or as a questionnaire. The organization of the SDH may help in conducting interviews and obtaining important historical information that may be beneficial in the diagnostic process.

The Student Observation System (SOS) is an observation tool developed to facilitate diagnosis and monitoring of intervention programs. Both adaptive and maladaptive behaviors are coded during a 15-minute classroom observation. An electronic version of the SOS is available for use on a laptop computer or personal digital assistant.

The SOS is divided into three parts. The first section, the Behavior Key and Checklist, is a list of 65 specific behaviors organized into 13 categories (4 categories of positive behavior and 9 categories of problem behavior). Following the 15-minute observation, the coder rates the child on the 65 items according to a 3-point frequency gradation ("never observed," "sometimes observed," and "frequently observed"). The rater can separately indicate whether the behavior is disruptive.

The second part, Time Sampling of Behavior, requires the informant to decide whether a behavior is present during a 3-second period following each 30-second interval of the 15-minute observation. Observers place a check mark in separate time columns next to any of the 13 categories of behavior that occur during any one interval. The third section, Teacher's Interaction, is completed following the 15-minute observation. The observer scores the teacher's interactions with the students on three aspects of classroom interactions: (1) teacher position during the observation, (2) teacher techniques to change student behavior, and (3) additional observations that are relevant to the assessment process.

Scores

The BASC-2 can be either hand or computer scored. A hand-scored response form can be used for the first three instruments (TRS, PRS, and SRP). The hand-scored protocols are constructed in a unique format, using pressure-sensitive paper that provides the examiner with an immediate translation of ratings to scores. After administration of the different rating forms, the administrator removes the outer page to reveal a scoring key. Scale and composite scores are totaled easily, and a behavior profile is available to represent the data graphically. Validity scores are tabulated to evaluate the quality of completed forms and to guard against response patterns that may skew the data profiles positively or negatively. Detailed scoring procedures that use a 10-step procedure for each of these scales are described in the administration manual.

Raw scores for each scale are transferred to a summary table for each individual measure. T-scores (mean = 50, standard deviation = 10), 90 percent confidence intervals, and percentile ranks are obtained after selecting appropriate norm tables for comparisons. In addition, a high/low column is provided to give the assessor a quick and efficient method for evaluating whether differences among composite scores for the individual are statistically significant.

The TRS produces three composite scores of clinical problems: Externalizing Problems, Internalizing Problems, and School Problems. Externalizing problems include aggression, hyperactivity, and conduct problems. Internalizing problems include anxiety, depression, and somatization. School problems are broken down into attention and learning problems. A broad composite score of overall problem behaviors is provided on the Behavioral Symptoms Index, which includes several of the subscales listed previously in addition to Atypicality and Withdrawal. In addition, positive behaviors are included in an adaptive skills composite; these include the Leadership, Social Skills, Study Skills, Adaptability, and Functional Communication subscales. An optional content scale can also be used, which provides information according to the following subscales: Anger Control, Bullying, Developmental Social Disorders, Emotional Self-Control, Executive Functioning, Negative Emotionality, and Resiliency. The PRS provides the same scoring categories and subscales, with the exception that the School Problems composite scores, composed of subscales for learning problems and study skills, are omitted, and Activities of Daily Living is added.

The SRP produces four composite scores—Inattention/Hyperactivity, Internalizing Problems, Personal Adjustment, and School Problems—and an overall composite score referred to as an Emotion Symptoms Index (ESI). The composite ESI score includes both negative and adaptive scales. Inattention/Hyperactivity includes the Attention Problems and Hyperactivity subscales. The Internalizing Problems composite includes atypicality, locus of control, social stress, anxiety, depression, and sense of inadequacy. Personal Adjustment groupings include relations with parents, interpersonal relations, self-esteem, and self-reliance. The School Problems composite includes attitude to school and attitude to teachers. Additional subscales, including Sensation Seeking, Alcohol Abuse, School Adjustment, and Somatization, are included in the ESI. An optional content scale is also available that includes the following subscales: Anger Control, Ego Strength, Mania, and Test Anxiety.

Three validity scores are provided. To detect either consistently negative bias or consistently positive bias in the responses provided by the student, there is an F index ("fakes bad") and an L index ("fakes good"). The V index incorporates nonsensical items (similar to "Spiderman is a real person"), such that a child who consistently marks these items "true" may be exhibiting poor reading skills, may be uncooperative, or may have poor contact with reality.

The SDH and SOS are not norm-referenced measures and do not provide individual scores of comparison. Rather, these instruments provide additional information about a child, which may be used to describe his or her strengths and weaknesses.

Norms

Standardization and norm development for the general and clinical norms on the TRS, PRS, and SRP took place between August 2002 and May 2004. Data were collected from more than 375 sites. The number of children who received or provided behavioral ratings across the different measures were, for the TRS, $N = 4,650$; for the PRS, $N = 4,800$; and for the SRP, $N = 3,400$. Efforts were made to ensure that the standardization sample was representative of the U.S. population of children ages 2 to 18 years, including exceptional children. The standardization sample was compared with census data for gender, geographic region, socioeconomic status (SES; as measured by mother's education level), placement in special education and gifted/talented programs, and race/ethnicity. Several cross-tabulations are provided (for instance, geographic region by gender by age, race by gender by age, and so forth). Data collected through Spanish versions of the PRS and SRP are included in the standardization sample. The authors present data to support mostly balanced norms; however, the 2- to 3-year-old sample tends to vary somewhat from the characteristics of the population. For instance, 2- to 3-year-old students of low SES (mother's education level) tend to be underrepresented, whereas 2- to 3-year-old students of high SES tend to be overrepresented. The authors claim that children with behavioral–emotional disturbances are represented appropriately at each grade level of each instrument, and the data provided in the manual support this claim.

A separate norm sample was collected for the college level of the SRP. This sample consisted of 706 students ages 18 to 25 years who were attending various postsecondary educational institutions. Information on the degrees sought by participants is presented, along with information on the frequency by age and gender of participants in this standardization sample. No comparisons to the U.S. population are presented. Females appear to be overrepresented in this sample.

Clinical population sample norms consist of data collected on children receiving school or clinical services for emotional, behavioral, or physical problems. Sample sizes were, for the TRS, $N = 1,779$; for the PRS, $N = 1,975$; and for the SRP, $N = 1,527$. The authors state that the clinical sample was not controlled demographically because this subgroup is not a random set of children. For example, significantly more males were included than females.

Reliability

The manual has a chapter devoted to the technical information supporting reliability and validity for each normed scale (TRS, PRS, and SRP). Three types of reliability are provided within the technical manual: internal consistency, test–retest, and interrater agreement.

Internal Consistency. Coefficient alpha reliabilities are provided for the TRS and PRS by gender according to the following six age levels: ages 2 to 3, ages 4 to 5, ages 6 to 7, ages 8 to 11, ages 12 to 14, and ages 15 to 18 years. Median reliabilities for the TRS subscales for these age/gender groups range from .84 to .89. Lower reliabilities are evident for subscales associated with the Internalizing Problems scale (including Anxiety, Depression, and Somatization) than for those associated with the Externalizing Problems scale. Median reliabilities for the PRS subscales range from .80 to .87 across these age/gender groups; reliabilities tend to be lower at the preschool-and-below ages. SRP coefficient alpha reliabilities are provided according to the following age levels: ages 8 to 11, ages 12 to 14, ages 15 to 18, and ages 18 to 25 years. Median subscale reliabilities for the SRP range from .79 to .83. The Sensation Seeking, Somatization, and Self-Reliance subscales tended to be particularly low ($<.70$) at certain age levels. Internal consistency reliabilities for the composite scales exceeded .80 across all three scales for each age/gender group. Coefficient alphas are also provided for certain disability groups within the clinical sample by gender (such as learning disabilities,

ADHD, and all clinical) and for those taking the Spanish version of the SRP and the PRS. Coefficient alpha reliabilities for the clinical groups are similar to those provided for the general norm sample; those for the Spanish version are slightly lower.

Test–Retest Reliability. TRS test–retest reliability was computed by having teachers rate the same child twice, with 8 to 65 days intervening between rating periods; this was done for a total of 240 students. Results are presented by age level (preschool, child, and adolescent) for each subscale and composite. Adjusted reliabilities ranged from .81 to .93 for composites and from .64 to .90 for the subscales. PRS test–retest reliability was determined based on parent ratings of 252 students, with an intervening time period of 9 to 70 days. Adjusted reliabilities for the PRS composites ranged from .78 to .92; those for the subscales ranged from .72 to .88. Test–retest reliabilities for the SRP were based on ratings provided by 279 students, for which there was an intervening time period of 13 to 66 days. Adjusted composite reliabilities ranged from .74 to .93; adjusted subscale reliabilities ranged from .61 to .99.

Interrater Reliability. A total of 170 students were rated according to the TRS by two teachers to determine interrater reliability of the TRS. Adjusted reliabilities ranged from .48 to .81 for the composite scales and from .19 to .82 for the subscales. Parents and caregivers completed the PRS for 134 students, such that two rating scales were completed for each student by different individuals. Adjusted reliabilities for the PRS composite scales ranged from .65 to .86; associated reliabilities for the PRS subscales ranged from .53 to .88. No interrater reliability study was conducted for the SRP, given that the scale is a self-report instrument.

Correlations were calculated across the PRS and the TRS by age level (preschool, child, and adolescent) for students in the standardization samples that had both forms completed ($N = 2,324$). Correlations for the related composites ranged from .17 to .52 for the preschool forms, from .22 to .50 for the child forms, and from .36 to .51 for the adolescent forms. The internalization composite scale tended to have the lowest correlations across forms. Correlations between the SRP and both the PRS and the TRS are also provided; however, the composites are substantially different for the SRP, making the presence of lower correlations among composites difficult to interpret.

Validity

The authors describe the procedures used to develop and select items for inclusion in the BASC-2. Many of the items included on the BASC-2 are taken directly from the original BASC. In the development of the original items, alternate behavior rating scales and related instruments were examined, and clinicians provided consultation in the selection of items to measure both problem and adaptive behaviors. Students and teachers were also involved in item development. The items went through several cycles of testing via expert and statistical review for inclusion in the original BASC. Several new items were developed for the BASC-2 to replace those with poor technical characteristics. More extensive revisions were conducted for the SRP, in which the item response format was altered from the previous edition, based on results of research studies examining internal consistency and factor loadings across the two formats. Confirmatory factor analysis was used to examine item characteristics to assist with decision making about inclusion in the final instrument. Items that correlated substantially with alternate composite scales that were not intended to be measured with the item, as well as those items that had low factor loadings on the intended composite scale, were eliminated. Analyses of partial correlations and differential item-functioning analyses were conducted to examine whether items were measuring appropriately across various student demographic groups (for instance, females versus males, African Americans versus non-Hispanics, and Hispanics versus non-Hispanics). A total of five items were eliminated based on bias reviews. Both exploratory and confirmatory factor analytic procedures were used to examine the appropriateness of the composite scale structure for the TRS, PRS, and SRP. These analyses supported the three-factor and four-factor child and adolescent composite scores.

Criterion-Related Validity. The TRS was compared with several related behavior rating scales, including various portions of the Achenbach System of Empirically Based Assessment (ASEBA; Achenbach & Rescorla, 2001), the Conners Teacher Rating Scale–Revised (Conners, 1997), and the original BASC TRS.

Ratings from the preschool form of the TRS were compared to an associated form of the ASEBA among 46 children ages 2 to 5 years. Fifty-seven children ages 6 to 11 years and 39 adolescents ages 12 to 18 years similarly had corresponding rating forms from the BASC and the ASEBA compared. Correlations for related subscales were primarily in the .60 to .90 range, with the exception of Somatization subscales, which tended to be very weakly correlated across rating scales. Correlations across composite scales were higher; however, Internalizing Problems composites tended to be lower than the other composite scale correlations.

Correlations with the Conners Teacher Rating Scale–Revised were based on teacher ratings for 59 children ages 6 to 11 years and 45 adolescents ages 12 to 18 years. Associated subscale adjusted correlations ranged from .26 (Anxiety scales for adolescents) to .94 (Aggression/Oppositional scales for adolescents). Composite behavior scale correlations (Conners Global Index and the BASC Behavioral Symptoms Index) were .84 at the child level and .69 at the adolescent level. Information is presented on the correlations with ratings from the original BASC for the standardization samples. As expected, the results for the BASC and the BASC-2 were very similar, with correlations exceeding .90 for the majority of composite and subscales.

The PRS was also compared to a variety of similar rating scales, including the following: related forms of the ASEBA, Conners Parent Rating Scale–Revised, the Behavior Rating Inventory of Executive Functioning (Gioia, Isquith, Guy, & Kenworthy, 2000), and the original BASC PRS. The associated parent rating forms for the ASEBA and the BASC-2 were completed for 53 young children, 65 school-age children, and 67 adolescents. Adjusted correlations for associated subscales ranged from .34 to .77; adjusted correlations for associated composites ranged from .67 to .84. Internalizing Problems composites tend to have weaker correlations than Externalizing Problems composites.

Correlations with the Conners Parent Rating Scale were determined based on 60 children ages 6 to 11 years and 55 adolescents ages 12 to 18 years. The Conners Global Index and the BASC-2 Behavioral Symptoms Index correlated .79 at the child level and .65 at the adolescent level. Subscale adjusted correlations ranged from .41 to .84 at the child level and .35 to .64 at the adolescent level. The BASC-2 and the Behavior Rating Inventory of Executive Functioning (Gioia et al., 2000) were administered to 51 children ages 6 to 11 years and 40 adolescents ages 12 to 18 years. Broad composite scores correlated .67 at the child level and .80 at the adolescent level. Finally, correlations with the original BASC PRS were primarily in the .80 to .95 range, as expected.

Criterion-related validity of the SRP was evidenced through correlations with the associated forms of the ASEBA, the Conners–Wells Adolescent Self-Report Scale (Conners, 1997), the Children's Depression Inventory (Kovacs, 1992), and the Revised Children's Manifest Anxiety Scale (Reynolds & Richmond, 2000). The associated scale of the ASEBA was administered concurrently with the SRP among 51 adolescents. Associated composite adjusted correlations were in the .75 to .80 range. All associated subscales of the Conners–Wells Adolescent Self-Report correlated positively (.52 to .67) with the BASC-2 scales among 54 adolescents, with an exception being the negative correlations showing up as expected for the relationship between "family problems" and "relations with parents" across these scales. Finally, the associated scales of the Children's Depression Inventory and the Children's Manifest Anxiety Scale correlated positively with the Depression and Anxiety scales on the BASC-2 SRP. Correlations for a group ($N = 86$) of students in postsecondary settings who took the college level of the SRP and the ASEBA self-report ranged from .38 to .61 for associated composite and subscales.

Evidence for criterion-related validity of the college level of the BASC-2 SRP is also presented using the Brief Symptom Inventory (Derogatis, 1993) and the Minnesota Multiphasic Personality Inventory–2 (Butcher, Graham, BenPorath, Tellegen, Dahlstrom, & Kaemmer, 2001). Correlations of the BASC-2 SRP with the original BASC SRP were lower than corresponding correlations for the TRS and PRS, but they were still positive.

Although there appears to be evidence of validity for using the BASC-2 in making diagnostic decisions, no evidence of validity for the purposes of program evaluation and treatment planning is provided.

Summary

The BASC-2 is a comprehensive instrument that may be used to evaluate the behavior and self-perception of children ages 2 to 25 years. The integrated system comprises five separate measures of behavior: (1) Teacher Rating Scale, (2) Parent Rating Scale, (3) Self-Report of Personality, (4) Structured Developmental History Inventory, and (5) Student Observation Scale. Although the multimethod and multidimensional approach should be commended, the TRS, PRS, and SRP are the only scales for which normative data are provided on which any classification statements can be made. Norms for the BASC are more than adequate, with general and clinical norm data provided. Reliability of the composite scales is good, although the internalizing composites tend to have lower reliability coefficients, along with lower reliability coefficients evident for very young children. The BASC-2, like the ASEBA, provides one of the most comprehensive assessment tools on the market today. Good evidence of reliability and validity is presented via analysis of standardization sample data and correlations with additional behavior rating scales; however, validity evidence is not present for all of the possible uses described by the authors.

CHAPTER COMPREHENSION QUESTIONS

Write your answers to each of the following questions, and then compare your responses to the text or the study guide.

1. What are four methods for assessing social–emotional functioning?

2. Describe two reasons for assessing social–emotional functioning.

3. Describe the steps that you would follow in conducting a functional behavioral assessment.

4. Name and describe one commonly used measure of social–emotional functioning. What evidence of reliability and validity is available for this measure?

17 Using Measures of Adaptive Behavior

Chapter Goals

1 Understand the concept of adaptive behavior, including the role of physical environment, social and cultural expectations, and age in the definition of adaptation.

2 Understand the concept of maladaptive behavior, including the role of the context in which behavior occurs and its frequency and amplitude.

3 Know how we assess adaptive behavior.

4 Be familiar with the second edition of the Vineland Adaptive Behavior Scales.

5 Be familiar with some of the current dilemmas we face in using adaptive behavior measures.

Key Terms

adaptive behavior	daily living skills	social skills and
maladaption	interrespondent	relationships
respondent	reliability	interinterviewer
		reliability

ADAPTIVE BEHAVIOR IS THE WAY INDIVIDUALS ADAPT THEMSELVES TO THE requirements of their physical and social environment (Schmidt & Salvia, 1984). In part, adaptation means survival: Adaptive behaviors are those that allow individuals to continue to live by avoiding dangers and by taking reasonable precautions to ensure their safety. Yet adaptivity refers to more than mere survival; it implies the ability to thrive in both good and adverse times.

Adaptive behavior also requires more than an appropriate response to the demands of the immediate environment; it requires preparation for responses to probable future environments. Certain current behaviors (for example, smoking or high-risk sexual activity) can have life-threatening future consequences. Similarly, acquiring more education or job training and saving money increase the likelihood of thriving in later years. Adaptive behavior, in the present and for the future, must also take into account the demands of a person's physical surroundings and the expectations of that person's culture.

1 Defining Adaptive Behavior

Physical Environment

The knowledge and skill required to avoid danger (or to react appropriately when in danger) vary considerably from environment to environment. For example, different environments require different protective clothing and different precautions against climatic conditions. Living in the desert Southwest in summer requires guarding against dehydration and heat stroke, whereas living in New England in the winter requires guarding against hypothermia and frostbite. Different environments have different dangerous wildlife: alligators in southeastern swamps, scorpions and Gila monsters in the Southwest, rats in many urban areas, and so forth. In addition to natural hazards, different environments present human-made hazards: automobiles, electrical appliances, cutting tools, chemicals, and so forth.

Social and Cultural Expectations

Social expectations vary considerably from culture to culture, and the ability to thrive in a culture requires some degree of conformity to that society's cultural norms. Societal expectations manifest themselves in language usage (for example, polite or respectful language, speaking distance, and speaking volume), role performance, personal responsibility, and independence.

Age and Adaptation

Sociocultural expectations are also a function of the person's age. In the United States, we have different expectations of infants, children, adolescents, and adults. For infants and young children, expectations center on maturational processes; at some points in these processes, reflexive behavior (for example, sucking) is a necessary component of survival. After infancy, maturational processes merely enable behavior. "Thus, goodness of vision and hearing, intactness of motor skills, neuromotor integrity, and similar characteristics are not adaptive behaviors of the individual; they are biological characteristics of the human species and provide the basis for behavior" (Salvia, Neisworth, & Schmidt, 1990, p. 57). Therefore, for older individuals, adaptive behavior is learned behavior.

We expect youngsters to use language socially, to play appropriately, to assume limited responsibilities (for example, picking up toys), and to function in increasingly independent ways (for example, self-feeding, self-dressing, and moving around in their homes and neighborhoods). As children get older, the expectations for independence and responsibility increase, both at home and in school. With adolescence come demands for making the transition to adulthood (for example, preparing for employment and accepting more complete personal responsibility).

Performance Versus Ability

The ability to behave in expected ways is not synonymous with the performance of adaptive behavior. Knowing how to survive and thrive does not ensure that people will behave accordingly. For example, children may know that they should look both ways before crossing streets, and they may know how to do so; however, the important consideration is whether they do look both ways. Not only must a behavior be performed regularly (habitually and customarily) but also it must be performed without prompting or assistance.

2 Maladaption

In their definitions of adaptive behavior, some theorists include an absence of marked maladaption. Although such a position may have intuitive appeal, there are at least two conceptual problems with including maladaptive behavior on formal tests. First, the absence of maladaptive behavior does not imply the presence of adaptive behavior. Second, except for suicidal behavior and a very few universally taboo behaviors (for example, adolescents' or adults' smearing human excrement on themselves), maladaptive behavior is determined by context, as well as by frequency and amplitude.

Context

The context of behavior refers to both social tolerance and the specific situation in which a behavior occurs. Social tolerance is an important qualifier because very few behaviors are universally taboo. For example, certain types of hallucinations may be prized as religious experiences in some societies but seen as psychotic in others; homosexuality is accepted in some societies but punished in others. The list of potential examples is very long. Within a society, taboo behavior is codified by custom, religion, and law.

Some behaviors are evaluated solely on the basis of context. For example, disrobing is usually considered deviant in a classroom full of students but normal before bathing; failure to disrobe is normal in classrooms but abnormal before bathing. Even when certain behaviors are proscribed, the circumstances in which those behaviors are demonstrated are important. For example, in the United States, killing another person is not necessarily murder. The context in which the death occurred determines whether it is a crime (murder or voluntary manslaughter) or not (self-defense or accidental death).

Finally, for a behavior to be considered deviant, either the behavior or its consequence must be observed. If no one witnesses the act or its consequence, it will not be considered maladaptive. Moreover, the person observing the behavior (or consequence) must be willing and must have the authority to label the behavior as deviant.

Frequency and Amplitude

The frequency and amplitude of behavior are also important in labeling a behavior as maladaptive. Some behavior will be tolerated or condoned if it occurs infrequently. For example, occasional drunkenness may be ignored, but chronic drunkenness is considered alcoholism. The boundaries separating tolerated occasional misbehavior from deviance vary with context, status of the person, and consequences of the behavior. The amplitude of behavior also affects social and cultural tolerance. For example, fingernail biting is seldom, in and of itself, considered significant. However, when fingernail biting produces bleeding, scarring, and deformity, the behavior has crossed a line into self-mutilation.

3 Assessing Adaptive Behavior

Historically, the assessment of adaptive behavior has relied on the report of a third person (typically designated as a "respondent"). Thus, we do not assess an individual's adaptive behavior directly; an examiner does not test or observe the individual being assessed. Instead, the examiner relies on the cumulative observations of a respondent who is both truthful and sufficiently familiar with the subject of the assessment to make a judgment about that subject's behavior.

This method of administration is susceptible to a variety of errors and biases. The student being evaluated may generally conceal behavior that is culturally taboo, or the student may conceal behavior from the respondent if the student knows that the respondent disapproves of the behavior. The student being evaluated may selectively demonstrate the behavior. For example, when the respondent (a parent or teacher) is present, the student may behave appropriately; when the respondent is absent, the student may not. Finally, when respondents have a stake in the outcome, they may be less than truthful or objective. For example, if a parent respondent does not want a student classified as mentally retarded, that parent may give the child the benefit of the doubt in every response.

Scenario in Assessment

Crina

Remember Crina from Chapter 4? She was the girl from Eastern Europe who was adopted by an American family when she was 10 years old. Crina was evaluated by a district multidisciplinary team that recommended placement in a life skills class because her scores on the English language intelligence test and achievement tests were in the retarded range. Crina's mother disagreed with the school's diagnosis and obtained an independent educational evaluation that included an assessment of her adaptive behavior. That assessment indicated that Crina was functioning within the average range for a person her age. Nonetheless, the district remained adamant about the recommended placement, and the dispute was eventually settled at a due process hearing that was won by the parents.

In her opinion, the hearing officer wrote the following:

The IDEA is clear with respect to the definition of mental retardation. It is "significantly subaverage general intellectual functioning, existing concurrently with deficits in adaptive behavior and manifested during the developmental period, that adversely affects a child's educational performance" (§300.7(c)(6)). The evidence in this case is overwhelming: Crina, while having severe academic problems, does not have deficits in adaptive behavior. Therefore, she cannot be classified as a student with mental retardation. The District has erred in its classification and this order will prohibit her classification as such a student.

The parents not only prevailed at the hearing but also the district was severely reprimanded for its failure to follow both state and federal law. Conclusion: To classify a student as mentally retarded, there must be an evaluation of adaptive behavior.

SPECIFIC TEST OF ADAPTIVE BEHAVIOR

In Table 17.1, we provide basic information about several commonly used adaptive behavior scales. Then we provide a detailed review of the Vineland Adaptive Behavior Scales, Second Edition (VABS II).

Vineland Adaptive Behavior Scales, Second Edition (VABS II)

The Vineland Adaptive Behavior Scales, Second Edition (VABS II; Sparrow, Cicchetti, & Balla, 2005), is an individually administered adaptive behavior scale for use with individuals from birth through 90 years of age. The VABS II is intended for use in diagnostic evaluations, monitoring a student's progress, planning educational and treatment plans, and research. The scale is completed by respondents who are familiar with the target individual's behavior. Respondents can either complete a rating form or participate in a structured third-party interview. The VABS II authors recommend using the interview form for diagnostic decisions and the rating form for program planning and evaluation. A Spanish translation and a teacher form are available, and available computer software can convert raw scores to derived scores and generate score reports.

The Survey Interview Form consists of 413 questions distributed among five domains:

■ *Communication.* This domain has two subdomains. Expressive Communication consists of 54 items, such as crying when wet or hungry

TABLE 17.1   Commonly Used Adaptive Behavior Scales (*continued*)

Test	Author	Publisher	Year	Ages	Individual/ Group	NRT/SRT/ CRT	Subtests
AAMD Adaptive Behavior Scale: Residential and Community Scale, 2nd Edition	Nihira, Leland, & Lambert	Pro-Ed	1993	18–79 years	Individual	NRT	Independent Functioning, Physical Development, Economic Activity, Language Development, Numbers and Time, Domestic Activity, Prevocational/Vocational Activity, Self-Direction, Responsibility, Socialization, Social Behavior, Conformity, Trustworthiness, Stereotyped and Hyperactive Behavior, Sexual Behavior, Self-Abusive Behavior, Social Engagement, Disturbing Interpersonal Behavior Factors: Personal Self-Sufficiency, Community Self-Sufficiency, Personal–Social Responsibility, Social Adjustment, Personal Adjustment
AAMR Adaptive Behavior Scale– School 2	Nihira, Leland, & Lambert	Pro-Ed	1993	3–21 years	Individual	NRT	Independent Functioning, Physical Development, Economic Activity, Language Development, Numbers and Time, Prevocational/Vocational Activity, Self-Direction, Responsibility, Socialization, Social Behavior, Conformity, Trustworthiness, Stereotyped and Hyperactive Behavior, Self-Abusive Behavior, Social Engagement, Disturbing Interpersonal Behavior Factors: Personal Self-Sufficiency, Community Self-Sufficiency, Personal–Social Responsibility, Social Adjustment, Personal Adjustment

continued on the next page

TABLE 17.1	Commonly Used Adaptive Behavior Scales *(continued)*						
Test	**Author**	**Publisher**	**Year**	**Ages**	**Individual/ Group**	**NRT/SRT/ CRT**	**Subtests**
Scales of Independent Behavior–Revised	Bruininks, Woodcock, Weatherman, & Hill	Riverside	1996	Infants to 90 years	Individual	NRT	Gross Motor Skills, Fine Motor Skills, Social Interaction, Language Comprehension, Language Expression, Eating and Meal Preparation, Toileting, Dressing, Personal Self-Care, Domestic Skills, Time and Punctuality, Money and Value, Work Skills, Home and Community Orientation Clusters: Broad Independence, Motor Skills, Social Interaction and Communication Skills, Personal Living Skills, Community Living Skills
Vineland Adaptive Behavior Scales, 2nd Edition	Sparrow, Cicchetti, & Balla	Pearson	2005	Birth to 90 years	Individual	NRT	Survey Interview Form: Expressive Communication, Written Communication, Personal Daily Living Skills, Domestic Daily Living Skills, Community Daily Living Skills, Interpersonal Relationships, Play and Leisure Time, Coping Skills, Gross Motor, Fine Motor, Internalizing, Externalizing, Other Maladaptive Behavior Domains: Communication, Daily Living Skills, Socialization, Motor Skills, Maladaptive Behavior Parent/Caregiver Rating: Listening and Understanding, Talking, Reading and Writing, Caring for Self, Caring for Home, Living in the Community, Relating to Others, Playing and Using Leisure Time, Adapting, Using Large Muscles, Using Small Muscles Internalizing, Externalizing, and Other Behaviors Domains: Communication, Daily Living, Social Skills and Relationships, Physical Activity, Maladaptive Behavior, Problem Behaviors

and saying one's complete home address when asked. Written Communication consists of 25 items, such as recognizing one's own name and writing business letters.

- *Daily Living Skills (DLS).* This domain has three subdomains. Personal DLS has 41 items, such as opening mouth when food is offered and making appointments for regular medical and dental checkups. Domestic DLS consists of 24 items, such as being careful with hot objects and planning and preparing the main meal of the day. Community DLS consists of 44 items, such as talking to familiar people on the telephone and budgeting for monthly expenses.

- *Socialization.* This domain has three subdomains. Interpersonal Relationships has 38 items, such as looking at a parent's (caregiver's) face and going on single dates. Play and Leisure Time has 31 items, such as responding to playfulness of a parent (or caregiver) and going to places in the evening with friends. Coping Skills consists of 30 items, such as apologizing for unintended mistakes and showing respect for coworkers.

- *Motor Skills.* This domain has two subdomains. Gross Motor consists of 40 items, such as holding head up for 15 seconds and pedaling a tricycle for 6 feet. Fine Motor consists of 36 items, such as reaching for a toy and using a keyboard to type 10 lines.

- *Maladaptive Behavior.* This domain has three subdomains. Internalizing consists of 11 items, such as being overly dependent and avoiding social interaction. Externalizing consists of 10 items, such as being impulsive and behaving inappropriately. Other Maladaptive Behavior consists of 15 items, such as sucking one's thumb, being truant, and using alcohol or illegal drugs during the school or work day. Critical Items consists of 14 items, such as engaging in inappropriate sexual behavior, causing injury to self, and being unable to complete a normal school or work day because of psychological symptoms.

The Parent/Caregiver Rating Form consists of 433 questions distributed among six domains.

- *Communication.* This domain has three subdomains. Listening and Understanding consists of 20 items, such as responding to one's

spoken name and listening to informational talk for 30 minutes. Talking consists of 54 items, such as crying or fussing when hungry or wet and using possessives in phrases or sentences to describing long-range goals. Reading and Writing consists of 25 items, such as recognizing one's name when printed and editing or correcting one's written work before handing it in.

- *Daily Living.* This domain has three subdomains. Caring for Self has 41 items, such as eating solid foods and keeping track of medications and refilling them as needed. Caring for Home has 24 items, such as cleaning up play or work area at the end of an activity and performing routine maintenance tasks. Living in the Community consists of 44 items, such as being aware and demonstrating appropriate behavior when riding in a car and holding a full-time job for a year.

- *Social Skills and Relationships.* This domain has three subdomains. Relating to Others consists of 38 items, such as showing two or more emotions, recognizing the likes and dislikes of others, and starting conversations about things that interest others. Playing and Using Leisure Time consists of 31 items, such as playing simple interaction games (for example, peekaboo), showing good sportsmanship, and planning fun activities requiring arrangements for two or more things. Adapting has 30 items, such as saying thank you and controlling anger or hurt feelings when not getting one's way.

- *Physical Activity.* This domain has two subdomains. Using Large Muscles has 40 items, such as climbing on and off an adult-sized chair and catching a tennis ball from 10 feet. Using Small Muscles has 36 items, such as picking up small objects, holding a pencil in proper position for writing or drawing, and tying a bow.

- *Maladaptive Behavior Part 1.* This domain contains 36 items divided into three parts: Internalizing, Externalizing, and Other Behaviors. Maladaptive behaviors include both states (for example, being overly anxious or nervous) and behaviors (for example, tantruming and being truant).

- *Problem Behaviors Part 2.* This domain has 14 "critical" items, such as obsessing with objects or activities and being unaware of things happening around oneself.

Scores

Individual items are scored on a 4-point scale: 2 = usually, 1 = sometimes or partially, 0 = never, and DK = don't know.[1] To speed administration of the VABS II, basal and ceiling rules are used in all subtests except those assessing maladaptive behavior.

Raw scores are converted to v-scale scores, a standard score with a mean of 10 and a standard deviation of 3. Summed v-scale scores can be converted to normalized standard scores (mean = 100, standard deviation = 15) and stanines for subdomains; subdomain scores can be summed and converted to domain indexes and to an Adaptive Behavior Composite. Raw scores can also be converted to age equivalents.[2] Percentiles are available for domain scores and the Adaptive Behavior Composite. Percentiles are based on the relationship between standard scores and percentiles in normal distributions.

Norms

Regardless of the method of assessment (that is, interview or rating scale), one set of norms is used to interpret VABS II scores. The decision to use a single set of norms was based on the results of a study comparing the results from both interviews and rating scales for 760 individuals. Three of the four analyses performed by the authors support the decision to use a single set of norms. However, the analysis of correlations between the two methods of assessment does not support that conclusion. For individuals 6 years of age or older, less than 10 percent of the correlations between the two assessment methods equal or exceed .90; almost half are less than .80. Clearly, the scores are not interchangeable.

The normative sample consists of 3,695 individuals selected to represent the U.S. population. The manual offers only the most cursory explanation of how these individuals were selected from a larger pool of potential subjects: Selections were made electronically "in a way that matched the demographic variable targets within each age group" (Sparrow et al., 2005, p. 93).

The number of persons within each age group varies considerably from age to age. Samples of children younger than 2 years of age, the sample of children 4 to 4.5 years old, the sample of individuals between 19 and 21 years, and samples of adults older than 31 years of age each contain fewer than 100 individuals. The norms are generally representative in terms of ethnicity (African American, Hispanic, and Caucasian), educational level of the respondents, and geographic region.

Reliability

Split-half estimates of internal consistency for adaptive behavior are provided for 19 age groups: 1-year age groups from 0 through 11 years, 2-year groups from 12 to 21 years, and four multiyear ranges from 22 through 90 years. The reliability of 18 of the 19 Adaptive Behavior Composites equals or exceeds .90; the exception is the 32- to 51-year-old age group. Domain scores are generally less reliable. In 6 of the 19 age groups, the reliability of the Communication domain is less than .90; in 9 of the 19 age groups, the reliability of the Daily Living Skills domain is less than .90; in 7 of the 19 age groups, the reliability of the Socialization domain is less than .90; and in 5 of the 9 age groups, the reliability of the Motor Skills domain is less than .90. Coefficient alpha is also reported for Part 1 Maladaptive Behavior for 5 age groups: 3 to 5, 6 to 11, 12 to 18, 19 to 30, and 40 to 90 years. No alpha for the Internalizing composite reaches .90, and only one (for 12- to 18-year-olds) equals .90. Only the alphas for the Maladaptive Behavior index for individuals 6 to 11 years old (.90) and for individuals 12 to 18 years old (.91) are large enough to use in making important individual decisions.

Test–retest estimates of reliability for adaptive behavior are provided for six age ranges.[3] Except for the 14- to 21-year-old age group, the obtained stability[4] of the Adaptive Behavior Composite equals or exceeds .90; stability for the same group is .81. Stabilities of

---

[1] If the number of items scored DK is greater than two, the subdomain should not be scored.

[2] Age equivalents are defined on the VABS II as representing "the age at which that score is average." It is unclear whether the average refers to the mean, the median, or the mode.

[3] Although it appears that standard scores were used to estimate the stability of domain scores, it is unclear what scores were used to estimate the stability of subdomain scores. We note that the use of raw scores would inflate stability estimates.

[4] The authors report both obtained and adjusted stability estimates. We prefer interpreting the reliability estimates that were actually obtained and therefore do not discuss adjusted estimates.

domains are lower; 11 of the 18 reported stability coefficients are less than .90. Stabilities of subdomain scores are generally less than those for the domains; 45 of the 50 subdomain stabilities reported are less than .90. Test–retest estimates are also provided for Part 1 Maladaptive Behavior for five age groups: 3 to 5, 6 to 11, 12 to 18, 19 to 39, and 40 to 71 years. Only the Externalizing and Maladaptive indexes for individuals between 40 and 71 years old reach the .90 level. All estimates of internalizing behavior and all other estimates of Externalizing and Maladaptive Behavior indexes are between .72 and .89.

Interinterviewer reliability was also evaluated for the interview form. Two interviewers interviewed the same respondent at different times. For adaptive behavior, two age ranges were used: 0 to 6 and 7 to 18 years. No VABS II score had an estimated reliability of .90 or higher, and most estimates were in the .40 to .60 range. For Part 1 Maladaptive Behavior, three age ranges were used: 3 to 11, 112 to 18, and 19 to 70 years. Estimated interinterviewer reliabilities ranged from .44 to .83.

Interrespondent reliability was evaluated by having two respondents rate the same individual. For adaptive behavior, two age ranges were again used: 0 to 6 and 7 to 18 years. In neither age group did the Adaptive Behavior Composite or any domain score reach an estimated reliability of .90. Most estimates were in the .60 to .80 range. For Part 1 Maladaptive Behavior, three age ranges were again used: 3 to 11, 112 to 18, and 19 to 70 years. Estimated interrater reliabilities ranged from .32 to .81.

Validity

Five types of information about the VABS II validity are included in the manual: test content, response process, test structure, clinical groups, and relationship with other measures. The description of content development lacks sufficient detail to allow a systematic analysis of that process. Similarly, the description of how items were selected is vague. In contrast, factor-analytic studies support the existence of separate domains and subdomains, whereas the examination of test content for sex bias, socioeconomic status bias, and ethnic bias indicates a lack of bias. Also, VABS II raw scores show a consistent developmental pattern, as would be expected with any measure of adaptive behavior.

Previously identified groups of individuals with mental retardation, autism, attention deficit hyperactivity disorder, emotional disturbance, learning disability, and vision and hearing impairments each earned the types of scores that would be expected for persons with those disabilities. For example, individuals with mental retardation all showed significant deficits on the Adaptive Behavior Composite and domain scores.

The VABS II correlates well with the previous edition of the scale. Correlations vary by age and domain, ranging from .65 (Communication for children 0 to 2 years of age) to .94 (Socialization for children 3 to 6 years of age). The VABS II correlates moderately with the Adaptive Behavior Assessment System, Second Edition, and the Behavior Assessment System for Children, Second Edition.

Summary

The VABS II is an individually administered, norm-referenced scale for evaluating the adaptive behavior of individuals from birth to 90 years of age. The scale can be administered as a structured interview or as a rating scale, but these two methods appear to yield somewhat different results (that is, they are not so highly correlated that they can be used interchangeably). Despite the differences in the results of the two administrations, one set of norms is used to convert raw scores to derived scores. Thus, although norms appear representative, their use for both methods of administration is problematic.

Reliability is generally inadequate for making important individual decisions about students, especially adolescents. Both interinterviewer and interrespondent reliability are too low to use the VABS II with confidence. The internal consistency of the Adaptive Behavior Composite is generally reliable enough to use in making important educational decisions for students. Domain, subdomain, and maladaptive reliabilities are not. Except for adolescents, the stability of the Adaptive Behavior Composite is adequate; the domain, subdomain, and maladaptive items stabilities are usually too low for making important individual decisions.

General indications of validity are adequate. However, no data are presented to indicate that the VABS II is valid for monitoring a student's progress or planning educational and treatment plans.

4 Why Do We Assess Adaptive Behavior?

There are two major reasons for assessing adaptive behavior: (1) identification of mental retardation and (2) program planning. First, mental retardation is generally defined, in part, as a failure of adaptive behavior. In theory, in order to classify a pupil as having mental retardation, for example, an evaluator needs to assess adaptive behavior. More important, however, are the federal regulations and state school codes requiring that adaptive behavior be assessed before a pupil can be considered mentally retarded.

Second, for program planning, educational objectives in the domain of adaptive behavior are frequently developed for individuals with moderate to severe retardation, as well as for students with other disabilities. Adaptive behavior is often important in planning habilitative and transition services for various students. Thus, scales of adaptive behavior are often the source of educational goals.

Dilemmas in Current Practice

There are three major problems in the use of currently available instruments to assess adaptive behavior: (1) lack of internal consistency, (2) poor norms, and (3) lack of interrater agreement.

The first problem is that there is no theoretical reason that adaptive behavior scales should not be internally consistent. That some scales are not homogeneous can reasonably be attributed to the lack of a clear definition of adaptive behavior, a problem to which we alluded previously in this chapter. There is no professional consensus about the types of behavior that are indicative of adaptation. Indeed, inspection of the behaviors sampled by the various devices suggests a lack of agreement about what adaptive behavior is—there is a broad range of behaviors sampled and of orientations toward measurement. Without a more precise concept of adaptive behavior, we should probably expect heterogeneous operationalizations of the definition (that is, heterogeneous scales of adaptive behavior) to continue.

The second problem is that scales of adaptive behavior frequently are poorly normed (sometimes normed only on individuals with disabilities). If its norm samples are unrepresentative, a scale should not be used.

The third and most vexing problem, both theoretically and practically, is the lack of agreement among raters. When reported at all for adaptive behavior scales, interrater agreement is often poor. Poor agreement indicates a lack of reliability. Thus, we would suspect at least three potential problems: (1) The specific items are difficult to understand or interpret, (2) the criteria used to rate the behavior are subjective, or (3) one or both of the raters are insufficiently familiar with the student. Lack of interrater agreement also leads to a lack of validity. In practice, examiners have few options beyond gathering more data when faced with rater disagreement.

CHAPTER COMPREHENSION QUESTIONS

Write your answers to each of the following questions, and then compare your responses to the text or the study guide.

1. How do the physical environment, age, and social and cultural expectations affect the definition of adaptation?

2. How do the context in which behavior occurs and its frequency and amplitude affect the definition of maladaption?

3. Why do we assess adaptive behavior?

4. Explain two potential problems in the assessment of adaptive behavior.

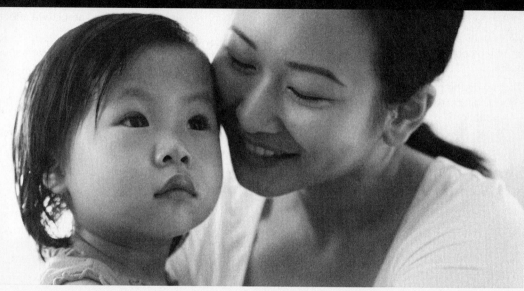

Chapter Goals

1 Know why we assess infants, toddlers, and preschoolers.

2 Understand unique challenges associated with measuring development among young children.

3 Understand methods that are commonly used for assessing young children.

4 Be familiar with several commonly used infant, toddler, and preschool measures.

Key Terms

developmental milestones

Individual Growth and
Developmental
Indicators (IGDIs)

Head Start/Early Head Start

Bayley Scales of Infant and
Toddler Development,
Third Edition (Bayley-3)

Developmental Indicators
for the Assessment of
Learning–Third Edition
(DIAL-3)

WITH THE PASSAGE OF PUBLIC LAW 99-457 IN 1986, STATES WERE REQUIRED TO serve children with disabilities between 3 and 5 years of age. In addition, this law extended services to children from birth to 3 years of age, provided that the children (1) have physical or mental conditions with a high probability of producing developmental delays (for example, cerebral palsy or trisomy); (2) are at risk medically or environmentally for developmental delay; or (3) have developmental delays in cognition, physical development, speech and language, or psychosocial behavior. Since the law's passage, it has no longer been legally acceptable to delay or deny school admission to children who are developmentally delayed or otherwise disabled. Emphasis has changed from testing young children for school readiness to comprehensively assessing infants, toddlers, and young children to address their educational and developmental needs. Furthermore, states must demonstrate that young children who are served through the associated funds are acquiring and using knowledge and skills, as well as developing positive social relationships.

Recently, interest in the assessment of all young children (including those without disabilities) has been on the rise. Recognizing the important role that early childhood programming can play in each student's future academic and social development, the federal government has provided substantial support for programs such as Head Start (ages 3 to 5 years) and Early Head Start (birth to 2 years) that are targeted to address the needs of students from low socioeconomic backgrounds. Accountability for family and child outcomes associated with early childhood programming has similarly increased. Early childhood initiatives such as "Good Start, Grow Smart," which was established in 2002, encourage states to develop early childhood standards for literacy and language on which to assess the performance and progress of young children.

According to a position statement on early childhood curriculum, assessment, and program evaluation put forth by the National Association for the Education of Young Children (2003), early childhood assessment should "use methods that are developmentally appropriate, culturally and linguistically responsive, tied to children's daily activities, supported by professional development, inclusive of families, and connected to specific, beneficial purposes" (p. 1). The assessment of young children is quite different from the assessment of older individuals. The types of behavior assessed differ from the behaviors of older individuals. Infants and young children are not miniature adults possessed of adult abilities and behavior. Infant behavior is undifferentiated, molar, and limited; for example, infants fuss with their bodies and their voices. Infant assessment frequently involves neurobiological appraisal in four areas: neurological integrity (for example, reflexes and postural responses), behavioral organization (for example, attention and response to social stimuli), temperament (for example, consolability and responsivity), and state of consciousness (for example, sleep patterns and attention). As infants develop into toddlers and preschoolers, their behavior differentiates, and broad domains of behavior emerge. Assessment of toddlers and preschoolers frequently involves appraisal of communication, cognition, personal–social behavior, and motor behavior.

The evaluation of toddlers and preschoolers generally relies on their attainment of developmental milestones (significant developmental accomplishments), such as using words and walking. Although children's development is quite variable, children are usually considered to be at risk for later problems when their attainment of developmental milestones is delayed. Thus, examiners must have a thorough understanding of normal development. Moreover, examiners must understand family systems and the role of culture in child-rearing practices so that they can understand the environments in which infants, toddlers, and preschoolers are developing. As is the case for school-age assessment practices, assessment tools are increasingly being designed to be aligned with the standards and curricula associated with early childhood programming, such that monitoring of child progress toward instructional targets is facilitated.

The Individual Growth and Development Indicators (IGDIs) represent sets of tools that have been developed at the infant, toddler, and preschool levels to monitor student progress and assist with intervention design and modification. At the infant and toddler levels, these include both child and family (that is, parent–child interaction) measures.

Finally, the procedures used to assess infants, toddlers, and preschoolers often differ from those used to evaluate older children and adults. Bailey and Rouse (1989) have reported a number of reasons why infants and young children are difficult to test. Infants between 6 and 18 months are distressed by unfamiliar adults. Although they may have better responses to strangers when held by their caregivers, they may still refuse to respond to an unfamiliar adult. Infants and preschoolers may be very active, inattentive, and distractible; they frequently perform inconsistently in strange situations. Because the language of these children is, by definition, undeveloped, they may not completely understand even simple questions and oral requests. Thus, traditional assessment formats in which students respond to examiner questions can be problematic. Not surprisingly, many toddlers and preschoolers are described as untestable. Rather than rely on traditional testing formats, assessment of young children typically involves observations of structured play activities and caregivers' ratings of the child's behavior. Having parents and caregivers complete a developmental history can be very helpful, and in some cases it is essential for appropriate decision making.

When assessing young children who are diagnosed as having severe disabilities, it is particularly important to recognize and show sensitivity to the family's emotional responses. Parents have many hopes and dreams for young children, and often they must go through a long grieving process as they recognize how these original hopes and dreams will not be actualized. Parents often need assistance in seeking out resources to help them cope with such grief.

1 Why Do We Assess Infants, Toddlers, and Preschoolers?

There are several reasons to assess young children. Assessments can play an integral role in guiding instructional planning decisions for early childhood programs, as well as in the development of individualized family service plans for students eligible to receive special education services. Delayed developmental areas may be targeted for intervention. Tests and rating scales are often used to conduct program evaluation and to monitor progress toward standards for children with and without disabilities. Many measures currently available for use with very young children were developed exclusively for measuring attainment of goals in Head Start (ages 3 to 5 years) and Early Head Start (birth to 2 years) programs. Meller, Ohr, and Marcus (2001) describe a dramatic increase in the development of tools to address young children since the 1980s. We use developmental tests with young children much as we use achievement and intelligence tests with students who have enrolled in schools: to facilitate eligibility decisions. Eligibility for special education programs is based on criteria, and these criteria are operationalized by tests and rating scales.

Scenario in Assessment

Olive Oyle

Olive Oyle is a 27-month-old toddler who was identified by her parents as seeming to be particularly slow in learning to talk. Upon expressing their concerns to their daughter's physician, Olive's parents were referred to a community-based program that provides services to young children in their home environments. In order to identify whether Olive is making appropriate progress through the program, an early childhood specialist uses the IGDIs, focusing on the Early Communication Indicator (ECI), to monitor her progress once each month.

The ECI requires the specialist to videotape a 6-minute play session in which the specialist attempts to engage Olive in play activities using a

particular set of toys. When viewing the recorded observation at a later time, the specialist tallies each gesture, vocalization, single word, and multiple word utterance that Olive displays in order to determine a rate for each of these behaviors per minute of the observation. These rates are then compared to Olive's rates from previous sessions as well as to those of typically developing children. A report that includes graphs displaying the child's progress over time, as well as a visual depiction of the reliability of the student's performance on the various tasks, is available to help determine whether Olive is making progress in the area of expressive language. The report is provided in Figure 18.1.

FIGURE 18.1
Sample IGDI Report for Early Communication Indicator

SOURCE: Juniper Gardens Children's Project, University of Kansas (www.igdi.ku.edu).

continued on the next page

Scenario in Assessment (*continued*)

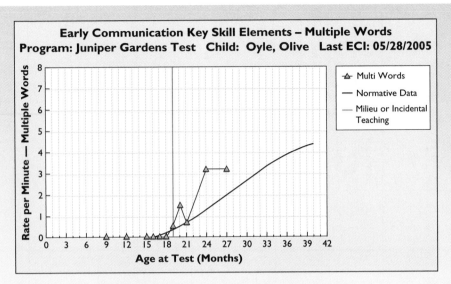

Early Communication Key Skill Elements – Multiple Words
Program: Juniper Gardens Test   Child: Oyle, Olive   Last ECI: 05/28/2005

SOURCE: www.igdi.ku.edu. Reprinted with permission.

TESTS USED WITH INFANTS, TODDLERS, AND PRESCHOOLERS

Table 18.1 provides information on several commonly used measures for assessing infants, toddlers, and preschoolers that are reviewed on the website for this book. Reviews for the Bayley Scales of Infant Development, Third Edition (Bayley-III) and the Developmental Indicators for the Assessment of Learning–Third Edition (DIAL-3) are provided following the table.

Bayley Scales of Infant Development, Third Edition (Bayley-III)

The Bayley Scales of Infant and Toddler Development, Third Edition (Bayley-III; Bayley, 2006), is a norm-referenced, individually administered test intended to assess the developmental functioning of children ages 1 to 42 months. The test takes 30 to 90 minutes to administer depending on the age of the child. The test is available in three formats: the Bayley-III Complete Kit, the Bayley-III Comprehensive Kit (which is the same as the complete kit but with a PDA Administration and Scoring Assistant), and the Bayley-III Screening Test.

The Bayley-III assesses development in five domains: Cognitive, Language, Motor, Socio-Emotional, and Adaptive Behavior. Data for the Cognitive, Language, and Motor domains are obtained by assessing the child; for the other two domains, data are obtained from caregiver responses to a questionnaire. The Language domain includes both receptive and expressive communication subtests, and the Motor subtest includes assessment of both fine and gross motor skills. The Socio-Emotional subtest (Greenspan, 2006) is new to the third edition of this test and is an adaptation of the Greenspan Social–Emotional Growth Chart: A Screening Questionnaire for Infants and Young Children (Greenspan, 2004). The Adaptive Behavior scale (Harrison, 2006) is composed of items and skill areas from the Adaptive Behavior Assessment System, Second Edition (Harrison & Oakland, 2003). The Adaptive Behavior scale includes measures of communication, functional preacademics (such as letter recognition and counting), self-direction, leisure time use, social functioning, community use, home living (helping with household tasks), health and safety, self-care, and motor skills (locomotion and getting around in the environment).

TABLE 18.1   Commonly Used Measures for Infants, Toddlers, and Preschoolers

Test	Author	Publisher	Year	Ages/ Grades	Individual/ Group	NRT/SRT/ CRT	Subtests
Bayley Scales of Infant and Toddler Development, Third Edition (Bayley-III)	Bayley	Pearson	2006	Ages 1–42 months	Individual	NRT	Cognitive, Language, Motor, Socio-Emotional, Adaptive Behavior
Boehm-3 Preschool	Boehm	Pearson	2001	Ages 3-0 to 5-11 years	Individual	NRT	Arithmetic, Information, Color, Copying Shapes, Block Assembly, Classification
Developmental Assessment of Young Children	Voress & Maddox	Pro-Ed	1998	Ages birth to 5 years	Individual	NRT	Cognitive, Communications, Social-Emotional, Physical Development, Adaptive Behavior
Developmental Indicators for the Assessment of Learning, Third Edition (DIAL-3)	Mardell-Czudnowski & Goldenberg	Pearson	1998	Ages 3–6 years	Individual	NRT	Motor, Concepts, Language, Self-Help, Social Development
Developmental Profile II	Alpern, Boll, & Shearer	Western Psychological Services	2000	Ages birth to 9-6 years	Individual	NRT	Physical, Social, Self-Help, Academic, Communication
Early Childhood Behavior Scale	S. B. McCarney	Hawthorne	1992	Ages 36–72 months	Individual	NRT	Academic Progress, Social Relationships, Personal Adjustment
Early Screening Inventory–Revised	Meisels, Marston, Wiske, & Henderson	Pearson	1997	Ages 3–6 years	Individual	CRT	Visual-Motor/Adaptive, Language and Cognition, Gross Motor Skills and Abilities

Test	Author	Publisher	Year	Ages/Grades	Administration	NRT/CRT	Areas Assessed
Metropolitan Readiness Tests, Sixth Edition	Nurss & McGauvran	Pearson	1995	Ages 4–7 years	Individual	NRT/CRT	Visual Discrimination, Beginning Consonants, Sound–Letter Correspondence, Aural Cloze, Story Comprehension, Quantitative Concepts and Reasoning
Preschool Evaluation Scale	S. B. McCarney	Hawthorne Educational Services	1992	Ages birth to 6 years	Individual	NRT	Large Muscle, Small Muscle, Cognitive Thinking, Expressive Language, Social–Emotional, Self-Help Skills
STAR Early Literacy (reviewed on website under Chapter 19)	Renaissance Learning	Renaissance Learning	2001	Ages 3–9	Individual	NRT	General Readiness, Phonemic Awareness, Phonics, Graphophonemic Knowledge, Structural Analysis, Vocabulary, Reading and Listening Comprehension
Test of Early Mathematics Abilites	Ginsburg & Baroody	Pro-Ed	2003	Ages 3-0 to 8-11	Individual	NRT	
Test of Early Reading Ability–Third Edition (TERA-3)	Reid, Hresko, & Hammill	Pro-Ed	2001	Ages 3-6 to 8-6 years	Individual	NRT	Alphabet, Conventions, Meaning
Work Sampling System, Fourth Edition	Meisels, Jablon, Marston, Dichtelmiller, Dorfman, & Marston	Pearson	1994	Grades pre-K to 6	Individual	CRT	Personal and Social Adjustment, Language and Literacy, Mathematical Thinking, Scientific Thinking, Social Studies, Arts, Physical Development and Health
Young Children's Achievement Test (YCAT)	Hresko, Peak, Herron, & Bridges	Pro-Ed	2000	Grades preschool–first grade	Individual	NRT	General Information, Reading, Mathematics, Writing, Spoken Language

Scores

Performance on the Bayley-III can be represented in the form of scaled scores, composite scores, percentile ranks, and growth scores. Developmental age equivalents are available for some subtests. The growth scores are used to plot individual child development over time.

Norms

There were several phases to standardization of the Bayley-III. First, a pilot study was conducted on 353 children. This pilot included items from the second edition of the Bayley, along with a subset of new items. Data were also collected from two clinical groups of children: those born prematurely and children with developmental delays. The data obtained from this pilot were used to construct a preliminary version of the test. This preliminary version was then applied with 1,923 children in a national tryout phase. Data obtained from this national tryout were used to construct a version of the test that was submitted to an additional minipilot with 20 children. Then a final version of the Bayley-III was developed.

The Bayley-III was standardized on a sample of 1,700 children ages 16 days to 43 months 15 days and to samples of children from "special groups." The sample was stratified on the basis of gender, geographic region, race/ethnicity, and parent education level. Norms for the Socio-Emotional scale were derived from 456 children in the standardization sample of the Greenspan Social-Emotional Growth Chart, whereas norms for the Adaptive Behavior scale were derived from 1,350 children who participated in the standardization of the Adaptive Behavior Assessment Scale–II. Data in the technical manual for the test show that each age group closely approximates the 2000 U.S. census in terms of race/ethnicity, geographic region, parental education, and gender.

Reliability

Alphas were used to estimate the internal consistency of the Cognitive, Language, and Motor scales at each age. For the Cognitive scale, alpha ranged from .79 to .97; 10 of the 17 coefficients equaled or exceeded .90. For the Motor scale, alpha ranged from .86 to .96; 14 of the 17 coefficients exceeded .90. Alphas for the Language scale ranged from .82 to .98. Across all three domains, internal consistency coefficients are lower for children younger than 1 year of age than they are for older children. Reliabilities for the Socio-Emotional and Adaptive Behavior scales generally are in the .70s for children younger than 1 year of age and .80s for older children.

Test–retest stability coefficients are generally in the .70s—too low for use in making important decisions for young children (those younger than 26 months of age). Some stability coefficients for children in the age range of 33 to 43 months are barely satisfactory for making important decisions.

Given the fact that it is very difficult to obtain stable performance over time for very young children, the Bayley-III is about as reliable as other measures designed for use with infants and toddlers.

Validity

Data are provided in the technical manual showing evidence for validity based on test content, evidence based on internal structure, and evidence based on relation with other variables. Evidence based on test content is limited to the author's argument that the test measures content consistent with theoretical conceptions of the development of infants and toddlers. Evidence based on internal structure consists of good evidence of the convergent and discriminant validity of the test. Evidence is provided that the Language subtests are more highly correlated with each other than with the Motor subtests and that they are moderately correlated with the Cognitive scale. There is also evidence for moderate correlations between the Motor and Cognitive scales. The author argues that the moderate correlation between scores on the Language and Cognitive scales reflects the close relationship between these domains.

Evidence for validity based on relation with other measures is based on examination of the relationship between performance on the Bayley-III and the second edition of the Bayley Scales of Infant Development, WPPSI-III, Preschool Language Scale 4, Peabody Developmental Motor Scales–II, and the Adaptive Behavior Assessment–2. The data presented provide reasonable evidence for the validity of the test.

There are several studies of the validity of the Bayley-III with special populations of students. Data are provided on the validity of the Bayley-III with children with Down syndrome and children identified as exhibiting "pervasive developmental disorder, children with cerebral palsy, those with specific language impairment, children with motor and physical impairments, those exposed prenatally or at birth to specific risks (asphyxiation at birth, prenatal alcohol exposure), and children born premature or with low birth weight." The scale is sensitive to performance differences between children in the normative sample and samples of children with various conditions that place them at risk for developmental delay.

Summary

The Bayley-III is a norm-referenced, individually administered test intended to assess developmental functioning of children between 1 and 42 months of age. The test has five subscales: the Cognitive scale, the Motor scale, the Language scale, a Socio-Emotional scale, and an Adaptive Behavior scale. The scales' norms appear representative in terms of race/ethnicity, geographic region, parental education, and gender, although cross-tabulations are not provided for these variables. There is good evidence for the reliability and validity of the scale, especially for children older than 1 year of age.

Developmental Indicators for the Assessment of Learning–Third Edition (DIAL-3)

The Developmental Indicators for the Assessment of Learning–Third Edition (DIAL-3; Mardell-Czudnowski & Goldenberg, 1998) is an individually administered, 30-minute screening test to assess the development of children between the ages of 3-0 and 6-11 years. Several new items were developed for this edition of the scale, and a Parental Questionnaire was added to assess self-help, social development, family background, and general developmental information. Finally, a short form (called the Speed DIAL) is now available. Both the DIAL-3 and the Speed DIAL can be administered in English or Spanish. Although individual children are screened, the testing procedures are designed to handle large numbers of children; different examiners (called operators) administer the Motor, Concepts, and Language subtests to a child, who moves from one testing area (and one tester) to another. There are no special qualifications for operators.

Subtests

Three subtests (called Areas on the DIAL-3) require direct observation of a child's performance on various items that may require multiple responses. The Speed DIAL includes eight of the DIAL-3 subtests.[1] Here, we describe the subtests and name and describe the items.

Motor.   This subtest includes catching a beanbag with one and two hands, jump–hop–skip, building with blocks, touching thumbs and fingers of the same hand in various sequences, cutting with scissors, copying four geometric shapes and four letters, and writing the child's own name.

Concepts.   This subtest includes pointing to body parts, identification of colors, rapid color naming, rote counting, using blocks to demonstrate relative positions (front, down, and so forth), concepts (for example, "big"), and sorting by shapes.

Language.   This subtest includes providing personal data (name, age, and so forth), articulation (repeating the names of objects), naming objects and actions, letters and sounds (saying the alphabet, naming letters presented in random order, and producing the sound of a letter), rhyming and "I Spy" (rhyming and alliteration), oral problem solving about social situations, and intelligibility rating by the examiner.

Self-Help.   Parents rate their children's development of eating, toileting, dressing, and other daily living skills. Parents indicate whether the child performs the skill most of the time with no help, sometimes or with help, not yet, or not allowed.

Social Development.   Parents rate the frequency with which their children exhibit feelings and behaviors that are related to successful relationships with family and peers.

Scores

Raw scores for each item are converted to an intermediate score called a scaled score for the areas/subtests of Motor, Concepts, and Language, as well as the Speed

---

[1]This item is also used in the Speed DIAL.

DIAL.[2] The scaled scores for each subtest can also be summed into the DIAL-3 Total score. Testers can look up children's ages (in 2-month intervals) in tables to convert scaled score sums to percentiles and cutoff levels for potential delay. Raw score sums for Self-Help and Social Development ratings can also be converted to percentiles and cutoff levels for potential delay.

The authors provide multiple ways to use the DIAL-3 scores to reach a decision and identify a child as needing further assessment. However, they offer users little guidance beyond the fact that more children can be identified with less stringent criteria and fewer children with criteria that are more rigorous.

Norms

The DIAL-3 was standardized on 1,560 children between the ages of 3-0 and 6-11 years who were tested between November 1995 and June 1997. The children resided in 36 states, the District of Columbia, Puerto Rico, and Panama. The proportions of individuals in the DIAL-3 norms are comparable to the 1994 census in terms of gender, race/ethnicity, geographic region, and parental educational level.

Reliability

Internal consistency was estimated using coefficient alpha for eight 6-month age groups (3-0 to 3-5, 3-6 to 3-11, and so forth). We consider .80 to be the minimum reliability for a screening device. The Motor, Language, and Self-Help subtests are usually not sufficiently reliable to use for screening decisions: For Motor, none of the alphas for the eight age groups equals or exceeds .80; for Language and Self-Help,

two of the eight alphas equal or exceed .80. The remaining two subtests have more age groups for which alphas equal or exceed .80: six age groups for Concepts and all eight for Social Development. The reliability of the Speed DIAL equals or exceeds .80 in half of the age groups, and the reliability of the DIAL-3 Total exceeds .80 except for the oldest group of children.

To estimate stability, 158 children were divided into two groups. A younger group contained 80 children between 3-6 and 4-5 years, and an older group contained 78 children between 4-6 and 5-10 years. The children were retested on average after approximately 28 days. For the younger group, two subtests had stability estimates that equaled or exceeded .80; stabilities for the DIAL-3 Total and the Speed DIAL both exceeded .80. For the older group, Social Development was the only subtest that exceeded .80; stabilities for the DIAL-3 Total and the Speed DIAL both exceeded .80.

Thus, only the DIAL-3 Total appears to have sufficient reliability for use in making screening decisions. It should also be noted that the age groups used to estimate reliability are not the same as the age groups used to convert raw scores to percentiles and delay ratings.

Validity

Some claim can be made for the content validity of the DIAL-3 because of the careful selection and field testing of the items. Some evidence for criterion-related validity comes from modest (that is, .25 to .45) correlations with similar subtests on the Early Screening Profile, moderate (that is, .30 to .55) correlations with similar subtests on the Battelle Screening Test, and fairly strong correlations of the total score on the Brigance Preschool Screen with Concepts Language and the DIAL-3 Total (that is, .53 to .79) and of Language with the Peabody Picture Vocabulary Test. The Self-Help and Social Development ratings were also correlated with parent ratings of social skills on the Social Skills Rating System. Finally, children with disabilities who were identified by means other than the DIAL-3 earned lower normalized standard scores. However, although this finding is interesting, it is difficult to interpret because no standard scores are available for the DIAL-3.

---

[2]*Scaled score* usually refers to a standard score with a predetermined mean and standard deviation. However, the DIAL-3 manual defines a scaled score as the median of an age distribution, so it is a developmental score. (A scaled score of 0 is the median for children younger than age 3 years, 1 is the median for 3-year-olds, 2 is the median for 4-year-olds, 3 is the median for 5-year-olds, and 4 is the median for 6-year-olds.) The manual provides no explanation for the ranges associated with each scaled score. For example, in Rapid Color Naming, a scaled score of 0 corresponds to raw scores of 0 to 4, a scaled score of 1 corresponds to raw scores of 5 to 9, a scaled score of 2 corresponds to raw scores of 10 to 19, and so forth. It appears that the scaled scores on the DIAL-3 are at best ordinal and cannot provide for equal weighting of items, as claimed on page 70 of the manual.

Dilemmas in Current Practice

There are three major dilemmas in assessing infants, toddlers, and preschoolers. The first is that the performances of children who are very young are so variable that long-term prediction (for example, 1 year) is not feasible. This inability to predict precisely is particularly pronounced with shorter, quickly administered (and less reliable) measures. Because there is relatively poor predictive validity, most inferences must be drawn with great care. If individuals wish to use these measures to predict school success, they should recognize that the closer the predicted measure (that is, the criterion) is to the predictor measure (that is, the test), the greater is the accuracy of the prediction. For example, language tests predict later language skills better than perceptual–motor tests do.

The second dilemma occurs when using preschool tests to measure current attainment and child progress. To use developmental measures in this way, educators must ensure that there is appropriate linkage between the curriculum and the content of the test.

The third dilemma is the fact that students must be labeled to be eligible for certain preschool programs, but the act of labeling may set up expectations for limited pupil performance. Those who assess infants, toddlers, and preschool children need to assess within a context of situational specificity. There is much situational variability in performance, and this must be taken into account when making predictions or planning interventions.

The validity of the Speed DIAL rests on the validity of the DIAL-3. There is a strong correlation (.94) between the two when scores are converted to normalized standard scores. However, no data are presented about frequency of false negatives and false positives.

Summary

The DIAL-3 is an individually administered screening device assessing development in motor, conceptual, language, self-help, and social development domains. The norms are generally representative, the reliability for the total score is generally adequate (although the reliabilities of the subtests usually are not), and the validity appears clearly established. Users are urged to make screening decisions based on the total score.

CHAPTER COMPREHENSION QUESTIONS

Write your answers to each of the following questions, and then compare your responses to the text or the study guide.

1. Describe four reasons why you might assess infants, toddlers, and preschoolers.

2. What characteristics of young children can make it particularly challenging to assess their skill development?

3. Describe a measure you might use to monitor the progress of a toddler.

4. Describe one commonly used measure for assessment of infant development. Include information on the reliability and validity of the measure.

19 Using Technology-Enhanced Assessments

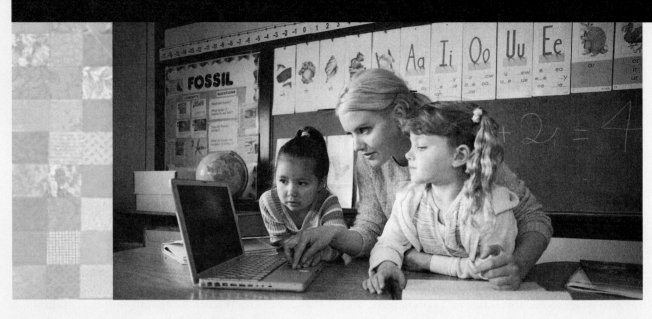

Chapter Goals

1 Understand the distinction between continuous and periodic progress monitoring.

2 Know the advantages of technology-enhanced progress monitoring and instructional management systems.

3 Understand representative technology-enhanced continuous progress monitoring measures.

4 Understand representative technology-enhanced periodic progress monitoring measures.

5 Understand how classroom response systems are used.

6 Understand representative classroom observation systems.

7 Know the advantages and limitations of computerized scoring and report-writing programs.

8 Understand examples of computer scoring systems for major tests.

Scenario in Assessment

Marcie Adams's Fourth-Grade Class

Each fall, students in Marcie Adams's fourth-grade class go to their Oakwood Elementary School media center where they take an individualized 15- or 20-minute math test, called STAR Math, on the computer. STAR Math is a computer adaptive test—one that starts each student with a math item of intermediate difficulty for fourth graders and then provides students who pass the item with a more difficult item and students who fail the item with a simpler item. The test adapts level of item difficulty based on student performance until a level of skill development in math is identified.

Ms. Adams receives a set of computer printouts listing the level of math performance of each of the 29 students in her class. The printouts provide her with information on the range of performance of students in her class, along with information on the numbers of students who are working at the various levels. This information enables her to provide individualized instruction matched specifically to each student's skill level. It enables her to group students who are at the same level and to use peer-assisted learning and small-group instruction. It enables her to adapt instruction and do a better job of meeting the needs of individual students.

Brandon Bollig is a student in Ms. Adams's class. Once she knows Brandon's instructional level, she assigns him to a specific level of a computerized math software program called Accelerated Math™. The computer in Ms. Adams's class generates sheets of math problems for Brandon, and these problems are

at his instructional level. Carlos Rodriquez is at the same instructional level as Brandon. The computer also generates sheets of math problems for Carlos, and the problems are different from those for Brandon. Brandon and Carlos each complete their individualized sheet of math problems, and they record their answers on a small bubble sheet (the kind of response sheet on which one darkens the circle next to what one believes is the correct answer). Both boys enter their bubble sheets into a small scanner, and the computer scores their responses and prints a corrective feedback sheet, called a TOPS (The Opportunity to Praise a Student) sheet. An example of a TOPS sheet that Brandon receives is shown in Figure 19.1. Notice that the sheet indicates that Brandon answered 16 of 20 problems correctly, which is 80 percent. Also indicated are Brandon's incorrect responses, his answers, and the correct answers. The feedback sheet also provides cumulative information, indicating in this case that Brandon has mastered 62 percent of the fourth-grade objectives at this point in the school year (March 21), and that he is averaging 75 percent correct on practice exercises to date. The computer also generates a new sheet of math problems at the same instructional level. Brandon and Carlos use their individual feedback sheets to review and discuss their performance. Together they rework items that either or both answered incorrectly, together they work the problems on the new sheets they have received, and as they have questions they seek assistance from Ms. Adams.

continued on the next page

Scenario in Assessment (*continued*)

FIGURE 19.1
Accelerated Math™ Practice
TOPS for Brandon Bollig

Accelerated Math™
Practice TOPS Report
for Brandon Bollig
Printed March 27, 2008 10:45:20 AM

The TOPS Report prints after each assignment is scored, giving the results for the current assignment and overall progress.

School: Oakwood Elementary School   Teacher: Mrs. M. Adams
Class: Math 4A   Grade: 4

Number Correct: 16/20 (80%)

Brandon had difficulty with these objectives on the assignment.

Incorrect Responses (4)

Objective	Problem	Your Answer	Correct Answer
90. Multiply money expressions by whole numbers	7	A	D
90. Multiply money expressions by whole numbers	12	D	A
91. WP: Figure change	15	B	C
91. WP: Figure change	18	A	B

Objectives on this Practice (5)

Objective	Results		Overall	
89. Count money and figure change	6/6	100%	9/12	75%
90. Multiply money expressions by whole numbers	4/6	67%	9/18	50%
91. WP: Figure change	4/6	67%	9/18	50%
39.ᶜ Multiply by powers of 10 (2-3 digits)	1/1	100%	4/4	100%
40.ᶜ Estimate products, round (1-4 digits)	1/1	100%	4/4	100%

The goal is 75% or above on practice.

Overall Progress

	Average Percent Correct		Objective Summary
	Marking Period (79% Complete)	**School Year** (70% Complete)	Ready to Test: 1
Practice %:	64	75	Goal for Marking Period: 32
Test %:	67	83	Total Mastered this Marking Period: 22 (69% of Goal)
Review %:	73	79	Total Mastered this Year: 89

The goal is 85% or above on tests.

Teacher   Parent

Comments:

SOURCE: Reprinted with permission, Renaissance Learning, Inc.

Brandon and Carlos continue working on sheets of math practice items that are tailored to their individual skill level until they consistently achieve 75 percent success rates on practice exercises for four objectives. The computer then signals Ms. Adams that the student is ready to take a test on the objective. She pushes a button to generate the test, and the computer generates the test. Brandon takes the test, records his answers on a bubble sheet, and scans his answers. The computer provides him with corrective feedback on the test. He continues to take tests until he achieves the required 85 percent accuracy. Once Brandon achieves 85 percent accuracy on a test, the computer moves him to the next objective and prints a sheet of practice items for that objective. The practice–practice–practice–test process is repeated.

Each morning, Ms. Adams uses the Accelerated Math™ software to print a Status of the Class Report. A copy of the kind of report she receives is illustrated in Figure 19.2. Notice that the computer lists the students in her class (we shortened the report to 12 students for purposes of illustration) and identifies students who need assignments and students who need help with two practice objectives. The Status of the Class Report indicates that Brandon needs help with practice items for two objectives that he is currently working on, and that he is not yet ready to test on any objectives. At the bottom of the sheet, Ms. Adams sees the specific objectives for which Brandon needs help: multiplying money expressions by whole numbers and word problems that require him to figure change. She is also able to see that Carlos is currently working but that she needs to print a test for him to take. Test printing is always under the control of the teacher.

The Status of the Class Report also alerts Ms. Adams to specific objectives that are causing difficulty for three or more students. She learns that Michelle, Lisa, and Tyler are having difficulty with telling time to the hour and minute, and she is alerted that she should provide small-group instruction on this objective to those three students. The report also gives her a summary of the status of the students in her class. She learns that one student needs to have a specific objective assigned, three students are ready to test, and two students need intervention.

Once a week, Ms. Adams prints a Diagnostic Report (an example is shown in Figure 19.3). The report gives her a snapshot of every student and the class as a whole. She reviews the report weekly to monitor student performance and look for students who may need help. She is able to see that on average, students in her class have completed 380 problems, are getting 83 percent correct on practice items, and are averaging 86 percent correct on regular tests. Note that she is also able to see that Brandon is performing below expectation (only achieving 64 percent correct on practice exercise and 67 percent correct on regular tests). Brandon is identified as a student at risk and one who is in need of intervention. The overall goal is to have fewer than 10 percent of the students in a class at risk. When students are persistently at risk, teachers can use this information to make informed decisions to refer students for additional assistance or psychoeducational evaluation.

School administrators can periodically review the Diagnostic Reports for the classes in their buildings or district. When they identify classes in which more than 10 percent of the students are at risk, they can intervene to assign additional resources (paraprofessionals or resource teachers) to these classes. Both teachers and administrators can use these technology-enhanced assessment systems to monitor student progress and make data-driven decisions about referral, instruction, program evaluation, and accountability.

These examples illustrate the ways in which technology is being used to enhance assessment and decision making. Ms. Adams uses the Accelerated Math™ software to manage practice and monitor individual student progress in math for each of the students in her class. She is able to shift her very valuable time from assigning instruction, grading papers, and providing feedback to provision of individualized and small-group instruction to students experiencing difficulty. Also, she receives information on the specific nature of the difficulty they are having, enabling her to provide precisely relevant remedial instruction.

Computer software is now available to assist teachers in continuous or periodic monitoring of student performance and progress. Compared to a static paper-and-pencil multiple-choice test where everyone takes a fixed set of items, computer adaptive testing requires fewer items to arrive at equally accurate scores.

continued on the next page

Scenario in Assessment (*continued*)

FIGURE 19.2
Accelerated Math™ Status
of the Class Report

Accelerated Math™
Status of the Class Report
Wednesday, March 28, 2008, 03:50 PM

This report provides a view of the entire class and identifies students who need assignments and those students who need help.

School: Oakwood Elementary School

Class: Math 4A
Teacher: Adams, Marcie

The Action Needed column alerts you to students who need attention.

Assignment Status

Student	Action Needed	Objectives Ready to Test	Last Assignment Completed		Outstanding Assignments		
			Type	Date	Practice	Exercise	Test
Anderson, Marcus		2	Practice	03/27/08	03/27/08		
Bell, Timothy		1	Regular Test	03/28/08		03/28/08	
Bollig, Brandon	I Intervene (2)	1	Practice	03/27/08	03/27/08		
Chang, Michelle		0	Practice	03/27/08	03/27/08		
Gonzales, Maria		3	Practice	03/28/08	03/28/08		
Halden, Susan	I Intervene (2)	1	Regular Test	03/27/08	03/28/08		
O'Neil, Sarah	Assign Objs	0	Practice	03/28/08			03/28/08[a]
Richmond, Angela		0	Practice	03/28/08	03/28/08		
Rodrigues, Carlos		4	Practice	03/28/08	03/28/08	03/28/08	
Stone, Lisa		0	Practice	03/27/08	03/27/08		
Tyler, Lawrence	Print Asssignment	3	Practice	03/27/08			
White, Jacob		0	Practice	03/28/08	03/28/08		

Provide individual instruction for students having problems with specific objectives.

I Intervention Needed

Student	Assignment Type	Objectives		Student	Library Objective Code	Overall Results
Bollig, Brandon	Practice	90. Multiply money expressions by whole numbers		Chang, Michelle	AMG4-090	11/18 (61%)
	Practice	91. WP: Figure change		Stone, Lisa	AMG4-091	12/18 (67%)
Halden, Susan	Regular Test	96. Measure customary length		Tyler, Lawrence	AMG4-096	6/10 (60%)
	Regular Test	97. Convert customary units of length			AMG4-097	5/10 (50%)

Objectives Causing Difficulties

Objectives	Assignment Type	Student	Library Objective Code	Overall Results
112. Intersecting, parallel, and perpendicular lines	Practice	Chang, Michelle	AMG4-112	8/12 (67%)
	Practice	Stone, Lisa	AMG4-112	7/12 (58%)
	Practice	Tyler, Lawrence	AMG4-112	5/10 (50%)

[a]Diagnostic Test

Scenario in Assessment (*continued*)

FIGURE 19.2
Accelerated Math™ Status of the Class Report (*continued*)

Status of the Class Report
Printed March 28, 2008 3:50 PM

School: Oakwood Elementary School
Class: Math 4A
Teacher: Adams, Marcie

Objectives Causing Difficulties

> Provide small-group instruction on objectives that are causing difficulty for three or more students.

Objectives	Assignment Type	Student	Library Objective Code	Overall Results
114. Identify polygons	Practice	Richmond, Angela	AMG4-114	6/10 (60%)
	Practice	Rodrigues, Carlos	AMG4-114	6/10 (60%)
	Practice	White, Jacob	AMG4-114	5/12 (42%)

Outstanding Assignments

Student	School Days Since Last Work Printed	Practice			Exercise			Test		
		Form	Problems	Date Printed	Form	Problems	Date Printed	Form	Problems	Date Printed
Anderson, Marcus	—	2431	1–18	03/27/08						
Bell, Timothy	Today				2487	1–8	03/28/08			
Bollig, Brandon	Today	2541	21–40	03/28/08	2453	1–16	03/27/08			
Chang, Michelle	—	2441	21–40	03/27/08						
Gonzales, Maria	Today	2509	1–20	03/28/08						
Halden, Susan	Today				2493	17–32	03/28/08			
O'Neil, Sarah	Today							2466[a]	1–20	03/28/08
Richmond, Angela	Today	2501	61–80	03/28/08						
Rodrigues, Carlos	Today	2476	21–48	03/28/08						
Stone, Lisa	—	2448	1–20	03/27/08						
White, Jacob	Today	2460	1–18	03/28/08						

Outstanding Assignments	Total
Practices	9
Exercises	2
Regular Tests	0
Diagnostic Tests	1

Class Summary

Action Summary	Total
Students Need Assignments Printed	1
Students Need Objs Assigned	1
Students Need Tests Printed	0
Students Need Intervention	2
Objectives with three or more students experiencing difficulty	2

SOURCE: Reprinted with permission, Renaissance Learning, Inc.

Scenario in Assessment (*continued*)

FIGURE 19.3
Accelerated Math™
Diagnostic Report

Diagnostic Report
Printed April 1, 2008 3:30 PM

Reporting Period: 1/29/2008–4/1/2008 (3rd Quarter)

> This report provides a snapshot of each student and the class as a whole. Review weekly to monitor performance and look for students who may need help.

School: Oakwood Elementary School

Report Options
Reporting Parameter Group: All Demographics [Default]
Group By: Class

Class: Math 4A
Teacher: Adams, Marcie

> Diagnostic codes alert you to students having trouble.

> The engaged time goal is 40 minutes per day. This indicates that students are on pace and are mastering an average of four objectives per week.

Student	Diagnostic Codes	Average Percent Correct							Objectives Mastered			
		Practice	Exercise	Regular Test	Diagnostic Test	Total Tests	Review	Engaged Time[a]	Average Number Per Week	Regular Test	Diagnostic Test	Total Tests	Average Objective Level
Anderson, Marcus		92	94	93	94	94	95	40	4.0	27	5	32	4.5
Bell, Timothy		80	77	85	82	84	83	29	2.9	15	8	23	4.4
Bollig, Brandon	I, P, T, R, I	64▼	69	67▼	72	70	73▼	28	2.8	12	10	22	4.0
Chang, Michelle		85	87	88	87	88	90	33	3.3	19	7	26	4.3
Gonzales, Maria		91	88	91	89	90	91	38	3.8	23	7	30	4.4
Halden, Susan	I, P, T, R, I	70▼	67	74▼	75	75	77▼	28	2.8	11	11	22	4.1
O'Neil, Sarah		95	96	95	96	96	97	44	4.4	31	4	35	4.8
Richmond, Angela		83	86	86	84	85	84	30	3.0	15	9	24	4.4
Rodrigues, Carlos		84	81	87	85	86	88	34	3.4	17	10	27	4.6
Stone, Lisa		89	87	88	86	87	90	35	3.5	18	10	28	4.5
Tyler, Lawrence		81	76	85	84	85	80	31	3.1	19	6	25	4.3
White, Jacob		86	89	90	88	89	88	30	3.0	16	8	24	4.5
Average		**(83)**	**83**	**(86)**	**85**	**86**	**86**	**33**	**3.3**	**19**	**8**	**27**	**4.4**

> The goal is 75% or above on practice.

> The goal is 85% or above on tests.

Diagnostic Code Summary

Number of Students	% of Students	Diagnostic Codes	Description
2	17	I	Teacher intervention needed (see Status of the Class Report)
2	17	P	Practice percentage lower than 75%
2	17	T	Regular test percentage lower than 85%
2	17	R	Review percentage lower than 80%
0	0	M	Less than 1/2 of the median objectives mastered (1/2 the median = 13)

Students At Risk: 2 of 12 (17%)

> Students at risk are those with at least one diagnostic code. The goal is to have 10% or fewer students at risk.

Class Summary

Objectives Mastered	Total
Regular Tests	223
Diagnostic Tests	95
All Tests	318
Students	
Total	12
Number who did not take any Regular Tests	0

▼Trouble value

[a]Engaged Time per Day: An estimate based on number of objectives mastered and an anticipated

SOURCE: Reprinted with permission, Renaissance Learning, Inc.

During the past 10 years, there have been major advances in the development of technology-enhanced assessment systems. These are designed to assist teachers in monitoring the progress of individuals or classes, and typically they are not specific to any one curriculum. In this chapter, we describe two kinds of technology-enhanced assessment systems: those intended to be used continuously during instruction and those that are administered periodically (for example, once every 10 days or every 2 weeks). The intent of both kinds of systems is the same: to provide teachers with information on the extent to which students are making progress toward instructional goals. The major reason why teachers choose to administer these tests is so that they can identify very early those students who are not on target for individual goals or school district goals and intervene to make changes in the students' instructional program. When education professionals use information to make changes in students' instruction, we often label this *formative assessment.*

At the same time, computerized scoring systems are available for individually administered assessments. These allow assessors to enter a student's raw score on subtests and to receive a variety of subtests scores, composite scores, confidence intervals, and computed significance of differences among scores. There are three parts to this chapter. In the first, we describe technology-enhanced assessment systems designed for use in continuous assessment of student progress. In the second part, we describe technology-enhanced assessment systems designed for use in periodic assessment of student progress. In the third part, we describe commonly used computerized scoring systems.

It is important to recognize that the measures described in this chapter are not computer-assisted instruction systems. Rather, they are *assessment* systems, designed to monitor pupil progress and help teachers manage instruction. They often provide guidance for decision making about what to teach, but they are certainly not a substitute for instruction. We have included reviews of assessment systems that are not linked directly to any one curriculum or textbook series.

CONTINUOUS TECHNOLOGY-ENHANCED ASSESSMENT SYSTEMS

Examples of commonly used technology-enhanced assessments designed for continuous progress monitoring are listed in Table 19.1. We describe one of these systems, Accelerated Math™, in the following section.

Accelerated Math™

Accelerated Math™ (AM) (Renaissance Learning, 1998) is a technology-enhanced system designed to monitor student progress toward instructional goals and manage student practice of relevant instructional tasks. We illustrated the system in the story

about students in Marcie Adams's class. Students are placed at an instructional level dependent on their level of skill development in math as determined by an assessment such as STAR Math (described later). They are taught at that level, and then they complete practice exercises that enable them to apply what they have learned. The computer is used to monitor accuracy and task completion, and students move at their own pace. The AM program is used to provide teachers with daily information on the progress of individual students, on the status of all students in the class, and to alert teachers when individual students are having difficulty. The program can be used by administrators to track

TABLE 19.1	Software Packages for Continuous Progress Monitoring	
Provider	**Product**	**Website**
Essential Solutions	Kid Compass	www.kid-compass.com
Hosts Learning	LearnerLink	www.hosts.com
LeapFrog SchoolHouse	LeapTrack	www.leaptrack.com
Princeton Review	Homeroom	www.k12.princetonreview.com
PRO-ED	Monitoring Basic Skills Progress	www.proedinc.com
Renaissance Learning	Accelerated Math™, Accelerated Reader, Accelerated Writer	www.renlearn.com
Riverdeep	Destination Success, Skill Detective, Skill Navigator	www.riverdeep.net
Scantron	Skills Connection, Classroom Wizard	www.scantron.com
Wireless Generation (and Harcourt Achieve)	e*assessment	www.wirelessgeneration.com

SOURCE: Adapted from Ysseldyke, J. E., & McLeod, S. (2007). Using technology tools to monitor response to intervention. In S. R. Jimerson, M. K. Burns, and A. M. VanDerHeyden (Eds.), *Handbook of Response to Intervention.* New York: Springer.

the progress of all students in classes, schools, or districts. Steps in the program are like those used by students in Marcie Adams's class. Students take STAR Math as a locator test; it identifies the appropriate library of instructional objectives toward which students should work. The computer generates worksheets of problems that students use to practice math skills. Students score their practice exercises using the computer, and once they achieve sufficient proficiency (typically 85 percent correct) the computer signals the teacher that they are ready for a test. When students pass tests, they proceed to the next objective. Teachers are able to get the kinds of reports shown previously for students in Marcie Adams's class. Administrators have available to them an Accelerated Math Dashboard, which is a web-based system that allows them to monitor the performance of all students in their school(s).

PERIODIC TECHNOLOGY–ENHANCED ASSESSMENT SYSTEMS

As their name implies, these are tests that are given periodically (typically once every 2 weeks) as monitors of student progress. In Table 19.2, we list examples of periodic progress monitoring measures. We then describe two measures, STAR Math and STAR Reading, as well as a set of measures available through AIMSweb.

TABLE 19.2	Software Packages for Periodic Progress Monitoring	
Provider	**Product**	**URL**
AIMSweb	Basic, Pro, RTI	www.aimsweb.com
Compass Learning	Explorer	www.compasslearning.com
CTB McGraw-Hill	i-know	www.ctb.com
McGraw-Hill Digital Learning	Yearly Progress Pro	www.mhdigitallearning.com
Northwest Evaluation Association	Measure of Academic Progress	www.nwea.org
Pearson Education	Pearson Prosper	www.pearsonncs.com
Pearson School Systems	Pearson Benchmark	www.personschoolsystems.com
PLATO Learning	eduTest	www.edutest.com
Renaissance Learning	AssessmentMaster, STAR Math, STAR Reading, STAR Early Literacy	www.renlearn.com
Riverside Publishing	Assess2Know	www.riverpub.com
Scantron	Achievement Series	www.scantron.com
ThinkLink Learning	Predictive Assessment Series	www.thinklinklearning.com
Vantage Learning	Learning Access!	www.vantagelearning.com
Wireless Generation	mCLASS DIBELS	www.wirelessgeneration.com

SOURCE: Adapted from Ysseldyke, J. E. & McLeod, S. (2007). Using technology tools to monitor response to intervention. In S. R. Jimerson, M. K. Burns, and A. M. VanDerHeyden (Eds.), *Handbook of Response to Intervention*. New York: Springer.

STAR Math

STAR Math (Renaissance Learning, 1998) is designed to provide teachers with quick and accurate estimates of students' math achievement levels relative to national norms. The test can also be used to monitor student progress in math over time. It is appropriate for use with students in grades 3 through 12. Using computer-adaptive procedures, a branching formula matches test items to students' ability and performance level. In other words, the specific test items that students receive depend on how well they perform on previous items. Thus, each test is unique, tailored to the individual student, and students can be given the test as many as five times in 1 year without being exposed to the same item more than once. The test is timed. Students have up to 3 minutes to solve each item and are given a warning when 30 seconds remain.

Items on STAR Math consist of some of the major strands of math content: numeration concepts, computation, word problems, estimation, statistics, charts, graphs, geometry, measurement, and algebra. Responses are four-item multiple-choice responses. The test consists of two parts: Concepts of numeration and computation are addressed in the first part, whereas the other content areas are addressed in the second part.

Scores

Users of STAR Math can obtain grade equivalents, percentile ranks, normal-curve equivalents, and scaled scores. The software provided with the test is used to score the test and give users immediate feedback on student performance.

Norms

STAR Math was standardized on 25,800 students who attended 256 schools in 42 states. Norming was completed in spring 1998 using a sample that was stratified on the basis of geographic region, school location (urban, rural, and suburban), gender, and ethnicity. The sample is representative of the U.S. population, as are the proportions of the various kinds of students in the sample.

Reliability

Reliability was calculated using a test–retest method with 1,541 students, who took alternative forms of the test because of its computer-adaptive nature. Reliabilities at grades 3 through 6 are in the high .70s, whereas at higher grades they are in the .80s. The test has sufficient reliability for use as a screening test but not for making eligibility decisions.

Validity

Performance on STAR Math was correlated with performance on a number of standardized math tests administered during standardization of the test. An extensive table in the manual reports these results. Comparison tests included the California Achievement Test, Comprehensive Test of Basic Skills, Iowa Tests of Basic Skills, and Metropolitan Achievement Test. Scores were moderately high and approximately as would be expected.

Summary

STAR Math is a norm-referenced, computer-adaptive math test that gives teachers information about students' instructional levels as well as their level of performance relative to a national sample. The test was standardized on a large representative sample. It provides teachers with immediate diagnostic profiles on student performance. Evidence for reliability is limited, but evidence for validity is good.

STAR Reading

STAR Reading (Renaissance Learning, 1997) is designed to provide teachers with quick and accurate estimates of students' instructional reading levels and estimates of their reading levels relative to national norms. The test is administered using computer software, so the specific test items each student receives are determined by his or her responses to previous test items. Using computer-adaptive procedures, a branching formula matches test items to student ability and performance level. The test uses a vocabulary-in-context format in which students must identify the best choice for a missing word in a single-context sentence. Correct answers fit both the semantics and the syntax of the sentence. All incorrect answers either fit the syntax of the sentence or relate to the meaning of something in the sentence.

Scores

Users of STAR Reading may obtain grade equivalents, percentile ranks, normal-curve equivalents, and scaled scores. In addition, they may obtain information about the zone of proximal development, an index of the low and high ends of the range at which students can read. The software used to administer the test provides the information, and scores are obtained immediately.

Norms

Items for STAR Reading were developed using 13,846 students from 59 schools. The development sample was stratified on the basis of gender, grade, geographic region, district socioeconomic status, school type, and district enrollment. The primary unit of selection was school rather than students. Tables in the manual contrast sample characteristics with national population characteristics. For the most part, sample characteristics approximate population characteristics. Notable exceptions include an underrepresentation of students from the Northeast (9 percent versus 20 percent in the population) and of schools with small (<2,500) and large (<25,000) enrollments.

STAR Reading was standardized on 42,000 students from 171 schools. The standardization sample was stratified on the basis of geographic region, school system and per-grade district enrollment, and socioeconomic status. Sample characteristics very closely approximate population characteristics. Students from all geographic regions, socioeconomic levels, and school sizes were selected in proportion to their presence in the population. Normative tables in the manual describe the close approximation of the sample to the U.S. population.

Reliability

STAR Reading is a computer-adaptive test that offers a virtually unlimited number of test forms, so traditional methods of conducting reliability analyses do not apply. The authors instead conducted reliability analyses using a test–retest methodology with alternative forms. Reliability was tested using both scaled scores and instructional reading levels. A total of 34,446 students were tested twice with STAR Reading, each taking the second test an average of 5 days after the first. Test–retest reliabilities ranged from .85 to .95 for scaled scores and from .79 to .91 for instructional reading level.

Validity

Performance on STAR Reading was correlated with performance on a number of different standardized measures of reading skills administered to those in the standardization group. An extensive table in the manual reports these results. Comparison tests included the California Achievement Test, Comprehensive Test of Basic Skills, Degrees of Reading Power, Gates–MacGinitie, Iowa Test of Basic Skills, Metropolitan Achievement Test, Stanford Achievement Test, and several state custom-built tests (Connecticut, Texas, Indiana, Tennessee, Kentucky, North Carolina, and New York). Performance on STAR Reading is closely related to performance on the other measures of reading.

Summary

STAR Reading is a norm-referenced, computer-adaptive reading test that provides teachers with information about students' instructional levels as well as their level of performance relative to a national sample. The test enables users to sample a wide range of reading behaviors in a relatively limited period of time. The test was standardized on a large and representative group of students. Evidence for reliability and validity is satisfactory. The test should be very useful to those who want immediate scoring and information about appropriate student instructional level.

AIMSweb

AIMSweb (Pearson, 2001) is a web-based tool designed to assist with the collection and management of formative evaluation data in a variety of academic areas. It facilitates the creation of graphs and reports for distribution to a variety of different stakeholders, including educators, administrators, and parents. Users can either download, administer, and enter results using curriculum-based measurement (CBM) probes provided on the AIMSweb website or enter results into the AIMSweb system that have been collected using the Dynamic Indicators of Basic Early Literacy Skills (DIBELS; reviewed in Chapter 11).

AIMSweb CBM benchmark and progress monitoring probes are available in the areas of early literacy (English and Spanish), early numeracy, reading (English and Spanish), math, spelling, and writing. Various tools are available for students from kindergarten to eighth grade. Data can be collected and managed through the AIMSweb system according to a three-tier response-to-intervention model, in which all students are screened a few times each year and those who are failing to meet benchmarks can be targeted for more frequent progress monitoring. Following data collection and entry, users can have the system create a variety of different graphs and reports to allow for analysis of performance and progress at the district, school, student group (that is, English language learners, students with disabilities, and so on), and individual student level.

The AIMSweb system provides assistance to ensure students' progress is monitored according to a determined schedule. Furthermore, program materials assist with setting goals and calculating individual student learning rates associated with specific changes in programming. The system also offers a method for documenting various activities that may occur as part of an intervention process (that is, communication with parents, documentation of intervention fidelity, and so on). Some example reports that can be generated using AIMSweb are provided in Figures 19.4 and 19.5.

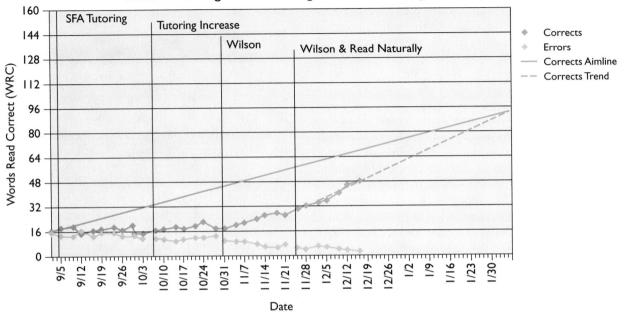

FIGURE 19.4
Student Progress Monitoring Chart
Created Using AIMSweb

SOURCE: AIMSweb. Copyright
© 2008 by NCS Pearson, Inc.
(Patent Pending.) Reproduced with
permission. All rights reserved.

FIGURE 19.5
District Report Created Using AIMSweb

SOURCE: AIMSweb. Copyright © 2008
by NCS Pearson, Inc. (Patent Pending.)
Reproduced with permission. All rights
reserved.

HANDHELD OBSERVATION SYSTEMS

Personal digital assistants (PDAs) represent another set of tools that are becoming more widely used in educational settings. They can be used to facilitate data collection for a variety of assessment purposes. PDAs can be particularly helpful in conducting structured classroom observations. Without them, structured observations require observers to pay close attention to both a stopwatch and the child they are observing, while at the same time recording their observations using paper and pencil. After collecting the data, the observer then needs to develop a way to organize, analyze, summarize, and display the results. Today, programs for PDAs have been developed that prompt observers at set time intervals to report on various conditions present in the classroom, as well as the behavior of target students and their peers. The observer can report the behaviors observed directly into the PDA, and the program then does the job of organizing, analyzing, and displaying the data. The data can be analyzed nearly instantaneously to determine the relationship between various teacher behaviors and how students behave in order to inform the development of an intervention plan. Overall, PDAs can allow the observer to conduct observations in an accurate, efficient, and unobtrusive manner.

We highlight two programs that are available to assist with structured observations. The Behavioral Observation of Students in Schools (Shapiro, 2003) is a program intended for use on PDAs that facilitates direct assessment of student behavior and is intended for use in school settings for children pre-K through twelfth grade. Observations can be set to run for 5 to 60 minutes and are used to determine the frequency with which students engage in particular appropriate or inappropriate behaviors. The Portable Observation Program is an ancillary to the Behavioral Assessment System for Children–2 (BASC-2; Reynolds & Kamphaus, 2004). It allows observers to design their own template for observation and to collect data on student behavior using a PDA that can likewise inform intervention planning and allow one to monitor the effects of an intervention on student behavior.

PDAs are also increasingly being used to assist with data collection associated with academic skill development. For instance, it is now possible to use a PDA to score and manage data associated with measures of oral reading fluency. AIMSweb has software called Palm Link that allows users to administer and score data from curriculum-based measurements directly on a PDA; the device can then be directed to immediately score, summarize, and save the results. The results can eventually be uploaded to AIMSweb to assist with further analysis and reporting.

Although PDAs offer many additional helpful features for keeping track of schedules, sending e-mail, and accessing the Internet, we chose to highlight those programs associated with the collection of assessment data. In the future, you should expect to find many more technological advances that facilitate the collection and analysis of data used to positively impact student learning.

CLASSROOM RESPONSE SYSTEMS

The days are gone when teachers have to call on individual students one by one to check on the extent to which they understand what they are being taught. New technological advances enable teachers to ask students questions and have them enter their responses on classroom responders or small computers. Results are transmitted wirelessly to the teacher's computer, and the teacher can view a graph showing the numbers of students who answered questions correctly/incorrectly. In this way, teachers obtain immediate feedback on the extent to which students comprehend lesson material, and teachers are able to personalize instruction. One such classroom response system is called 2Know! (Renaissance Learning, 2007). The system consists of a wireless handheld responder (see Figure 19.6), software, and a receiver that plugs into the classroom computer.

Teachers generate test questions prior to class and then use those questions during instruction. Teachers pause at periodic times during instruction to have students respond to the questions on their handheld responders. Students select their answers and the teacher obtains a graph showing the numbers of students who selected each response. Provision of this information allows teachers to know the numbers of students choosing each of several answers.

Teachers can also use software, called AccelTest Software, to create a nearly endless number of reusable test items, quizzes, and so on. Data banks can be used to input end-of-unit or other questions directly from popular textbooks. Teachers can also download the state standards for their state and can align their test questions to the standards. The 2Know! system can then be used to monitor progress toward meeting standards. All tests are scored automatically, so teachers do not have to use valuable time scoring tests.

The 2Know! product is linked directly to Accelerated Math™ so that students can respond to test questions on their responders.

When you were in elementary or secondary school, you may have used small computers called Alpha Smart Computers to write papers or take notes in class. The latest versions of Alpha Smart computers are called NEO[2] (Renaissance Learning, 2006) and DANA (Renaissance Learning, 2007) computers. The NEO[2] computer is shown in Figure 19.6. The use of NEO[2] has been expanded from writing to classroom assessment activities. Teachers can now use NEOs as classroom responders. Students can take Accelerated Reader quizzes on NEOs, and teachers can use AccelTest software to create multiple-choice, true–false, and yes–no questions. As with the 2Know! responders, students can respond to teacher questions directly on NEO[2] computers. Responses are transmitted wirelessly to teachers' computers and provide teachers with immediate feedback about the performance of the class and individual students.

FIGURE 19.6
2Know! Responder and NEO[2] Computer

Classroom Response Systems

COMPUTER SCORING SYSTEMS

In addition to providing efficient ways to monitor progress and manage targeted practice opportunities, advances in technology have also made scoring of several other measures, including those commonly used for diagnostic and eligibility decisions, much more efficient. In the past, test users spent countless hours adding, subtracting, and converting test scores. Today, computerized scoring programs are available to ease this burden so that test users can spend more time interpreting scores and identifying appropriate instructional interventions.

Computerized scoring programs offer several advantages to traditional paper-and-pencil scoring. Most notably, they reduce the time needed to compute and convert test scores. In addition, they may reduce error associated with calculating scores and misreading conversion tables. They can also assist with calculating scores associated with more sophisticated statistical and measurement techniques, such as the W-scores that are used in the Woodcock–Johnson

Scales; calculating these scores by hand could be tedious. See Table 19.3.

Computer scoring programs (which are developed and used by humans, of course) are certainly not perfect, and they need to be carefully developed and applied by test users. On more than one occasion, even after test developers have conducted numerous demonstration trials and the product has gone to market, glitches in computer scoring have been identified. Unfortunately, in some cases, this has led to misinformed decision making such that students have been denied services that they otherwise should have received. Also, even though computers may help to eliminate computation and table-reading errors, it is essential that the user enters scores and other information (for example, date of birth, grade, form, and norms to be used) accurately for correct scoring. It is recommended that users carefully check results even when using a computer and always use multiple sources of data

TABLE 19.3	Assessment Tools with Computerized Scoring and Reporting Programs			
Tool	**Name of Associated Product(s)**	**Hand Scoring**	**Computer Scoring**	**Report Writing**
Wechsler Scales	WISC-IV Writer and Scoring Assistant	X	X	X
Kaufman Scales	Assist	X	X	X
Stanford Binet	SB5 ScoringPro	X	X	X
BASC-2	BASC-2 Assist and Assist Plus	X	X	X
Achenbach	Assessment Data Manager	X	X	X
Woodcock–Johnson Scales	WJ III Compuscore and Profiles Program Report-Writer for the WJ III	No	X	X
Vineland Adaptive Behavior Scales	Vineland-II Survey Forms Assist	X	X	X

when making important decisions. Storing electronic copies of scoring records can also pose challenges. It is important to ensure that only those individuals with a need to know the given test score results have access to such data. This may require the development of special electronic passwords known only to those who administer the test.

When first learning a new test that has both a hand and a computer scoring option, it may be beneficial to learn how to hand score the test in order to understand how the scores are derived. This can allow you to better understand the nature of the scores that you interpret. However, once you have a good understanding of how the test scores are calculated, use of a computer scoring program can help you score more quickly and accurately.

With advances in technology, computer programs are becoming more widely available to not only assist with calculating and converting scores but also discriminate correct and incorrect responses. Whereas it may be relatively simple to design a computer program to score selected response items, it is more difficult to design programs that can accurately score constructed response items and essay responses. Yet, such programs are being created. Although such software may help reduce problems associated with poor interrater reliability, it may be difficult for such programs to accurately score unique and creative responses.

In addition to offering automated scoring, some test packages that are used to make special education eligibility decisions offer computer-generated reports. These make use of predetermined language and table formats that are intended to facilitate communication of score results to parents and educators. Although it may be appropriate to incorporate some of the language and tables from a computer-generated report program, it is important to recognize how such reports, when used in their entirety and without editing, may lead users away from incorporating multiple assessment methods and measures in their overall evaluation. Because a report-writing program is often specific to a given test, it will focus on presenting scores obtained through the given test alone, and it may not easily allow a user to incorporate additional data collected from multiple sources. Furthermore, standard language presented through a computer-generated report may not optimally convey the information to certain audiences; users should edit such information in order to communicate most effectively with the individuals with whom they are working. We discourage the use of computer-generated reports and instead encourage assessors to write reports that are tailored specifically to the students they test.

CHAPTER COMPREHENSION QUESTIONS

Write your answers to each of the following questions, and then compare your responses to the text or the study guide.

1. What is the distinction between continuous and periodic progress monitoring?

2. What are the advantages of using technology-enhanced assessment systems?

3. How does a technology-enhanced continuous progress monitoring measure work?

4. Identify representative technology-enhanced periodic progress monitoring measures.

5. Identify two handheld observation systems, and indicate how they might be used in today's classrooms.

6. Identify two ways in which you might use classroom responders in your class.

7. What are the advantages and limitations of computerized scoring and report-writing programs?

8. Give examples of computer scoring systems for major tests.

PART 4

Using Assessment Results to Make Educational Decisions

Assessment is the process of collecting data for the purpose of making decisions about students. The fourth part of this text is about using assessment information to make decisions.

We began this text by developing the basic foundations of assessment. In the first part we provided an overview of assessment in special and inclusive education (the context for assessment in schools and current assessment practices, legal and ethical considerations in assessment, test scores and how to use them, and an overview of technical adequacy) before turning to a chapter on test accommodations and adaptations. In the second part we described assessment in classrooms, with attention to observation as a form of assessment, teacher-made tests, and the management of classroom assessments. In Part 3 we first described how to evaluate a test, and then described commercially available tests that are commonly used with students with disabilities. These tests and procedures deal with testing academic achievement (multiple skill tests and measures of specific skills in reading and mathematics), psychological processes (intelligence perceptual motor skills, language), socio-emotional behavior, and adaptive behavior. Because the behavior of infants and toddlers tends to be undifferentiated and its measurement fraught with difficulties, we provided a separate chapter on this topic. Increasingly, school personnel are using technology-enhanced assessments as continuous and periodic measures of student performance and progress, so we provided a separate chapter on these measures.

Part 4 returns to the assessment of students. It contains chapters that discuss how, in practice, decisions are made. Chapter 20 discusses various instructional decisions and the assessment information used to make those decisions. We differentiate those classroom instructional decisions that are made prior to referral and those that are made for students who receive special education. Chapter 21 discusses decisions related to special education eligibility and how they are made. Specifically, we discuss how to determine whether a student has a disability and whether a disabled student needs special education. We provide examples of how specific test results are used in making these decisions. Chapter 22 describes current legal requirements and practices in developing and using standards-based large-scale accountability measures. We include a discussion of alternate assessments linked to grade-level content standards, modified achievement standards, and alternate achievement standards. Chapter 23 addresses best practices in communicating assessment information to multiple audiences. We include a description of team decision-making practices and describe the kinds of teams that communicate assessment information. We include a section on the collection, maintenance, and dissemination of written records on student assessment performance.

20

Making Instructional Decisions

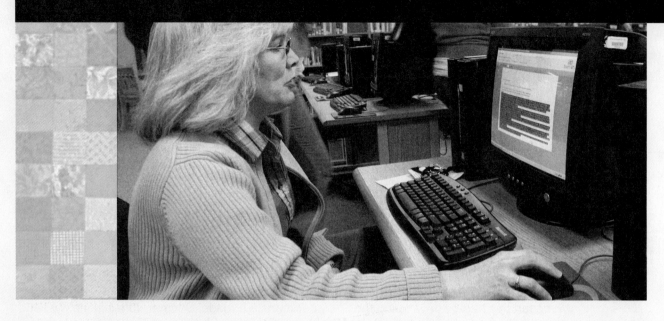

Chapter Goals

1 Understand the decisions that are made prior to a student's referral for special education (for example, recognizing problems, intervention planning, and inadequate progress academically and behaviorally).

2 Understand the decisions that are made in special education (for example, individualized educational program content, inclusion in general education, and program effectiveness).

Key Terms

child find

audiologist

ophthalmologist

graphomotor skills

prereferral assessment

prereferral intervention

EACH REGULAR AND SPECIAL EDUCATION TEACHER MAKES LITERALLY HUNDREDS of professional decisions every day. Some decisions affect classroom management; others affect instructional management. Some types of decisions occur infrequently; others occur several times each day. In this chapter, we are primarily concerned with the decisions that teachers make about the adequacy and appropriateness of instruction for students who need special assistance, students who are at risk, and students who have disabilities.

Both general and special educators share responsibility for students who are disabled. General educators are largely responsible for identifying students with sufficiently severe learning or behavior problems to be referred for special education services. General and special educators share responsibility for the education of students with disabilities who are included in general education classrooms. Special educators are responsible for students whose disabilities are so severe that they cannot be educated in general education settings even with a full complement of related services and classroom adaptations and accommodations.

1 Decisions Prior to Referral

The overwhelming majority of children enter school under the presumption that they do not have disabilities, and most complete their schooling under the same presumption. Approximately 40 percent of all students will experience difficulty during their school career. Here, we deal with those decisions that precede entitlement to special education. Before referring students for possible identification as exceptional, general educators take several steps, some of which are mandated by federal and state regulations. The first step is to recognize that a problem exists; the remaining steps may vary in sequence, depending on the state or district.

Decision: Are There Unrecognized Problems?

Federal regulations (§300.125) require that all states have policies and procedures to ensure all children with disabilities who need special education and related services are identified, located, and evaluated. This requirement is generally referred to as *child find*. In practice, this means that local school districts and other agencies inform parents of available services through strategically placed flyers, notices in local newspapers, and so forth. Children with moderate or severe disabilities are usually recognized before the age of 3 or 4 years and identified as disabled upon enrolling in school.

However, some children have undiagnosed sensory difficulties that may not have been readily apparent to parents, physicians, or teachers. Therefore, schools routinely screen all children to identify these hidden or unrecognized hearing and vision problems as a first step in providing services for them. Sensory screening is usually conducted by a school nurse with the intention of finding children who require diagnosis by a health care professional—a hearing specialist such as an audiologist or a vision specialist such as an optometrist or ophthalmologist. The critical point is that screening, by itself, cannot be used to identify a student as disabled. There must be follow-up.

Decision: Is the Student Making Adequate Progress in Regular Education?

General educators may recognize that some students are not making adequate progress toward individual, classroom, or state goals. These students may require additional assistance to help them achieve the desired educational outcomes. The threshold of recognition varies from teacher to teacher and may be a function of several factors: teacher skill and experience, class size, availability of alternative materials and curriculum, ability and behavior of other students in the class, and the teacher's tolerance for atypical progress or behavior. Generally, when a student is performing at a rate that is between 20 and 50 percent of the rate of other students, a teacher has reason to be concerned.

Academic Needs

The following might signal that students are having academic difficulty:

- Students ask questions that indicate that they do not understand new material.
- Students do not know material that was previously taught and presumed to be mastered.
- Students make numerous errors and few correct responses.
- Students do not keep up with peers, in general or in their instructional groups.
- Students' work is so far behind that of their peers that they cannot be maintained in the lowest instructional group in a class—that is, the students become instructionally isolated.
- Student work deteriorates from good or acceptable to poor or unacceptable.
- Students perform adequately in most academic areas but have extreme difficulty in one or more important core skill areas.

Why a student is having difficulty is seldom clear at this point in the decision-making process. There are multiple reasons for school failure, and these reasons may often interact with one another. The reasons for these differences generally fall into two broad categories: ineffective instruction or individual differences.

Some students make progress under almost any instructional conditions. When students with emerging skills and a wealth of information enter a learning situation, such students merely need the opportunity to continue learning and developing skills. These students often learn despite ineffective instructional methodology. However, some students enter a learning situation with poorly developed skills and require much more effective instruction. Without good instruction, these students are in danger of becoming casualties of the educational system. This situation can occur in at least five ways.

1. *Students' lack of prerequisite knowledge or skill.* Some students may lack the prerequisites for learning specific content. In such cases, the content to be learned may be too difficult because the student must learn the prerequisites and the new content simultaneously. For example, Mr. Santos may give Alex a reader in which he knows only 70 percent of the words. Alex will be forced

Scenario in Assessment

Alex and Jenna

Example 1. Alex is a third grader whose teacher is worried that he is falling behind his peers. Assessment information is of two types. First, his teacher notices that he has not kept up with the slowest students in the class and that he has not acquired reading skills as fast as those students. Second, his teacher assesses Alex and some of his peers and finds that the students in the lowest reading group are reading preprimer materials orally at a rate of 50 words per minute or more, with no more than two errors per minute. Alex reads the same materials at a rate of 20 words per minute with four errors per minute. The reading materials used by the lowest group are too difficult for Alex; easier reading materials are needed for effective instruction.

Example 2. Jenna is a fourth grader whose teacher is concerned about her writing skills. Assessment information is of two types. First, her teacher notes that Jenna has been placed in the classroom's highest instructional group for arithmetic, reading, social science, and music, where her performance is among the best in the class. However, her teacher notices that she struggles in her written work. Her writing is messy and often indecipherable. Her written work is like that of the least able students in the class. Second, her teacher assesses Jenna and some of her peers using timed writings with story starters. Jenna's writings contain relatively few words (7 words per minute), whereas peers judged to be progressing satisfactorily write almost twice as many (13) words per minute. Jenna has frequent misspellings (approximately 30 percent of her words), whereas peers progressing satisfactorily misspell approximately 10 percent of their words). Although not quantified, Jenna's writing demonstrates poor graphomotor skills (for example, letter formation, spacing within and between words, and text lines that move up and down as they go across the page), whereas her peers' writing is much neater and more legible.

to learn sight vocabulary that he lacks while trying to comprehend what he is reading. The chances are that he will not comprehend the material because he must read too many unknown words (Salvia & Hughes, 1990).

2. *Insufficient instructional time.* The school curriculum may be so cluttered with special events and extras that sufficient time cannot be devoted to core content areas. Students who need more extensive and intensive instruction in order to learn may suffer from the discrepancy between the amounts of instruction (or time) they need and the time allocated to teaching them.

3. *Teachers' lack of subject matter knowledge.* The teacher may lack the skills to teach specific subject matter. For example, in some rural areas, it may not be possible to attract physics teachers, so the biology teacher may have to teach the physics course and try to stay one or two lectures ahead of the students.

4. *Teachers' lack of pedagogical knowledge.* A teacher may lack sufficient pedagogical knowledge to teach students who are not independent learners. Although educators have known for a very long time about teaching methods that promote student learning (see Stevens & Rosenshine, 1981), this information is not as widely known to teachers and supervisors as one would hope. Thus, some educators may not know how to present new

material, structure learning opportunities, provide opportunities for guided and independent practice, or give effective feedback. Also, given the number of families in which all adults work, there is less opportunity for parents to provide supplementary instruction at home to overcome ineffective instruction at school.

5. *Teachers' commitment to ineffective methods.* A teacher may be committed to ineffective instructional methods. A considerable amount of effort has gone into the empirical evaluation of various instructional approaches. Yet much of this research fails to find its way into the classroom. For example, a number of school districts have rejected systematic instruction in phonics. However, the empirical research is more than clear that early and systematic phonics instruction leads to better reading (Adams, 1990; Foorman, Francis, Fletcher, Shatschneider, & Mehta, 1998; Pflaum, Walberg, Karegianes, & Rasher, 1980; Stanovich, 1986).

Before investing in expensive and extensive assessment of the student, it is almost always preferable to examine the effectiveness of the curriculum and the instruction. If students begin to make better progress with more effective instructional procedures, there is no need to refer them.

A few students make little progress despite systematic application of sound instructional principles that have been shown to be generally effective. There are at least three reasons for this.

1. Student ability may affect instruction. Obviously, instruction that relies heavily on visual or auditory presentation will be less effective with students who have severe visual or auditory impairments.[1] Just as obviously, slow learners require more practice to acquire various skills and knowledge.

2. Some students may find a particular subject inherently interesting and be motivated to learn, whereas other students may find the content to be boring and require additional incentives to learn.

3. Cultural differences can affect academic learning and behavior. For example, reading is an interactive process in which an author's writing is interpreted on the basis of a reader's experience and knowledge. To the extent that students from different cultures have different experiences, their comprehension of some written materials may differ. Thus, students from different cultural groups may have different understandings of, for example, "all men are created equal." Similarly, cultural norms for instructional dialogues between teacher and student may also vary, especially when the teacher and student are of different genders. Boys and girls may be raised differently, with different expectations, in some cultures. Thus, it may be culturally appropriate for women and girls to be reticent in their responses to male teachers. Similarly, teachers may feel ill equipped to teach students from different cultures. For example, teachers may be hesitant to discipline students from another culture, or they may not have culturally relevant examples to illustrate concepts and ideas.

---

[1]The instructional importance of other abilities has been asserted; however, there is scant evidence to support such assertions. There is limited and dated support for the notion that intelligence interacts with teaching methods in mathematics. Maynard and Strickland (1969) found that students with high IQs tended to learn mathematics somewhat better when discovery methods were used, although more direct methods were equally effective with students with lower IQs.

Scenario in Assessment

Nick

Example 3. Nick is a fifth grader who is earning unsatisfactory grades in all instructional areas. Assessment data are again of two types. First, his teacher notices that Nick frequently does not understand new material and seldom turns in homework. His teacher notices that he frequently stares into space or watches the tropical fish in the class aquarium at inappropriate times. He occasionally seems startled when his teacher calls on him. Although he usually begins seatwork, unlike the other students in class, he usually fails to complete his assignments. He seldom brings his homework to school even when his mother says that he has

done it. Second, his teacher systematically observes Nick and two of his peers who are progressing satisfactorily for their attention to task. Specifically, once each minute during language arts and arithmetic seatwork, the teacher notes if the boys are on task (that is, looking at their work, writing, or appear to be reading). After a week of observation, the teacher summarizes the data and finds that Nick is off task in both language arts and arithmetic approximately 60 percent of the time. His peers are off task less than 5 percent of the time. It is not surprising, given Nick's lack of attention, that he is doing poorly in school.

Behavioral Needs

General educators may also come to believe that a student has such different behavioral needs that he or she will require special assistance to achieve desired educational outcomes. As discussed in Chapter 6, any behavior that falls outside the range typically expected—too much or too little compliance, too much or too little assertiveness, too much or too little activity, and so forth—can be problematic in and of itself. In other cases, a behavior may be problematic because it interferes with learning.

As is true with academic learning problems, why a student is having behavioral difficulty may be unclear. The problem may lie in the teacher's inability to manage classroom behavior, the individual student's distinctive behavior, or a combination of both.

A teacher may lack sufficient knowledge, skill, or willingness to structure and manage a classroom effectively. Many students come to school with well-developed interpersonal and intrapersonal skills, and such students are well behaved and easily directed or coached in almost any setting. Other students enter the classroom with far less developed skills. For these students, a teacher needs much better management skills. In a classroom in which the teacher lacks these skills, the behavior of such students may interfere with their own learning and the learning of their peers. Thus, a teacher must know how to manage classroom behavior and be willing to do so. Classroom management is one of the more emotional topics in education, and often teachers' personal values and beliefs affect their willingness to control their classrooms. Although for some time there has been extensive empirical research supporting the effectiveness of various management techniques (see Alberto & Troutman, 2005; Sulzer-Azaroff & Mayer, 1986), these techniques may be rejected by some teachers on philosophical grounds. Occasionally, teachers may

Nick

Example 4. Because Nick has trouble paying attention, his teacher moves him to the front of class and away from the class aquarium. When his attention seems to wander, she taps his desk unobtrusively with her index finger; this usually brings him back to task. The teacher also has a conference with Nick's mother, and they agree that the teacher will send the parents each homework assignment via e-mail. The mother agrees to check Nick's book bag each morning to make sure that his completed homework is taken to school. It is important that the teacher monitors the effect of these interventions on Nick's attention and learning—that is, determine if the intervention improves Nick's behavior. The assessment data used by the teacher consist of the frequency of homework turned in before and after the homework intervention is introduced. The teacher also notes the duration of Nick's redirected attention.

know how to manage behavior and be willing to do so generally but be unwilling to deal with specific students for some reason. For example, some European American teachers may be hesitant to discipline minority students.

Even when teachers use generally effective management strategies, they may be unable to control some students effectively. For example, some students may be difficult to manage because they have never had to control their behavior before, because they reject women as authority figures, or because they seek any kind of attention—positive or negative. Other students may not get enough sleep or nutritious food to be alert and ready to participate and learn in school. Thus, generally effective management strategies may be ill suited to a particular student. Because there is seldom a perfect relationship between undesirable behavior and its cause, it is impossible to know a priori whether a student's difficulties are the result of different values, lack of learning, or flawed management techniques without modifying some of the management strategies and observing the effect of the modifications. If a student begins to behave better with the modifications, the reasons for the initial difficulties are not particularly important (and no one should assume that the teacher has found the cause of the difficulty).

Decision: What Can We Do to Enhance Competence and Build Capacity?

Many academic and behavioral problems can be remediated or eliminated when classroom teachers intervene quickly and effectively. When teachers recognize that students are experiencing difficulties, they usually provide those students with a little extra help. Frequently, this special assistance will take the form of more of the same instruction and attempts to obtain parental help; occasionally, assistance involves informal consultation with other teachers or building specialists. The special help can also take the form of Title I services. If the student responds to the extra help and the problems are solved, no further action is required (with the exception of perhaps more careful monitoring).

Scenario in Assessment

Nick

Example 5. The data on the effectiveness of the interventions on Nick's on-task behavior showed mixed results. Nick's rate of homework completion immediately jumped to 100 percent. Thus, Nick's completion problem was solved by providing the parents with each homework assignment and having them make sure that Nick actually brought his homework to school. Moving Nick to the front of the class, nearer to the teacher, stopped him from staring at the aquarium but had little effect on his staring into space in general. The tapping cue to redirect

Nick's attention worked 100 percent of the time, but the duration of his redirected attention was short, averaging approximately 30 seconds. Moreover, the teacher found that increasingly harder tapping was required, and that this intervention had become intrusive and distracting to the students seated next to Nick. Because the teacher's classroom interventions had met with little success and because Nick's lack of attention was still affecting his learning, the teacher decided to consult with the building's child study team to find out if they had other suggestions.

Decision: Should the Student Be Referred to an Intervention Assistance Team?

When teachers are unable to address a student's academic or behavioral problems effectively, they often seek formal help from a specialist or staff support team to discuss issues related to their specific needs or the student's, to get suggestions, or to obtain follow-up assistance.

A team can respond to requests in a variety of ways. It can provide immediate crisis intervention, short-term consultation, continuous support, or the securing of information, resources, or training for those who request its services. By providing problem-specific support and assistance to individuals and groups, the team can help teachers and other professionals to become more skillful, gain confidence, and feel more efficacious in their work with students. Although the team's makeup and job titles vary by state, team members should be skilled in areas of learning, assessment, behavior management, curriculum modification, and interpersonal communication.

Obviously, students should not receive special education simply because they are casualties of a certain teaching style or curriculum. Nor should students receive special education when better teaching or management would allow them to make satisfactory progress in regular education. Thus, when a teacher seeks help in addressing the special needs of a student, the first form of help offered should be providing the general education classroom teacher with additional strategies and materials. The goals of prereferral assessment and intervention are (1) to remediate, if possible, student difficulties before they become disabling; (2) to provide remediation in the least restrictive environment; and (3) to verify that if the problems cannot be resolved effectively, they are not caused by the school (that is, to establish that the problems reside within the child or the family). Typically, there are five stages of prereferral activities (Graden, Casey, & Bonstrom, 1983): (1) making a formal request for services, (2) clarifying the problem, (3) designing the interventions, (4) implementing the interventions, and (5) evaluating the interventions' effects.

Making the Request

Because prereferral intervention is a formalized process, a formal request for services may be required and might be made on a form similar to that shown in Figure 20.1.

FIGURE 20.1
Request for Prereferral
Consultation

Request for Prereferral Consultation

Student _____ Gender _____ Date of Birth _____

Referring Teacher _____ Grade _____ School _____

Specific Educational/Behavioral Problems:
_____
_____
_____
_____

Current Level or Materials in Deficit Areas:
_____
_____
_____

Specific Interventions to Improve Performance in Deficit Areas and
Their Effectiveness:
_____
_____
_____
_____

What Special Services Does the Student Receive
(e.g., Title I Reading, Speech Therapy)?
_____
_____

Most Convenient Days and Times for Consultation:
_____
_____

When a prereferral[2] form is used, it should contain identifying information (such as teacher and student names), the specific problems for which the teacher is seeking consultation, the interventions that have already been attempted in the classroom, the effectiveness of those interventions, and current academic instructional levels. This information allows those responsible for providing consultation to decide whether the problem warrants their further attention.

Clarifying the Problem

In the initial consultation, the team works with the classroom teacher to specify the nature of a problem or the specific areas of difficulty. These difficulties should be stated in terms of observable behavior, not hypothesized causes of the problem. For example, the teacher may specify a problem by saying that "Jenna does not write legibly" or that "Nick does not complete homework assignments as regularly as other students in his class." The focus is on the discrepancy between actual and desired performance.

The team may seek additional information. For example, the referring teacher may be asked to describe in detail the contexts in which problems occur, the student's curriculum, the way in which the teacher interacts with or responds to the student, the student's interactions with the teacher and with classmates, the student's instructional groupings and seating arrangements, and antecedents and consequences of the student's behaviors. The referring teacher may also be asked to specify the ways in which the student's behavior affects the teacher or other students and the extent to which the behavior is incongruent with the teacher's expectations. When multiple problems are identified, they may be ranked in order of importance for action.

Finally, as part of the consultation, a member of the staff support team may observe the pupil in the classroom to verify the nature and extent of the problem. In relevant school settings, a designated member of the team observes the student, notes the frequency and duration of behaviors of concern, and ascertains the extent to which the student's behavior differs from that of classmates. At this point (or later in the process), the perceptions of the student and the student's parents may also be sought.

Designing the Interventions

Next, the team and the referring teacher design interventions to remediate the most pressing problems. The team may need to coach the referring teacher on how to implement the interventions. Initially, the interventions should be based on empirically validated procedures that are known to be generally effective. In addition, parents, other school personnel, and the student may be involved in the intervention.

A major factor determining whether an intervention will be tried or implemented by teachers is feasibility. Those who conduct assessments and make recommendations

[2]Early on, special educators adopted the term *referral* to designate a request that a student be evaluated for special education eligibility and entitlement. Subsequently, an additional step was inserted into the process. Because referral had already gained widespread acceptance, the new step was called "prereferral," although this step clearly involves referral, too. We use the term *prereferral* to describe assessment and intervention activities that occur prior to formal referral to determine eligibility for special education.

about teaching must consider the extent to which the interventions they recommend are doable. (Unfortunately, too often feasibility is determined on the basis of how much of a hassle the intervention planning will be or how much work it will take to implement a given program.) Phillips (1990) identifies eight major considerations in making decisions about feasibility, which we suggest that assessors address.

1. *Degree of disruption.* How much will the intervention the teacher recommends disrupt school procedures or teacher routines?

2. *Side effects.* To what extent are there undesirable side effects for the student (for example, social ostracism), peers, home and family, and faculty?

3. *Support services required.* How readily available are the support services required, and are the costs reasonable?

4. *Prerequisite competencies.* Does the teacher have the necessary knowledge, motivation, and experience to be able to implement the intervention? Does the teacher have a philosophical bias against the recommended intervention?

5. *Control.* Does the teacher have control of the necessary variables to ensure the success of the intervention?

6. *Immediacy of results.* Will the student's behavioral change be quick enough for the teacher to be reinforced for implementing the intervention?

7. *Consequences of nonintervention.* What are the short- and long-term prognoses for the student if the behaviors are left uncorrected?

8. *Potential for transition.* Is it reasonable to expect that the intervention will lead to student self-regulation and generalize to other settings, curriculum areas, or even to other students who are experiencing similar difficulties?

The intervention plan should include a clear delineation of the skills to be developed or the behavior to be changed, the methods to be used to effect the change, the duration of the intervention, the location of the intervention, and the names of the individuals responsible for each aspect of the intervention. Moreover, the criteria for a successful intervention should be clear. At a minimum, the intervention should bring a student's performance to an acceptable or tolerable level. For academic difficulties, this usually means accelerating the rate of acquisition. For an instructional isolate, achievement must improve sufficiently to allow placement in an instructional group. For example, if Bernie currently cannot read the material used in the lowest reading group, the team would need to know the level of the materials used by the lowest instructional group. In addition, the team would need to know the probable level of materials that the group will be using when Bernie's intervention has been completed. For students with more variable patterns of achievement, intervention is directed toward improving performance in areas of weakness to a level that approximates performance in areas of strength.

Setting the criterion for a behavioral intervention involves much the same process as setting targets for academic problems. When the goal is to change behavior, the teacher should select two or three students who are behaving appropriately. These students should not be the best behaved students but, rather, those in the middle of the range of acceptable behavior. The frequency, duration, latency, or amplitude of their behavior should be used as the criterion. Usually, the behavior of the appropriate students is stable, so the team does not have to predict where they will be at the end of the intervention.

Implicit in this discussion is the idea that the interventions will reach the criterion for success within the time allotted. Thus, the team not only desires progress toward the criterion but also wants that progress to occur at a specific rate—or faster. Finally, it is generally a good idea to maintain a written record of these details. This record might be as informal as a set of notes from the team meeting, or it might be a formal document such as the Prereferral Intervention Plan shown in Figure 20.2.

Implementing the Interventions

The interventions should then be conducted as planned. To ensure that the intervention is being carried out faithfully, a member of the team may observe the teacher using the planned strategy or special materials, or careful records may be kept and reviewed in order to document that the intervention occurred as planned.

FIGURE 20.2
Prereferral Intervention Plan

Prereferral Intervention Plan

Complete one form for each targeted problem.

Student _____ Gender _____ Date of Birth _____

Referring Teacher _____ Grade _____ School _____

Intervention Objectives

Behavior to be changed:

Criterion for success/termination of intervention:

Duration of intervention:

Location of intervention:

Person responsible for implementing the intervention:

Strategies

Instructional methods:

Instructional materials:

Special equipment:

Signatures

_____   _____
            (Referring Teacher)   (Date)

_____   _____
    (Member, Teacher Assistance Team)   (Date)

Evaluating the Effects of the Interventions

The effects of the interventions should be evaluated frequently enough to allow fine-tuning of the teaching methods and materials. Frequently, student performance is graphed to create learning pictures (Salvia & Hughes, 1990). Effective programs designed to increase desired behavior produce results like those shown in Figure 20.3: The student usually shows an increase in the desired behavior (correct responses) and a decrease in the number of errors (incorrect responses). It is also possible for successful programs to produce only increasingly correct responses or only a decrease in errors. Ineffective programs show no increase in the desired correct responses, no decrease in the unwanted errors, or both.

To assess a student's rate of behavior change, we graph the acceleration of a desired behavior (or the deceleration of an undesired behavior) as a separate line, called an "aimline," as shown in Figure 20.4. The aimline connects the student's current level of performance with the point that represents both the desired level of behavior and the time at which the behavior is to be attained. The student's progress is compared with the aimline. When behavior is targeted for increase, we expect the student's progress to be above the aimline (as shown in Figure 20.4); when behavior

FIGURE 20.3
A Successful Learning
Intervention

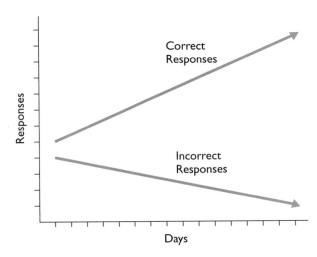

FIGURE 20.4
Student Progress
with an Aimline

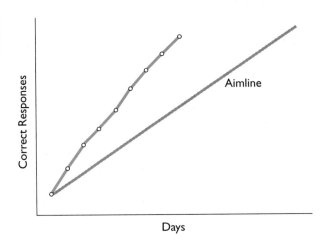

is targeted for decrease, we expect the student's progress to be below the aimline (not shown). Thus, a teacher, the intervention assistance team, or the student can look at the graph and make a decision about the adequacy of progress.

When adequate progress is being made, the intervention should obviously be continued until the criterion is reached. When better than anticipated progress is being made, the teacher or team can decide to set a more ambitious goal (that is, raise the level of desired performance) without changing the aim date, or they can set an earlier target for achieving the criterion without changing the level of performance.

When inadequate progress is being made, teachers can take several steps to fine-tune the student's program. Salvia and Hughes (1990, pp. 121–122) offer various suggestions for instructional modification, depending on the pattern of student performance in relation to the aimline. Although a discussion of instructional methods is beyond the scope of this text, some examples can illustrate the kinds of things a teacher might do when faced with inadequate progress. When a student demonstrates no correct responses (or too few), the goal may be too difficult; the team should consider changing the goal to include attainment of a prerequisite skill. When a student demonstrates correct responses but too many errors, the teacher should consider modeling or prompting and more closely monitoring practice. When a student demonstrates accurate but slow responding, the teacher can encourage faster performance by providing incentives or additional practice. When performance is consistently below the aimline (3 or 4 days are generally considered a significant amount of time), the teacher might consider varying the instructional methods or incentives. Finally, when a student's performance worsens, the teacher should question the motivational value of the task, vary any drill or practice activities, or discuss the performance directly with the student.

Decision: Should the Student Be Referred for Multidisciplinary Evaluation?

When several attempted interventions have not led to sufficient success, the student is likely to be referred for psychoeducational evaluation to ascertain eligibility for special education.

2 Decisions Made in Special Education

Approximately 10 to 12 percent of all students who enter school will experience sufficient difficulty to be identified as having a disability at some time during their school career. Most of these students will receive special education services because they need special instruction. Some students with disabilities (such as students with certain chronic health impairments) will not need special education but will require special related services that must be provided under Section 504 of the Rehabilitation Act of 1973.

After students have been determined to be eligible for special education, special education decisions revolve around design and implementation of their individualized education plans (IEPs). An IEP is a blueprint for instruction and specifies the goals, procedures, and related services for an individual eligible student.

Alex

Example 6. Alex's teacher found an easier reader for him and read individually with him for 5 minutes each day. During this time, he corrected his errors and showed him how to sound out words. Although Alex could read the lower level materials more fluently, he was unable to advance to more grade-appropriate reading materials (that is, his fluency and error rate were below an instructional level). The building assistance team recommended that the teacher assess Alex's knowledge of letter–sound associations. Alex was found to know all long vowel sounds, the short *a* sound, and hard consonant sounds. Consequently, the team developed a program that targeted the sounds of the consonants and vowels that he had not yet mastered. One of the district's reading specialists administered the intervention daily and evaluated his progress every other day. Assessment data to ascertain the effectiveness of the intervention consisted of Alex's progress in learning letter–sound associations and his oral reading fluency. The reading specialist administered a letter–sound probe after each day's instruction. After 4 weeks of intervention, Alex had learned half of the unknown soft consonant sounds as well as the short *e* and *i* sounds. A retest of his oral reading fluency indicated that he had become fluent in the next higher reading level. At the rate he was improving, he would fall at least another half-year behind his peers at the end of the current school year. Because the intervention selected had support in the research literature but had not proved sufficiently effective with Alex, he was referred for multidisciplinary evaluation to ascertain if there were nonschool factors that could be impeding his learning (for example, a disability). Determination of eligibility requires further assessment by specialists, such as school psychologists, who use commercially prepared instruments.

Assessment data are important for such planning. Numerous books and hundreds of articles in professional and scientific journals discuss the importance of using assessment data to plan instructional programs for students. The Individuals with Disabilities Education Act (IDEA) requires a thorough assessment that results in an IEP. Pupils are treated differentially on the basis of their IEPs. Moreover, most educators would agree that it is desirable to individualize programs for students in special and remedial education because the general education programs have not proved beneficial to them.

Decision: What Should Be Included in a Student's IEP?

The Individuals with Disabilities Education Act of 1997 and subsequent revisions to the Act and its regulations set forth the requirements for IEPs. Instructionally, an IEP is a road map of a student's 1-year trip from point A to point B. This road map is prepared collaboratively by an IEP team composed of the parents and student (when appropriate), at least one general education teacher, at least one of the student's special education teachers, a representative of the school administration, an individual who can interpret the instructional implications of evaluation results, and other individuals who have knowledge or special expertise regarding the student.

The IEP begins with a description of the student's current educational levels—the starting point of the metaphoric trip. Next, the IEP specifies measurable,

Scenario in Assessment

Alex and Nick

Example 7. For the sake of this example, assume that Alex has been found eligible for special education services as a student with a learning disability in reading. To ascertain Alex's current level of performance in oral reading, he was again assessed by having him read from the materials actually used in his school. Two passages of 300 to 400 words that were representative of the beginning, middle, and end of each grade-level reading text were selected. Because Alex was already known to be reading only slightly above the preprimer level, he was asked to start reading at that level. He read passages of increasing difficulty until he was no longer reading at an instructional level (that is, reading with 85 to 95 percent accuracy).[3] Alex read beginning first-grade material with 95 percent accuracy, but he read middle second-grade material with only 87 percent accuracy. Thus, his current instructional level in oral reading was determined to be middle third grade.

[3]To calculate accuracy, first find the number of words with two or more letters. Then count the number of errors; for example, words a reader cannot decode correctly and words a reader incorrectly adds to the text. See Chapter 13 for a discussion of errors in oral reading.

Current educational level in behavioral areas should also be quantified. Frequency, duration, latency, and amplitude can be quantified, and the results can be compared to those of a peer who is performing satisfactorily on the target skill or behavior.

Example 8. For the sake of this example, assume that Nick has also been found eligible for special education services as a student with other health impairments (attention deficit disorder without hyperactivity). To ascertain the duration of Nick's attention to task during academic instruction, the school counselor systematically observed Nick and another student who was not reported to be having attention problems. Observations occurred between 10:00 and 10:45 for a week during reading and arithmetic instruction. Nick's teacher did not use the tapping cue during this time period. The counselor sat behind and to Nick's side and used an audio signal tape with beeps at a fixed interval of 30 seconds. The counselor calculated that Nick was on task 35 percent of the time, whereas his peer was on task 93 percent of the time. Nick's current level of attention to academic tasks is 35 percent.

annual, academic, and functional goals (the student's destination). The IEP must include a description of how progress toward meeting annual goals will be measured and when progress reports will be provided to parents. The IEP must identify the special education and related services that are based on peer-reviewed research (to the extent practicable) needed by the student in order to reach the goals (the method of transportation and provisions that make the trip possible). Finally, the IEP requires measurement, evaluation, and reporting of the student's progress toward the annual goals (periodic checks to make sure the student is on the correct road and traveling fast enough).

Current Levels

A student's current level of performance is not specifically defined in the regulations. However, because current levels are the starting points for instruction, a current level must be instructionally relevant and expressed quantitatively. Although legally permissible, scores from standardized achievement are not particularly useful. The fact that a student is reading less well than 90 percent of students in the grade is not useful information about where the teacher should begin instruction. If a student is physically aggressive in the third-grade classroom, that alone is too vague to allow a teacher, parents, and the student to tell whether progress toward acceptable behavior is being made. We think a current educational level in an academic area should be the level at which a student is appropriately instructed.

Annual Goals

IEPs must contain a statement of measurable annual goals, which meet each educational need arising from the student's disability and ensure the student's access to the general education curriculum (or appropriate activities, if a preschooler). Thus, for each area of need, parents and schools must agree on what should be a student's level of achievement after 1 year of instruction.

In part, the selection of long-term goals is based on the aspirations and prognosis for a student's postschool outcomes. Although these are not formally required by federal law until a special education student reaches 16 years of age, the expected or desired postschool outcomes shape the special education a student receives. For students with pervasive and severe cognitive disabilities, the prognosis may be assisted living with supported employment. With this prognosis, educational goals are likely to center on daily living, social skills, and leisure rather than academic areas. For students with moderate disabilities, the prognosis may be independent living and unskilled or semiskilled employment. With this prognosis, educational goals are likely to be basic academics and vocational skills. For students with mild disabilities, the prognosis may be professional or skilled employment. For these students, educational goals can prepare students for college or technical schools.

In part, the selection of long-term goals is based on the degree to which the educational deficit caused by the disability is remediable. All students receiving special education will lag significantly behind their nondisabled peers.[4] Except when students have severe and pervasive disabilities, special educators and parents generally try to remediate the educational deficits first. The benefit of this approach is that it allows the student the fullest access to later school and postschool opportunities. When remediation repeatedly fails, parents and teachers usually turn to compensatory mechanisms so that the student can attain the more generally desired educational outcomes. For example, if Cliff just cannot learn math facts, he may be allowed to use a calculator. The advantage of this option is that it allows Cliff to move to higher curricular goals; the disadvantage is that the deficits will always be with Cliff, and he will always behave to compensate for them. When a student cannot master the curriculum with compensatory mechanisms, parents and teachers may adapt the curriculum by reducing the complexity of some components. For example, in social studies all students might be required to learn about taxes, but LeShaun might not have to learn about the constitutional issues surrounding the creation of the federal income tax. If reducing the complexity is not appropriate, areas of the curriculum may be eliminated for individual students with disabilities. Obviously, this option is the last resort, but it may be appropriate when a child's disabilities are profound. For example, we would not expect all

---

[4]Some gifted students have learning disabilities. Thus, these gifted students will also have significant deficits.

deaf students to be fluent oral communicators, although we would expect them to attain other generally prescribed educational outcomes; we would not expect quadriplegics to pass a swimming test, although we might well expect them to meet other educational outcomes.

Annual goals are derived directly from a student's curriculum and a student's current instructional levels. When continued academic integration is the desired educational outcome, a student's goals are mastery of the same content at the same rate as nondisabled peers. Thus, after 1 year, the student would be expected to be instructional in the same materials as his or her peers. When reintegration is the desired educational outcome, a student's goal depends on where the regular class peers will be in 1 year. For students pursuing alternative curricula, the IEP team makes an educated guess about where the student should be after 1 year of instruction.

Specially Designed Instruction

IDEA defines special education, in part, as specially designed instruction that is provided in classrooms, the home, or other settings (see 34 CFR §300.26). It includes the adaptation of instructional content, methods, or delivery to meet the needs of a student with disabilities.

Currently, the best way to teach handicapped learners appears to rely on generally effective procedures.[5] Teachers can do several things to make it easier for their pupils to learn facts and concepts, skills, or behavior. They can model the desired behavior. They can break down the terminal goal into its component parts and teach each of the steps and their integration. They can teach the objective in a variety of contexts with a variety of materials to facilitate generalization. They can provide time for practice, and they can choose the schedule on which practice is done (in other words, they can offer distributed or massed practice). Several techniques that are under the direct control of the teacher can be employed to instruct any learner effectively. To help pupils recall information that has been taught, teachers may organize the material that a pupil is to learn, provide rehearsal strategies, or employ overlearning or distributed practice. There are also a number of things that teachers can do to elicit responses that have already been acquired: Various reinforcers and punishers have been shown to be effective in the control of behavior.

Assessment personnel can help teachers identify specific areas in which instructional difficulties exist, and they can help teachers plan interventions in light of information gained from assessments. Certain procedures (Ysseldyke & Christenson,

---

[5]Historically, some psychologists and educators have believed that students learn better when instruction is matched to test-identified abilities. This approach led to the development of instructional procedures that capitalized on areas of strength or avoided weaker abilities. For example, test scores from the first edition of the Developmental Test of Visual Perception (Frostig, Maslow, Lefever, & Whittlesey, 1964), the Illinois Test of Psycholinguistic Abilities (Kirk, McCarthy, & Kirk, 1968), and the Purdue Perceptual–Motor Survey (Roach & Kephart, 1966) were at one time believed to be instructionally useful. In part because test-identified abilities were frequently unreliable and in part because special instructional methods did not result in better learning, this approach to instruction gradually lost favor, although some educators today still cling to a belief in it. In the 1980s, attempts to match instruction to specific student attributes resurfaced. However, hypothetical cognitive structures and learning processes replaced the hypothetical abilities of the 1960s (for example, see Resnick, 1987). This approach is interesting but has yet to be validated.

Alex

Example 9. Alex is finishing third grade, so his annual goal specifies his desired performance near the end of fourth grade. If he were to be completely caught up with his peers, Alex would read independently in his fourth-grade materials. (If his teacher or school uses different levels of reading materials for different tracks of students, he would need to read independently the materials used by the lowest track in regular education.) For the sake of this example, let us assume that the lowest group will use reading materials written at the middle third-grade level at the end of fourth grade. Thus, for Alex to be "caught up" with his peers, he would need to complete approximately 3.3 years in 1 year. Because this much growth in reading could not likely be attained without omitting instruction in other key curricular areas (such as science and written language), the IEP team decides to take 2 years to try to catch Alex up to his age peers. Thus, his annual goal becomes "At the end of 1 year of instruction in oral reading Alex will read material written at the end of second-grade difficulty level with 95 percent accuracy."

1987; Ysseldyke, Christenson, & Kovaleski, 1994) can aid assessment personnel in determining the nature of students' instructional environments. Procedures such as the Functional Assessment of Academic Behavior (Ysseldyke & Christenson, 2002) may be used both to pinpoint the extent to which a student's academic or behavioral problems are a function of factors in the instructional environment and to identify likely starting points for designing appropriate interventions for individual students. Yet there is no way to know for certain ahead of time how best to teach a specific student.

There should be good evidence that the instructional interventions are generally effective with students who are at the same age and grade as the student being assessed. [Under the requirements of No Child Left Behind, school personnel are expected to be putting in place evidence-based treatments.] Information about the extent to which treatments are generally effective is found by reviewing the research evidence in support of the treatments. The What Works Clearinghouse (WWC) can provide direction as to what treatments might be particularly effective. At the WWC website (http://ies.ed.gov/ncee/wwc), you can look up interventions for middle school math and find a topic report listing the kinds of interventions that WWC reviewed on middle school math. Information on the extent to which there is good empirical support for a particular intervention can be obtained from the website.

However, always remember that efficacy is local. We recommend that teachers first rely on general principles that are known and demonstrated to be effective in facilitating learning for students with disabilities. However, even when we find studies that demonstrate that a particular application of a learning principle worked for a research sample, we still cannot be certain that it will work for specific students in a specific classroom. The odds are that it will, but we cannot be sure. Consequently, we must treat our translation of these principles, known to be effective, as tentative.

In a real sense, we hypothesize that our treatment will work, but we need to verify that it has worked. The point was made years ago by Deno and Mirkin (1977) and remains true today:

> At the present time we are unable to prescribe specific and effective changes in instruction for individual pupils with certainty. Therefore, changes in instructional programs that are arranged for an individual child can be treated only as hypotheses that must be empirically tested before a decision can be made about whether they are effective for that child. (p. 11)

Teaching is often experimental in nature. When there is no database to guide our selection of specific tasks or materials, decisions must be tentative. The decision maker makes some good guesses about what will work and then implements an instructional program. We do not know whether a decision is correct until we gather data on the extent to which the instructional program actually works. We never know if the program will work until it has worked.

Tests do provide some very limited information about how to teach. Tests of intelligence, for example, yield information that gives a teacher some hints about teaching. Generally, the lower a pupil's intelligence, the more practice the student will require for mastery. A score of 55 on the Wechsler Intelligence Scale for Children–IV does not tell the teacher whether a pupil needs 25 percent or 250 percent more practice, but it does alert the teacher to the likelihood that the pupil will need more practice than the average student will need. Other tenuous hints can be derived, but we believe that it is better to rely on direct observation of how a student learns in order to make adjustments in the learning program. Thus, to determine whether we had provided enough practice, we would observe Sally's recall of information rather than looking at Sally's IQ. We cannot do anything about Sally's IQ, but we can do something about the amount of practice she gets.

Related Services

In addition to special instruction, eligible students are entitled to developmental, corrective, and other supportive services if such services are needed in order for the students to benefit from special education; federal legislation uses the term *related services*, which has been widely adopted by states and school districts. Related services include both those not typically provided by schools and those typically provided (34 CFR §300.24).

Schools must provide to students with disabilities a variety of services to which nondisabled students are seldom entitled. Services described in 34 CFR §300.24 include, but are not limited to, the following types:

1. *Audiology.* Allowable services include evaluation of hearing, habilitation (for example, programs in auditory training, speech reading, and speech conservation), amplification (including the fitting of hearing aids), and hearing conservation programs.

2. *Psychological services.* Psychological services allowed include testing, observation, and consultation.

3. *Physical and occupational therapy.* These therapies can be used to (a) improve, develop, or restore functional impairments caused by illness, injury, or deprivation; and (b) improve independent functioning. These therapies

Scenario in Assessment

Nick and Alex

Example 10. The assessment data pointed to areas where Nick needed specially designed instruction. Although Nick's physician prescribed Ritalin, Nick also needed systematic behavioral intervention to minimize the effects of his attention deficit disorder on school functioning.[6] The team developed a program of specially designed instruction that included systematic reinforcement for appropriate attention and systematic instruction in self-monitoring his attention. The district behavior management specialist will be responsible for

[6]Assume that Nick's psychoeducational evaluation did not reveal other intellectual, physical, or cognitive problems beyond his lack of attention.

training Nick to self-monitor accurately, and Nick's teacher will be trained to implement the plan developed by the district specialist.

Example 11. The assessment data also indicated that Alex needs specially designed instruction in reading. Although he had now mastered all of the sounds of consonants and vowels, he was slow and inaccurate in reading grade-appropriate materials. To improve Alex's accuracy, the IEP team decided that Alex should be taught the basic site vocabulary needed to read the words in his language arts text as well as content-area curricula. To improve Alex's reading fluency, the IEP team decided to use the strategy of rereading.

may also be used with preschool populations to prevent impairment or further loss of function.

4. *Recreation.* Allowable programs include those located in the schools and community agencies that provide general recreation programs, therapeutic recreation, and assessment of leisure functioning.

5. *Counseling services.* Either group or individual counseling may be provided for students and their parents. Student counseling includes rehabilitation counseling that focuses on career development, employment preparation, achievement of independence, and integration in the workplace and community; it also includes psychological counseling. Parental counseling includes therapies addressing problems in the student's living situation (that is, home, school, and community) that affect the student's schooling. Parental counseling also includes assistance to help parents understand their child's special needs, as well as information about child development.

6. *Medical services.* Diagnostic and evaluative services required to determine medically related disabilities are allowed.

The schools must also provide to students with disabilities the services they typically provide to all children. Thus, schools must provide to students with disabilities, as needed, speech and language services, school health and school social work services, and transportation. School-provided transportation includes whatever is needed to get students to and from school, as well as between schools or among school buildings, including any required special equipment such as ramps. Although these related services are mandatory for students who need them to profit from their special education, there is nothing to prohibit a school from offering other services. Thus, schools may offer additional services free of charge to eligible students.

Although federal law is very clear about the need to provide related services to students with disabilities, how that need should be established remains unclear. In practice, most schools or parents seek an evaluation by a specialist. The specialist notes a problem and expresses a belief that a specific therapy could be successful and benefit the student. Thus, need is frequently based on professional opinion. We must also note that related services can be very costly, and some school districts try to avoid providing them. We have heard of districts maintaining that they do not offer a particular service even though federal law mandates that service should be provided to students who need it.

Decision: What Is the Least Restrictive Appropriate Environment?

Federal law expresses a clear preference for educating students with disabilities as close as possible to their home and with their nondisabled peers to the maximum extent appropriate. Education in "special classes, separate schooling or other removal of children with disabilities from the regular educational environment occurs only if the nature or severity of the disability is such that education in regular classes with the use of supplementary aids and services cannot be achieved satisfactorily" (34 CFR §300.550).

Placement Options

A hierarchy of placements ranges from the least restrictive (educating students with disabilities in a general education classroom with a general education teacher who receives consultative services from a special education teacher) to the most restrictive (educating students with disabilities in segregated residential facilities that provide services only to students with disabilities). Between these two extremes are at least five other options:

1. *Instructional support from a special education teacher in the general education classroom.* In this arrangement, eligible students remain in the general education classroom in their neighborhood schools, and the special education teacher comes to the student to provide whatever specialized instruction is necessary.

2. *Instructional support from a special education teacher in a resource room.* In this arrangement, eligible students remain in a general education classroom for most of the day. When they need specialized instruction, they go to a special education resource room to receive services from a special education teacher. Because districts may not have enough students with disabilities in each school to warrant establishing a resource room program at each school, a student may be assigned to a general education classroom that is not in the student's neighborhood school.

3. *Part-time instruction in a special education classroom.* In this arrangement, eligible students have some classes or subject matter taught by the special education teacher and the rest taught in the general education classroom. As is the case with resource rooms, the general education classroom may not be in the student's neighborhood school.

4. *Full-time instruction in a special education classroom, with limited integration.* In this arrangement, eligible students receive all academic instruction from a special education teacher in a special classroom. Eligible students may be integrated with nondisabled peers for special events or activities (such as lunch, recess, and assemblies) and nonacademic classes (such as art and music).

5. *Full-time instruction in a special education classroom, without integration.* In this arrangement, eligible students have no interaction with their nondisabled peers, and their classrooms may be in a special day school that serves only students with disabilities.

Factors Affecting the Placement Choice

The selection of a particular option should be based on the intensity of education needed by the eligible student: The less intensive the intervention needed by the student, the less restrictive the environment; the more intensive the intervention needed by the student, the more restrictive the environment. The procedure for determining the intensity of an intervention is less than scientific. Frequently, there is some correspondence between the severity of disability and the intensity of service needed, but that correspondence is not perfect. Therefore, special education teachers and parents should consider the frequency and duration of the needed interventions. The more frequent an intervention is (for instance, every morning versus one morning per week) and the longer its duration (for example, 30 minutes versus 15 minutes per morning), the more likely it is that the intervention will be provided in more, rather than less, restrictive settings. When frequent and long interventions are needed, the student will have less opportunity to participate with nondisabled peers, no matter what the student's placement. Obviously, if students require round-the-clock intervention, they cannot get what they need from a resource room program.

In addition to the nature of needed interventions, parents and teachers may also reasonably consider the following factors when deciding on the type of placement:

1. *Disruption.* Bringing a special education teacher into or pulling a student out of a general education classroom may be disruptive. For example, some students with disabilities cannot handle transitions: They get lost between classrooms, or they forget to go to their resource rooms. When eligible students have a lot of difficulty changing schedules or making transitions between events, less restrictive options may not be appropriate.

2. *Well-being of nondisabled individuals.* Eligible students will seldom be integrated when they present a clear danger to the welfare of nondisabled peers or teachers. For example, assaultive and disruptive students are likely to be placed in more restrictive environments.

3. *Well-being of the student who has a disability.* Many students with disabilities require some degree of protection—in some cases, from nondisabled peers who may tease or physically abuse a student who is different; in other cases, from other students with disabilities. For example, the parents of a seriously withdrawn student may decide not to place their child in a classroom for students with emotional disabilities when those students are assaultive.

Nick and Alex

Example 12. Although Nick's behavior was not disruptive or detrimental to the learning of his peers, the interventions that his regular class teacher had used were distracting to the other students. However, the team believed that the specially designed instruction (systematic reinforcement for appropriate attention and self-monitoring) that had been approved by the team would be much less intrusive. Therefore, the team believed that the impact of the intervention on Nick's peers would not be a consideration in where the special education services would be provided.

The classroom teacher, once properly trained by the behavior management specialist, can administer the positive reinforcement correctly. Although the behavior management specialist will remove Nick from class when teaching him to self-monitor, the special education teacher and the behavior specialist will evaluate Nick's use of the self-monitoring system in his classroom. Thus, Nick's needs can readily be met in the regular classroom; he will not be instructed in a special education setting.

Example 13. Because the reading interventions designed by the IEP team were not being used in Alex's classroom and because Alex required more instruction in reading than could be provided in his regular classroom, the IEP team recommended placement in a special education resource room for 1 hour per day. The team decided that Alex would go to the resource room when the rest of his class was being instructed in social studies and art.

4. *Labeling.* Many parents, especially those of students with milder handicaps, reject disability labels. They desire special education services, but they want these services without having their child labeled. Such parents often prefer consultative or itinerant services for their children.

5. *Inclusion.* Some parents are willing to forgo the instructional benefits of special education for the potential social benefits of having their children educated exclusively with nondisabled peers. For such parents, full inclusion is the only option.

There are also pragmatic considerations in selecting the educational setting. One very real consideration is that a school district may, for economic reasons, not be able to provide a full range of options. In such districts, parents are offered a choice among existing options unless they are willing to go through a due process hearing or a court trial. A second consideration is instructional efficiency. When several students require the same intervention, the special education teacher can often form an instructional group. Thus, it will probably cost less to provide the special education services. A third consideration is the specific teachers. Some teachers are better than others, and parents may well opt for a more restrictive setting because the teacher there is highly regarded.

Parents and special education teachers must realize that selecting a placement option is an imprecise endeavor. Thus, although federal regulations are clear in their preference for less restrictive placements, the criteria that guide the selection of one option over another are unclear. Choices among placement options should be regarded as best guesses.

Decision: Is the Instructional Program Effective?

IEPs are supposed to result in effective instruction for students with disabilities. IDEA requires that each student's IEP contain a statement detailing the way in which progress toward annual goals will be measured and how parents will be informed of their child's progress (34 CFR §300.347). In addition, IDEA requires IEP teams to review each student's IEP "periodically, but not less than annually, to determine whether the annual goals for the child are being achieved." (34 CFR §300.343). If adequate progress is not being made, IEP teams are required to revise the IEPs of students who are not making expected progress toward their annual goals. An exception to this rule is that according to IDEA 2004, some states may put in place comprehensive multiyear IEPs for those students who have milder disabilities and for whom parents agree a multiyear IEP is sufficient.

Throughout this book, we have discussed procedures that are useful in collecting information about students' achievement and behavior. We have also discussed how that information can be systematized using graphs and charts. We have offered guidelines about how to reach decisions about a student's progress. All of these discussions are relevant to the decision about the effectiveness of each component of a student's instructional program. Judgments about the simultaneous effectiveness of all of the components of an instructional program are geometrically more complicated. Based on our personal experience, a program is effective if the most important goals are achieved. What makes a goal important varies by student. For an aggressive, acting-out student, self-control may be more important than quadratic equations. For a bright student with a learning disability, learning to read may be more important than improvement in spelling.

CHAPTER COMPREHENSION QUESTIONS

Write your answers to each of the following questions, and then compare your responses to the text or the study guide.

1. List and explain three instructional decisions that are made prior to a student being found eligible for special education.

2. List and explain three instructional decisions that are made after a student has been found eligible for special education.

21

Making Special Education Eligibility Decisions

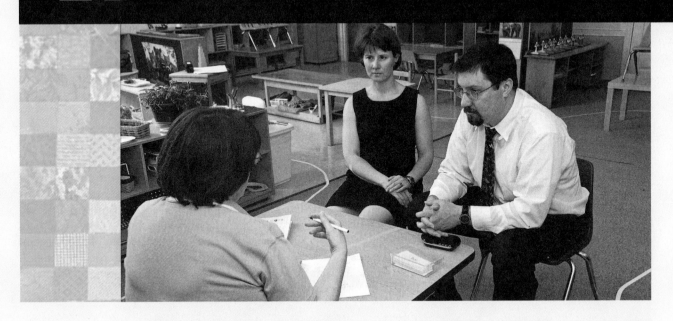

Chapter Goals

1 Understand the disabilities recognized by the Individuals with Disabilities Education Improvement Act.

2 Understand how the need for special education is established.

3 Understand multidisciplinary teams (their composition and responsibilities).

4 Understand the process for determining eligibility (including procedural safeguards, the requirements for valid assessment, and the team process).

5 Understand common problems in determining eligibility.

Key Terms

autism

mental retardation

specific learning disability

severe discrepancy

response to instruction

emotional disturbance

traumatic brain injury

speech or language impairment

deafness and hearing impairment

visual impairment

orthopedic impairments

other health impairments

deaf–blindness

multiple disabilities

developmental delay

need for special education

multidisciplinary team

procedural safeguards

THE ISSUE OF ELIGIBILITY FOR SPECIAL EDUCATION HINGES ON TWO QUESTIONS: (1) Does the student have a disability? and (2) If so, does the student need special education? Both questions must be answered in the affirmative to be eligible for special education and related services. Students who have disabilities but do not need special education are not eligible (although they may well be eligible for services under Section 504 of the Rehabilitation Act of 1973). Students who do not have disabilities but need (or would benefit from) special education services are not eligible. Once students have been determined to be eligible for special education, they are automatically entitled to procedural safeguards, special services, altered outcome expectations, and special fiscal arrangements, as discussed in Chapter 2.

1 Official Student Disabilities

Students are classified as having a disability under several laws; three are particularly important: The Americans with Disabilities Act (Public Law 101-336), Section 504 of the Rehabilitation Act of 1973, and the Individuals with Disabilities Education Improvement Act (IDEA; 34 CFR §300.7). In the schools and other educational settings, the following disabilities, enumerated in regulations of IDEA (34 CFR §300.7), are the most frequently used: autism, mental retardation, specific learning disability, emotional disturbance, traumatic brain injury, speech or language impairment, visual impairment, deafness and hearing impairment, orthopedic impairments, other health impairments, deaf–blindness, multiple disabilities, and developmental delay.[1] Identification under §300.8 of the IDEA requires that

■ a group of qualified professionals and the parent(s) of the child determine whether the child has a disability, and the public agency provides a copy of the evaluation report and the documentation of determination of eligibility at no cost to the parent(s); and

■ a child cannot be determined to have a disability if the determinant factor for that determination is lack of appropriate instruction in reading, lack of appropriate instruction in math, or limited English proficiency, or if the child does not otherwise meet the eligibility criteria.

[1]The definitions in IDEA (excluding the need for special education) are generally used for entitlements under Section 504.

In addition, the identification must

- draw upon information from a variety of sources, including aptitude and achievement tests, input from parents, and teachers, as well as information about the child's physical condition, social or cultural background, and adaptive behavior; and

- ensure that information obtained from all of these sources is documented and carefully considered.

§300.8 of the IDEA regulations define the specific disabilities. These definitions are given below.

Autism

Autistic students are those who demonstrate "developmental disability significantly affecting verbal and nonverbal communication and social interaction, generally evident before age 3, that adversely affects a child's educational performance. Other characteristics often associated with autism are engagement in repetitive activities and stereotyped movements, resistance to environmental change or change in daily routines, and unusual responses to sensory experiences. Autism does not apply if a child's educational performance is adversely affected primarily because the child has an emotional disturbance."

Students with suspected autism are usually evaluated by speech and language specialists and psychologists after it has been determined that some aspects of their educational performance fall outside the normal range and various attempts to remedy the educational problems have failed. Frequently, a speech and language specialist would look for impaired verbal and nonverbal communication. A large proportion of autistic children are mute, an impairment that is readily apparent. Autism in students with speech and language might manifest itself as overly concrete thinking. For example, an autistic student might react to a statement such as "don't cry over spilled milk" quite literally ("I didn't spill any milk"). Another manifestation would be a lack of conversational reciprocity (usually long, often tedious, orations about a favorite subject) and failure to recognize a listener's waning interest. Moreover, this impaired social communication would be a consistent feature of the student's behavior rather than an occasional overexuberance. A psychologist looks for behavior that defines the condition: repetitive activities (for example, self-stimulating behavior, spinning objects, aligning objects, and smelling objects), stereotyped movements (for example, hand flapping, rocking, and head banging), resistance to change (for example, eating only certain foods or tantruming when activities are ended). A psychologist may also administer a behavior rating scale (for example, the Gilliam Autism Rating Scale) as an aid to diagnosis. Finally, a psychologist rules out emotional disturbance as a cause of the student's behavior and impairments.

Mental Retardation

Students with mental retardation are those who demonstrate "significantly subaverage general intellectual functioning, existing concurrently with deficits in adaptive behavior and manifested during the developmental period, that adversely affects a child's educational performance." Students who are eventually labeled "mentally retarded" are often referred because of generalized slowness: They lag behind their age mates in most areas of academic achievement, social and emotional development, language ability, and, perhaps, physical development.

Usually, a psychologist will administer a test of intelligence that is appropriate in terms of the student's age, acculturation, and physical and sensory capabilities. In most states, students must have an IQ that is two standard deviations or more below the mean (usually 70 or less) on a validly administered test. However, a test of intelligence is not enough. The pupil must also demonstrate impairments in adaptive behavior. There is no federal requirement that a test or rating scale be used to assess adaptive behavior psychometrically. In practice, most school psychologists will administer an adaptive behavior scale (for example, the Vineland Adaptive Behavior Scale II). However, when it is not possible to do so appropriately, a psychologist will interview parents or guardians and make a clinical judgment about a student's adaptive behavior.

Specific Learning Disability

Students with learning-disabilities are those who demonstrate "a disorder in one or more of the basic psychological processes involved in understanding or in using language, spoken or written, that may manifest itself in the imperfect ability to listen, think, speak, read, write, spell, or to do mathematical calculations, including conditions such as perceptual disabilities, brain injury, minimal brain dysfunction, dyslexia, and developmental aphasia. . . . Specific learning disability does not include learning problems that are primarily the result of visual, hearing, or motor disabilities, of mental retardation, of emotional disturbance, or of environmental, cultural, or economic disadvantage."

Students who are eventually labeled as having a learning disability do not achieve adequately or meet state-approved grade-level standards in one or more of the core achievement areas when provided with learning experiences and instruction appropriate for the child's age or state-approved grade-level standards.

Regardless of the approach used, the committee responsible for making the actual determination that a student has a learning disability must rule out other causes for poor achievement in oral expression, listening comprehension, written expression, basic reading skill, reading comprehension, mathematics calculation, and mathematics reasoning. IDEA specifically forbids that the student's achievement problem be the result of a visual, hearing, or motor impairment; mental retardation; emotional disturbance; or environmental, cultural, or economic disadvantage.

The formal evaluation of students suspected of having a learning disability begins after it has been determined that the student's educational performance in the specified areas (for example, basic reading skill) falls outside the normal range and various attempts to remedy the educational problems have failed. The evaluation of these students must include an observation of each student in the student's learning environment to document the student's academic performance and behavior in the areas of concern (§300.310). The student may also be evaluated by a speech and language specialist who would look for manifestations of a disorder in producing or understanding language. This specialist may conduct an assessment of a student's spontaneous or elicited language during an interview or play situation; the specialist may administer a formal test such as the Test for Auditory Comprehension of Language–Third Edition or the Test of Language Development–Primary, Fourth Edition. There are no quantitative guidelines in the regulations to indicate a language disorder, but a child with a disability in language would be expected to earn scores that are substantially below average. The evaluations to determine special education eligibility can take one of two paths—severe discrepancy or response to intervention.

- *Severe discrepancy.* In this approach, students suspected of having a learning disability are evaluated by psychologists. All psychologists should look for manifestations of a disorder in the areas specified in IDEA. This search requires the results from a current individually administered test of intelligence to rule out mental retardation (as required by the federal definition of learning disability) and to establish the level of ability that was needed to ascertain if a student had a significant discrepancy between ability and achievement. Psychologists usually administered a standardized achievement test such as the Woodcock–Johnson Psychoeducational Battery–III: Tests of Achievement or the Wechsler Individual Achievement Test in all areas of possible learning disability. The results of the achievement tests served two purposes. First, they verified that the student was indeed having difficulties in oral expression, listening comprehension, written expression, basic reading skill, reading comprehension, mathematics calculation, or mathematics reasoning. Second, the standard scores in these areas were systematically compared to the student's IQ to determine if a significant discrepancy existed between the scores. Because IDEA does not specify the number of standard score points required for a difference in scores to be considered a significant discrepancy, practice is inconsistent from state to state—and from district to district within a state.[2] Some psychologists may also administer tests to assess basic psychological processes such as visual perception (for example, the Developmental Test of Visual Perception).

- *Response to intervention.* In this approach, students suspected of having a learning disability receive more intensive instruction using methods of proven effectiveness (that is, by objective, empirical research). The student's progress is repeatedly and appropriately monitored to ascertain if achievement has improved. Lack of improvement is evidence of a learning disability. There are multiple models for assessing response to intervention. Interested readers should read the material related to response to intervention on the student website.

[2]Some psychologists will define a severe discrepancy as a difference greater than chance fluctuation. Psychologists who use this approach may use the reliability of an obtained difference or the reliability of the predicted difference to reach their decision. Some psychologists will use the rarity of a difference, which is often provided by test authors when they have normed both the intelligence and the achievement tests on the same sample.

Emotional Disturbance

Emotional disturbance means "a condition exhibiting one or more of the following characteristics over a long period of time and to a marked degree that adversely affects a child's educational performance: (1) an inability to learn that cannot be explained by intellectual, sensory, or health factors; (2) an inability to build or maintain satisfactory interpersonal relationships with peers and teachers; (3) inappropriate types of behavior or feelings under normal circumstances; (4) a general pervasive mood of unhappiness or depression; (5) a tendency to develop physical symptoms or fears associated with personal or school problems." This disability includes schizophrenia but excludes "children who are socially maladjusted, unless it is determined that they have an emotional disturbance." Students who are eventually labeled as having an emotional disorder are often referred for problems in interpersonal relations (for example, fighting or extreme noncompliance) or unusual behavior (for example, unexplained episodes of crying or extreme mood swings).

Students suspected of being emotionally disturbed are evaluated by a psychologist after it has been determined that some of their school performance falls outside the normal range and various attempts to remedy the school problems have failed. Requirements for establishing a pupil's eligibility as a student with emotional disturbance vary among the states. However, multidisciplinary teams usually obtain a developmental and health history from a student's parent or guardian to rule out sensory and health factors as causes of a student's inability to learn. A parent or guardian is usually interviewed about the student's relationships with peers, feelings (for example, anger, alienation, depression, and fears), and physical symptoms (for example, headaches or nausea). Parents or guardians may also be asked to complete a behavior rating scale such as Achenbach's Child Behavior Checklist to obtain normative data on the student's behavior. Teachers will likely be interviewed about their relationships with the student and the student's relationships with peers at school. They may also be asked to complete a rating scale (for example, the Walker–McConnell Scale of Social Competence and School Adjustment) to obtain normative data for in-school behavior. In addition, a psychologist might be asked to administer a norm-referenced achievement battery to verify that the student's educational performance has been negatively affected by the student's emotional problems.

Traumatic Brain Injury

Students with traumatic brain injury have "an acquired injury to the brain caused by an external physical force, resulting in total or partial functional disability or psychosocial impairment, or both, that adversely affects a child's educational performance. Traumatic brain injury applies to open or closed head injuries resulting in impairments in one or more areas, such as cognition; language; memory; attention; reasoning; abstract thinking; judgment; problem solving; sensory, perceptual, and motor abilities; psychosocial behavior; physical functions; information processing; and speech. Traumatic brain injury does not apply to brain injuries that are congenital or degenerative, or to brain injuries induced by birth trauma." Students with traumatic brain injury have normal development until they sustain a severe head injury. As a result of this injury, they have a disability. Most head injuries are the result of an accident (frequently an automobile accident), but they may also occur as a result of physical abuse or intentional harm (for example, being shot).

Traumatic brain injury will be diagnosed by a physician, who is usually a specialist (a neurologist). The need of a student with brain injury for special education will be based first on a determination that the student's school performance falls outside the normal range and various attempts to remedy the educational problems have failed. Next, a school psychologist will likely administer a standardized achievement battery to verify that the student's achievement has been adversely affected.

Speech or Language Impairment

A student with a speech or language impairment has "a communication disorder, such as stuttering, impaired articulation, a language impairment, or a voice impairment, that adversely affects a child's educational performance." Many children will experience some developmental problems in their speech and language. For example, children frequently have difficulty with the *r* sound and say "wabbit" instead of "rabbit." Similarly, many children will use incorrect grammar, especially with internal plurals; for example, children may say, "My dog has four foots." Such difficulties are so common as to be considered a part of normal speech development. However, when such speech and language errors continue to occur beyond the age when most children have developed correct speech or language, there is cause for concern. Not all students who require intervention for speech or language problems are eligible for special education. A student may be eligible for speech or language services but not have a problem that adversely affects his or her school performance. Thus, for a student to be eligible for special education as a person with a speech or language impairment, that student must not only have a speech/language impairment but also need special education.

The identification of students with speech and language impairments proceeds along two separate paths. School personnel identify the educational disability in the same way that other educational disabilities are identified. When extra help from a teacher does not solve the problem, the student is referred to a child study team for prereferral intervention. If those interventions fail to remedy the achievement problem, the student is referred for multidisciplinary evaluation. A psychologist or educational diagnostician will likely administer a norm-referenced achievement test to verify the achievement problem. At the same time, speech and language specialists will use a variety of assessment procedures (norm-referenced tests, systematic observation, and criterion-referenced tests) to identify the speech and language disability. If the student has both need and disability, the student will be eligible for special education and related services.

Visual Impairment

A student with a visual impairment has "an impairment in vision that, even with correction, adversely affects a child's educational performance. The term includes both partial sight and blindness." Students with severe visual impairments are usually identified by an ophthalmologist before they enter school. Many students who are partially sighted will be identified by routine vision screening that usually takes place in the primary grades; others will be identified when visual demands increase (for example, when font size is reduced from the larger print used in beginning reading materials). Severe visual impairment is always presumed to adversely affect their educational development, and students with this disability are presumed to require special education services and curricular adaptations (for example, mobility training, instruction in Braille, and talking books). A vision specialist usually assesses functional vision through systematic observation of a student's responses to various types of paper, print sizes, lighting conditions, and so forth. For more information about vision screening, see the material on sensory screening on the student website.

Deafness and Hearing Impairment

Deafness is an impairment in hearing "that is so severe that the child is impaired in processing linguistic information through hearing, with or without amplification, and that adversely affects a child's educational performance." A student with a hearing impairment has "an impairment in hearing, whether permanent or fluctuating, that adversely affects educational performance but that is not included under the definition of deafness."

Most students classified as deaf will be identified before they enter school. Deafness will be presumed to adversely affect a student's educational development, and students with this disability are presumed to require special education services and curricular adaptations. However, even severe hearing impairments may be difficult to identify in the first years of life, and students with milder hearing impairments may not be identified until school age. Referrals for undiagnosed hearing-impaired students may indicate expressive and receptive language problems, variable hearing performance, problems in attending to aural tasks, and perhaps problems in peer relationships. Diagnosis of hearing impairment is usually made by audiologists, who identify the auditory disability, in conjunction with school personnel, who identify the educational disability. For more information about vision screening, see the material on sensory screening on the student website.

Orthopedic Impairments

An orthopedic impairment is "a severe impairment that adversely affects a child's educational performance. The term includes impairments caused by a congenital anomaly, impairments caused by disease (such as poliomyelitis and bone tuberculosis), and impairments from other causes (such as cerebral palsy, amputations, and fractures or burns that cause contractures)."

Physical disabilities are generally identified prior to entering school. However, accidents and disease may impair a student who previously did not have a disability. Medical diagnosis establishes the presence of the condition. The severity of the condition may be established in part by medical opinion and in part by systematic observation of the particular student. For many students with physical disabilities, the ability to learn is not affected. These students may not require special education classes, but they will need accommodations and modifications to the curriculum—and perhaps the school building—that can be managed through a 504 plan. For example, a student may require a personal care aide to help with positioning, braces, and catheterization; educational technology (for example, a voice-activated computer); and transportation to and from school that can accommodate a wheelchair. When such adaptations and accommodations are insufficient to allow adequate school progress, special education is indicated. The specially designed instruction can include alternate assignments, alternative curricula, alternative testing procedures, and special instruction.

Other Health Impairments

Other health impairment "means having limited strength, vitality, or alertness, including a heightened alertness to environmental stimuli, that results in limited alertness with respect to the educational environment that (i) is due to chronic or acute health problems such as asthma, attention deficit disorder or attention deficit hyperactivity disorder, diabetes, epilepsy, a heart condition, hemophilia, lead poisoning, leukemia, nephritis, rheumatic fever, sickle cell anemia, and Tourette syndrome; and (ii) adversely affects a child's educational performance." Diagnosis of health impairments is usually made by physicians, who identify the health problems, and school personnel, who identify the educational disability. For some students with other health impairments, the ability to learn is not affected. These students may not require special education classes, but they will need accommodations and modifications to the curriculum that can be managed through a 504 plan. For example, a student may require nursing services to administer medication, times and places to rest during the day, and provisions for instruction in the home. When health impairments adversely affect educational progress even with the curricular adaptations and modifications, special education is indicated.

Deaf–Blindness

Deaf–blindness means "concomitant hearing and visual impairments, the combination of which causes such severe communication and other developmental and educational needs that they cannot be accommodated in special education programs solely for children with deafness or children with blindness."

Only a small number of students are deaf–blind, and their assessment is typically complex. Tests that compensate for loss of vision usually rely on auditory processes; tests that compensate for loss of hearing usually rely on visual processes. Psychological and educational evaluations of students who are both deaf and blind rely on observations as well as interviews of and ratings by individuals sufficiently familiar with the student to provide useful information. For more information about vision screening, see the material on sensory screening on the student website.

Multiple Disabilities

Multiple disabilities "means concomitant impairments (such as mental retardation–blindness or mental retardation–orthopedic impairment), the combination of which causes such severe educational needs that they cannot be accommodated in special education programs solely for one of the impairments. The term does not include deaf–blindness."

Developmental Delay

Although not mandated by IDEA, states may use the category of developmental delay for children between the ages of 3 and 9 years who need special education and are "(1) experiencing developmental delays, as defined by the state and as measured by appropriate diagnostic instruments and procedures, in one or more of the following areas: physical development, cognitive development, communication development, social or emotional development, or adaptive development; and (2) . . . need special education and related services." Diagnosis of developmental delay is usually made by school personnel, who identify the educational disability, and other professionals (such as speech and language specialists, physicians, and psychologists), who identify the delays in the developmental domains.

2 Establishing Educational Need for Special Education

In addition to having one (or more) of the disabilities specified in IDEA, a student must experience a lack of academic success. This criterion is either implicit or explicit in the IDEA definitions of disabilities. Autism, hearing impairment, mental retardation, and six other disabling conditions are defined as "adversely affecting a child's educational performance." Multiple disabilities (such as deaf–blindness) cause "severe educational needs." Learning disability results in an "imperfect ability" to learn basic academic skills.

Most students without obvious sensory or motor disabilities are presumed to not have disabilities when they enter school. However, during their education, it becomes clear to school personnel that these students have significant problems. They fail to behave appropriately or to meet state-approved grade-level standards in one or more core achievement areas when provided with appropriate instruction. In short, they demonstrate marked discrepancies from mainstream expectations or from the achievement and behavior of typical peers. The magnitude of the discrepancy necessary to consider a student for special education is not codified, and there are many opinions on this issue. Whereas some say that a student should be performing at half the level of his or her peers, others believe that only a 20 percent discrepancy demonstrates educational need. Marston and Magnusson (1985) recommend that students receive special education services when they are 2 years behind their peers.

The presence of a discrepancy alone does not establish need, because there are many causes for a discrepancy. Thus, school personnel usually should engage in a number of remedial and compensatory activities designed to reduce or eliminate the discrepancy. As discussed in Chapter 20, interventions initially may be designed and implemented by the classroom teacher. When the teacher's interventions are unsuccessful, the student is referred to a teacher assistance team that designs and may help implement further interventions. Need for special educational services for students is established when one of two conditions is met. First, if a student fails to respond to validated and carefully implemented interventions, need for special education is indicated. We address the specifics of decision making at greater length in the response-to-intervention materials on the student website. Second, successful interventions may be too intensive or extensive for use in regular education. That is, the interventions needed to remediate the student's academic or behavioral deficits are so intrusive, labor-intensive, or specialized that a general education classroom teacher cannot implement them without the assistance of a special education teacher or without seriously detracting from the education of other students in the classroom.

Some students have such obvious sensory or motor problems that they are identified as having a disability before they enter school. From accumulated research and professional experience, educators know that students with certain disabilities (for example, blindness, deafness, and severe mental retardation) will not succeed in school without special education. Thus, educators (and relevant regulations) assume that the presence of a severe disability is sufficient to demonstrate the need for special educational services.

3 The Multidisciplinary Team

The determination that a student has a disability is made by a team of professionals called a multidisciplinary team (MDT). The team conducts a multidisciplinary evaluation (MDE) by collecting, assembling, and evaluating information to determine whether a student meets the conditions that define a handicap as set forth in IDEA and state law.[3]

Composition of the MDT

IDEA requires that the team have members with the same qualifications as those who must serve on IEP teams and "other qualified professionals, as appropriate" (34 CFR §300.533). Thus, the team must include the student's parents (and the student, if appropriate), a general education teacher, a special education teacher, a representative of the school administration, and an individual who can interpret the instructional implications of evaluation results. If the student is suspected of having a learning disability, the team must also include "at least one person qualified to conduct individual diagnostic examinations of children, such as a school psychologist, speech–language pathologist, or remedial reading teacher" (34 CFR §300.540). In practice, school psychologists are usually members of most MDTs.

Responsibilities of the MDT

The team is responsible for gathering information and determining if a student has a disability. In theory, the decision-making process is straightforward. The MDT assesses the student to determine whether he or she meets the criteria for a specific disability. Thus, the MDT must collect, at a minimum, information required by the definition of the disability being considered. Moreover, federal regulations (34 CFR §300.532) require that a student be "assessed in all areas related to the suspected disability, including, if appropriate, health, vision, hearing, social and

---

[3]Note that there are two types of teams required under special education law, and the same people may or may not serve on the two types of teams: evaluation teams (usually called MDTs) and individualized educational program (IEP) teams (always called IEP teams). In addition, many schools have teacher teams (often called child study teams) that deal with student difficulties before a student is referred for evaluation.

emotional status, general intelligence, academic performance, communicative status, and motor abilities."

In reaching its decision about eligibility, the team must do two things. First, it must draw upon information from a variety of sources, including aptitude and achievement tests, parent input, and teacher recommendations, as well as information about the child's physical condition, social or cultural background, and adaptive behavior. Second, it must ensure that information obtained from all of these sources is documented and carefully considered [§300.306(c)].

4 The Process of Determining Eligibility

IDEA has established rules that MDTs must follow in determining whether a student is eligible for special education and related services. The first set of rules provide a variety of procedural safeguards intended to provide students and their parents the right to full and meaningful participation in the evaluation process.

Procedural Safeguards

As specified in §300.504, school districts and other public agencies must give parents a copy of the procedural safeguards relating to

- independent educational evaluation;
- prior written notice in the native language of the parent or other mode of communication used by the parent;
- parental consent;
- access to educational records;
- opportunity to present complaints to initiate due process hearings;
- the child's placement during pendency of due process proceedings;
- procedures for students who are subject to placement in an interim alternative educational setting;
- requirements for unilateral placement by parents of children in private schools at public expense;
- mediation;
- due process hearings, including requirements for disclosure of evaluation results and recommendations;
- state-level appeals (if applicable in that state);
- civil actions;
- attorneys' fees; and
- the state complaint procedures.

Valid Assessments

The next set of rules require valid and meaningful assessments. School districts and other public agencies must ensure that students are assessed in all areas related to their suspected disabilities, including, if appropriate, health, vision, hearing, social and emotional status, general intelligence, academic performance, communicative status, and motor abilities. The evaluations must be sufficiently comprehensive to identify all of the child's special education and related services needs, whether or not they are commonly linked to the disability category in which the child has been classified.

School districts and other public agencies must ensure that the assessment includes a variety of techniques, including information provided by the parent, that provide relevant information about

- whether the student is a student with a disability; and
- the student's involvement and progress in the general curriculum.

The assessments must be conducted by trained and knowledgeable personnel in accordance with any instructions provided by the producer of the tests (and if an assessment is not conducted under standard conditions, a description of the extent to which it varied from standard conditions must be provided in the evaluation report). As specified in §300.304(c), only tests or other evaluation materials may be used that are

- "not racially or culturally discriminatory";
- "administered in the child's native language or other mode of communication" (In addition, for students with limited English proficiency, districts and other public agencies must select and use materials and procedures that measure the extent to which the child has a disability and needs special education, rather than measuring the child's English language skills.);
- "selected and administered so as best to ensure that if a test is administered to a child with impaired sensory, manual, or speaking skills, the test results accurately reflect the child's aptitude or achievement level or whatever other factors the test purports to measure, rather than reflecting the child's impaired sensory, manual, or speaking skills (unless those skills are the factors that the test purports to measure)";
- technically sound instruments that may assess the relative contribution of cognitive and behavioral factors, in addition to physical or developmental factors;
- "tailored to assess specific areas of educational need and not merely designed to provide a single general intelligence quotient"; and
- relevant in assisting persons determining the educational needs of the student.

Team Process

The final set of requirements sets forth the process for determining a student's eligibility for special education and related services. The MDT team follows four basic steps as specified in §§300.305/306:

1. The team reviews existing evaluation data to determine if additional data are needed.
2. The team gathers any additional data that are needed, ensuring that information obtained from all sources is documented.
3. The team determines if the student is a child with a disability by considering information from a variety of sources (that is, aptitude and achievement tests, parent input, teacher recommendations (including response to intervention), physical condition, social or cultural background, and adaptive behavior)

and comparing this information to the state and federal standards for the suspected disability.

4. The team prepares an evaluation report.

In practice, deciding whether a student is entitled to special education can be complex. Sometimes, the problems a student is experiencing can suggest a specific disability to team members. For example, having problems maintaining attention, being fidgety, and being disorganized may suggest the possibility of attention deficit disorder; persistent and major difficulties learning letter–sound correspondences despite many interventions may suggest a learning disability. MDTs should do more than simply confirm a disability. MDTs should adopt a point of view that is, in part, disconfirmatory—a point of view that seeks to disprove the working hypothesis.

Many behaviors are indicative of different disabilities. For example, stereotypies such as hand flapping are associated with autism, severe retardation, and some emotional disturbances. Assessors must be open to alternative explanations for the behavior and, when appropriate, collect information that will allow them to reject a working hypothesis of a particular disability. For example, if Tom was referred for inconsistent performance in expressive language, even though his other skills—especially math and science—were average, an MDT might suspect that he could have a learning disability. What would it take to reject the hypothesis that he has such a disability? He would not be considered to have a learning disability if it could be shown that his problem was caused by a sensorineural hearing loss, his problem arose because his primary language is a dialect of English, he suffered from recurrent bouts of otitis media (middle ear infections), and so forth. Therefore, the MDT would have to consider other possible causes of his behavior. Moreover, when there is evidence that something other than the hypothesized disability is the cause of the educational problems, the MDT would need to collect additional data that would allow it to evaluate these other explanations. Thus, MDT evaluations frequently (and correctly) go beyond the information required by the entitlement criteria to rule out other possible disabling conditions or to arrive at a different diagnosis.

Finally, in attempting to establish that a student should be classified with a disability, we often must choose among competing procedures and tests. However, as indicated in Chapter 14, individual tests of intelligence are not interchangeable. They differ significantly in the behaviors they sample and in the adequacy of their norms and reliability and slightly in their standard deviations. A dull, but normal, person may earn an IQ of less than 70 on one or two tests of intelligence but earn scores greater than 70 on two others. Thus, if we had to assess such a student, we could be caught in a dilemma of conflicting information.

The routes around and through the eligibility process are easier to state than to accomplish. First, we should choose (and put the most faith in) objective, technically adequate (reliable and well-normed) procedures that have demonstrated validity for the particular purpose of classification. Second, we must consider the specific validity. For example, we must consider the culture in which the student grew up and how that culture interacts with the content of the test. A test's technical manuals may contain information about the wisdom of using the test with individuals of various cultures, or the research literature may have information for the particular cultural group to which a student belongs. Often, theory can guide us in the absence of research. Sometimes it is just not possible to test validly, and we must also recognize that fact.

Scenario in Assessment

Cheryl

Cheryl was the youngest of the three children of Jack and Melinda Stenman. Cheryl was a full-term baby but weighed only 1800 grams (4 pounds) at birth. In addition to her significantly low birth weight, she was placed in the neonatal intensive care unit for almost 3 days and was not released from the hospital until she was 10 days old. Although her health during her early years was unremarkable, she was slower to attain the common developmental milestones (walking and talking) than her older siblings.

Cheryl entered a local daycare center at the age of 3 years. Little information is available from the center except the general perception that Cheryl did not engage in developmentally appropriate play activities. The daycare center provided no interventions because its philosophy was that each child developed uniquely and there was plenty of time for intervention.

Mrs. Stenman enrolled Cheryl in the local school district's half-day kindergarten the September when she was 5 years and 8 months of age. Cheryl was slow compared to her peers. She still had toileting accidents, had immature speech and language, and did not engage in cooperative play, preferring parallel play instead. At the end of the first semester of kindergarten, she had not learned her colors, whereas her peers had mastered the primary and additive colors (that is, red, green, blue, yellow, violet, blue-green, brown, black, and white); she recognized only five capital letters (that is, A, B C, D, and S), whereas most of her peers recognized and could write all upper- and lowercase letters. Her teacher characterized her as following other children around but not joining in the various activities. In January, Cheryl's teacher sought the help of the school's student assistance team. The team met with Mr. and Mrs. Stenman and agreed that some interventions would be appropriate to try to accelerate her academic progress. They agreed that Cheryl should attend all-day kindergarten and developed a program in which the teachers or the reading

specialist provided individual direct instruction in the recognition and writing of all letters of the alphabet; they also developed a behavior plan that reinforced Cheryl for successive approximations of cooperative play. From the very beginning, the classroom interventions did not work. Cheryl would seem to have learned one or two new letters but forget them the next day. The team met with the teacher several times and modified the instructional program, but Cheryl's progress was slow. She could not seem to master more than two letters per week, and that rate of progress was simply not enough to get her ready for first grade. The results of the behavioral interventions were similarly unsuccessful. At the end of the year, all kindergartners received a district screening test. Cheryl scored at or below the first percentile in all academic areas.

The teacher and the student assistance team (which included the parents) weighed various options for Cheryl's next year: retention, promotion with help from the student assistance team, and referral for an MDE to determine if Cheryl had a disability that required special education and related services. After some discussion, the team was unanimous in its recommendation that Cheryl should be evaluated for eligibility for special education.

An MDT was appointed and consisted of Cheryl's kindergarten teacher, a special education teacher who worked with children of Cheryl's age, the school principal (who chaired the meetings), and the school psychologist assigned to Cheryl's school. At the first team meeting, the principal gave the parents a copy of the procedural safeguards guaranteed by IDEA and the state. The principal also explained each element carefully and answered all of the parents' questions to their satisfaction. Next, the team reviewed all relevant documents: attendance records, data from the interventions developed by the student assistance team, the results of the district's routine hearing and vision

continued on the next page

Scenario in Assessment, (*continued*)

screening (which indicated Cheryl was normal), and the results from the district's first-grade readiness assessment. After reviewing the data and discussing Cheryl's strengths and weaknesses, the MDT decided that additional data would be necessary to determine if Cheryl was eligible for special education and related services. The team discussed the possibility of special language or cultural considerations and concluded there were none. The team then decided that it needed (1) the results of a valid, individually administered test of intelligence; (2) the results of a valid, individually administered test of achievement; (3) ratings from a validly administered scale of social and emotional development; and (4) the ratings from a valid evaluation of adaptive behavior. The principal would be responsible for distributing and collecting the results from the social–emotional rating scale; the school psychologist would be responsible for administering and scoring the test of intelligence and the adaptive behavior scale and also for scoring and interpreting the social–emotional ratings provided by the teachers.

The testing went smoothly. Teachers completed the Behavior Assessment System for Children, Second Edition; the parents completed the Vineland Adaptive Behavior Scales, Second Edition; and the school psychologist administered the Wechsler Intelligence Scale for Children–Fourth Edition and the Stanford–Binet Intelligence Scale, Fifth Edition. The school psychologist drafted an evaluation report and distributed copies to each team member. The MDT then met to consider the results of their evaluation and to decide if additional data might be needed to make sure that their evaluation examined all areas of potential disability. If the evaluation results were complete and sufficient, the team would decide if Cheryl was a student with a disability under IDEA and state law. The school psychologist affirmed that all of the instruments were administered under standard conditions and that she believed the results to be valid. She next interpreted the evaluation results and answered all of the questions posed by the parents and educators. The results indicated that Cheryl's level of general intellectual functioning was 59 ± 4 points. Her achievement in Reading, Mathematics, and Written Language was at the second percentile. Her parent's ratings of adaptive behavior resulted in a composite (total) score of 64, with Daily Living her area of highest functioning and Communication her lowest area. Although the evaluation results suggested that Cheryl was a student with mental retardation, the parents believed that Cheryl was too young to be diagnosed with such a stigmatizing diagnosis. After some discussion, the team unanimously agreed that a diagnosis of developmental delay would be appropriate at that time. Cheryl met the criteria for that disability, and she would not be 9 years of age for almost 3 years.

The MDT next turned to the question of need for special education. The team relied heavily on Cheryl's lack of progress when she was given the maximum amount of intervention services within the regular education curriculum. Clearly, she needed more services. The MDT added recommendations for special education and related services to the evaluation report. The team noted that Cheryl needed direct instruction in the core academic areas of reading, writing, and mathematics. The team recommended that Cheryl's social interactions be monitored for possible intervention later in the first semester. The MDT also recommended that Cheryl be evaluated by a speech and language therapist to determine if the teacher should have ongoing consultations with the therapist about curriculum or methods and/or if Cheryl would benefit from direct speech and language services. The team also recommended that Cheryl should be included in all nonacademic activities with her same-age peers. Finally, it recommended that Cheryl receive her special education services from an itinerant special education teacher in the general education classroom who would also consult with the regular education teacher, who would also be implementing portions of Cheryl's educational program.

5 Problems in Determining Special Education Eligibility

Four problems with the criteria used to determine eligibility for special services are especially noteworthy. First, we find the prevalent (but mistaken) belief that special educational services are for students who could benefit from them. Thus, in many circles, educational need is believed to be sufficient for entitlement. Clearly, this belief is contradicted by pertinent law, regulations, and litigation. Students must need the services *and* meet the criteria for a specific disability. Nonetheless, some educators have such strong humanitarian beliefs that when they see students with problems, they want to get those students the services that they believe are needed. Too often, the regulations may be bent so that students fit entitlement criteria.

Second, the definitions that appear in state and federal regulations are frequently very imprecise. The imprecision of federal regulations creates variability in standards among states, and the imprecision of state regulations creates variability in standards among districts within states. Thus, students who are eligible in one state or district may not be eligible in other states or districts. For example, some states and school districts may define a learning disability as a severe discrepancy between measured intellectual ability and actual school achievement. However, there is no consensus about the meaning of "severe discrepancy"; certainly, there is no widely accepted mathematical formula to ascertain severe discrepancy. To some extent, discrepancies between achievement and intelligence are determined by the specific tests used. Thus, one test battery might produce a significant discrepancy, whereas another battery would not produce such a discrepancy for the same student. Other states and school districts may define a learning disability by an inadequate response to intervention. Yet, what constitutes an inadequate response is ambiguous.

Third, the definitions treat disabilities as though they were discrete categories. However, most diagnosticians are hard-pressed to distinguish between primary and secondary mental retardation or between primary and secondary emotional disturbance. Also, for example, distinctions between individuals with autism and individuals with severe mental retardation and autistic-like behaviors are practically impossible to make with any certainty.

Fourth, parents may often prefer the label associated with one disability (for example, autism or learning disability) over the label associated with another (for example, mental retardation). Because of the procedural safeguards afforded students with special needs and their parents, school districts may become embroiled in lengthy and unnecessarily adversarial hearings in which each side has an expert testifying that a particular label is correct even though those labels are contradictory and sometimes mutually exclusive. School personnel find themselves in a no-win situation because the definitions and their operationalizations are so imprecise. As a result, school districts frequently give parents the label they want rather than what educators, in their best professional judgments, believe to be correct. Districts may be reluctant to risk litigation because parents can frequently find an expert to contradict the district staff members. In some states, special educational services are noncategorical. In these states, a label qualifies a student for special education but does not determine the nature of the special education; that is determined by the individual student's needs, not label.

CHAPTER COMPREHENSION QUESTIONS

Write your answers to each of the following questions, and then compare your responses to the text or the study guide.

1. List and define each disability recognized by IDEA.

2. How is the need for special education established?

3. What are the responsibilities of the MDT?

4. What procedural safeguards are guaranteed by IDEA?

5. What constitutes a valid assessment under IDEA?

22 Making Accountability Decisions

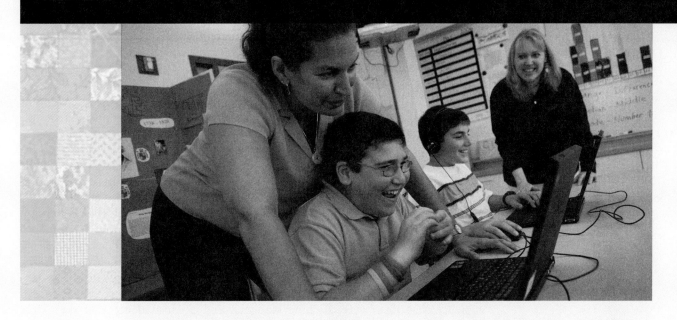

Chapter Goals

1 Understand the legal requirements for state and school district assessment and accountability systems specified in the No Child Left Behind Act and the Individuals with Disabilities Education Improvement Act.

2 Know the important terms associated with assessment for the purpose of making accountability decisions.

3 Distinguish between grade-level achievement standards, modified achievement standards, and alternate achievement standards.

4 Be able to distinguish between alternate assessment based on grade-level achievement standards, alternate assessment based on modified achievement standards, and alternate assessment based on alternate achievement standards.

5 Know the steps in developing a standards-based accountability system.

6 Know the important considerations in assessment for purposes of making accountability decisions.

Key Terms

accountability

adequate yearly progress

modified achievement
   standards

content standards

performance standards

alternate achievement
   standards

assessment alignment

alternate assessment

benchmarks

cut scores

out-of-level testing

ARE OUR SCHOOLS PRODUCING THE RESULTS WE WANT? TO WHAT EXTENT ARE individual students meeting the goals, standards, or outcomes that their schools have set for them? What goals or standards should we expect students and schools to meet? How should we assess progress toward meeting standards? During the past 15 years, there has been an increased focus on the results of education for all students, including students with disabilities. In this chapter, we examine the collection and use of assessment information for the purpose of making accountability decisions.

A powerful idea dominates policy discussions about schools: the notion that "students should be held to high, common standards for academic performance and that schools and the people who work in them should be held accountable for ensuring that students—all students—are able to meet those standards" (Elmore, 2002, p. 3). It has not always been that way. Until the early to mid-1990s, school personnel focused on the *process* of providing services to students. They provided evidence that they were teaching students, and often evidence that they were teaching specific types of students (for example, Title 1, mentally retarded, deaf, or disadvantaged students). When administrators were asked about special education students or services, typically they described the numbers and kinds of students who were tested or taught, the settings in which they were taught, or the numbers of special education teachers who tested and taught them (for example, "We have 2,321 students with disabilities in our district; 1,620 are educated in general education classes with special education supports, and the remainder are in resource rooms, self-contained classes and out-of-school settings; the students are served by 118 special education teachers and 19 related services personnel"). Few administrators could provide evidence for the results or outcomes of the services being provided. Since the early 1990s, there has been a dramatic shift in focus from serving students with disabilities to measuring the results of the services provided. This shift has paralleled the total quality management (TQM; Deming, 1994, 2000), results-based management, and management by objectives (Olson, 1964) movements in business and, more recently, in federal and state government.

Much of the impetus for this shift to a focus on results was the publication of *A Nation at Risk: The Imperative for Educational Reform* (National Commission of Excellence in Education, 1983). In this document, the then-secretary of education revealed the low status of U.S. schoolchildren relative to their counterparts in other nations and reported that "the educational foundations of our society are presently being eroded by a rising tide of mediocrity that threatens our very future as a nation and a people" (p. 5). In this report, the secretary argued that the nation was at risk because mediocrity, not excellence, was the norm in education. Recommendations included more time for learning; better textbooks and other materials; more homework; higher expectations; stricter attendance policies; and improved standards, salaries, rewards, and incentives for teachers. The entire nation began to focus on raising educational standards, measuring performance, and achieving results. Policymakers and bureaucrats, who had been spending a great deal of money to fund special education, began demanding evidence of its effectiveness. In essence, they employed the old saw, "The proof of the pudding is in the eating"—arguing that it matters little what you do if it does not produce what you want.

In 1994, the Clinton administration specified a set of national education goals. Called "Goals 2000," these were a list of goals that students should achieve by the year 2000. The 1994 reauthorization of the Elementary and Secondary Education Act, known as the Improving American Schools Act, included a requirement that in Title I schools, disadvantaged students should be expected to attain the same challenging standards as all other students. The 1997 reauthorization of the Individuals with Disabilities Education Act (IDEA) included provisions specifying that students with disabilities should participate in states' assessment and accountability systems; that states needed to specify standards to be attained by *all* students; and that states would report each year on the extent to which *all* students, including students with disabilities, met state-specified standards. In 2004, Congress again amended IDEA and reaffirmed those requirements. The No Child Left Behind Act of 2001 (NCLB; a portion of the Improving America's Schools Act) included requirements that states report annually on the performance and progress of *all* students. All states now have accountability systems and are required by law to report on the participation and performance of students with disabilities on their state assessments. Within state or district systems, there may be two kinds of accountability. One kind assigns responsibility to the student (student accountability) and the other assigns responsibility to the educational system or individuals within that system (system accountability). System accountability is designed to improve educational programs, whereas student accountability is designed to motivate students to do their best. System accountability is the focus of federal education reform efforts. All states have some type of system accountability, but not all states have student accountability. *Accountability systems* hold schools responsible for helping all students reach high challenging standards, and they provide rewards to schools that reach those standards and sanctions to schools that do not. States or school districts specify goals they aim to achieve and then apply certain positive or negative consequences meant to promote reform to schools that meet certain performance criteria in specific areas (Marion & Gong, 2003).

Today, the consequences of accountability systems are becoming more significant, often referred to as "high stakes." States are relying on evidence from state and district assessments to determine high stakes. The most common high-stakes use of assessment evidence for individual students is to determine whether a student receives a standard high school diploma or some other type of document. Another type of student accountability, appearing with increasing frequency, is the use of test scores to determine whether a student will move from one grade to another. All states are required to have an accountability system with sanctions and rewards. Imposing sanctions to schools or administrators is slightly more prevalent than providing rewards. Among the sanctions that states commonly use are assigning negative labels to schools, removing staff, and firing principals. Rewards include assigning positive labels to schools and giving extra funding to schools or cash awards to staff.

Scenario in Assessment

Steven

Steven is a third-grade student diagnosed with autism. Steven receives instruction in the general education setting for most of his day, although he needs a teacher assistant to assist with implementation of his comprehensive behavior plan. This plan involves providing him with a variety of cues and reminders about the daily classroom schedule and how he is expected to behave during various activities. He has a very difficult time behaving appropriately when there are changes in the classroom schedule; in such cases, he often becomes very anxious, sometimes throws tantrums, and rarely completes his work.

This is the first year that Steven is expected to complete the statewide assessment used for accountability purposes, and his individualized education program team must determine how he can best participate. At first, Steven's parents are very concerned that he will have an anxious reaction to testing, and they do not want him to participate. His general education teacher is also fearful that he will not be able to focus and complete the test.

Steven's school district has been warned by the state that it needs to increase its rates of participation of students with disabilities in the statewide assessment; in the past, many students with disabilities were excluded from statewide testing. Steven's school is under considerable pressure to show that it is including all students, particularly those with disabilities, in the accountability program. At the meeting, the administrator, special educator, and school psychologist explain how important it is for Steven to participate, in order for the education that he and students like him receive to be of concern to

those who help in determining how resources will be allocated throughout the district. They also point out how he is working toward all the same grade-level achievement standards as other students, and that his participation may help them determine what he can and cannot do. They explain the variety of ways in which Steven can be accommodated during testing. For instance, they can continue to have the teacher assistant implement his behavior management plan. They can role play in the days prior to the test what the test will be like. Also, they can develop a picture schedule that is similar to the one he uses in the classroom to go along with the testing schedule.

After presenting the underlying rationale for having Steven participate, as well as the ways in which he could be accommodated during testing, the team agrees that it is appropriate to have Steven attempt the statewide assessment toward grade-level achievement standards. His teacher assistant is provided specific training on how she can and cannot assist Steven during testing in order to ensure that his results are as accurate as possible.

The day of the test was considerably draining for Steven and his teacher assistant, but Steven managed to complete the test. Although his total score fell below the proficiency standard, and his teachers questioned whether it is an optimal measure of his skills and knowledge, his teachers and parents were impressed with the fact that he did not score in the lowest proficiency category. In fact, Steven was able to correctly answer many of the items on the test; he was able to demonstrate some of what he knew when provided appropriate accommodations during testing.

1 Legal Requirements

The 1997 reauthorization of IDEA challenged all states to develop accountability systems that were sensitive to the educational progress of all students. The law was based on the beliefs that all children can learn, all students are to be held to the same high standards, and schools should be held accountable to ensure that all students are achieving to the same high standards. IDEA 1997 introduced the requirement for alternate assessments. The law led to a push for specification of standards, development of assessments to measure student progress toward standards, and annual reporting on how schools and students are doing. It required alternate assessments for all students unable to participate in statewide assessments even with accommodations. The 2004 reauthorization of IDEA contains those same requirements.

NCLB included the requirement that states have assessment and accountability systems, report annually on the performance and progress of all students, and have alternate assessments in place for reporting on the annual yearly progress of all students in reading, math, and science. In 2003, the U.S. Department of Education issued a set of guidelines for alternate assessments that included the concept of alternate achievement standards. States, school districts, and individual schools are required by law to measure the performance and progress of all students, and school personnel need to know much about how assessment information is used by State Education Agency personnel to make accountability decisions. The law requires that school systems consider not only how their students are doing as a whole but also how particular groups of students are doing. To be considered successful, schools must succeed with all students.

2 Important Terminology

The standards-based assessment and accountability movement and the federal laws that accompany it have brought a new assessment vocabulary that includes terms such as "alternate achievement standards," "modified achievement standards," "adequate yearly progress," and "schools in need of improvement." Some of these terms are used in many different ways in the professional and popular literature. In fact, the multiple uses of the terms cause confusion. The Council of Chief State School Officers publishes a *Glossary of Assessment Terms and Acronyms Used in Assessing Special Education*, which is a good source of definitions for terms used in assessment and accountability systems. We include an adapted version of this glossary in Table 22.1.

3 It's All About Meeting Standards

Assessments completed for accountability purposes involve measuring the extent to which students are learning what we want them to learn, or the extent to which school systems are accomplishing what we want them to accomplish. To do this, state education agency personnel must specify the standards that schools and students will work toward. They typically do so by specifying a set of *academic content standards*, which are statements of the subject-specific knowledge and skills that schools are expected to teach students, indicating what students should know and be able to do. States are required by law to specify academic content standards in reading, math, and science. Many states specify academic content standards in other areas. States must also specify *academic achievement standards* (sometimes called *performance standards*), which are statements of the levels at which or the

TABLE 22.1	Glossary of Assessment Terms Used Within Accountability Systems

Academic standards. There are two types of standards: content and performance.

- ■ *Academic content standards.* Statements of the subject-specific knowledge and skills that schools are expected to teach students, indicating what students should know and be able to do in reading/language arts, math, and science. Many states have content standards in other academic areas as well. These standards must be the same for all schools and all students within a state.
- ■ *Academic achievement (performance) standards.* Specifications of how well students need to know the academic content standards. They must have the following components:
   1. Specific levels of achievement: States are required to have at least three levels of achievement—basic, proficient, and advanced. Many states have more than three levels and may use different names for the levels.
   2. Descriptions of what students at each particular level must demonstrate relative to the task.
   3. Examples of student work at each level illustrating the range of performance within each level.
   4. Cut scores clearly separating each performance level.

Accommodations. Changes in the administration of an assessment, such as setting, scheduling, timing, presentation format, response mode, or others, including any combination of these that does not change the construct intended to be measured by the assessment or the meaning of the resulting scores. Accommodations are used for equity, not advantage, and serve to level the playing field. To be appropriate, assessment accommodations must be identified in the student's individualized education plan (IEP), limited education proficiency document, or Section 504 plan and used regularly during instruction and classroom assessment.

Accountability. The use of assessment results and other data to ensure that schools are moving in desired directions. Common elements include standards, indicators of progress toward meeting those standards, analysis of data, reporting procedures, and rewards or sanctions.

Accountability system. A plan that uses assessment results and other data outlining the goals and expectations for students, teachers, schools, districts, and states to demonstrate the established components or requirements of accountability. An accountability system typically includes rewards for those who exceed the goals and sanctions for those who fail to meet the goals.

Achievement data by subgroup. Performance results for schools broken out by important student groups, such as students from major racial/ethnic groups, economically disadvantaged, limited English proficiency, and those with disabilities.

Adaptations. A generalized term that describes a change made in the presentation, setting, response, or timing or scheduling of an assessment that may or may not change the construct of the assessment.

Adequate yearly progress (AYP). The annual improvement that school districts and schools must make each year in order to reach the NCLB goal of having every student proficient by the year 2014. In order to meet AYP requirements, schools must test at least 95 percent of their students in each of the subgroups, and high poverty schools must demonstrate sufficient progress for students in each of eight subgroups (for example, students with disabilities, students with limited English proficiency, and students who are members of specific racial/ethnic groups). Nontest indicators, such as attendance or high school graduation rate, are also used as indicators of AYP.

Alignment. The similarity or match between or among content standards, performance standards, curriculum, instruction, and assessments in terms of knowledge and skill expectations.

Alternate achievement standards. Expectations for performance that differ in complexity from a grade-level achievement standard but are linked to the content standards.

Alternate assessment based on alternate achievement standards (AA-AAS). An alternate assessment for which the expectation of performance differs in complexity from grade-level achievement standards and that is designed for use with students whose significant cognitive disabilities preclude their participation in the regular grade-level assessment.

Alternate assessment based on grade-level academic achievement standards (AA-GLAS). An instrument in a different format than the regular test, but it defines for students with disabilities a level of "proficient" performance as equivalent to grade-level achievement and same difficulty as on the state's regular grade-level assessment.

TABLE 22.1	Glossary of Assessment Terms Used Within Accountability Systems, *continued*

Alternate assessment based on modified academic achievement standards (AA-MAS). An instrument whose content is aligned to grade-level content standards for the grade in which a student is enrolled, that is challenging for eligible students, but that may be less difficult than the regular test.

Benchmark. A specific statement of knowledge and skills within a content area's continuum that a student must possess to demonstrate a level of progress toward mastery of a standard.

Body of evidence. Information or data that establish that a student can perform a particular skill or has mastered a specific content standard and that was either produced by the student or collected by someone who is knowledgeable about the student.

Cut score. A specified point on a score scale. Scores at or above that point are interpreted differently from scores below that point.

Disaggregation. The collection and reporting of student achievement results by particular subgroups (e.g., students with disabilities and limited English-proficient students) to ascertain a subgroup's academic progress. Disaggregation makes it possible to compare subgroups or cohorts.

Modified academic achievement standards. Expectations for performance that are lower than the grade-level achievement standards but that must be aligned with the content standards. States can modify their academic achievement standards in a number of ways, and they can design a totally different assessment or adapt the regular assessment by reducing the total number of test questions, simplifying the language of test questions, using pictures to aid understanding, and so on.

Norm-referenced test. A standardized test designed, validated, and implemented to rank a students' performance by comparing that performance to the performance of that student's peers.

Opportunity to learn. The provision of learning conditions, including suitable adjustments, to maximize a student's chances of attaining the desired learning outcomes, such as the mastery of content standards.

Out-of-level testing (off-grade or off-level). Administration of a test at a level above or below a student's present grade level to enable the student to be assessed at the level of instruction rather than the level of enrollment. According to federal education law, this practice is not allowed for accountability purposes.

Standards-referenced test (sometimes called a criterion-referenced test). A standardized test designed, validated, and implemented to rank a students' performance by comparing that performance to the specific standards for the state in which the student resides. Students are said to have met or not met the state standards.

Student accountability. Consequences exist for individual students and are based on their individual assessment performance. For example, students might not be promoted to the next grade or graduate if their assessment results do not meet a prespecified level.

System accountability. Consequences exist for school systems and are based on the assessment performance of a group of individuals (for example, the school building, district, or state education agency). For example, a school might receive a financial award or special recognition for having a large percentage of students meeting a particular assessment performance level.

SOURCE: Adapted from "Policy to Practice Study Group: Assessing Special Education Students," from Cortelia, C. (2007). *Learning opportunities for your child through alternate assessments: Alternate assessments based on modified academic achievement standards.* Minneapolis, MN: University of Minnesota, National Center on Educational Outcomes. Reprinted by permission.

proficiency with which students will show that they have mastered the academic content standards. Academic achievement standards use language drawn directly from the NCLB law, and they have the force of law. States are required to define at least three levels of proficiency (usually called basic, proficient, and advanced). Some states specify more than three levels of proficiency (for example, they may choose to indicate that a student's level of performance is below basic). The law requires that all students be assessed related to the state content and achievement standards. The state must provide for students with disabilities reasonable adaptations and accommodations necessary to measure their academic achievement relative to state academic content and state student academic achievement standards.

Two other kinds of standards apply specifically to students with disabilities: alternate achievement standards and modified achievement standards. *Alternate achievement standards* are expectations for performance that differ in complexity from grade-level achievement standards, but they are linked to those general education standards. States are permitted to define alternate achievement standards to evaluate the achievement of students with the most significant cognitive disabilities. *Modified achievement standards* are intended to provide reliable and valid information about the academic achievement and progress of a unique group of students. These students are pursuing grade-level academic content standards and attend general education classes with their peers, but they have "persistent academic disabilities"—that is, their performance may be hampered by significant learning disabilities and other cognitive limitations. These students' IEP teams are reasonably certain they are not likely to achieve grade-level proficiency within the school year covered by the IEP. Although the meaning of the term "modified achievement standards" is still being debated, and although the concept may well change by the time this book appears in print, modified standards are specified for students who have not responded to appropriate instruction and for whom an IEP team believes will not learn grade-level academic content with the same depth and breadth as other students and whose learning is likely to progress more slowly. These are students whose cognitive academic functioning and instructional programs make them ineligible for the alternate assessments based on alternate achievement standards that are intended for students with significant cognitive disabilities, and for whom general education grade-level assessments are considered inappropriate, even with test accommodations. The National Center on Educational Outcomes (NCEO) has produced some very helpful documents on alternate assessments based on modified achievement standards, including the following:

▧ *States' Alternate Assessments Based on Modified Achievement Standards* (AA-MAS) (Synthesis Report 67)

▧ *Identifying Students with Disabilities Who Are Eligible to Take an Alternate Assessment Based on Modified Academic Achievement Standards*

▧ *A Technical Design and Documentation Workbook for Assessments Based on Modified Achievement Standards*

All three documents are available at the NCEO website (www.cehd.umn. edu/nceo/).

Standards-based assessment is characterized by specifying what all students can be expected to learn and then expecting that time will vary but that all will achieve the standards. States are required to have in place assessments of student proficiency relative to academic content standards. The following are reasons why school personnel would want to assess student performance and progress relative to standards in addition to the state tests:

▧ To ascertain the extent to which individual students are meeting state standards—that is, accomplishing what it is that society wants them to accomplish

- To identify student strengths and weaknesses for instructional planning
- To allocate supports and resources
- To ascertain the extent to which specific schools within states are providing the kinds of educational opportunities and experiences that enable their students to achieve state-specified standards
- To provide data on student or school performance that can be helpful in making instructional policy decisions (curricula or instructional methodologies to use)
- To decide who should receive a diploma as indicated by performance on tests that measure whether standards are met
- To inform the public on the performance of schools or school districts
- To know the extent to which specific subgroups of students are meeting specified standards

Alternate Assessment

Regardless of where students receive instruction, all students with disabilities should have access to, participate in, and make progress in the general curriculum. Thus, all students with disabilities must be included in state assessment systems and in state reporting of AYP toward meeting the state's standards. We have noted that states must specify academic content standards and academic achievement standards, and they must have assessments aligned to those standards. To address the needs of students with substantial concerns, states may choose to develop alternate achievement standards and modified achievement standards that are based on the expectations for all students.

States must include all students in their assessment and accountability systems. However, not all students can participate in the general state assessments, even with assessment accommodations designed to compensate for their specific needs. IDEA 1997 included a provision that by the year 2000 states would have in place alternate assessments intended for use with those students who evidenced severe cognitive impairments. In August 2002, the U.S. Secretary of Education proposed a regulation to allow states to develop and use alternate achievement standards for students with the most significant cognitive disabilities for the purpose of determining the AYP of states, local education agencies, and schools. In August 2003, the secretary specified that the number of students considered proficient using alternate assessments toward alternate achievement standards could not exceed 1 percent of all students, and on April 7, 2005, the Secretary of Education issued a rule that states could have an alternate assessment for an additional group of students who evidence persistent academic difficulties and thus are working toward "modified achievement standards." Although there is no limit on the number of students to whom an AA-MAS can be given, states cannot count as proficient more than 2 percent of students based on the AA-MAS. The term "modified achievement standards" was not defined. States thus may count as proficient up to 1 percent of students in the alternate assessment intended for students with significant cognitive disabilities who are working toward alternate achievement standards and 2 percent of students in an alternate assessment intended for students with "persistent academic difficulties" who are working toward modified achievement standards.

An *alternate assessment* is defined in the NCLB federal regulations as "an assessment designed for the small number of students with disabilities who are unable to participate in the regular state assessment, even with appropriate accommodations." It is further indicated that "an alternate assessment may include materials collected under several circumstances, including (1) teacher observation of the student, (2) samples of student work produced during regular classroom instruction that demonstrate mastery of specific instructional strategies . . . , or (3) standardized performance tasks produced in an 'on demand' setting, such as completion of an assigned task on test day" (p. 7). The assessments must yield results separately in both reading/language arts and mathematics, and they must be designed and implemented in a manner that supports use of the results as an indicator of AYP.

Alternate assessments are not simply compilations of student work, sometimes referred to as box or folder stuffing. Rather, they must have a clearly defined structure, specific participation guidelines, and clearly defined scoring criteria and procedures; must meet requirements for technical adequacy; and must have a reporting format that clearly communicates student performance in terms of the academic achievement standards specified by the state. They must meet the same standards for technical adequacy as does the general assessment. It has been a struggle for some states to satisfy this NCLB requirement. Alternate assessments may be needed for students with a broad array of disabling conditions, so a state may use more than one alternate assessment.

Alternate assessments can be designed to measure student performance toward grade-level standards, alternate achievement standards, or modified achievement standards. Recall that an alternate achievement standard is an expectation of performance that differs in complexity from a grade-level standard. For example, the Massachusetts Curriculum Frameworks include the following content standard: "Students will identify, analyze, and apply knowledge of the purpose, structure, and elements of nonfiction or informational materials and provide evidence from the text to support their understanding." A less complex demonstration of this standard is "to gain information from signs, symbols, and pictures in the environment"; a more complex demonstration is to "gain information from captions, titles, and table of contents in an informational text" (Massachusetts Department of Education, 2001). As previously mentioned, modified achievement standards are a very new concept, and many are only in the very beginning stages of considering what these standards might look like (Figure 22.1).

4 Developing Standards-Based Accountability Systems

Nationally, there is no consensus on educational standards. States have been developing standards-based accountability systems, and these are revised and rewritten regularly. There is also much debate about whether alternate assessments must be aligned to the general education standards or simply linked to those standards. The National Center on Educational Outcomes developed a self-study guide for states and school districts to use in the development of accountability systems (Ysseldyke & Thurlow, 1993). In this section, we rely on the content of the self-study guide and describe the process that a school or school district would go

Regualar grade-level assessment measures student progress on the same state grade-level content standards as all students, *with or without* appropriate accommodations

or

Alternate assessment based on grade-level academic achievement standards (AA-GLAS) is usually in a different format than the regular test, but it defines a level of "proficient performance equivalent to grade-level achievement and same difficulty as on the state's regular grade-level assessment.

Alternate assessment based on modified achievement standards (AA-MAS) is aligned to grade-level content standards for the grade in which a student is enrolled and challenging for eligible student, but may be less difficult than the grade-level achievement standard.

Alternate assessment based on alternate achievement standards (AA-AAS) represents an expectation of performance that differs in complexity from a grade-level achievement standard usually based on a very limited sample of content that is linked to but does not fully represent grade-level content.

FIGURE 22.1 Most/Some/Few Assessment

through in developing a system to assess the extent to which it is achieving desired results. We describe ways to accomplish the following:

- Establish a solid foundation for educators' assessment efforts
- Develop, adopt, or adapt a conceptual model of outcomes and indicators
- Establish a data collection and reporting system
- Install a standards-based accountability system

Establish a Solid Foundation for Assessment Efforts

Accountability systems must be carefully thought out and comply with current federal legislation. It is important that stakeholders be involved up front and throughout the entire process, with their involvement carefully documented and reported, and that they give considerable thought to why they want to measure and report results. Considerable confusion exists in this field, so it is very important to define terms and consider the assumptions that underlie efforts to account for educational results. Finally, it is critical to resolve some fundamental issues before beginning.

Involve Stakeholders Up Front

Stakeholders are those individuals in a community who have a personal interest in the measurement of educational results: teachers, supervisors, providers of related services, parents, representatives of community agencies, and students. Involving stakeholders up front in the process of developing standards and desired results enhances their feeling of investment in the assessment process and their desire to participate in it. Involvement up front empowers those individuals or groups to chart their own activities and futures.

Decide Why We Measure and Account for Results

There are four major reasons why stakeholders want to measure educational results: instructional improvement, public accountability, public information, and policy formulation. First, data on the results of service provision can be useful in improving instructional programs for students. In fact, to improve instructional practices, it is imperative that school personnel have data illustrating the extent to which what they are doing is achieving the desired results. For example, school personnel might want to know the extent to which the math curriculum they are using is resulting in students earning high scores on math tests. Knowledge of results enables professionals to consider making changes in instructional programs. For instructional improvement, it is important that stakeholders reach agreement on assessment goals.

Second, data on results are important for accountability—to document for people in authority that desired goals are being met. Tests are regularly given to students, and data indicating how pupils are doing are provided to state agencies and school districts within states. The test scores can be used by legislators and policymakers to decide whether they are getting their money's worth from funds invested in education.

Third, data on educational results are useful in providing public information on the outcomes of schooling. You may have seen reports in newspapers indicating how the nation's youth is doing in math, reading, science, or other forms of literacy.

Fourth, data on results are useful in policy formulation. Those who formulate educational policy repeatedly indicate the need to have information about outcomes of schooling in order to allocate resources and establish instructional processes.

Consider the Assumptions That Underlie an Accountability System

Any accountability system is based on a number of assumptions. Those who want to assess educational results will have to consider carefully the assumptions that underlie the system they develop. There is general agreement on the following:

- Accountability systems are needed for all students and, at the broadest level, should apply to all students, regardless of the characteristics of individuals.
- Accountability systems should primarily focus on intended outcomes but be sensitive to unintended outcomes of schooling.
- Indicators of results for students receiving special education services should be related, conceptually and statistically, to those identified for students without disabilities.
- Indicators should reflect the diversity of gender, culture, race, and other characteristics of the students in today's school population.
- An accountability system should provide the data needed to make policy decisions at the national, state, and local levels.
- An accountability system should be flexible, dynamic, and responsive to review and criticism. It should also change to meet identified needs and future developments in the measurement of educational inputs, contexts, processes, and results.

Decide What Data Will Be Collected and What Rewards and Sanctions Will Be Used

Specify Content Domains for Data Collection

School personnel typically restrict data collection to academic content domains. In some instances, states specify both academic and functional literacy domains.

Specify Rewards and Sanctions

Educational professionals must decide the kinds of rewards that will be provided for students, teachers, schools, and districts who provide evidence of making annual yearly progress for all students. Also, they must specify the kinds of sanctions that will be given to those who fail to show progress.

Establish a Data Collection and Reporting System

Stakeholders should give considerable thought to sources of information or data that can be used to illustrate educational results. Decisions need to be made about where data will come from, how they will be collected, and how results will be reported to and used by the general community.

Identify Data Sources

Those who engage in standards-based accountability will necessarily have to identify sources from which they can get data or the extent to which results are being achieved. A fundamental premise to guide the data collection process is that it should rely as much as possible on the use of existing information.

Define the Population of Students for Whom Alternate Assessments Will Be Used

States must have general assessments and may have three kinds of alternate assessments: those aligned to grade-level standards, those aligned to modified achievement standards, and those aligned to alternate achievement standards. Particularly among those states that choose to have multiple alternate assessments, it is necessary to specify the kinds of students for whom each of the kinds of alternate assessments will be used. It is expected that students assessed relative to modified achievement standards are the approximately 2 percent of students whose persistent academic difficulties preclude their learning at the same speed and with the same depth as other students. It is expected that students assessed relative to alternate achievement standards are the approximately 1 percent of students with significant cognitive disabilities.[1]

---

[1]The percentages specified are percentages of all students, not percentages of students with disabilities. Remember that approximately 13 percent of students have disabilities. Those eligible for alternate assessments are the most severely disabled but represent 1 percent of the total population of students rather than 1 percent of the 13 percent who have disabilities. Two of the authors of this text have attended administrative speeches in which administrators mistakenly informed school personnel that alternative assessments were for "1 percent of students with disabilities." Both administrators also argued that this was "not many kids so the policy changes were not all that important."

Develop Rules or Guidelines for IEP Teams to Use in Deciding Who Takes What Kind of Assessment

It is expected that all students will participate in state assessments. That does not mean that all students take the regular state assessment. Rather, decisions about the kind of assessment to be taken (AA-GLAS, AA-MAS, or AA-AAS), and any assessment accommodations to be provided, are made by IEP teams. It will be necessary to give teams guidelines to work with. Failure to do so could result in different kinds of students taking the different kinds of tests with or without accommodations.

Develop or Adapt Data Collection and Analysis Mechanisms

School personnel find that they have to create new data collection mechanisms to address new indicators or to include new populations that have not been included before. Data collection systems must be designed in such a way that they are sensitive to cultural differences during sampling, instrument development, data collection, and data analysis.

Decide How Information Will Be Reported and Used

Information on educational results (accountability systems) needs to be reported in ways that are meaningful to the intended audience. It is important to ask members of the audience (for instance, administrators and school board members) what would help them make decisions consistent with the stated purpose of the accountability system (such as program improvement, public information, or policy formulation). Probably the most important decision to be made is how the data will be used. Will rewards and consequences be given as a result of educational outcomes? Other reporting decisions to be made include levels of reporting (system versus individual), formats and types of reports, types of comparisons to be reported, ways of presenting and grouping data, and vehicles for dissemination of information.

Install a Standards-Based Accountability System

An accountability system cannot be installed overnight. Those who use the information on results will need to see personal and programmatic benefits before the system can be considered fully in place. There must be incentives for teachers, parents, and administrators who will ultimately ensure the success of the system.

Two commonly used incentives are public comparisons and sanctions for failure to meet standards or goals. Public comparisons formally display schools, districts, or states side by side. Sanctioning involves negative techniques such as withdrawal of accreditation, takeovers of schools, and reduction of funding based on identification of inadequate outcomes. Both comparisons and sanctions are high-stakes uses of any accountability system. They can lead to overemphasis on appearances, without substantive changes.

Change in measurement and accountability systems occurs in the same way as it occurs in any system. State or governmental agencies fund research and demonstration projects, establish networking and recognition systems, and provide technical assistance and resources for use of outcomes-based accountability systems. Personnel in state departments of education provide technical assistance to local school districts that are trying to implement accountability systems.

Once an outcomes-based accountability system is in place and being used, we may be able to identify the extent to which the interventions used with individuals who have disabilities are working as we would like them to work. Systemwide accountability assessment should enable us to make judgments about the extent of the system's success.

Current State Assessment and Accountability Practices

State assessment and accountability systems change often and rapidly. State education agency personnel are always working on refinement of academic content standards and working to improve their assessment systems. In Appendix 3 (available on the website) we provide the list of tests/assessments used in each of the states that provide this information on their websites. The information is from the 2005–2006 academic year, the most recent available at the time of publication of this edition. Refer to that appendix and look at the kinds of tests used in the various states. What tests are used most often? Are states using primarily off-the-shelf norm-referenced tests such as the Stanford Achievement Tests, or are they using primarily standards-based measures that they or others design? What tests were used in your state in 2005–2006? How does the system used in your state compare to the systems used in the states that border yours? NCEO regularly publishes the results of their surveys of state assessment practices. Go to the NCEO website (www.cehd.umn.edu/nceo) and review the most recent state survey results. Discuss with your classmates the changes that have taken place in your assessment system since 2005–2006. NCEO also provides a "data viewer." The NCEO Data Viewer lets you view information related to students with disabilities and create individualized reports based on criteria that you can choose. Two major databases are currently available for your use:

1. State Policies on Assessment Participation and Accommodations for Students with Disabilities (this lists the kinds of accommodations that are permitted in your state)
2. Annual Performance Reports (this is a detailed summary of the report that your state submitted to the federal government on performance of students in the state)

You should also visit the website www.schoolmatters.com, where you can obtain detailed information on the numbers of students classified as disabled, the kinds of disabilities they have, and data on how students perform on tests.

5 Important Considerations in Assessment for the Purpose of Making Accountability Decisions

As a result of accountability system implementation, student assessment data have become much more readily available to the public. Although this public reporting is intended to promote better student instruction and learning, it is important that those who have access to the data know how to appropriately interpret the information. Without these skills, poor judgments and decisions may be made that are harmful to students. For instance, it is important for consumers of accountability information to understand that most tests used for accountability purposes are intended to measure performance of an entire group of students, and that the tests do not necessarily provide reliable data on the skills of individual students. Without this knowledge, consumers may make unwarranted judgments and decisions about individual students based on their test scores.

In addition, it is important for people to recognize that not all students need to be tested in the same way; it is often important for students to be tested using different formats. Some students have special characteristics that make it difficult for them to demonstrate their knowledge on content standards in a traditional paper-and-pencil format. These students may need accommodations to demonstrate their true knowledge. What is most important is that students' knowledge and skill toward the identified achievement standards are measured. Those with assessment expertise can help determine what accommodations or alternate assessments might be necessary for students to best demonstrate their skills and knowledge.

6 Best Practices in High-Stakes Assessment and Accountability

It is critical that accountability systems include and report on the performance of all students, including those with disabilities and limited English proficiency. Personnel at the NCEO (Thurlow, Quenemoen, Thompson, & Lehr, 2001) specified a set of principles of inclusive assessment and accountability systems. These are listed in Table 22.2. The principles address who should participate, the kinds of guidelines states should have, how scores should be reported, the use of scores in accountability systems, and the fundamental belief system that should guide practice.

TABLE 22.2	NCEO Best Practices in Inclusive Assessment and Accountability

Principle 1: All students with disabilities are included in the assessment and accountability system.

Principle 2: Decisions about how students with disabilities participate in the assessment and accountability system are the result of clearly articulated participation, accommodations, and alternate assessment decision-making processes.

Principle 3: All students with disabilities are included when student scores are publicly reported, in the same frequency and format as all other students, whether they participate with or without accommodations, or in an alternate assessment.

Principle 4: The assessment performance of students with disabilities has the same impact on the final accountability index as the performance of other students, regardless of how the students participate in the assessment system (that is, with or without accommodations, or in an alternate assessment).

Principle 5: There is improvement of both the assessment system and the accountability system over time, through the processes of formal monitoring, ongoing evaluation, and systematic training in the context of emerging research and best practice.

Principle 6: Every policy and practice reflects the belief that *all students* must be included in state and district assessment and accountability systems.

SOURCE: Thurlow, M., Quenemoen, R., Thompson, S., & Lehr, C. (2001). *Principles and characteristics of inclusive assessment and accountability systems* (Synthesis Report 40), Table 1. Minneapolis, MN: University of Minnesota, National Center on Educational Outcomes. Reprinted by permission.

CHAPTER COMPREHENSION QUESTIONS

Write your answers to each of the following questions, and then compare your responses to the text or the study guide.

1. What legal requirements for state and school district assessment and accountability systems are specified in NCLB and IDEA 2004?

2. Distinguish between grade-level achievement standards, modified achievement standards, and alternate achievement standards.

3. Distinguish between alternate assessment based on grade-level achievement standards, alternate assessment based on modified achievement standards, and alternate assessment based on alternate achievement standard.

4. What are the steps in developing a standards-based accountability system?

5. State two important considerations in assessment for purposes of making accountability decisions.

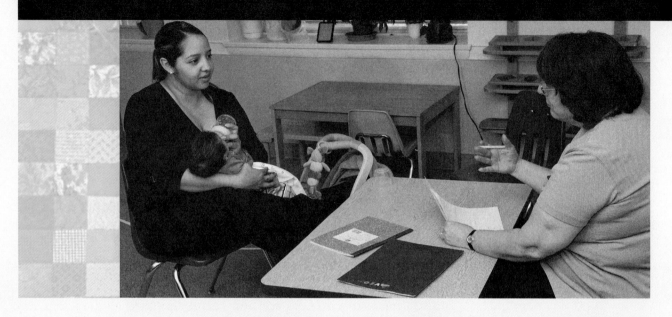

Chapter Goals

1 Understand several characteristics of effective school teams.

2 Be familiar with various teams that are commonly formed in school settings.

3 Know strategies for effectively communicating assessment information to parents.

4 Know a variety of ways in which assessment information is communicated and maintained in written formats, and various related rules about data collection and record keeping.

Key Terms

school wide assistance teams	child study teams	Family Educational Rights and Privacy Act (FERPA)
problem-solving teams	groupthink	

THE EXTENT TO WHICH ASSESSMENT INFORMATION HAS A POSITIVE IMPACT ON student learning ultimately depends on your ability to (1) be an informed consumer of assessment information and (2) effectively communicate that knowledge to those responsible for decision making. In schools, important decisions are made by teams of individuals. Although some team members may be well-versed in assessment concepts, others may need considerable support to understand and effectively use assessment data. Research conducted through the Center for Research on Evaluation, Standards, and Student Testing suggests that many educational professionals do not know how to carefully examine and use assessment data (Baker, Bewley, Herman, Lee, & Mitchell, 2001; Baker & Linn, 2002). Parents may need considerable support to understand and make appropriate use of assessment information that is collected. Some professional associations (for example, the American Psychological Association, the Council for Exceptional Children, and the National Association of School Psychologists) specify in their ethical standards or principles that their members are responsible for accurate and sensitive communication of assessment information.

In this chapter, we provide information on the many different teams that may be formed to examine assessment data and suggestions for making appropriate team decisions. We offer guidelines for communicating assessment information in both oral and written formats, as well as rules concerning record keeping and the dissemination of information collected in school settings.

1 Characteristics of Effective School Teams

Many individuals play important roles in promoting student learning; each brings unique expertise that can be useful in the process of decision making. In using assessment data to make decisions, you will work with special and general educators, administrators, speech/language pathologists, school psychologists, social workers, nurses, physicians, physical therapists, occupational therapists, audiologists, counselors, curriculum directors, attorneys, child advocates, and probably many others. Effective communication and collaboration is essential to promoting positive student outcomes. Although the expertise each individual offers can be an asset to decision making, it is important to recognize that group decision making does not necessarily result in better decisions than individual decision making. Unfortunately, there are many ways in which group dynamics can hinder appropriate decision making. Gutkin and Nemeth (1997) summarize ways in which group decision making can go awry, including (1) the tendency for groups to concede to the majority opinion regardless of whether it is accurate, and (2) group polarization, in which groups tend to become more extreme in their decision making than what any individual originally intended (which could either hinder or promote best practice). In order to avoid making poor decisions, it is important to adhere to several principles when working as a team. Although the goals and purposes of school teams may vary, certain principles of effective teaming appear to be universal. These are described next.

Have shared goals and purpose. Unnecessary conflict and inefficiencies in decision making occur when team members do not understand the team's purpose and when their activities do not reflect that purpose. For example, some members of prereferral intervention teams may view the team's purpose as "just one more hoop to jump through" before a referral for evaluation to determine special education eligibility is made, whereas others may view it as an opportunity to identify the conditions under which a student learns best. Those holding the former perspective may be less inclined to put forth substantial effort in associated team activities, which may reduce team effectiveness. It is important for the team's purpose and function to be clearly articulated when the team is formed and for all team members to be committed to working toward that goal.

Clearly articulate the roles and functions of team members. Team composition needs to be determined carefully, balancing the need for unique expertise and the need for a team to efficiently complete commissioned tasks. More team members is not always better; managing large teams can be overwhelming and may intimidate important members of the team (for example, some parents may be intimidated when they walk into a team meeting that includes many school professionals). In addition, large teams may lead to decisions that are informed by just one or two particularly dominant team members (Moore, Fifield, Spira, & Scarlato, 1989). Those team members who are selected for participation need to be fully aware of the unique expertise that they bring as well as their knowledge limitations. The appointment of a team meeting facilitator can be helpful in assisting the team in following appropriate organizational procedures and ensure that all team members are fully able to share their expertise and knowledge in ways that facilitate progress toward the team's goal.

Listen to and respect each team member's contributions. Teams sometimes gravitate toward "groupthink" (that is, agreeing with the majority opinion) despite the fact that group decisions can be inaccurate (Gutkin & Nemeth, 1997). It is important for those with minority opinions to be given the opportunity to express their positions and for their ideas to be respected and considered within the group's functioning. Creative and effective problem solving can occur when all individuals are encouraged to contribute.

Balance structure and flexibility within team meetings. It can often be helpful for teams to develop and implement systematic procedures for operation. In many cases, teams may have forms that facilitators use to guide team meetings (see Figure 23.1 for an example of such a form). The facilitator might create a written agenda for team meetings, in which there is time for those who have collected information to present their findings, time for additional input from team members, and time for group decision making. Such procedures and structures can help teams maintain attention to task and promote efficiency toward addressing the team's goals. When team members want to discuss important issues that are not associated with the specific decisions to be made, it is important to know how to tactfully

FIGURE 23.1
Completed Example Form to
Guide Initial Problem-Solving
Team Meeting

Date of meeting: 01/30/08
Student name: Jesse Johansen
Student's grade: 3
Teacher's name: Darcy Dunlap
School: Eastern Elementary
Name and title of those attending the meeting (note facilitator and recorder):
Carrie Court (3rd grade lead teacher), Darcy Dunlap (recorder), Greg Gorter (guidance counselor), Jackie Johansen (mother), Eric Enright (principal, facilitator)

A. Student Strengths (Provide brief summary of student strengths; 2–3 minutes)
Jesse has many friends and gets along really well with all the other students. He likes to play soccer, and is very good at math.

B. Nature of Difficulties (In 2 minutes, circle all that apply)

<u>Academic</u>

(Reading)   Writing   Spelling   Math   Social Studies   History   Other: _____

<u>Behavioral</u>

Aggression Attention Task Completion Homework Attendance Tardiness Other: _____

<u>Social/Emotional</u>

Depression   (Anxiety)   Peer Relationships   Social Skills   Other: _____

<u>Physical</u>

Body Odor   Headaches   Nausea   Fatigue/Sleeping in Class   Other: _____

C. Summary of Data Collected to Support Difficulties Circled Above (2–3 minutes per area)
Jesse performed in the at-risk range on the Fall and Winter DIBELS benchmarking tasks during third grade. When asked to read in class, his voice becomes shaky, and he shuts down, and he refuses to read. His mother reports that he is beginning to not like going to school, and doesn't eat his breakfast (most likely due to his nervousness about having to go to school).

D. Prioritization of Difficulties (2–3 minutes)
#1 Most Problematic of the Above Listed Difficulties: Reading (the team believes that his poor skills in reading are what are contributing to his anxiety).

#2 Most Problematic of the Above Listed Difficulties: Anxiety

#3 Most Problematic of the Above Listed Difficulties: _____

E. Problem Definition in Observable and Measurable Terms (2 minutes)
Currently when presented with a third grade DIBELS benchmark passage, Jesse reads a median of 60 words correctly in one minute.

F. Goal (2 minutes)
Eight weeks from now when presented with a third grade DIBELS benchmark passage, Jesse will read a median of 75 words correctly in one minute.

(*continued*)

FIGURE 23.1
(Continued)

G. Suggested Intervention Ideas for Addressing #1 of Prioritized Difficulties (15 minutes)

Intervention Idea #1: After school tutoring with an eighth grade student.

Intervention Idea #2: Flashcards of phonics patterns that Jesse's teacher would administer after school two days per week, and Jesse's mom would administer at home the other three days each week

Intervention Idea #3: Read Naturally® program that would be administered after school.

H. Description of Final Intervention Selected (10 minutes)

i. What will the student do? Jesse will be taught how to use the Read Naturally® program, and will practice listening to and reading aloud with the tapes.

ii. How often and when will this occur? Two times a week for 45 minutes after school (Tues./Thurs.).

iii. Who is responsible for implementing the intervention? Jesse's mom and teacher

iv. How will progress be measured? DIBELS progress monitoring probes will be administered once a week.

v. Who is responsible for measuring progress? Jesse's teacher

vi. How, when, and to whom will progress be reported? Progress will be reported at the follow-up meeting, unless four consecutive data points fall below the aim line, in which case an earlier meeting will be convened.

I. Date and Time of Follow-Up Meeting (2 minutes): April 9, 2008

address those concerns. We have found the following statement to be helpful in such circumstances: "That's an important issue, but it will take us away from the decision that we are trying to make now. Can we discuss it later or at another meeting?" Some decisions that school teams make are associated with a substantial amount of conflicting opinion and emotionality. For example, discussing certain disability labels such as "student with mental retardation" and "student with an emotional disturbance" can be very troubling to parents. It is important that team meeting facilitators be willing to shuffle the agenda or even stop and reschedule meetings when the emotional nature of the meeting is such that progress toward the team's goals cannot be made.

Use objective data to guide decision making. Often, educational decisions are made without appropriate attention to relevant student data (Ysseldyke, 1987). Without the appropriate collection of and adherence to using data to guide team decision making, the subjective preferences of team members may take precedence over what is truly in the best interest of the student being served. The appropriate use of data to inform decision making can (1) ensure that appropriate practices are put into place and (2) help eliminate conflicting viewpoints on how to proceed.

Work to ensure confidentiality. Those who study team decision making find that eventually confidentiality breaks down. When this happens and a member learns that someone betrayed confidentiality, the team ceases to function well. It is suggested that this be handled by regular reminders from an administrator, school psychologist, or other team leader that meeting discussions are confidential. We suggest that the leader tell members at the very first meeting that confidentiality is critical and that he or she will be reminding members of this regularly. Then the reminders do not raise questions of "I wonder who talked inappropriately about what we are discussing."

Regularly evaluate team outcomes and processes to promote continuous improvement in team functioning. Team processes and procedures can always be improved. It is important for the team to engage in periodic self-evaluation in order to ensure that it is meeting identified goals and objectives and that it is respectful of all team members' contributions. In some cases, it may be helpful to ask someone uninvolved in the team functioning to do an evaluation of a team's functioning. This can help to ensure that all team members are able to contribute their skills and knowledge in a way that is most beneficial to students.

2 Types of School Teams

There are many different teams created to examine assessment data and inform decision making in schools. These teams may have very different names and be composed of professionals with varying expertise. Although all the teams described here are typically involved in examination of data for the purpose of decision making, the teams vary considerably in the types of decisions made and, therefore, the nature of data collected, analyzed, and interpreted. Although we provide titles for these teams, it is important to recognize that there may be a variety of different terms used to describe similarly functioning teams in the schools and districts you encounter.

Schoolwide Assistance Teams

With the development of technology for managing large amounts of student data, as well as increased attention to accountability for student outcomes, teams of educational professionals are more frequently being formed to collect, analyze, and interpret data on students across the entire school or district. The ultimate purpose of these teams is to inform instructional planning and resource allocation at school and district levels such that student achievement is optimized. Sometimes these teams are referred to as "resource teams." Team members may consist of those with special expertise in data analysis, curriculum, and instruction. These individuals come together to examine statewide assessment data, results from school-wide screening efforts, and information on existing educational programming, with the purpose of identifying strategies for improving student achievement. In some cases, such teams may be created by grade level, such that all teachers from a particular grade meet on a regular basis with the administrator and someone with expertise in assessment in order to identify areas for instructional improvement.

Following a systematic analysis of data, the team may make recommendations for professional development and changes in school programming.

Participants on these teams who have specialized expertise in assessment can contribute to the team by (1) helping the school identify methods for collecting relevant data on all students effectively and efficiently, (2) creating and interpreting visual displays of assessment data for the purpose of decision making, (3) recognizing areas in which additional assessment is needed prior to making substantial changes in school programming, and (4) identifying methods for monitoring the effectiveness of any associated changes in school programming.

Problem-Solving Teams

Problem-solving teams are formed to address difficulties that small groups of students or individual students experience within general education classrooms. The purpose of the team is to define the specific problem, analyze the problem in order to develop a targeted intervention plan, implement the intervention plan, monitor the plan implementation and student progress, and evaluate the effectiveness of the plan. Initially, the team may simply consist of a general education teacher and parents of the child involved. However, if the problem is not solved, additional school professionals may be added to the team in order to more systematically define and analyze the problem and to inform the development of interventions that are of increasing intensity. The parent–teacher team might be expanded to include other teachers or the school guidance counselor; these individuals could help conduct a more in-depth problem analysis and brainstorm additional ideas for intervention. If that plan does not lead to progress, other personnel, such as the school psychologist, social worker, or special education teacher, might be added to the problem-solving team to provide additional support for assessment and intervention. Names for teams with a function similar to that of the problem-solving teams described previously include "teacher assistance teams," "student assistance teams," "building assistance teams," and "instructional consultation teams."

Those with expertise in assessment can assist these teams by helping to select and administer assessment tools that can assist with defining and analyzing the problem, as well as select tools for monitoring intervention integrity and student progress.

Child Study Teams

These teams are typically developed to examine specific difficulties that an individual child is experiencing prior to referral for special education evaluation. Although in some places these teams may function similarly to problem-solving teams, there tends to be a greater focus on identifying child characteristics that are contributing to the difficulties rather than on instructional variables that may be altered to eliminate those difficulties. Child study teams are composed of parents, teachers, and other specialists that may include a school psychologist, special educator, speech/language pathologist, counselor, nurse, social worker, and principal. Together, these individuals identify prereferral intervention strategies to put into place prior to initiating a formal special education eligibility evaluation. Although not every student who is initially referred for consideration by a child study team goes through the special educational evaluation process, such has been the case for a large percentage of these students (Algozzine, Christenson, & Ysseldyke, 1982).

Multidisciplinary Teams

These teams are convened when a child is being considered for special education evaluation; the function and activities of these teams are more fully discussed in Chapter 20. They are charged with the responsibility of determining whether a student has a disability and is in need of special education services according to the Individuals with Disabilities Education Act (IDEA).

Individual Education Plan Teams

After a student is found eligible for special education services under IDEA, the individualized education program is developed by a team of individuals who have specialized knowledge in the specific areas of the child's disability, as well as those who will be responsible for carrying out the plan and the child's parents. These teams typically meet on an annual basis to review the progress and programming for each student receiving special education services individually.

3 Communicating Assessment Information to Parents

Parents and guardians are often the members of teams who have the least knowledge and skill in understanding assessment. Given the influential role that they play in the lives of their children, it is important for them to be equipped with knowledge to assist with interpreting assessment results. Parents need to be empowered to be active and helpful members of school decision-making teams.

A variety of things can limit parent understanding of assessment information and participation in team decision making. Language barriers can clearly hinder effective communication. Many parents may not have a schedule that permits participation in meetings as scheduled by school professionals. They may feel intimidated by various school professionals. They may not recognize the important knowledge that they can bring to the team or not understand how to effectively communicate that knowledge to the team. They may have strong emotional reactions to data that are presented about their child's academic successes and failures, which may hinder rational decision making. They may have strong feelings and opinions about the quality of educational services provided to their child and about how their child's needs might best be met by educational professionals. Unfortunately, parents' unique knowledge about their child is often disregarded or ignored by school professionals, who often make decisions prior to team meetings.

Schools can take several steps to make communication with parents more effective. Better communication should result in more effective parental participation in associated team decision making.

■ *Communicate with parents frequently.* Often, parents are not made aware of difficulties that their child is having until the child is being considered for special education evaluation. When this happens, it can lead to strong emotional reactions and frustration among parents. It can also lead to unnecessary conflict if parents do not think that special education services would be in the best interest of their child. It is important that parents are provided frequent and accurate information on the progress of their child from the very beginning of their child's enrollment in school. By providing this information, parents of those students who are consistently low performing may become more involved in helping to develop intervention plans that may reduce their child's difficulties. Furthermore, when parents receive frequent communication about their child's progress (or lack thereof), they may more readily understand why a referral for special education eligibility evaluation is made.

■ *Communicate both the child's strengths and the child's weaknesses.* Parents of students with special needs are often reminded of their child's weaknesses and difficulties in school and may rarely be alerted to their child's successes and strengths. Other parents may overvalue their child's relative strengths and ignore or minimize their child's weaknesses. In order to work effectively with parents, and to facilitate creative problem solving as a part of a team, it is important to recognize and communicate about a child's specific strengths as well as weaknesses.

■ *Translate assessment information and team communications as needed.* Assessment data that are reported to all parents (for example, statewide assessment results and screening results) should be made available in the parent's primary language or mode of communication. To facilitate participation in team meetings, interpreters should be provided. In order to interpret well, they may need special training in how to communicate the pertinent information to parents, as well as how to ensure that parents' questions, concerns, and contributions have a voice within team meanings.

■ *Be aware of how cultural differences may impact the understanding of assessment information.* It is also suggested that when cultural differences exist, a person who understands both the student's culture and educational matters be present. This may be necessary even when language differences are nonexistent (for example, the student is Amish and the culture of the school is not Amish). This can help a team identify issues that may be cultural in nature.

■ *Schedule meetings to facilitate parent attendance.* Efforts should be made to schedule meetings at a time when parents can be present. Challenges associated with transportation should be addressed. In certain circumstances, it may be necessary for school professionals to meet at a location that is more convenient for parents than the school setting. It may also be necessary for school personnel to communicate directly with an employer, encouraging the employer to allow the parent to be excused from work. This is especially true in communities in which one company (for example, a paper mill, an automobile factory, or a meat packing plant) is the employer of many parents. In this case, a blanket arrangement could be made in which the company agrees to release the parent for school meetings if a request is made by the school.

■ *Clearly explain the purpose of any assessment activities, as well as the potential outcomes.* Whereas school professionals may be very familiar with assessment-related processes and procedures, and associated decisions that are made, parents often are new to the process. It is important to prepare them for what to expect as it relates to using the results of assessment data that are collected. Sometimes, it can be helpful for school professionals to contact parents before a meeting to explain the purpose of the meeting and what they can expect to happen at the meeting. Parents should be informed of all potential outcomes of a particular meeting (for example, development of an intervention plan,

Scenario in Assessment

Amelia

Ineffective Communication of Assessment Information with Parents

In early November, Mr. and Mrs. Martinez were notified that a meeting was being scheduled to discuss their third-grade daughter Amelia's failure to make progress in reading. The meeting was scheduled as part of a series of child study team meetings, in which a total of seven children from her elementary school would be discussed by a team of individuals who included the principal, guidance counselor, and the students' general education teachers. General educators were rotated into the meeting at 10-minute intervals, as each child was being discussed. Although Mr. and Mrs. Martinez were notified by Amelia's teacher that the meeting would be held, they were told that it was not important for them to attend, and that it would probably be better for them to plan to attend the meeting that would likely be held in mid-December to discuss Amelia's need for special education services. A few days later, Amelia's parents received a letter and consent form in the mail asking them to sign for permission to conduct an assessment to determine whether Amelia was eligible to receive special education services. Amelia's parents, although discouraged and confused about what this meant, promptly signed and returned the form, assuming that the school knew what was in Amelia's best academic interests.

On December 15, a multidisciplinary team meeting was held. Mr. Martinez could not make it to the early afternoon meeting, given his work schedule. Mrs. Martinez was able to catch a bus and arrive at the school with her two young children 30 minutes prior to the meeting. At the meeting, several different professionals shuffled into the room at different times, with each presenting results from speech/language testing, intelligence testing, achievement testing, and classroom observations of Amelia. Toward the end of the meeting, a special education teacher asked Mrs. Martinez to sign some forms, which she was told would allow Amelia to get the services she needed, given that Amelia was in the words of her teacher "clearly a student with a learning disability."

Effective Communication of Assessment Information with Parents

In January of Amelia Martinez's first-grade year, Mr. and Mrs. Martinez received a phone call from her teacher. The teacher indicated that although Amelia was making many friends in first grade and seemed to get along very well with her classmates, she was performing below expectations in her development of early literacy skills as measured by the early literacy screening measures administered to all students in the fall and winter. The teacher invited Amelia's parents to attend a meeting in which they would discuss strategies for targeting instruction to Amelia's needs and discuss the possibility of implementing strategies at home for helping her develop early literacy skills.

At the meeting, Mr. and Mrs. Martinez, along with the classroom teacher and a more experienced kindergarten teacher, discussed the fact that Amelia did not demonstrate adequate letter–sound correspondence. They developed a plan that allowed her to receive additional instruction and practice in this area at both home and school (with the teacher assistant) each day for 6 weeks, after which they would reconvene as a team to examine the progress that she had made. After 6 weeks, the two teachers and Amelia's parents met, and an additional person (that is, an intervention specialist) was added to the team to help identify any additional assessment and intervention that might be applied, given that Amelia had not made the progress needed to put her on track for learning how to read by the end of third grade. After reviewing Amelia's progress together, and recognizing that she had made small gains as a result of the intervention, they decided to intensify the support she was receiving by providing her more intervention time during

continued on the next page

the school day, and they continued to monitor her progress. Her mother was provided simple phonemic awareness development activities to practice with Amelia at home in the evening.

Soon after spring break of her first-grade year, the team reconvened to examine Amelia's progress, which continued to be below expectations. Together, the team decided that an evaluation for special education services was warranted. Mr. and Mrs. Martinez were provided information on their rights as parents of a child undergoing evaluation to determine special education eligibility. They were briefly told about the types of testing that would occur and how this would help determine whether Amelia might be in need of and benefit from special education services. At the end of her first-grade year, the team was brought together to examine the assessment results. Based on the information collected, it was clear that Amelia met the state criteria for having a specific learning disability in reading, and the team identified instructional strategies that were beneficial to include as part of an individualized education program for Amelia.

decision to collect more data, and decision that the student is eligible to receive special education services) so that they are not caught off guard.

■ *Communicate using nontechnical language as much as possible.* By now, you have most certainly recognized that language used in educational circles is full of acronyms. It is important for these, as well as all of the other technical terms that may be used, to be fully explained to parents so that they can be in dialog with team members. Whereas some parents may understand technical terms associated with assessment data, others may not. It is more appropriate to err on the side of using language that is easier to understand than to assume that parents understand terminology that is used by school professionals.

■ *Maintain a solution-focused orientation and avoid pointing blame.* Just about every school team meeting is intended to promote student achievement, whether directly or indirectly. Making this goal happen requires that individual team members focus on alterable rather than unalterable variables and on what can be changed in the future to promote student learning rather than dwelling on what has happened in the past. Unfortunately, there can be a tendency to focus on what people may have done or failed to do in the past rather than making plans for the future. Although it is important to learn from past mistakes, team members should focus on what can be done in the future to improve student learning. Focusing on past failure can decrease morale and contribute to unnecessary conflict among team members.

4 Communicating Assessment Information Through Written Records

Although presentation of assessment information and related decision making is frequently done verbally and in team meetings, assessment data are also collected, summarized, and interpreted in written form. Policies and standards for the collection, maintenance, and dissemination of information in written formats must balance two sometimes conflicting needs. Parents and children have a basic right to privacy; schools need to collect and use information about children (and sometimes parents) in order to plan appropriate educational programs. Schools and parents have a common goal: to promote the welfare of children. In theory, schools and parents should agree on what constitutes and promotes a child's welfare, and in practice, schools and parents generally do work cooperatively.

In 1974, many of these recommended guidelines became federal law when the Family Educational Rights and Privacy Act (Public Law 93-380, commonly called FERPA) was enacted. The basic provisions of the act are quite simple. All educational agencies that accept federal money (preschools, elementary and secondary schools, community colleges, and colleges and universities) must grant parents the opportunity to inspect and challenge student records. Regardless of whether the school decides to change the records according to parent input, parents have the right to supplement the records with what they understand to be true or an explanation as to why they believe the file to be inaccurate. The only records to which parental access may be denied are the personal notes of teachers, supervisors, administrators, and other educational personnel that are kept in the sole possession of the maker of the records. Also, educational agencies must not release identifiable data without the parents' written consent. However, at age 18 years, the student becomes the individual who has the authority to provide consent for his or her data to be released to others. Violators of the provisions of FERPA are subject to sanctions; federal funds may be withheld from agencies found to be in violation of the law.

The following section discusses specific issues and principles in the collection, maintenance, and dissemination of pupil information through written records and reports.

Collection of Pupil Information

Schools routinely collect massive amounts of information about individual pupils and their parents, and not all of this information requires parental permission to collect or maintain. As discussed in Chapter 1, information can be used for a number of legitimate educational decisions: screening, progress monitoring, instructional planning and modification, resource allocation, special education eligibility determination, program evaluation, and accountability. Considerable data must be collected if a school system is to function effectively, both in delivering educational services to children and in reporting the results of its educational programs to the various community, state, and federal agencies to which it may be responsible.

Schoolwide Screening

Many schools systematically collect and keep written records of hearing, vision, and basic skill development across all students. The associated screening measures are intended to identify all students who have the potential for additional difficulties very early in time, and they are purposely developed to overidentify students. This can help to ensure that true difficulties are not missed, and that difficulties can be addressed earlier rather than later in time. When students fail to meet minimum thresholds of performance on screening measures, they may be referred for additional assessment to determine whether true difficulties exist. Vision and hearing screening records are typically maintained at the school for a substantial amount of time; review of this information can help determine that basic abilities such as hearing and vision are not contributing to difficulties that a student may experience.

Vision   Most schools have vision screening programs, but the effectiveness of these programs varies. Two fundamentally different kinds of tests are used: those that screen only central visual acuity at a distance and those that assess both central visual acuity and a number of other visual capabilities. Most preschool screening programs also include screening for amblyopia, often called "lazy eye."

Schools conduct vision screening, whereas vision testing is done clinically by ophthalmologists and optometrists. When a student experiences learning difficulties, or when routine vision screening indicates visual difficulties, the child is referred for a clinical vision exam. If the clinical exam indicates 20/20 vision, no additional visual assessment needs to be done by educational personnel. Similarly, if visual acuity is limited but can be corrected by glasses, no visual assessments need be conducted by education personnel. However, if vision is 20/70 or less with best correction, or if there is a limited visual field, educational personnel must ensure that a clinical low vision exam, functional vision assessment, or learning-media assessment is conducted. The purpose of these tests is intervention planning.

Hearing   The identification of preschool and school-age children with hearing problems usually falls within the realm of a hearing screening program, which may also be called a "hearing conservation program," a "hearing loss identification program," or "identification audiometry." All states have laws requiring hearing screening of school-age children. Unfortunately, hearing screening for many children in preschool programs is not mandated by state or federal laws. Therefore, many preschool children who have educationally significant hearing losses are not being identified and may become educationally delayed. Hearing-screening programs generally have three components: the actual hearing screening, follow-up hearing threshold tests for those who fail the screening, and referral for those diagnosed with hearing impairment.

Early detection of hearing problems in preschool and school-age children is imperative so that appropriate remedial or compensatory procedures can be instituted. Children with hearing problems characteristically fail to pay attention, provide wrong answers to simple questions, frequently ask to have words or sentences repeated, and hear better in quiet conditions and when watching the teacher's face. Such children often function below their educational potential, are withdrawn, or exhibit behavior problems. Children who are repeatedly sick, having frequent earaches, colds, or other upper respiratory infections, allergies, or fluid draining from their ears, may also have a concomitant hearing problem. Furthermore, children who do not speak clearly or who show other types of speech or language problems, and children who fail to discriminate between sounds or words with similar vowels but different consonants, may also have hearing problems. Finally, some preschool and school-age children are more at risk for hearing problems, including children with craniofacial anomalies such as cleft palate or Down syndrome; children from a lower socioeconomic class; Native Americans and Eskimos, who may not receive appropriate and routine health care (Northern & Downs, 1991, pp. 22–24); and children with mental retardation or severe disabilities who cannot express that they have trouble hearing.

Any child, regardless of age, who has one or more of the aforementioned hearing loss symptoms and any child at risk for hearing loss should be referred for a hearing test. Depending on the school system, the hearing test may be given by the school nurse, a speech/language pathologist, a hearing therapist, an audiologist, or a trained technician. In a preschool setting, support personnel for assessing hearing problems may not be available. Children in such a setting should be referred to their family physician or directly to a hearing specialist.

If a hearing problem is detected or if the child is difficult to test, making the results questionable, the child should be referred to a physician specializing in disorders of the ear, called an otologist or an otolaryngologist, or to a specialist in hearing evaluation and rehabilitation, called an audiologist. The otologist and the audiologist often work together as a team. An otologist has expertise in physical examination of the ears and in diagnosing and treating ear disorders. If a child has a correctable hearing loss, the otologist can provide the appropriate treatment (such as drug therapy or surgery). The audiologist has expertise in hearing assessment and rehabilitation. If a child has an educationally significant and noncorrectable hearing loss, the audiologist can prescribe, fit, and monitor the use of hearing aids. Furthermore, the audiologist can make recommendations to teachers, hearing therapists, speech/language pathologists, and parents concerning the child's hearing ability in different listening environments.

Academic Screening and Monitoring Increasingly, schools are implementing universal screening and monitoring in order to ensure early identification of academic problems. Programs such as DIBELS, AIMSweb, and others described in Chapter 8 may be used to screen for academic problems and monitor student progress. Some screening is done schoolwide; however, other screening may occur for individual students who are initially identified as having difficulties. Students who do not meet benchmark levels on screening measures and fail to make expected levels of progress toward meeting proficiency may be identified for additional assessment and referred to a school problem-solving team. Although it is best practice to remain in frequent communication with parents about data that are collected about their children, it is not always necessary to get their explicit permission for data collection. For example, prior to holding a problem-solving team meeting, a school professional may collect data to inform the selection of an intervention that would target a student's individual academic deficits. Such assessment would not necessarily require explicit parent permission.

Consent for Additional Data Collection

Although it is best practice to communicate with parents frequently about student progress, and to alert them to any academic difficulties that the student is having as soon as possible, schools are not required to have parent consent for additional data collection unless a change in educational placement or the provision of a free and appropriate public education according to the Individuals with Disabilities Education Act (IDEA) is being considered.[1] In the section on procedural safeguards, IDEA mandates that prior written notice be given to the parents or guardians of

---

[1]This is also the case if data are to be collected for the purpose of research. The collection of research data requires the individual informed consent of parents. Various professional groups, such as the American Psychological Association and the National Association of School Psychologists, consider the collection of data without informed consent to be unethical; according to the Buckley amendment, it is illegal to experiment with children without prior informed consent. Typically, informed consent for research-related data collection requires that the pupil or parents understand (1) the purpose of and procedures involved in the investigations, (2) any risks inherent in participation in the research, (3) the fact that all participants will remain anonymous, and (4) the participants' option to withdraw from the research at any time.

a child whenever an educational agency proposes to initiate or change (or refuses to initiate or change) either the identification, evaluation, or educational placement of the child or the provision of a free and appropriate education to the child. It further requires that the notice fully inform the parent, in the parent's native language, regarding all appeal procedures available. Thus, schools must inform parents of their right to present any and all complaints regarding the identification, evaluation, or placement of their child; their right to an impartial due process hearing; and their right to appeal decisions reached at a due process hearing, if necessary, by bringing civil action against a school district.

Verification

Verifying information means ascertaining or confirming the information's truth, accuracy, or correctness. Depending on the type of information, verification may take several forms. For observations or ratings, verification means confirmation by another individual. For standardized test data, verification means conducting a reliable and valid assessment. (The concepts of reliability and validity are defined and discussed in detail in Chapter 4.)

Unverified information can be collected, but every attempt should be made to verify such information before it is retained in a student's records. For example, serious misconduct or extremely withdrawn behavior is of direct concern to the schools. Initial reports of such behavior by a teacher or counselor are typically based on observations that can be corroborated by other witnesses. Behavior that cannot be verified can still provide useful hints, hypotheses, and starting points for diagnosis. Ultimately, when the data are not confirmable, they should not be collected and must not be retained. We believe that this requirement should also apply to unreliable or invalid test data that cannot otherwise be substantiated.

Summarization and Interpretation

When additional assessment data are collected as a part of an evaluation to determine whether a student is eligible to receive special education services under IDEA, a written report is typically developed prior to the multidisciplinary team meeting that is held to determine whether a student is eligible for services. The purpose of the report is to summarize the assessment data collected. Written reports communicate information to both existing team members and those who may review the child's file in the future. Although the content of these reports will vary depending on the nature of data needed to determine eligibility, certain principles should be used to promote effective written communication about the data that are collected. These are discussed here.

Organize the report. In general, an eligibility evaluation report will include the following information: a reason for referral, identifying and background information about the student, a description of the assessment methods and instruments used, information on observations conducted while assessment data were being collected (that is, to substantiate that test results represent accurate measures of typical student behavior), assessment results, recommendations, and a summary of the assessment procedures and results. In order for readers to easily access the information presented, it can be helpful to present assessment results in tables and figures.

Use language that is easily understood by team members. As when communicating assessment information orally, it is important that your language is accessible to parents and other school professionals. Avoid jargon, and carefully explain all terminology that may be unfamiliar to any members of your audience. When reporting scores, it is important to use scores (like percentiles) that are easily interpreted by those who will read your report. When you are not sure whether readers will understand reported scores, explain them clearly. It is always best to err on the side of "overexplaining" than "underexplaining."

Focus on the reporting of observed behaviors. In report writing, it is important to be transparent in how you describe assessment tasks and results. In your writing, clearly communicate that scores represent performance on particular tasks rather than innate student qualities or characteristics. In doing so, you will more accurately reflect the nature of the data collected and help to avoid misinterpretations and high-level inferences based on collected data.

> *Poor example of a report statement*: John is average in his short-term memory capabilities.
>
> *Better example of a report statement*: On tasks that required John to listen to and recall numbers in the order that were verbally communicated to him by the examiner, John performed in the average range in comparison to his same-grade peers.

However, it is important to ensure that the specific content of test items remains secure. When offering example items in written reports, avoid providing the exact content of test items and/or paraphrasing or revising an item in such a way that the item is essentially the same as the original.

Focus on relevant information. You will likely sift through and collect a large amount of information in the process of conducting a special education eligibility evaluation. Instead of reporting on all information examined and collected, it is important to report only the most relevant information. In order to determine whether the information is relevant, ask yourself the following: (1) To what extent is the given information needed to answer the specific referral question? and (2) To what extent will the given information promote the provision of better educational services to the student? Include only those data that address these questions.

Clearly convey your level of certainty. The potential for error is always present. When reporting the results of tests, it is important to convey this potential. In the presentation of test scores, we suggest explaining and providing confidence intervals for reported scores in order to appropriately communicate the existence of error in testing.

Make data-based recommendations. The assessment summary and recommendations sections are by far the most frequently read sections of assessment reports. Recommendations are perhaps the most important aspect of reports; it is important that they are made very carefully and are clearly supported by the data collected. Although it is expected that the recommendation section will document what students need in order to ensure that they receive a free and appropriate public education, recommendations that are made carelessly and without adequate support can result in inefficient use of educational resources.

Maintenance of Pupil Information

The decision to keep test results and other information should be governed by three principles: (1) retention of pupil information for limited periods of time, (2) parental rights of inspection and amendment, and (3) assurance of protection against inappropriate snooping. First, the information should be retained only as long as there is a continuing need for it. Only verified data of clear educational value should be retained. A pupil's school records should be periodically examined, and information that is no longer educationally relevant or no longer accurate should be removed. Natural transition points (for example, promotion from elementary school to junior high) should always be used to remove material from students' files.

The second major principle in the maintenance of pupil information is that parents have the right to inspect, challenge, and supplement student records. Parents of children with disabilities or with special gifts and talents have had the right to inspect, challenge, and supplement their children's school records for some time. Parents or guardians must be given the opportunity to examine all relevant records with respect to the identification, evaluation, and educational placement of the child and the free and appropriate public education of the child, and they must be given the opportunity to obtain an independent evaluation of the child. Again, if parents have complaints, they may request an impartial due process hearing to challenge either the records or the school's decision regarding their child.

The third major principle in the maintenance of pupil records is that the records should be protected from snoopers, both inside and outside the school system. In the past, secretaries, custodians, and even other students have had access, at least potentially, to pupil records. Curious teachers and administrators who had no legitimate educational interest had access. Individuals outside the schools, such as credit bureaus, have often found it easy to obtain information about former or current students. To ensure that only individuals with a legitimate need have access to the information contained in a pupil's records, it is recommended that pupil records be kept under lock and key. Adequate security mechanisms are necessary to ensure that the information in a pupil's records is not available to unauthorized personnel.

Dissemination of Pupil Information

Educators need to consider both access to information by officials and dissemination of information to individuals and agencies outside the school. In both cases, the guiding principles are (1) the protection of pupils' and parents' rights to privacy and (2) the legitimate need to know particular information, as demonstrated by the person or agency to whom the information is disseminated.

Access Within the Schools

Those desiring access to pupil records must sign a form stating why they need to inspect the records. A list of people who have had access to their child's files and the reasons that access was sought should be available to parents. The provisions of FERPA as well as IDEA state that all persons, agencies, or organizations desiring access to the records of a student shall be required to sign a written form that shall be kept permanently with the file of the student, but only for inspection by the parents or student, indicating specifically the legitimate educational or other interest that each person, agency, or organization has in seeking this information (§438, 4A; §300.563).

When a pupil transfers from one school district to another, that pupil's records are also transferred. FERPA is very specific with regard to the conditions of transfer. When a pupil's file is transferred to another school or school system in which the pupil plans to enroll, the school must (1) notify the pupil's parents that the records have been transferred, (2) send the parents a copy of the transferred records if the parents so desire, and (3) provide the parents with an opportunity to challenge the content of the transferred data.

Access for Individuals and Agencies Outside the Schools

School personnel collect information about pupils enrolled in the school system for educationally relevant purposes. There is an implicit agreement between the schools and the parents that the only justification for collecting and keeping any pupil data is educational relevance. However, because the schools have so much information about pupils, they are often asked for pupil data by potential employers, credit agencies, insurance companies, police, the armed services, the courts, and various social agencies. To divulge information to any of these sources is a violation of this implicit trust unless the pupil (if older than 18 years) or the parents request that the information be released. Note that the courts and various administrative agencies have the power to subpoena pupil records from schools. In such cases, FERPA requires that the parents be notified that the records will be turned over in compliance with the subpoena.

Except in the case of the subpoena of records or the transfer of records to another school district, no school personnel should release any pupil information without the written consent of the parents. FERPA states that no educational agency may release pupil information unless "there is written consent from the student's parents specifying records to be released, the reasons for such release, and to whom, and with a copy of the records to be released to the student's parents and the student if desired by the parents" (§438, b2A).

CHAPTER COMPREHENSION QUESTIONS

Write your answers to each of the following questions, and then compare your responses to the text or the study guide.

1. Describe four characteristics of effective school teams.

2. Name and describe the functions of four types of teams commonly formed in school settings.

3. What are some potential barriers to communicating effectively about assessment with parents? What are some ways to overcome these barriers?

4. What are some ways in which assessment information is communicated in written form in schools? What are the rules governing who has access to this information?

Glossary

abscissa The horizontal axis of a graph, representing the continuum on which individuals are measured

access Availability of an assessment to consumers

accommodation A change in testing materials or procedures that enables students to participate in assessments in ways that reflect their skills and abilities rather than their disabilities

accommodative ability The automatic adjustment of the eyes for seeing at different distances

accountability, accountability system The use of assessment results and other data to ensure that schools are moving in desired directions; common elements include standards, indicators of progress toward meeting those standards, analysis of data, reporting procedures, and rewards or sanctions

acculturation A child's particular set of background experiences and opportunities to learn in both formal and informal educational settings

accuracy Usually the percentage of a student's attempted responses that are correct; accuracy is most important during a student's acquisition of new information

achievement What has been learned as a result of instruction

achievement-standards referenced A type of test that involves ascertaining the degree to which students are meeting state and national standards, which specify the qualities and skills that competent learners need to demonstrate

achievement test A measure of what students have been taught and learned

acquisition deficit Failure to learn a particular skill

adaptations A generalized term that describes a change made in the presentation, setting, response, or timing or scheduling of an assessment that may or may not change the construct of the assessment

adaptive behavior Behavior that allows individuals to adapt themselves to the expectations of nature and society

adequate yearly progress (AYP) A provision of the federal No Child Left Behind (NCLB, 2001) legislation requiring schools, districts, and states to demonstrate that students are making academic progress based on test scores; each state was required by NCLB to submit by January 31, 2003, a specific plan for monitoring AYP

affective comprehension A reader's personal and emotional responses to the reading material

age equivalent A derived score that expresses a person's performance as the average (the median or mean) performance for that age group; age equivalents are expressed in years and months, with a hyphen used in age scores (e.g., 7-1 is 7 years, 1 month); an age-equivalent score is interpreted to mean that the test taker's performance is equal to the average performance of an X-year-old

aid An error in oral reading, recorded when a student hesitates for more than ten seconds and the word or words are supplied by the teacher

aided observation Use of recording devices to allow for review of observations

aimline On a progress monitoring chart, a line that connects a student's baseline performance level with a goal performance level to show an expected rate of growth over time

algorithm The steps, processes, or procedures used for solving a problem or reaching a goal

alignment The similarity or match between or among content standards, performance standards, curriculum, instruction, and assessments in terms of knowledge and skill expectations

alternate assessment Substitute way of gathering data, often by means of portfolio or performance measures; alternate assessments are intended for students with significant disabilities that keep them from participating in the regular assessment

alternate form reliability The correlation of student performance on multiple equivalent forms of the test

alternate forms Two tests that measure the same trait or skill to the same extent and that are standardized on the same population; alternate forms offer essentially equivalent tests and are sometimes called "equivalent forms"

alternative achievement standard Expectations for performance that differ in complexity from a grade-level achievement standard, but are linked to the content standards

amplitude The intensity of a behavior

assessment The process of collecting data for the purpose of (1) specifying and verifying problems, and (2) making decisions about students

attainment What an individual has learned, regardless of where it has been learned

audiogram A graph of the results of the pure-tone threshold test

basal That item in a test below which it is assumed the student will get all items correct

behavioral contexts The array of setting events and discriminative stimuli that may be associated with demonstration of a particular behavior

behavioral observation Observation of spontaneous behavior, which has not been elicited by a predetermined and standardized set of stimuli (that is, not test behavior)

behavioral topography The way in which a behavior is performed

benchmark A specific statement of knowledge and skills within a content area's continuum that a student must possess to demonstrate a level of progress toward mastery of a standard

beneficence Responsible caring; educational professionals do things that are likely to maximize benefit to students, or at least do no harm

bimodal distribution A distribution that has two modes

biserial correlation coefficient An index of association between two variables, one of which has been forced into an arbitrary dichotomy (e.g., smart/dull) and one of which is equal interval (e.g., grade point average)

body of evidence Information or data that establish that a student can perform a particular skill or has mastered a specific content standard and that was either produced by the student or collected by someone who is knowledgeable about the student

capacity building Working with systems (community agencies, schools, families, churches, businesses, related services personnel) to help enhance student competence

cash validity The notion that frequently used tests are valid tests

Category A data The basic, minimum information schools need in order to operate an educational program, including identifying information, as well as information about a student's educational progress

Category B data Test results and other verified information useful to the schools in planning a student's educational program or maintaining a student safely in school

Category C data Information that may be potentially useful to schools, including any unverified information, scores on personality tests, etc.

Cattell-Horn-Carroll (CHC) theory A theory of intelligence that articulates intelligence as being composed of several factors

ceiling That item in a test above which it is assumed the student will fail all items

celeration charts Charts based on the principle that changes (increases or decreases) in the frequency of behavior within a specified time (e.g., number of correct responses per minute) are multiplicative not additive; also called standard behavior charts, semilogarithmic charts, or seven cycle charts

classification A type of decision that concerns a pupil's eligibility for special services, special education services, remedial education services, speech services, etc.

classroom response systems Handheld devices, often called "clickers," that are used in class to simultaneously assess all students: students are presented with a multiple choice question, and click the responder to indicate their answer; teachers get an immediate graph or table showing all students' responses

coefficient alpha The average split-half correlation based on all possible divisions of a test into two parts; coefficient alpha can be computed directly from the variances of individual test items and the variance of the total test score

competence enhancement Helping students build those skills and behaviors that enable them to meet standards or achieve desired outcomes; basically, this involves helping students get better at what they do

computer adaptive testing An assessment method whereby items are selected for administration based on the student's performance on earlier items within the test

computer-generated reports A feature of many standardized tests in which a report is generated based on data about the student that the examiner enters into the computer; when used to inform special education eligibility, these decisions may not allow for appropriate tailoring based on individual characteristics and needs

computerized scoring A feature of many standardized tests that has the potential to increase efficiency and accuracy in scoring; an examiner enters student responses and the computer calculates scores

concurrent criterion-related validity A measure of how accurately a person's current test score can be used to estimate a score on a criterion measure

conductive hearing loss Abnormal hearing associated with poor air-conduction sensitivity but normal bone-conduction sensitivity

confidence interval The range of scores within which a person's true score will fall with a given probability

construct validity   A measure of the extent to which a test measures a theoretical trait or characteristic

consultation   A meeting between a resource teacher or other specialist and a classroom teacher to verify the existence of a problem, specify the nature of the problem, and develop strategies that might relieve the problem

content standard   Statement of the specific content or skills that students are expected to have mastered at a specific point in time

content validity   A measure of the extent to which a test is an adequate measure of the content it is designed to cover; content validity is established by examining three factors: the appropriateness of the types of items included, the comprehensiveness of the item sample, and the way in which the items assess the content

continuous recording   A way to record behavior in which the observer counts each occurrence of a behavior in the observation session; the duration or latency of each occurrence within the observation session can be timed

continuous technology-enhanced measures   Computer-administered tests that are used in continuous (ongoing or daily) progress monitoring

contrived observations   An observation in which a situation is set up before a student is introduced into it

correlation   A measure of the degree of relationship between two or more variables; a correlation indicates the extent to which any two variables go together—that is, the extent to which changes in one variable are reflected by changes in the second variable

correlation coefficient   A numerical index of the relationship between two or more variables

criterion-referenced test   Test that measures a person's skills in terms of absolute levels of mastery

criterion-related validity   A measure of the extent to which a person's score on a criterion measure can be estimated from that person's score on a test of unknown validity

critical comprehension   Analyzing, evaluating, and making judgments about material read

crystallized intelligence (*gc*)   General knowledge and skill that an individual acquires over time (compare with **fluid intelligence**)

curriculum-based assessment   Use of assessment materials and procedures that mirror instruction in order to ascertain whether specific instructional objectives have been accomplished, and monitor progress directly in the curriculum being taught

cut score   A specified point on a score scale; scores at or above that point are interpreted differently from scores below that point (also called a cutoff score)

daily living skills   A domain measured within the Vineland Adaptive Behavior Scales, 2nd edition, that consists of personal, domestic, and community living skills

decile   A band of percentiles that is ten percentile ranks in width; each decile contains 10 percent of the norm group

decision-making rules   Rules commonly applied to progress monitoring results to inform the need for instructional change

derived score   A general term for a raw score that is transformed to a developmental score or to a score of relative standing

descriptive statistics   Numerical values, such as mean, standard deviation, or correlation, that describe a data set

developmental age   A test score expressed as an age equivalent; the score represents the average score earned by individuals of a specific age

developmental equivalent   A type of derived score in which raw scores are converted to the mean or median for a particular age or grade (e.g., a grade equivalent expresses a test taker's raw score as the mean of a school grade; a grade equivalent of 7.0 means that the raw score was the mean of students in the beginning of seventh grade. An age equivalent of 7-0 means that the raw score was the mean of seven-year-old test takers. Age equivalents are also sometimes divided by chronological age to create a developmental quotient.)

developmental milestones   Significant developmental accomplishments (such as using words and walking) commonly used to determine whether infants and toddlers are developing as expected

developmental score   A raw score that has been transformed into age equivalent (AE) (e.g., mental age), grade equivalent, or developmental quotient

deviation IQ   A standard score with a mean of 100 and a standard deviation of 15 or 16 (depending on the test)

deviation score   The distance between an individual's score and the average score for the group, such as *z*-scores and *T*-scores

diagnostic achievement test   A test designed to identify a student's specific skill development strengths and weaknesses

diagnostic report   A report commonly generated by technology-enhanced assessment programs that can provide data on individual students, classrooms, schools, and districts

disaggregation   The collection and reporting of student achievement results by particular subgroups (e.g., students with disabilities, limited-English-proficient students) to ascertain the subgroup's academic progress; disaggregation makes it possible to compare subgroups or cohorts

discriminative stimulus   A stimulus that is consistently present when a behavior is reinforced and that elicits the behavior even in the absence of the original reinforcer

disregard of punctuation   An error in oral reading in which a student fails to give appropriate inflection in response to punctuation; e.g., a student may not pause for a comma, stop for a period, or indicate voice inflection at a question mark or exclamation point

distractor   An incorrect option contained in a response set

distribution   The way in which scores in a set array themselves; a distribution may be graphed to demonstrate visually the relations among the scores in the group or set

due process provisions   A set of legal provisions specifying that schools and the personnel who work in schools must respect all the rights that students are entitled to as persons; specifically, IDEA includes specification of steps school personnel must go through before assessing or changing the placement of students, or resolving conflicting opinion between school personnel and parents

duration   The length of time a behavior lasts

ecobehaviorial assessment   Observations of functional relationships between student behavior and ecological or environmental factors (What environmental factors are related to specific student behaviors?); enables educators to identify natural instructional conditions that are associated with academic success, behavioral competence, or problem behaviors

ecobehavioral observation   Observation targeting the interaction among student behavior, teacher behavior, time allocated to instruction, physical grouping structures, the types of tasks being used, and instructional content

ecology   Mutual relationships between organisms and their environments

efficiency   The speed and economy with which data are collected

English language accommodation   A change in a test for an English language learner that involves providing support using the English language

English language learner (ELL)   An individual who is acquiring the English language and has a non-English primary language

entitlement   In special education, the right to a free and appropriate education, related services, and due process

equal-interval scale   A scale in which the differences between adjacent values are equal, but in which there is no absolute or logical zero

error   Misrepresentation of a person's score as a result of failure to obtain a representative sample of times, items, or scorers

ethnographic observation   Observation in which the observer does not participate in what is occurring

etiology   The cause of a disorder

evidence-based   An assessment or instructional approach that has been shown through research to be effective

expectancy   The tendency of an observer to see behaviors consistent with her or his beliefs about what should happen

expressive language   The production of language

extended responses   A testing format in which student response is in the form of an essay; typically it is most useful for testing comprehension, application, analysis, synthesis, and evaluation objectives

externalizing problems   Problems in social-emotional functioning that are characterized by aggressive and acting-out behavior

fluency   The rate and automaticity with which an individual can complete a given task

fluid intelligence (*gc*)   The efficiency with which an individual learns and completes various tasks (compare with **crystallized intelligence**)

focal points   A small number of mathematical topics that should be focused on at each grade level and serve as areas teachers should focus on; the National Council of Teachers of Mathematics published a document detailing these

formative assessment   Administration of a continuous or periodic tests and use of the test results to adjust teaching or learning while they are happening

formative evaluation   Ongoing frequent evaluation as the thing being evaluated is occurring; in instructional evaluation, collection of data as instruction is occurring

free operant   A test situation that presents more problems than a student can answer in the given time period

frequency   The tabulation of the number of behaviors with discrete beginnings and endings that occur in a predetermined time frame; when the time periods in which the behavior is counted vary, frequencies are usually converted to rates

frustration level   Usually accuracy that is less than 85 percent correct; when a student is performing at frustration level, the material is too difficult

functional behavioral assessment   Collecting data in order to identify the function of a student's problematic behavior, which is then used to inform the development of an intervention

function of behavior   The reason a person behaves as he or she does, or the purpose the behavior serves

goal line   On a progress monitoring chart, a line that connects a student's baseline performance level with a goal performance level to show an expected rate of growth over time

grade equivalent   A derived score that expresses a student's performance as the average (the median or mean) performance for a particular grade; grade equivalents are expressed in grades and tenths of grades, with a decimal point used in grade scores (e.g., 7.1 is grade 7 and one-tenth)

gross mispronunciation   An error in oral reading in which a student's pronunciation of a word is in no way similar to the word in the text

halo effect   The tendency of an observer to make subjective judgments on the basis of general attributes, such as race or social class

handheld observation system   Observational systems available for personal digital assistants (PDA) that can facilitate observation of classroom behavior

hesitation   An error in oral reading in which a student pauses for two or more seconds before pronouncing a word

histogram   A representation of frequency distribution by means of rectangles whose widths are class intervals and whose areas are proportional to corresponding frequencies

historical information   Information that describes how a person has functioned in the past

inclusive education   Education of people with and without disabilities in the same classes or school environments

independent level   Usually accuracy that is 95 percent or higher

indicator   The symbolic representation of one or more outcomes that can be used to make comparisons among students or schools

individual consent   Consent by parent (or pupil) required for the collection of family information (religion, income, occupation, and so on), personality data, and other noneducational information

individualized education plan (IEP)   A document that specifies the long-term and short-term goals of an instructional program, where the program will be delivered, who will deliver the program, and how progress will be evaluated

inferential comprehension   Interpreting, synthesizing, or extending the information that is explicit in the reading material

informal assessment   Any assessment that involves collection of data by anything other than a norm-referenced (standardized) test

informal reading inventory (IRI)   Usually a test without a normative sample, consisting of graded reading passages and vocabulary words that span a wide range of skill levels; IRIs are used to assess decoding and comprehension in order to locate the level at which a student reads at an instructional level (with about 90 percent accuracy)

informed consent   Consent that a parent or a student gives for the collection or dissemination of information not directly relevant and essential to the child's education; the assumption underlying the notion of informed consent is that the parent (or pupil) is "reasonably competent to understand the nature and consequences of his [or her] decision" (Goslin, 1969, p. 17)

insertion   An error in oral reading in which a student inappropriately adds one or more words to the sentence being read

instructional ecology   Relationships between students and their instructional environments

instructional environment   Those contexts in which learning takes place (schools, classrooms, homes), as well as the interface of essential contexts for children's learning (home-school relationships)

instructional level   Usually accuracy that is between 85 and 95 percent correct

instructional match   Instruction that is matched to a student's specific level of skill development

intelligence   An inferred ability; a term or construct used to explain differences in present behavior and to predict differences in future behavior

intelligence factors   Components that are considered to be part of intelligence

inter-interviewer reliability   The extent to which multiple interviewers who rate behavior of an individual based on interviews with a respondent at different times rate the individual's behavior similarly

internal consistency   A measure of the extent to which items in a test correlate with one another

internalizing problems   Problems in social-emotional functioning that are characterized by withdrawn, anxious, or depressed behaviors

inter-observer agreement   The extent to which results can be generalized to different observers, which is determined by having two observers provide scores/ratings, and then determining either percent agreement or the correlation between scores/ratings

inter-respondent reliability   The extent to which multiple respondents who indirectly rate behavior of an individual based on cumulative exposure to the individual rate the behavior similarly

interscorer reliability   An estimate of the degree of agreement between two or more scores on the same test

intervention assistance team (IAT)   A group of teachers (and sometimes other professionals, such as school psychologists or speech-language pathologists) who meet to review student difficulties, try to ascertain the kinds of interventions to implement to try to alleviate difficulties in the regular classroom, and monitor the extent to which the interventions work; sometimes called "mainstream assistance team" or "prereferral team"

inversion   An error in oral reading in which a student says the words in an order different from the order in which they are written

Iowa problem-solving model   A systematic process used to assess and intervene on behalf of students with academic and behavioral problems

item reliability   The extent to which one can assume that performance on a set of items can generalize to performance on other items within the domain

keyed response   The correct answer in a response set

KR-20   An estimate of the internal consistency of a test when test items are scored dichotomously

kurtosis   The peakedness of a curve, or the rate at which a curve rises

language   A code for conveying ideas; although there is some variation, language theorists propose five basic components to describe the code: phonology, semantics, morphology, syntax, and pragmatics

language mechanics   Punctuation and capitalization

latency   The amount of time between a signal to initiate the behavior and the actual beginning of the behavior

least restrictive environment   The specification in IDEA that to the maximum extent appropriate students with disabilities are to be educated with children who are not disabled, and that they should be removed to separate classes, schools, or elsewhere only when the nature or severity of their disability is such that education in regular classes with the use of supplementary aids and services cannot be achieved satisfactorily

leptokurtic curve   A fast-rising curve; tests that do not spread out (or discriminate among) those taking the test are typically leptokurtic

lexical comprehension   Knowing the meaning of key vocabulary words

Likert scale   A technique in which a set of attitude statements is presented and respondents are asked to express degree of agreement or disagreement, usually on a five- or seven-point scale ranging from *strongly agree* to *strongly disagree*; each degree of agreement is given a numerical value, and a total numerical value can be calculated from all the responses

limited English proficiency (LEP)   Used to describe an individual who has a native language other than English, such that it affects the individual's ability to learn in an English-speaking classroom

literal comprehension   Understanding information that is explicit in the reading material

maladaption   Behavior that does not promote surviving and thriving as an individual; often, it is determined based on context, age, and social/cultural expectations; an absence of this is sometimes used in definitions of adaptive behavior

mandated tests   Tests that are administered as a result of legislation

mastery   Usually accuracy that equals or exceeds 90 to 95 percent correct

mean   The arithmetic average of scores in a distribution

measurement error   The difference between observed score and true score; the distribution of measurement error can be determined using the test's standard deviation and reliability

median   A score that divides the top 50 percent of test takers from the bottom 50 percent; the point on a scale above which 50 percent of the cases (not the scores) occur and below which 50 percent of the cases occur

metalinguistic   Relating to the direct examination of the structural aspects of language

mixed hearing loss   Abnormal hearing attributed to abnormal bone conduction and even more abnormal air conduction

mode   The most frequently obtained score in a distribution

modified achievement standards   Expectations for performance that are lower than the grade-level achievement standards, but linked to or aligned with the content standards; this term will be further defined by policy makers in the near future

momentary time sampling   A procedure used in systematic observation to determine when observations will occur; a behavior is scored as an occurrence if it is present at the last moment of an observation interval; if the behavior is not occurring at the last moment of the interval, a nonoccurrence is recorded

morphology   The use of affixes (prefixes and suffixes) to change the meaning of words used in sentences

multiple gating   A method for conducting assessment that involves screening, followed by increasingly comprehensive assessment for students who are identified to be at-risk

multiple-skill battery   A test that measures skill development in several achievement areas

native language accommodation   A change in a test for an English language learner that involves providing support using a student's native language

naturalistic observations   Observations that occur in settings that are not contrived

NCTM Standards   Math standards and results specified by the National Council of Teachers of Mathematics

negatively skewed distribution   An asymmetric distribution in which scores tail off to the low end of the continuum; a distribution in which there are more scores above the mean than below it

nominal scale   A scale of measurement in which there is no inherent relationship among adjacent values

nonsystematic observation   Observation in which the observer notes behaviors, characteristics, and personal interactions that seem of significance

nonverbal tests   Tests, such as some intelligence tests, where students can understand and respond to items without verbal language

normal-curve equivalent   Standard score with a mean equal to 100 and a standard deviation equal to 21.06

normative sample (norm group)   A group of subjects of known demographic characteristics (age, gender, grade in school, and so on) to whom a person's performance may be compared

normative update   The re-standardization of a test by giving it to a new norm sample without changing the test items

norm group   See **standardization sample**

norm-referenced device   Test that compares an individual's performance to the performance of his or her peers

objective-referenced assessment   Tests referenced to specific instructional objectives rather than to the performance of a peer group or norm group

objective scoring   Scoring that is based on observable qualities and not influenced by emotion, guess, or personal bias

observation   The process of gaining information through one's senses—visual, auditory, etc.; observation can be used to assess behavior, states, physical characteristics, and permanent products of behavior (such as a child's poem)

obtrusive observations   Observations in which it is obvious to the person being observed that they are being observed

omission   An error in oral reading in which a student skips a word or a group of words

operationalize   To define a behavior or event in terms of the operations used to measure it; e.g., an operational definition of intelligence would be a score on a specific intelligence test

oral reading   A skill often measured in diagnostic reading tests; students are asked to read a series of passages and the examiner takes note of fluency, accuracy, errors, and other characteristics of reading quality

oral reading errors   Instances in which a student misreads a printed word

ordinal scale   A scale on which values of measurement are ordered from best to worst or from worst to best; on ordinal scales, the differences between adjacent values are unknown

ordinate   The vertical axis of a graph of a distribution, showing the frequency (or the number) of individuals earning any given score

outcome   The result of interactions between individuals and schooling experiences

out-of-level test   A lower- or higher-level test that is judged appropriate for the student's developmental level rather than the student's age/grade level

partial-interval recording   A procedure used in systematic observation in which an occurrence is scored if the behavior occurs during any part of the interval

partial mispronunciation   One of several kinds of errors in oral reading, including partial pronunciation, phonetic mispronunciation of part of the word, omission of part of the word, or insertion of elements of words

participant-observer observation   Observation in which the observer joins the target social group and participates in its activities

Pearson product-moment correlation coefficient (r)   An index of the straight-line (linear) relationship between two or more variables measured on an equal-interval scale

peer acceptance nomination scales   Scales that provide an indication of an individual's social status and may help describe the attitude of a particular group (such as the class) toward a target student

penmanship   The formation of individual letters and letter sequences that make up words

percentile rank (percentile)   Derived score that indicates the percentage of people whose scores are at or below a given raw score; percentiles are useful for both ordinal and equal-interval scales

perception   Any ability or skill involving the interaction of perception and voluntary movement (e.g., typing)

performance deficit   A particular skill that has been learned, but is not used appropriately

performance standard   A statement of the degree of mastery (such as "with 80 percent accuracy") that students are expected to demonstrate

periodic technology-enhanced measures   Computer-administered tests that are used in periodic (bi-weekly, monthly, quarterly) progress monitoring

phi coefficient   An index of linear correlation between two sets of naturally dichotomous variables (e.g., male/female, dead/alive)

phonology   The hearing and production of speech sounds

platykurtic curve   A curve that is flat and slow rising

point biserial correlation coefficient   An index of linear correlation between one naturally occurring dichotomous variable (such as gender) and a continuous, equal-interval variable (such as height measured in inches)

point-to-point agreement   A method of determining inter-observer agreement, calculated by dividing the number of observations where both observers agree (occurrence and nonoccurrence) by the total number of observations and multiplying the quotient by 100

portfolio   A collection of products that provide a basis for judging student accomplishment; in school settings, portfolios typically contain extended projects and may also contain drafts, teacher comments and evaluations, and self-evaluations

positively skewed distribution   An asymmetrical distribution in which scores tail off to the higher end of the continuum; a distribution in which there are more scores below the mean than above it

power test   An untimed test in which the interest is in how many items a student can complete correctly

pragmatics   The social context in which language occurs

predictive criterion-related validity   A measure of the extent to which a person's current test scores can be used to estimate accurately what that person's criterion scores will be at a later time

prereferral   Activities that occur prior to formal referral, assessment, and consideration for placement; the goal of prereferral and intervention is twofold: (1) verification and specification of the nature of a student's difficulties and (2) provision of services in the least restrictive environment

presentation accommodation   A change in how a test is presented that facilitates appropriate testing of an individual student

probe   A special testing format that is well suited to the assessment of direct performances; probes are brief (usually three minutes or less), timed, frequently administered assessments that can be used for any purpose

processing deficits   Deficits in cognitive functioning that are sometimes used in definitions of learning disabilities

process standards   Statements of the specific processes students should go through in solving problems

prognosis   A prediction of future performance

progress monitoring   The collection of data that is used to determine the impact of instruction and intervention over a short period of time

protection in evaluation procedures provisions   The specification in IDEA that assessment procedures and activities must be fair, equitable, and non-discriminatory

qualitative data   Information consisting of nonsystematic and unquantified observations

qualitative observation   A description of behavior, its function, and its context; the observer begins without preconceived ideas about what will be observed and describes behavior that seems important

quantitative data   Observations that have been tabulated or otherwise given numerical values

quantitative observation   A type of observation that is focused on quantification of a specific behavior, with procedures for recording that behavior at selected times and in selected places

quartile   A band of percentiles that is 25 percentile ranks in width; each quartile contains 25 percent of the norm group

random error   In measurement, sources of variation in scores that make it impossible to generalize from an observation of a specific behavior observed at a specific time by a specific person to observations conducted on similar behavior, at different times, or by different observers

range   The distance between the extremes in a set of scores, including those extremes; the highest score less the lowest score, plus one

rate   The number of responses per minute; rate measures are thought to indicate a student's fluency or automaticity of response

rate of reading   Often used to measure reading skill; tells how quickly and automatically a student can decode words

rating scale   A standardized assessment procedure whereby behavior, states, or feelings are quantified; most rating scales rely on ordinal measurement of recalled observations

ratio IQ   A derived score based on mental age (MA), in relation to chronological age (CA), in which IQ equals

$$\frac{\text{MA (in months)}}{\text{CA (in months)}} \times 100$$

ratio scale   A scale of measurement in which the difference between adjacent values is equal and in which there is a logical and absolute zero

raw score   The quantified evaluation of a test item or group of test items such as right or wrong on a specific item, or the number of right or wrong items on a student's test; in standardized testing, raw scores are usually transformed to derived scores

readiness   The extent of preparation to participate in an activity; most often refers to readiness to enter school, but applies to all levels

receptive language   The comprehension of language

referral   A request for help from a specialist; e.g., a teacher or parent may refer a student to a specialist who can provide the student with an appropriate educational program

reliability   In measurement, the extent to which it is possible to generalize from an observation of a specific behavior observed at a specific time by a specific person to observations conducted on similar behavior, at different times, or by different observers

reliability coefficient   An index of the extent to which observations can be generalized; the square of the correlation between obtained scores and true scores on a measure r_{xt}^2

repetition   An error in oral reading in which a student repeats words or groups of words

representational consent   Consent to collect data, given by appropriately elected officials such as members of a state legislature

respondent   A person who is relied on to provide judgment about behavior based on cumulative observations

RTI (response to instruction)   How students respond to core instruction or universal programming (the everyday instruction that occurs for students)

response accommodation   A change in how a student may respond to a test that facilitates appropriate testing of that student

response to intervention   Students' responses when substantial changes are made in regular classroom instruction

retention   The percentage of correct responses recalled following learning; also called "maintenance," "recall," or "memory"

sample   A representative subset of a population

scheduling accommodation   A change in the scheduling of a test that facilitates appropriate testing of an individual student

scoring rubric   An ordinal scale used to rate a product; rubrics typically use verbal descriptions to anchor the end intermediate points of the scale

scotoma   A visionless spot in the eye

screening   An initial stage of assessment in which those who may exhibit a particular problem, disorder, disability, or disease are discriminated from the general population

selection format   A method of presenting test questions in which students indicate their choice from an array of the possible test answers (usually called "response options"); true-false, multiple-choice, and matching are the three most common selection formats

semantics   The study of word meanings; although the scope of the term can extend beyond individual words to include sentence meaning, the term generally applies to words

sensitivity   An assessment procedure's capacity to detect small differences among or within students

sensorineural hearing loss   Abnormal hearing associated with both poor bone-conduction sensitivity and poor air-conduction sensitivity

setting accommodation   A change in the testing environment that facilitates appropriate testing of an individual student

setting event   An environmental event that sets the occasion for the performance of an action

simple agreement   A method of determining inter-observer agreement, calculated by dividing the smaller number of occurrences by the larger number of occurrences and multiplying the quotient by 100

single-skill test   A test designed to measure skill development in one specific content area (e.g., reading)

skew   Asymmetry in a distribution; the distribution of scores below the mean is not a mirror image of the distribution above the mean

social comparison   Observing a peer whose behavior is considered to be appropriate and using the peer's rate of behavior as the standard against which to evaluate the target student's rate of behavior

social skills and relationships   A domain measured within the Vineland Adaptive Behavior Scales, 2nd edition, that consists of Relating to Others, Playing and Using Leisure Time, and Adapting

social tolerance   The threshold above which behaviors are viewed as undesirable by others

social validity   A consumer's access to and satisfaction with an intervention or assessment

sociometric ranking   Provides an indication of an individual's social status and may help describe the attitude of a particular group (such as the class) toward a target student

Spearman rho   An index of correlation between two variables measured on an ordinal scale

speed test   A timed test

spelling   The formation of words from letters according to accepted usage

split-half reliability estimate   An estimate of internal-consistency reliability derived by correlating people's scores on two halves of a test

stability coefficient   Another name for test-retest reliability coefficient; quantifies the consistency of scores over time

standard deviation   A measure of the degree of dispersion in a distribution; the square root of the variance

standard error of measurement (SEM)   The standard deviation of error around a person's true score

standardization sample   The group of individuals on whom a test is standardized; also called "the norm group"

standards Statements of desired goals or outcomes

standard score The general name for a derived score that has been transformed to produce a distribution with a predetermined mean and standard deviation

stanine Short for *standard nines*; a standard-score band that divides a distribution into nine parts; the middle seven stanines are each 0.50 standard deviation wide, and the fifth stanine is centered on the mean

stem In selection formats, the part of a problem that contains the question

student accountability The idea that consequences exist for individual students, and are based on their individual assessment performance; for example, students might not be promoted to the next grade or graduate if their assessment results do not meet a pre-specified level

subjective scoring Scoring that is not based on observable qualities but relies on personal impressions and private criteria

substitution An error in oral reading in which a student replaces one or more words in the passage with one or more meaningful words (synonyms)

supply format A method of presenting test questions in which a student is required to produce a written or oral response; this response can be as restricted as a number or a word and can be as extensive as a sentence, a paragraph, or several pages of written response

supralinguistics A second order of analysis required to understand the meaning of words or sentences

syntax Word order of sentences; includes a description of the rules for arranging the words into a sentence

system accountability The idea that consequences exist for school systems, and are based on the assessment performance of a group of individuals (e.g., school building, district, or state education agency); for example, a school might receive a financial award or special recognition for having a large percent of students meeting a particular assessment performance level

systematic bias A type of error that can threaten validity; it can consist of the method of measurement, enabling behaviors, differential item effectiveness, systematic administration errors, and unrepresentative norms

systematic error A consistent error that can be predicted; bias

systematic observation Observation in which an observer specifies or defines the behaviors to be observed and then counts or otherwise measures the frequency, duration, magnitude, or latency of the behaviors

test A predetermined set of questions or tasks to which predetermined types of behavioral responses are sought

testing Administering a particular set of questions to an individual or group of individuals in order to obtain a score

testing formats The methods by which test items are presented and responded to

test-retest reliability An index of stability over time

test translation A test that was developed in one language and converted into another language

tetrachoric correlation coefficient An index of correlation between two arbitrarily dichotomized variables (e.g., tall/short, smart/dull)

topography of behavior The way a behavior is performed

transformed score A special form of *z*-score that allows the transformation of a *z*-score to a distribution defined by the user:

Transformed score = Mean + (*z* * Standard deviation)

where the *z*-score is computed from existing data and the mean and standard deviation are defined according to the needs of the user

trendline On a progress monitoring chart, a line that represents the student's actual growth

true score The score that a student would earn if the entire domain of items was assessed

T-**score** A standard score with a mean of 50 and a standard deviation of 10

tunnel vision Normal central visual acuity with a restricted peripheral field

universal design for assessment The design of assessment programs that involves consideration of the needs of all participants

unobtrusive observations An observation in which the people being observed do not realize they are being watched

validity The extent to which a test measures what its authors or users claim it measures; specifically, test validity concerns the appropriateness of the inferences that can be made on the basis of test results

validity coefficient A coefficient that measures the correlation between a test of unknown validity and an established criterion measure

variance A numerical index describing the dispersion of a set of scores around the mean of the distribution; specifically, the average squared distance of the scores from the mean

visual acuity The clarity or sharpness with which a person sees

whole-interval recording A procedure used in systematic observation in which an occurrence is scored if the behavior is present throughout the entire observation interval

word-attack skills   Skills used to derive the pronunciation or meaning of a word through phonic analysis, structural analysis, or context cues

word recognition skills   Used to refer to skills in recognizing words by sight rather than through use of word attack skills

writing style   Rule-governed writing, which includes grammar (e.g., verb tense and use) and mechanics (e.g., punctuation and capitalization)

z-**score**   Standard score with a mean of 0 and a standard deviation of 1

Achenbach, T. M. (1986). *The Direct Observation Form (DOF)*. Burlington: University of Vermont, Department of Psychiatry.

Achenbach, T. M., & Rescorla, L. A. (2000). *Manual for the ASEBA Preschool Forms and Profiles*. Burlington: University of Vermont, Department of Psychiatry.

Achenbach, T. M., & Rescorla, L. A. (2001). *Manual for the ASEBA School-Age Forms and Profiles*. Burlington: University of Vermont, Department of Psychiatry.

Adams, M. (1990). *Beginning to read: Thinking and learning about print*. Cambridge, MA: MIT Press.

Alberto, P. A., & Troutman, A. C. (2005). *Applied behavior analysis for teachers* (7th ed.). Upper Saddle River, NJ: Prentice-Hall.

Algozzine, B. A., Christenson, S. L., & Ysseldyke, J. E. (1982). Probabilities associated with the referral to placement process. *Teacher Education and Special Education, 5*, 19–23.

American Association for the Advancement of Science. (1987). *Science for all Americans*. New York: Oxford University Press.

American Association for the Advancement of Science. (1993). *Benchmarks for science literacy*. New York: Oxford University Press.

American Educational Research Association (AERA), American Psychological Association, & National Council on Measurement in Education. (1997). *Standards for educational and psychological testing*. Washington, DC: American Educational Research Association.

American Educational Research Association (AERA), American Psychological Association, & National Council on Measurement in Education. (1999). *Standards for educational and psychological testing*. Washington, DC: American Educational Research Association.

American Psychological Association. (1992). *Ethical principles of psychologists and code of conduct*. Washington, DC: Author.

Ames, W. (1965). A comparison of spelling textbooks. *Elementary English, 42*, 146–150, 214.

Armbruster, B., & Osborn, J. (2001). *Put reading first: The research building blocks for teaching children to read*. Jessup, MD: Partnership for Reading. Available from the National Institute for Literacy website: www.nifl.gov.

Ayers, A. (1981). *Sensory integration and the child*. Los Angeles, CA: Western Psychological Services.

Bachor, D. (1990). The importance of shifts in language level and extraneous information in determining word-problem difficulty: Steps toward individual assessment. *Diagnostique, 14*, 94–111.

Bachor, D., Stacy, N., & Freeze, D. (1986). *A conceptual framework for word problems: Some preliminary results*. Paper presented at the conference of the Canadian Society for Studies in Education, Winnipeg, Manitoba.

Bailey, D. B., & Rouse, T. L. (1989). Procedural considerations in assessing infants and preschoolers with handicaps. In D. B. Bailey & M. Wolery (Eds.), *Assessing infants and preschoolers with handicaps*. Columbus, OH: Merrill.

Baker, E. L., Bewley, W. L., Herman, J. L., Lee, J. J., & Mitchell, D. S. (2001). *Upgrading America's use of information to improve student performance* (Proposal to the U.S. Secretary of Education). Los Angeles: University of California, National Center for Research on Evaluation, Standards, and Student Testing.

Baker, E. L., & Linn, R. L. (2002). *Validity issues for accountability systems*. Los Angeles, CA: University of California, National Center for Research on Evaluation, Standards, and Student Testing.

Bandura, A. (1969). *Principles of behavior modification*. Oxford: Holt, Rinehart, & Winston.

Barsch, R. (1966). Teacher needs—motor training. In W. Cruickshank (Ed.), *The teacher of brain-injured children*. Syracuse, NY: Syracuse University Press.

Baumgardner, J. C. (1993). *An empirical analysis of school psychological assessments: Practice with students who are deaf and bilingual*. Unpublished doctoral dissertation, University of Minnesota, Minneapolis.

Bayley, N. (2006). *Bayley Scales of Infant and Toddler Development*. San Antonio, TX: Psychological Corporation.

Beery, K. E. (1982). *Revised administration, scoring, and teaching manual for the Developmental Test of Visual-Motor Integration*. Cleveland, OH: Modern Curriculum Press.

Beery, K. E. (1989). *The Developmental Test of Visual-Motor Integration*. Cleveland, OH: Modern Curriculum Press.

Beery, K. E., & Beery, N. (2004). *Beery VMI.* Minneapolis, MN: NCS Pearson.

Bender, L. (1938). *Bender Visual-Motor Gestalt Test.* New York: Grune & Stratton.

Boehm, A. E. (2001). *Boehm Test of Basic Concepts—Third Edition.* Bloomington, MN: Pearson.

Bond, G., & Dykstra, R. (1967). The cooperative research program in first-grade reading instruction (1967). *Reading Research Quarterly, 2,* 5–142.

Bracken, B., & McCallum, R. S. (1998). *Universal Nonverbal Intelligence Test.* Itasca, IL: Riverside Publishing Company.

Brannigan, G., & Decker, S. (2003). *Bender Visual-Motor Gestalt Test* (2nd ed.). Itasca, IL: Riverside Publishing.

Breland, H. (1983). *The direct assessment of writing skill: A measurement review* (College Board Report No. 83-6). New York: College Entrance Examination Board.

Breland, H., Camp, R., Jones, R., Morris, M. M., & Rock, D. (1987). *Assessing writing skill.* New York: The College Board.

Briggs, A., & Underwood, G. (1984). Phonological coding in good and poor readers. *Reading Research Quarterly, 20,* 54–66.

Broderick, C. B. (1993). *Understanding family process: Basics of family systems theory.* Newbury Park, CA: Sage.

Brown, L., & Hammill, D. (1990). *Behavior Rating Profile* (2nd ed.). Austin, TX: Pro-Ed.

Brown, L., Hammill, D., & Wiederholt, J. L. (1995). *Test of Reading Comprehension–3.* Austin, TX: Pro-Ed.

Brown, L., Sherbenou, R., & Johnsen, S. (1997). *Test of Nonverbal Intelligence–3.* Austin, TX: Pro-Ed.

Brown, R., & Bellugi, U. (1964). Three processes in the child's acquisition of syntax. *Harvard Educational Review, 34,* 133–151.

Brown, V., Wiederholt, J. L., & Hammill, D. D. (2009). *Test of reading comprehension* (4th ed.). Austin, TX: PRO-ED.

Bruininks, R., Woodcock, R., Weatherman, R., & Hill, B. (1996). *Scales of Independent Behavior, Revised, comprehensive manual.* Chicago: Riverside Publishing Company.

Butcher, N. N., Graham, J. R., Ben-Porath, Y. S., Tellegen, Y. S., Dahlstrom, W. G., & Kaemmer, B. (2001). *Minnesota Multiphasic Personality Inventory–2.* Minneapolis, MN: University of Minnesota Press.

Caldwell, J., & Goldin, J. (1979). Variables affecting word problem difficulty in elementary school mathematics. *Journal of Research in Mathematics Education, 10,* 323–335.

Campbell, D., & Fiske, D. (1959). Convergent and discriminate validation by the multi-trait–multi-method matrix. *Psychological Bulletin, 56,* 81–105.

Carr, E. (1994). Emerging themes in functional analysis of problem behavior. *Journal of Applied Behavioral Analysis, 27,* 393–400.

Carrow-Woolfolk, E. (1995). *Manual for the Listening Comprehension and Oral Language Subtests of the Oral and Written Language Scales.* Circle Pines, MN: American Guidance Service.

Carrow-Woolfolk, E. (1999a). *Comprehensive Assessment of Spoken Language.* Circle Pines, MN: American Guidance Service.

Carrow-Woolfolk, E. (1999b). *Test for Auditory Comprehension of Language* (3rd ed.). San Antonio, TX: Harcourt.

Center for Universal Design. (1997). *The principles of universal design, version 2.0.* Raleigh: North Carolina State University.

Chall, J. (1967). *Learning to read: The great debate.* New York: McGraw-Hill.

Conners, C. K. (1997). *Conners Parent Rating Scale–Revised.* New York: Psychological Corporation.

Connolly, J. (2007). *KeyMath 3 Diagnostic Assessment (KeyMath 3 DA).* Minneapolis, MN: Pearson.

Cooper, C. (1977). Holistic evaluation of writing. In C. Cooper & L. Odell (Eds.), *Evaluating writing: Describing, measuring, judging.* Buffalo, NY: National Council of Teachers of English.

Crocker, L. M., Miller, M. D., & Franks, E. A. (1989). Quantitative methods for assessing the fit between test and curriculum. *Applied Measurement in Education, 2*(2), 179–194.

Cronbach, L. (1951). Coefficient alpha and the internal structure of tests. *Psychometrika, 16,* 297–334.

CTB/McGraw-Hill. (2004). *Guidelines for inclusive test administration 2005.* Monterey, CA: Author.

CTB/McGraw-Hill. (2008). *TerraNova—Third Edition.* Monterey, CA: Author.

Cummins, J. (1984). *Bilingual special education: Issues in assessment and pedagogy.* San Diego, CA: College Hill.

Das, J., & Naglieri, J. (1997). *Cognitive Assessment System.* Itasca, IL: Riverside Publishing.

Deming, W. E. (1994). *The new economics for industry, government and education.* Cambridge, MA: MIT, Center for Advanced Educational Services.

Deming, W. E. (2000). *The new economics for industry, government and education* (2nd ed.). Cambridge, MA: MIT Press.

Deno, S. L. (1985). Curriculum-based assessment: The emerging alternative. *Exceptional Children, 52,* 219–232.

Deno, S. L., & Fuchs, L. S. (1987). Developing curriculum-based measurement systems for data-based special education problem solving. *Focus on Exceptional Children, 19,* 1–16.

Deno, S. L., & Mirkin, P. (1977). *Data-based program modification: A manual.* Reston, VA: Council for Exceptional Children.

Derogatis, L. R. (1993). *Brief Symptom Inventory.* Minneapolis, MN: National Computer Systems.

Diana v. State Board of Education, 1970 (*Diana v. State Board of Education*, C-70: 37RFT) (N.D. Cal., 1970).

Doman, R., Spitz, E., Zuckerman, E., Delacato, C., & Doman, G. (1967). Children with severe brain injuries: Neurological organization in terms of mobility. In E. C. Frierson & W. B. Barbe (Eds.), *Educating children with learning disabilities.* New York: Appleton-Century-Crofts.

Dunn, L. M., & Dunn, M. (2007). *Peabody Picture Vocabulary Test* (4th ed.). San Antonio, TX: Pearson Assessment.

Dunn, L. M., & Markwardt, F. C. (1970). *Peabody Individual Achievement Test.* Circle Pines: MN: American Guidance Service.

Dunn, L. M., & Markwardt, F. C. (1998). *Peabody Individual Achievement Test—Revised/Normative Update.* Circle Pines, MN: American Guidance Service.

Edformation (2006). *AIMSweb.* Available at www.edformation.com.

Educational Testing Service. (1990). *Exploring new methods for collecting students' school-based writing: NAEP's 1990 portfolio study* (ED 343154). Washington, DC: U.S. Department of Education.

Elmore, R. (2002). *Bridging the gap between standards and achievement.* Washington, DC: The Albert Shanker Institute.

Englemann, S., Granzin, A., & Severson, H. (1979). Diagnosing instruction. *Journal of Special Education, 13,* 355–365.

Englert, C., Cullata, B., & Horn, D. (1987). Influence of irrelevant information in addition word problems on problem solving. *Learning Disabilities Quarterly, 10,* 29–36.

Epstein, M. H. (2004). *Examiner's manual for the Behavioral and Emotional Rating Scale* (2nd ed.). Austin, TX: Pro-Ed.

Ervin, S. M. (1964). Imitation and structural change in children's language. In E. H. Lenneberg (Ed.), *New directions in the study of language.* Cambridge, MA: MIT Press.

Figueroa, R. (1990). Assessment of linguistic minority group children. In C. R. Reynolds & R. W. Kamphaus (Eds.), *Handbook of psychological assessment of children.* New York: Guilford Press.

Flesch, R. (1955). *Why Johnny can't read.* New York: Harper & Row.

Foorman, B., Francis, D., Fletcher, J., Schatschneider, C., & Mehta, P. (1998). The role of instruction in learning to read: Preventing reading failure in at-risk children. *Journal of Educational Psychology, 90,* 1–13.

Freeland, J., Skinner, C., Jackson, B., McDaniel, C., & Smith, S. (2000). Measuring and increasing silent reading comprehension rates: Empirically validating a related reading intervention. *Psychology in the Schools, 37*(5), 415–429.

Frostig, M. (1968). Education for children with learning disabilities. In H. Myklebust (Ed.), *Progress in learning disabilities.* New York: Grune & Stratton.

Frostig, M., Maslow, P., Lefever, D. W., & Whittlesey, J. R. (1964). *The Marianne Frostig Developmental Test of Visual Perception: 1963 standardization.* Palo Alto, CA: Consulting Psychologists Press.

Fuchs, D., & Fuchs, L. S. (1989). Effects of examiner familiarity on black, Caucasian, and Hispanic children: A meta-analysis. *Exceptional Children, 55*(4), 303–308.

Fuchs, L. S., Deno, S. L., & Mirkin, P. (1984). The effects of frequent curriculum based measurement and evaluation on pedagogy, student achievement and student awareness of learning. *American Educational Research Journal, 21,* 449–460.

Fuchs, L. S., & Fuchs, D. (1986). Effects of systematic formative evaluation: A meta-analysis. *Exceptional Children, 53,* 199–208.

Fuchs, L. S., & Fuchs, D. (1987). The relation between methods of graphing student performance data and achievement: A meta-analysis. *Journal of Special Education Technology, 8*(3). 5–13.

Fuchs, L. S., Fuchs, D., Hamlett, C. L., Walz, L., & Germann, G. (1993). Formative evaluation of academic progress: How much growth can we expect? *School Psychology Review, 22,* 27–48.

Fuchs, L. S., Fuchs, D., & Maxwell, L. (1988). The validity of informal reading comprehension measures. *Remedial and Special Education,* 20–28.

Gilliam, J. E. (2001). *Manual for the Gilliam Asperger Disorder Scale.* Circle Pines, MN: American Guidance Service.

Ginsburg, H., & Baroody, A. (2003). *Test of Early Mathematics Ability* (3rd ed.). Austin, TX: Pro-Ed.

Gioia, G. A., Isquith, P. K., Guy, S. C., & Kenworthy, L. (2000). *Behavior Rating Inventory of Executive Functioning (BRIEF).* Lutz, FL: Psychological Assessment Resources.

Goldman, R., & Fristoe, M. (2000). *Goldman-Fristoe Test of Articulation* (2nd ed.). Circle Pines, MN: American Guidance Service.

Good, R. H., & Kaminski, R. A. (Eds.). (2002). *Dynamic Indicators of Basic Early Literacy Skills* (6th ed.). Eugene, OR: Institute for the Development of Educational Achievement. Available at dibels.uoregon.edu. Also available in print form from Sopris West Educational Publishers (sopriswest.com).

Good, R. H., & Salvia, J. A. (1988). Curriculum bias in published norm-referenced reading tests: Demonstrable effects. *School Psychology Review, 17*(1), 51–60.

Gottesman, I. (1968). Biogenics of race and class. In M. Deutsch, I. Katz, & A. Jensen (Eds.), *Social class, race, and psychological development*. New York: Holt, Rinehart, & Winston.

Graden, J., Casey, A., & Bonstrom, O. (1983). *Prereferral interventions: Effects on referral rates and teacher attitudes* (Research Report No. 140). Minneapolis: Minnesota Institute for Research on Learning Disabilities.

Greenspan, S. I. (2004). *Greenspan Social Emotional Growth Chart: A Screening Questionnaire for Infants and Young Children*. San Antonio, TX: Harcourt Educational Measurement.

Greenspan, S. I. (2006). *Bayley Scales of Infant and Toddler Development: Socio-Emotional Subtest*. San Antonio, TX: Harcourt Educational Measurement.

Gresham, F., & Elliott, S. N. (1990). *Social Skills Rating System*. Circle Pines, MN: American Guidance Service.

Grimes, J., & Kurns, S. (2003, December). Response to intervention: Heartland's model of prevention and intervention. National Research Center on Learning Disabilities Responsiveness to Intervention Symposium, Kansas City.

Gronlund, N. E. (1985). *Measurement and evaluation in teaching* (5th ed.; Part 2: Constructing classroom tests). New York: Macmillan.

Guilford, J. P. (1967). *The nature of human intelligence*. New York: McGraw-Hill.

Gutkin, T. B., & Nemeth, C. (1997). Selected factors impacting decision making in prereferral intervention and other school-based teams: Exploring the intersection between school and social psychology. *Journal of School Psychology, 35*, 195–216.

Hammill, D. (1998). *Examiner's manual: Detroit Tests of Learning Aptitude*. Austin, TX: Pro-Ed.

Hammill, D., & Larsen, S. (2008). *Examiner's manual for the Test of Written Language, Fourth Edition*. Austin, TX: PRO-ED.

Hammill, D. D., & Larsen, S. C. (2009). *Written language observation scale*. Austin, TX: Hammill Institute on Disabilities.

Hammill, D., Mather, H., & Roberts, R. (2001). *Illinois Test of Psycholinguistic Abilities* (3rd ed.). Austin, TX: Pro-Ed.

Hammill, D., & Newcomer, P. (2008). *Test of Language Development–Intermediate* (4th ed.). Austin, TX: PRO-ED.

Hammill, D., Pearson, N., & Voress, J. (1993). *Examiner's manual: Developmental Test of Visual Perception* (2nd ed.). Austin, TX: Pro-Ed.

Hammill, D., Pearson, N., & Voress, J. (1996). *Test of Visual-Motor Integration*. Austin, TX: Pro-Ed.

Hammill, D., Pearson, N., & Wiederholt, L. (1997). *Comprehensive Test of Nonverbal Intelligence*. Austin, TX: Pro-Ed.

Hanna, P., Hanna, J., Hodges, R., & Rudoff, E. (1966). *Phoneme-grapheme correspondence as cues to spelling improvement*. Washington, DC: U.S. Department of Health, Education, and Welfare.

Harcourt Assessment, Inc. (2004). *Stanford Achievement Test series, Tenth Edition technical data report*. San Antonio, TX: Author.

Harcourt Brace Educational Measurement. (1996). *Stanford Diagnostic Mathematics Test 4*. San Antonio, TX: Psychological Corporation.

Harcourt Educational Measurement. (2002). *Metropolitan Achievement Test* (8th ed.). San Antonio, TX: Author.

Harcourt Educational Measurement. (2003). *Otis Lennon School Ability Test* (8th ed.). San Antonio, TX: Author.

Harrison, P. (2006). *Bayley Scales of Infant and Toddler Development: Adaptive Behavior Subtest*. San Antonio, TX: Harcourt Educational Measurement.

Harrison, P., & Oakland, T. (2003). *Adaptive Behavior System, Second Edition*. San Antonio, TX: Harcourt Educational Measurement.

Herrnstein, R., & Murray, C. (1994). *The bell curve: Intelligence and class structure in American life*. New York: The Free Press.

Hintze, J., Christ, T., & Methe, S. (2005). Curriculum-based assessment. *Psychology in the Schools, 43*(1), 45–56.

Horn, E. (1967). *What research says to the teacher: Teaching spelling*. Washington, DC: National Education Association.

Hosp, M. K., & Hosp, J. L. (2003). Curriculum-based measurement for reading, spelling, and math: How to do it and why. *Preventing School Failure, 48*(1), 10–17.

Howell, K. W., & Nolet, V. (2000). *Curriculum-based evaluation* (3rd ed.). Atlanta, GA: Wadsworth.

Hresko, W., Peak, P., Herron, S., & Bridges, D. L. (2000). *Young Children's Achievement Test*. Austin, TX: Pro-Ed.

Hresko, W. P., Schlieve, P. L., Herron, S. R., Swain, C., & Sherbenou, R. J. (2003). *Comprehensive Mathematical Abilities Test*. Austin, TX: Pro-Ed.

Isaacson, S. (1988). Assessing the writing product: Qualitative and quantitative measures. *Exceptional Children, 54*, 528–534.

Jenkins, J., & Pany, D. (1978). Standardized achievement tests: How useful for special education? *Exceptional Children, 44*, 448–453.

Jensen, A. R. (1980). *Bias in mental testing*. New York: The Free Press.

Johnson, D., & Myklebust, H. (1967). *Learning disabilities: Educational principles and practices*. New York: Grune & Stratton.

Kaplan, E., Fein, D., Kramer, J., Morris, R., Delis, D., & Maerlender, A. (2004). *Wechsler Intelligence Scale for Children* (4th ed., Integrated). San Antonio, TX: Psychological Corporation.

Kaufman, A. S. & Kaufman, N. L. (1998). *Kaufman Test of Educational Achievement—Second Edition.* Circle Pines, MN: American Guidance Service.

Kaufman, A., & Kaufman, N. (2004). *Kaufman Assessment Battery for Children, Second Edition.* Bloomington, MN: Pearson.

Kephart, N. (1971). *The slow learner in the classroom.* Columbus, OH: Merrill.

Kirk, S., & Kirk, W. (1971). *Psycholinguistic disabilities.* Urbana: University of Illinois Press.

Kirk, S., McCarthy, J., & Kirk, W. (1968). *Illinois Test of Psycholinguistic Abilities.* Urbana: University of Illinois Press.

Koppitz, E. M. (1963). *The Bender Gestalt Test for Young Children.* New York: Grune & Stratton.

Kovacs, M. (1992). *Children's Depression Inventory: Manual.* North Tonawanda, NY: Multi-Health Systems.

Kovaleski, J., & Glew, M. (2006). Bringing instructional support teams to scale: Implications of the Pennsylvania experience. *Remedial and Special Education, 27,* 16–25.

LaBerge, D., & Samuels, S. (1974). Toward a theory of automatic information processing in reading. *Cognitive Psychology, 6,* 293–323.

Larsen, S., Hammill, D. D., & Moats, L. (1999). *Test of Written Spelling–4.* Austin, TX: Pro-Ed.

Linn, R., Graue, E., & Sanders, N. (1990). Comparing state and district test results to national norms: The validity of claims that "everyone is above average." *Educational Measurement: Issues and Practice, 9*(3), 5–14.

Loeding, B. L., & Crittenden, J. B. (1993). Inclusion of children and youth who are hearing impaired and deaf in outcomes assessment. In J. E. Ysseldyke & M. L. Thurlow (Eds.), *Views on inclusion and testing accommodations for students with disabilities.* Minneapolis: University of Minnesota, National Center on Educational Outcomes.

Lohman, D., & Hagan, E. (2001). *Cognitive Abilities Test.* Chicago: Riverside Publishing.

Maddox, T. (Ed.). (2008). *Tests, sixth edition—A comprehensive reference for assessments in psychology, education, and business.* Austin, TX: PRO-ED.

Mardell-Czudnowski, C., & Goldenberg, D. (1998). *Manual: Developmental indicators for the assessment of learning* (3rd ed.). Circle Pines, MN: American Guidance Service.

Marion, S., & Gong, B. (2003, October). *Evaluating the validity of state accountability systems.* Paper presented at the Ed Reidy, Jr. Interactive Lecture Series, Nashua, NH.

Markwardt, F. (1998). *Peabody Individual Achievement Test–Revised–Normative update.* Circle Pines, MN: American Guidance Service.

Marston, D., & Magnusson, D. (1985). Implementing curriculum-based measurement in special and regular education settings. *Exceptional Children, 52,* 266–276.

Marston, D., Muyskens, P., Lau, M., & Canter, A. (2003). Problem-solving model for decision making with high-incidence disabilities: The Minneapolis experience. *Learning Disabilities Research and Practice, 18*(3), 187–200.

Martin, R. P. (1988). *Assessment of personality and behavior problems: Infancy through adolescence.* New York: Guilford Press.

Massachusetts Department of Education. (2001). *Resource Guide to the Massachusetts Curriculum Frameworks for Students with Significant Disabilities– English Language Arts Section.* Retrieved April 5, 2005, from www.doe.mass.edu/mcas/alt/rg/ela.pdf

Mather, N., Hammill, D., Allen, E., & Roberts, R. (2004). *Test of Silent Word Reading Fluency.* Austin, TX: Pro-Ed.

Maynard, F., & Strickland, J. (1969). *A comparison of three methods of teaching selected mathematical content in eighth and ninth grade general mathematics courses* (ED 041763). Athens, GA: University of Georgia.

McCarney, S. B. (1992a). *Early Childhood Behavior Scale: Technical manual.* Columbia, MO: Hawthorne Educational Services.

McCarney, S. B. (1992b). *Preschool Evaluation Scale.* Columbia, MO: Hawthorne Educational Services.

McGraw-Hill Digital Learning. (2004). *Yearly Progress Pro.* Columbus, OH: Author.

McGrew, K., Thurlow, M. L., Shriner, J., & Spiegel, A. N. (1992). *Inclusion of students with disabilities in national and state data collection programs* (Technical Report 2). Minneapolis: University of Minnesota, National Center on Educational Outcomes.

McGrew, K. S., & Woodcock, R. W. (2001). *Woodcock-Johnson III: Technical manual.* Itasca, IL: Riverside Publishing Company.

McNamara, K. (1998). Adoption of intervention-based assessment for special education: Trends in case management variables. *School Psychology International, 19,* 251–266.

Meller, P. J., Ohr, P. S., & Marcus, R. A. (2001). Family-oriented, culturally sensitive (FOCUS) assessment of young children. In L. A. Suzuki, J. G. Ponterotto, & P. J. Meller (Eds.), *Handbook of multicultural assessment: Clinical, psychological, and educational applications* (2nd ed., pp. 461–496). San Francisco: Jossey-Bass.

Mercer, C., & Mercer, A. (1985). *Teaching students with learning problems* (2nd ed.). Columbus, OH: Merrill.

Merrell, K. W. (1994). *Assessment of behavioral, social, and emotional problems.* New York: Longman.

Miller, J. (1981). *Assessing language production in children.* Austin, TX: Pro-Ed.

Moore, K. J., Fifield, M. B., Spira, D. A., & Scarlato, M. (1989). Child study team decision making in special education: Improving the process. *Remedial and Special Education, 10,* 50–58.

Mullen, E. (1995). *Mullen Scales of Early Learning: AGS Edition.* Circle Pines, MN: American Guidance Service.

Myles, B., Bock, S., & Simpson, R. (2001). *Examiner's manual for the Asperger Syndrome Diagnostic Scale.* Circle Pines, MN: American Guidance Service.

Naglieri, J. (2008). *Naglieri Nonverbal Ability Test* (2nd ed.). San Antonio, TX: Pearson Assessment.

National Association for the Education of Young Children. (2003). *Position statement on early childhood curriculum, assessment, and program evaluation.* Washington, DC: Author. [Retrieved June 14, 2008, at www.naeyc.org/about/positions/pdf/pscape.pdf]

National Association of School Psychologists. (2002). *Principles for professional ethics.* Bethesda, MD: Author.

National Commission of Excellence in Education. (1983). *A nation at risk: The imperative for educational reform.* Washington, DC: U.S. Government Printing Office.

National Council of Teachers of Mathematics. (2000). *Principles and standards for school mathematics.* Reston, VA: Author.

National Institute of Child Health and Human Development. (2000a). Report of the National Reading Panel. *Teaching children to read: An evidence-based assessment of the scientific research literature on reading and its implication for reading instruction* (NIH Publication 00-4). Washington, DC: U.S. Government Printing Office.

National Institute of Child Health and Human Development. (2000b). Report of the National Reading Panel. *Teaching children to read: An evidence-based assessment of the scientific research literature on reading and its implication for reading instruction: Reports of the Subgroups* (Chapter 2, Part II). Available at www.nichd.hih.gov/publications/nrp/ch2-II.pdf

Neisworth, J., Bagnato, S., Salvia, J. A., & Hunt, F. (1999). *Temperament and Atypical Behavior Scale.* Baltimore, MD: Paul H. Brookes.

Newcomer, P. (2001). *Diagnostic Achievement Battery* (3rd ed.). Austin, TX: Pro-Ed.

Newcomer, P., & Hammill, D. (2008). *Test of Language Development–Primary* (4th ed.). Austin, TX: Pro-Ed.

Nihira, K., Leland, H., & Lambert, N. (1993a). *AAMR Adaptive Behavior Scale–School* (2nd ed.). Austin, TX: Pro-Ed.

Nihira, K., Leland, H., & Lambert, N. (1993b). *Examiner's manual, AAMR Adaptive Behavior Scale–Residential and Community* (2nd ed.). Austin, TX: Pro-Ed.

Northern, J. L., & Downs, M. P. (1991). *Hearing in children* (4th ed). Baltimore, MD: Williams & Wilkens.

Nunnally, J. (1967). *Psychometric theory.* New York: McGraw-Hill.

Nurss, J., & McGauvran, M. (1995). *The Metropolitan Readiness Tests: Norms book* (6th ed.). San Antonio, TX: Harcourt Brace.

Olson, D. (1964). *Management by objectives.* Auckland, NZ: Pacific Book Publishers.

Otis, A. S., & Lennon, R. T. (2003). *Otis-Lennon School Ability Test* (8th ed.). San Antonio, TX: Harcourt Educational Measurement.

Paul, D., Nibbelink, W., & Hoover, H. (1986). The effects of adjusting readability on the difficulty of mathematics story problems. *Journal of Research in Mathematics Education, 17,* 163–171.

Pearson. (2001). *AIMSweb.* San Antonio, TX: Author.

Pflaum, S., Walberg, H., Karegianes, M., & Rasher, S. (1980). Reading instruction: A quantitative analysis. *Educational Researcher, 9,* 12–18.

Phillips, K. (1990). *Factors that affect the feasibility of interventions.* Workshop presented at Mounds View Schools, unpublished.

Prutting, C., & Kirshner, D. (1987). A clinical appraisal of the pragmatic aspects of language. *Journal of Speech and Hearing Disorders, 52,* 105–119.

Psychological Corporation. (2001). *Wechsler Individual Achievement Test* (2nd ed.). San Antonio, TX: Author.

Rayner, K., Foorman, B., Perfetti, C., Pesetsky, D., & Seidenberg, M. (2001). How psychological science informs the teacher of reading. *Psychological Science in the Public Interest, 2,* 31–73.

Reid, D., Hresko, W., & Hammill, D. (2001). *Test of Early Reading Ability* (3rd ed.). Austin, TX: Pro-Ed.

Renaissance Learning. (1997). *Standardized Test for the Assessment of Reading.* Wisconsin Rapids, WI: Author.

Renaissance Learning. (1998). *STAR Math.* Wisconsin Rapids, WI: Author.

Renaissance Learning. (2006). NEO-2. Wisconsin Rapids, WI: Author.

Renaissance Learning. (2007). DANA. Wisconsin Rapids, WI: Author.

Resnick, L. (1987). *Education and learning to think.* Washington, DC: National Academy Press.

Reynolds, C. R. (2007). *Koppitz Developmental Scoring System for the Bender Gestalt Test–Second Edition (Koppitz-2).* Austin, TX: Pro-Ed.

Reynolds, C. R., & Kamphaus, R. W. (2004). *Behavior Assessment System for Children–Second Edition–Manual.* Circle Pines, MN: American Guidance Service.

Reynolds, C. R., & Richmond, B. O. (2000). *Revised Children's Manifest Anxiety Scale.* Los Angeles: Wester Psychological Services.

Roach, E. F., & Kephart, N. C. (1966). *The Purdue Perceptual-Motor Survey.* Columbus, OH: Merrill.

Roid, G. (2003). *Stanford-Binet Intelligence Scale* (5th ed.). Chicago, IL: Riverside Publishing.

Roid, G., & Miller, N. (1997). *Leiter International Performance Scale–Revised.* Chicago: Stoelting.

Salvia, J. A., & Hughes, C. (1990). *Curriculum-based assessment: Testing what is taught.* New York: Macmillan.

Salvia, J. A., Neisworth, J., & Schmidt, M. (1990). *Examiner's manual: Responsibility and Independence Scale for Adolescents.* Allen, TX: DLM.

Schmidt, M., & Salvia, J. A. (1984). Adaptive behavior: A conceptual analysis. *Diagnostique, 9*(2), 117–125.

Shapiro, E. S. (2003). *BOSS—Behavioral Observation of Students in Schools.* San Antonio, TX: Psychological Corporation. [Software for PDA platform]

Shapiro, E. S. (2004). *Academic skills problems workbook.* New York: Guilford Press.

Shapiro, E. S., & Derr, T. (1987). An examination of overlap between reading curricula and standardized reading tests. *Journal of Special Education, 21*(2), 59–67.

Shapiro, E. S., & Kratochwill, T. (Eds.). (2000). *Behavioral assessment in schools: Theory, research, and clinical foundations* (2nd ed.). New York: Guilford Press.

Share, D., & Stanovich, K. (1995). Cognitive processes in early reading development: A model of acquisition and individual differences. *Issues in Education: Contributions from Educational Psychology, 1,* 1–57.

Shinn, M. (1998). *Advanced applications of curriculum-based measurement.* New York: Guilford Press.

Shinn, M. R. (Ed.). (1989). *Curriculum-based measurement: Assessing special children.* New York: Guilford.

Shinn, M., Tindall, G., & Stein, S. (1988). Curriculum-based measurement and the identification of mildly handicapped students: A review of research. *Professional School Psychology, 3*(1), 69–85.

Shriner, J., & Salvia, J. A. (1988). Content validity of two tests with two math curricula over three years: Another instance of chronic noncorrespondence. *Exceptional Children, 55,* 240–248.

Sindelar, P., Monda., L., & O'Shea, L. (1990). Effects of repeated readings on instructional- and mastery-level readers. *Journal of Educational Research, 83*(4), 220–226.

Slobin, D. I., & Welsh, C. A. (1973). Elicited imitation as a research tool in developmental psycholinguistics. In C. Ferguson & D. Slobin (Eds.), *Studies of child language development.* New York: Holt, Rinehart, and Winston.

Snow, C., Burns, M., & Griffin, P. (1998). *Preventing reading difficulties in young children.* Washington, DC: National Academy Press.

Sparrow, S., Cicchetti, D., & Balla, D. (2005). *Vineland Adaptive Behavior Scales* (2nd ed.). Circle Pines, MN: American Guidance Service.

Stanovich, K. (1986). Matthew effects in reading: Some consequences of individual differences in the acquisition of literacy. *Reading Research Quarterly, 21,* 360–406.

Stanovich, K. (2000). *Progress in understanding reading: Scientific foundations and new frontiers.* New York: Guilford Press.

Stevens, R., & Rosenshine, B. (1981). Advances in research on teaching. *Exceptional Education Quarterly, 2*(1), 1–9.

Stevens, S. S. (1951). Mathematics, measurement, and psychophysics. In S. S. Stevens (Ed.), *Handbook of experimental psychology* (p. 23). New York: Wiley.

Suen, H., & Ary, D. (1989). *Analyzing quantitative behavioral observation data.* Hillsdale, NJ: Lawrence Erlbaum Associates.

Sulzer-Azaroff, B., & Mayer, G. Roy (1986). *Achieving educational excellence: Using behavior strategies.* New York: Holt, Rinehart, and Winston.

Taylor, B., Harris, L., Pearson, P. D., & Garcia, G. (1995). *Reading difficulties: Instruction and assessment* (2nd ed.). New York: McGraw-Hill.

Tharp, R. G., & Wetzel, R. J. (1969). *Behavior modification in the natural environment.* New York: Academic Press.

Therrien, W. (2004). Fluency and comprehension gains as a result of repeated reading: A meta-analysis. *Remedial and Special Education, 25*(4), 252–261.

Thompson, S., & Thurlow, M. (2001). *State special education outcomes: A report on state activities at the beginning of the new decade.* Minneapolis: University of Minnesota, National Center on Educational Outcomes.

Thompson, S. J., Johnstone, C. J., & Thurlow, M. L. (2002). *Universal design applied to large scale assessments* (Synthesis Report 44). Minneapolis: University of Minnesota, National Center on Educational Outcomes. [Retrieved April 9, 2008, at http://cehd.umn.edu/NCEO/OnlinePubs/Synthesis44.html]

Thorndike, R. L., & Hagen, E. (1978). *Measurement and evaluation in psychology and education.* New York: Wiley.

Thurlow, M. L., Elliott, J. L., & Ysseldyke, J. E. (2003). *Testing students with disabilities: Practical strategies for complying with district and state requirements* (2nd ed.). Thousand Oaks, CA: Corwin Press.

Thurlow, M. L., Elliott, J. L., & Ysseldyke, J. E. (2003). *Testing students with disabilities: Procedures for complying with district and state requirements.* Thousand Oaks, CA: Corwin Press.

Thurlow, M. L., Quenemoen, R., Thompson, S., & Lehr, C. (2001). *Principles and characteristics of inclusive assessment and accountability systems* (Synthesis Report 40). Minneapolis, MN: National Center on Educational Outcomes, University of Minnesota.

Thurlow, M. L., & Thompson, S. (2004). *2003 state special education outcomes.* Minneapolis: University of Minnesota, National Center on Educational Outcomes.

Thurstone, T. G. (1941). Primary mental abilities in children. *Educational and Psychological Measurement, 1,* 105–116.

Tindal, G., & Hasbrouck, J. (1991). Analyzing student writing to develop instructional strategies. *Learning Disabilities: Research and Practice, 6,* 237–245.

Torgesen, J., & Bryant, B. (2004). *The Test of Phonological Awareness, Second Edition: Plus, Examiner's Manual.* Austin, TX: Pro-Ed.

U.S. Census Bureau. (1998). *Current population survey.* Washington, DC: Author.

Voress, J., & Maddox, T. (1998). *Developmental Assessment of Young Children.* Austin, TX: Pro-Ed.

Wagner, R., Torgesen, J., & Rashotte, C. (1999). *Comprehensive Test of Phonological Processing.* Austin, TX: Pro-Ed.

Walker, D. K. (1973). *Socioemotional measures for preschool and kindergarten children.* San Francisco: Jossey-Bass.

Walker, H. M., & McConnell, S. R. (1988). *Walker-McConnell Scale of Social Competence.* Austin, TX: Pro-Ed.

Walker, H. M., & Severson, H. H. (1992). *Systematic screening for behavior disorders* (2nd ed.). Longmont, CO: Sopris West.

Wallace, G., & Hammill, D. (2002). *Comprehensive Receptive and Expressive Vocabulary Test* (2nd ed.). Austin, TX: Pro-Ed.

Wechsler, D. (1939). *Wechsler-Bellevue Intelligence Scale.* New York: Psychological Corporation.

Wechsler, D. (1974). *Manual for the Wechsler Intelligence Scale for Children–Revised.* Cleveland, OH: Psychological Corporation.

Wechsler, D. (2001). *Wechsler Individual Achievement Test—Second Edition.* San Antonio, TX: Psychological Corporation.

Wechsler, D. (2002). *Wechsler Preschool and Primary Scale of Intelligence* (3rd ed.). San Antonio, TX: Pearson Assessment.

Wechsler, D. (2003). *Wechsler Intelligence Scale for Children* (4th ed.). San Antonio, TX: Psychological Corporation.

Wechsler, D. (2004). *Wechsler Intelligence Scale for Children, Fourth Edition–Integrated: Technical and interpretive manual.* San Antonio, TX: Psychological Corporation.

Wechsler, D. (2008). *Wechsler Adult Intelligence Scale* (4th ed.). San Antonio, TX: Pearson Assessment.

White, O., & Haring, N. (1980). *Exceptional teaching* (2nd ed.). Columbus, OH: Merrill.

Wiederholt, L., & Bryant, B. (2001). *Gray Oral Reading Tests–4.* Austin, TX: Pro-Ed.

Wiederholt, L., & Bryant, B. (2001). *Examiner's manual: Gray Oral Reading Tests–3.* Austin, TX: Pro-Ed.

Wilkinson, G. S., & Robertson, G. J. (2007). *Wide Range Achievement Test 4 (WRAT 4).* Lutz, FL: Psychological Assessment Resources.

Williams, K. (2001). *Group reading assessment and diagnostic evaluation.* Circle Pines, MN: American Guidance Service.

Williams, K. T. (2004). *Group Mathematics Assessment and Diagnostic Evaluation.* Circle Pines, MN: AGS Publishing.

Woodcock, R. W. (1998). *Woodcock Reading Mastery Tests–Revised: Normative update.* Circle Pines, MN: American Guidance Service.

Woodcock, R. W., Mather, N., & Schrank, F. A. (2004). *Woodcock-Johnson III Diagionistic Reading Battery.* Itasca, IL: Riverside Publishing.

Woodcock, R. W., McGrew, K. S., & Mather, N. (2001). *WJ-III Tests of Cognitive Abilities and Tests of Achievement.* Itasca, IL: Riverside Publishing.

Woodcock, R. W., McGrew, K. S., & Mather, N. (2003). *Woodcock-Johnson III Tests of Cognitive Abilities.* Itasca, IL: Riverside Publishing.

Woodcock, R. W., Schrank, F. A., McGrew, K. S., & Mather, N. (2007). *Woodcock–Johnson III Normative Update.* Itasca, IL: Riverside.

Ysseldyke, J. E. (1987). Classification of handicapped students. In M. C. Wang, M. Reynolds, & H. J. Walberg (Eds.), *Handbook of special education: Research & practice* (vol. 1, pp. 253–271). New York: Pergamon.

Ysseldyke, J. E., & Christenson, S. L. (1987). *The Instructional Environment Scale.* Austin, TX: Pro-Ed.

Ysseldyke, J. E., & Christenson, S. L. (2002). *Functional assessment of academic behavior: Creating successful learning environments.* Longmont, CO: Sopris West.

Ysseldyke, J. E., Christenson, S. L., & Kovaleski, J. F. (1994). Identifying students' instructional needs in the context of classroom and home environments. *Teaching Exceptional Children, 26*(3), 37–41.

Ysseldyke, J. E., & McLeod, S. (2007). Using technology tools to monitor response to intervention. In S. R. Jimerson, M. K. Burns, and A. M. VanDerHeyden (Eds.), *Handbook of response to intervention.* New York: Springer.

Ysseldyke, J. E., & Salvia, J. A. (1974). Diagnostic-prescriptive teaching: Two models. *Exceptional Children, 41,* 181–186.

Ysseldyke, J. E., & Thurlow, M. L. (1993). *Self-study guide to the development of educational outcomes and indicators.* Minneapolis: University of Minnesota, National Center on Educational Outcomes.

CREDITS

p. 213, Figure 12.1: Concepts and Communication Example 1 from Levels M and H from *Group Mathematics Assessment and Diagnostic Evaluation (G•MADE): Technical Manual ALL Levels*, Figure 2.1, p. 18 by Kathleen T. Williams, Ph.D., NCSP © 2004 American Guidance Service, Inc., 4201 Woodland Road Circle Pines, MN 55014-1796. Reproduced with permission. All rights reserved.

p. 213, Figure 12.2: Operations and Computation Example 1 from Level 4 from *Group Mathematics Assessment and Diagnostic Evaluation (G•MADE): Technical Manual ALL Levels*, Figure 2.2, p. 20 by Kathleen T. Williams, Ph.D., NCSP © 2004 American Guidance Service, Inc., 4201 Woodland Road Circle Pines, MN 55014-1796. Reproduced with permission. All rights reserved.

p. 213, Figure 12.3: Process and Applications Example 1 from Level 1 from *Group Mathematics Assessment and Diagnostic Evaluation (G•MADE): Technical Manual ALL Levels*, Figure 2.3, p. 22 by Kathleen T. Williams, Ph.D., NCSP © 2004 American Guidance Service, Inc., 4201 Woodland Road Circle Pines, MN 55014-1796. Reproduced with permission. All rights reserved.

p. 391, Figure 22.1: Alternate Assessment Based on Modified Academic Achievement, August 2007, Minneapolis, MN: University of Minnesota, National Center on Educational Outcomes. Reprinted by permission. http://cehd.umn.edu/nceo/OnlinePubs/AAMASParentGuide.pdf

Index

Note: Page numbers followed by *n* indicate footnotes.